The Christ Conspiracy

The Greatest Story Ever Sold

by Acharya S

Adventures Unlimited

The Christ Conspiracy

©1999 Acharya S

ISBN 0-932813-74-7

Printed in Canada

Published by
Adventures Unlimited Press
One Adventure Place
Kempton, Illinois 60946 USA
auphq@frontiernet.net

Few books present so smooth a blend of clarity and erudition as *The Christ Conspiracy*. This is a well-crafted, thought-provoking work that belongs in the library of every thinking individual. It should be read by every person concerned about the moral, ethical, and spiritual aspects of our culture; it should be read particularly by those who profess belief in any of the numerous varieties of Christianity. It is a book of true enlightenment.

—Barbara G. Walker, author of
The Woman's Encyclopedia of Myths and Secrets, The Crone, Amazon, The Woman's Dictionary of Symbols and Sacred Objects, Women's Rituals, Feminist Fairytales, The Skeptical Feminist, etc.

For two millennia, a spurious tale has enslaved the human mind and spirit. It still does. Acharya S's *The Christ Conspiracy* may well be the most dangerous and important book of our time, for it reveals beyond a shadow of a doubt that Jesus Christ is not a historical figure but simply a mythological toehold by which powermongers provide the dope of hope to the needy, malleable and violent masses.

—Adam Parfrey, author of
Cult Rapture, editor of *Apocalypse Culture*

The Christ Conspiracy
The Greatest Story Ever Sold

Table of Contents

Preface

The liberation of the human mind has never been furthered by dunderheads; it has been furthered by gay fellows who heaved dead cats into sanctuaries and then went roistering down the highways of the world, proving to all men that doubt, after all, was safe—that the god in the sanctuary was finite in his power and hence a fraud. One horse-laugh is worth ten thousand syllogisms. It is not only more effective; it is also vastly more intelligent.

H.L. Mencken

The search for the conspiratorial origins of the name of this book's author takes a circuitous route. "Acharya" means "teacher," but the title conjures an image of a little old man in India. Mahatma Gandhi, for instance, bestowed the title onto his spiritual heir, Acharya Vinoba Bhave, who began the Bhoodan land movement in India in the early 1950s. More strictly, the word means "preceptor," the head-master or principal of a school. A student could further fine-tune that definition by discovering, only in some dictionaries, that "preceptory" includes reference to the Knights Templar, an order ostensibly founded in 1119 CE to protect Holy Land pilgrims during the Second Crusade until it was banned and went underground two centuries later. Today, Freemasonry continues to claim descent from this medieval brotherhood.

None of this rumination suggests that Acharya S claims title as a preceptor or direct kinship to the Freemasons, although she has helped re-popularize an essay by Thomas Paine regarding Masonic sun-worship. Acharya's preceptory resides in cyberspace, on the web at www.truthbeknown.com, on her discussion list, through her posts in such e-places as konformist.com and Steamshovel Press, of which I am the publisher, and through her non-profit Institute for Historical Accuracy. Acharya S is also not a kindly little old guru. Her writing reflects a wicked wit and the intelligence of a person who does not suffer fools gladly. Under the flashing head of Bob Dobbs on her website and the words "God is BORG" are essays/rants on Earth and the cosmos, the existence or nonexistence of "God," the spiritual paucity of organized religion, as well as conspiracy and UFO/alien realities. "The believers/theists feel my views are intolerant," she writes, "while the nonbelievers/atheists object to the mysticism and perceive me as creating new beliefs . . . While I do not wish to live in a world where everyone is deluded by blind belief, I also do not want to totally dismiss all imagination or color."

A certain contemporary, straight-talking style distinguishes the work of Acharya S, which is surprising in that her scholarship sets out to recover ancient understanding from the relatively modern corruption of Judeo-Christian culture. Her style and perception are reminiscent of the late novelist and satirist William S. Burroughs, and she no doubt agrees with this assessment of his: "Perhaps the most basic concept in my writing is a belief in the magical universe, a universe of many gods often in conflict. The paradox of an all-powerful, all-seeing God who nonetheless allows suffering, evil and death, does not arise." Indeed, Acharya S likes to say, "There is no single giant male god in charge. There are six billion little gods all jockeying for position."

What is most interesting, perhaps, about Acharya S's work is that, while a rabblerousing rebel, she has an impressive set of academic credentials. She belongs to one of the world's most exclusive institutes for the study of ancient Greek civilization, the American School of Classical Studies at Athens, Greece. She has taught on Crete and worked on archaeological excavations in Corinth, site where legend holds Paul addressed the Corinthians, and in New England. She has also traveled extensively around Europe and has a "working knowledge" of Greek, French, Spanish, Italian, German, Portuguese and other languages. She has read Euripides, Plato and Homer in ancient Greek and Cicero in Latin, as well as Chaucer in Middle English, and has clearly sat down with the Bible – in English, as well as in the original Hebrew and Greek – long enough to understand it more than most clergy.

So, as entertaining and edifying as is the dharma combat carried on by Acharya S via her expository cyberprose, this book, *The Christ Conspiracy: The Greatest Story Ever Sold*, reflects the scholarship from which her fiery perspective comes. Some readers may find different aspects of it familiar. For instance, her survey of the lack of evidence for the existence of the historical Jesus contains information that has become increasingly accepted even by Christian revisionist groups such as the Jesus Seminary. As inflammatory as that material remains in many circles, it serves only as the beginning for Acharya S. She takes hammer and tong to many other non-historical figures, fraudulent church scams and misrepresented history in a matter of fact way, with chapters containing mythological character cross-references and details of legends. She recovers astronomical and cosmological elements in biblical texts that are far older than the corrupted versions revered in churches. The thesis of her work, that Christianity was created artificially out of older religions to consolidate Roman state control over those religions, as well as various mystery schools and secret societies, is a wellspring of awareness for students of conspiracy. Acharya S also makes a clear case yet for the existence of an ancient global civilization.

While some may wonder about her motives for creating such a monumental work that will no doubt shake up many people's perceptions of reality, Acharya S told me in no uncertain terms that "one of the reasons for doing this work is that I spent the first decade of my life literally becoming ill at war, violence, death and man's inhumanity to man and other creatures. Such vile behavior has all too often occurred because of religion and unfounded beliefs. The deception of the religion business is appalling, and it's high time it is exposed." Amen.

Kenn Thomas
January 1, 1999
Beginning the last year of the second Common-Era millennium

Introduction

Believe not because some old manuscripts are produced, believe not because it is your national belief, believe not because you have been made to believe from your childhood, but reason truth out, and after you have analyzed it, then if you find it will do good to one and all, believe it, live up to it and help others live up to it.

"Buddha"

The history of religious belief on Earth is long and varied, with concepts, doctrines and rituals of all sorts designed to propitiate and beseech any number of gods and goddesses. Although many people believe religion to be a good and necessary thing, no ideology is more divisive than religion, which rends humanity in a number of ways through extreme racism, sexism and even speciesism. Religion, in fact, is dependent on division, because it requires an enemy, whether it be earthly or in another dimension. Religion dictates that some people are special or chosen while others are immoral and evil, and it too often insists that it is the duty of the "chosen" to destroy the others. And organized religion puts a face on the divine itself that is sectarian, sexist and racist, portraying a male god of a particular ethnicity, for example. The result is that, over the centuries, humankind has become utterly divided among itself and disconnected from nature and life around it, such that it stands on the verge of chaos.

More horrors have been caused in the name of God and religion than can be chronicled, but some examples can be provided, as well as an assessment of how religions function:

The fires of Moloch in Syria, the harsh mutilations in the name of Astarte, Cybele, Jehovah; the barbarities of imperial Pagan Torturers; the still grosser torments which Roman-Gothic Christians in Italy and Spain heaped on their brother-men; the fiendish cruelties to which Switzerland, France, the Netherlands, England, Scotland, Ireland, America, have been witnesses, are none too powerful to warn man of the unspeakable evils which follow from mistakes and errors in the matter of religion, and especially from investing the God of Love with the cruel and vindictive passions of erring humanity, and making blood to have a sweet savor in his nostrils, and groans of agony to be delicious to his ears. Man never had the right to usurp the unexercised prerogative of God, and condemn and punish another for his belief. Born in a Protestant land, we are of that faith. If we had opened our eyes to the light under the shadows of St. Peter's in Rome, we should have been devout Catholics; born in the Jewish quarter of Alepp, we should have condemned Christ as an impostor; in Constantinople, we should have cried

"Allah il Allah, God is great and Mahomet is his prophet!" Birth, place and education give us our faith. Few believe in any religion because they have examined the evidences of its authenticity, and made up a formal judgment, upon weighing the testimony. Not one man in ten thousand knows anything about the *proofs* of his faith. We believe what we are taught; and those are most fanatical who know least of the evidences on which their creed is based.[1]

Even today, when humankind likes to pretend it has evolved, battles go on around the world over whose god is bigger and better, and religious fanatics of any number of faiths repeatedly call for and receive the blood of "unbelievers" and "infidels." Few religions of any antiquity have escaped unscathed by innumerable bloodbaths, and, while Islam is currently the source of much fear in the world today, Christianity is far and away the bloodiest in history:

> . . . the briefest glance at the history of the Christian churches— the horrible rancours and revenges of the clergy and the sects against each other in the fourth and fifth centuries A.D., the heresy-hunting crusades at Beziers and other places and the massacres of the Albigenses in the twelfth and thirteenth centuries, the witch-findings and burnings of the sixteenth and seventeenth, the hideous science-urged and bishop-blessed warfare of the twentieth—horrors fully as great as any we can charge of the Aztecs or the Babylonians—must give us pause.[2]

Defenders claim that Christianity ended human sacrifice. This may be true, but to do so, it had to sacrifice millions of humans. Christians also claim Christianity ended slavery, an assertion that is not true, as not only did Christians widely practice slavery, but the ideology itself serves as oppression and soul-enslavement: "Believe or go to hell. Submit your will to God or suffer eternally." As Barbara Walker relates, "Anthropologist Jules Henry said, 'Organized religion, which likes to fancy itself the mother of compassion, long ago lost its right to that claim by its organized support of organized cruelty.'"[3]

To deflect the horrible guilt off the shoulders of their own faith, religionists have pointed to supposedly secular ideologies such as Communism and Nazism as oppressors and murderers of the people. However, few realize or acknowledge that the originators of Communism were Jewish (Marx, Lenin, Hess, Trotsky)[4] and that the most overtly violent leaders of both bloody movements were Roman Catholic (Hitler, Mussolini, Franco) or Eastern Orthodox Christian (Stalin), despotic and intolerant ideologies that breed fascistic dictators. In other words, these movements were not "atheistic," as religionists maintain. Indeed, Hitler proclaimed himself a "Christian" and fighter for "his Lord and Savior," using the famous temple scene with Jesus driving out the "brood of vipers and adders" as a motivation for his evil deeds.[5] Said Hitler:

> It is of no matter whether or not the individual Jew is decent. He possesses certain characteristics given to him by nature, and he can never rid himself of those characteristics. The Jew is harmful to us . . . My feeling as a Christian leads me to be a fighter for my Lord and Savior. It leads me to the man who, at one time lonely and with only a few followers, recognized the Jews for what they were, and called on men to fight against them . . . As a Christian, I owe something to my own people.

Hitler also remarked to one of his generals: "I am now as before a Catholic and will always remains so." Whether or not Hitler was a "true" Christian is debatable, as he also reputedly considered Christianity a Jewish invention and part of the conspiracy for world domination. In addition, Hitler's paternal grandmother was allegedly Jewish. But Hitler himself was raised a Roman Catholic, and he was very much impressed by the power of the Church hierarchy. He pandered to it and used it and religion as a weapon. All during his regime, Hitler worked closely with the Catholic Church, quashing thousands of lawsuits against it and exchanging large sums of money with it. In addition, thousands of Nazis were later given safe passage by the Vatican, as well as by multinational governmental agencies, to a number of locales, including North and South America, via the "Ratline" from Germany through Switzerland and Italy.[6]

In reality, Hitler was only building on a long line of imputation against the Jews as "Christkillers," a charge used numerous times over the centuries whenever the Catholic Church wanted to hold a pogrom against common Jews and seize their assets. The events of WWII, in fact, were the grisly culmination of a centuries-old policy, started by the Church and continued by Martin Luther, as was well known by Hitler. Indeed, Hitler was embraced as a Christian instrument, as Walker relates:

> The rise of Hitler's Germany provides an interesting case in point, showing a nation swept by militaristic sentiment coupled with a sense of divine mission. The churches accepted Hitler's warmongering with religious joy. In April 1937, a Christian organization in the Rhineland passed a resolution that Hitler's word was the law of God and possessed "divine authority." Reichsminister for Church Affairs Hans Kerrl announced: "There has arisen a new authority as to what Christ and Christianity really are—that is Adolf Hitler. Adolf Hitler . . . is the true Holy Ghost." And so the pious gave him their blessing, and the churches gave him God's.[7]

But Hitler and the Church's behavior was not an aberration in
the history of Christianity, as from its inception, the religion was
intolerant, zealous and violent, with its adherents engaging in
terrorism. For example, while blessing peacemakers and
exhorting love and forgiveness of enemies and trespassers, the
"gentle Jesus" also paradoxically declares:

> Do not think that I have come to bring peace on earth; I have not
> come to bring peace, but a sword. For I have come to set man
> against his father, and a daughter against her mother, and a
> daughter-in-law against her mother-in-law; and a man's foes will
> be those of his own household. (Mt. 10:34)

Jesus further states that "nation will rise up against nation,
and kingdom against kingdom"; thus, with a few sentences, Jesus
has seeded extreme division, sedition and enmity wherever
Christianity is promulgated. In thus exhorting his followers to
violence, however, Jesus himself was building on centuries-old
Jewish thought that called for the "extermination" of non-Jews,
i.e., "unbelievers," in Christian parlance. As an example of
this Judeo-Christian fanaticism, the apostle Paul was a violent
zealot who as a Jew first persecuted the Christians and as a
Christian subsequently terrorized the Pagans. As Joseph Wheless
says in *Forgery in Christianity*:

> And [Paul], the tergiversant slaughter-breathing persecutor-for-
> pay of the early Christians, now turned for profit their chief
> apostle of persecution, pronounces time and again the anathema
> of the new dispensation against all dissenters from his
> superstitious, tortuous doctrines and dogmas, all such "whom I
> have delivered unto Satan" (I Tim. i, 20), as he writes to advise
> his adjutant Timothy. He flings at the scoffing Hebrews this
> question: "He that despised Moses's law died without mercy . . . :
> Of how much sorer punishment, suppose ye, shall he be thought
> worthy, who hath trodden under foot the Son of God?" (Heb. x,
> 28, 29). All such "are set forth for an example, suffering the
> vengeance of eternal fire" (Jude 7); "that they might all be
> damned who believed not the truth" (2 Thess. ii, 12); and even
> "he that doubteth is damned" (Rom. xiv, 23). This Paul, who with
> such bigoted presumption "deals damnation 'round the land on
> all he deems the foe" of his dogmas, is first seen "consenting to
> the death" of the first martyr Stephen (Acts viii, 1); then he
> blusters through the country "breathing out threatenings and
> slaughter against the disciples of the Lord" (Acts ix, 1), the new
> converts to the new faith. Then, when he suddenly professed
> miraculous "conversion" himself, his old masters turned on him
> and sought to kill him, and he fled to these same disciples for
> safety, to their great alarm (Acts ix, 23-26), and straightway
> began to bully and threaten all who would not now believe his
> new preachments. To Elymas, who "withstood them," the
> doughty new dogmatist "set his eyes on him," and thus blasted

him with inflated vituperation: "O full of all subtilty and all mischief, thou child of the devil, thou enemy of all righteousness, wilt thou not cease to pervert the right ways of the Lord?" (Acts xiii, 8-10). Even the "meek and loving Jesus" is quoted as giving the fateful admonition: "Fear him which is able to destroy both soul and body in hell" (Matt. x, 28)—here first invented and threatened by Jesus the Christ himself, for added terror unto belief. Paul climaxes the terror: "It is a fearful thing to fall into the hands of the living God' (Heb. x, 31)."[8]

The Myth of Massive Martyrdom

Along with the tale that Christianity began with a "Prince of Peace" comes the myth that the early Christians were gentle "lambs" served up in large numbers as "martyrs for the faith" by the diabolical Romans. The myth of martyrdom starts with the purported passage of the Roman historian Tacitus in which he excoriated Nero for killing a "great multitude" of Christians at Rome in 64 CE; however, this passage is a forgery, one of many made by the conspirators in the works of ancient authors, and there is little other evidence of such a persecution under either Nero or Domitian, the alleged notorious persecutor of Christians. As GA Wells says in *Did Jesus Exist?*:

> . . . the earliest unambiguous Christian reference to persecution under Nero is a statement made by Melito, bishop of Sardis, about AD 170. It would be surprising if a "great multitude" of Christians lived at Rome as early as AD 64 . . . The evidence for persecution under Domitian is [also] admitted to be very slight indeed.[9]

What persecutions the Christians did suffer were not as gross as portrayed by propagandists in either number or severity:

> These punishments [of Christians] lacked the public finality of the death sentence: until, 180, no governor in Africa was known to have put a Christian to death. In the late 240s, Origen insisted with rare candour that "few" Christians had died for the faith . . . They were "easily numbered," he said.[10]

And, as the editor of Eusebius's *The History of the Church* states:

> In fact, up to the persecution under the Emperor Decius (250-51) there had been no persecution of Christians ordered by the Emperor on an imperial scale.[11]

To bolster their claims of massive martyrdom, pious Christians began around the ninth century to forge the martyrdom traditions. As Walker relates:

> The martyrs of the famous Roman "persecutions" under such emperors as Nero and Diocletian, seven centuries earlier, were largely invented at this time, since there were no records of any

such specific martyrdoms. Names were picked at random from ancient tombstones, and the martyr-tales were written to order. In reality, it was the Christian church that did much more persecuting and made many more martyrs than Rome had ever done, because religious tolerance was the usual Roman policy.[12]

To weave their martyr-tales, the conspirators used the Jewish apocryphon the Fourth Book of Maccabees, which described gruesome "martyrdom" by torture: "The tale told in the *4 Maccabees* was widely read by Greeks and early Christians and served as a model for Christian martyrdom stories."[13] The methods described in Fourth Maccabees are disturbingly similar to those used by the later Catholic Church:

> . . . the guards had produced wheels, and joint-dislocators, and racks, and bone-crushers, and catapults, and cauldrons, and braziers, and thumb-screws, and iron claws, and wedges, and branding irons . . . [14]

The author of Fourth Maccabees goes on to describe the most foul torture imaginable, including the infamous "racks" being used to tear limbs from the body, as well as the flesh being stripped off and tongues and entrails ripped out, along with the obligatory death by burning. These techniques were later adopted with tremendous enthusiasm by the Christians themselves, who then became the persecutors. As Wheless says:

> When the Christians were weak and powerless and subjected to occasional persecutions as "enemies of the human race," they were vocal and insistent advocates of liberty of conscience and freedom to worship whatever God one chose; the Christian "Apologies" to the Emperors abound in eloquent pleas for religious tolerance; and this was granted to them and to all by the Edict of Milan and other imperial Decrees. But when by the favor of Constantine they got into the saddle of the State, they at once grasped the sword and began to murder and despoil all who would not pretend to believe as the Catholic priest commanded them to believe.[15]

The melodramatic portrayal of the early Christian movement as consisting of righteous "Mom and Pop" Christians being driven underground and ruthlessly persecuted is not reality, nor are the stories of massive martyrdom. What is reality is that from the fourth century onward, *it was the Christians who were doing the persecution.*

The Myth of the Rapid Spread of Christianity

It is widely believed that Christianity spread because it was a great idea desperately needed in a world devoid of hope and faith. Indeed, the myth says that Christianity was such a great idea that it caught on like wildfire in a lost world barren of spiritual enlightenment and crying out "like a voice in the wilderness." It is further maintained that Christianity spread because of the "martyrdom" of its adherents, which purportedly so impressed a number of the early Church fathers that they cast off their Pagan roots to join the "true faith." In reality, Christianity was not a new and surprising concept, and the impression of the ancient world given in this story is incorrect, as the ancient cultures possessed every bit of wisdom, righteousness and practically everything else found in Christianity.

Furthermore, according to noted historian Gibbon, as related by Taylor, by the middle of the 3rd century, there were at Rome—the hotbed of Christianity—only "'*one* bishop, *forty-six* presbyters, *fourteen* deacons, *forty-two* acolytes and *fifty* readers, exorcists and porters. We may venture, (concludes the great historian) to estimate the Christians at Rome, at about *fifty thousand*, when the total number of inhabitants cannot be taken at less than a *million* . . .' It should never be forgotten, that miraculously rapid as we are sometimes told the propagation of the gospel was, it was first preached in England by Austin, the monk, under commission of Pope Gregory, towards the end of the seventh century. So that the *good news* of salvation, in travelling from the supposed scene of action to this favoured country, may be calculated as having posted at the rate of almost an inch in a fortnight."[16] And as Robin Lane Fox says:

> . . . in the 240s, Origen, the Christian intellectual, did admit that Christians were only a tiny fraction of the world's inhabitants . . . If Christians were really so numerous, we could also expect some evidence of meeting places which could hold so many worshippers. At this date, there were no church buildings on public ground . . . [17]

If the rest of the Empire is factored in, it is estimated that by the middle of the third century Christians constituted only perhaps two percent of the total population.[18]

Also, as noted, there were in fact few martyrs, and the early forgers of Christianity were impressed not by such alleged martyrdom but by the position of power they would earn by their "conversion." In actuality, Christianity did not spread because it was a great idea or because it was under the supernatural guidance of the resurrected "Lamb of God." Were that so, he would have to be held accountable, because Christianity was promulgated by the sword, with a bloody trail thousands of mile long, during an era called by not a few a "shameless age."

Like so much else about Christianity, the claims of its rapid spread are largely mythical. In reality, in some places it took many blood-soaked centuries before its opponents and their lineage had been sufficiently slaughtered so that Christianity could usurp the reigning ideology. Pagan Europeans and others fought it tooth and nail, in an epic and heroic effort to maintain their own cultures and autonomy, in the face of an onslaught by those whom the Pagans viewed as "idiots" and "bigots." As Walker says:

> Christian historians often give the impression that Europe's barbarians welcomed the new faith, which held out a hope of immortality and a more kindly ethic. The impression is false. The people didn't willingly give up the faith of their ancestors, which they considered essential to the proper functioning of the earth's cycles. They had their own hope of immortality and their own ethic, in many ways a kinder ethic than that of Christianity, which was imposed on them by force. Justinian obtained 70,000 conversions in Asia Minor by methods that were so cruel that the subject populations eventually adopted Islam in order to rid themselves of the rigors of Christian rule. As a rule, heathen folk resisted Christianity as long as they could, even after their rulers had gone over to the new faith for its material rewards. . . . Certain words reveal by their derivation some of the opposition met by missionaries. The pagan Savoyards called Christians "idiots," hence *crétin*, "idiot," descended from *Chrétian*, "Christian." German pagans coined the term *bigot*, from *bei Gott*, an expression constantly used by the monks.[19]

Christianity was thus fervently resisted wherever it invaded, as nation after nation died under the sword fighting it off, because its doctrines and proponents were repugnant and blasphemous. As Walker also relates:

> Radbod, king of the Frisians, refused to abandon this faith when a Christian missionary informed him that Valhala was the same as the Christians' hell. Where were his own ancestors, Radbod wanted to know, if there was no Valhala? He was told they were burning in hell because they were heathens. "Dastardly priest!" Radbod cried. "How dare you say my ancestors have gone to hell? I would rather—yes, by their god, the great Woden, I swear—I would ten thousand times rather join those heroes in their hell, than be with you in your heaven of priests!"[20]

Some of the "barbarians" who resisted Christianity were actually far more advanced than those who followed what the Pagans considered a vulgar ideology. For example, "The Irish Fenians, whose rule was never to insult women, were said to have gone to hell for denying Christian anti-feminist doctrines."[21]

When the "great idea," threats of hell and other sweet talk failed to impress the Pagans, the Christian conspirators began turning the screws by establishing laws banning Pagan priests, holidays and "superstitions." Pagans were barred from being palace guards or holding civil and military office. Their properties and temples were destroyed or confiscated, and people who practiced "idolatry" or sacrifices were put to death. As Charles Waite says in *History of the Christian Religion to the Year Two Hundred*:

> Under Constantine and his sons, commissions had been issued against heretics, especially against the Donatists, who were visited with the most rigorous punishment. . . . The decrees for the extirpation of heathenism were even more severe. Jerome and Leo the Great were in favor of the death penalty.[22]

Under the "great Christian" Constantine, the "followers of Mithra were hounded with such pertinacity that no one even dared to look at the sun, and farmers and sailors dared not observe the stars for fear of being accused of the heresy."[23] And where hellfire, repressive laws and bribery did not work, force was used. Leaders who were tolerant of religions other than Christianity, such as Emperor Julian, were murdered. In *Bible Myths and Their Parallels in Other Religions*, Doane relates how this "great faith" was in reality propagated by the most atrocious methods:

> In Asia Minor the people were persecuted by orders of [Christian emperor] Constantius . . . "The rites of baptism were conferred on women and children, who, for that purpose, had been torn from the arms of their friends and parents; the mouths of the communicants were held open by a wooden engine, while the consecrated bread was forced down their throats; the breasts of tender virgins were either burned with red-hot egg-shells, or inhumanly compressed between sharp and heavy boards." . . . Persecutions in the name of Jesus Christ were inflicted on the heathen in most every part of the then known world. Even among the Norwegians, the Christian sword was unsheathed. They clung tenaciously to the worship of their forefathers, and numbers of them died real martyrs for their faith, after suffering the most cruel torments from their persecutors. It was by sheer compulsion that the Norwegians embraced Christianity. The reign of Olaf Tryggvason, a Christian king of Norway, was in fact entirely devoted to the propagation of the new faith, by means the most revolting to humanity. . . . the recusants were tortured to death with fiend-like ferocity, and their estates confiscated. These are some of the reasons "why Christianity prospered."[24]

The standard excuse for this vile behavior has been that Christian proponents had the right to purge the earth of "evil" and to convert the "heathen" to the "true faith." Over a period of more than a millennium, the Church would bring to bear in this "purification" and "conversion" to the religion of the "Prince of Peace" the most horrendous torture methods ever devised, in the end slaughtering tens of millions worldwide.

These "conversion" methods by Catholics against men, women and children, Christians and Pagans alike, included burning, hanging and torture of all manner, using the tools described in Fourth Maccabees. Women and girls had hot pokers and sharp objects slammed up their vaginas, often after priests had raped them. Men and boys had their penises and testicles crushed or ripped or cut off. Both genders and all ages had their skin pulled off with hot pincers and their tongues ripped out, and were subjected to diabolical machinery designed for the weakest parts of the body, such as the knees, ankles, elbows and fingertips, all of which were crushed. Their legs and arms were broken with sledgehammers, and, if there was anything left of them, they were hanged or burned alive. Nothing more evil could possibly be imagined, and from this absolute evil came the "rapid" spread of Christianity.

So far this despicable legacy and crime against humanity remains unavenged and its main culprit unpunished, not only standing intact but inexplicably receiving the undying and unthinking support of hundreds of millions, including the educated, such as doctors, lawyers, scientists, etc. This acquiescence is the result of the centuries of destruction and degradation of their ancestors' cultures, which demoralized them and ripped away their spirituality and heritage. In annihilating these cultures, the Christian conspirators also destroyed countless books and much learning, prizing the subsequent illiteracy and ignorance, which assisted in allowing for Christianity to spread. Wheless recounts the state of the world under Christian dominance:

> With the decline and fall of the Roman Empire the Christian religion spread and grew, among the Barbarian destroyers of Rome. The Dark Ages contemporaneously spread their intellectual pall over Europe. Scarcely any but priests and monks could read. Charlemagne learned to wield the pen only to the extent of scrawling his signature. The barons who wrested Magna Carta from John Lackland signed with their marks and seals. The worst criminals, provided they were endowed with the rare and magic virtue of knowing how to read even badly, enjoyed the "benefit of clergy" (i.e., of clerical learning), and escaped immune or with greatly mitigated punishment. There were no books save painfully-written manuscripts, worth the ransom of princes, and utterly unattainable except by the very wealthy and by the Church; not till about 1450 was the first printed book known in Europe. The Bible existed only in Hebrew, Greek, and Latin, and the ignorant masses were totally ignorant of it other than what they heard from the priests, who told them that they must believe it or be tortured and killed in life and damned forever in the fires of hell after death. It is no wonder

that faith flourished under conditions so exceptionally favorable.[25]

Such is the disgraceful history of the religion of the "gentle Prince of Peace." Yet, there are those today who not only support its monstrous edifice, built on the blood and charred bones of tens of millions, as well as on the death of learning in the Western world, but, unbelievably, wish it to be restored to its full "glory," with the whole bloody works, witchburnings, persecution, annihilation of unbelievers and all. The fact is that too much trauma and bloodshed have been caused throughout the millennia strictly on the basis of unfounded faith and excessive illogic, and too much knowledge and wisdom has been lost, such that human history has been rife with ignorance and misunderstanding. It is for these reasons, among others, including the restoration of humanity, that we hope the oppressive and exploitative conspiracy behind religion in general and Christianity in particular will be exposed. As it is said, those who do not remember the past are doomed to repeat it, and humans as a species are prone to amnesia. It is thus imperative that these all-important matters of religious ideology and doctrine be thoroughly explored and not left up to blind faith.

---

1. Pike, 164-5.
2. Carpenter, 118.
3. Walker, *WEMS*, 447.
4. *Jewish Encyclopedia*, 1905, 418; *Universal Jewish Encyclopedia*, 1943, "Hess, Moses," "Soviet Russia."
5. Walker, *WEMS*, 474.
6. Aarons and Loftus, xiii.
7. Walker, *WEMS*, 1061.
8. Wheless, *IIGW*.
9. Wells, *DJE*, 41.
10. Fox, 434.
11. Eusebius, xxvi.
12. Walker, *WDSSO*, 271-2.
13. Barnstone, 154.
14. *The Forgotten Books of Eden*, 187.
15. Wheless, *FC*, 303.
16. Taylor, 82-3.
17. Fox, 269.
18. Fox, 317.
19. Walker, *WEMS*, 760.
20. Walker, *WEMS*, 1039.
21. Walker, *WEMS*, 771.
22. Waite, 528.
23. Larson, 191.
24. Doane, 448-9.
25. Wheless, *IIGW*.

Jews of Trent, Italy, burned in 1475 on accusations of sacrificing Christian children. (Haught)

Protestants of Haarlem, Holland, executed in 1573 by Catholic troops. (Haught)

The Quest for Jesus Christ

In exploring the origins of Christianity, our focus naturally is turned to its purported founder and object of worship, Jesus Christ, whose story is told in the New Testament. So much interest and fascination have circulated around this wonderworker over the centuries that numerous and sizable tomes have been composed to fill out the New Testament tale by digging into the few clues as to Jesus's nature and historical background in order to produce a biographical sketch that either bolsters faith or reveals a more human side of this godman to which all can relate. Obviously, considering the time and energy spent on them, the subjects of Christianity and its legendary founder are very important to the Western mind and culture, and, increasingly to the Eastern as well. Nevertheless, little has come of all these efforts, as the "real" Jesus remains a phantom, mutating to suit the needs of the era and beholder.

In fact, it has been said that Jesus is all things to all people. This assertion is certainly true, as from the earliest times his nature and character have been interpreted and reinterpreted to fit the cultural context of his proponents and representatives. As Burton Mack says in *The Lost Gospel of Q*:

> In the course of Christian history, to take one example of a series of social and cultural shifts, the Christ has been refigured many times over. In the period before Constantine, when bishops were taking their place as the leaders of the churches, the Christ was commonly depicted as the good shepherd who could guide the flock to its heavenly home. After Constantine, the Christ was pictured as the victor over death and the ruler of the world. During the medieval period, when the church was the primary vehicle of both social and cultural tradition, the story of Christ's ascent from the cross (or the tomb) to the seat of sovereignty, judgment, and salvation in heaven focused the Christian imagination on a Christ of a truly comprehensive, three-decker world. Somewhat later we see the Gothic Christ appear, and then the Christ of the crucifix, the man of Galilee, the cosmic Christ, the feminine Christ, and so on. In every case, the rearrangements were necessary in order to adjust the mythic world to new social constraints and cultural systems of knowledge.[1]

In fact, Jesus began his omnipotent reign when sons of God and sacred kings were all the rage. After the shocking and bloody turmoil of the Middle Ages, however, he became in the minds of the desperate a compassionate yet human teacher of morality, since it was obvious he could not possibly have been supernaturally in charge of the church in his name, which was torturing and slaughtering by the millions. During the political upheavals of the 20th century, Jesus was considered a heroic revolutionary striving against oppression, as well as a communist. When various Indian gurus and yogis with their magic tricks became famous, it was fashionable to locate Jesus in India and/or Tibet. At that time too was the psychedelic explosion, such that Jesus soon became a magic mushroom. Within the "New Age" movement that began with the renaissance of spiritualism last century, he has become the "Cosmic Christ" and "Christ Consciousness." He has also of late become a black, a white supremacist, a gay, a woman, a heretic, a "Mediterranean peasant," an orthodox butcher whose name wasn't Jesus, a "Cynic-sage," an Arab, as well as the husband of Mary Magdalene and father of many children, from whom are descended at least one European royal family. Now, with the popular subject of UFOs and extraterrestrials, Jesus is an alien with extraordinary powers because he is of a superior race, with any number of "alien" groups laying claim to his parentage. As commander of an enormous spaceship, this alien Jesus is waiting in the wings to rapture true believers off the earth in the nick of time during the coming earth changes. In a sense, Jesus *is* an alien, in that people are so alienated from the actual history of the planet they cannot grasp his true nature.

Wells adds to the list of "biographies" of Jesus:

> In the past generation, the "real" Jesus has been variously a magician (Smith), a Galilean rabbi (Chilton), a marginal Jew (Meyer), a bastard (Schaberg), a cipher (Thiering), a Qumran dissident (Allegro, et al.), a gnosticising Jew (Koester), a dissident Jew (Vermes), a happily married man and father of sons (Spong), a bandit (Horsley), an enthusiastic (possible Zealot?) opponent of the Temple cult (Sanders). Perhaps most remarkable of all is the "real" Jesus of the Westar Project/Jesus Seminar whose existence has been pinned on just over thirty "authentic" sayings, derived from an eclectic application of biblical-critical axioms and confirmed by vote of the seminar members.[2]

Despite all of this literature continuously being cranked out, it is obvious that we are dealing not with biography but with speculation, and there remains in the public at large a serious and unfortunate lack of education regarding religion and mythology, particularly that of Christ. Indeed, the majority of people are taught in most schools and churches that Jesus Christ was an actual historical figure and that the only controversy regarding him is that some people accept him as the Son of God and the Messiah, while others do not. However, whereas this is the raging debate most evident today, it is not the most important. Shocking as it may seem to the general populace, *the most enduring and profound controversy in this subject is whether or not a person named Jesus Christ ever really existed.*

History and Positions of the Debate

The debate as to whether or not Jesus Christ is a historical character may not be apparent from publications readily found in popular bookstores; however, beginning over two centuries ago, a significant group of scholars started springing up to challenge long-held beliefs. In more recent times, this controversy erupted when GA Wells published *Did Jesus Exist?* and *The Historical Evidence for Jesus*, among others, which sought to prove that Jesus is a non-historical character. An attempt to repudiate Wells was made in *Jesus: The Evidence*, an entire (slim) volume written to establish that Jesus did exist. It should be noted that no such book would be needed if the existence of Jesus Christ as a historical figure were a proven fact accepted by all. In addition, it is not uncommon to hear in a discussion about Jesus something to the effect, "Don't get me wrong—I believe he existed," a strange declaration, since, according to popular belief, "Everybody knows he existed." Were the last assertion true, this type of doubtful "don't get me wrong" comment would not be necessary. No one discussing Abraham Lincoln, for example, needs to clarify her/his position by expressing the belief that Lincoln existed.

Indeed, it is such doubt, which has existed since the beginning of the Christian era, that has led many seekers of truth over the centuries to research thoroughly this important subject from an independent perspective and to produce an impressive volume of literature that, while hidden, suppressed or ignored, nevertheless has demonstrated logically and intelligently that Jesus Christ is a mythological character along the same lines as the gods of Egypt, England, Greece, India, Phoenicia, Rome, Sumeria and elsewhere, entities presently acknowledged by mainstream scholars and the masses alike as myths rather than historical figures. Delving deeply into this large body of work, one uncovers evidence that the Jesus character is in fact based upon these much older myths and heroes. One discovers that the gospel story is not, therefore, a historical representation of a Jewish rebel carpenter who had physical incarnation in the Levant 2,000 years ago. In other words, it has been demonstrated continually for centuries that the story of Jesus Christ was invented and did not depict a real person who was either a superhuman "son of God" or a man who was "evemeristically" built up into a superhuman fairytale by enthusiastic followers.

Within this debate regarding the nature and character of Jesus Christ, then, there have been three main schools of thought: the believers and the evemerists, both of which are historicizers, and the mythicists.

The Believers

The believers take the Judeo-Christian bible as the literal "Word of God," accepting "on faith" that everything contained within it is historical fact infallibly written by scribes "inspired by God." As we shall see, this position is absolutely untenable, and requires blind and unscientific devotion, since, even if we discount the countless mistakes committed over the centuries by scribes copying the texts, the so-called infallible "Word of God" is riddled with inconsistencies, contradictions, errors and yarns that stretch the credulity to the point of non-existence. In order to accept the alleged factuality of the Christian tale, i.e., that a male God came down from the heavens as his own son through the womb of a Jewish virgin, worked astonishing miracles, was killed, resurrected and ascended to heaven, we are not only to suspend critical thinking and integrity, but we must be prepared to tolerate a rather repulsive and generally false portrayal of the ancient world and peoples. In particular, we must be willing to believe fervently that the "gentle Jesus"—who was allegedly the all-powerful God—was mercilessly scourged, tortured and murdered by Romans and Jews, the latter of whom possess the ignominy and stigma of being considered for eternity as "vipers," "serpents," "spawn of Satan" and "Christkillers" guilty of deicide who gleefully shouted "Crucify him!" and "Let his blood be upon us and our children!"

In addition to this hideous notion, we are also expected to believe that the omnipotent and perfect God could only fix the world, which he created badly in the first place, by the act of blood-atonement, specifically with his own blood; yet, we know that such blood-atonement is rooted in the ancient custom of sacrificing humans and animals, serving basically as a barbaric, scapegoat ritual. Indeed, the sacrifice of God seems far worse than that of either animals or humans, yet this deicide is supposed to be one of the highest "religious" concepts. In fact, it is "God's plan!" As Kersey Graves says in *The World's 16 Crucified Saviors*:

> And hereafter, when they laugh at the Jewish superstition of a scape-goat, let them bear in mind that the more sensible and intelligent people may laugh in turn at their superstitious doctrine of a scape-God. . . . The blood of God must atone for the sins of the whole human family, as rams, goats, bullocks and other animals had atoned for the sins of families and nations under older systems. . . . Somebody must pay the penalty in blood, somebody must be slaughtered for every little foible or

peccadillo or moral blunder into which erring man may chance to stumble while upon the pilgrimage of life, while journeying through the wilderness of time, even if a God has to be dragged from his throne in heaven, and murdered to accomplish it. . . . Whose soul—possessing the slightest moral sensibility—does not inwardly and instinctively revolt at such a doctrine? . . . We hold the doctrine to be a high-handed insult to the All-Loving Father—who, were are told, is "long suffering in mercy," and "plentiful in forgiveness"—to charge *Him* with sanctioning such a doctrine, much less originating it.

In embracing Christianity as reality, we are also required to assume that, in order to get "his" important message across, "God" came to Earth in a remote area of the ancient world and spoke the increasingly obscure language of Aramaic, as opposed to the more universally spoken Greek or Latin. We must also be prepared to believe that there is now an invisible man of a particular ethnicity omnipresently floating about in the sky. In addition, we are asked to ridicule and dismiss as fiction the nearly identical legends and tales of many other cultures, while happily receiving the Christian fable as fact. This dogmatic stance in effect represents cultural bigotry and prejudice. All in all, in blindly believing we are faced with what can only appear to be an abhorrent and ludicrous plan on the part of "God."

The Evemerists

It is because of such irrational beliefs and prejudicial demands that many people have rejected Christian claims as being incredible and unappealing. Nevertheless, numerous such dissidents have maintained that behind the fabulous fairytales found in the gospels there *was* a historical Jesus Christ somewhere, an opinion usually based on the fact that it is commonly held, not because its proponents have studied the matter or seen clear evidence to that effect. This "meme" or mental programming of a historical Jesus has been pounded into the heads of billions of people for nearly 2,000 years, such that it is assumed *a priori* by many, including "scholars" who have put forth an array of clearly speculative hypotheses hung on highly tenuous threads regarding the "life of Jesus." Such speculators often claim that a historical Jewish master named Jesus was deified or "evemerized" by his zealous followers, who added to his mundane "history" a plethora of supernatural qualities and aspects widely found in more ancient myths and mystery religions.

This school of thought, called "Evemerism" or "Euhemerism," is named after Evemeras, or Euhemeros, a Greek philosopher of the 4th century BCE who developed the idea that, rather than being mythical creatures, as was accepted by the reigning intellectuals, the gods of old were in fact historical characters, kings, emperors and heroes whose exploits were later deified. Of these various evemerist "biographies," the most popular are that Jesus was a compassionate teacher who irritated the Romans with his goodness, or a political rebel who annoyed the Romans with his incitement of discord, for which he was executed. Wells comments upon the theory du jour:

> As political activism is today à la mode, it is widely felt that a revolutionary Jesus is more "relevant" than the Jesus of the nineteenth century liberal theologians who "went about doing good" (Acts, 10:38). Both these Jesuses simply reflect what in each case the commentators value most highly rather than the burden of the texts. If Jesus had been politically troublesome, his supporters would have been arrested with him. But there is no suggestion of this in any of the gospels.[3]

He further states:

> There are . . . three obvious difficulties against the supposition that a historical Jesus was actually executed as a rebel:
>
> (ii) All Christian documents earlier than the gospels portray him in a way hardly compatible with the view that he was a political agitator . . .
>
> (ii) If his activities had been primarily political, and the evangelists were not interested in—or deemed it inexpedient to mention—his politics, then what was the motive for their strong interest in him? How did they come to suppose that a rebel, whose revolutionary views they tried to suppress in their gospels, was the universal saviour?
>
> (iii) If such an episode as the cleansing of the temple was not a religious act (as the gospels allege) but an armed attempt to capture the building and to precipitate a general insurrection, then why does Josephus say nothing of it? As Trocmé has observed . . . a military attack on the temple would not have been ignored by this writer who was so concerned to show the dangers of revolt and violence. Josephus' silence is corroborated by the positive affirmation of Tacitus that there was no disturbance in Palestine under Tiberius (AD 14-37), whereas the preceding and following reigns were characterized by rebellion and unrest there . . . [4]

Of these various "lives of Jesus," Wells also says:

> It is now customary to dismiss with contempt many nineteenth-century lives of Jesus on the grounds that their authors simply found in him all the qualities which they themselves considered estimable. But the wide circulation today of books which portray

him as a rebel seems yet another illustration of the same phenomenon.[5]

Evemerist scholar Shaye Cohen, professor of Judaic and Religion Studies at Brown University, admits the desperate situation of trying to find this "historical" reformer/rebel under the accreted layers of miracles:

> Modern scholars have routinely reinvented Jesus or have routinely rediscovered in Jesus that which they want to find, be it rationalist, liberal Christianity of the 19th century, be it apocalyptic miracle workers in the 20th, be it revolutionaries, or be it whatever it is that they're looking for, scholars have been able to find in Jesus almost anything that they want to find. Even in our own age scholars are still doing this. People are still trying to figure out the authentic sayings of Jesus. . ., all our middle class liberal Protestant scholars. . . will take a vote and decide what Jesus should have said, or might have said. And no doubt their votes reflect their own deep-seated, very sincere, very authentic Christian values, which I don't gainsay for a moment. But their product is, of course, bedeviled by the problem that we are unable to have any secure criteria by which to distinguish the real from the mythic or what we want to be so from what actually was so. . . .

These various theories in the end constitute wheel-spinning in a futile effort to rescue historicity, *any* historicity, in the gospel tale. Because of the dearth of personality in the gospels and the irrationality of the tale, historicizers must imbue the character with their own personalities and interpretations of reality, such as: "When Jesus said, 'Blessed are the poor,' he surely didn't mean that poverty is a blessing but that those who lived with poverty are good, because they are not resorting to robbery."[6] And in order to pad out the "real" Jesus after most of his "life" is removed, scholars must resort to reasoning of the most tortured kind:

> While the miracles of Jesus could easily be created and multiplied by the credulity of His followers, [the followers] could never have devised ethical, speculative, or soteriological doctrines, which, although *in no instance original*, presented new combinations of established religious concepts and ethical principles.[7]

Thus, we have an admission that Jesus brought nothing new, but an insistence nevertheless that Jesus deserved merit because he novelly combined his unoriginal concepts. In reality, this type of eclecticism also was not new but quite common long before the Christ character arose. In *The Historical Jesus and the Mythical Christ*, Gerald Massey says of these scholars' efforts:

It is pitiful to track the poor faithful gleaners who picked up every fallen fragment or scattered waif and stray of the mythos, and to watch how they treasured every trait and tint of the ideal Christ to make up the personal portrait of their own supposed real one.[8]

In *Ancient History of the God Jesus*, Edouard Dujardin remarks of Evemerism:

> This doctrine is nowadays discredited except in the case of Jesus. No scholar believes that Osiris or Jupiter or Dionysus was an historical person promoted to the rank of a god, but exception is made only in favour of Jesus. . . . It is impossible to rest the colossal work of Christianity on Jesus, if he was a man.

Indeed, evemerist scholars will admit that this humanized Jesus stripped of all miracles would not have "made a blip on Pilate's radar screen," being insignificant as one of the innumerable rabblerousers running about Palestine during this time. If we were to take away all the miraculous events surrounding the story of Jesus to reveal a human, we would certainly find no one who could have garnered huge crowds around him because of his preaching. And the fact is that this crowd-drawing preacher finds his place in "history" only in the New Testament, completely overlooked by the dozens of historians of his day, an era considered one of the best documented in history. Such an invisible character, then, could never have become a god worshipped by millions.

In fact, the standard Christian response to the evemerists has been that no such Jesus, stripped of his miracles and other supernatural attributes, could ever "have been adored as a god or even been saluted as the Messiah of Israel." This response is quite accurate: No mere man could have caused such a hullabaloo and hellish fanaticism, the product of which has been the unending spilling of blood and the enslavement of the spirit. The crazed "inspiration" that has kept the Church afloat merely confirms the mythological origins of this tale. Furthermore, the theory of Evemerism has served the Catholic Church, as Higgins remarks:

> . . . that the gods of the ancients were nothing but the heroes or benefactors of mankind, living in very illiterate and remote ages, to whom a grateful posterity paid divine honors . . . appears at first sight to be probable; and as it has served the purpose of the Christian priests, to enable them to run down the religion of the ancients, and, in exposing its absurdities, to contrast it disadvantageously with their own, [Evemerism] has been, and continues to be, sedulously inculcated, in every public and private seminary. . . . Although the pretended worship of Heroes appears at first sight plausible, very little depth of thought or

learning is requisite to discover that it has not much foundation
in truth. . . .[9]

In *Pagan Christs*, JM Robertson states of Evemerism:

> It is not the ascription of prodigies to some remarkable man that
> leads us to doubt his reality. Each case must be considered on
> its merits when we apply the tests of historical evidence. We
> must distinguish between what the imagination has added to a
> meager biography, and those cases in which the biography itself
> has been added to what has grown out of a ritual or doctrine.[10]

The bottom line is that when one removes all the elements of
those preceding myths that contributed to the formation of the
Jewish godman, there remains no one and nothing historical left
to which to point. As Walker says, "Scholars' efforts to eliminate
paganism from the Gospels in order to find a historical Jesus
have proved as hopeless as searching for a core in an onion."
Massey remarks, ". . . a composite likeness of twenty different
persons merged in one . . . is not *anybody*." And, it is clear that in
their desperate attempts, evemerist scholars have added their
own likenesses to the composite.

The Mythicists

This missing core to the onion has been recognized by many
individuals over the centuries who have thus been unable to
accept the historical nature of Jesus Christ, because not only is
there no proof of his existence but virtually all evidence points to
him being a mythological character. As stated, this "Mythicist
School" began to flourish starting a few hundred years ago,
propelled by archaeological and linguistical discoveries and
studies, as well as by the reduction of the Church's power and
vicious persecution of its critics. This group has consisted of a
number of erudite and daring individuals who have overcome the
conditioning of their culture to peer closely and with clear eyes
into the murky origins of the Christian faith. Massey elucidates
the mythicists' perspective:

> The general assumption concerning the canonical gospels is that
> the historic element was the kernel of the whole, and that the
> fables accreted round it; whereas the mythos, being pre-extant,
> proves the core of the matter was mythical, and it follows that
> the history is incremental. . . . It was the human history that
> accreted round the divinity, and not a human being who became
> divine.[11]

While the mythicist school has only made real inroads in the
past couple of centuries, and even though its brilliant work and
insight have been ignored by mainstream "experts" in both the
believing and evemerist camps, the mythicist arguments have

been built upon a long line of Bible criticism. Indeed, this controversy has existed from the very beginning as is evidenced by the writings of the Church fathers themselves, i.e., those who founded the Christian Church, who revealed that they were constantly forced by the "Pagan" intelligentsia to defend what the non-Christians and other Christians ("heretics") alike saw as a preposterous and fabricated yarn with absolutely no evidence of it ever having taken place in history. As Rev. Robert Taylor says in *The Diegesis*, "And from the apostolic age downwards, in a never interrupted succession, but never so strongly and emphatically as in the most primitive times, was the existence of Christ as a man most strenuously denied." In fact, as Taylor also states:

> Those who denied the *humanity* of Christ were the first class of professing Christians, and not only first in order of time, but in dignity of character, in intelligence, and in moral influence. . . . The deniers of the humanity of Christ, or, in a word, professing Christians, who denied that any such man as Jesus Christ ever existed at all, but who took the name Jesus Christ to signify only an abstraction, or prosopopoeia, the *principle of Reason* personified; and who understood the whole gospel story to be a sublime allegory . . . these were the first, and (it is not dishonour to Christianity to pronounce them) the best and most rational Christians.

Again, this denial of Christ in the flesh is found numerous times in the writings of the day, including the New Testament itself, yet it is ignored by historicizers, believers and evemerists alike. Indeed, in their "exhaustive" research into this all-important subject, historicizers have either wilfully and unreasonably ignored the great minds of the mythicist school or have never come across them. If we assume that the historicizers' disregard of these scholars is deliberate, we can only conclude that it is because the mythicists' arguments have been too intelligent and knifelike to do away with. Of course, the works of the mythicists have not been made readily available to the public, no doubt fearfully suppressed because they are somewhat irrefutable, so we cannot completely fault the "experts" for having never read them. The arguments of these particular mythicists are, however, the most important work done in this field to date, so any refutation that has not dealt with them properly is neither exhaustive nor convincing.

Those historicizers who have acknowledged the mythicists' contentions, not being able to refute the voluminous amount of evidence as to Christ's mythical nature, are forced to dismiss the mythicists' research and conclusions by claiming their work to be "outdated." Yet, the mythicist argument has existed from the beginning of the Christian era, and there is still no cogent argument that demonstrates it to be "outdated." Also, if it is "outdated" merely because it comes before, how much more outdated is the Bible, which came even more so before?

It is also claimed that the mythicists make too much of the Pagan origins and ignore the Jewish aspects of the Gospel tale. The Jewish elements, argue historicizers, must be historical and, therefore, Jesus existed. Specious and sophistic though it may be, since anyone can interpolate quasi-historical data into a fictional story—and many people have done so, from the composers of *The Iliad* to those of the Old Testament and any number of other novels—this historicizer argument has conveniently allowed for the dismissal of the entire mythicist school, despite the overwhelming evidence in its favor and absolute dearth thereof in the historical camp.

The fact is that it is historicizing scholars themselves who do not pay enough attention to the Jewish aspects, because if they did, they would discover that these elements are frequently erroneous, anachronistic and indicative of a lack of knowledge about geography and other details that would not have been so, had the writers been indigenous to the era and eyewitnesses to the events.

Massey summarizes the mythicist position:

> It can be demonstrated that Christianity pre-existed without the Personal Christ, that it was continued by Christians who entirely rejected the historical character in the second century, and that the supposed historic portraiture in the Canonical Gospels was extant as mythical and mystical before the Gospels themselves existed.[12]

And he further states, "Whether considered as the God made human, or as man made divine, this character never existed as a person."[13] Moreover, the claim of preexistence of the gospel portraiture was repeatedly confirmed by Christians, as shall be seen. According to the mythicist school, then, the New Testament could rightly be called, "Gospel Fictions" and the Christian religion could be termed the "Christ Conspiracy."

---

1. Mack, 210.
2. Wells, *JL*, viii.
3. Wells, *WWJ*, 137.
4. Wells, *DJE*, 160.
5. Wells, *DJE*, 176.
6. Larson.
7. Larson, 352.
8. Massey, *HJMC*, 170.
9. Higgins, I, 44.
10. Robertson, 96.
11. Massey, *HJMC*.

12. Massey, *GHC*, 2.
13. Massey, *GHC*, 22.

The Holy Forgery Mill

J'accuse!

From the very beginning of our quest to unravel the Christ conspiracy, we encounter suspicious territory, as we look back in time and discover that the real foundation of Christianity appears nothing like the image provided by the clergy and mainstream authorities. Indeed, far more rosy and cheerful than the reality is the picture painted by the vested interests as to the origins of the Christian religion: To wit, a miracle-making founder and pious, inspired apostles who faithfully and infallibly recorded his words and deeds shortly after his advent, and then went about promulgating the faith with great gusto and success in "saving souls." Contrary to this popular delusion, the reality is that, in addition to the enormous amount of bloodshed which accompanied its foundation, Christianity's history is rife with forgery and fraud. So rampant is this treachery and chicanery that any serious researcher must immediately begin to wonder about the story itself. In truth, the Christian tale has always been as difficult to swallow as the myths and fables of other cultures; yet countless people have been able to overlook the rational mind and to willingly believe it, even though they may equally as easily dismiss the nearly identical stories of these other cultures.

Indeed, the story of Jesus as presented in the gospels, mass of impossibilities and contradictions that it is, has been so difficult to believe that even the fanatic Christian "doctor" and saint, Augustine (354-430), admitted, "I should not believe in the truth of the Gospels unless the authority of the Catholic Church forced me to do so."[1] Nevertheless, the "monumentally superstitious and credulous Child of Faith" Augustine must not have been too resistant, because he already accepted "as historic truth the fabulous founding of Rome by Romulus and Remus, their virgin-birth by the god Mars, and their nursing by the she-wolf . . ."[2]

Apparently unable to convince himself rationally of the validity of his faith, early Church father Tertullian (c. 160-200) made the notorious statement, *"Credo quia incredibilis est—I believe because it is unbelievable."*[3] An "ex-Pagan," Tertullian vehemently and irrationally defended his new faith, considered fabricated by other Pagans, by acknowledging that Christianity was "a shameful thing" and "monstrously absurd":

> . . . I maintain that the Son of God was born; why am I not ashamed of maintaining such a thing? Why! but because it is itself a shameful thing. I maintain that the Son of God died: well, that is wholly credible because it is monstrously absurd. I

maintain that after having been buried, he rose again: and that I take to be absolutely true, because it was manifestly impossible.[4]

In addition to confessions of incredulity by Pagans and Christians alike, we also encounter repeated accusations and admissions of forgery and fraud. While the masses are led to believe that the Christian religion was founded by a historical wonderworker and his devoted eyewitnesses who accurately wrote down the events of his life and ministry in marvelous books that became "God's Word," the reality is that none of the gospels was written by its purported author and, indeed, no mention of any New Testament text can be found in writings prior to the beginning of the second century of the Common Era ("CE"), long after the purported events. These "holy" books, then, so revered by devotees, turn out to be spurious, and since it is in them that we find the story of Christ, we must be doubtful as to its validity as well.

Regarding the canonical gospels, Wheless states:

The gospels are all priestly forgeries over a century after their pretended dates. . . . As said by the great critic, Salomon Reinach, "With the exception of Papias, who speaks of a narrative by Mark, and a collection of sayings of Jesus, no Christian writer of the first half of the second century (i.e., *up to* 150 A.D.) quotes the Gospels or their reputed authors."[5]

Bronson Keeler, in *A Short History of the Bible*, concurs:

They are not heard of till 150 A.D., that is, till Jesus had been dead nearly a hundred and twenty years. No writer before 150 A.D. makes the slightest mention of them.[6]

In *The Book Your Church Doesn't Want You to Read*, John Remsburg elucidates:

The Four Gospels were unknown to the early Christian Fathers. Justin Martyr, the most eminent of the early Fathers, wrote about the middle of the second century. His writings in proof of the divinity of Christ demanded the use of these Gospels, had they existed in his time. He makes more than 300 quotations from the books of the Old Testament, and nearly one hundred from the Apocryphal books of the New Testament; but none from the four Gospels. Rev. Giles says: "The very names of the Evangelists, Matthew, Mark, Luke and John, are never mentioned by him (Justin)—do not occur once in all his writings."[7]

And Waite says:

At the very threshold of the subject, we are met by the fact, that nowhere in all the writings of Justin, does he once so much as mention any of these gospels. Nor does he mention either of their supposed authors, except John. Once his name occurs; not, however, as the author of a gospel, but in such a connection as raises a very strong presumption that Justin knew of no gospel of John the Apostle.[8]

Waite further states:

No one of the four gospels is mentioned in any other part of the New Testament. . . . No work of art of any kind has ever been discovered, no painting, or engraving, no sculpture, or other relic of antiquity, which may be looked upon as furnishing additional evidence of the existence of those gospels, and which was executed earlier than the latter part of the second century. Even the exploration of the Christian catacombs failed to bring to light any evidence of that character. . . . The four gospels were written in Greek, and there was no translation of them into other languages, earlier than the third century.[9]

In *The Woman's Encyclopedia of Myths and Secrets*, Barbara Walker relates:

The discovery that the Gospels were forged, centuries later than the events they described, is still not widely known even though the Catholic Encyclopedia admits, "The idea of a complete and clear-cut canon of the New Testament existing from the beginning . . . has no foundation in history." No extant manuscript can be dated earlier than the 4th century A.D.; most were written even later. The oldest manuscripts contradict one another, as also do even the present canon of synoptic Gospels.[10]

In fact, as Waite says, "Nearly every thing written concerning the gospels to the year 325, and all the copies of the gospels themselves to the same period, are lost or destroyed."[11] The truth is that very few early Christian texts exist because the autographs, or originals, were destroyed after the Council of Nicea and the "retouching" of 506 CE under Emperor Anastasius, which included "revision" of the Church fathers' works,[12] catastrophic acts that would be inconceivable if these "documents" were truly the precious testaments of the very Apostles themselves regarding the "Lord and Savior," whose alleged advent was so significant that it sparked profound fanaticism and endless wars. Repeating what would appear to be utter blasphemy, in the 11th and 12th centuries the "infallible Word of God" was "corrected" again by a variety of church officials. In addition to these major "revisions" have been many others, including copying and translation mistakes and deliberate mutilation and obfuscation of meaning.

It has never been only nonbelieving detractors who have made such allegations of falsification and deceit by the biblical writers. Indeed, those individuals who concocted some of the hundreds of "alternative" gospels and epistles being circulated during the first several centuries even admitted that they forged the texts. Of these numerous manuscripts, the *Catholic Encyclopedia* acknowledges, as quoted by Wheless:

> Enterprising spirits responded to this natural craving *by pretended gospels* full of romantic fables, and fantastic and striking details; their fabrications were eagerly read and *accepted as true* by common folk who were *devoid of any critical faculty* and who *were predisposed to believe* what so luxuriously fed their pious curiosity. Both Catholics and Gnostics were concerned in writing these fictions. The *former* had no motive other than that of a PIOUS FRAUD.[13]

Forgery during the first centuries of the Church's existence was thus admittedly rampant, so common in fact that this phrase, "pious fraud," was coined to describe it. Furthermore, while admitting that the Catholics were engaged in fraud, the *Catholic Encyclopedia* is also implying that the Gnostics were truthful in regard to the fictitious and allegorical nature of their texts. Regarding this Catholic habit of fraud, Mangasarian states in *The Truth about Jesus*:

> The church historian, Mosheim, writes that, "The Christian Fathers deemed it a pious act to employ deception and fraud." . . . Again, he says: "The greatest and most pious teachers were nearly all of them infected with this leprosy." Will not some believer tell us why forgery and fraud were necessary to prove the historicity of Jesus. . . . Another historian, Milman, writes that, "Pious fraud was admitted and avowed by the early missionaries of Jesus." "It was an age of literary frauds," writes Bishop Ellicott, speaking of the times immediately following the alleged crucifixion of Jesus. Dr. Giles declares that, "There can be no doubt that great numbers of books were written with no other purpose than to deceive." And it is the opinion of Dr. Robertson Smith that, "There was an enormous floating mass of spurious literature created to suit party views."[14]

So fundamental to "the faith" was fraud that Wheless remarked:

> The clerical confessions of lies and frauds in the ponderous volumes of the *Catholic Encyclopedia* alone suffice . . . to wreck the Church and to destroy utterly the Christian religion. . . . The Church exists mostly for wealth and self-aggrandizement; to quit paying money to the priests would kill the whole scheme in a couple of years. This is the sovereign remedy.[15]

According to Christian father and Church historian Eusebius (260?-340?), Bishop of Corinth Dionysius lashed out against forgers who had mutilated not only his letters but the gospels themselves:

> When my fellow-Christians invited me to write letters to them I did so. These the devil's apostles have filled with tares, taking

away some things and adding others. . . . Small wonder then if
some have dared to tamper even with the word of the Lord
Himself, when they have conspired to mutilate my own humble
efforts.[16]

These statements by Dionysius imply that the letters and
gospels were mutilated by his "fellow-Christians" themselves, as
the letters were presumably in their possession, unless they were
hijacked along the way by some other "devil's apostles," and as
the "the word of the Lord" certainly was in the possession of
Christians and no others.

In addition, a number of the fathers, such as Eusebius
himself, were determined by their own peers to be unbelievable
liars who regularly wrote their own fictions of what "the Lord"
said and did during "his" alleged sojourn upon the earth. In one
of his works, Eusebius provides a handy chapter entitled: "How it
may be Lawful and Fitting to use Falsehood as Medicine, and for
the Benefit of those who Want to be Deceived." Of Eusebius,
Waite writes, "Not only the most unblushing falsehoods, but
literary forgeries of the vilest character, darken the pages of his
apologetic and historical writings."[17]

Wheless also calls Justin Martyr, Tertullian and Eusebius
"three luminous liars."[18] Keeler states, "The early Christian
fathers were extremely ignorant and superstitious; and they were
singularly incompetent to deal with the supernatural." Larson
concludes that many early bishops "like Jerome, Antony, and St.
Martin, were definitely psychotic. In fact, there was scarcely a
single Father in the ancient Church who was not tainted with
heresy, mental aberration, or moral enormity."[19] Thus, deceiving,
mentally ill individuals basically constitute the genesis of
Christianity.

Of their products, Wheless further remarks:

If the pious Christians, confessedly, committed so many and so
extensive forgeries and frauds to adapt these popular Jewish
fairy-tales of their God and holy Worthies to the new Christian
Jesus and his Apostles, we need feel no surprise when we
discover these same Christians forging outright new
wonder-tales of their Christ under the fiction of the most noted
Christian names and in the guise of inspired Gospels, Epistles,
Acts and Apocalypses. . . . [20]

He continues:

Half a hundred of false and forged Apostolic "Gospels of Jesus
Christ," together with more numerous other "Scripture" forgeries,
was the output, so far as known now, of the lying pens of the
pious Christians of the first two centuries of the Christian "Age of
Apocryphal Literature" . . . [21]

Wheless also reports the Protestant *Encyclopedia Biblica* as stating, "Almost every one of the Apostles had a Gospel fathered upon him by one early sect or another."[22]

Doane relates the words of Dr. Conyers Middleton on the subject of biblical forgery:

> There never was any period of time in all ecclesiastical history, in which so many rank heresies were publicly professed, nor in which so many spurious books were forged and published by the Christians, under the names of Christ, and the Apostles, and the Apostolic writers, as in those primitive ages. Several of these forged books are frequently cited and applied to the defense of Christianity, by the most eminent fathers of the same ages, as true and genuine pieces.[23]

Wheless demonstrates how low the fathers and *doctors* of texts were willing to stoop:

> . . . If the Gospel tales were true, why should God need pious lies to give them credit? Lies and forgeries are only needed to bolster up falsehood: "Nothing stands in need of lying but a lie." But Jesus Christ must needs be propagated by lies upon lies; and what better proof of his actuality than to exhibit letters written by him in his own handwriting? The "Little Liars of the Lord" were equal to the forgery of the signature of their God—false letters in his name, as above cited from that exhaustless mine of clerical falsities, the *Catholic Encyclopedia* [CE].[24]

Indeed, Christian tradition pretends that Christ was extremely renowned even during his own time, having exchanged correspondence with King Abgar of Syria, who was most pleased to have the Christian savior take refuge in his country. Of course this story and the silly letters alleged to have been exchanged between the two are as phony as three-dollar bills, illustrating the ridiculous mendacity to which historicizers had to resort to place their invented character and drama at this time.

Furthermore, the forgers were not very skilled or conscientious, such that they left many clues as to their underhanded endeavors. As Wheless states, ". . . the Hebrew and Greek religious forgers were so ignorant or careless of the principles of criticism, that they 'interpolated' their fraudulent new matter into old manuscripts without taking care to erase or suppress the previous statements glaringly contradicted by the new interpolations."[25]

We have established the atmosphere of the foundation of Christianity: conspiracy, forgery and fraud, the result of which are its sacred texts, falsely alleged to be infallible accounts by eyewitnesses to the most extraordinary events in human "history." Let us now examine the "evidence" left to us by these pious forgers as to the "historicity" of the great savior and godman Jesus Christ.

---

1. Steiner, 168.
2. Wheless, *FC*, 163.
3. Wheless, *FC*, 145.
4. Doane, 412.
5. Wheless, *FC*, 94.
6. Keeler, 23.
7. Leedom, 173.
8. Waite, 307.
9. Waite, 346.
10. Walker, *WEMS*, 469.
11. Waite, 461.
12. Higgins, I, 680.
13. Wheless, *FC*, 99-100.
14. www.infidels.org
15. Wheless, xxxi.
16. Eusebius, 132.
17. Waite, 328.
18. Wheless, *FC*, 105.
19. Larson, 506.
20. Wheless, *FC*, 67.
21. Wheless, *FC*, 101.
22. Wheless, 102.
23. Doane, 459.
24. Wheless, *FC*, 109.
25. Wheless, *FC*, 178.

Biblical Sources

The story of Jesus Christ can be found only in the forged books of the New Testament, an assortment of gospels and epistles that required many centuries and hands to create. As Dr. Lardner said, ". . . even so late as the middle of the sixth century, the canon of the New Testament had not been settled by any authority that was decisive and universally acknowledged. . ."[1] Mead describes the confused compilation of the "infallible Word of God":

> The New Testament is not a single book but a collection of groups of books and single volumes, which were at first and even long afterwards circulated separately. . . . the Gospels are found in any and every order. . . . Egyptian tradition places Jn. first among the Gospels.[2]

In fact, it took well over a thousand years to canonize the New Testament, and the Old Testament canon remains different to this day in the Catholic and Protestant versions. This canonization also required many councils to decide which books were to be considered "inspired" and which "spurious." Contrary to the impression given, these councils were not peaceful gatherings of the "good shepherds of Christ" but raucous free-for-alls between bands of thugs and their arrogant and insane bishops. As Keeler says:

> The reader would err greatly did he suppose that in these assemblies one or two hundred gentlemen sat down to discuss quietly and dignifiedly the questions which had come before them for settlement. On the contrary, many of the bishops were ignorant ruffians, and were followed by crowds of vicious supporters who stood ready on the slightest excuse to maim and kill their opponents.[3]

In fact, at the Council of Ephesus in 431 mobs consisting of the dregs of society and representing the warring factions of Antioch and Alexandria broke out in riots and killed many of each other. This melee was merely one of many, and this shedding of blood by Christian followers was only the beginning of a hideous centuries-long legacy.

Church historian Eusebius admits the chaotic atmosphere of the Christian foundation:

> But increasing freedom transformed our character to arrogance and sloth; we began envying and abusing each other, cutting our own throats, as occasion offered, with weapons of sharp-edged words; rulers hurled themselves at rulers and laymen waged party fights against laymen, and unspeakable hypocrisy and dissimulation were carried to the limit of wickedness. . . . Those

of us who were supposed to be pastors cast off the restraining influence of the fear of God and quarrelled heatedly with each other, engaged solely in swelling the disputes, threats, envy, and mutual hostility and hate, frantically demanding the despotic power they coveted.[4]

Such were the means by which the New Testament was finally canonized. Concerning the NT as it stands today, Wheless says:

> The 27 New Testament booklets, attributed to eight individual "Apostolic" writers, and culled from some 200 admitted forgeries called Gospels, Acts, and Epistles, constitute the present "canonical" or acceptedly inspired compendium of the primitive history of Christianity.[5]

The various gospels, of which only four are now accepted as "canonical" or "genuine," are in actuality not the earliest Christian texts. The earliest canonical texts are demonstrably the Epistles of Paul, so it is to them that we must first turn in our investigation.

The Epistles

The various Pauline epistles contained in the New Testament form an important part of Christianity, yet these "earliest" of Christian texts never discuss a historical background of Jesus, even though Paul purportedly lived during and after Jesus's advent and surely would have known about his master's miraculous life. Instead, these letters deal with a spiritual construct found in various religions, sects, cults and mystery schools for hundreds to thousands of years prior to the Christian era. As Dujardin points out, the Pauline literature "does not refer to Pilate or the Romans, or Caiaphas, or the Sanhedrin, or Herod or Judas, or the holy women, or any person in the gospel account of the Passion, and that it also never makes any allusion to them; lastly, that it mentions absolutely none of the events of the Passion, either directly or by way of allusion."[6]

Mangasarian notes that Paul also never quotes from Jesus's purported sermons and speeches, parables and prayers, nor does he mention Jesus's supernatural birth or any of his alleged wonders and miracles, all of which would presumably be very important to Jesus's followers, had such exploits and sayings been known prior to Paul. Mangasarian then understandably asks:

> Is it conceivable that a preacher of Jesus could go throughout the world to convert people to the teachings of Jesus, as Paul did, without ever quoting a single one of his sayings? Had Paul known that Jesus had preached a sermon, or formulated a prayer, or said many inspired things about the here and the hereafter, he could not have helped quoting, now and then, from

the words of his master. If Christianity could have been established without a knowledge of the teachings of Jesus, why then, did Jesus come to teach, and why were his teachings preserved by divine inspiration?. . . If Paul knew of a miracle-working Jesus, one who could feed the multitude with a few loaves and fishes, who could command the grave to open, who could cast out devils, and cleanse the land of the foulest disease of leprosy, who could, and did, perform many other wonderful works to convince the unbelieving generation of his divinity—is it conceivable that either intentionally or inadvertently he would have never once referred to them in all his preaching?. . . The position, then, that there is not a single saying of Jesus in the gospels which is quoted by Paul in his many epistles is unassailable, and certainly fatal to the historicity of the gospel Jesus.

In fact, even though the "Lord's Prayer" is clearly spelled out in the gospels as being given directly from Jesus's mouth, Paul expresses that he does not know how to pray. Paul's Jesus is also very different from that of the gospels. As Wells says:

. . . these epistles are not merely astoundingly silent about the historical Jesus, but also that the Jesus of Paul's letters (the earliest of the NT epistles and hence the earliest extant Christian documents) is in some respects incompatible with the Jesus of the gospels; that neither Paul, nor those of his Christian predecessors whose views he assimilates into his letters, nor the Christian teachers he attacks in them, are concerned with such a person. . .[7]

So it appears that Paul, even though he speaks of "the gospel," had never heard of the canonical gospels or even an orally transmitted life of Christ. The few "historical" references to an actual life of Jesus cited in the epistles are demonstrably interpolations and forgeries, as are the epistles themselves, not having been written by the Pharisee/Roman "Paul" at all, as related by Wheless:

The entire "Pauline group" is the same forged class . . . says *E.B.* [*Encyclopedia Biblica*] . . . "With respect to the canonical Pauline Epistles, ... there are *none of them by Paul*; neither fourteen, nor thirteen, nor nine or eight, nor yet even the four so long 'universally' regarded as unassailable. They *are all, without distinction, pseudographia* (false-writings, forgeries). . ." They are thus all uninspired anonymous church forgeries for Christ's sweet sake![8]

In *The Myth of the Historical Jesus*, Hayyim ben Yehoshua evinces that the orthodox dates of the Pauline epistles (c. 49-70) cannot be maintained, also introducing one of the most important individuals in the formation of Christianity, the Gnostic-Christian "heretic" Marcion of Pontus (c. 100-160), a well-educated "man of letters" who entered the brotherhood and basically took the reins of the fledgling Gnostic-Christian movement:

> We now turn to the epistles supposedly written by Paul. The *First Epistle of Paul to Timothy* warns against the Marcionist work known as the *Antithesis*. Marcion was expelled from the Church of Rome in c. 144 C.E. and the *First Epistle of Paul to Timothy* was written shortly afterwards. Thus we again have a clear case of pseudepigraphy. The *Second Epistle of Paul to Timothy* and the *Epistle of Paul to Titus* were written by the same author and date to about the same period. These three epistles are known as the "pastoral epistles." The ten remaining "non-pastoral" epistles written in the name of Paul, were known to Marcion by c. 140 C.E. Some of them were not written in Paul's name alone but are in the form of letters written by Paul in collaboration with various friends such as Sosthenes, Timothy, and Silas. . . . The non-canonical *First Epistle of Clement to the Corinthians* (written c. 125 C.E.) uses the *First Epistle of Paul to the Corinthians* as a source and so we can narrow down the date for that epistle to c. 100-125 C.E. However, we are left with the conclusion that all the Pauline epistles are pseudepigraphic. (The semi-mythical Paul was supposed to have died during the persecutions instigated by Nero in c. 64 C.E.) Some of the Pauline epistles appear to be have been altered and edited numerous times before reaching their modern forms. . . . We may thus conclude that they provide no historical evidence of Jesus.

It is clear that the epistles do not demonstrate a historical Jesus and are not as early as they are pretended to be, written or edited by a number of hands over several decades during the second century, such that the "historical" Jesus apparently was not even known at that late point. As is also evidenced, these texts were further mutilated over the centuries.

The Gospels

Although they are held up by true believers to be the "inspired" works of the apostles, the canonical gospels were forged at the end of the 2nd century, all four of them probably between 170-180, a date that just happens to correspond with the establishment of the orthodoxy and supremacy of the Roman Church. Despite the claims of apostolic authorship, the gospels were not mere translations of manuscripts written in Hebrew or Aramaic by Jewish apostles, because they were originally written in Greek. As Waite relates:

> It is noticeable that in every place in the gospels but one (and the total number is nearly a hundred) where Peter is mentioned, the Greek name "Petros" is given, which is supposed to be used by Jews as well as others. This would indicate that all the canonical gospels, Matthew included, are original Greek productions.[9]

Of these Greek texts and their pretended apostolic attribution, Wells states:

> . . . a Galilean fisherman could not have written what Kümmel calls such "cultivated Greek," with "many rhetorical devices," and with all the Old Testament quotations and allusions deriving from the Greek version of these scriptures, not from the Hebrew original.[10]

Furthermore, as stated and as is also admitted by the writer of Luke when he says that there were many versions of "the narrative," there were numerous gospels in circulation prior to the composition of his gospel. In fact, of the dozens of gospels that existed during the first centuries of the Christian era, several once considered canonical or genuine were later rejected as "apocryphal" or spurious, and vice versa.

Out of these numerous gospels the canonical gospels were chosen by Church father and bishop of Lyons, Irenaeus (c. 120-c. 200), who claimed that the number four was based on the "four corners of the world." In reality, this comment is Masonic, and these texts represent the four books of magic of the Egyptian Ritual,[11] facts that provide hints as to where our quest is heading.

According to some early Christians, the gospel of Matthew is the earliest, which is why it appears first in the canon. However, as noted, the gospels have been arranged in virtually every order, and scholars of the past few centuries have considered Mark to be the earliest, used by the writers/compilers of Matthew and Luke. Going against this trend, Waite evinced that Luke was first, followed by Mark, John and Matthew. In fact, these gospels were written not from each other but from common source material, including the narrative, or *Diegesis*, as it is in the original Greek. The first gospel of the "narrative" type, in actuality, appears to have been the proto-Lukan text, the "Gospel of the Lord," published in Rome by the Gnostic-Christian Marcion, as part of his "New Testament." As Waite relates:

> The first New Testament that ever appeared, was compiled and published by Marcion. It was in the Greek language. It consisted of "The Gospel," and "The Apostolicon." No acts—no Revelation, and but one gospel. The Apostolicon comprised ten of Paul's Epistles, as follows: Galatians, 1st and 2nd Corinthians, Romans, except the 15th and 16th chapters, 1st and 2nd Thessalonians, Ephesians, Colossians, Philemon and Philippians; arranged in the order as here named. This canon of the New Testament was prepared and published shortly after his arrival in Rome; probably about 145 A.D. Baring-Gould thinks he brought the gospel from Sinope. . . . [Marcion's] gospel resembles the Gospel of Luke, but is much shorter.[12]

It is interesting to note that the two missing chapters of Romans are historicizing, whereas the rest of the epistle is not. Furthermore, the gospel referred to by Paul in this epistle and others has been termed the "Gospel of Paul," presumed lost but in reality claimed by Marcion to be a book he found at Antioch, along with 10 "Pauline" epistles, and then edited, bringing it around 139-142 to Rome, where he translated it into both Greek and Latin.

The Gospel of the Lord

Originally in the Syro-Chaldee or Samaritan language, Marcion's Gospel of the Lord, which predated the canonical gospels by decades, represents the basic gospel narrative, minus key elements that demonstrate the conspiracy. Although much the same as the later Gospel of Luke, Marcion's gospel was Gnostic, non-historical, and did not make Jesus a Jewish man, i.e., he was not born in Bethlehem and was not from Nazareth, which did not even exist at the time. In Marcion's gospel there is no childhood history, as Marcion's Jesus was not born but "came down at Capernaum," i.e., appeared, in "the fifteenth year of the reign of Tiberius Caesar," the very sentence used in Luke to "prove" Jesus's historicity. Marcion's original, non-historicizing and non-Judaizing New Testament was a thorn in the side of the carnalizing conspirators, who were compelled to put a spin on the facts by claiming that the "heretic" had expurgated the gospel of Luke, removing the genealogies and other "historical" and "biographical" details, for example. Thus, Marcion was accused of "purging the letters of Paul and Luke of 'Jewish traits,'" an allegation that served as a subterfuge to hide the fact that Marcion's Jesus was indeed not a Jewish man who had incarnated a century before. However, as demonstrated by Waite and others, Marcion's gospel was first, and Luke was created from it. Thus, it was not Marcion who had mutilated the texts but the historicizers who followed and added to his.

The Gospel of Luke (170 CE)

The Gospel of Luke is acknowledged by early church fathers to be of a late date. As Waite states:

> . . . Jerome admits that not only the Gospel of Basilides, composed about A.D. 125, and other gospels, admitted to have been first published in the second century, were written before that of Luke, but even the Gospel of Apelles also, which was written not earlier than A.D. 160.[13]

Like the rest of the gospels Luke fits into the timeframe of having been written between 170-180, as admitted by the *Catholic Encyclopedia*:

... according to the *Catholic Encyclopedia* the book of Luke was not written till nearly two hundred years after this event [of Jesus's departure]. The proof offered is that the Theophilus to whom Luke addressed it was bishop of Antioch from 169-177 A.D.[14]

The Gospel of Luke is a compilation of dozens of older manuscripts, 33 by one count, including the Gospel of the Lord. In using Marcion's gospel, the Lukan writer(s) interpolated and removed textual matter in order both to historicize the story and to Judaize Marcion's Jesus. In addition to lacking the childhood or genealogy found in the first two chapters of Luke, Marcion also was missing nearly all of the third chapter, save the bit about Capernaum, all of which were interpolated into Luke to give Jesus a historical background and Jewish heritage. Also, where Marcion's gospel speaks of Jesus coming to Nazareth, Luke adds, "where he had been brought up," a phrase missing from Marcion that is a further attempt on Luke's part to make Jesus Jewish.

Another example of the historicizing and Judaizing interpolation of the compiler(s) of Luke into Marcion can be found in the portrayal of Christ's passion, which is represented in Marcion thus:

Saying, the Son of Man must suffer many things, and be put to death, and after three days rise again.[15]

At Luke 9:22, the passage is rendered thus:

Saying, "The Son of man must suffer many things, *and be rejected by the elders and the chief priests and scribes*, and be killed, and on the third day be raised."

The inclusion of "elders and the chief priests and scribes" represents an attempt to make the story seem as if it happened one time in history, as opposed to the recurring theme in a savior-god cult and mystery school indicated by Marcion.

Of this Lukan creation, Massey says:

It can be proved how passage after passage has been added to the earlier gospel, in the course of manufacturing the later history. For example, the mourning over Jerusalem (Luke xiii. 29-35) is taken verbatim from the 2nd Esdras (i. 28-33) without acknowledgement, and the words previously uttered by the "Almighty Lord" are here assigned to Jesus as the original speaker.[16]

The Gospel of Mark (175 CE)

After the final destruction of Jerusalem and Judea by the Romans in 135, the Jerusalem church was taken over by non-Jews. Of this destruction and appropriation, Eusebius says:

> When in this way the city was closed to the Jewish race and
> suffered the total destruction of its former inhabitants, it was
> colonized by an alien race, and the Roman city which
> subsequently arose changed its name, so that now, in honour of
> the emperor then reigning, Aelius Hadrianus, it is known as
> Aelia. Furthermore, as the church in the city was now composed
> of Gentiles, the first after the bishops of the Circumcision to be
> put in charge of the Christians there was Mark.[17]

This devastation and changeover occurred in the 18th year of
Hadrian's rule, i.e., 135 CE; thus, we see that *this* Mark of whom
Eusebius speaks could not have been the disciple Mark. The date
is, however, perfect for the Gnostic *Marcion*. Eusebius
provides confirmation of this association of Mark with Marcion
when he immediately follows his comment about Mark with a
discussion of "Leaders at that time of *Knowledge* falsely so
called," i.e., Gnostics and *Gnosis*. Indeed, legend held that Mark
wrote his gospel in Rome and brought it to Alexandria, where he
established churches, while Marcion purportedly published his
gospel in Rome and no doubt went to Alexandria at some point.

Like Waite, Mead also does not put Mark first: "It is very
evident that Mt. and Lk. do not use *our* Mk., though they use
most the material contained in our Mk. . . ."[18] In fact, all three
manuscripts used Marcion as one of their sources.

Like Marcion, Mark has no genealogy; unlike Marcion, he
begins his story with John the Baptist, the hero of the
Nazarenes/Mandaeans, added to incorporate that faction. The
Gospel of Mark was admittedly tampered with, as is noted in the
New Testament, with several verses (16:9-20) regarding the
resurrected apparition and ascension added to the end. Here we
have absolute proof of the gospels being changed to fit the
circumstances, rather than recording "history."

Mark also provides an example of how interpolation was used
to set the story in a particular place:

> For instance, Mk. 1:16 reads: "And passing along by the sea of
> Galilee he saw Simon and Andrew . . ." Almost all commentators
> agree that the words "by the sea of Galilee" were added by Mark.
> They are placed quite ungrammatically in the Greek syntax . . .
> Mark, then, has interpolated a reference to *place* into a report
> which lacked it . . . [19]

As to the authorship of Mark, ben Yehoshua says, ". . . the
style of language used in *Mark* shows that it was written
(probably in Rome) by a Roman convert to Christianity whose first
language was Latin and not Greek, Hebrew or Aramaic." It would
seem, then, that the compiler of Mark used the Latin version of
Marcion's gospel, while Luke and Matthew used the Greek
version, accounting for the variances between them. Indeed, the

author of Mark was clearly not a Palestinian Jew, as Wells points out that Mark "betrays in 7:31 an ignorance of Palestinian geography."[20]

The Gospel of John (178 CE)

The Gospel of John is thought by most authorities to be the latest of the four, but Waite provides a compelling argument to place it third and reveals its purpose not only in refuting the Gnostics but also in establishing the primacy of the Roman Church:

> So strong is the evidence of a late date to this gospel, that its apostolic origin is being abandoned by the ablest evangelical writers. . . . Both Irenaeus and Jerome assert that John wrote against Cerinthus. Cerinthus thus flourished about A.D. 145. [T]here is evidence that in the construction of this gospel, as in that of Matthew, the author had in view the building up of the Roman hierarchy, the foundations of which were then (about A.D. 177-89) being laid. . . . There is a reason to believe that both [John and Matthew] were written in the interest of the supremacy of the Church of Rome.[21]

The tone of this gospel is anti-Jewish, revealing that it was written/compiled by a non-Jew, possibly a "Gentile" or an "exiled" Israelite of a different tribe, such as a Samaritan, who not only spoke of "the Jews" as separate and apart from him but also was not familiar with the geography of Palestine. As Waite also says:

> There are also many errors in reference to the geography of the country. The author speaks of Aenon, near to Salim, in Judea; also of Bethany, beyond Jordan, and of a "city of Samaria, called Sychar." If there were any such places, they were strangely unknown to other writers. The learned Dr. Bretschneider points out such mistakes and errors of geography, chronology, history and statistics of Judea, as no person who had ever resided in that country, or had been by birth a Jew, could possibly have committed.[22]

In addition, as Keeler states:

> The Gospel of John says that Bethsaida was in Galilee. There is no such town in that district, and there never was. Bethsaida was on the east side of the sea of Tiberias, whereas Galilee was on the west side. St. John was born at Bethsaida, and the probability is that he would know the geographical location of his own birthplace.[23]

Furthermore, the writer of John relates several events at which the apostle John was not depicted as having appeared and does not record others at which he is said to have been present. Moreover, John is the only gospel containing the story of the raising of Lazarus from the dead, which is an Egyptian myth.

That the Gospel of John served as a refutation of the Gnostics, or an attempt to usurp their authority and to bring them into the "fold," is obvious from its Gnostic style. In fact, it has been suggested that the author of John used Cerinthus's own gospel to refute the "heretic." As Waite relates:

> The history as well as the writings of Cerinthus are strangely blended with those of John the presbyter, and even with John the apostle. . . . A sect called the Alogi attributed to him [Cerinthus] (so says Epiphanius), the gospel, as well as the other writings of John.[24]

The Gospel of Matthew (180 CE)

Although it was claimed by later Christian writers to be a "translation" of a manuscript written in Hebrew by the apostle Matthew, the Gospel of Matthew did not exist prior to the end of the second century and was originally written in Greek. As Waite says:

> The Greek Gospel of Matthew was a subsequent production, and either originally appeared in the Greek language, or was a translation of the Gospel of the Hebrews, with extensive changes and additions. There is reason to believe it to have been an original compilation, based upon the Oracles of Christ, but containing, in whole, or in part, a number of other manuscripts.[25]

The gospel of Matthew is particularly noteworthy in that it contains the interpolation at 16:17-19 not found in either Mark or Luke that gives authority to the Roman Church: To wit, the statement by Jesus that Peter is the rock upon which the church is to be built and the keeper of the keys to the kingdom of heaven. The appearance of this gospel determining Roman dominance corresponds to the violent schism of 180-190 between the branches of the Church over the celebration of Easter.

It is clear that the canonical gospels are of a late date, forged long after the alleged time of their purported authors. Such they are, and, as Doane says, "In these four spurious Gospels . . . we have the only history of Jesus of Nazareth."[26]

The Narrative

Even knowing this fact of falsity, some believers will claim the gospels are nonetheless inspired by the omnipotent God and represent an infallible representation of the life of "the Lord." Far from being "infallible," these spurious gospels contradict each other in numerous places. As noted by Otto Schmiedel, considered one of the greatest authorities on the "life of Jesus": "If John possesses the genuine tradition about the life of Jesus, that of the first three Evangelists (the Synoptists) is untenable. If the

Synoptists are right, the Fourth Gospel must be rejected as a historical source."[27]

In fact, as Wheless says:

> The so-called "canonical" books of the New Testament, as of the Old, are a mess of contradictions and confusions of text, to the present estimate of 150,000 and more "variant readings," as is well known and admitted.[28]

In regard to these "variant readings," Waite states:

> Of the 150,000 variant readings which Griesbach found in the manuscripts of the New Testament, probably 149,500 were *additions and interpolations.*[29]

In this mess, the gospels' pretended authors, the apostles, give conflicting histories and genealogies. The birthdate of Jesus is depicted as having occurred at different times, in Matthew about two years *before* and in Luke more than nine years *after* Herod's death. Jesus's birth and childhood are not mentioned in Mark, and although he is claimed in Matthew and Luke to have been "born of a virgin," his lineage is also traced through Joseph to the house of David, so that he may "fulfill prophecy." Furthermore, the genealogies presented in Luke and Matthew are irreconcilable. In fact, as Wheless says, "Both genealogies are false and forged lists of mostly fictitious names."[30] A number of the names, in reality, are not "patriarchs" but older gods.

Regarding the contradictory chronology found in the NT, ben Yehoshua states:

> The New Testament story confuses so many historical periods that there is no way of reconciling it with history. The traditional year of Jesus's birth is 1 C.E. Jesus was supposed to be not more than two years old when Herod ordered the slaughter of the innocents. However, Herod died before 12 April 4 B.C.E. This has led some Christians to redate the birth of Jesus to 6-4 B.C.E. However, Jesus was also supposed have been born during the census of Quirinius. This census took place after Archelaus was deposed in 6 C.E., ten years after Herod's death. Jesus was supposed to have been baptised by John soon after John had started baptising and preaching in the fifteenth year of the reign of Tiberias, i.e., 28-29 C.E., when Pontius Pilate was governor of Judaea, i.e., 26-36 C.E. According to the New Testament, this also happened when Lysanias was tetrarch of Abilene and Annas and Caiaphas were high priests. But Lysanias ruled Abilene from c. 40 B.C.E. until he was executed in 36 B.C.E. by Mark Antony, about 60 years before the date for Tiberias and about 30 years before the supposed birth of Jesus! Also, there were never two joint high priests; in particular, Annas was not a joint high priest with Caiaphas. Annas was removed from the office of high priest in 15 C.E. after holding office for some nine years. Caiaphas only became high priest in c. 18 C.E., about three years after Annas. . . .

Many of these chronological absurdities seem to be based on misreadings and misunderstandings of Josephus's book *Jewish Antiquities* which was used as reference by the author of *Luke* and *Acts*.

Thus, the few incidents useful for dating are found mainly in Luke and turn out to be false. Doane states:

> Luke ii. 1, shows that the writer (whoever he may have been) lived long after the events related. His dates, about the fifteenth year of Tiberius, and the government of Cyrenius (the only indications of time in the New Testament), are manifestly false. The general ignorance of the four Evangelists, not merely of the geography and statistics of Judea, but even of its language— their egregious blunders, which no writers who had lived in that age could be conceived of as making—prove that they were not only no such persons as those who have been willing to be deceived have taken them to be, but that they were not Jews, had never been in Palestine, and neither lived at, or at anywhere near the times to which their narratives seem to refer.[31]

As concerns Jesus's birthplace, while the synoptics place it in Bethlehem, such that he is from David's village, John says he is from Galilee and that the Jews rejected him because was *not* from Bethlehem, whence the Messiah must come to "fulfill scripture" (Jn. 7:41-42). Also, in the conflicting and illogical gospel account, Jesus's birth is heralded by a star, angels, and three Magi or wise men travelling from afar, and represents such a danger to Herod that he takes the heinous and desperate act of slaughtering the male infants in Bethlehem. Yet, when Jesus finally appears in his hometown, he is barely acknowledged, as if the inhabitants had never heard of his miraculous birth with all the fanfare, or of Herod's dreadful deed, or of any of Jesus's "wisdom" and "mighty works," not even the purportedly astounding temple-teaching at age 12. Even his own family, who obviously knew of his miraculous birth and exploits, rejects him. In addition, in the Christian tale, the three wise men are represented as following the star until they arrive near Herod's house, whereupon he tells them to continue following the star until they reach the place where the baby Jesus lies. The wise men then go off and find the baby, but Herod cannot, so he must put to death the firstborn male of every family. One must ask, how is it that the "wise men" needed Herod's help to know that the star would lead them to the babe, when they were already following it in the first place? And why wouldn't Herod simply have followed the star himself and killed only Jesus, rather than all the boys? In reality, the terrible story of Herod killing the infants as portrayed only in Matthew is based on ancient mythology, not found in any histories of the day, including Josephus, who does otherwise chronicle Herod's real abuses.

In the gospel story, practically nothing is revealed of Jesus's childhood, and he disappears completely from the age of 12 to about 30, when he suddenly reappears to begin his ministry. After this dramatic and unhistorical appearance out of nowhere, Jesus is said in the synoptics to have taught for one year before he died, while in John the number is around three years. Furthermore, in Matthew, Mark and Luke, Jesus's advent takes place in Galilee, except for the end in Jerusalem, while John places the story for the most part in Jerusalem and other sites in Judea, discrepancies that reveal two important forces at work in the gospels, i.e., the northern kingdom of Israel and the southern of Judah.

ben Yehoshua continues the critique as to the purported "history" of the New Testament:

> The story of Jesus's trial is also highly suspicious. It clearly tries to placate the Romans while defaming the Jews. The historical Pontius Pilate was arrogant and despotic. He hated the Jews and never delegated any authority to them. However, in Christian mythology, he is portrayed as a concerned ruler who distanced himself from the accusations against Jesus and who was coerced into obeying the demands of the Jews. According to Christian mythology, every Passover, the Jews would ask Pilate to free any one criminal they chose. This is, of course, a blatant lie. Jews never had a custom of freeing guilty criminals at Passover or any other time of the year. According to the myth, Pilate gave the Jews the choice of freeing Jesus the Christ or a murderer named Jesus Barabbas. The Jews are alleged to have enthusiastically chosen Jesus Barabbas. This story is a vicious antisemitic lie, one of many such lies found in the New Testament (largely written by antisemites).

Walker points out other errors of fact and perception about the part of the world in question during the era of Jesus's alleged advent:

> The most "historical" figure in the Gospels was Pontius Pilate, to whom Jesus was presented as "king" of the Jews and simultaneously as a criminal deserving the death penalty for "blasphemy" because he called himself Christ, Son of the Blessed. . . . This alleged crime was no real crime. Eastern provinces swarmed with self-styled Christs and Messiahs, calling themselves Sons of God and announcing the end of the world. None of them was executed for "blasphemy."[32]

Mangasarian concurs that the story is implausible:

> A Roman judge, while admitting that he finds no guilt in Jesus deserving of death, is nevertheless represented as handing him

over to the mob to be killed, after he has himself scourged him. No Roman judge could have behaved as this Pilate is reported to have behaved toward an accused person on trial for his life.

And Massey states:

> The account of Pilate's shedding the blood the Galileans and mingling it with their sacrifices (Luke xiii. 1) has been added by some one so ignorant of the Hebrew history, that he has ascribed to Pilate an act which was committed when Quirinius was governor, twenty-four years earlier than the alleged appearance of Jesus.[33]

In order to shore up their fallacious claims of Christ being crucified under Pilate, Christian forgers even went so far as to produce the "Acts of Pilate," which at one point was considered "canonical." After the canon was formalized, the book was deemed "spurious," thus demonstrating that it was merely an opinion as to what was "inspired" and what was "forged." The Acts of Pilate purports to relate the trial of Jesus before Pilate, in accordance with the canonical gospel accounts but in greater detail. Some of the scenes of this book were lifted from *The Iliad*:

> . . . Pilate has been turned into Achilles, . . . Joseph is the good old Priam, begging the body of Hector, and the whole story is based upon the dramatic passages of the twenty-fourth book of the Iliad.[34]

The Acts of Pilate, also called the Gospel of Nicodemus, even goes so far as to purport to be a record of the actual conversations of the astonished faithful and prophets of old, such as David and Enoch, who have been resurrected from the dead after Jesus's own resurrection and ascension! This "true" gospel also contains a ludicrous conversation between Satan and his "prince" in Hell. The fictitious nature of such writings is obvious, as is, ultimately, that of the gospels.

Furthermore, the gospel accounts of Jesus's passion and resurrection differ utterly from each other, and none states how old he was when he died. In fact, the early Church fathers were constantly bickering over how old "the Lord" was when he died, with Irenaeus—who was widely respected by his peers as a highly educated establisher of doctrine—fervently insisting that Jesus was at least 50 years old, rather than the 30 or 33 held by other traditions, including the four gospels he helped canonize. Indeed, Irenaeus "flatly den[ied] as 'heresy' the Gospel stories as to his crucifixion at about thirty years of age."[35]

If the gospel narrative as found in the canon had existed earlier than 170-80, and if it constituted a true story, there would be no accounting for the widely differing traditions of "the Savior's" death: To wit, "By the third century A.D., there were no fewer than 25 versions of Jesus' death and resurrection! Some have him not being put to death at all, some have him revived back to life, and some have Jesus living on to an old age and dying in Egypt."[36] These various details of the lives of Christ and his apostles should have been "set in stone," had the story been true and these books been written by the apostles, or even had an orally transmitted "life of Christ" been widespread during the decades that followed.

Various other aspects of the gospel accounts reveal their non-historical nature, including faulty geography, as mentioned, and incidents such as Jesus's preaching in Galilee, which allegedly occurred precisely during the time Herod was building the city of Tiberias. Of this incident, Dujardin says:

> We should here note the total lack of historic verity as to facts and places in the gospels. With the methods then available a town was not built rapidly, and the work would not have been completed in A.D. 27 or even 30. The gospel writers were therefore unaware that they were placing in a countryside overturned by demolition and rebuilding the larger part of the teaching of Jesus.
>
> If the stories are historical, it is in the middle of timber-yards that one must picture the divine precepts delivered, with the accompaniment of the noise of pikes and mattocks, the grinding of saws, and the cries of the workers.[37]

Furthermore, in the gospels Jesus himself makes many illogical contradictions concerning some of his most important teachings. First he states that he is sent only "to the lost sheep of Israel" and forbids his disciples to preach to the Gentiles. Then he is made to say, "Go ye therefore, and teach *all nations* . . ."

Next, Jesus claims that the end of the world is imminent and warns his disciples to be prepared at a moment's notice. He also tells them to build a church from which to preach his message, an act that would not be necessary if the end was near. This doomsday "prophecy" in fact did not happen; nor has Jesus returned "soon," as was his promise. Even if he had been real, his value as a prophet would have been very little, as his most important "prophecies" have not occurred, thus proving that he was no more prophetic or divine than the average newspaper astrologer or palmreader.

In reality, the contradictions in the gospels are overwhelming and irreconcilable by the rational mind. In fact, the Gospel was not designed to be rational, as the true meaning of the word "gospel" is "God's Spell," as in magic, hypnosis and delusion.

As Mack says:

> The narrative gospels can no longer be viewed as the trustworthy accounts of unique and stupendous historical events at the

foundation of the Christian faith. The gospels must now be seen as the result of early Christian mythmaking.[38]

The Acts of the Apostles (177 CE)

In addition to the hundreds of epistles and gospels written during the first centuries were many "Acts" of this apostle or that. The canonical Acts of the Apostles cannot be dated earlier than the end of the second century, long after the purported events. Acts purports to relate the early years of the Christian church, yet in it we find a well-established community that could not have existed at the time this book was alleged to have been written, i.e., not long after the death of Christ. In Acts we read that the first "Christians" are found at Antioch, even though there was no canonical gospel there until after 200 CE. Taylor calls Acts "a broken narrative," and Higgins states that it was fabricated by monks, "devil-drivers" and popes, who wished to form an alliance by writing the book, "the Latin character of which is visible in every page . . ."[39] According to Wheless, even the Protestant *Encyclopedia Biblica* admits Acts to be "untrustworthy."

The purpose of Acts was not, in fact, to record the history of the early Church but to bridge the considerable gap between the gospels and the epistles. Like Matthew and John, it was also designed to empower the Roman hierarchy. As Waite says:

> It is plain that the Acts of the Apostles was written in the interest of the Roman Catholic Church, and in support of the tradition that the Church of Rome was founded by the joint labors of Peter and Paul.[40]

The author(s) of Acts used text from Josephus and, evidently, from the writings of Aristides, a Sophist of the latter part of the second century, to name a couple of its sources, which also purportedly included the life of Apollonius of Tyana, the quasi-mythical Cappadocian/Samaritan/Greek miracle-worker of the first century CE.

Bible Prophecy

Many people believe that the biblical tale of Jesus must be true because the Bible itself predicted his advent and because so many other Old Testament "prophecies" had come true, demonstrating that the book was indeed "God's word." First of all, much of the biblical "prophecy" was written after the fact, with merely an appearance of prophecy. Secondly, the book has served as a blueprint, such that rulers have deliberately followed to some degree its so-called prophecies, thus appearing to bring them to fulfillment. Thirdly, very few if any "prophecies," particularly of the supernatural kind, have indeed come true. Fourthly, biblical interpreters claim that records of events centuries in the past somehow refer to the future. As concerns purported prophetic references to Jesus in the OT, Wells says:

> Nearly all New Testament authors twist and torture the most unhelpful Old Testament passages into prophecies concerning Christianity. Who, ignorant of Mt. 2:16-9, could suppose that Jeremiah 31:15 (Rachel weeping for her children) referred to Herod's slaughter of the Innocents?[41]

To demonstrate that their Messiah was predicted, Christians have also grabbed onto the brief reference made at Psalms 2 to "the Lord and his *Anointed*," a word that in the Greek translation of the Hebrew bible, the Septuagint, is "Christos." In fact, the Septuagint, allegedly translated and redacted during the second and third centuries BCE at Alexandria, Egypt, contains the word "Christos" at least 40 times.[42] This *title* "Christos" or "anointed," however, referred only to an Israelite king or priest, not a superhuman savior. This Christian defense, in fact, proves that there were other Christs long before Jesus, including David, Zadok and Cyrus. The title "Christ" or "Anointed" ("Mashiah") was in reality held by all kings of Israel, as well as being "so commonly assumed by all sorts of impostors, conjurers, and pretenders to supernatural communications, that the very claim to it is in the gospel itself considered as an indication of imposture . . ."[43]

As to the reliability of both Old and New Testaments, Hilton Hotema declared, "Not one line of the Bible has a known author, and but few incidents of it are corroborated by other testimony."[44] Thus, Christianity is based upon a false proposition, and, without the inspired authorship of apostles under an infallible god, the Church is left with little upon which to base its claims. Regarding this state of affairs, Wheless declared:

> The Gentile Church of Christ has therefore no divine sanction; was never contemplated nor created by Jesus Christ. The Christian Church is thus founded on a forgery of pretended words of the pretended Christ.[45]

---

1. Taylor, 108.
2. Mead, *GG*, 59, 123.
3. Keeler, 101.
4. Eusebius, 258.
5. Wheless, *FC*, 91.
6. Dujardin, 33.
7. Wells, *DJE*, 3.
8. Wheless, *FC*, 231.
9. Waite, 32.
10. Wells, *WWJ*, 198.
11. Massey, *HJMC*, 161.

12. Waite, 274-5.
13. Waite, 80.
14. Graham, 284.
15. Waite, 294.
16. Massey, *GHC*, 19.
17. Eusebius, 108.
18. Mead, *GG*, 128.
19. Wells, *DJE*, 71.
20. Wells, *DJE*, 78.
21. Waite, 400-1.
22. Waite, 397-8.
23. Keeler, 16.
24. Waite, 265.
25. Waite, 75.
26. Doane, 459.
27. Steiner, 119.
28. Wheless, *FC*, 174. See also Wells, esp. *WWJ*.
29. Waite, 213.
30. Wheless, *FC*, 207.
31. Doane, 462.
32. Walker, *WEMS*, 470.
33. Massey, *GHC*, 19.
34. Mead, *DJL*, 66.
35. Wheless, *FC*, 173.
36. Notovich, 6.
37. Dujardin, 100.
38. Mack, 10.
39. Higgins, II, 131-2.
40. Waite, 417-19.
41. Wells, *HEJ*, 36.
42. Carpenter, 202.
43. Taylor, 7.
44. Hotema, *EBD* by Massey, intro., 26.
45. Wheless, *FC*, 224.

Non-Biblical Sources

We have seen that the gospel accounts are utterly unreliable as history and cannot serve as evidence that Jesus Christ ever existed. Now we shall examine if there are any non-biblical, non-partisan records by historians during the alleged time of the astonishing events: To wit, a virgin-born "son of God" who was famed widely as a great teacher and wonderworker, miraculously healing and feeding multitudes, walking on water and raising the dead; who was transfigured on a mount into a shining sun; whose crucifixion was accompanied by great earthquakes, the darkening of the sun and the raising from their graves of numerous "saints"; and who himself was resurrected from the dead. Of these alleged events, Eusebius asserts:

> Because of His power to work miracles the divinity of our Lord and Saviour Jesus Christ became in every land the subject of excited talk and attracted a vast number of people in foreign lands very remote from Judaea . . . [1]

Surely these extraordinary events known far and wide were recorded by one or more competent historians of the time! As noted, the centuries surrounding the beginning of the Christian era, the periods of Tiberias and Augustus, were, in fact, some of the best-documented in history, as admitted even by Christian apologists.[2] For example, the Roman historian under Augustus, Livy (59 BCE-17 CE), alone composed 142 volumes, over a hundred of which were subsequently destroyed by the conspirators trying to cover their tracks.

Despite this fact, however, there are basically *no non-biblical references to a historical Jesus* by any known historian of the time during and after Jesus's purported advent. As Walker says, "No literate person of his own time mentioned him in any known writing." Eminent Hellenistic Jewish historian and philosopher Philo (20 BCE-50 CE), alive at the purported time of Jesus, was silent on the subject of the great Jewish miraclemaker and rabblerouser who brought down the wrath of Rome and Judea. Nor are Jesus and his followers mentioned by any of the some 40 other historians who wrote during the first and second centuries of the Common Era, including Plutarch, the Roman biographer, who lived at the same time (46-120 CE) and in the same place where the Christians were purportedly swarming yet made no mention of them, their founder or their religion. As is related in *McClintock and Strong's Cyclopedia of Theological Literature*:

> Enough of the writings of [these] authors . . . remain to form a library. Yet in this mass of Jewish and Pagan literature, aside from two forged passages in the works of a Jewish author, and

two disputed passages in the works of Roman writers, there is to
be found no mention of Jesus Christ.[3]

Flavius Josephus, Jewish Historian, (37-@ 95 CE)

Flavius Josephus is the most famous Jewish historian,
especially because he wrote during the first century. His father,
Matthias, was a reputable and learned member of a priestly
family, and lived in Jerusalem contemporaneously with Pilate.
Certainly he would have told his historian son about the bizarre
and glorious events depicted in the gospels, had they occurred
just years earlier. Josephus himself was appointed to Galilee
during the Jewish Wars and was in Rome at the same time Paul
was supposed to have been there incurring the wrath of the
authorities upon him and his community of Christians. Yet, in
the entire works of the Josephus, which constitute many volumes
of great detail encompassing centuries of history, there is no
mention of Paul or the Christians, and there are only two brief
paragraphs that purport to refer to Jesus. Although much has
been made of these "references," they have been dismissed by
scholars and Christian apologists alike as forgeries, as have been
those referring to John the Baptist and James, "brother of Jesus."
No less an authority than Bishop Warburton of Gloucester (1698-
1779) labeled the Josephus interpolation regarding Jesus "a rank
forgery, and a very stupid one, too."[4] Of Josephus and this stupid
forgery, Wheless says:

> The fact is, that with the exception of this one incongruous
> forged passage, section 3, the wonder-mongering Josephus
> makes not the slightest mention of his wonder-working
> fellow-countryman, Jesus the Christ—though some score of
> other Joshuas, or Jesuses, are recorded by him, nor does he
> mention any of his transcendent wonders. . . . The first mention
> ever made of this passage, and its text, are in the Church History
> of that "very dishonest writer," Bishop Eusebius, in the fourth
> century. . . CE [*Catholic Encyclopedia*] admits . . . the above cited
> passage *was not known to Origen and the earlier patristic
> writers.*[5]

Wheless, a lawyer, and Taylor, a minister, agree with many
others, including Christian apologists such as Dr. Lardner, that it
was Eusebius himself who forged the passage in Josephus. In any
case, the Josephus passages are fraudulent, leaving his sizable
works devoid of the story of Jesus Christ. Of this absence, Waite
asks:

> . . . Why has Josephus made no mention of Jesus, called Christ?
> . . . It is true that Josephus was not contemporary with Jesus if
> the latter was crucified at the time commonly supposed. But
> during the administration of Josephus in Galilee, the country

must have been full of traditions of the crucified Galilean. But a single generation had passed, and the fame of Jesus being now spread abroad in other lands, could it have been any less in Galilee? Paul was contemporary with Josephus, and in his travels, if the accounts in the Acts of the Apostles can be at all relied upon, he must, more than once, have crossed the track of the Jewish priest and magistrate.[6]

Thus, Josephus is silent on the subject of Christ and Christianity.

Pliny the Younger (@ 62-113 CE)

One of the pitifully few "references" held up by Christians as evidence of Jesus's existence is the letter to Trajan supposedly written by the Roman historian Pliny the Younger. However, in this letter there is but one word that is applicable, "Christians," and that has been demonstrated to be spurious, as is also suspected of the entire "document." It has been suggested on the basis of Pliny's reportage of the Essenes that, if the letter is genuine, the original word was "Essenes," which was later changed to "Christians" in one of the many "revisions" of the works of ancient authorities by Christian forgers.

Tacitus (@ 55-120 CE)

Like Pliny, the historian Tacitus did not live during the purported time of Jesus but was born two decades after "the Savior's" alleged death; thus, if there were any passages in his work referring to Christ or his immediate followers, they would be secondhand and long after the alleged events. This fact matters not, however, because the purported passage in Tacitus regarding Christians being persecuted under Nero is also an interpolation and forgery, as noted. Zealous defender of the faith Eusebius never mentions the Tacitus passage, nor does anyone else prior to the 15th century CE. As Taylor says:

> This passage, which would have served the purposes of Christian quotation better than any other in all the writings of Tacitus, or of any Pagan writer whatever, is not quoted by any of the Christian fathers. . . . It is not quoted by Tertullian, though he had read and largely quotes the works of Tacitus. . . . There is no vestige or trace of its existence anywhere in the world before the 15th century.[7]

Suetonius (@ 69-140 CE)

Christian defenders also like to hold up as evidence of their godman the minuscule and possibly interpolated passage from the Roman historian Suetonius referring to someone named "Chrestus" or "Chrestos" at Rome. Obviously, Christ was not alleged to have been at Rome, so this passage is not applicable to him. Furthermore, while some have speculated that there was a Roman man of that name at that time, the title "Chrestus" or "Chrestos," meaning "good" and "useful," was frequently held by freed slaves, among others, including various gods.

Regarding these "historical references," Taylor says, "But even if they are authentic, and were derived from earlier sources, they would not carry us back earlier than the period in which the gospel legend took form, and so could attest only the legend of Jesus, and not his historicity." In any case, these scarce and brief "references" to a man who supposedly shook up the world, can hardly serve as proof of his existence, and it is absurd that the purported historicity of the Christian religion is founded upon them.

There were indeed at the time of Christ's alleged advent dozens of relatively reliable historians who generally did not color their perspectives with a great deal of mythology, cultural bias and religious bigotry—where are their testimonies to such amazing events recorded in the gospels? As Mead relates, "It has always been unfailing source of astonishment to the historical investigator of Christian beginnings, that there is not a single word from the pen of any Pagan writer of the first century of our era, which can in any fashion be referred to the marvellous story recounted by the Gospel writer. The very existence of Jesus seems unknown."[8] The silence of these historians is, in fact, deafening testimony against the historicizers.

Talmudic or Jewish References

One might think that there would at least be reference to the "historical" Jesus in the texts of the Jews, who were known for record-keeping. Yet, such is not the case, despite all the frantic pointing to the references to "Jesus ben Pandira," who purportedly lived during the first century BCE, or other "Jesuses" mentioned in Jewish literature. Unfortunately, these characters do not fit either the story or the purported timeline of the gospel Jesus, no matter how the facts and numbers are fudged.

The story of Jesus ben Pandira, for example, related that, a century before the Christian era, a "magician" named "Jesus" came out of Egypt and was put to death by stoning or hanging. However, ritualistic or judicial executions of this manner were common, as were the name "Jesus" and the magicians flooding out of Egypt. In addition, there is in this story no mention of Romans, among other oversights. Even if ben Pandira were real, it is definitely *not* his story being told in the New Testament.

Massey explains the difficulty with the ben Pandira theory:

It has generally been allowed that the existence of a Jehoshua, the son of Pandira . . . acknowledged by the Talmud, proves the personal existence of Jesus the Christ as an historical character in the gospels. But a closer examination of the data shows the theory to be totally untenable. . . . Jehoshua ben Pandira must have been born considerably earlier than the year 102 B.C. . . . The Jewish writers altogether deny the identity of the Talmudic Jehoshua and the Jesus of the gospels. . . . The Jews know nothing of Jesus as the Christ of the gospels . . . [9]

Of the Pandira/Pandera story, Larson states, "Throughout the middle ages, the legend of Pandera and Yeshu, *considered by most scholars a Jewish invention*, continued to persist."[10] This Jewish invention may have been created in order to capitulate to the Christian authorities, who were persecuting "unbelievers." Thus we find the tale in the Talmud, written after the Christ myth already existed.

To quote Wells:

Klausner's very full survey of the relevant material in [the Talmud] led him to the conclusion that the earliest references to Jesus in rabbinical literature occur not earlier than about the beginning of the second century . . . If there had been a historical Jesus who had anything like the career ascribed to him in the gospels, the absence of earlier references becomes very hard to explain. When Rabbis do begin to mention him, they are so vague in their chronology that they differ by as much as 200 years in the dates they assign to him. . . . It is clear from this that they never thought of testing whether he had existed, but took for granted that this name stood for a real person. . . . But let us see what modern Jewish scholarship, as represented by Sandmel and Goldstein, has to say about Jesus' historicity. Sandmel concedes that what knowledge we have of him "comes only from the NT", "since he went unknown in the surviving Jewish and pagan literature of his time"; and that passages about him in the ancient rabbinical literature of reflect NT material and give no information that is independent of Christian tradition. That the Talmud is useless as a source of reliable information about Jesus is conceded by most Christian scholars.[11]

Other Talmudic references to Jesus, cloaked by the name "Balaam," are derogatory condemnations written centuries after the purported advent, thus serving as commentary on the tradition, not testimony to any "history."

Wells further states:

Now that so much in the NT has fallen under suspicion, there is a natural tendency to exaggerate the importance of non-Christian material that seems to corroborate it—even though

Christian scholars past and present have admitted that, on the matter of Jesus' historicity, there is no pagan or Jewish evidence worth having . . .[12]

To reiterate, "The forged New Testament booklets and the foolish writings of the Fathers, are the sole 'evidence' we have for the alleged facts and doctrines of our most holy Faith," as, adds Wheless, is admitted by the *Catholic Encyclopedia* itself.[13]

As it is said, "Extraordinary claims require extraordinary proof"; yet, no proof of any kind for the historicity of Jesus has ever existed or is forthcoming.

---

1. Eusebius, 30.
2. Jackson, 186.
3. Wheless, *FC*.
4. Mangasarian.
5. Wheless, *FC*, 115-6.
6. Waite, 506-7.
7. Taylor, 395-6.
8. Mead, *DJL*, 48.
9. Massey, *HJMC*, 186-197.
10. Larson, 281.
11. Wells, *DJE*, 12.
12. Wells, *DJE*, 207.
13. Wheless, *FC*, 125.

Further Evidence of a Fraud

There is basically no textual evidence of the existence of Jesus Christ, other than forged biblical books and epistles. In our quest we will now examine what proponents and opponents of the Christian religion were claiming beginning in the second century, during which the "new faith" actually arose. Little of the actual works of most opponents survives, unfortunately, because the Christian conspirators went on a censorship rampage for centuries. However, in their refutations the Christians themselves preserved their opponents' main points of contention, the most important of which was that the whole story was fabricated. In fact, from their own admissions the early Christians were incessantly under criticism by scholars of great repute whom the Christians at first viciously impugned and later murdered by the thousands. Yet, it was not only the dissenters and Pagans who apprehended the truth, as the Christians themselves continuously disclosed that they knew the story and religion of Jesus Christ were not original but were founded upon more ancient myths and ideologies throughout the known world.

For example, the eminent Church doctor Augustine readily confessed that Christianity was a rehash of what already existed long prior to the Christian era:

> That which is known as the Christian religion existed among the ancients, and never did not exist; from the beginning of the human race until the time when Christ came in the flesh, at which time the true religion, which already existed, began to be called Christianity.[1]

In addition, in the face of criticism that Christianity was fabricated, Eusebius sought to demonstrate it was not "novel or strange" by claiming it was based on older ideas. Says he:

> . . . although we certainly are a youthful people and this undeniably new name of Christians has only lately become known among all nations, nevertheless our life and mode of conduct together with our religious principles, have not been recently invented by us, but from almost the beginnings of man were built on the natural concepts of those whom God loved in the distant past . . .

Eusebius thus admitted not only that Christianity was built upon earlier ideologies but also that the name "Christian" was still "undeniably new" by his time, 300 years after the purported beginning of the Christian era, in spite of the New Testament tales that the gospel had been "preached to all the nations" and that a vast church network had sprung up during the first century.

Regarding these Christian admissions, Doane states:

> Melito (a Christian bishop of Sardis), in an *apology* delivered to the Emperor Marcus Atoninus, in the year 170, claims the patronage of the emperor, for the *now*-called Christian religion, which he calls "*our philosophy,*" "on account of its *high antiquity,* as having been *imported* from countries lying beyond the limits of the Roman empire, in the region of his ancestor Augustus, who found its *importation* ominous of good fortune to his government." This is an absolute demonstration that Christianity did *not* originate in Judea, which was a Roman province, but really was an exotic oriental fable, *imported* from India . . . [2]

As this exotic oriental fable settled in, it was placed in Judea and based on Old Testament tales as well, as is affirmed by Tertullian in his *Against Praxeas*, in which he gives the following ludicrous argument, when confronted with the similarities between Christ and a number of OT characters, such as Joshua, or *Jesus*, as his name is in Greek:

> Early Manifestations of the Son of God, as Recorded in the Old Testament; Rehearsals of His Subsequent Incarnation. . . . Thus was He ever learning even as God to converse with men upon earth, being no other than the Word which was to be made flesh. But He was thus learning (or rehearsing), in order to level for us the way of faith, that we might the more readily believe that the Son of God had come down into the world, if we knew that in times past also something similar had been done.

It is more than a little odd that the "omniscient" God would need to learn how to be a human, especially when humans themselves do not receive such an opportunity to "rehearse." In reality, Tertullian's pitiful "excuse" sounds more as if "God" is acting in a *play* (and as if Tertullian has a screw loose).

In his First Apology, Christian father Justin Martyr (c. 100-165) acknowledged the similarities between the older Pagan gods and religions and those of Christianity, when he attempted to demonstrate, in the face of ridicule, that Christianity was no more ridiculous than the earlier myths:

> ANALOGIES TO THE HISTORY OF CHRIST. And when we say also that the Word, who is the first-birth of God, was produced without sexual union, and that He, Jesus Christ, our Teacher, was crucified and died, and rose again, and ascended into heaven, we propound nothing different from what you believe regarding those whom you esteem sons of Jupiter. For you know how many sons your esteemed writers ascribed to Jupiter: Mercury, the interpreting word and teacher of all; Aesculapius, who, though he was a great physician, was struck by a thunderbolt, and so ascended to heaven; and Bacchus too, after he had been torn limb from limb; and Hercules, when he had committed himself to the flames to escape his toils; and the sons

of Leda, and Dioscuri; and Perseus, son of Danae; and Bellerophon, who, though sprung from mortals, rose to heaven on the horse Pegasus. For what shall I say of Ariadne, and those who, like her, have been declared to be set among the stars? And what of the emperors who die among yourselves, whom you deem worthy of deification, and in whose behalf you produce some one who swears he has seen the burning Caesar rise to heaven from the funeral pyre?

In his endless apologizing, Justin reiterates the similarities between his godman and the gods of other cultures:

As to the objection of our Jesus's being crucified, I say, that suffering was common to all the aforementioned sons of Jove [Jupiter] . . . As to his being born of a virgin, you have your Perseus to balance that. As to his curing the lame, and the paralytic, and such as were cripples from birth, this is little more than what you say of your Aesculapius.[3]

In making these comparisons between Christianity and its predecessor Paganism, however, Martyr sinisterly spluttered:

It having reached the Devil's ears that the prophets had foretold the coming of Christ, the Son of God, he set the heathen Poets to bring forward a great many who should be called the sons of Jove. The Devil laying his scheme in this, to get men to imagine that the *true* history of Christ was of the same characters the prodigious fables related of the sons of Jove.[4]

In his *Dialogue with Trypho the Jew*, Martyr again admits the pre-existence of the Christian tale and then uses his standard, irrational and self-serving apology, i.e., "the devil got there first":

Be well assured, then, Trypho, that I am established in the knowledge of and faith in the Scriptures by those counterfeits which he who is called the devil is said to have performed among the Greeks; just as some were wrought by the Magi in Egypt, and others by the false prophets in Elijah's days. For when they tell that Bacchus, son of Jupiter, was begotten by [Jupiter's] intercourse with Semele, and that he was the discoverer of the vine; and when they relate, that being torn in pieces, and having died, he rose again, and ascended to heaven; and when they introduce wine into his mysteries, do I not perceive that [the devil] has imitated the prophecy announced by the patriarch Jacob, and recorded by Moses? And when they tell that Hercules was strong, and travelled over all the world, and was begotten by Jove of Alcmene, and ascended to heaven when he died, do I not perceive that the Scripture which speaks of Christ, "strong as a giant to run his race," has been in like manner imitated? And when he [the devil] brings forward Aesculapius as the raiser of the dead and healer of all diseases, may I not say that in this matter likewise he has imitated the prophecies about Christ? . . . And when I hear, Trypho, that Perseus was begotten of a virgin, I understand that the deceiving serpent counterfeited also this.

This "devil did it" response became de rigeur in the face of persistent and rational criticism. As Doane relates:

> Tertullian and St. Justin explain all the conformity which exists between Christianity and Paganism, by asserting "that a long time before there were Christians in existence, the devil had taken pleasure to have their future mysteries and ceremonies copied by his worshipers."[5]

Christian author Lactantius (240-330), in his attempts to confirm the emperor Constantine in his new faith and to convert the "Pagan" elite, also widely appealed to the Pagan stories as proof that Christianity was not absurd but equally viable as they were, even though naturally he dismissed these earlier versions as works of the devil. As Wheless says, "In a word, Christianity is founded on and proved by Pagan myths."[6]

Other Christians were more blunt in their confessions as to the nature and purpose of the Christian tale, making no pretense to being believers in higher realms of spirituality, but demonstrating more practical reasons for fanatically adhering to their incredible doctrines. For example, Pope Leo X, privy to the truth because of his high rank, made this curious declaration, **"What profit has not that *fable* of Christ brought us!"** As Wheless also says, "The proofs of my indictment are marvellously easy."

The Gnostics

Although the Christian conspirators were quite thorough in their criminal destruction of the evidence, especially of ancient texts, such that much irreplaceable knowledge was lost, from what remains we can see that the scholars of other schools and sects never gave up their arguments against the historicizing of a very ancient mythological creature. This group of critics included many Gnostics, who strenuously objected to the carnalization and Judaization of their allegorical texts and characters by the Christians.

The impression has been cast that the philosophy or religion of Gnosticism began only during the Christian era and that the former was a corruption of the latter. However, Gnosticism is far older than Christianity, extending back thousands of years. The term Gnosticism, in fact, comes from the Greek word *gnosis*, which means knowledge, and "Gnostic" simply means "one who knows," rather than designating a follower of a particular doctrine. From time immemorial, those who understood "the mysteries" were considered "keepers of the gnosis." The Greek philosophers Pythagoras and Plato were "Gnostics," as was the historian Philo, whose works influenced the writer of the Gospel of John.

Nevertheless, during the early centuries of the Christian era, "Gnosticism" became more of a monolithic movement, as certain groups and individuals began to amalgamate the many religions, sects, cults, mystery schools and ideologies that permeated the Roman Empire and beyond, from England to Egypt to India and China. This latest infusion of Gnosticism traced its roots to Syria, oddly enough the same nation in which Christians were first so called, at Antioch. Of this development, Massey says:

> We are told in the Book of Acts that the name of the *Christiani* was first given at Antioch; but so late as the year 200 A.D. no canonical New Testament was known at Antioch, the alleged birth-place of the Christian name. There was no special reason why "the disciples" should have been named as Christians at Antioch, except that this was a great centre of the Gnostic Christians, who were previously identified with the teachings and works of the mage Simon of Samaria.[7]

These Antiochan Gnostic-Christians were followers of "Simon the Magus," who was impugned as the "heresiarch" or originator of all Christian heresies. Yet, this Simon Magus appears to have been a mythical character derived from two mystical entities, Saman and Maga, esteemed by the Syrians prior to the Christian era. This religion could be called Syro-Samaritan Gnostic Christianity. Syro-Judeo-Gnosticism, on the other hand, was originally a Jewish heresy, starting with Mandaeanism, a highly astrological ideology dating to the fourth century BCE that tried to bridge between Judaism and Zoroastrianism and that was very influential on Christianity. The Gnostic tree of thought thus had many branches, such that it was not uniform and was colored by the variety of cultures and places in which it appeared, a development that created competition. Pagels says, "These so-called gnostics, then, did not share a single ideology or belong to a specific group; not all, in fact, were Christians."[8] Indeed, the various Gnostic "Christian" texts from Chenoboskion were found in non-Christian, Pagan tombs.[9] Thus, we find in the ancient world Syrian or Samaritan Gnosticism, Jewish Gnosticism, Christian Gnosticism and Pagan Gnosticism.

Yet, as stated, Gnosticism was eclectic, gathering together virtually all religious and cultic ideologies of the time, and constituting a combination of "the philosophies of Plato and Philo, the Avesta and the Kabbala, the mysteries of Samothrace, Eleusis and of Orphism."[10] Buddhism and Osirianism were major influences as well. The Gnostic texts were multinational, using terms from the Hebrew, Persian, Greek, Syriac/Aramaic, Sanskrit and Egyptian languages.

Although there now seems to be a clear-cut distinction between Gnostics and Christians, there was not one at the beginning, and the fact is that Gnosticism was proto-Christianity. The distinction was not even very great as late as the third century, when Neoplatonic philosopher and fierce Christian critic Porphyry attacked "Gnostics," whom he considered to be Christians, as did Plotinus (205-270), both of whom indicted the Christians/Gnostics for making up their texts. Pagels describes the murky division between the "Gnostics" and the "Christians":

> . . . one revered father of the church, Clement of Alexandria . . . writing in Egypt c. 180, identifies himself as orthodox, although he knows members of gnostic groups and their writings well: some even suggest that he was himself a gnostic initiate.[11]

In fact, Bishop Irenaeus was a Gnostic and had a zodiac on the floor of his church at Lyons.[12] Furthermore, the great "Christian" saint Augustine was originally a Mandaean, i.c., a Gnostic, until after the Council of Nicea, when he was "converted," i.e., promised a prominent place in the newly formed Catholic Church, such that he then excoriated his former sect.

Concerning this confusion between the Christians and Gnostics, Waite relates, "Most of the Christian writers of the second century who immediately succeeded the apostolic fathers, advocated doctrines which were afterward considered heretical."[13] Yet, the orthodox Christians used whatever doctrine they could to benefit their cause, exalting these same "heretics," including Origen (@ 185-254) and Tertullian, as founding fathers.

Many "Christian" concepts are in fact "Gnostic," such as the disdain for the flesh and for matter in general. In actuality, the Gnostic-Christian ideology deemed as evil both matter and the god of the material world, the "Demiurge," also called the "god of this world," or the "prince of this world," as well as "Ialdabaôth," the jealous god. Jesus's own Gnosticism is revealed at John 7:7: "The world cannot hate you, but it hates me because I testify of it that its works are evil." And Paul's Gnostic thought appears where he reveals his abhorrence of the flesh and at 2 Corinthians 4:4, for example, where he speaks gnostically about the "god of this world" being evil. In this passage, the apostle also reveals that the scriptures were tampered with and suggests that he and his cohorts themselves were at some point guilty of "underhanded ways," apparently including such mutilation of texts, which they were thereafter giving up:

> We have renounced disgraceful, underhanded ways; we refuse to practice cunning or to tamper with God's word . . . And even if our gospel is veiled, it is veiled only to those who are perishing. In their case *the god of this world* has blinded the minds of the

unbelievers, to keep them from seeing the light of the gospel of the glory of Christ . . .

Concerning these sentiments, Massey comments:

> Speaking from his Gnostic standpoint, Paul declared to the historic Christians who followed John and Peter, that God had sent them a working of error, that they should believe a lie, because they rejected the truth as it was according to his spiritual Gospel![14]

Not only was Paul propounding a "veiled" or "spiritual" gospel, he was a classic Gnostic, called, in fact, the "Apostle of the Gnostics," in that he did not acknowledge a historical Christ. As Massey further says:

> . . . Paul opposed the setting up of a Christ carnalized, and fought the Sarkolaters [carnalizers] tooth and nail. . . . If the writings of Paul were retouched by the carnalizers, that will account for the two voices heard at times in his Epistles and the apparent *duplicity* of his doctrine . . . Paul passed away and his writings remained with the enemy, to be withheld, tampered with, reindoctrinated, and turned to account by his old opponents who preached the gospel of Christ carnalized.[15]

The Gnostic Christ of Paul is also reflected at Galatians 3:27-8: "For as many of you as were baptized into Christ have put on Christ. There is neither Jew nor Greek, there is neither slave nor free, there is neither male nor female; for you are all one in Christ Jesus." Regarding this concept, Massey says:

> The Christ of the Gnostics was a mystical type continued from mythology to portray a spiritual reality of the interior life. Hence the Christ in this human phase could be female as well as male; for such to become historical, or be made so, except by ignorantly mistaking a mythical Impersonation for a Hermaphrodite in Person![16]

The Gnostic focus on attaining gnosis, or the "kingdom of God within," is also a concept that made it into the Christian religion and bible but that is widely ignored in favor of "a-gnosis," or ignorance, and "pistis," or blind faith.

The fact is that Gnosticism existed first and was eventually changed into orthodox Christianity around 220 CE. As time went on, the carnalizing Christians created distance between themselves and their Gnostic roots by rewriting texts for their own benefit. As Jackson says, "It will be noticed that generally speaking the earlier Epistles show signs of Gnostic influence, while the later show signs of anti-Gnostic bias."[17]

In turn, the Gnostics likened the orthodox Christians to "dumb animals" and stated that it was the orthodoxy, not the Gnostics themselves, who were the blasphemers, because the orthodoxy did not know "who Christ is."[18] As Pagels relates, "Gnostic Christians . . . castigated the orthodox for making the mistake of reading the Scriptures—and especially Genesis—literally, and thereby missing its 'deeper meaning.'"[19] In fact, as Massey says:

> Historic Christianity originated with turning the Gnostic and Esoteric teachings inside out and externalising the mythical allegory in a personal human history.[20]

As stated, many of the Gnostics were fervently "anti-material," such that when the historicizers appeared and began to insist that the Christian savior had indeed "come in the flesh," the Gnostics equally zealously held that *their* Christ could never take human form. These, in fact, were the Christian "heretics" noted by Taylor as the "first class of professing Christians."

This denial of Christ "come in the flesh" was called "Docetism," a term used by the conspirators to gloss over the disbelief in the incarnation by saying it meant that Christ existed but had never taken a material body, rather than serving as a rejection of the gospel story. While later Gnostics may have followed this opinion, the pioneers did not, nor did the Pagans, who were more blunt in their assessment as to the historical nature of Christ. Of Docetism, Massey says:

> The Docetae sects, for example, are supposed to have held that the transactions of the gospel narrative *did occur*, but in a phantasmagoria of unreality. This, however, is but a false mode of describing the position of those who denied that the Christ could be incarnated and become human to suffer and die upon the cross. The Christians who report the beliefs of the Gnostics, Docetae, and others, always *assume the actual history and then try to explain the non-human interpretation as an heretical denial of the alleged facts.* But the docetic interpretation was first, was pre-historical . . . [21]

In *Against Heresies*, Irenaeus speaks of the followers of the Gnostic-Christian Valentinus (2nd cent.), who preceded Irenaeus and was so orthodox that he was nearly elected bishop:

> For, according to them, the Word did not originally become flesh. For they maintain that the Saviour assumed an animal body, formed in accordance with a special dispensation by an unspeakable providence, so as to become visible and palpable. . . . At the same time, they deny that He assumed anything material [into His nature], since indeed matter is incapable of salvation.

Irenaeus further complains about and threatens the Docetics, while acknowledging them as followers of the Master, i.e., Christians:

He shall also judge those who describe Christ as [having become man] only in [human] opinion. For how can they imagine that they do themselves carry on a real discussion, when their Master was a mere imaginary being? Or how can they receive anything steadfast from Him, if He was a merely imagined being, and not a verity? And how can these men really be partaken of salvation, if He in whom they profess to believe, manifested Himself as a merely imaginary being?

In addition to denying that Christ came in the flesh, the early followers were extremely confused as to the "history" of their savior, depicting his death, for example, in dozens of different ways, even though such astounding events should have been seared into memory. Irenaeus recounts other Gnostic-Christian "heresies," beginning with the Samaritan belief that it was not Christ who had died on the cross but "Simon," a peculiar development if Jesus's "history" had been based in fact and widely known from the time of his alleged advent.

In his diatribe against the Gnostics Valentinus, Marcion, Basilides and Saturninus, in particular, Irenaeus recapitulates their diverse beliefs and doctrines:

But according to Marcion, and those like him, neither was the world made by Him; nor did He come to His own things, but to those of another. And, according to certain of the Gnostics, this world was made by angels, and not by the Word of God. But according to the followers of Valentinus, the world was not made by Him, but by the Demiurge. . . . For they say that he, the Lord and Creator of the plan of creation, by whom they hold that this world was made, was produced from the Mother; while the Gospel affirms plainly, that by the Word, which was in the beginning with God, all things were made, which Word, he says, "was made flesh, and dwelt among us." But, according to these men, neither was the Word made flesh, nor Christ, nor the Saviour (Soter) . . . For they will have it, that the Word and Christ never came into this world; that the Saviour, too, never became incarnate, nor suffered, but that He descended like a dove upon the dispensational Jesus; and that, as soon as He had declared the unknown Father, He did again ascend into the Pleroma. . . . But *according to the opinion of no one of the heretics was the Word of God made flesh.*

Other sects, such as the followers of Apelles, held that Christ's body was made of "star stuff," and the Ebionites claimed that Christ was a "type of Solomon" or "type of Jonah," appropriate designations, as we shall see. Obviously, the Gnostics were not uniform in their beliefs and doctrines, despite their attempts at harmonization, mainly because Gnosticism encouraged creativity and freedom of expression. The most disturbing of these heresies, of course, was the denial of Christ's historicity.

In his "Twelve Topics of the Faith," Gregory Thaumaturgus (205-265), head of the Alexandrian school, wrote:

> If any one says that the body of Christ is uncreated, and refuses to acknowledge that He, being the uncreated Word (God) of God, took the flesh of created humanity and appeared incarnate, even as it is written, let him be anathema.

As Topic I, this subject was obviously the most important and once again reveals that the fathers were under incessant charges of fraud in presenting Jesus Christ as a historical personage.

Doresse reveals the ultimate "heresy" of the Gnostics, although he is interpreting it as if the history were first:

> Firstly, a flood of light is thrown upon the strange figure that the Gnostics made of Jesus. . . . For them, his incarnation was fictitious, and so was his crucifixion.[22]

In other words, they denied Jesus Christ ever existed; in fact, the earliest Gnostic-Christians were not even aware of the claims that he had. As noted, others were revolted by the concept. Concerning one of the most widespread and influential Gnostic-Christian sects, Manichaeism, Doane relates:

> The Manichaean Christian Bishop Faustus expresses himself in the following manner:
>
> > "Do you receive the gospel? (ask ye). Undoubtedly I do! Why then, you also admit that Christ was born? Not so; for it by no means follows that believing in the gospel, I should therefore believe that Christ was born! Do you think that he was of the Virgin Mary? Manes hath said, 'Far be it that I should ever own that Our Lord Jesus Christ [descended by scandalous birth through a woman].'"[23]

Faustus's gospel was apparently the same in concept as Paul's "spiritual gospel" and Marcion's non-historicizing Gospel of the Lord. Like Marcion, Faustus expresses an extreme manifestation of the Gnostic distaste of "flesh" and "matter," i.e., misogyny, the contempt for women, which was reasoned because the word "matter" or "mater," as in "material," was also the word for "mother," and matter was deemed female. Thus, the absolute separation of spirit and matter found within the Christian religion has its roots in Gnosticism, as does the attendant sexism. Yet, other Gnostic sects were more balanced and addressed the feminine aspect of the divine.

Graves summarizes the Manicheans' perspective:

"One of the most primitive and learned sects," says a writer, "were the Manicheans, who denied that Jesus Christ ever existed in flesh and blood, but believed him to be a God in spirit only . . ."[24]

These "heretics" were so common that the conspirators had to forge the two Epistles of John to combat and threaten them: ". . . every spirit which confesses that Jesus Christ has come in the flesh is of God, and every spirit which does not confess Jesus is not of God." (1 Jn. 4:2-3) And again at 2 John 7: "For many deceivers have gone out into the world, *men who will not acknowledge the coming of Jesus Christ in the flesh*; such a one is the deceiver and the antichrist." Of these Johannine passages, Higgins says:

> This is language that could not have been used, if the reality of Christ Jesus's existence as a man could not have been denied, or, it would certainly seem, if the apostle himself had been able to give any evidence whatever of the claim.

Massey comments:

> We see from the Epistle of John how mortally afraid of Gnostic Spiritualism were the founders of the historical fraud. "Many deceivers are gone forth into the world that confess not that Jesus Christ cometh in the flesh." These words of John state the Gnostic position. Their Christ had not so come, and could not be carnalized. These Gnostics were in the world long before they heard of such a doctrine; but when they did they denied and opposed it. This, says John, is anti-Christ.[25]

Ignatius, Bishop of Antioch

It was evidently the task of Antiochan bishop Ignatius (c. 50-98/117) to convince those inclined to Docetism that "Christ really and truly lived," by way of writing letters to the churches of Asia Minor and Rome. Of Ignatius, Wheless says:

> He was the subject of very extensive forgeries; fifteen Epistles bear the name of Ignatius, including one to the Virgin Mary, and her reply; two to the apostle John, others to the Philippians, Tarsians, Antiocheans, Ephesians, Magnesians, Trallians, Romans, Philadelphians, Smyrnaeans, and to Polycarp, besides a forged *Martyrium*; the clerical forgers were very active with the name of Saint Ignatius.[26]

As Waite says, "It is now established that the only genuine writings of Ignatius extant, are the Cureton Epistles. These consist of about twelve octavo pages. They were written A.D. 115."[27] By a few decades later, some 100 pages had been forged in his name. The Cureton epistles comprised the three Syriac texts: the Epistles to Polycarp, to the Romans and to the Ephesians. The other epistles, then, are late forgeries, and those that were "original," not necessarily from the hand of Ignatius but of the early second century, were interpolated after the beginning of Roman dominance at the end of that century. The older elements reflect Gnosticism, which, as noted, preceded orthodox, historicizing Christianity and which emanated out of Syria, in particular Antioch, where Ignatius was alleged to have been a bishop. For example, the gnosticizing Ignatius makes reference to the delusion-inducing "prince of this world," such as in Ephesians, in which he says, "So you must never let yourselves be anointed with the malodorous chrism of the *prince of this world*'s doctrines . . ." The "malodorous chrism" of which Ignatius speaks is apparently the mystery of the lingam or phallus, practiced in a variety of mystery schools for centuries prior to the Christian era, including by Old Testament characters. By the term "malodorous," Ignatius is also evidently addressing the highly esoteric chrism or anointing that used semen.

The purpose of many of the epistles attributed to Ignatius was to deal with those "blasphemers" who denied his Lord "ever bore a real human body" (Smyrnaeans) and to program his followers into believing Jesus's "history." In his (forged) Epistle to the Magnesians, "Ignatius" exhorts his followers to resist such "heresies":

> . . . but be ye fully persuaded concerning the birth and the passion and the resurrection, which took place in the time of the governorship of Pontius Pilate; for these things were truly and certainly done by Jesus Christ our hope . . .

And again, in the letter to the Smyrnaeans, "Ignatius" begins by emphatically protesting that:

> . . . suffer He did, verily and indeed; just as He did verily and indeed raise Himself again. His Passion was no unreal illusion, as some sceptics aver who are all unreality themselves. . . . For my own part, I know and believe that He was in actual human flesh . . .

Further in Smyrnaeans he reiterates:

> . . . our Lord . . . is truly of the race of David according to the flesh, but Son of God by the Divine will and power, truly born of a virgin and baptized by John that [all righteousness might be fulfilled] by Him, truly nailed up in the flesh for our sakes under Pontius Pilate and Herod the tetrarch (of which fruit are we—that is, of His most blessed passion) . . .

In his Epistle to the Trallians, "Ignatius" repeats the conditioning of his "flock":

> Close your ears, then, if anyone preaches to you without speaking of Jesus Christ. Christ was of David's line. He was the son of Mary; He was verily and indeed born, and ate and drank;

> He was verily persecuted in the days of Pontius Pilate, and verily and indeed crucified . . . He was also verily raised up again from the dead . . .

And in his Epistle to Mary, "Ignatius" does continue to protest too much, and reveals how prevalent were the denials of the history:

> Avoid those that deny the passion of Christ, and His birth according to the flesh: and *there are many at present* who suffer under this disease.

Next, Ignatius programs the Philippians against the unbelievers and Gnostics, ironically using a Gnostic concept to threaten them, and sets the stage for centuries-long persecution with his calumny against the Jews:

> CHRIST WAS TRULY BORN, AND DIED, For there is but One that became incarnate . . . the Son only, [who became so] not in appearance or imagination, but in reality. For "the Word became flesh." . . . And God the Word was born as man, with a body, of the Virgin, without any intercourse of man. . . . He was then truly born, truly grew up, truly ate and drank, was truly crucified, and died, and rose again. He who believes these things, as they really were, and as they really took place, is blessed. He who believeth them not is no less accursed than those who crucified the Lord. For *the prince of this world* rejoiceth when any one denies the cross, since he knows that the confession of the cross is his own destruction. . . . And thou art ignorant who really was born, thou who pretendest to know everything. If any one celebrates the passover along with the Jews, or receives the emblems of their feast, he is a partaker with those that killed the Lord and His apostles.

In all his protestation, Ignatius offers no proof whatsoever of his claims and heinous accusations except his word that "Jesus the Lord was truly born and crucified . . ." This utterly unscientific habit occurs repeatedly throughout the Christian fathers' works, without a stitch of tangible proof and hard evidence. It is upon this fanatic protestation and not factual events that Christianity's "history" is founded.

Obviously, if everyone in the early Christian movement had known and/or believed that Jesus Christ had existed "in the flesh," the authors of the Ignatian epistles would not have needed continually to make known their historicizing contentions. Regarding "Ignatius's" assorted historicizing elements, Earl Doherty says, *The Jesus Puzzle*:

> Before Ignatius, not a single reference to Pontius Pilate, Jesus' executioner, is to be found. Ignatius is also the first to mention Mary; Joseph, Jesus' father, nowhere appears. The earliest reference to Jesus as any kind of a teacher comes in 1 Clement,

just before Ignatius, who himself seems curiously unaware of any of Jesus' teachings. To find the first indication of Jesus as a miracle worker, we must move beyond Ignatius to the Epistle of Barnabas.

Despite "Ignatius's" attempts, by Irenaeus's time, around 170, the Gnostics were still so powerful that Irenaeus felt compelled to spend a great deal of effort refuting them, even though he himself was Gnostic. In his attacks, Irenaeus was forced to take on the most influential of all Gnostics, Marcion.

Marcion of Pontus

The Cappadocian/Syrian/Samaritan Marcion had an enormous impact on Christianity, publishing the first New Testament, upon which the canon was eventually based. Although he was considered a Christian even by his adversaries, Marcion was one of those "heretics" who vehemently denied that Christ had come in the flesh, died and been resurrected. Marcion was "anti-matter," and his Gnostic god was not the same as the violent, angry YHWH of the Old Testament, a book Marcion rejected. Like others before and after him, Marcion viewed as evil the "god of this world," a notion reflected in the works of Paul, whom Marcion considered the truest apostle.

As stated, the one "historical" fact from Marcion's gospel used by the later historicizers was: "In the fifteenth year of the reign of Tiberius Caesar, Jesus came down to Capernaum, a city of Galilee, and taught them on the sabbath days." This "coming down at Capernaum" was not considered a historical event by Marcion, who denied the incarnation, so it was interpreted through the minds of Christian historicizers as meaning that Marcion claimed "the Lord" had been a "phantom" or spiritual being who literally "came down from the heavens" at that time. Massey interprets this passage in its proper mythological, allegorical and Gnostic context:

> Tertullian says, "According to the gospel of Marcion, in the fifteenth year of Tiberius, Christ Jesus *deigned to emanate from heaven, a salutary spirit.*" But, he also says, according to this "Great Anti-Christian," the Christ was a phantom, who appeared suddenly at the synagogue of Capernaum in the likeness of a full-grown man for the purpose of protesting against the law and the prophets! But it is certain that the Lord or Christ of Marcion is entirely non-historical. He has no genealogy or Jewish line of descent; no earthly mother, no father no mundane birthplace or human birth.[28]

In his "On the Flesh of Christ," spinmeister Tertullian repeats his charges that Marcion expurgated Luke by removing historicizing and Judaizing elements:

Marcion, in order that he might deny the flesh of Christ, denied also His nativity, or else he denied His flesh in order that he might deny His nativity; because, of course, he was afraid that His nativity and His flesh bore mutual testimony to each other's reality, since there is no nativity without flesh, and no flesh without nativity. . . .

He will not brook delay, since suddenly (without any prophetic announcement) did he bring down Christ from heaven. "Away," says he, "with that eternal plaguey taxing of Caesar, and the scanty inn, and the squalid swaddling-clothes, and the hard stable. We do not care a jot for that multitude of the heavenly host which praised their Lord at night. Let the shepherds take better care of their flock, and let the wise men spare their legs so long a journey; let them keep their gold to themselves. Let Herod, too, mend his manners, so that Jeremy may not glory over him. Spare also the babe from circumcision, that he may escape the pain thereof; nor let him be brought into the temple, lest he burden his parents with the expense of the offering; nor let him be handed to Simeon, lest the old man be saddened at the point of death. Let that old woman also hold her tongue, lest she should bewitch the child." After such a fashion as this, I suppose you have had, O Marcion, the hardihood of blotting out the original records (of the history) of Christ, that His flesh may lose the proofs of its reality. . . .

In actuality, Marcion did not "do away with" these various historicizing and Judaizing elements, as they were not attached to the story until after Marcion's death.

Tertullian continues his fact-bending and illogical diatribe:

Chapter V.—Christ Truly Lived and Died in Human Flesh. Incidents of His Human Life on Earth, and Refutation of Marcion's Docetic Parody of the Same. There are, to be sure, other things also quite as foolish (as the birth of Christ), which have reference to the humiliations and sufferings of God. . . . But Marcion will apply the knife to this doctrine also, and even with greater reason. . . . Have you, then, cut away all sufferings from Christ, on the ground that, as a mere phantom, He was incapable of experiencing them? *We have said above that He might possibly have undergone the unreal mockeries of an imaginary birth and infancy.* But answer me at once, you that murder truth: Was not God really crucified? And, having been really crucified, did He not really die?

Here Tertullian is actually conceding that Jesus's birth and infancy may have been imaginary and "unreal mockeries."

To repeat, the Gnostic texts were non-historicizing, allegorical and mythological. In other words, they did not tell the story of a "historical" Jewish master. As a further example, regarding the Gnostic texts dating from the fourth century and found at Nag Hammadi in Egypt, Frank Muccie exclaims, "Still another interesting fact recorded in this same Coptic collection of Gospel fragments is that the disciples did not refer to themselves as Jews, but were from other nations—and that Jesus was also not a Jew!"29

Several other Gnostic texts were non-historicizing and non-Judaizing, such as the Diatessaron of the Marcionite-Christian Tatian (fl. 170), a gospel purportedly compiled from the four canonical gospels and of which 200 copies were in use in Syrian churches as late as the time of "church superintendent" Theodoret (435), who removed them, no doubt violently, because they had no genealogies and did not declare Jesus to be "born of the seed of David." Thus, following Marcion, Tatian did not believe that Jesus Christ was a historical person, nor did he perceive of "the Savior" as being Jewish. In reality, Tatian's gospel was compiled not from the four canonical gospels but in the manner of the four Egyptian books of magic, using the same sources as the evangelists. This episode concerning Theodoret and the 200 texts in the Syrian churches also reveals that well into the 5th century there were still plenty of Christians who did not believe in the incarnation.

The Pagans

In addition to the non-carnalizing Gnostics were many non-Gnostic "Pagan" detractors, although "Pagan" was a pejorative term used to describe illiterate country folk and applied by Christians in a fraudulent attempt to demonstrate that they were more learned than their critics. These "Pagan" critics were, in fact, highly erudite in their own right, much more scientific than their adversaries and, as noted, frequently more moral.

As non-Christians, the Pagans were less euphemistic than the Gnostics in their denial of Christ's appearance in the flesh, calling it a blatant fabrication and subjecting the Christians to endless ridicule, such that a number of Christian apologists were forced to write long, rambling and illogical rants in attempts to silence their critics. One of the harshest critics of Christianity was the Epicurean and Platonist philosopher Celsus, who was so potent in his arguments that Gnostic-Christian Origen was compelled to compose his refutation *Against Celsus*. Regarding Celsus's opinions of the Christian religion and its adherents, Doane relates:

> Celsus (an Epicurean philosopher, towards the end of the second century) . . . in common with most of the Grecians, looked upon Christianity as a *blind faith*, that shunned the light of reason. In speaking of the Christians, he says:

"They are forever repeating: 'Do not examine. *Only believe*, and thy *faith* will make thee blessed. *Wisdom* is a bad thing in life; *foolishness* is to be preferred.'"

He jeers at the fact that *ignorant men* were allowed to preach, and says that "weavers, tailors, fullers, and the most illiterate and rustic fellows," were set up to teach strange paradoxes. "They openly declared that none but the ignorant (were) fit disciples for the God they worshiped," and that one of their rules was, "let no man that is learned come among us."[30]

Doane also relates Celsus's general impression of Christianity, one reflected by many others and admitted by Christians:

The Christian religion contains nothing but what Christians hold in common with heathens; nothing new, or truly great.[31]

Regarding Celsus's indictment of Christianity, Doresse remarks:

In this he asserts that the teaching of the Gospel derives, in part, from Plato, from Heraclitus, from the Stoics, the Jews, from the Egyptians and Persians myths and the Cabiri![32]

Being educated in such philosophies, Celsus had no difficulty determining the biblical narratives as fiction. As Bowersock says, in *Fiction as History*:

The fiction and mendacity that Celsus wished to expose in his *True Discourse* were nothing less than the Christian representation of the life and death of Jesus Christ.[33]

Bowersock continues:

Origen strained every nerve in the third century to confute Celsus's elaborate attempt to expose the Gospel narratives as fiction . . . For any coherent and persuasive interpretation of the Roman empire it becomes obvious that fiction must be viewed as a part of its history.[34]

Under Nero fiction thrived, as the emperor had an insatiable appetite for Greek and Roman literature, such that he sparked a renaissance, no doubt with numerous poets, playwrights and novelists vying for imperial favor and patronage. Such was the atmosphere into and out of which Christianity was born. Bowersock also states:

Parallels in form and substance between the writings of the New Testament and the fictional production of the imperial age are too prominent to be either ignored or dismissed as coincidental. Both Celsus, in his attack on the Christians, and Origen, in his defense of them, recognize the similarities, particularly . . . where apparent miracles—such as the open tomb or resurrection of the dead—were at issue.[35]

Over the centuries, ancient texts were reworked in order to explain the founding of nations and other auspicious events, as was the case with the Roman book *Trojan War*, which was suddenly "discovered" centuries after its pretended date and which is a rewriting of *The Iliad* designed to glorify the foundation of the Roman state.[36] Every culture and nation had its heroic epics and legendary foundations, including Greece and Rome. Israel was no exception, and its legendary foundation related in the Old Testament is as fictitious as the tale of Romulus and Remus, the mythical founders of Rome. The foundation of Christianity is no less fictitious, except in the minds of the people who have been told otherwise.

Celsus was not the only vocal and erudite critic of "the new superstition," as Christianity was called. Another detractor, ironically also Origen's teacher after Origen defected from orthodox Christianity, was Ammonius Saccas, a Greek philosopher and founder of the Alexandrian Neoplatonic school of the third century, who taught that "Christianity and Paganism, when rightly understood, differ in no essential points, but had common origin, *and are really one and the same thing.*"[37] Higgins reveals another group of "Pagan" critics: ". . . Brahmins constantly tell [Christian] missionaries that [the Christian] religion is only corrupted Brahminism."[38]

So widespread was the criticism and ridicule that Christian elder Arnobius (4th cent.) complained, "The Gentiles make it their constant business to laugh at our faith and to lash our credulity with their facetious jokes."[39] In fact, as Massey states, "The total intelligence of Rome [treated] the new religion as a degrading superstition founded on a misinterpretation of their own dogmas."[40] Indeed, in his "On the Incarnation," Saint and Alexandrian Bishop Athanasius (c. 293-373) fretted endlessly about being mocked, particularly for believing that Jesus Christ was historical:

> We come now to the unbelief of the Gentiles; and this is indeed a matter for complete astonishment, for they laugh at that which is no fit subject for mockery, yet fail to see the shame and ridiculousness of their own idols. . . . First of all, what is there in our belief that is unfitting or ridiculous? *Is it only that we say that the Word has been manifested in a body?*

Another vocal critic of Christianity was the Pagan Emperor Julian, who, coming after the reign of the fanatical and murderous "good Christian" Constantine, returned rights to Pagan worshippers, for which he was murdered. Julian expressed his objections to the Christian religion thus:

If anyone should wish to know the truth with respect to you Christians, he will find your impiety to be made up partly of the Jewish audacity, and partly of the indifference and confusion of the Gentiles, and that you have put together not the best, but the worst characteristics of them both.

In fact, the Christians were not just mocked, they were considered criminals. As Pagels relates:

In an open letter addressed to "rulers of the Roman Empire," Tertullian acknowledges that pagan critics detest the movement: "You think that a Christian is a man of every crime, an enemy of the gods, of the emperor, of the law, of good morals, of all nature."[41]

The early Christians were thus accused of heinous behavior, including infanticide and orgies, imputations that Christians themselves later used against their enemies. In the face of such charges, Justin Martyr was forced to say, "Do you also . . . believe that we eat human flesh and that after our banquets we extinguish the lights and indulge in unbridled sensuality?"[42] And Tertullian was compelled to write, "We are accused of observing a holy rite in which we kill a little child and then eat it . . . after the feast, we practise incest . . . This is what is *constantly* laid to our charge."[43]

Pagels also relates:

The Christian group bore all the marks of conspiracy. First, they identified themselves as followers of a man accused of magic and executed for that and treason; second, they were "atheists," who denounced as "demons" the gods who protected the fortunes of the Roman state . . . Besides these acts that police could identify, rumor indicated that their secrecy concealed atrocities: their enemies said that they ritually ate human flesh and drank human blood . . . [44]

Another of the Pagan criticisms, as we have seen, was that the Christians were plagiarists (and degraders) of old ideologies and concepts, an accusation that the Christians were compelled to confirm as they attempted to gain respectability for their "new superstition." Thus, the Christians admitted the superlative nature and morality of those "Pagan" ideologies. In his Apology, Justin Martyr aligned himself with several ideologies that existed long prior to the Christian era:

In saying all these things were made in this beautiful order by God, what do we seem to say more than Plato? When we teach a general conflagration, what do we teach more than the Stoics? By opposing the worship of the works of men's hands, we concur with Menander, the comedian; and by declaring the Logos, the first begotten of God, our master Jesus Christ, to be born of a virgin, without any human mixture, to be crucified and dead,

and to have risen again, and ascended into heaven: we say no
more in this, than what you say of those whom you style the
sons of Jove.[45]

In fact, Plato was widely studied by the Christian
fathers/forgers, as is obvious from their writings, particularly
those pontificating about "the Word," an ancient concept refined
by the Greek philosopher. Indeed, Justin Martyr was originally a
Platonist. As to the purported difference between "Pagans" and
"Christians," Doane states:

> The most celebrated Fathers of the Christian church, the most
> frequently quoted, and those whose names stand the highest
> were nothing more or less than Pagans, being born and educated
> Pagans.[46]

These celebrated Pagan-Christian fathers included Pantaenus,
Origen, Clemens Alexandrinus, Gregory and Tertullian.

The Jews

Naturally, orthodox Jews also denied the reality of Christ,
although, like other cultures, they were eventually forced through
violence to recite that the tale had at least some historicity. In his
debate with Trypho the Jew, Justin depicts Trypho as saying:

> If, then, you are willing to listen to me (for I have already
> considered you a friend), first be circumcised, then observe what
> ordinances have been enacted with respect to the Sabbath, and
> the feasts, and the new moons of God; and, in a word, do all
> things which have been written in the law: and then perhaps you
> shall obtain mercy from God. *But Christ—if He has indeed been
> born, and exists anywhere—is unknown, and does not even know
> Himself, and has no power until Elias come to anoint Him, and
> make Him manifest to all.* And you, having accepted a groundless
> report, invent a Christ for yourselves, and for his sake are
> inconsiderately perishing.

Trypho's argument reveals not only that the Jews did not
accept Christ as a historical person but also Christ's true nature,
as his "anointer," Elias, is not only a title for John the Baptist but
also *Helios*, the sun. To such accusations, Justin attempts to
respond in a chapter titled, "The Christians Have Not Believed
Groundless Stories," but he offers no proof at all, merely
groundless protestations.

As to the origins of Christianity, Massey spells it out:

> Christianity began as Gnosticism, refaced with falsehoods
> concerning a series of facts alleged to have been historical, but
> which are demonstrably mythical. By which I do not mean
> mythical as exaggerations or perversions of historic truth, but
> belonging to the pre-extant Mythos. . . It is obvious that the
> Roman Church remained Gnostic at the beginning of the second

century, and for some time afterwards. Marcion, the great Gnostic, did not separate from it until about the year 136 A.D. Tatian did not break with it until long after that. In each case the cause of quarrel was the same. They left the Church that was setting up the fraud of Historic Christianity. They left it as Gnostic Christians, who were anathematized as heretics, because they rejected the Christ made flesh and the new foundations of religion in a spurious Jewish history.[47]

Thus, we can see that the veracity of the gospel story and the historicity of its main character have been called into question since the tale was released upon an unsuspecting public.

---

1. Jackson, 1.
2. Doane, 409.
3. Doane, 411-12.
4. Wheless, *FC*, 32.
5. Doane, 231.
6. Wheless, *FC*, 152.
7. Massey, *GHC*, 12.
8. Pagels, *AES*, 60.
9. Doresse, 133-5.
10. Doresse, 2.
11. Pagels, *GG*, 67.
12. Higgins, II, 129.
13. Waite, 251.
14. Massey, *GHC*, 25-26.
15. Massey, *HJMC*, 193-7.
16. Massey, *GHC*, 21.
17. Jackson, 119.
18. Pagels, *GG*, 102-3.
19. Pagels, *AES*, 63.
20. Massey, *GHC*, 25.
21. Massey, *HJMC*, 177.
22. Doresse, 305.
23. Doane, 512.
24. Graves, *WSCS*, 101.
25. Massey, *GHC*, 24-5.
26. Wheless, *FC*, 133.
27. Waite, 212.
28. Massey, *GHC*, 18.
29. Notovich, 6.
30. Doane, 272.
31. Doane, 411.
32. Doresse, 62.
33. Bowersock, 3.
34. Bowersock, 9-12.
35. Bowersock, 124.
36. Bowersock, 60ff.
37. Doane, 411.
38. Higgins, I, 663.
39. Doane, 275.
40. Massey, *HJMC*, 180.
41. Pagels, AES, 32.

42. Larson, 298.
43. Larson, 298.
44. Pagels, *GG*, 76.
45. Doane, 411-12.
46. Doane, 412.
47. Massey, *GHC*, 12-13.

Physical Evidence

It has been demonstrated that there is no reliable textual evidence for the existence of Jesus Christ and that, in fact, his existence and the historicity of the gospel tale were denied from the earliest times by Pagans and Christians ("heretics") alike. What about the physical remains? What does archaeology tell us about the historicity of the Christian story? In order to determine the evidence, we must look to architecture, monuments, coins, medals, inscriptions, pottery, statues, frescoes and mosaics, among other things. Unfortunately, much of the evidence has been completely destroyed, mostly due to "religious" fervor; however, there remains enough to reveal the conspiracy and fraud.

Jesus's Physical Appearance

There is no physical description of Jesus in the New Testament, other than that which resembles the sun, such as at his transfiguration at Matthew 17:2: "And he was transfigured before them, and his face shone like the sun, and his garments became white as light," a fitting description for the "light of the world that every eye can see." The androgynous character at Revelation 1:13-15 has also been interpreted to refer to Jesus: "And in the midst of the seven candlesticks, one like unto the Son of Man, clothed in a garment down to the foot, and girt about his paps [breasts]. His head and his hair were white as white wool, white as snow . . ." A number of people have claimed that the "wooly" hair reference means Christ was a black man, and they cite black crucifixes and bambinos as evidence. As can be seen, the scriptural "evidence" of Jesus's physicality creates more problems than it solves.

In fact, early Christian fathers admitted that Jesus's appearance was unknown. For example, as St. Augustine said of Christ, according to the *Catholic Encyclopedia*, "in his time there was no authentic portrait of Christ, and . . . the type of features was still undetermined, so that we have *absolutely no knowledge of His appearance.*"[1] This deficiency would appear to be very strange, particularly since it was claimed that Jesus was "known throughout the world." How, pray tell, did anyone recognize him? Despite the lack of any gospel description, Jesus was alternately described by the early Christian fathers as either "the most beautiful of the sons of men" or "the ugliest of the sons of men"— another highly strange development, if this character were real. But, as Augustine admitted, this debate existed before the "type of features" was determined, i.e., fabricated and standardized. Fox relates the ambiguity of Christ's appearance:

> Nobody remembered what Jesus had looked like. Citing Isaiah, one wing of Christian opinion argued that he had chosen a mean and ugly human form. By c. 200, he was being shown on early Christian sarcophagi in a stereotyped pagan image, as a philosopher teaching among his pupils or a shepherd bearing sheep from his flock.[2]

It is beyond belief that had Jesus existed and been seen by "the multitudes," no one would remember what he looked like. The authors of the gospels, pretending to be the apostles, professed to remember Jesus's exact deeds and words, verbatim, yet they couldn't recall what he looked like!

Many people think that the standard image with the long, dark hair is how Jesus's early followers saw him. In reality, the earliest images of Christ portray a young, beardless boy, at times with blond hair. As Carpenter relates:

> The Christian art of [the first three to four centuries] remained delightfully pagan. In the catacombs we see the Saviour as a beardless youth, like a young Greek god; sometimes represented, like Hermes the guardian of the flocks, bearing a ram or lamb round his neck; sometimes as Orpheus tuning his lute among the wild animals.[3]

Of these early depictions of Christ, Doane states:

> One of the favorite ways finally, of depicting him, was, as Mr. Lundy remarks: "Under the figure of a beautiful and adorable youth, of *about fifteen or eighteen years of age*, beardless, with a sweet expression of countenance, and long and abundant hair flowing in curls over his shoulders. His brow is sometimes encircled by a diadem or bandeau, *like a young priest of the Pagan gods*; that is, in fact, the favorite figure. On sculptured sarcophagi, in fresco paintings and Mosaics, Christ is thus represented as a graceful youth, *just as Apollo was figured by the Pagans*, and as angels are represented by Christians . . ."[4]

According to the gospel story, Jesus disappeared between the ages of around 12 and 29 before he began his ministry, so this depiction of him at "about fifteen to eighteen years of age" certainly would be odd, since his followers never saw him at that age.

These depictions demonstrate that Jesus's appearance was arbitrary, allegorical, unhistorical and not based on a single individual. Dujardin says:

> As to archaeological evidence, the oldest paintings in the Catacombs not only display no features that confirm the gospel legend, but represent Jesus under forms that are inconsistent with it.[5]

Furthermore, the Christian crucifix originally held the image of a lamb instead of a man, up until the eighth to ninth centuries, at which time Christ was nevertheless depicted as a young, pagan god:

> The earliest artists of the crucifixion represent the Christian Saviour as *young and beardless,* always without the crown of thorns, alive, and erect, apparently elate; no signs of bodily suffering are there.[6]

Moreover, some of the earliest images associated with Christ include not only a lamb but also a fish, rather than a man:

> The fish, in the opinion of antiquarians generally, is the symbol of Jesus Christ. The fish is sculptured upon a number of Christian monuments, and more particularly upon the ancient sarcophagi. It is also upon medals, bearing the name of our Saviour and also upon engraved stones, cameos and intaglios. The fish is also to be remarked upon the amulets worn suspended from the necks by children, and upon ancient glasses and sculptured lamps.
>
> Baptismal fonts are more particularly ornamented with the fish. The fish is constantly exhibited placed upon a dish in the middle of the table, at the Last Supper, among the loaves, knives and cups used at the banquet.[7]

The fish is in fact representative of the astrological age of Pisces, symbolized by the two fishes.

In addition, the archaeological evidence reveals the existence of the dark-haired and bearded "Jesus" image long *before* the Christian era. Indeed, Higgins describes a medal of "the Savior" found in pre-Christian ruins with the image of a bearded man with long hair on one side and an inscription in Hebrew on the other. He then exclaims:

> And now I wish to ask any one how a coin with the head of Jesus Christ and a legend, *in a language obsolete in the time of Jesus Christ,* should arrive in Wales and get buried in an old Druidical monument?[8]

The image held today of a white man with long, dark hair and a beard is also that of Serapis, the syncretic god of the Egyptian state religion in the third century BCE, who was by the fourth century CE the most highly respected god in Egypt. Serapis was in fact considered to be the "peculiar god of the Christians." As Doane relates:

> There can be no doubt that the head of Serapis, marked as the face is by a grave and pensive majesty, *supplied the first idea for the conventional portraits of the Saviour.*[9]

Coins

Coin evidence is one of the more underrated methods of archaeology, yet it provides a superior dating system for a number of reasons, including that coins do not disintegrate over time. Unfortunately for Christian propagandists, the coin evidence for early Christianity is nil:

> "[T]he close consideration of coin evidence may shake the foundations of the literary narrative. This is because coins are produced with immediacy in response to events, whereas the literary record is composed after the event, often much after, and can suffer from bias if not outright distortion or suppression of facts." Why, no Christian coins [dating to the] 1st, 2nd, 3rd centuries C.E.? Because the "events," were literary events (Fiction!)—only![10]

Birth Caves, Tombs, Sundry Sites

Many people point to "Calvary Hill," Jesus's tomb, the stations of the cross, and other tourist spots in Jerusalem and Israel as evidence that there must have been *somebody* there and *some* drama must have taken place. It is an unfortunate fact that, because of this belief, hundreds of unstable people have been running about these so-called sacred sites trying to get themselves "crucified" even to this day. It is this same religious madness that has allowed to flourish not only stories such as the Christian myth, et al., but also the booming business of relics, holy sites, etc. Of these purported sacred sites, Wells says:

> There is not a single existing site in Jerusalem which is mentioned in connection with Christian history before 326, when Helena (Mother of Constantine) saw a cave that had just been excavated, and which was identified with Jesus' tomb.[11]

Indeed, it is reported that when Helena's representative inquired in Jerusalem as to the "Lord and Savior Jesus Christ," no one had ever heard of him except, reputedly, one old man, who promptly showed Helena's envoy a field of buried crucifixes, which was apparently evidence satisfactory enough for these great minds and honest characters to settle the matter, such that they claimed to have found the "true cross."

Doherty addresses the problem of these so-called sacred sites:

> In all the Christian writers of the first century, in all the devotion they display about Christ and the new faith, not one of them ever expresses the slightest desire to see the birthplace of Jesus, to visit Nazareth his home town, the sites of his preaching, the upper room where he held his Last Supper, the tomb: where he was buried and rose from the dead. These places are never mentioned! Most of all, there is not a hint of pilgrimage to

Calvary itself, where humanity's salvation was consummated. How could such a place not have been turned into a shrine? Is it conceivable that Paul would not have wanted to run to the hill of Calvary, to prostrate himself on the sacred ground that bore the blood of his slain Lord? Surely he would have shared such an intense emotional experience with his readers! Would he not have been drawn to the Gethsemane garden, where Jesus was reported to have passed through the horror and the self-doubts that Paul himself had known? Would he not have gloried in standing before the empty tomb, the guarantee of his own resurrection? Is there indeed, in this wide land so recently filled with the presence of the Son of God, any holy place at all, any spot of ground where that presence still lingers, hallowed by the step, touch or word of Jesus of Nazareth? Neither Paul nor any other first century letter writer breathes a whisper of any such thing.

It is in reality inconceivable, particularly in consideration of the religious fanaticism evident even today, that such zealots as Paul and the other early Christians who were purportedly "dying for the faith" in droves were completely disinterested in such sacred sites and relics.

As to the value of the present sites claimed to provide evidence of the Christian story, it should be noted that, much to the dismay of the Christian orthodoxy, the Kashmir vale in India lays claim to the grave sites of both Moses and Jesus, who, as the wandering prophet Yuz Asaf, allegedly lived there for many years following his resurrection. The evidence may seem convincing to the uninitiated; however, "Yuz Asaf" is basically the same as "Joseph," which was often a title of a priest and not a name. In addition, some have attempted to place Jesus's "lost years" in India and/or Tibet, where the traveler Nicholas Notovitch purportedly received a text by Tibetan monks concerning Jesus's life and times. Notovich claimed that the contents of this text were written "immediately after the Resurrection." The manuscript itself was purported to date from the second or third century after the Christian Era and was certainly was not composed "immediately after the Resurrection." Even if it genuinely dated from the early centuries, the text itself says at the beginning, "*This is what is related on this subject by the merchants who have come from Israel,*" thus demonstrating not that "Jesus"—or "Issa," as he is called there—lived in India but that the Jesus *tradition* was brought to India and Tibet by the extensive trading and brotherhood network that readily allowed for such stories to spread. The Notovich text has a cheery view of the Jews, throws the entire onus of the crucifixion on Pilate and the Romans, and was apparently written as not only Jewish but Buddhist propaganda, as evidenced by the following passage, designed to elevate Buddha above Jesus: "Six years later, Issa, whom the Buddha had chosen to spread his holy word, could perfectly explain the sacred rolls." One notable aspect of the text, however, is its pro-women exhortations, which are surely neither Jewish nor Christian.

Furthermore, it should be noted that there were innumerable "traveling prophets" throughout the ancient world, spouting the same parables and platitudes and doing the standard bag of magic tricks as Jesus, as do the countless Indian yogis of today. It is difficult to believe that the Indians or Tibetans would be very impressed by such stories, since their own traditions are full of countless such godmen. Nor is it possible that the Hindus would not have recognized in the "life of Christ" that of Christna/Krishna; indeed, they did.

In addition, concerning the Indian "grave of Moses," the name "Mousa," or Moses, is common in Kashmir, as are graves. Along with the Moses and Jesus graves, there are also at least *two* tombs of the apostle "Thomas" in India.

In fact, over the millennia, the establishment of such revered tombs has been routine. Japan also lays claim to the tombs of both Moses and Jesus. The villagers of Shingo insist that Jesus and his brother were buried there, and they have the graves to prove it. As do the Indians and Tibetans with their nations, the Shingoese assert that Jesus was educated by religious masters in Japan during his "lost years." The Japanese tale goes further than the Indian and maintains that, after escaping crucifixion when his brother was mistakenly executed in his place, Jesus fled with the remains of his brother and with followers to Shingo, where he married a Japanese woman, fathered three daughters and lived to be 106. Although some locals will swear the story is true, it turns out that the Shingo graves are those of Christian missionaries dating from the 16th century.

This type of confusion between the gods and their messengers is behind many of the tales about this or that god or godman having been real, and having walked or lived here or there. Often the person who is preaching about the foreign or "alien" god is called by the same name as the god; hence, his exploits are confused with the mythology he is presenting. For example, a "priest of Apollo," becomes "priest Apollo" and may then be shortened to "Apollo." In cases of culture clash, an entire culture or place may be called by the name of a god. When there are migrations, tradition may be garbled such that it seems to be that of an individual rather than a whole culture. Confusion happens as well when a number of individuals hold the same name or title, as in Buddhism, where the exploits and sayings of many Buddhas, mythical and historical, are rolled into one.

The existence of "tombs" or other sacred sites proves little in itself, since it is a common practice to set up symbolic sites, the symbolism of which no doubt becomes lost to the masses. Sacred site-making is also great business—imagine owning the piece of property where God himself was born, walked and died! Providing an example of this type of profiteering, Fox states:

> . . . just outside [Athens], they claimed, was the very cave in which the infant Zeus had been nursed. Claiming the infant Zeus, the city gained honour, visitors and a temple of particular design. The claim, naturally, was contested by other cities that had caves: Zeus's birthplace, like his tomb, became a topic of keen intercity rivalry . . .[12]

The island of Crete also laid claim to both Zeus's birth and death caves. At Delphi, Greece, there are purported graves of Dionysus and Apollo, and Osiris had his tomb at Sais in Egypt. Orpheus had his tomb in Thrace. There are also several places where the Virgin Mary rested and/or died, including Bethlehem, Ephesus and Gethsemane, the latter of which did not even exist at the time. Just recently a place in Nepal laid claim to being "Buddha's birthplace." Are we to suppose these deities were really born or buried in these places? The pillars of Hercules are celestial, yet they were given geographical location. Does this mean that Hercules was a real man? In the case of the various gods and their locations, the abstract is first, the historical second.

Again, sites where this god or that allegedly was born, walked, suffered, died, etc., are found around the world, revealing a common and unremarkable occurrence that is not monopolized by and did not originate with Christianity. As Walker states:

> All over India the "footprints of Buddha" are still worshipped at holy shrines; but some of these Buddhist feet were originally worshipped as the feet of Vishnu. Even earlier, some may have been the red, henna-dyed feet of the Goddess. In antiquity, stones dedicated to Isis and Venus were marked with footprints, meaning "I have been here." The custom was copied later on Christian tombs, where the footprint bore the legend *In Deo*.[13]

Such footprints are found over the purported grave of Jesus in Srinagar, India, as well.

If proof of the historicity of a god lies in graves, birthplaces and such, then all of these gods must also have been historical, which would mean that Jesus is a johnny-come-lately in a long line of historical godmen. In reality, this relic- and site-fabrication is standard behavior in the world of mythmaking and is not indication or evidence of historicity. As noted, these birthplaces, graves and relics of gods, godmen and saints have been hyped in fact for purposes of tourism, i.e., for money.

The Shroud of Turin and Other "Holy Relics"

In its quest to create a religion to gain power and wealth, the Church forgery mill did not limit itself to mere writings but for centuries cranked out thousands of phony "relics" of its "Lord," "Apostles" and "Saints." Although true believers desperately keep attempting to prove otherwise, through one implausible theory after another, the Shroud of Turin is counted among this group of frauds:

> There were at least 26 "authentic" burial shrouds scattered throughout the abbeys of Europe, of which the Shroud of Turin is just one. . . . The Shroud of Turin is one of the many relics manufactured for profit during the Middle Ages. Shortly after the Shroud emerged it was declared a fake by the bishop who discovered the artist. This is verified by recent scientific investigation which found paint in the image areas. The Shroud of Turin is also not consistent with Gospel accounts of Jesus' burial, which clearly refer to multiple cloths and a separate napkin over his face.[14]

As Gerald Larue says:

> Carbon-14 dating has demonstrated that the Shroud is a 14th-century forgery and is one of many such deliberately created relics produced in the same period, all designed to attract pilgrims to specific shrines to enhance and increase the status and financial income of the local church.[15]

Walker comments on the holy relic mill:

> About the beginning of the 9th century, bones, teeth, hair, garments, and other relics of fictitious saints were conveniently "found" all over Europe and Asia and triumphantly installed in the reliquaries of every church, until all Catholic Europe was falling to its knees before what Calvin called its anthill of bones. . . . St. Luke was touted as one of the ancient world's most prolific artists, to judge from the numerous portraits of the Virgin, painted by him, that appeared in many churches. Some still remain, despite ample proof that all such portraits were actually painted during the Middle Ages.[16]

And Wells states:

> About 1200, Constantinople was so crammed with relics that one may speak of a veritable industry with its own factories. Blinzler (a Catholic New Testament scholar) lists, as examples: letters in Jesus' own hand, the gold brought to the baby Jesus by the wise men, the twelve baskets of bread collected after the miraculous feeding of the 5000, the throne of David, the trumpets of Jericho, the axe with which Noah made the Ark, and so on. . . . [17]

At one point, a number of churches claimed the one foreskin of Jesus, and there were enough splinters of the "True Cross" that Calvin said the amount of wood would make "a full load for a good ship."[18] The disgraceful list of absurdities and frauds goes on, and, as Pope Leo X exclaimed, the Christ fable has been enormously profitable for the Church. Again, it must be asked why force, forgery and fraud were needed to spread the "good news" brought by a "historical son of God."

The relic business was not limited to the Christian faith, however, as there have always been relics associated with other luminaries of the vast pantheon found around the world. As Hislop says:

> If, therefore, Rome can boast that she has sixteen or twenty holy coats, seven or eight arms of St. Matthew, two or three heads of St. Peter, this is nothing more than Egypt could do in regard to the relics of Osiris. Egypt was *covered* with sepulchres of its martyred god; and many a leg and arm and skull, all vouched to be genuine, were exhibited in the rival burying-places for the adoration of the Egyptian faithful.[19]

As regards other "evidence" of Christianity, such as weeping or bleeding statues, so much in vogue these days, or visions, voices, or miracles, etc., these too have their Pagan predecessors:

> False prophecies and miracles and fraudulent relics were the chief reliance among the Pagans, as among the Christians, for stimulating the faith, or credulity, of the ignorant and superstitious masses. The images of the gods were believed to be endowed with supernatural power. Of some, the wounds could bleed; of others, the eyes could wink; of others, the heads could nod, the limbs could be raised; the statues of Minerva could brandish spears, those of Venus could weep; others could sweat; paintings there were which could blush. The Holy Crucifix of Boxley, in Kent, moved, lifted its head, moved its lips and eyes; it was broken up in London, and the springs exposed, and shown to the deriding public; but this relation is out of place—this was a pious Christian, not Pagan, fake. One of the marvels of many centuries was the statue of Memnon, whose divine voice was heard at the first dawn of day . . . Other holy relics galore were preserved and shown to the pious: The Aegis of Jove . . . the very tools with which the Trojan horse was made . . . the Cretans exhibited the tomb of Zeus, which earned for them their reputation as Liars. But Mohammedans show the tomb of Adam and Christians that of Peter! There were endless shrines and sanctuaries at which miracle-cures could be performed . . . The gods themselves came down regularly and at the fine feasts spread before their statues. . . . [20]

In establishing their "holy relics," the Catholics were merely building on a long line of priestly hoaxing. If such "relics" are "evidence" of the reality of Jesus and Mary, are they not also "evidence" of the reality of Venus, whose statue also wept, or of the Indian elephant-headed god Ganesha, whose images drink milk by the bucket? A truly pious person, then, would do well to worship them all and not just these meager few from Palestine.

Doane sums up the quest thus:

> In vain do the so-called disciples of Jesus point to the passages in Josephus and Tacitus; in vain do they point to the spot on which he was crucified; to the fragments of the true cross, or the nails with which he was pierced, and to the tomb in which he was laid. Others have done as much for scores of mythological personages who never lived in the flesh. Did not Damis, the beloved disciple of Apollonius of Tyana, while on his way to India, see, on Mt. Caucasus, the identical chains with which Prometheus had been bound to the rocks? Did not the Scythians say that Hercules had visited their country? and did not they show the print of his foot upon a rock to substantiate their story? Was not his tomb to be seen at Cadiz, where his bones were shown? Was not the tomb of Apollo to be seen at Delphi? Was not the tomb of Achilles to be seen at Dodona . . . ? Was not the tomb of Aesculapius to be seen in Arcadia . . . ? Was not the tomb of Deucalion—he who was saved from the Deluge—long pointed out . . . in Athens? Was not the tomb of Osiris to be seen in Egypt . . . ? . . . Of what value, then, is such evidence of the existence of such an individual as Jesus of Nazareth?[21]

Basically, there is no physical evidence for the existence of Jesus Christ. In addition, since there are sacred sites all over the globe, for every culture, it is merely cultural bias that allows so many to claim that theirs are the only true ones, that their land is *the* "Holy Land" or some other designation.

The Bible as History?

Furthermore, if we look to the archaeological evidence to support the Old Testament, we will find much less than expected. Although the texts make the Jewish people appear to have been a force to be reckoned with in the region, there is no evidence of grand buildings, navies or militaries of the Jews. In fact, during the centuries prior to the Christian era, the Greeks barely noticed the Jews, and the famous historian Herodotus could not find the "great" kingdom of Judah: ". . . Solomon, *whose magnificent empire was invisible to Herodotus*, when searching for kingdoms in Judea . . ."[22] As Hazelrigg relates:

> "Where is the empire of Solomon the Magnificent? It is not noticed by Herodotus, Plato, or Diodorus Siculus. It is a most extraordinary fact that the Jewish nation, over whom . . . the mighty Solomon had reigned in all his glory and magnificence scarcely equaled by the greatest monarchs, spending nearly *eight*

thousand millions of gold on a temple, was overlooked by the historian Herodotus writing of Egypt on one side and of Babylon on the other—visiting both places, and of course almost necessarily passing within a few miles of the splendid capital of the national Jerusalem. How can this be accounted for? Suleyman was a Persian title equivalent to the Greek Aiolos, and meant universal emperor. Like Pharaoh, it was not a name, but a designation of rank. The Jews, aiming at universal empire, feigned that one of their kings bare this name; and it is with this petty pilfered thane (for in a little place like Judea he could be no other), that the mighty Suleymans of the Orient are confounded alike by the civilized European and the ignorant Bedoween."—Kenealy, *The Book of God*. One need not search very diligently in order to find similar disparities between biblical statement and the inferences of historical evidence.[23]

This dearth of evidence for such an empire was noticed at least 2,000 years ago, and eventually provoked the Jewish historian Josephus to write his *Antiquities of the Jews* to demonstrate that the Hebrew culture was very old. While the Hebrew culture may have been old, the "nation of Israel" in fact was not a "great empire" but a group of warring desert tribes with grandiose stories "borrowed" from other cultures. Out of this fertile imagination and opportunism came an even more grandiose tale to end all tales: the Christian myth.

---

1. Wheless, *FC*, 112.
2. Fox, 392.
3. Carpenter, 180-1.
4. Doane, 502.
5. Dujardin, 2.
6. Doane, 203.
7. Levi, 4.
8. Higgins, II, 154.
9. Doane, 501.
10. P. J. Casey, *Understanding Ancient Coins An Introduction for Archaeologists and Historians*, Batsford, 1986, 43. (www.christianism.com)
11. Wells, *HEJ*, 194.
12. Fox, 69.
13. Walker, *WDSSO*, 309.
14. Freethought Datasheet #5, Atheists United.
15. Leedom, 164.
16. Walker, *WEMS*, 880-1.
17. Wells, *HEJ*, 184.
18. Walker, *WEMS*.
19. Hislop, 179.
20. Wheless, *FC*, 11-12.
21. Doane, 511.
22. Higgins, I, 668.
23. Hazelrigg, 178.

The Myth of Hebrew Monotheism

As demonstrated, the historical and archaeological record fails to provide any evidence whatsoever that the New Testament story is true. Nor does it bear out important Old Testament tales, such that the religion Christianity is purportedly based on is unsubstantiated as well. In fact, the very notion of the monotheistic Hebrew God, as allegedly depicted in the Old Testament, who could produce a son, is baseless.

It is a common belief that the Hebrew people, beginning with Moses, were monotheists whose one god, Yahweh, was the only true god, as revealed exclusively to Hebrew prophets. These original monotheists, it is believed, were superior to and had the right to destroy the polytheistic cultures around them by killing their people and stealing their towns, booty and virgin girls, which is what "God's chosen" are recorded as doing throughout the Old Testament. This monotheist versus polytheist scenario is the common perception, but it is incorrect, as the Hebrews were latecomers to the idea of monotheism and were originally themselves polytheists. In actuality, the Hebrews were by no means the originators of the concept of monotheism, as the Egyptians, for one, had the One God at least a thousand years before the purported time of Moses, by orthodox dating. As Wheless says:

> [T]his finally and very late evolved monotheism is neither a tardy divine revelation to the Jews, nor a novel invention by them; it was a thousand years antedated by Amenhotep IV and Tut-ankh-amen in Egypt—nor were even they pioneers. We have seen the [Catholic] admission that the Zoroastrian Mithra religion was "a divinely revealed Monotheism" (*CE.* ii, 156).[1]

The monotheism of the Persian religion of Zoroastrianism, in fact, is virtually identical to that of Judaism, or Yahwism, which is, in part, an offshoot of Zoroastrianism:

> Ormuzd says to Zoroaster, in the Boundehesch: "I am he who holds the Star-Spangled Heaven in ethereal space; who makes this sphere, which once was buried in darkness, a flood of light. Through me the Earth became a world firm and lasting—the earth on which walks the Lord of the world. I am he who makes the light of Sun, Moon, and Stars pierce the clouds. I make the corn seed, which perishing in the ground sprouts anew . . . . I created man, whose eye is light, whose life is the breath of his nostrils. I placed within him life's unextinguishable power."[2]

Prior to the intrusion of monotheistic Yahwism, the Hebrews were not monotheists separate and apart from their polytheistic "Gentile" neighbors, either before or after Moses. This Hebrew polytheism is why in the Old Testament "the chosen" are constantly depicted as "going after" other gods and why "the LORD God" himself changes from hero to hero, king to king and book to book. As to the polytheism of the Hebrews and the supposed superiority of monotheism, Robertson says:

> There is overwhelming testimony to the boundless polytheism of the mass of people even in Jerusalem, the special seat of Yahweh, just before the Captivity. Monotheism did not really gain a hold in the sacred city until a long series of political pressures and convulsions had built up a special fanaticism for one cult. . . . Monotheism of this type is in any case morally lower than polytheism since those who held it lacked sympathy for their neighbors. Most of the Jewish kings were polytheists. What I am concerned to challenge is the assumption—due to the influence of Christianity—that Jewish monotheism is essentially higher than polytheism, and constitutes a great advance in the progress of religion. . . . If the mere affirmation of a Supreme Creator God is taken to be a mark of superiority, certain primitive tribes who hold this doctrine and yet practice human sacrifice must be considered to have a "higher" religion than the late Greeks and Romans.[3]

The Hebrew polytheism is reflected in the various biblical names for "God," the oldest of which were the plural Elohim, Baalim and Adonai, representing both male and female deities. In order to make the Hebrews appear monotheistic, the biblical writers and translators obfuscated these various terms and translated them as the singular "God" (Elohim), "the Lord" (Adonai), "the LORD God" (Elohim YHWH) or "the LORD" (YHWH/IEUE). As Higgins states:

> In the original, God is called by a variety of names, often the same as that which the Heathens gave to their Gods. To disguise this, the translators have availed themselves of a contrivance adopted by the Jews in rendering the Hebrew into Greek, which is to render the word . . . *Ieue* [YHWH], and several of the other names by which God is called in the Bible, by the word . . . Lord . . . The fact of the names of God being disguised in all the translations tends to prove that no dependence can be placed on any of them. The fact shows very clearly the temper or state of mind with which the translators have undertaken their task. God is called by several names. How is the reader of a translation to discover this, if he find them all rendered by one name? He is evidently deceived. It is no justification of a translator to say it is of little consequence. Little or great, he has no right to exercise any discretion of this kind. When he finds God called Adonai, he has no business to call him Jehovah or Elohim. . . . The fact that Abraham worshipped several gods, who were, in reality, the same as those of the Persians, namely, the creator, preserver, and the destroyer, has been long asserted,

and the assertion has been very unpalatable both to Jews and
many Christians; and to obviate or disguise what they could not
account for, they have had recourse, in numerous instances, to
the mistranslation of the original . . .⁴

The Biblical Writers

Although many people still believe that the Bible is a
monolithic product of the Almighty Himself, infallibly recorded by
the authors purported, the reality is that "Moses" did not write
the Pentateuch, or first five books, and that the other OT texts
are, like those of the NT, pseudepigraphical, i.e., not written by
those in whose names they appear. Also like the NT, over the
centuries the various texts of the OT were "redacted" many times,
which is a polite way of saying they were interpolated, mutilated
and forged. As Wheless says of the Old Testament:

> It may be stated with assurance that not one of them bears the
> name of its true author; that every one of them is a composite
> work of many hands "interpolating" the most anachronistic
> and contradictory matters into the original writings, and often
> reciting as accomplished facts things which occurred many
> centuries after the time of the supposed writer . . . ⁵

The Pentateuch, for example, had at least four authors or
schools of writers. Even though they are of different authors,
these separate segments, some of which were written centuries
apart, were interwoven in a confusing yet clever manner. The
oldest section of these books is called "E," for "Elohist," so-named
because the writer mostly uses the word "Elohim" for "God,"
although it should be rendered "Gods." The next section is the
"Yahwist/Jahwist" or "J" account wherein God is called
"Yahweh," designated by the tetragrammaton YHWH. The major
portion of the Pentateuch was created by "P," for Priestly, who
refers to God mostly as Elohim and less often as Yahweh. The
next discernible influence is "D," the Deuteronomist, who
apparently cobbled together J and E, along with the laws of
Deuteronomy, then wrote the "history" books that follow,
including Joshua, Judges, 1 and 2 Samuel, and 1 and 2 Kings.
The Deuteronomist is fanatically Yahwist and writes his
"histories" of the kings from a biased perspective, judging their
reigns based on whether or not they had "done right in the sight
of Yahweh." Finally, someone or a school called by scholars the
Redactor ("R"), possibly the author of "Ezra," pulled together the
various works during or after the "Babylonian captivity" (586-538
BCE).
These various texts and their authors represent different
schools of thoughts and influences, as well as competing
priesthoods, explaining why the harried folk of the Levant were

constantly falling out of favor with their God(s). The Elohist's stories are often silly and nonsensical, when taken literally, because they actually represent the mythologies of a variety of cultures from Canaan/Phoenicia to Egypt, Persia and India. The Yahwist, who portrays some of the same anthropomorphic myths as E, is, of course, very concerned with the Jealous God, Yahweh, as opposed to the various Elohim. P dispenses with the tall tales and portrays his Elohim, now a unified entity, as very cosmic and impersonal, rather than walking about in the Garden of Eden, for example. D and R are, of course, Yahwistic.

As stated, in order to represent the polytheistic Hebrews as monotheists the biblical writers mutilated texts and reinterpreted history, while the translators used the trick of rendering these many gods and goddesses as the singular "God," "Lord," or "LORD." For example, the word YHWH, transliterated as Jehovah, appears over 6,700 times in each of the Darby and Young's Literal (YLT) translations, while it is used only four times in the King James Version (KJV) and not once in the most modern versions such as the RSV and NIV. Of these versions, only the Darby retains the word "Elohim" for "God(s)," and this word almost always is accompanied by "Jehovah," even though "the LORD God" was not called YHWH until the time of Moses. In this way, translators have given the appearance of uniformity where there was none.

Elohim

The plural term Elohim appears over 2500 times in the Old Testament but is falsely translated in most versions. This fact of plurality explains why in Genesis "Gods" said, "Let *us* make man in *our* image." As stated, Elohim refers to both "gods" and "goddesses," and its singular form, El, served as a prefix or suffix to names of gods, people and places, whence Emmanu-El, Gabri-El, Beth-El, etc. Even "Satan" was one of the Elohim, as Walker relates:

> In the original wording, Satan was one of the *bene ha-elohim*, sons of "the gods"; but Bible translators always singularized the plurals to conceal the facts that the biblical Jews worshipped a pantheon of multiple gods.[6]

Of the Elohim, Taylor says:

> The Jewish *Elohim* were the decans of the Egyptians; the same as the genii of the months and planets among the Persians and Chaldeans; and Jao, or Yahouh, considered merely as one of the beings generically called Elohim or Alehim, appears to have been only a national or topical deity.[7]

The Elohim were in reality a number of "El" gods, such as El Elyon, the "God Most High"; El Sabaoth, the "God of the Heavenly Hosts"; El Chay, the "Living God"; El Neqamah, the "God of Vengeance"; El Ma'al, the "God Above"; and El Shaddai, the "Almighty God." El Shaddai was the name of the god of Abraham, or the "God of the fathers," who was replaced by Yahweh in the 6th chapter of Exodus:

> And God spake unto Moses and said unto him, I am Yahweh: and I appeared unto Abraham, unto Isaac, and unto Jacob, by the name of El Shaddai, but by my name Yahweh I was not known unto them.[8]

Charles Potter relates that El Shaddai was later demonized in Psalms 106:37, condemned as one of the "devils"—the Canaanite *Shedim*, to whom the Israelites sacrificed their sons and daughters. Psalms 106, in fact, provides a concise chronicle of how the "chosen people" "whored after" other gods, i.e., were polytheistic.

In a somewhat common development of the human mind, which allows for polytheism, pantheism, monotheism and atheism at once, the Elohim became perceived as one "EL." The word El also represented a deity both male and female, but the later Jews generally interpreted it exclusively as male. El was the sun or "day star," as well as the planet Saturn, which at one point was considered the "central and everlasting sun" of the night sky. El/Saturn's worship is reflected in the fact that the Jews still consider Saturday as the Sabbath or "God's Day." Furthermore, El is Elias, "the sun god Helios to whom Jesus called from the cross. . ."[9] Since El is the sun, the many Elohim of the Bible also represent the stars.

The Elohim were not only Phoenician and Canaanite gods but as "Ali" were originally Egyptian. The Ali were considered the "associated gods" or "members, i.e. the lips, the limbs, the joints, the hands, etc., of Atum, or Amen, the son of Ptah."[10] Therefore, as in the Indian system, we have a sort of polytheistic monotheism in the Elohim. The "son of Ptah" is also called Iao/Iau/Iahu/Iu, the same as Yahweh. Therefore, the two accounts of Genesis, the Elohist and Jahwist, may be understood as reflecting the older Egyptian religion: "Thus the Elohim are represented in the first creation of man by the maker, Ptah, and in the second by Iu, the son of Ptah; and Iu, the son of Ptah, is Iahu-Elohim [the biblical LORD God], who becomes the creator of the second Adam [Atum] in the second chapter of the Hebrew Genesis."[11]

Baalim and Adonai

The god "Baal" and gods "Baalim" are mentioned dozens of times in the Old Testament, as the Israelites are frequently castigated or murdered by "their own" priests for "going after Baal." Like the Elohim, the plural Baalim or Baals were often represented by the singular "Baal," or "Ba'al," an Egyptian term combining "Ba," the symbol of the planet and goddess Venus, with "al" or "el," the designation of the sun. Thus, Baal was the name for the sun in the Age of Taurus (Bull), which was ruled by Venus. The Taurean age is one of 12 ages representing the astrological phenomenon called the "precession of the equinoxes," whereby the sun rising at the vernal or spring equinox is backdropped by a different constellation every 2,150 years. The precession takes nearly 26,000 years to move through the 12 constellations, a cycle called the "Great Year." The knowledge of the precession goes back many thousands of years and is found around the globe from China to Mexico,[12] reflecting that the so-called primitive ancients were in reality extraordinarily advanced. In addition, when the sun was in Taurus, beginning about 6,500 years ago, the bull motif sprang up in many parts of the world, including the Levant, where it symbolized Baal.

Like the other epithets for "God," Baal is a title meaning "Lord" or "husband"; it is, in fact, a very old appellation for the Deity, and can be found not only in Egypt but also in India as Bala.[13] In the ancient languages of Ireland and Sri Lanka, "Baal" means "sun."[14] Baal is in reality the earlier name of the character later known as Yahweh, as is stated at Hosea 2:16:

> And in that day, says YHWH, you will call me, "My husband,"
> and no longer will you call me "My Baal."

Walker relates that Baal was "'The Lord' among ancient Semites; consort of the goddess Astarte . . . Every god was a Baal. The title was introduced into Ireland via Phoenician colonies from Spain . . . Old Testament Jews worshipped many *baalim* as past or present consorts of the Goddess Zion (Hosea 2:2-8). Yahweh shared these other gods' temples for a long time, until his priesthood managed to isolate his cult and suppress the others."[15] And Blavatsky says, "The *Baal* of the Israelites (the Shemesh of the Moabites and the Moloch of the Ammonites) was the identical 'Sun-Jehovah,' and he is till now 'the King of the Host of Heaven,' the Sun, as much as Astoreth [Astarte] was the 'Queen of Heaven'—or the moon."[16] The other Baalim worshipped by the Israelites included "Baal Peor," the "Lord of the Gap," and "Baal Berith," "Lord of the Covenant." Another was "Baal Jehoshua," also Joshua or Jesus, the "Lord of Salvation," long before the Christian era.

Another word basically the same as Baal is Adonis, which in the plural is Adonai, a term used for "Lord" over 400 times in the Hebrew bible. Adonis, like Baal and El, is an epithet for the sun.

Yahweh

The attempted changeover from Elohim/Baalim/Adonai to Yahweh "coincided" with the arrival on the main stage of the Levitical priesthood, as Moses, to whom Yahweh purportedly first appeared, was said to have been a "son of Levi." Among other things, the Levites were fanatic priests obsessed in moving Israel from the Age of Taurus into that of Aries, the Ram/Lamb. In fact, in Exodus 12 Moses resets the precessional clock by changing the beginning of the year and instituting the passover and "the feast of the lamb and the salvation of Israel by the *blood* of the lamb."[17]

As stated, prior to being labeled Yahweh, the Israelite god was called "Baal," signifying the sun in the Age of Taurus. When the sun passed into Aries, "the Lord's" name was changed to the Egyptian Iao,[18] which became YHWH, IEUE, Yahweh, Jahweh, Jehovah and Jah. This ancient name "IAO/Iao" represents the totality of "God," as the "I" symbolizes unity, the "a" is the "alpha" or beginning, while the "o" is the "omega" or end.

In fact, the name Yahweh, Iao, or any number of variants thereof can be found in several cultures:

> In Phoenicia the Sun was known as Adonis . . . identical with Iao, or, according to the Chinese faith, Yao (Jehovah), the Sun, who makes his appearance in the world "at midnight of the twenty-fourth day of the twelfth month."[19]

YHWH/IEUE was additionally the Egyptian sun god Ra:

> Ra was the father in heaven, who has the title of "Huhi" the eternal, from which the Hebrews derived the name "Ihuh."[20]

Thus, the tetragrammaton or sacred name of God IAO/IEUE/YHWH is very old, pre-Israelite, and can be etymologically linked to numerous gods, even to "Jesus," or "Yahushua," whose name means "salvation" or "Iao/YHWH saves." As Higgins says:

> The pious Dr. Parkhurst . . . proves, from the authority of Diodorus Siculus, Varro, St. Augustin, etc., that the Iao, Jehovah, or *ieue*, or *ie* of the Jews, was the Jove of the Latins and Etruscans. . . . he allows that this *ie* was the name of Apollo . . . He then admits that this *ieue* Jehovah is Jesus Christ in the following sentences: "It would be almost endless to quote all the passages of scripture wherein the name . . . (*ieue*) is applied to Christ . . . they cannot miss of a scriptural demonstration that Jesus is Jehovah." But we have seen it is admitted that Jehovah is Jove, Apollo, Sol, whence it follows that Jesus is Jove, etc.[21]

Yahweh had yet another aspect to "his" persona, as at some early stage the "sacred tetragrammaton" of "God" was bi-gendered. As Walker states:

> Jewish mystical tradition viewed the original Jehovah as an androgyne, his/her name compounded as Jah (*jod*) and the pre-Hebraic name of Eve, Havah or Hawah, rendered *he-vau-he* in Hebrew letters. The four letters together made the sacred tetragrammaton, YHWH, the secret name of God. . . . The Bible contains many plagiarized excerpts from earlier hymns and prayers to Ishtar and other Goddess figures, with the name of Yahweh substituted for that of the female deity.[22]

Thus, even Yahweh was at one time plural, but "he" eventually became an all-male, sky god. This singular Yahweh was a warrior god, representing the sun in Aries, which is ruled by the warlike Mars and symbolized by the Ram—the same symbolic ram "caught in a thicket" near Abraham and used by him as a replacement sacrifice for his son Isaac. This warrior god Yahweh was not only Jealous but also *Zealous*, as his name is rendered in Young's Literal Translation:

> . . . for ye do not bow yourselves to another god—for Jehovah, whose name [is] *Zealous*, is a *zealous* God. (Exodus 34:14)

In fact, the same word in Hebrew is used for both jealous and zealous, although is transliterated differently, "qanna" being jealous and "qana," zealous.

As El Elyon was but one of the Canaanite Elohim, the Most High God, so was "Yahweh," as "El Qanna," the Jealous/Zealous God, which is why in the Old Testament he keeps sticking his nose in and shouting at everyone. The title "Jealous/Zealous" is also appropriate for a god represented by a volcano, as was Yahweh by the smoky and fiery Mt. Sinai. Hence, Yahweh's followers themselves were intolerant and hot-headed zealots.

As we have seen, Yahweh represented not only the sky but the sun, the heat, energy and fire of which were localized on the earth in the Jewish Yahweh, whose priests claimed dominance over all other gods and priests by using a volcano to frighten the Hebrews into submission. The word Yahweh or Yahveh in the Sanskrit means "overflowing," an apt description for a volcano god imposed upon the natives by the use of its eruptions and lava flows. In regard to Yahweh's volcanic nature, Stone relates:

> In the Exodus account of the "mountain of God" we read these descriptions: "On the third day when the morning came, there were peals of thunder and flashes of lightning, dense cloud on the mountain and a loud trumpet blast; the people in the camp were all terrified." (Exod. 19:16). And in Exod. 20:18-21: "When all the people saw how it thundered and the lightning flashed,

when they heard the trumpet sound and saw the mountain smoking, they trembled and stood at a distance."[23]

Deuteronomy 9:21 relates that Moses took the golden calf, ground it into dust and threw it "into the torrent that flowed down the mountain." Moreover, Numbers 11 and Psalms 11, 18 and 97 speak of the Lord's fire and volcanic activity. As Stone also states:

> Surely the most vivid description of Yahweh as a volcanic mountain occurs in Ps. 18. Here we read, "The earth heaved and quaked, the foundations of the mountain shook; they heaved, because He was angry. Smoke arose from his nostrils, devouring fire came out of His mouth, glowing coals and searing heat . . . Thick clouds came out of the radiance before Him, hailstones and glowing coals. . . He shot forth lightning shafts and sent them echoing." The imagery is hard to ignore.[24]

Furthermore, a representation of the Jewish "Feast of the giving of the law" has an image of an erupting volcano—Mt. Sinai—with the two tablets of the Ten Commandments above it. As Jordan Maxwell points out, the benediction or blessing sign of the Feast is the same as the split-fingered, "live long and prosper" salutation of the Vulcan character Spock on "Star Trek." Vulcan, of course, is the same word as volcano, and the Roman god Vulcan was also a lightning and volcano god. In volcano cults, the thunderous noise coming from the mountain is considered the "voice of God," the same voice that "spoke" to Moses in the myth.

Indeed, if Yahweh were not a volcano god, his violent and angry persona would be doubly repulsive. As Taylor relates:

> Sometimes he is described as roaring like a lion, at others as hissing like a snake, as burning with rage, and unable to restrain his own passions, as kicking, smiting, cursing, swearing, smelling, vomiting, repenting, being grieved at his heart, his fury coming up in his face, his nostrils smoking, etc.[25]

As stated, Yahweh the volcano god made his entrance at the same time as Moses and Aaron, brothers and "sons of Levi." Moses and Aaron were in reality only made to appear to be Levites, a tribe that, it is posited, were actually "Indo-Europeans invaders" who took over the desert tribes and forced a centralized religion on them in order to gain power and wealth. These zealots, however, need not have been "invaders" as such, since Indo-European/Aryans already dwelled among the Semites. Although the "house of Levi" is purported to descend from the "sons of Shem," i.e., to be Semites, it appears that at least some of the Levites may have been "sons of Japheth," known as Assyrians, Persians, Babylonians and assorted other "Chittim," "Kittim" or "Kittaeans," a generic Jewish term for Aryans. Both of these groups, Semites and Aryans, are claimed in the Bible to have been "sons of Noah" who were to "share the same tent" and to enslave the descendants of Noah's third son, the Hamites; thus, at some point their distinction could not have been very pronounced. In fact, the Aryans and Semites are more intermingled than suspected, as some of the "sons of Japheth" became Ashkenazi, or "European Jews," as stated at Genesis 10:2-3. Indeed, the distinction was made long afterwards, when the Yahwists were compiling their books and attempting to promote themselves as strict segregationists. Furthermore, these Yahweh zealots incorporated Egyptian mythology, such that they were "Indo-Aryan-Egyptians," precisely the mix found in the Levant. Wherever they were from, the Levites certainly represented a break from the old, polytheistic Semitic/Hebrew tribes.

This break is thus reflected in the story of Moses, where the Hebrews are portrayed as having a difficult time turning from their ancient worship of the Egyptian god Horus as the golden calf, son of the Egyptian mother goddess, Hathor, who was represented as a cow. As Walker states:

> Egypt revered Mother Hathor as the heavenly cow whose udder produced the Milky Way, whose body was the firmament, and who daily gave birth to the sun, Horus-Ra, her Golden Calf, the same deity worshipped by Aaron and the Israelites: "These be thy gods, O Israel, which brought thee up out of the land of Egypt" (Exodus 32:4).[26]

Even though Yahweh was also identified with the sun, the Golden Calf was so horrifying to the Judean Levites that they wrote diatribes against its worship, such as the book of Hosea, whose author rails against the Baals and the "calf of Samaria," the nation also called Israel, as well as Ephraim, after the "son of Joseph." Moses's Levitical/Yahwist law, however, evidently didn't stick, as even the exalted Hebrew patriarch Solomon set up for his foreign wives altars to the Moabite sun god Chemosh and the Tyrian sun and fire god Moloch, Molech, Melech or Melek. Although he was purportedly vilified by "the Lord," Chemosh was, as Walker relates, the "Hebrew form of Shamash, the sun god of Sippar and Moab, worshipped in the temple of Solomon (1 Kings 11:17). Because Chemosh was one of Yahweh's rivals, called an 'abomination' by later priests attempting to suppress all cults but their own, he was adopted into the still later Christian pantheon of hell as a demon."[27]

Like that of India and Egypt, the Levantine pantheon of the first millennium BCE was in fact burgeoning with deities. As noted, even Yahweh himself was not a single god, nor is "he" found in any one culture. In fact, Yahweh was at one point associated with the Indian elephant-headed god Ganesha, whose title was "Lord of Hosts," also a biblical epithet for Yahweh. As Yahweh is purported to have done in the later gospel story, in Indian mythology Ganesha "impregnated the Virgin Goddess Maya, who subsequently gave birth to Buddha."[28] If Yahweh is the monotheistic father god who gave birth to Jesus, he must also have given birth to Buddha. However, as the Hebrew god Behemoth, Ganesha was later demonized by the Christians.[29] Yahweh also took many of his attributes from the Babylonian god Marduk, who "created the world by separating the celestial and the abyssal waters."[30] In fact, Marduk and Ishtar were worshipped by the Jews at Elam.[31] Among these many gods revered by the Hebrews was also the Sumero-Babylonian goddess Aruru, who was worshipped in the Jewish temple.[32]

Furthermore, the word Israel itself is not a Jewish appellation but comes from the combination of three different reigning deities: Isis, the goddess revered throughout the ancient world; Ra, the Egyptian sun god; and El. As Hazelrigg says:

> . . . Israel, meaning a belt or land of the heavens, the twelve tribes of which compare to the number of constellations that environ the ecliptic, and through which the Sun makes his annual circuit. . . . Issa-ra-el, the kingdom of the moon (Isis), Sun (Ra), and stars (El).[33]

In addition, the Syrian savior Tammuz was the god or genius of Jerusalem, where also the Greek god Dionysus was worshipped "under his Phrygian name of Zeus Sabazius."[34] In fact, Jewish coins have been found with the images of Dionysus on one side and the word YHWH on the other. Walker relates that "Jews living in Asia Minor said their Jehovah was another form of Zeus Sabazius."[35] The Hebrews are also reported to have sacrificed rams to Jupiter.[36]

Thus, as Wheless says, "The Hebrew-Christian One-God is a patent Forgery and Myth . . ."[37]

The Imposition of Monotheism

The myth of Hebrew monotheism comes from the Yahweh propagandists who set about to formulate "the" Jewish religion. While the Elohim were the special gods of the northern tribes and kingdom of Israel, the Levitical Yahweh was in fact the local god of the southern kingdom of Judah. As such, Yahweh is made to elevate Judah above all the other tribes by making it the progenitor of the kings of Israel. In fact, Yahweh and Judah are basically the same word, as Judah is "Yahuda," which means "Yahweh, I will praise." This name Judah is also the same as Judas, which was thus likewise the name of the tribal god.

Hence, it was the Jews and not all Hebrews and Israelites who were Yahweh-fanatics. The other nations, in fact, were frequently both disinterested in and repulsed by the violent, angry, jealous, zealous god that Yahweh became. As Knight and Lomas say:

> For many, Yahweh was no more than the Israelite war god, useful in time of battle but a fairly lowly figure when viewed against the full pantheon of the gods. The names given to notable Israelites down the ages shows a strong respect for Baal, and even the most ardent Yahwist would not pretend that the Jews of this period believed in only one god.[38]

The Yahwists were in reality a rude bunch of marauders who pretended to speak for their "Lord" and who then spent centuries destroying the ancient Hebrew polytheism so they could hold total power over the people. Their favorite targets were the followers of the Great Goddess, who were ubiquitous in the ancient world. Larson illustrates how prevalent and long-lived was the worship of the Goddess and how great the zeal to destroy it:

> The Old Testament contains at least forty passages in which the Yahweh prophets denounce the temple groves of Ashtoreth (Ishtar) with their sacred prostitution; and it is obvious that the Israelites celebrated her ritual almost universally until the middle of the seventh century.[39]

The much-vilified biblical character Jezebel was in reality a refined priestess of Baal and Astoreth, the Goddess, while her main nemesis, Elijah, a Yahweh zealot, as evidenced by his name, was a crude, dirty and hairy wildman. Except in the eyes of the Yahwists, Jezebel was considered Hebrew royalty, and her worship of the Great Goddess was consistent with what had existed prior to the Yahwist invasion. In fact, in the Old Testament the Yahwist priests are depicted as virtually foaming at the mouth in describing "their" people as worshipping Baal and Astoreth, but many of "their" people at this time were virgin girls who had been the only ones spared as the Yahwist thugs captured town after town, slaughtering the inhabitants, stealing their property and raping their young (Num. 31:17-18, et al.). These surviving girls continued their ancient tradition of worship, including that of the Goddess and assorted Baals, much to the constant frustration and outrage of the sexist, patriarchal and virgin-enslaving Yahwists.

In order to establish their supremacy, the creed and duty of the Yahwists were as follows:

> You shall surely destroy all the places where the nations whom you shall dispossess served their gods, upon the high mountains and upon the hills and under every green tree; you shall tear down their altars, and dash in pieces their pillars, and burn their

Asherim with fire; you shall hew down the graven images of their
gods, and destroy their name out of that place. (Deut. 12:2-3)

Part of the Hebrews' ancient worship included the
establishment of "high places" where they set up altars and other
religious accoutrements, including the "Asherim," or singular
Asherah, "the stylized multibranched tree symbolizing the Great
Goddess of Canaan."[40] The Asherim were erected by Hebrews
such as the patriarch Abraham in Beer-Sheba, yet later Yahwist
fanatics destroyed them.[41] These Asherim in sacred groves served
as "astronomical instruments," reflecting the connection between
trees and the stars, which possessed the names of trees.[42]

These sacred high places were specially constructed all over
the Levant as sites of sacrifice, both animal and human, by non-
Semites and Semites alike, the latter of whom were, in fact, the
last people to maintain human sacrifice, into Hadrian's time,
when it was banned.[43] These sacrifices on high places, however,
served not only for the propitiation of the Gods but also to provide
food, and this was the major reason the monopolizing Yahwists
went after the high places: So that they could control the Hebrews
down to the food they ate, giving the priests tremendous power.
Obviously, it is more than unreasonable to insist that, in order to
eat, the people of a nation must all go to a centralized place,
where they are compelled to pay a priest to sacrifice their food
animals; thus, the people relentlessly rebuilt the high places and
ignored the centralizing priests. When the threats and destruction
of the high places failed to end the polytheism, however, the
Yahwists repeatedly butchered "their own" people (Num. 25, Ezek.
9), demonstrating that the repressive, despotic monotheism is no
more "moral" than other religious or secular ideologies and
governing systems. In the face of such unbearable oppression as
having their food controlled, the people not only rebelled against
the imposed Jealous/Zealous God, YHWH, they turned to other
gods to get rid of him.

In fact, according to the biblical story it was this oppression
that split the kingdom in two after Solomon's death, at which
time the northern kingdom of Israel returned to the old
polytheism under the Ephraimite king Jeroboam. Jeroboam, it
should be noted, was appointed by Solomon to be the foreman
over the *slaves* of the "house of Joseph," i.e., Ephraim/Manasseh
(1 Kings 11:28), who had originally inhabited the northern lands
but whom the genocidal tribe of Judah had been unable to
exterminate (1 Kings 9:20). The division actually occurred after
the people, including Jeroboam, asked Solomon's son Rehoboam
to "lighten the yoke" of his father. Jeroboam then made two
golden calves at the Hebrew sacred sites of Dan and Beth-El and

said to the northern Israelites, "*You have gone up to Jerusalem long enough.* Behold your gods, O Israel, who brought you out of the land of Egypt." Jeroboam was thus expressing the frustration of the people, "Jews" and "Gentiles" alike, who had been slaves to the Jerusalemite priests. The king was also stating that it was the golden calf of Horus/Baal/Iusa, as opposed to the volcanic Yahweh, who brought Israel out of Egypt. According to the story, Jeroboam's efforts were doomed to failure, however, because a couple of centuries later two "reformer" kings, Hezekiah and Josiah, arose to reinstate the repressive and exploitative centralized worship. Hezekiah (715-687 BCE), in fact, "purged" Judah and Ephraim of their high places and Asherim in a frenzied rampage that destroyed centuries-old religious sanctuaries. Friedman says of this purge:

> The religious reform meant more than breaking idols and cleansing the Temple. It also meant destroying the places of worship of *Yahweh* outside of the Temple in Jerusalem. In addition to the Temple, there had been various local places where people could go to sacrifice to God. These places of worship in the local communities were called "high places." Hezekiah eliminated them. He promoted the centralization of the religion at the Temple in Jerusalem.[44]

The high priest of Jerusalem, therefore, came to hold enormous power, as Jerusalem was the only "Jewish" religious center left. Hezekiah also purportedly destroyed the bronze serpent of Moses, a 500-year-old religious relic, striking a blow at the Levitical priesthood traced through Moses ("Mushites"), an act that leaves one to wonder how Hezekiah could represent a "great" exemplar of the Mosaic law and religion.

After Hezekiah's death, his son Manasseh returned the local "pagan" worship to the people, but the reformers struck back with their favorite king Josiah, who was even more vehement than Hezekiah in his assaults on the old religion. In order to explain why the Hebrews kept going after other gods, the biblical writers pretended that the "book of the Law" of Moses had been "lost" and found 600 years later (622 BCE) by Josiah's high priest, Hilkiah, a "son of Zadok" or Sadducee. After reading the law, or before, depending on which of the contradictory accounts in the "infallible word" one reads, Josiah goes on a rampage and purges the high places.

The tale is obviously fictitious, as, in reality, it cannot be explained why, if Moses had been real and had such a dramatic and impactful life, his Law would have been "lost" in the first place. And if it had been lost, how did Hezekiah know to follow it when he made his purges and reforms? It is also inexplicable as to why "the Lord" would have gone to so much trouble to talk regularly with Moses and Aaron, give them an enormous amount of detailed instructions, and then just let "his chosen" put it all away for 600 years. Where was "the Lord" during this time? He was purportedly involved in every little detail of Israelite life, yet he never reminded them of the long-lost law?

The truth is that Hilkiah's book of law was created in his time or afterward in order to consolidate the power of the priesthood, in particular that of the Judean Levites. Shortly thereafter, Jerusalem was destroyed because it was considered troublesome, an oppressive atmosphere that may have been one of the reasons the majority of "Jews" did not return to Palestine after the end of the "Babylonian captivity."

This important incident of Josiah and the new law provides an example of how the Old Testament was not produced in the manner commonly portrayed but represents the work of several hands or schools. The early stories basically constitute ancient myths mixed with the tribal "histories," with a number of people over the centuries re-writing them for propagandistic purposes, long after their purported era. The fact is that the Hebrews/ Israelites were polytheists before and after the supposed finding of the law, and that the law itself was variously interpreted by the different tribes/nations. In addition to the variety of gods and doctrines represented by the biblical writers are these various tribes, with the Elohist, for example, affiliated with the kingdom of Israel and the Jahwist, Judah. The differing accounts, then, were combined in an attempt to unify the kingdoms, and the tribe/god whose scribes wrote the stories was elevated above the rest. As Robertson says, "Yahweh (or Yah, or Yaha) was simply a local worship aggrandized by the [tribal] king and imposed on the fictitious history of the Hebrews long afterwards."[45]

Doane sums up the state of Israel during biblical times:

> It is supposed by many—in fact, we have heard it asserted by those who should know better—that the Israelites were always *monotheists*, that they worshiped One God only—*Jehovah*. This is altogether erroneous; they were not different from their neighbors—the Heathen, so-called—in regard to their religion. In the first place, we know that [the Israelites] revered and worshiped a *Bull*, called *Apis*, just as the ancient Egyptians did. They worshiped the *sun*, the *moon*, and the *stars* and all the host of heaven. They worshiped *fire*, and kept it burning on an altar, just as the Persians and other nations. They worshiped *stones*, revered an *oak tree*, and "bowed down to *images*." They worshiped a "Queen of Heaven" called the goddess *Astarte* or *Mylitta*, and "burned incense" to her. They worshiped *Baal*, Moloch, and *Chemosh, and offered up human sacrifices to them,* after which in some instances, *they ate the victim.*[46]

The Hebrews were thus not distinct from their polytheistic neighbors, except after centuries of programming and conditioning that eventually caused them to become a "race separate and apart from the rest of the world." Stone relates:

> As George Mendenhall writes, "Ancient Israel can no longer be treated as an isolated independent object of study; its history is inseparably bound up with ancient oriental history, whether we are concerned with religion, political history or culture."[47]

The Levant, in fact, was a melting-pot of ideologies and gods of all sorts from around the known world, out of which would arise a "king of kings" and "lord of lords" to beat them all.

---

1. Wheless, *FC*, 70.
2. Pike, 612.
3. Roberston, 17-18.
4. Higgins, I, 62.
5. Wheless, 69.
6. Walker, *WEMS*, 895.
7. Taylor, 21.
8. Potter, 42.
9. Walker, *WEMS*, 84, 125, 271-2.
10. A. Churchward, 318.
11. A. Churchward, 318.
12. Jackson, 183-4.
13. Higgins, I, 238.
14. Higgins, II, 289.
15. Walker, *WEMS*, 84.
16. Blavatsky, *SD*, i, 397fn.
17. Anderson, 79.
18. Higgins, I, 259.
19. Hazelrigg, 20.
20. A. Churchward, 280.
21. Higgins, I, 327.
22. Walker, *WDSSO*, 202.
23. Stone, 122-3.
24. Stone, 123.
25. Taylor, 22.
26. Walker, *WEMS*, 180-1.
27. Walker, *WEMS*, 163.
28. Walker, *WDSSO*, 372.
29. Walker, *WDSSO*, 236.
30. Walker, *WEMS*, 581.
31. Walker, *WEMS*, 829.
32. Walker, *WEMS*, 815.
33. Hazelrigg, 20-21.
34. Walker, *WEMS*, 236-7.
35. Walker, *WEMS*, 874.
36. Carpenter, 47.
37. Wheless, FC, 78.
38. Christopher Knight & Robert Lomas, *The Hiram Key: Pharaohs, Freemasons and the Discovery of the Secret Scrolls of Jesus,*
    marlowe.wimsey.com/~rshand/streams/thera/canaan.html

39. Larson, 210.
40. Walker, *WDSSO*, 196.
41. Higgins, II, 194.
42. Higgins, II, 193.
43. Walker, *WEMS*, 464.
44. Friedman, 91-92.
45. Robertson, 17.
46. Doane, 108.
47. Stone, 103.

The Characters

We have seen that there is no evidence for the historicity of the Christian founder, that the earliest Christian proponents were as a whole either utterly credulous or astoundingly deceitful, and that said "defenders of the faith" were compelled under incessant charges of fraud to admit that Christianity was a rehash of older religions. It has also been demonstrated that the world into which Christianity was born was filled with assorted gods and goddesses, as opposed to a monotheistic vacuum. In fact, in their fabulous exploits and wondrous powers many of these gods and goddesses are virtually the same as the Christ character, as attested to by the Christian apologists themselves. In further inspecting this issue we discover that "Jesus Christ" is in fact a compilation of these various gods, who were worshipped and whose dramas were regularly played out by ancient peoples long before the Christian era.

Although many people have the impression that the ancient world consisted of unconnected nations and tribes, the truth is that during the era Jesus allegedly lived there was a trade and brotherhood network that stretched from Europe to China. This information network included the library at Alexandria and had access to numerous oral traditions and manuscripts that told the same narrative portrayed in the New Testament with different place names and ethnicity for the characters. In actuality, the legend of Jesus nearly identically parallels the story of Krishna, for example, even in detail, with the Indian myth dating to at least as far back as 1400 BCE. Even greater antiquity can be attributed to the well-woven Horus myth of Egypt, which also is practically identical to the Christian version but which preceded it by thousands of years.

The Jesus story incorporated elements from the tales of other deities recorded in this widespread area of the ancient world, including several of the following world saviors, most or all of whom predate the Christian myth. It is not suggested that all of these characters were used in the creation of the Christian myth, as some of them are found in parts of the world purportedly unknown at the time; however, it is certain that a fair number of these deities were utilized. Thus, we find the same tales around the world about a variety of godmen and sons of God, a number of whom also had virgin births or were of divine origin; were born on or near December 25th in a cave or underground; were baptized; worked miracles and marvels; held high morals, were compassionate, toiled for humanity and healed the sick; were the basis of soul-salvation and/or were called "Savior, Redeemer,

Deliverer"; had Eucharists; vanquished darkness; were hung on trees or crucified; and were resurrected and returned to heaven, whence they came. The list of these saviors and sons of God includes the following:

- Adad and Marduk of Assyria, who was considered "the Word" (Logos)
- Adonis, Aesclepius, Apollo (who was resurrected at the vernal equinox as the lamb), Dionysus, Heracles (Hercules) and Zeus of Greece
- Alcides of Thebes, divine redeemer born of a virgin around 1200 BCE[1]
- Attis of Phrygia
- Baal or Bel of Babylon/Phoenicia
- Balder and Frey of Scandinavia
- Bali of Afghanistan
- Beddru of Japan
- Buddha and Krishna of India
- Chu Chulainn of Ireland
- Codom and Deva Tat of Siam
- Crite of Chaldea
- Dahzbog of the Slavs
- Dumuzi of Sumeria
- Fo-hi, Lao-Kiun, Tien, and Chang-Ti of China, whose birth was attended by heavenly music, angels and shepherds[2]
- Hermes of Egypt/Greece, who was born of the Virgin Maia and called "the Logos" because he was the Messenger or Word of the Heavenly Father, Zeus.
- Hesus of the Druids and Gauls
- Horus, Osiris and Serapis of Egypt
- Indra of Tibet/India
- Ieo of China, who was "the great prophet, lawgiver and savior" with 70 disciples[3]
- Issa/Isa of Arabia, who was born of the Virgin Mary and was the "Divine Word" of the ancient Arabian Nasara/Nazarenes around 400 BCE[4]
- Jao of Nepal
- Jupiter/Jove of Rome
- Mithra of Persia/India
- Odin/Wodin/Woden/Wotan of the Scandinavians, who was "wounded with a spear."[5]
- Prometheus of Caucasus/Greece
- Quetzalcoatl of Mexico
- Quirinius of Rome

- Salivahana of southern India, who was a "divine child, born of a virgin, and was the son of a carpenter," himself also being called "the Carpenter," and whose name or title means "cross-borne" ("Salvation")[6]
- Tammuz of Syria, the savior god worshipped in Jerusalem
- Thor of the Gauls
- Universal Monarch of the Sibyls
- Wittoba of the Bilingonese/Telingonese
- Zalmoxis of Thrace, the savior who "promised eternal life to guests at his sacramental Last Supper. Then he went into the underworld, and rose again on the third day"[7]
- Zarathustra/Zoroaster of Persia
- Zoar of the Bonzes

This list does not pretend to be complete, nor is there adequate room here to go into detail of all these mythological characters. It should be noted that, as with Jesus, a number of these characters have been thought of in the past as being historical persons, but today almost none of them are considered as such.

The Major Players

Attis of Phrygia

The story of Attis, the crucified and resurrected Phrygian son of God, predates the Christian savior by centuries, in the same area as the gospel tale. Attis shares the following characteristics with Jesus:

- Attis was born on December 25th of the Virgin Nana.
- He was considered the savior who was slain for the salvation of mankind.
- His body as bread was eaten by his worshippers.
- His priests were "eunuchs for the kingdom of heaven."
- He was both the Divine Son and the Father.
- On "Black Friday," he was crucified on a tree, from which his holy blood ran down to redeem the earth.
- He descended into the underworld.
- After three days, Attis was resurrected on March 25th (as tradition held of Jesus) as the "Most High God."

Doane provides detail of the Attis drama, which was a recurring blood atonement:

Attys, who was called the "*Only-Begotten Son*" and "*Saviour*" was worshiped by the Phrygians (who were regarded as one of the oldest races of Asia Minor). He was represented by them as *a man tied to a tree*, at the foot of which was a *lamb*, and, without

doubt also *as a man nailed to the tree, or stake,* for we find
Lactantius making . . . Apollo of Miletus . . . say that: "He was a
mortal according to the flesh; wise in miraculous works; but,
being arrested by an armed force by command of the Chaldean
judges, *he suffered a death made bitter with nails and stakes.*"[8]

And in *Christianity Before Christ* Jackson relates:

In the Attis festival a pine tree was felled on the 22nd of March
and an effigy of the god was affixed to it, thus being slain and
hanged on a tree. . . . At night the priests found the tomb
illuminated from within but empty, since on the third day Attis
had arisen from the grave.[9]

The drama or passion of Attis took place in what was to
become Galatia, and it was the followers of Attis to whom Paul
addressed his Epistle to the Galatians at 3:1: "O foolish
Galatians! Who has bewitched you, before whose eyes Jesus
Christ was publicly portrayed as crucified?" Since the
Galatians presumably were not in Jerusalem when Christ was
purportedly crucified, we may sensibly ask just who this was
"publicly *portrayed* as crucified" before their eyes? This
"portrayal" certainly suggests the recurring passion of the cult
of Attis.

Again, in addressing the Galatians, Paul brings up what is
obviously a recurring event: "Christ redeemed us from the curse
of the law, having become a curse for us—for it is written, 'Cursed
be every one who hangs on a tree.'" (Gal. 3:13) As followers of
Attis, the addressees would understand the part about "every one
who hangs on a tree," since they, like other biblical peoples,
annually or periodically hung a proxy or effigy of the god on a
tree. As is the case in the Old Testament with ritualistic hangings,
this "cursing" is in fact a blessing or consecration.

Attis was popular not only in Phrygia/Galatia but also in
Rome, where he and Cybele, the Great Mother of the Gods, had a
temple on Vatican Hill for six centuries.[10] So similar was the Attis
myth to the Christian story that the Christians were forced to
resort to their specious argument that the devil had created the
Attis cult first to fool Christ's followers.

Buddha

Although most people think of Buddha as being one person
who lived around 500 BCE, the character commonly portrayed as
Buddha can also be demonstrated to be a compilation of godmen,
legends and sayings of various holy men both preceding and
succeeding the period attributed to *the* Buddha (Gautama/
Gotama), as was demonstrated by Robertson:

. . . Gotama was only one of a long series of Buddhas who arise at intervals and who all teach the same doctrine. The names of twenty-four of such Buddhas who appeared before Gotama have been recorded. . . . It was held that after the death of each Buddha, his religion flourishes for a time and then decays. After it is forgotten, a new Buddha emerges and preaches the lost Dhamma, or Truth. . . .

It seems quite probable in the light of these facts that any number of teachings attributed to "the Buddha" may have been in existence either before or at the time when Gotama was believed to have lived. . . .

The name Gotama is a common one; it is also full of mythological associations. There was admittedly *another* Gotama known to the early Buddhists, who founded an order. So what proof is there that the sayings and doings of different Gotamas may not have been ascribed to one person? . . .[11]

Because of this non-historicity and of the following characteristics of the Buddha myth, which are not widely known but which have their hoary roots in the mists of time, we can safely assume that Buddha is yet another personification of the ancient, universal mythos being revealed herein.

The Buddha character has the following in common with the Christ figure:

- Buddha was born on December 25th[12] of the virgin Maya, and his birth was attended by a "Star of Announcement,"[13] wise men[14] and angels singing heavenly songs.[15]
- At his birth, he was pronounced ruler of the world and presented with "costly jewels and precious substances."[16]
- His life was threatened by a king "who was advised to destroy the child, as he was liable to overthrow him."[17]
- Buddha was of royal lineage.
- He taught in the temple at 12.[18]
- He crushed a serpent's head (as was traditionally said of Jesus) and was tempted by Mara, the "Evil One," when fasting.
- Buddha was baptized in water, with the "Spirit of God" or "Holy Ghost" present.[19]
- He performed miracles and wonders, healed the sick, fed 500 men from a "small basket of cakes," and walked on water.[20]
- Buddha abolished idolatry, was a "sower of the word," and preached "the establishment of a kingdom of righteousness."[21]
- His followers were obliged to take vows of poverty and to renounce the world.[22]

- He was transfigured on a mount, when it was said that his face "shone as the brightness of the sun and moon."[23]
- In some traditions, he died on a cross.[24]
- He was resurrected, as his coverings were unrolled from his body and his tomb was opened by supernatural powers.[25]
- Buddha ascended bodily to Nirvana or "heaven."
- He was called "Lord," "Master," the "Light of the World," "God of Gods," "Father of the World," "Almighty and All-knowing Ruler," "Redeemer of All," "Holy One," the "Author of Happiness," "Possessor of All," the "Omnipotent," the "Supreme Being," the "Eternal One."[26]
- He was considered the "Sin Bearer," "Good Shepherd,"[27] the "Carpenter,"[28] the "Infinite and Everlasting,"[29] and the "Alpha and Omega."[30]
- He came to fulfill, not destroy, the law.[31]
- Buddha is to return "in the latter days" to restore order and to judge the dead."[32]

In addition to the characteristics of the "teaching/savior god" as outlined above, the Buddhistic influence in Christianity includes: Renouncing the world and its riches, including sex and family; the brotherhood of man; the virtue of charity and turning the cheek; and conversion. That Buddhism preceded Christianity is undeniable, as is its influence in the world long prior to the beginning of the Christian era. As Walker relates:

> Established 500 years before Christianity and widely publicized throughout the Middle East, Buddhism exerted more influence on early Christianity than church fathers liked to admit, since they viewed Oriental religions in general as devil worship. . . . Stories of the Buddha and his many incarnations circulated incessantly throughout the ancient world, especially since Buddhist monks traveled to Egypt, Greece, and Asia Minor four centuries before Christ, to spread their doctrines. . . . Many scholars have pointed out that the basic tenets of Christianity were basic tenets of Buddhism first; but it is also true that the ceremonies and trappings of both religions were more similar than either has wanted to acknowledge.[33]

As to Buddhistic influence in the specific area where the Christ drama purportedly took place, Larson states:

> Buddhist missionaries penetrated every portion of the then known world, including Greece, Egypt, Baktria, Asia Minor, and the Second Persian Empire. Palestine must have been permeated by Buddhist ideology during the first century. . . . The literature of India proves that Jesus drew heavily upon Buddhism, directly or indirectly, to obtain not simply the content of His ethics, but

the very form in which it was delivered. Both Gautama and Jesus found parable effective.[34]

Indeed, it seems that a number of Jesus's parables were direct lifts from Buddhism; for example, that of the prodigal son.[35]

The existence of Buddhism in the Middle East during the Christian era is acknowledged by Christian apologists themselves such as Cyril and Clement of Alexandria, who said the Samaneans or Buddhists were priests of Persia.[36]

Furthermore, a number of scholars have pushed back the origins of Buddhism many thousands of years prior to the alleged advent of Gautama Buddha. Albert Churchward also traces the Buddha myth originally to Egypt:

> The first Buddha was called Hermias, and can be traced back to Set of the Egyptians; he originated in the Stellar Cult. Later, however, the Solar Cult was carried to India, and the Buddha is there the representative of Ptah of the Egyptians. . . . . Sakya-Muni or Gautama, whose life and history were evolved from the pre-extant mythos, the true Buddha, . . . could become no more historical than the Christ of the gnosis. If Buddhism could but explicate its own origins, it would become apparent that it is both natural and scientific, i.e. the old Stellar Cult of Egypt. But the blind attempt to make the Buddha historical in one person will place it ultimately at the bottom of a dark hole.[37]

Higgins also evinced that true "Buddhism" is much more ancient than the legends of *the* Buddha, since in ancient Indian temples long predating the era of "Gautama" are depictions of the Buddha as a *black* man, not only in color but in feature.[38] In Higgins's opinion, Buddhism has been the most widespread religion on the planet, also found in England, where it was the religion of the Druids. He also states that the "Hermes of Egypt, or Buddha, was well known to the ancient Canaanites," i.e., the people who preceded and in large part became the Israelites. Therefore, Buddhism was no doubt an early influence on Hebrew thought and religion.

Dionysus/Bacchus

Dionysus or Bacchus is thought of as being Greek, but he is a remake of the Egyptian god Osiris, whose cult extended throughout a large part of the ancient world for thousands of years. Dionysus's religion was well-developed in Thrace, northeast of Greece, and Phrygia, which became Galatia, where Attis also later reigned. Although Dionysus is best remembered for the rowdy celebrations in his name, which was Latinized as Bacchus, he had many other functions and contributed several aspects to the Jesus character:

- Dionysus was born of a virgin on December 25th[39] and, as the Holy Child, was placed in a manger.
- He was a traveling teacher who performed miracles.
- He "rode in a triumphal procession on an ass."[40]
- He was a sacred king killed and eaten in an eucharistic ritual for fecundity and purification.
- Dionysus rose from the dead on March 25th.
- He was the God of the Vine, and turned water into wine.
- He was called "King of Kings" and "God of Gods."
- He was considered the "Only Begotten Son," "Savior," "Redeemer," "Sin Bearer," "Anointed One," and the "Alpha and Omega."[41]
- He was identified with the Ram or Lamb.[42]
- His sacrificial title of "Dendrites" or "Young Man of the Tree" intimates he was hung on a tree or crucified.[43]

As Walker says, Dionysus was "a prototype of Christ with a cult center at Jerusalem," where during the 1st century BCE he was worshipped by Jews, as noted. Dionysus/Bacchus's symbol was "IHS" or "IES," which became "Iesus" or "Jesus." The "IHS" is used to this day in Catholic liturgy and iconography. As Roberts relates:

"IES," the Phoenician name of the god Bacchus or the Sun personified; the etymological meaning of that title being, "I" the one and "es" the fire or light; or taken as one word "ies" the one light. This is none other than the light of St. John's gospel; and this name is to be found everywhere on Christian altars, both Protestant and Catholic, thus clearly showing that the Christian religion is but a modification of Oriental Sun Worship, attributed to Zoroaster. The same letters IHS, which are in the Greek text, are read by Christians "Jes," and the Roman Christian priesthood added the terminus "us". . .

And Larson states:

Dionysus became the universal savior-god of the ancient world. And there has never been another like unto him: the first to whom his attributes were accredited, we call Osiris; with the death of paganism, his central characteristics were assumed by Jesus Christ.[44]

Like Jesus the Nazarene, Dionysus is the "true Vine," and the grape imagery is important to both cults. As Walker says:

[The grapevine] was preeminently an incarnation of Dionysus, or Bacchus, in his role of sacrificial savior. His immolation was likened to the pruning of the vine, necessary to its seasonal rebirth. . . . In Syria and Babylon the vine was a sacred tree of life. Old Testament writers adopted it as an emblem of the chosen people, and New Testament writers made it an emblem of

Christ (John 15:1, 5). When accompanied by wheat sheaves in sacred art, the vine signified the blood (wine) and body (bread) of the savior: an iconography that began in paganism and was soon adopted by early Christianity.[45]

On Crete, Dionysus was called Iasius,[46] a title also of the godman of the Orphic mysteries of Samothrace, who has been identified with Dionysus and who was promulgated by the "apostle" Orpheus in his missionary work as he took the same route later purportedly traveled by Paul. Iasius, Iesius or Jason is in fact equivalent to Jesus.

Hercules/Heracles

Heracles, or Hercules, is well-known for his 12 labors, which correspond to the 12 signs of the zodiac and are demonstrations of his role as "Savior." Born of a virgin, he was also known as the "Only Begotten" and "Universal Word."[47] The virgin mother of Heracles/Hercules was called Alcmene, whose name in Hebrew was "almah," the "moon-woman," who, as Walker says, "mothered sacred kings in the Jerusalem cult, and whose title was bestowed upon the virgin Mary. Parallels between earlier myths of Alcmene and later myths of Mary were too numerous to be coincidental. Alcmene's husband refrained from sexual relations with her until her god-begotten child was born."[48]

Walker also recounts the story of Hercules and its relationship to the Christian tale:

His Twelve Labors symbolized the sun's passage through the twelve houses of the zodiac . . . After his course was finished, he was clothed in the scarlet robe of the sacred king and killed, to be resurrected as his own divine father, to ascend to heaven . . . The influence of Heracles's cult on early Christianity can hardly be overestimated. St. Paul's home town of Tarsus regularly reenacted the sacred drama of Heracles's death by fire, which is why Paul assumed there was great saving virtue in giving one's body to be burned, like the Heracles-martyrs (1 Corinthians 13:3). Heracles was called Prince of Peace, Sun of Righteousness, Light of the World. He was the same sun greeted daily by the Persians and Essenes with the ritual phrase, "He is risen." The same formula announced Jesus's return from the underworld (Mark 16:6). He was sacrificed at the spring equinox (Easter), the New Year festival by the old reckoning. He was born at the winter solstice (Christmas), when the sun reaches his *nadir* and the constellation of the Virgin rises in the east. As Albert the Great put it centuries later, "The sign of the celestial virgin rises above the horizon, at the moment we find fixed for the birth of our Lord Jesus Christ."[49]

Horus/Osiris of Egypt

The legends of Osiris/Horus go back thousands of years, and many people over the millennia have thought Osiris to be a real person, some claiming he lived up to 22,000 years ago. The cult of Osiris, Isis and Horus was widespread in the ancient world, including in Rome. In the Egyptian myth, Horus and his once-and-future Father, Osiris, are frequently interchangeable, as in "I and my Father are one." Concerning Osiris, Walker says:

> Of all savior-gods worshipped at the beginning of the Christian era, Osiris may have contributed more details to the evolving Christ figure than any other. Already very old in Egypt, Osiris was identified with nearly every other Egyptian god and was on the way to absorbing them all. He had well over 200 divine names. He was called the Lord of Lords, King of Kings, God of Gods. He was the Resurrection and the Life, the Good Shepherd, Eternity and Everlastingness, the god who "made men and women to be born again." Budge says, "From first to last, Osiris was to the Egyptians the god-man who suffered, and died, and rose again, and reigned eternally in heaven. They believed that they would inherit eternal life, just as he had done. . . ."
>
> Osiris's coming was announced by Three Wise Men: the three stars Mintaka, Anilam, and Alnitak in the belt of Orion, which point directly to Osiris's star in the east, Sirius (Sothis), significator of his birth. . . .
>
> Certainly Osiris was a prototypical Messiah, as well as a devoured Host. His flesh was eaten in the form of communion cakes of wheat, the "plant of Truth.". . . The cult of Osiris contributed a number of ideas and phrases to the Bible. The 23rd Psalm copied an Egyptian text appealing to Osiris the Good Shepherd to lead the deceased to the "green pastures" and "still waters" of the *nefer-nefer* land, to restore the soul to the body, and to give protection in the valley of the shadow of death (the Tuat). The Lord's Prayer was prefigured by an Egyptian hymn to Osiris-Amen beginning, "O Amen, O Amen, who are in heaven." Amen was also invoked at the end of every prayer.[50]

As Col. James Churchward naively exclaims, "The teachings of Osiris and Jesus are wonderfully alike. Many passages are identically the same, word for word."[51]

Massey provides other details as to the similarity between Osirianism and Christianity:

> For instance, in one of the many titles of Osiris in all his forms and places he is called "*Osiris in the monstrance*". . . In the Roman ritual the monstrance is a transparent vessel in which the host or victim is exhibited. . . . Osiris in the monstrance should of itself suffice to show that the Egyptian Karast (Krst) is the original Christ, and that the Egyptian mysteries were continued by the Gnostics and Christianized in Rome.[52]

Osiris was also the god of the vine and a great travelling teacher who civilized the world. He was the ruler and judge of the dead. In his passion, Osiris was plotted against and killed by Set and "the 72." Like that of Jesus, Osiris's resurrection served to provide hope to all that they may do likewise and become eternal.

Osiris's "son" or renewed incarnation, Horus, shares the following in common with Jesus:

- Horus was born of the virgin Isis-*Meri* on December 25th in a cave/manger with his birth being announced by a star in the East and attended by three wise men.
- His earthly father was named "Seb" ("Joseph").
- He was of royal descent.[53]
- At age 12, he was a child teacher in the Temple, and at 30, he was baptized, having disappeared for 18 years.
- Horus was baptized in the river Eridanus or Iarutana (Jordan)[54] by "Anup the Baptizer" ("John the Baptist"),[55] who was decapitated.
- He had 12 disciples, two of whom were his "witnesses" and were named "Anup" and "Aan" (the two "Johns").
- He performed miracles, exorcised demons and raised El-Azarus ("El-Osiris"), from the dead.
- Horus walked on water.
- His personal epithet was "Iusa," the "ever-becoming son" of "Ptah," the "Father."[56] He was thus called "Holy Child."[57]
- He delivered a "Sermon on the Mount" and his followers recounted the "Sayings of Iusa."[58]
- Horus was transfigured on the Mount.
- He was crucified between two thieves, buried for three days in a tomb, and resurrected.
- He was also the "Way, the Truth, the Light," "Messiah," "God's Anointed Son," the "Son of Man," the "Good Shepherd," the "Lamb of God," the "Word made flesh," the "Word of Truth," etc.
- He was "the Fisher" and was associated with the Fish ("Ichthys"), Lamb and Lion.
- He came to fulfill the Law.[59]
- Horus was called "the KRST," or "Anointed One."[60]
- Like Jesus, "Horus was supposed to reign one thousand years."[61]

Furthermore, inscribed about 3,500 years ago on the walls of the Temple at Luxor were images of the Annunciation, Immaculate Conception, Birth and Adoration of Horus, with Thoth announcing to the Virgin Isis that she will conceive Horus; with Kneph, the "Holy Ghost," impregnating the virgin; and with the infant being attended by three kings, or magi, bearing gifts. In addition, in the catacombs at Rome are pictures of the baby Horus being held by the virgin mother Isis—the original "Madonna and Child." As Massey says:

> It was the gnostic art that reproduced the Hathor-Meri and Horus of Egypt as the Virgin and child-Christ of Rome . . . *You poor idiotai,* said the Gnostics [to the early Christians], *you have mistaken the mysteries of old for modern history, and accepted literally all that was only meant mystically.*[62]

Moreover, A. Churchward relates another aspect of the Egyptian religion found in Catholicism:

> We see in the ancient Catholic churches, over the main altar, an equilateral triangle, and within it an eye. The addition of the eye to the triangle originated in Egypt—"the all seeing eye of Osiris."[63]

Krishna of India

The similarities between the Christian character and the Indian messiah Krishna number in the hundreds, particularly when the early Christian texts now considered apocryphal are factored in. It should be noted that a common earlier English spelling of Krishna was "Christna," which reveals its relation to "Christ." Also, in Bengali, Krishna is reputedly "Christos," which is the same as the Greek for "Christ" and which the soldiers of Alexander the Great called Krishna. It should be further noted that, as with Jesus, Buddha and Osiris, many people have believed and continue to believe in a historical Krishna. The following is a partial list of the correspondences between Jesus and Krishna:

- Krishna was born of the Virgin Devaki ("Divine One") on December 25th.[64]
- His earthly father was a carpenter,[65] who was off in the city paying tax while Krishna was born.[66]
- His birth was signaled by a star in the east and attended by angels and shepherds, at which time he was presented with spices.
- The heavenly hosts danced and sang at his birth.[67]
- He was persecuted by a tyrant who ordered the slaughter of thousands of infants.
- Krishna was anointed on the head with oil by a woman whom he healed.[68]
- He is depicted as having his foot on the head of a serpent.
- He worked miracles and wonders, raising the dead and healing lepers, the deaf and the blind.

- Krishna used parables to teach the people about charity and love, and he "lived poor and he loved the poor."[69]
- He castigated the clergy, charging them with "ambition and hypocrisy. . . Tradition says he fell victim to their vengeance."[70]
- Krishna's "beloved disciple" was Arjuna or Ar-jouan (John).
- He was transfigured in front of his disciples.
- He gave his disciples the ability to work miracles.[71]
- His path was "strewn with branches."[72]
- In some traditions he died on a tree or was crucified between two thieves.
- Krishna was killed around the age of 30,[73] and the sun darkened at his death.[74]
- He rose from the dead and ascended to heaven "in the sight of all men."[75]
- He was depicted on a cross with nail-holes in his feet, as well as having a heart emblem on his clothing.[76]
- Krishna is the "lion of the tribe of Saki."[77]
- He was called the "Shepherd God" and considered the "Redeemer," "Firstborn," "Sin-Bearer," "Liberator," "Universal Word."[78]
- He was deemed the "Son of God" and "our Lord and Savior," who came to earth to die for man's salvation.[79]
- He was the second person of the Trinity.
- His disciples purportedly bestowed upon him the title "Jezeus," or "Jeseus," meaning "pure essence."[80]
- Krishna is to return to judge the dead, riding on a white horse, and to do battle with the "Prince of Evil," who will desolate the earth.[81]

The story of Krishna as recorded in the ancient Indian legends and texts penetrated the West on a number of occasions. One theory holds that Krishna worship made its way to Europe as early as 800 BCE, possibly brought by the Phoenicians. Higgins asserts that Krishna-worship in Ireland goes back even further, and he points to much linguistic and archaeological evidence of this early migration. Krishna was reinjected into Western culture on several other occasions, including by Alexander the Great after the expansion of his empire and his sojourn in India. It is also claimed that his worship was reintroduced during the first century CE by Apollonius of Tyana, who carried a fresh copy of the Krishna story in writing to the West, where it made its way to Alexandria, Egypt. Graham relates the tale:

The argument runs thus: There was in ancient India a very great sage called Deva Bodhisatoua. Among other things he wrote a mythological account of Krishna, sometimes spelled Chrishna. About 38 or 40 A.D., Apollonius while traveling in the East found this story in Singapore. He considered it so important he translated it into his own language, namely, Samaritan. In this he made several changes according to his own understanding and philosophy. On his return he brought it to Antioch, and there he died. Some thirty years later another Samaritan, Marcion, found it. He too made a copy with still more changes. This he brought to Rome about 130 A.D., where he translated it into Greek and Latin.[82]

Thus, we have the apparent origins of Marcion's Gospel of the Lord, which he claimed was the Gospel of Paul. In addition to the gospel story, the moralistic teachings purportedly introduced by Jesus were established long before by Krishna. These similarities constitute the reason why Christianity has failed, despite repeated efforts for centuries, to make headway in India, as the Brahmans have recognized Christianity as a relatively recent imitation of their much older traditions, which they have considered superior as well. Higgins relates:

> The learned Jesuit Baldaeus observes that every part of the life of Cristna [Krishna] has a near resemblance to the history of Christ; and he goes on to show that the time when the miracles are supposed to have been performed was during the Dwaparajug, which he admits to have ended 3,100 years before the Christian era. So that, as the Cantab says, *If there is meaning in words, the Christian missionary admits that the history of Christ was founded upon that of Crishnu* [Krishna].[83]

Mithra of Persia

Mithra/Mitra is a very ancient god found both in Persia and India and predating the Christian savior by hundreds to thousands of years. In fact, the cult of Mithra was shortly before the Christian era "the most popular and widely spread 'Pagan' religion of the times," as Wheless says. Wheless continues:

> Mithraism is one of the oldest religious systems on earth, as it dates from the dawn of history before the primitive Iranian race divided into sections which became Persian and Indian . . . When in 65-63 B.C., the conquering armies of Pompey were largely converted by its high precepts, they brought it with them into the Roman Empire. Mithraism spread with great rapidity throughout the Empire, and it was adopted, patronized and protected by a number of the Emperors up to the time of Constantine.[84]

Indeed, Mithraism represented the greatest challenge to Christianity, which won out by a hair over its competitor cult. Mithra has the following in common with the Christ character:

- Mithra was born of a virgin on December 25th in a cave, and his birth was attended by shepherds bearing gifts.
- He was considered a great traveling teacher and master.
- He had 12 companions or disciples.
- Mithra's followers were promised immortality.
- He performed miracles.
- As the "great bull of the Sun," Mithra sacrificed himself for world peace.[85]
- He was buried in a tomb and after three days rose again.
- His resurrection was celebrated every year.
- He was called "the Good Shepherd" and identified with both the Lamb and the Lion.
- He was considered the "Way, the Truth and the Light," and the "Logos," "Redeemer," "Savior" and "Messiah."
- His sacred day was Sunday, the "Lord's Day," hundreds of years before the appearance of Christ.
- Mithra had his principal festival on what was later to become Easter.
- His religion had a eucharist or "Lord's Supper," at which Mithra said, "He who shall not eat of my body nor drink of my blood so that he may be one with me and I with him, shall not be saved."[86]
- "His annual sacrifice is the passover of the Magi, a symbolical atonement or pledge of moral and physical regeneration."[87]

Furthermore, the Vatican itself is built upon the papacy of Mithra, and the Christian hierarchy is nearly identical to the Mithraic version it replaced. As Walker states:

> The cave of the Vatican belonged to Mithra until 376 A.D., when a city prefect suppressed the cult of the rival Savior and seized the shrine in the name of Christ, on the very birthday of the pagan god, December 25.[88]

Walker also says:

> Christians copied many details of the Mithraic mystery-religion, explaining the resemblance later with their favorite argument that the devil had anticipated the true faith by imitating it before Christ's birth.[89]

Shmuel Golding states, in *The Book Your Church Doesn't Want You to Read*:

> Paul says, "They drank from that spiritual rock and that rock was Christ" (I Cor. 10:4). These are identical words to those found in the Mithraic scriptures, except that the name Mithra is used instead of Christ. The Vatican hill in Rome that is regarded as sacred to Peter, the Christian rock, was already sacred to

Mithra. Many Mithraic remains have been found there. The merging of the worship of Attis into that of Mithra, then later into that of Jesus, was effected almost without interruption.[90]

In fact, the legendary home of Paul, Tarsus, was a site of Mithra worship.

Of Mithraism the *Catholic Encyclopedia* states, as related by Wheless, "The *fathers* conducted the worship. The chief of the fathers, a sort of *pope, who always lived at Rome*, was called 'Pater Patratus.'" The Mithraic pope was also known as Papa and Pontimus Maximus.

Virtually all of the elements of the Catholic ritual, from miter to wafer to altar to doxology, are directly taken from earlier Pagan mystery religions. As Taylor states, "That Popery has borrowed its principal ceremonies and doctrines from the rituals of Paganism,' is a fact which the most learned and orthodox of the established church have most strenuously maintained and most convincingly demonstrated."

Prometheus of Greece

The Greek god Prometheus is said to have migrated from Egypt, but his drama traditionally took place in the Caucasus mountains. Prometheus shares a number of striking similarities with the Christ character:

- Prometheus descended from heaven as God incarnate to save mankind.
- He had a "especially professed" friend, "Petraeus" (Peter), the fisherman, who deserted him.[91]
- He was crucified, suffered and rose from the dead.
- He was called the Logos or Word.

Quetzalcoatl of Mexico

Modern scientific orthodoxy allows neither for the date provided by Graves, i.e., that the Mexican Quetzalcoatl originated in the 6th century BCE, nor for pre-Columbian contact between the "Old" and "New" Worlds. The evidence, however, reveals that the mythos was indeed in Mexico long before the Christian era, suggesting such contact between the Worlds. In fact, tradition holds that the ancient Phoenicians, expert navigators, knew about the "lost land" to the West. One would therefore not be surprised to discover that the stories of the New World were contained in ancient libraries prior to the Christian era, such as at Alexandria, as was averred by Graves.[92]

However it got there, there can be no doubt as to the tremendous similarity between the Mexican religion and Catholicism. As Doane remarks:

> For ages before the landing of Columbus on its shores, the inhabitants of ancient Mexico worshiped a "Saviour"—as they called him—(*Quetzalcoatle*) who was *born of a pure virgin. A messenger from heaven announced to his mother that she should bear a son without connection with man.* Lord Kingsborough tells us that the annunciation of the *virgin Sochiquetzal,* mother of Quetzalcoatle—who was styled the "*Queen of Heaven*"—was the subject of a Mexican hieroglyph.[93]

Quetzalcoatl was also designated the morning star, was tempted and fasted for 40 days, and was consumed in a eucharist using a proxy, named after Quetzalcoatl. As Walker says:

> This devoured Savior, closely watched by his ten or twelve guards, embodied the god Quetzalcoatl, who was born of a virgin, slain in atonement for primal sin, and whose Second Coming was confidently expected. He was often represented as a trinity signified by three crosses, a large one between the smaller ones. Father Acosta naively said, "It is strange that the devil after his manner hath brought a Trinity into idolatry." His church found it all too familiar, and long kept his book as one of its secrets.[94]

The Mexicans revered the cross and baptized their children in a ritual of regeneration and rebirth long before the Christian contact.[95] In one of the few existing Codices is an image of the Mexican savior bending under the weight of a burdensome cross, in exactly the same manner in which Jesus is depicted. The Mexican crucifix depicted a man with nail holes in feet and hands, the Mexican Christ and redeemer who died for man's sins. In one crucifix image, this Savior was covered with suns.[96] Furthermore, the Mexicans had monasteries and nunneries, and called their high priests *Papes.*[97]

The Mexican savior and rituals were so disturbingly similar to the Christianity of the conquering Spaniards that Cortes was forced to use the standard, specious complaint that "the Devil had positively taught to the Mexicans the same things which God had taught to Christendom."[98] The Spaniards were also compelled to destroy as much of the evidence as was possible, burning books and defacing and wrecking temples, monuments and other artifacts.

Serapis of Egypt

Another god whose story was very similar to that of Christ, the evidence of which was also destroyed, was the Egyptian god Serapis or Sarapis, who was called the "Good Shepherd" and considered a healer. Walker says of Sarapis:

> Syncretic god worshipped as a supreme deity in Egypt to the end of the 4th century A.D. The highly popular cult of Sarapis used many trappings that were later adopted by Christians: chants,

lights, bells, vestments, processions, music. Sarapis represented a final transformation of the savior Osiris into a monotheistic figure, virtually identical to the Christian god. . . . This Ptolemaic god was a combination of Osiris and Apis. . . As Christ was a sacrificial lamb, so Sarapis was a sacrificial bull as well as god in human form. He was annually sacrificed in atonement for the sins of Egypt. . . .[99]

As we have seen, the image of Serapis, which once stood tall in the Serapion/Serapeum at Alexandria, was adopted by the later Christians as the image of Jesus, and the cult of Serapis was considered that of the original Christians. As Albert Churchward states:

The Catacombs of Rome are crowded with illustrations that were reproduced as Egypto-gnostic tenets, doctrines, and dogmas which had served to Persian, Greek, Roman, and Jew as evidence of the non-historic origins of Christianity. In the transition from the old Egyptian religion to the new Cult of Christianity there was no factor of profounder importance than the worship of Serapis. As the Emperor Hadrian relates, in his letter to Servianus, "Those who worship Serapis are likewise Christians: even those who style themselves the Bishops of Christ are devoted to Serapis."[100]

Zoroaster/Zarathustra

As they do concerning the founders of other religions and sects, many people have believed that Zoroaster was a single, real person who spread the Persian religion around 660 BCE. However, Zoroastrianism is asserted to have existed 10,000 years ago, and there have been at least "seven Zoroasters . . . recorded by different historians."[101] Thus, it is clear that Zoroaster is not a single person but another rendering of the ubiquitous mythos with a different ethnicity and flavor. Zoroaster's name means "son of a star," a common mythical epithet, which Jacolliot states is the Persian version of the more ancient Indian "Zuryastara (who restored the worship of the sun) from which comes this name of Zoroaster, which is itself but a title assigned to a political and religious legislator." Zoroaster has the following in common with the Christ character:

- Zoroaster was born of a virgin and "immaculate conception by a ray of divine reason."[102]
- He was baptized in a river.
- In his youth he astounded wise men with his wisdom.
- He was tempted in the wilderness by the devil.
- He began his ministry at age 30.
- Zoroaster baptized with water, fire and "holy wind."
- He cast out demons and restored the sight to a blind man.

- He taught about heaven and hell, and revealed mysteries, including resurrection, judgment, salvation and the apocalypse.[103]
- He had a sacred cup or grail.
- He was slain.
- His religion had a eucharist.
- He was the "Word made flesh."
- Zoroaster's followers expect a "second coming" in the virgin-born Saoshyant or Savior, who is to come in 2341 CE and begin his ministry at age 30, ushering in a golden age.

That Zoroastrianism permeated the Middle East prior to the Christian era is a well-known fact. As Mazdaism and Mithraism, it was a religion that went back centuries before the purported time of the "historical" Zoroaster. Its influence on Judaism and Christianity is unmistakable:

> When John the Baptist declared that he could baptize with water but that after him would come one who would baptize with fire and with Holy Ghost, he was uttering words which came directly from the heart of Zoroastrianism.[104]

"Zoroaster" considered nomads to be evil and agriculturalists good, and viewed Persia, or Iran, to be the Holy Land. Like his Christian missionary counterparts, he believed that the devil, Angra Mainyu or Ahriman, "sowed false religions," which his followers later claimed to be Judaism, Christianity, Manichaeism, and Islam.[105] And, like its offspring Yahwism, Zoroastrianism was monotheistic and forbade images or idols of God, who was called in Zoroastrianism "Ormuzd" or "Ahura-Mazda." Thus, religious intolerance may also be traced to its doctrines. Larson relates the influence of Zoroastrianism on Christianity:

> Among the basic elements which the Synoptics obtained from Zoroastrianism we may mention the following: the intensely personal and vivid concepts of hell and heaven; the use of water for baptism and spiritual purification; the savior born of a true virgin-mother; the belief in demons who make human beings impure and who must be exorcised; the Messiah of moral justice; the universal judgment, based upon good and evil works; the personal immortality and the single life of every human soul; the apocalyptic vision and prophecy; and the final tribulation before the Parousia. . . . In addition, Paul, Revelation, and the Fourth Gospel drew heavily upon Zoroastrianism for elements which are absent from the Synoptics: e.g., the doctrine of absolute metaphysical dualism, the Logos concept, transformation into celestial spirits, the millennial kingdom, Armageddon, the final conflagration, the defeat of Satan, the renovation of the universe,

and the celestial city to be lowered from the Supreme Heaven to the earth.[106]

As Wheless states:

All these divine and "revealed" doctrines of the Christian faith we have seen to be originally heathen Zoroastrian mythology, taken over first by the Jews, then boldly plagiarized by the ex-Pagan Christians.[107]

Other Saviors and Sons of God

Many of the other sons of God, and several "daughters of God" and goddesses such as Diana Soteira as well, share numerous aspects with the Christian savior, such as the following notable examples.

The Arabian Issa purportedly lived around 400 BCE in the western Arabian region of Hijaz, where also existed places called Galilee, Bethsaida and Nazareth, a town that was not founded in Palestine until *after* "Jesus of Nazareth's" alleged era. The similarities between the Arabian Issa and the Palestinian Jesus are many and profound.

Aesclepius is the great healing god of the Greeks who had long, curly hair, wore robes and did miracles, including raising the dead. Of Aesclepius, Dujardin relates:

The word Soter has not only the meaning of Saviour, but also of Healer; it is the title given to Esculapius . . . it is interesting to realize that the same men who carried to the world the revolutionary message of salvation by union with the god were at the same time an organized group of healers, who day by day earned their living by the practice of healing.[108]

It has also been demonstrated that the Orphic religion is similar to Christianity. In *Jesus Christ: Sun of God*, David Fideler relates of the Greek hero/god Orpheus:

Orphism promulgated the idea of eternal life, a concept of "original sin" and purification, the punishment of the wicked in the afterlife, and the allegorical interpretation of myth, which the early church fathers applied to the Christian scriptures. Orpheus was known as the Good Shepherd, and Jesus was frequently represented as Orpheus, playing music and surrounded by animals, a symbol of the Peaceable Kingdom or Golden Age, representing the ever-present harmony of the Logos. Like Orpheus, Jesus descended to Hell as a savior of souls.[109]

Indeed, as Werner Keller relates:

In Berlin . . . there is a small amulet with a crucified person, the Seven Sisters and the moon which bears the inscription ORPHEUS BAKKIKOS. It has a surprisingly Christian appearance. The same can be said of a representation of the hanging Marsyas in the Capitoline Museum in Rome.[110]

Conclusion

It is evident that Jesus Christ is a mythical character based on these various ubiquitous godmen and universal saviors who were part of the ancient world for thousands of years prior to the Christian era. As Massey says:

> The same legend was repeated in many lands with a change of name, and at times of sex, for the sufferer, but none of the initiated in the esoteric wisdom ever looked upon the Kamite Iusa, a gnostic Horus, Jesus, Tammuz, Krishna, Buddha Witoba, or any other of the many saviours as historic in personality for the simple reason that they had been more truly taught.[111]

The existence and identity of all these mysterious characters who are so identical in their persona and exploits, constituting the universal mythos, have been hidden from the masses as part of the Christ conspiracy.

---

1. Graves, *WSCS*.
2. Graves, *WSCS*, 36.
3. Higgins, II, 421.
4. Lockhart, 116.
5. Graham, 351.
6. Higgins, I, 662-9.
7. Walker, *WEMS*, 1100.
8. Doane, 190-1.
9. Jackson, 67.
10. Walker, *WEMS*, 77.
11. Robertson, 75-6.
12. Doane, 363.
13. A. Churchward, 334.
14. Doane, 290.
15. Larson, 136; Doane, 147, 290.
16. Doane, 290.
17. Doane, 168.
18. Doane, 291.
19. Doane, 292.
20. Mead, *GG*, 133.
21. Mead, *GG*, 133.
22. Doane, 294.
23. Doane, 292.
24. Pike, 290; Higgins, I, 159, 444.
25. Doane, 293.
26. Doane, 116.
27. Blavatsky, *IU*, II, 209, 537-538.
28. Massey, HJMC, 150.
29. Mead, 134.
30. Doane, 292.
31. Doane, 294.
32. Doane, 293.
33. Walker, *WEMS*, 123.
34. Larson, 142-8.
35. Larson, 149.

36. Higgins, I, 163.
37. A. Churchward, 331, 339.
38. Higgins, I, 161.
39. Carpenter, 52; Doane, 364; Higgins, II, 102.
40. Higgins, II, 102.
41. Doane, 193.
42. Carpenter, 52.
43. Walker, *WEMS*, 237.
44. Larson, 82.
45. Walker, *WDSSO*, 456.
46. Pike, 357.
47. Doane, 193.
48. Walker, *WEMS*, 22.
49. Walker, *WEMS*, 393-4.
50. Walker, *WEMS*, 748-754.
51. J. Churchward, *CM*, 254.
52. Massey, *EBD*, 54-5.
53. Doane, 163.
54. Jackson, 168.
55. A. Churchward, 397.
56. A. Churchward.
57. Walker, *WEMS*, 1054.
58. Jackson, 118.
59. Massey, *EBD*, 126.
60. A. Churchward, 397; viz. Massey, *EBD*, 13, 64; MC.
61. Higgins, I, 217.
62. Massey, *EBD*.
63. J. Churchward, *LCM*, 320.
64. Graves, *WSCS*, 257.
65. Leedom, 185; viz. Taylor.
66. Jackson, 81.
67. Doane, 147.
68. Graves, *WSCS*, 261, 280.
69. Jacolliot, 250.
70. Blavatsky, II, 538.
71. Pike, 277.
72. Jacolliot, 241.
73. Graves, *WSCS*, 261.
74. Jackson, 80.
75. Leedom, 137.
76. Graves, *WSCS*, 104-5.
77. Graves, *WSCS*, 258.
78. Blavatsky, Walker.
79. Jacolliot, 56.
80. Jacolliot, 251.
81. Jacolliot, 282.
82. Graham, 290.
83. Higgins, I, 197.
84. Wheless, *FC*, 20.
85. O'Hara, 65.
86. Lockhart, 65.
87. Pike, 613.
88. Walker, *WEMS*, 155.
89. Walker, *WEMS*, 663.
90. Leedom, 203.
91. Doane, 193.

92. Graves, *WSCS*.
93. Doane, 129.
94. Walker, *WEMS*, 47.
95. Higgins, II, 30-31.
96. Doane, 200.
97. Doane, 404.
98. Carpenter, 25.
99. Walker, *WEMS*, 893.
100. A. Churchward, 367.
101. Higgins, 591.
102. Graves, 45.
103. Larson, 88.
104. Larson, 89.
105. Larson, 91.
106. Larson, 105.
107. Wheless, *FC*, 90.
108. Dujardin, 53.
109. Fideler, 175.
110. Keller, 392.
111. Massey, *EBD*, 51.

An Egyptian goddess
piercing the serpent's
head. (Hislop)

The Indian Krishna crushing the
serpent's head. (Hislop)

The Babylonian dual God
(the Egyptian Horus and Set).
(A. Churchward)

Hesus the "wood cutter,"
Celtic/Druid Sun God,
1st century BCE.

The god Hermes as
the Good Shepherd,
6th century BCE.
(Walker, *WDSSO*)

Astrology and the Bible

> For everything there is a season, and a time for every matter
> under heaven: a time to be born, and a time to die; a time to
> plant, and time to pluck up what is planted . . . (Ecclesiastes
> 3:1-2)

The Christian religion was thus founded upon the numerous
gods, goddesses, religions, sects, cults and mystery schools that
thrived around the globe prior to the Christian era, even in the
Hebrew world, where the Israelites worshipped numerous gods,
including "the sun, the moon, and the stars and all the host of
heaven." In order to determine the framework upon which the
Christian conspirators hung their myths, in fact, we will need to
turn to that ancient body of knowledge which in almost every
culture has been considered sacred and which the priests have
wished to keep to themselves: the science of astrology.

The Christian masses, of course, are repeatedly taught to
reject all forms of "astrology" or "star-gazing" as the "work of the
Devil," and any number of biblical texts are held up to assert that
astrology is an "evil" to be avoided at all costs. This animosity
towards studying the heavenly bodies and their interrelationships
is in reality propaganda designed to prevent people from finding
out the truth about the Bible, which is that it is loaded with
astrological imagery, as evidenced by the fact that the Hebrew
gods were in large part celestial bodies. The Bible is, in actuality,
basically an astrotheological text, a reflection of what has been
occurring in the heavens for millennia, localized and historicized
on Earth. This fact is further confirmed by numerous biblical
passages concerning the influences of the heavenly bodies, but it
also becomes clear through exegesis of the texts from an informed
perspective.

Although the Catholic Church has feverishly discouraged
star-gazing by its flock—so frightened in fact were the people of
the Church's wrath in regard to astrology that sailors would not
look up at the stars, a habit crucial to their occupation—the truth
is that the Church has been a longtime practitioner of astrology.
Many of the Church hierarchy have not only "looked to the stars"
but have been regular, secret adepts of the same "magical arts"
widely practiced by Pagans but publicly condemned by
Christians,[1] and it would be safe to assume that this practice
continues to this day behind the scenes. Numerous churches and
cathedrals, such as Notre Dame in Paris, have abundant
astrological symbols, full zodiacs, etc. In the 19th century the
papal throne, St. Peter's chair, was cleaned, only to reveal upon it

the 12 labors of Hercules,[2] who, as we have seen, was a sun god. As Walker states:

Astrology survives in our own culture because Christianity embraced it with one hand, while condemning it as a devilish art with the other. Church fathers like Augustine, Jerome, Eusebius, Chrystostom, Lactantius, and Ambrose all anathematized astrology, and the great Council of Toledo prohibited it for all time. Nevertheless, six centuries later the consistory and the dates of popes' coronations were determined by the zodiac; aristocratic prelates employed their own personal astrologers; and signs of the zodiac appeared all over church furnishings, tiles, doorways, manuscripts, and baptismal fonts. The traditional Twelve Days of Christmas were celebrated by taking astrological omens each day for the corresponding months of the coming year.[3]

Despite its outward vilification by the clergy, astrology has also been used by countless kings and heads of state privy to the astrological, as opposed to literal, nature of the Bible. Not being thus privy, biblical literalists claim that everything in the Bible occurred literally and factually upon the earth, including the talking snake, Noah's ark, the parting of the Red Sea, the raising of the dead and numerous other incredible miracles that apparently occurred only to the biblical people at that time in that part of the world. The miraculous and implausible exploits of other cultures, however, are to be tossed aside as being unhistorical, mythological and downright ridiculous. As we have seen and will continue to see, these other cultures had the identical stories as those found in the Bible; therefore, following the "logic" of biblical proponents, we should also toss out the Judeo-Christian versions as "merely" mythological and allegorical at best, and diabolical at worst. As history, these various biblical tales are no more factual than the stories of the Greek gods or the Arabian knights. As allegory, however, they record an ancient wisdom that goes back well beyond the founding of the Hebrew nation, into the deepest mists of time.

In ascertaining the astrology of the Bible we should first properly define the word astrology. Although many people think astrology is meaningless mumbo-jumbo, it is not merely casting horoscopes but is in fact a science, as "astrology" means the study of the celestial bodies (astronomy) and their influences on each other and on life on Earth. The only difference between the well-respected astronomy and the vilified astrology is that astronomy charts the movements and constitution of the celestial bodies, while astrology attempts to determine their interrelationships and meaning. The sacred science of astrology began with astronomy, when humans noticed that they could determine some regularity in life by observing the skies and heavenly bodies, both nighttime and daytime. They could thus predict the seasons, including the time of planting and harvest, as well as the annual flooding of the Nile, for example. They also noticed the sun's effects on plants, as well as the moon's waxing and waning and effect on the tides. The knowledge of the heavens was also essential in seafaring, as stated, and a variety of ancient peoples were extraordinary seafarers for millennia, an impossible feat without a precise and detailed knowledge of the heavens, which in turn was not possible without the understanding that the earth was round and revolved around the sun, crucial information suppressed by the conspirators, to be seemingly re-discovered late in history. Such information, however, has always been known by those behind the scenes.

Thus, in reading the stars, humans could make sense of the universe and find lessons applicable to daily life. Higgins explains:

> Among all the ancient nations of the world, the opinion was universal that the planetary bodies were the disposers of the affairs of men. Christians who believe in Transubstantiation, and that their priests have an unlimited power to forgive sins, may affect to despise those who have held that opinion . . . ; but their contempt is not becoming, it is absurd. . . . It was thought that the future fortunes of every man might be known, from a proper consideration of the state of the planets at the moment of his birth. . . . This produced the utmost exertion of human ingenuity to discover the exact length of the periods of the planetary motions: that is, in other words, to perfect the science of astronomy. In the course of the proceedings it was discovered, or believed to be discovered, that the motions of the planets were liable to certain aberrations, which it was thought would bring on ruin to the whole system, at some future day.[4]

As time went on, this science became increasingly complicated, as the infinite stars were factored in and as the heavens changed. Recognizing the interaction between the planetary bodies and their influence on Earth, the ancients began to give the heavens shape and form, persona and attitude. In order to pass along this detailed information, which was, and continues to be, so important to all aspects of life, the ancients personified the heavenly bodies and wove stories about their "exploits," giving them unique personalities and temperaments that reflected their particular movements and other qualities, such as color and size. These stories were passed down over the many millennia basically by a priesthood, because they were esteemed for their sacred astronomical, astrological and mathematical value. As Higgins says, ". . . astrology was so connected with religion that it was impossible to separate them."[5] These celestial movements and/or the revered stories about them were recorded in stone all over the world, in great monuments and in city layouts. These monuments constitute much of our proof that the ancients possessed this amazingly intricate knowledge, but we can also find enormous evidence of it in the legends and writings of the ancients, including the Judeo-Christian bible, which is rife with symbolism and allegory.

Those individuals who believe the Bible to be the "literal word of God" are not only unaware of its symbolism, they are also ignorant of the passages within the Bible itself which clearly reflect that at least certain aspects of the biblical tales are *allegory*. For example, at Ezekiel 23, the author(s) tells a long story about two sisters, Oholah and Oholibah, and their "faithless harlotry" when "their breasts were pressed and their virgin bosoms handled." Just as we get to the good stuff, "Ezekiel" springs it on us that he is speaking **allegorically** about the cities of Samaria and Jerusalem, which are accused of having "played harlot in Egypt"; in other words, they worshipped other gods. It is rather evident that Ezekiel is enjoying this sexual allegory, as he goes into gleeful detail about the transgressions of the "sisters" and their "nakedness" and "bed of love." It is also evident that this type of allegorical speech is used more often in the Bible than its writers and proponents would wish to admit. As in the lusty Ezekiel tale, a number of other biblical places, nations and tribes are frequently referred to allegorically as "he" or "she," which makes it difficult to figure out whether the speaker is talking about a person, group, place or thing.

The Christian cheerleader "Paul" also knew that there was allegory in the Bible, as he so stated at Galatians 4:22-5, in reference to the story of Abraham having sons by two women. As to these women, who we are led in the Old Testament to believe are real, historical characters, Paul clarifies what they actually represent:

> Now this is **allegory**: these two women are two covenants. One is from Mount Sinai, bearing children for slavery; she is Hagar. Now Hagar is Mount Sinai in Arabia; she corresponds to the present Jerusalem, for she is in slavery with her children.

Thus, again, we discover that biblical characters are not actual persons but allegory for places. We also discover that certain places are allegory for other places:

> . . . and their dead bodies will lie in the street of the great city which is **allegorically** called Sodom and Egypt, where their Lord was crucified. (Rev. 11:8)

Of course, this fact is hidden by some translators, who render the word "allegorically" as "spiritually."

Other early Christians also knew about the allegorical nature of the Bible, but their later counterparts began in earnest the profitable push for utter historicization, obliterating millennia of human study and knowledge, and propelling the Western world into an appalling Dark Age. St. Athanasius, bishop and patriarch of Alexandria, was not only aware of the allegorical nature of biblical texts, but he "admonishes us that 'Should we understand sacred writ according to the letter, we should fall into the most enormous blasphemies.'"6 In other words, *it is a sin to take the Bible literally!*

Christian father Origen, called the "most accomplished biblical scholar of the early church," admitted the allegorical and esoteric nature of the Bible: "The Scriptures were of little use to those who understood them literally, as they are written."7 St. Augustine, along with Origen, was forceful in his pronouncement of Genesis as allegory:

> There is no way of preserving the literal sense of the first chapter
> of Genesis, without impiety, and attributing things to God
> unworthy of him.

Thus, it is understood that there is allegory and symbolism in the Bible. What is also understood is that, despite protestations to the contrary, the stars, sun and moon are described and utilized repeatedly within an allegorical or astrological context by biblical writers. In fact, in examining biblical texts closely, we further discover that various places and persons, portrayed as actual, historical entities, are in fact allegory for the heavens and planetary bodies. In reality, virtually all Hebrew place-names have astronomical meanings.8 So prevalent is this custom of creating "as above, so below," it is obvious that the "chosen" were as enchanted with the heavens as their adversaries and neighbors, such as the Chaldeans, master astrologers jealously reviled by their Hebrew counterparts. Contrary to popular belief, the reverence displayed by other peoples for "God's heavens" is also exhibited by the Israelites, whose very name, as we have seen, is astrotheological. Indeed, from the very beginning, the biblical people were encouraged to study the stars and signs in the heavens, as at Genesis 1:14, which basically describes the zodiac:

> And God [Elohim] said, Let there be lights in the firmament of
> the heaven to divide the day from the night; and let them be for
> signs, and for seasons, and for days, and years . . .

Despite the negative comments and exhortations found in the Bible against astrology, star-gazing, soothsaying and divination, we discover various passages that clearly refer to these magical arts and their objects of reverence with fondness. In fact, at several points the heavens are personified and appear as wondrous characters whose praises are sung by biblical characters, in precisely the same manner as their Pagan counterparts. The author(s) of Job is one such character, and it is in this book we find unambiguous references to astrology. In Job, "the Lord" personifies the "morning stars"—the "sons of God"— and has them "joyfully crying out." In trying to make Job feel small and obey him, the Lord presents a list of his own godly attributes, including the ability to command the happy heavens:

> Can you bind the chains of the Pleiades, or loose the cords of Orion? Can you lead forth the Mazzaroth in their season, or can you guide the Bear with its children? Do you know the ordinances of the heavens? Can you establish their rule on the earth? (Job 38:31-33)

The "Mazzaroth" is, in fact, the Zodiac. Orion is a prominent player on the cosmic stage, as is the Bear. The Pleiades, or "Seven Sisters," have been since very ancient times elements of many mythologies and astrotheologies, including the Egyptian, Babylonian, Indian, Greek and Mexican. The presentation of the seven sisters as "judges" is a common theme, and it was thought at times that they required sacrifice as propitiation. The Pleiades factor into Judaism more than is admitted, as some of the numerous "sevens" mentioned throughout the Bible refer to these "sisters," as Walker relates:

> [The Pleiades] were probably represented in pre-patriarchal Jerusalem by the holy Menorah (seven-branched candlestick) symbolizing the sevenfold Men-horae or Moon-priestesses, as shown by its female-genital decorations, lilies and almonds (Exodus 25:33).[9]

After the patriarchy took over, it would seem, the menorah came to represent only the sun, moon and five inner planets, as will be seen.

Also in Job, a book replete with celestial imagery, the author portrays the Lord as he who "described a circle upon the face of the waters at the boundary between light and darkness. The pillars of heaven tremble . . . his hand pierced the fleeing serpent." In mythology the heavens are depicted as an "abyss of waters," so this scripture is reference to the zodiacal circle, "described" or drawn by God. The "boundary between light and darkness" is, naturally, the horizon, and the trembling "pillars of heaven" are the same held up by Samson, the "bright sun." In addition, "his hand piercing the fleeing serpent" could refer to the Egyptian god Set/Seth, the constellation of Serpens, or the sky itself; however, this last part could also be translated as the "crooked serpent" who does not flee but is *formed* by the Lord's hand, representing Scorpio. Of this mysterious and clearly astrological work attributed to Job, Anderson says, ". . . the whole book is a complete description of the Masonic ceremonies or Egyptian Masonry, or trial of the dead by Osiris . . ."[10]

In Psalms 19, we hear about the heavens "telling the glory of God . . . there is no speech, nor are there words; their voice is not heard; yet their voice goes out through all the earth, and their words to the end of the world." To the uninitiated, this sounds strange—how can the heavens tell the "glory of God?" And how do their "voice" and "words" go out to the end of the world without speech or words? The word for "voice" in the Hebrew is properly translated as "line." This line or lines are the cosmic rays coming off the various planetary bodies, lines that were perceived by the ancients to penetrate the earth as well, a perception that caused them to be anxious about establishing the "kingdom of heaven on Earth" by emulating what was happening in the heavens. Anderson explains the importance of the lines or rays:

> Among the Eastern nations it was taught that all spiritual life first came from the sun, and its magnetic descent to the earth, becoming earth-bound, or dwelling in the earth, and after passing through a series of evolutions, and different births and changes from the mineral, vegetable, and animal kingdoms, ascending or descending the scale [like Jacob's angels], according to the good or evil magnetic rays at its births and its various probationary existences, at last purified and intellectually refined, and master of itself, the *pure* Ra, or *astral* body, at last was drawn back into the bosom of the father, sun, from whence it was first originated.[11]

Thus, astrology, or astro*logos* in the Greek, has been considered the "word of God," as is evidenced by the biblical singing stars and heavens passing along their "voice" and "words" through the earth.

The Psalms passage continues: "In [the heavens] he has set a tent for the sun." This "tent" or "tabernacle" represents a holy sanctuary or house of worship; thus, the heavens are truly the temple of the sun, as well as of the other celestial bodies. This heavenly temple was, however, continuously recreated all over the planet, as continues to this day, unbeknownst to the masses.

At Job 9, it is explicit that God is the Divine Architect of the Zodiac "who made the Bear and Orion, the Pleiades and the chambers of the south . . ." And again at Amos 5:8: "He who made the Pleiades and Orion, and turns deep darkness into the morning and darkens the day into night." The Lord "builds his upper chambers in the heavens and founds vaults upon the earth." (Amos 9:6) And he is praised for his astrological creation:

"Thou has made the moon to mark the seasons; the sun to know its time." Like the Lord himself, his creations such as the sun, moon and skies are considered righteous and eternal, as is reflected at Psalms 89:37 and at Daniel 12:3; thus, the heavenly bodies served as sacred symbols and representatives of God.

From these various biblical passages, it is obvious that the Lord is not only the architect of the heavens but is pleased with both his stellar creations and his ability to command them. That being the case, it is equally obvious that astrology is not evil, unless the Lord is evil, an idea widely subscribed to by the Gnostics, who made the assessment that anyone in charge of this chaotic and crude "lower" world must be a villain. But, if "God" is good, then "his" creation must be good, and the biblical writers make it clear that astrology and the zodiac are their Lord's creation.

That the stars, moon and sun were considered to have personality is also explicit from biblical texts. Early Church father Origen opined, and was ridiculed by "heretics" and "heathens" for his opinion, that "all the stars and heavenly bodies are living, rational beings, having souls," and he quotes Isaiah 14:12 in his proof of this, saying that the Lord has "given commandments to all the stars."[12]

At Psalms 147:4, the stars have names, given to them by "the Lord." That biblical writers were aware of the constellations is also clear from Isaiah 13:10: "For the stars of the heavens and their constellations will not give their light." The fact that the Hebrews believed the sun and moon had personality and animation is further reflected at Isaiah 24:23: "Then the moon will be confounded, and the sun ashamed." The sun and moon are again anthropomorphized or personified at Psalms 148:3, when they are asked to praise the Lord.

The importance of the skies is repeatedly emphasized throughout the Old Testament, with the sun and moon even considered the "rulers" of the day and night, made out of the Lord's "steadfast love" (Ps. 136:9). In the Song of Solomon, an embarrassment to God-fearing Christians for its overt sexuality, "Solomon" uses celestial imagery to describe his beloved: "Who is this that looks forth like the dawn, fair as the moon, bright as the sun . . ." (Sol. 6:10)

The sun and moon are also considered to be healing, as is reflected at Isaiah 30:26, in which the light of the sun and moon increase "in the day when the Lord binds up the hurt of his people, and heals the wounds inflicted by his blow." (And this from a "loving" God!) Furthermore, the arts of medicine and astrology were inextricably linked, because medicines were frequently dispensed not only based upon symptoms but also on natal charts and other astrological castings; hence, "physicians" or "doctors" were also astrologers, as well as priests and prophets. As Allegro says:

> To know the correct dosages in these cases required an appreciation of the susceptibility of the patient to the drug's effects, perhaps the most difficult calculation of all. Much depended on the recipient's "fate" allotted him at his birth, the factor that determined his individuality, his physical stature, the colour of his eyes, and so on. Only the astrologer could tell this, so the art of medicine was itself dependent for success on astrology and the considerable astronomical knowledge this presupposed. . . . The combined arts of medicine and astrology were known and practised by the Sumerians and their Mesopotamian successors, as we know from their cuneiform records as well as the repute they enjoyed in this respect in the ancient world. . . . These traits of character and bodily constitution could be determined by astrological means, so the early doctors were also astrologers. [The early doctor] was also a prophet, a prognosticator. The arts of healing and religion were inseparable.[13]

Biblical Sun- and Moon-Worshippers

Thus, we can see that astrology is not at all "evil" but a sacred science, as acknowledged abundantly by biblical writers. In fact, as noted, the polytheistic Hebrews and Israelites worshipped a variety of Elohim, Baalim and Adonai, many of which were aspects of the sun, such as El Elyon, the Most High God. In addition, at Amos 5:26 is a verse concerning the mysterious "Kaiwan," the "star-god" of the house of Israel. This star-god is El, the sun, or Saturn, the "central sun," whom, as stated, the Hebrews worshipped, as reflected by their sabbath on Saturday. As also noted, Yahweh, or Iao, was likewise a sun god. Furthermore, we have already seen that Solomon, for one, worshipped in the manner of the pre-Yahwist cultures, revering Chemosh, the Moabite sun god, for example.

The Hebrews were also "moon-worshippers" in that many of their feasts and holidays revolved around the movements and phases of the moon. Such moon-worship is found repeatedly in the Old Testament (Ps. 8:13, 104:19; Is. 66:23), and to this day Jews celebrate holidays based on the lunar calendar. At Isaiah 47, these moon-worshippers are equated with astrologers, i.e., ". . . those who divide the heavens, who gaze at the stars, who at the new moons predict what shall befall you."

The Jewish nighttime worship is also reflected in the noncanonical Epistle to Diognetus, an early Christian writing which further demonstrates that astrology was important to Christians, as, while the author obviously does not like the way in which the Jews are consulting the heavens, he does consider the "cycle of the seasons" to be "divinely appointed":

> As for the way [the Jews] scrutinize the moon and stars for the purpose of ritually commemorating months and days, and chop up the divinely appointed cycle of the seasons to suit their own fancies, pronouncing some to be times for feasting and others for mourning. . .

As we can see, the Hebrews/Israelites, like the other peoples around the world, revered a number of aspects of the heavens, both the night sky and the day. Also clear from biblical texts is that the Hebrew people were constantly confused as to who "the Lord" really was and what he wanted from "his chosen," as they are endlessly being bounced to and fro in their reverence for the heavens. In fact, as is written in the Book of Jasher, which is given scriptural authority at Joshua 10:13 and 2 Samuel 1:18 but which was suppressed in large part because of its obvious astrological imagery, Abraham's father Terah "had twelve gods of large size, made of wood and stone, after the twelve months of the year, and he served each one monthly" (Jas. 9:8). Abram himself is also represented as first worshipping the sun, until it set, and then the moon: "And Abram served the sun in that day and he prayed to it . . . and Abram served the moon and prayed to it all that night" (9:14-17). Abram eventually realizes that "these are not gods that made the earth and mankind but the servants of God . . ." This epiphany is no great thing, actually, as the intelligentsia of virtually all cultures viewed the planetary bodies as divine proxies or "limbs" of the Almighty Itself. Abraham then goes on to destroy his father's gods, yet the Hebrews did not give up their astrotheology, which was, in fact, what the Hebrews/ Israelites were constantly "whoring after." As noted, by the time of reformer king Josiah, the kings of Judah reportedly erred terribly when they established the worship of the heavens, even though their predecessors were applauded for doing the same:

> And he deposed the idolatrous priests whom the kings of Judah had ordained to burn incense in the high places at the cities of Judah and round about Jerusalem; those also who burned incense to Baal, to the sun, and the moon, and the constellations, and all the host of heavens. (2 Kings 23:5)

These kings of Judah were sun-worshippers, as is made clear at 2 Kings 23:11, when Josiah "removed the horses that the kings of Judah had dedicated to the sun. . ."

It is evident that there are a number of characters or factions in the OT depicting themselves as "the Lord," since in one book, the heavens are to be praised as creations of the Almighty himself, but, in another, to do so is considered idolatrous. On the contradictions within the Judeo-Christian scriptures, eminent freethinker Robert Ingersoll commented, "If a man would follow, today, the teachings of the Old Testament, he would be a criminal. If he would strictly follow the teachings of the New, he would be insane."

Ezekiel

Likewise, if he were to attempt to make literal the enigmatic passages in Ezekiel, he might go mad. Ezekiel, in fact, provides an interesting testimonial to the practice of polytheism and astrology by the Hebrews/Jews as in a "vision" he is given by Yahweh a tour of Israel's "abominations" that includes a trip into the Jerusalem Temple's "inner court that faces north, where was the seat of the image of jealousy, which provokes to jealousy." The "image of jealousy," of course, is Yahweh, El Qanna, the jealous god; however, it seems that the "living God" was even jealous of his own image, apparently considering it an idol. Next, Ezekiel is shown a hole in the north court wall, which he excavates to find a door:

> And [God] said to me, "Go in, and see the vile abominations that they are committing here." So I went in and saw; and there, portrayed upon the wall round about, were all kinds of creeping things, and loathsome beasts, and all the idols of the house of Israel. And before them stood seventy men of the elders of the house of Israel, with Jaazaniah the son of Shaphan standing among them. Each had his censer in his hand, and the smoke of the cloud of incense went up. Then he said to me, "Son of man, have you seen what the elders of the house of Israel are doing in the dark, every man in his room of pictures? For they say, 'The LORD does not see us, the LORD has forsaken the land.'" He said also to me, "You will see even greater abominations which they commit."

Thus we find the elders of Israel performing in the hidden chamber of the temple their secret, esoteric religion, which was basically astrological. This Shaphan, father of Jaazaniah, evidently and ironically was the scribe of Hilkiah, the Zadokite priest who purportedly "found" the law that caused Josiah to go berserk and destroy the other gods and high places. It should also be noted that El Qanna's inner court to the north was reserved only for the Zadokite priesthood, which became the Sadducees.

Ezekiel then goes on to describe the Hebrew women at the entrance of the Temple's north gate who were weeping for Tammuz, the Syrian/Samaritan savior/fertility/sun god who annually died and was resurrected. Ezekiel is next shown "between the porch and the altar" of the "temple of the Lord" some 25 men, "with their backs to the temple of the Lord, and their faces toward the east, worshipping the sun to the east." Such were the "abominations" of the house of Israel, for which the jealous/zealous god commanded a group of Yahwist thugs to slaughter the Hebrews, smiting "old men outright, young men and maidens, little children and women," who were not worshipping properly, according to the Yahwist bias. Consequently, El Qanna, the jealous/zealous god, orders the extermination of Jews and Hebrews who were worshipping other Elohim, as their fathers had before them.

Despite "the Lord's" purported hatred of these "abominations," he then goes on to show Ezekiel the zodiacal circle, the celebrated "wheel within a wheel," about which so much tortured speculation has been put forth, including the latest that the wheel represents a spaceship. Unfortunately for the X-philes, Ezekiel's allegories—and *he is commanded by the Lord to speak in allegory* (17:1-2; 24:3)—are a bit less mysterious, as the wheel is nothing more cryptic than the zodiac, with the four "cherubim," the man, ox, lion and eagle, representing the cardinal points and four elements: Aquarius (air), Taurus (earth), Leo (fire) and Scorpio (water). Walker elucidates upon these creatures:

> Ezekiel's four-faced creature composed of eagle, lion, bull, and man, was piously interpreted as prophesying the four evangelists; but the original biblical description was copied from the fabulous composite beasts of Assyria, who represented the four seasons of the year.[14]

Biblical Diviners and Astrologers

In addition to these examples of astrology in the Bible can be found a number of references to esteemed biblical characters using the "arts of divination" to their and their Lord's benefit. Naturally, where characters are favored by biblical writers, these astrological and magical arts are perfectly good, but when used by those not favored, they are "evil." Regardless of this prejudice, there is no doubt that "good" biblical characters practiced the magical arts. In fact, in the earliest parts of the Bible, divination is praised as a way to commune with God or *divine* the future (Genesis 30:27). Indeed, the word "divination" comes from the word "divine," which is a demonstration that divination was originally considered *godly* and not evil.

Divination does not fall out of favor until later books, eventually being considered as "sin" in the first book of Samuel, in which the Israelite king Saul uses a diviner to "divine for me by a spirit and bring up for me whomever I shall name to you." The diviner or medium, whom Saul is approaching in disguise, objects to his request, saying, "Surely you know what Saul has done, how he has cut off the mediums and the wizards from the land. Why then are you laying a snare for my life to bring about my death?" It is interesting that *this* Saul, like the Saul of the New Testament, is notorious for persecuting people of a different faith.

Moreover, when describing the men who joined David in his fight against Saul, biblical writers obfuscate the occupation of the men of the tribe of Issachar: "Of Issachar men who had understanding of the times, to know what Israel ought to do, two hundred chiefs, and all their kinsmen under their command." (1 Chr. 12:32) In reality, these "men who had understanding of the times" are astrologers, and quite a lot of them at that. It is obvious that, despite protestations to the contrary, the Israelites used astrologers to "know what Israel ought to do." Furthermore, from the repeated biblical exhortations against these magical arts, it is clear that large numbers of people in Israel and Judah were practicing astrology and divination, as indicated at Isaiah 3:2, for example, where "the Lord" takes away from Judah and Jerusalem "the judge and prophet, the diviner and elder." The "judges" in the OT are also priests and, in fact, judicial astrologers.[15]

Furthermore, although Abraham in Jasher is represented as turning away from the sun and moon, his title "of the Chaldeans" was a reference to his status as an astrologer, a fact confirmed by Church historian Eusebius who claimed that Abraham "taught the science to the priests of Heliopolis or On."[16]

Moses and the Tabernacle

For centuries, the character Moses has been held in high esteem, his every word studied and each move charted. Yet, few have understood the true nature of his "covenant with the Lord," as reflected by the esoteric or mystical meaning of Moses's tabernacle, which, in fact, is the "tent of the sun." Respected Jewish historian Josephus, who was an initiate of several secret societies, elucidates upon Moses's tabernacle:

> And when [Moses] ordered twelve loaves to be set on the table, he denoted the year, as distinguished into so many months. By branching out the candlestick into seventy parts he secretly intimated the *Decani,* or seventy divisions of the planets; and as to the seven lamps upon the candlesticks, they referred to the course of the planets, of which that is the number. . . . Now the vestment of the high priest being made of linen, signified the earth; the blue denoted the sky, being like lightning in its pomegranates, and in the noise of the bells resembling thunder. . . . Each of the sardonyxes declares to us the sun and the moon; those, I mean, that were in the nature of buttons on the high priest's shoulders. And for the twelve stones, whether we understand by them the months, or whether we understand the

like number of the signs of that circle which the Greeks call the Zodiac, we shall not be mistaken in their meaning.

The 12 stones, of course, are the tribes or "sons" of Jacob, which Josephus firmly establishes as the constellations.[17] Josephus is also explicit in relating other aspects of Jewish "history" as being astrological. Therefore, this astrological or astrotheological meaning of the Bible has been known a very long time. As Higgins says:

> . . . the Mosaic account . . . is allowed by all philosophers, as well as most of the early Jews and Christian fathers, to contain a mythos or allegory—by Philo, Josephus, Papias, Pantaenus, Irenaeus, Clemens Alex., Origen, the two Gregories of Nyssa and Nazianzen, Jerome, Ambrose . . .[18]

Jacob and his Sons and Ladder

The "father" of these 12 constellations or tribes, Jacob, is "the supplanter" (Iakovo), which was a title for the adversary and twin of the sun, Set, or Seth, the night sky. Each of the 12 tribes had its own totem, god and religious accoutrements, brought "out of Egypt." As demonstrated by the biblical texts, these groups did not reside peacefully with each other but fought constantly among themselves and with outsiders over whose god was superior and whose rituals and symbols were divinely inspired and correct.

As to their zodiacal designations, Jacob's first-born, Reuben, is Aquarius, the "the beginning of my strength . . . unstable as water." Simeon and Levi, "the brothers," are Gemini. Judah, the "lion's whelp," is Leo. Zebulun, who ". . . shall be for an haven of ships," may correspond to Libra, "the ship sign, or arc, or ark."[19] Issachar is a "strong ass, crouching between the sheepfold's burdens," possibly corresponding to the bull of Taurus, the "workhorse." Of Jacob's son Dan, Anderson relates:

> "Dan shall be the serpent by the way, an adder in the path, that biteth the horse heels, so that his rider shall fall backwards." This is . . . the scorpion, or serpent, and alludes to that constellation which is placed next to the centaur or armed horseman, or Sagittarius, which *falleth* backward into the winter solstice of [Capricorn].[20]

Jacob's son Gad is a reversal of Dag, the fish god, possibly representing Pisces. It was said of Asher that he would have "rich food" or "fat bread;" thus, he would correspond to Virgo, the bread-giver or fall harvest. Naphtali is "a hind let loose," representing Capricorn, the goat. Joseph, who was fiercely attacked by archers, is Sagittarius. The son of Rachel the "Ewe," Benjamin, the "ravenous wolf" who "divides the spoil," would be

Aries, who "comes in like a lion" and divides spring and winter. According to Anderson, the "fruitful bough" of Joseph representing his sons, Ephraim and Manasseh, could share the "portion divided between them" of the "double-sign" of Cancer. Joseph himself, of course, is "an interpreter of dreams and a noted magician" with a magical "silver cup," by which he divines.

Jacob's ladder with the 72 angels ascending and descending represents the 72 decans, or portions of the zodiac of five degrees each. The same ladder story is found in Indian and Mithraic mythology, as Doane relates:

> Paintings representing a scene of this kind may be seen in works of art illustrative of *Indian Mythology*. Manrice speaks of one, in which he says:
>
>> "The souls of men are represented as ascending and descending (on a ladder), according to the received opinion of the sidereal Metempsychosis."
>
> . . . And Count de Volney says:
>
>> "In the cave of Mithra *was a ladder with seven steps*, representing the seven spheres of the planets by means of which *souls ascended and descended.* This is precisely the ladder of Jacob's vision."[21]

In addition, the name "Jacob" is a title for a priest of the Goddess Isis,[22] which is fitting, since she is the Queen of Heaven who rules over the night sky, or Set the supplanter.

Joshua/Jesus, Son of Nun

Joshua, or *Jesus*, son of Nun (the "fish"), was the second great prophet after Moses, leading the Israelites to the promised land in Jericho, first encamping at Gilgal, or *Galilee*. Like Jacob, Joshua also sets up twelve stones representing the tribes and the signs of the zodiac. It is said that in Joshua's day, the sun stood still, an event about which has been put forth much tortured speculation as to how and when it could have occurred. In reality, it occurred quite frequently and still does, at the solstices, as the meaning of the word "solstice" is "sun stands still," the time when "the sun changes little in declination from one day to the next and appears to remain in one place north or south of the celestial equator."[23] The sun also stood still at the death of Krishna, centuries earlier: "1575 years before Christ, after the death of Cristna (Boodh the son of Deirca), the sun stood still to hear the pious ejaculations of Arjoon."[24] This solstice motif likewise appears in the mythologies of China and Mexico.[25]

Of the book of Joshua, Higgins relates:

> Sir William Drummond has shown that the names of most of the places in Joshua are astrological; and General Vallancey has

shown that Jacob's prophecy is astrological also, and has a direct reference to the Constellations.[26]

As to Joshua and various other aspects of the Old Testament, Higgins sums it up:

> The pretended genealogy of the tenth chapter of Genesis [from Noah on down] is attended with much difficulty. It reads like a genealogy: it is notoriously a chart of geography. . . . I have no doubt that the allotment of lands by Joshua was astronomical. It was exactly on the same principle as the nomes of Egypt, which every one knows were named astronomically, or rather, perhaps, I should say, astrologically. The double meaning is clear . . . Most of the names . . . are found in the mystic work of Ezekiel. . . . [Genesis's tenth] chapter divides the world into 72 nations. Much ingenuity must have been used to make them agree with the exact number of dodecans into which the great circle was divided.[27]

Daniel

In the famous scene where Daniel interprets the dreams of Cyrus and Nebuchadnezzar, it is implied that while the others who attempted to do likewise were astrologers, soothsayers and the like, Daniel himself was not. On the contrary, Daniel too was an astrologer, and we also discover he is not a historical character, as Walker relates:

> Writers of the Old Testament disliked the Danites, whom they called serpents (Genesis 49:17). Nevertheless, they adopted Dan-El or Daniel, a Phoenician god of divination, and transformed him into a Hebrew prophet. His magic powers were like those of the Danites emanating from the Goddess Dana and her sacred serpents. He served as court astrologer and dream-interpreter for both the Persian king Cyrus, and the Babylonian king Nebuchadnezzar (Daniel 1:21, 2:1), indicating that "Daniel" was not a personal name but a title, like the Celtic one: "a person of the Goddess Dana."[28]

Graham states that, "The story of Daniel was taken from a northern Syrian poem written before 1500 B.C. The hero, Daniel by name, was a son of El or God—the source of the Hebrew El. He was a mighty judge and lawgiver, also a provider for his people. This poem about him became so widely known that many races used its hero as a model for their own."[29]

As for his "visions," Larson says, "It is evident that the apocalyptic tribulations of Daniel and those described in the New Testament are appropriated from the literature of the Zoroastrians . . ."[30] Furthermore, although Daniel's "prophecies" are frequently held up to have been astoundingly accurate, proving the Bible to be the inspired Word of God, they were actually written after the fact. In particular, the so-called prophecy at Daniel 9:24-27, referring to the "coming of an anointed one," has been fervently interpreted to mean Jesus's advent. However, in the next paragraph, Daniel reveals whom he is really discussing: King Cyrus. Cyrus, in fact, is called the "Lord's Christ," as at Isaiah 45:1: "Thus says the Lord to his *Christ*, to Cyrus . . ."

Esther

In the story of the heroine Esther, her husband-to-be, King Ahasuerus, becomes enraged by the behavior of his current wife, Queen Vashti, so he takes council with "the wise men who knew the times—for this was the king's procedure toward all who were versed in law and judgment . . ." These "wise men who knew the times" were astrologers, whom the king evidently considered "versed in law and judgment" and indispensable to the workings of his domain. This book is, however, not historical, as "Esther" is a remake of the Goddess and Queen of Heaven Ishtar, Asherah, Astarte, Astoreth or Isis, from whom comes "Easter." Of Esther, Walker relates:

> "Star," the Hebrew rendering of Ishtar or Astarte. The biblical book of Esther is a secularized Elamite myth of Ishtar (Esther) and her consort Marduk (Mordecai), who sacrificed to the god Hammon, or Amon (Haman). Yahweh was never mentioned, because the Jews of Elam worshipped Marduk, not Yahweh. . . . Even the Bible story admits that Esther-Ishtar was not the real name of the Elamite-Jewish queen. Her real name was Hadassah (Esther 2:7).[31]

Walker continues:

> The story of Esther is an allegorical tale of the intercession of Ishtar, whom the Jews worshipped at the time, with the king who was supposed to be her consort, on behalf of the subject Jewish tribes. Interwoven with this theme is that of the ritual sacrifice.[32]

The Dial of Ahaz

In the second book of Kings and in Isaiah, the reformer king Hezekiah on his death bed calls upon the Lord, who adds 15 years onto Hezekiah's life by making "the shadow cast by the declining sun on the dial of Ahaz turn back ten steps,' So the sun turned back on the dial the ten steps by which it had declined." This story represents the correction of the calendar to align with the changing heavens. Higgins elucidates:

> The cycles would require correcting again after several revolutions, and we find Isaiah making the shadow go back ten degrees on the dial of Ahaz. This would mean nothing but a

second correction of the Neros [600-year cycle], or a correction of some cycle of a planetary body, to make it agree with some other. In the annals of China, in fact of the Chinese Buddhists, in the reign of Emperor Yau (a very striking name, being the name of the God of the Jews), it is said that the sun was stopped ten days, that is, probably, ten degrees of Isaiah, a degree answering to a year, 360 degrees and 360 days.[33]

Deborah

The great biblical prophet Deborah is also an astrologer, who, in order to defeat Sisera's armies, uses the stars: "From heaven fought the stars, from their courses they fought against Sisera." (Judges 5:20) Naturally, like Daniel, Esther, et al., Deborah is a deity of an older age rendered human:

> "Queen Bee," a ruler of Israel in the matriarchal period, bearing the same name as the Goddess incarnate in early Mycenaean and Anatolian rulers as "the Pure Mother Bee." . . . The Bible called her a "prophetess" or "judge" to disguise the fact that she was one of the governing matriarchs of a former age (Judges 4:4).[34]

In addition to the biblical texts, there is direct evidence of the Jewish use of astrology in the scrolls found at the Dead Sea, specifically the "Horoscopes" dated to the first century BCE. These horoscopes are similar to those used today but combine astrology with physiognomy, or the study of physical features. The Dead Sea horoscopes seem basically to be templates to determine who will be a "good" man and who will be "bad," rather than castings for particular individuals. Also, as Zecharia Sitchin reports:

> Earlier in this century archaeologists uncovered in the Galilee, in northern Israel, the remains of synagogues dating to the decades and centuries immediately following the destruction of the Second Temple in Jerusalem by the Romans (in A.D. 70). To their surprise, a common feature of those synagogues was the decoration of their floors with intricate mosaic designs that included the signs of the zodiac.[35]

Astrology in the New Testament

The biblical astrological imagery does not end with the Old Testament, however, as the New Testament is also an astrotheological text. Although the biblical and Christian admonitions against astrology are pitched and hysterical, from the beginning of the gospel tale we encounter astrology, as the "three wise men" or "magi" who used the stars to find the babe in the manger represent astrologers. Of this event, ben Yehoshua says:

It should be noted that the centre of astrological superstition in the Roman Empire was the city of Tarsus in Asia Minor—the place where the legendary missionary Paul came from. The idea that a special star had heralded the birth of Jesus, and that a solar eclipse occurred at his death, is typical of Tarsian astrological superstition.

Furthermore, at John 14:2 Jesus says, "In my Father's house are many rooms," which is also translated "many mansions." Walker explains:

> The original meaning of these mansions was "houses of the moon," that is, the zodiacal constellations through which the Moon Goddess passed on her monthly round.[36]

These "houses," of course, are also applicable in the story of the sun. As Paul says at 1 Corinthians 15:41, revealing his astrotheological thinking: "There is one glory of the sun, and another glory of the moon, and another glory of the stars; for star differs from star in glory."

In the gospels, Jesus refers to different "ages," which are in fact the divisions that constitute the precession of the equinoxes. As Moses was created to usher in the Age of Aries, so was Jesus to serve as the Avatar of the Age of Pisces, which is evident from the abundant fish imagery used throughout the gospel tale. This zodiacal connection has been so suppressed that people with the fish symbol on the back of their cars have no idea what it stands for, although they are fallaciously told it represents "ICHTHYS," an anagram for "Jesus Christ, Son of God, Savior," ichthys also being the Greek word for fish. The residual symbols of the previous Age of Aries can be found in the "Lamb" designations of Jesus, including the "Agnus Dei," or "Lamb of God." In addition, Jesus makes mention of the precession of the equinoxes or the change of the ages when he says to the disciples, who are asking about how to prepare for the "passover," "Behold, when you have entered the city, a man carrying a pitcher of water will meet you; follow him into the house which he enters . . ." (Lk. 22:10) This famous yet enigmatic passage refers to the "house" or Age of Aquarius, the Water-Bearer, and Jesus is instructing his disciples to pass over into it. Furthermore, the "upper room" where Jesus sends his disciples to "make ready" is the same "upper chambers in the heavens" found in Amos.

That the ancients, including Christians, were well aware of astrology and its influence is evident not only from the canonical biblical texts but also from those that did not make the final cut. For example, the noncanonical Epistle of Barnabas (c. 100-120 CE) speaks of a 2,000-year eon, clearly referring to one of the equinoctial ages, and the author of First Clement also expresses his knowledge of astrology, as well as his love for it:

> The heavens are moved by His direction and obey Him in peace. Day and night accomplish the course assigned to them by Him, without hindrance one to another. The sun and the moon and the dancing stars according to His appointment circle in harmony within the bounds assigned to them, without any swerving aside. The earth, bearing fruit in fulfillment of His will at her proper seasons, putteth forth the food that supplieth abundantly both men and beasts and all living things which are thereupon, making no dissension, neither altering anything which He hath decreed.

In fact, the earliest "Christians," the Gnostics, also were astrologers, and their texts are permeated with astrological imagery. The Gnostics developed the ages-old notion that the celestial bodies represented guides and levels through which the soul must pass after death, some paying penance in a temporary hell and others going directly to peace or "heaven." As Allegro says:

> Thus for the gnostic, as for religionists all over the world, the heavenly bodies were imbued with divinity and honoured as angelic bodies.[37]

The Gnostics also knew the allegorical and astrotheological nature of the "life of Christ," as admitted by Christian father Irenaeus, and which was at the root of their denial of the "historical" Christ. As Graham relates:

> Irenaeus said: "The Gnostics *truly* declared that all the supernatural transactions asserted in the gospels were counterparts of what took place above."[38]

The astrological imagery was the major difference between Gnosticism and Christianity, and the primary reason the Gnostics were refuted and their texts destroyed or mutilated.

There are many references to astrology in the canonical scriptures that are not as clear as those examined herein. What is clear is that the Hebrews and Christians were no more "astrology-free" than any of their contemporaries or predecessors, although said predecessors, such as the Chaldeans and Babylonians, were in general far more skilled and gnostic in the astrological arts. Indeed, Karl Anderson, master navigator and author of *Astrology in the Old Testament*, calls the Bible "that greatest of all astrological works . . ."[39] Jordan Maxwell concurs:

> The bible is nothing more than the greatest astrological, astronomical story ever told. It is pure astrology, based on the zodiac. The fact of the matter is, if you've done your homework,

you're going to find out that the Bible is nothing more than astrotheology, the worship of God's heaven.[40]

Astrology is no more "evil" than are the sky and the heavenly bodies, which biblical writers claimed were divine emanations of the Grand Architect. The vilification of astrology is not merely a sign of ignorance but, by insisting that its adherents were either lacking in wisdom or led astray by the devil, of cultural bigotry, as astrology has been appreciated and utilized in countless cultures around the globe. The ancients were, in fact, constantly reenacting the heavens, a reenactment that was eventually literalized and carnalized as "The Greatest Story Ever Sold."

---

1. Wheless, *FC*, 164.
2. Higgins, I, 691.
3. Walker, *WEMS*, 287.
4. Higgins, I, 207-8.
5. Higgins, I, 559.
6. Pike, 266.
7. Higgins, II, 270.
8. Higgins, I, 423; II, 136.
9. Walker, *WEMS*, 804.
10. Anderson, 113.
11. Anderson, 20.
12. Wheless, *FC*, 150-1.
13. Allegro, *SMC*, 31-5.
14. Walker, *WEMS*, 401.
15. Anderson, 105.
16. Higgins, I, 85, 593.
17. Jackson, 151; A. Churchward, 348.
18. Higgins, I, 34.
19. Anderson, 66.
20. Anderson, 66.
21. Doane, 45.
22. Anderson, 66.
23. Webster's.
24. Higgins, I, 197.
25. Doane, 91.
26. Higgins, I, 370.
27. Higgins, I, 265.
28. Walker, *WEMS*, 207.
29. Graham, 256.
30. Larson, 99.
31. Walker, *WEMS*, 286.
32. Walker, *WEMS*, 829.
33. Higgins, I, 197.
34. Walker, *WEMS*, 217.
35. Sitchin, *WTB*, 183.
36. Walker, *WDSSO*, 144.
37. Allegro, *DSSCM*, 112.
38. Graham, 354.
39. Anderson, 10.
40. "The Naked Truth."

The Grand Architect of the Universe.
French manuscript of the 13th Century CE.
(*Mysteries of the Past.*)

Zodiac with 12 signs and four cardinal points.
Mosaic from the floor of a synagogue in
Bet-Alpha, Galilee, 1-2 centuries BCE-CE.
(Sitchin, *WTB*)

The Son of God is the Sun of God

... there is nothing new under the sun. (Ecclesiastes 1:9)

Over the ages, the ancients did not simply observe the movements of the celestial bodies but personified them and created stories about them that were recreated upon the earth. Out of this polytheistic, astrological atmosphere came the "greatest story ever told," as the gospel tale is, in fact, astrotheological and non-historical, recording the mythos found around the globe for eons. Thus, the Christian religion, created and shored up by forgery, fraud and force, is in reality astrotheological and its founder mythical, based on many thousands of years of observation by the ancients of the movements and interrelationships of the celestial bodies and the earth, one of the favorite of which was, understandably, the sun.

The sun figured in the stories of virtually every culture worldwide. In many places and eras, the sun was considered the most visible proxy of the divine and the most potent bestower of Spirit. It was regarded as the first entity in "the Void" and the progenitor of all life and matter. The sun also represented the Archetypal Man, as human beings were perceived as "solar entities." In addition to being a symbol of the spirit because it rises and sinks, the sun was the "soul of the world," signifying immortality, as it is eternally resurrected after "dying" or setting. It was also considered the purifier of the soul, as noted. Hence, from at least the Egyptian age down to the Gnostic Christians, the sun, along with the moon and other celestial bodies, was viewed as a "guide" into the afterlife. By the Gnostic Zoroastrians, the sun was considered "the Archimagus, that noblest and most powerful agent of divine power, who 'steps forth as a Conqueror from the top of the terrible Alborj to rule over the world which he enlightens from the throne of Ormuzd'."[1] Long before the Christian era, the sun was known as the "Son of Ormuzd," the "Mediator," while his adversary, Ahriman, represented the darkness, which caused the fall of man.[2]

The sun was considered the "Savior of the World," as it rose and brought light and life to the planet. It was revered for causing seeds to burst and thus giving its life for plants to grow; hence, it was seen to sacrifice itself in order to provide fertility and vegetation. The sun is the "tutelary genius of universal vegetation,"[3] as well as the god of cultivation and the benefactor of humankind. When the sun "dies" in winter, so does the vegetation, to be "resurrected" in the spring. The first fruits, vine and grain were considered symbols of the sun's strength and were ritualistically offered to the divine luminary. The solar heroes and gods were said to be teachers as well, because agriculture, a science developed out of astronomy, freed mankind to pursue something other than food, such as other sciences and the arts.

The various personifications of the sun thus represent the "image of fecundity which perpetuates and rejuvenates the world's existence."[4] In their fertility aspects, the sun was the phallus, or lingam, and the moon was the vulva, or yoni, the male and female generative principles, the generators of all life on Earth.

In the mythos, the two pillars or columns of the Celestial Temple, the mysterious Jachin and Boaz, are the sun and moon.[5] Of the relationship between the sun and moon, Hazelrigg adds: "The Sun may be likened to a wire through which the planetary messages are electrically transmitted, and of which the lunar moisture is the insulation."[6]

In the ancient world, light was the subject of awe, and the sunlight's ability to make plants grow was considered magical and miraculous. So special is light that the writer of Ecclesiastes waxes, "Light is sweet, and it is pleasant for the eyes to behold the sun." We know that it is *not* pleasant for the eyes to behold the direct *light* of the sun; it is, however, pleasant for humanity to behold the sun as it rises in the morning, bringing light and life. Indeed, the sun itself is the "face of the divine" upon which it is impossible to look.

Thus, the sun was very important to the ancients, so much so that around the world for millennia a wide variety of peoples have built solar temples, monuments and entire religions with priestesses and priests of the Sun, along with complex rituals and accoutrements. Within these religions is contained the ubiquitous mythos, a template or archetypical story that personifies the heavens and Earth, and rolls them into a drama about their interrelationship. Rather than being an entertaining but useless "fairytale," as myths are erroneously considered to be, the mythos is designed to pass along from generation to generation information vital to life on Earth, so that humans do not have to learn it repeatedly but can progress. Without the knowledge, or gnosis, of the celestial mythos, humankind would still be in caves.

The celestial mythos is complicated because the solar myth is intertwined with the lunar, stellar and terrestrial myths. In addition, some of the various celestial players were introduced later than others, and many of them took on new functions as the focus switched from stars to moon to sun to other planets, and back again. For example, Horus is not only the sun but also the North Pole star, and his twin brother-cum-adversary, Set, represents not only darkness but also the South Pole star.

Furthermore, as time progresses and the skies change, as with the precession of the equinoxes and the movements of the sun annually through the zodiac and daily through its "houses," as well as with cataclysm, the attributes of the planetary bodies within the mythos also change. Moreover, the incorporation of the phases of moon into the mythos adds to its complexity:

> The Moon, like the Sun, changed continually the track in which she crossed the Heavens, moving ever to and fro between the upper and lower limits of the Zodiac; and her different places, phases, and aspects there, and her relations with the Sun and the constellations, have been a fruitful source of mythological fables.[7]

An example of the complexity of the mythos is provided by the story of the "Queen of Heaven," the goddess Isis, mother of Horus, who is not only the moon that reflects the sun, she is the original creator, as well as the constellation of Virgo. As the moon, she is the "woman clothed with the sun," and as the Virgin, she is the sun's mother. She is also Stella Maris, the "Star of the Sea," as she regulates the tides, a fact known of the moon beginning eons ago, as were the facts of the roundness of the earth and of the heliocentricity of the solar system—again, knowledge never actually "lost" and "rediscovered," as popularly portrayed.

The sun and moon were deemed to be one being in some cultures or twins in others. When eclipses occurred, it was said that the moon and sun were uniting to create lesser gods. Thus, the pantheon kept growing.

Although it is generally now considered to be "male," the sun was also regarded as female in several places, including Alaska, Anatolia, Arabia, Australia, Canaan, England, Germany, India, Japan, North America and Siberia. The sun's feminine side was, naturally, suppressed by the patriarchy. As Walker says:

> The popular European tradition usually made the sun male and the moon female, chiefly to assert that "his" light was stronger, and that "she" shone only by reflected glory, symbol of the position of women in patriarchal society. However, Oriental and pre-Christian systems frequently made the sun a Goddess.[8]

When one factors into this complexity the fertility aspect of the gods and goddesses of the grape and grain, along with the sexual imagery found in all mythologies and religions, one can understand why it has been so difficult to sort it all out.

The Zodiac

As the mythos developed, it took the form of a play, with a cast of characters, including the 12 divisions of the sky called the signs or constellations of the zodiac. The symbols that typified these 12 celestial sections of 30° each were not based on what the constellations actually look like but represent aspects of earthly life. Thus, the ancient peoples were able to incorporate these earthly aspects into the mythos and project them onto the all-important celestial screen.

These zodiacal designations have varied from place to place and era to era over the tens of thousands of years during which the skies have been observed, for a number of reasons, including the changes in the skies brought on by the precession. For example, Scorpio is not only the eagle but also the scorpion. It is difficult to determine absolutely all of their origins, but the current zodiacal symbols or totems are or may have been devised as follows, based on the formula made by inhabitants of the northern hemisphere:

- Aries is represented as the Ram/Lamb because March/April is the time of the year when lambs are born.
- Taurus is the Bull because April/May is the time for ploughing and tilling.
- Gemini is the Twins, so-called for Castor and Pollux, the twin stars in its constellation, as well as because May/June is the time of the "increase" or "doubling" of the sun, when it reaches its greatest strength.
- After the sun reaches its strength at the summer solstice and begins to diminish in Cancer (June/July), the stars are called the Crab, who "backslides."
- Leo is the Lion because, during the heat of July/August, the lions in Egypt would come out of the hot desert.
- Virgo, originally the Great Mother Earth, is the "Gleaning Virgin, who holds a sheath of wheat," symbolizing August/September, the time of the harvest.
- Libra (September/October) is the Balance, reflecting the autumnal equinox, when the days and night are again even in length.
- Scorpio is the Scorpion because in the desert areas the fierce storms of October/November were called "scorpions" and because this time of the year is the "backbiter" of the sun as it begins to wane.
- Sagittarius is the "vindictive Archer" who side-wounds and weakens the sun during its approach in November/December towards the winter solstice.
- In Capricorn, the weakened sun encounters the "filthy, ill-omened He-goat," who drags the solar hero down in December/January.
- Aquarius is the Water-Bearer because January/February is the time of winter rains.

- Pisces is represented by the Fishes because February/ March is the time when the thinning ice is broken and the fattened fish are plucked out.[9]

The story of the skies was so important to the ancients that they were singularly focused on it and their lives in effect revolved around it. As we have seen, however, the heavens were revered not only by so-called Pagans but also by biblical peoples, including the Israelites, whose name and various Elohim were also stars and aspects of the solar-celestial mythos. In the Bible, the sun is worshipped in various forms by the Hebrews and "kings of Judah." It is also overtly personified and imbued with divine and ethical qualities, as in Deuteronomy: "But thy friends be like the sun as he rises in his might." Throughout the Old Testament important deeds are done "in the sight of this sun," "before the sun," or "under the sun," revealing the ages-old perception of the sun as God's proxy, judge or "eye." So significant was the solar orb that it was ever a grave concern that the sun would "go down on the prophets."

At Psalms 113:3, the chosen are instructed to praise the Lord from the "rising of the sun to its setting." Psalms 85:11 states, "Faithlessness will spring up from the ground, and righteousness will look down from the sky." Psalms 84:11 reads, "For *the Lord God is a sun* and shield." At Psalms 68:32-32, the faithful are instructed to "sing praises to Jah, to him who rides in the heavens, the ancient heavens . . . whose majesty is over Israel, and his power is in the skies," exactly as was said about the ubiquitous solar hero.

At Psalms 72:17, we read, "May his name endure for ever, his fame continue as long as the sun," and, at Malachi 1:11: "For from the rising of sun to its setting my name is great among the nations." The Lord's name is not said to be great *after* the setting of the sun, during the night, because his "name" *is* the sun, as we have seen Iao, Jah, YHWH and so on, to mean. Thus, the esteem of the sun by the Hebrews is evident; yet, the story of the solar hero is also found in numerous places in the Old Testament, but these stories are masked by carnalization and historicization. Indeed, so important was the sun to the ancients, including the Israelites, that they created a "Sun Book," a "Helio Biblio," or "Holy Bible,"[10] the original of which can be found in the myths encoded in stone and story around the ancient world millennia before the Judeo-Christian bible was compiled.

The word "Bible" itself comes from the City of the Great Mother: Byblos, in Phoenicia. As Walker relates, "'Bibles were named after her city because the earliest libraries were attached to her temple."[11] As noted, the Judeo-Christian bible was written by a number of hands, edited numerous times and contains countless errors and inaccuracies. It is a rehash of ancient legends and myths, and is not, therefore, the "infallible Word of God." "Such," says Graham, "is the Bible's 'revealed truth'—other races' mythology, the basis of which is cosmology."[12] The cosmology or celestial mythos has in reality been hidden from the masses for many centuries for the purposes of enriching and empowering the ruling elite. Its conspiring priest-kings have ruled empires in full knowledge of it since time immemorial and have "lorded" it over the heads of the "serfs."

The Sun of God

Within the Sun Book or Holy Bible was incorporated by such priestcraft the most consolidated version of the celestial mythos ever assembled, the story of the "son of God." First, we have seen that "God" is the sun. Second, in Job 38 the stars are called "sons of God"; hence, one star would be a "son of God," as well as the "son of the Sun." Thus, *the son of God is the sun of God.* The solar mythos, in fact, explains why the narratives of the sons of God previously examined are so similar, with a godman who is crucified and resurrected, who does miracles and has 12 disciples, etc.: To wit, these stories were in actuality based on the movements of the sun through the heavens. In other words, Jesus Christ and the others upon whom he is predicated are personifications of the sun, and the gospel fable is merely a repeat of a mythological formula revolving around the movements of the sun through the heavens.

For example, many of the world's crucified godmen have their traditional birthdays on December 25th ("Christmas"). This date is set because the ancients recognized that (from a geocentric perspective in the northern hemisphere) the sun makes an annual descent southward until after midnight of December 21st, the winter solstice, when it stops moving southerly for three days and then starts to move northward again. During this time, the ancients declared that "God's sun" had "died" for three days and was "born again" after midnight of December 24th. Thus, these many different cultures celebrated with great joy the "sun of God's" birthday on December 25th. The following are the main characteristics of the "sun of God":

- The sun "dies" for three days at the winter solstice, to be born again or resurrected on December 25th.
- The sun of God is "born of a virgin," which refers to both the new or "virgin" moon and the constellation of Virgo.

- The sun's "birth" is attended by the "bright Star," either Sirius/Sothis or the planet Venus, and by the "Three Kings," representing the three stars in the belt of Orion.
- The sun at its zenith, or 12 noon, is in the house or heavenly temple of the "Most High"; thus, "he" begins "his Father's work" at "age" 12. Maxwell relates, "At that point, all Egypt offered prayers to the 'Most High' God!"[13]
- The sun enters into each sign of the zodiac at 30°; hence, the "Sun of God" begins his ministry at "age" 30. As Hazelrigg states, ". . . the Sun of the visible heavens has moved northward 30° and stands at the gate of Aquarius, the Water-bearer, or John the Baptist of the mystic planisphere, and here begins the work of ministry in the Palestine . . ."[14]
- The sun is the "Carpenter" who builds his daily "houses" or 12 two-hour divisions.
- The sun's "followers" or "disciples" are the 12 signs of the zodiac, through which the sun must pass.
- The sun is "anointed" when its rays dip into the sea.[15]
- The sun "changes water into wine" by creating rain, ripening the grape on the vine and fermenting the grape juice.
- The sun "walks on water," referring to its reflection.[16]
- The sun "calms the sea" as he rests in the "boat of heaven."[17] (Mt. 8:23-7)
- When the sun is annually and monthly re-born, he brings life to the "solar mummy," his previous self, raising it from the dead.
- The sun triumphantly "rides an ass and her foal" into the "City of Peace" when it enters the sign of Cancer, which contains two stars called "little asses," and reaches its fullness.[18]
- The sun is the "Lion" when in Leo, the hottest time of the year, called the "throne of the Lord."
- The sun is "betrayed" by the constellation of the Scorpion, the backbiter, the time of the year when the solar hero loses his strength.
- The sun is "crucified" between the two thieves of Sagittarius and Capricorn.
- The sun is hung on a cross, which represents its passing through the equinoxes, the vernal equinox being Easter.
- The sun darkens when it "dies": "The solar god as the sun of evening or of autumn was the suffering, dying sun, or the dead sun buried in the nether world."[19]

- The sun does a "stutter-step" at the winter solstice, unsure whether to return to life or "resurrect," doubted by his "twin" Thomas.
- The sun is with us "always, to the close of the age" (Mt. 28:20), referring to the ages of the precession of the equinoxes.
- The sun is the "Light of the World," and "comes on clouds, and every eye shall see him."
- The sun rising in the morning is the "Savior of mankind."
- The sun wears a corona, "crown of thorns" or halo.
- The sun was called the "Son of the Sky (God)," "All-Seeing," the "Comforter," "Healer," "Savior," "Creator," "Preserver," "Ruler of the World," and "Giver of Daily Life."[20]
- The sun is the Word or Logos of God.
- The all-seeing sun, or "eye of God," was considered the judge of the living and dead who returned to Earth "on a white horse."[21]

A. Churchward demonstrates the complex yet poetic celestial mythology of the Egyptians, developed around the core mythos long prior to the Christian era:

> The Sun was not considered human in its nature when the Solar force at dawn was imaged by the Lion-faced Atum, the flame of the furnace by the fiery serpent Uati, the Soul of its life by the Hawk, the Ram, or the Crocodile. Until Har-ur the elder Horus was depicted as the child in the place of the calf or lamb, fish, or shoot of papyrus plant, which now occurred in the Solar Cult, no human figure was personalized in the Mythology of Egypt. . . . Isis in this Cult takes the place of Hathor as the Mother-Moon, the reproducer of light in the underworld. The place of conjunction and of rebegettal by the Sun-god was in the underworld, when she became the woman clothed with the sun. At the end of lunation the old Moon died and became a corpse; it is at times portrayed as a mummy in the underworld and there it was revivified by the Sun-god, the Solar fecundation of the Moon representing the Mother, resulting in her bringing forth the child of light the "cripple deity," who was begotten in the dark.[22]

Massey provides another sketch of the mythos as applied to Horus, who, like Baal, was the sun in the Age of Taurus:

> . . . [The] infant Horus, who sank down into Hades as the suffering sun to die in the winter solstice and be transformed to rise again and return in all his glory and power in the equinox at Easter.[23]

As we have seen, the story of Jesus is virtually identical in numerous important aspects to that of Horus, a solar myth. Higgins spells it out:

> The history of the sun . . . is the history of Jesus Christ. The sun is born on the 25th of December, the birthday of Jesus Christ. The first and greatest of the labours of Jesus Christ is his victory over the serpent, the evil principle, or the devil. In his first labor Hercules strangled the serpent, as did Cristna, Bacchus, etc. This is the sun triumphing over the powers of hell and darkness; and, as he increases, he prevails, till he is crucified in the heavens, or is decussated in the form of a cross (according to Justin Martyr) when he passes the equator at the vernal equinox.[24]

At Malachi 4:2, YHWH says, "But for you who fear my name the sun of righteousness shall rise, with healing on its wings." Who is this sun of righteousness with healing on its wings? Malachi is the last book of the Old Testament, and this scripture is one of the last in that book, which leads directly into the story of Jesus, who was indeed called by the Church fathers the "sun of righteousness." Malachi's sun of righteousness rising with "healing on its wings" is, in reality, the saving light that ends the gloom of night, the daily resurrection of sunrise, and the birth of the sun of a new age, who was carnalized and historicized in Jesus Christ. As "shamash," which is the Hebrew word for sun and the name of the Babylonian sun god, Malachi's righteous sun is also Solomon's Moabite god Chemosh, which is the same as shamash in Hebrew, an ironic development considering Chemosh was later demonized by the Christians.

Jesus's solar attributes are also laid plain by the story of his followers waiting to go to his "tomb" until *sunrise*, when "he is risen." In John 2, Jesus says, "Destroy this temple, and in three days I will raise it up"; however, as John relates, ". . . he spoke of the temple of his body," an admission of biblical allegory. In this statement Jesus describes his own *solar* resurrection, not that of the Jerusalem Temple, although the original "Temple of the Most High" is indeed the same Temple of the Sun that is Jesus's "body." In fact, Jesus is called the "son of the Most High God" (Lk. 8:28; Mk. 5:7) and a priest after the order of Melchizedek, who was the priest of the Most High, El Elyon, or Helios, the sun. At Acts 26:13, regarding his conversion Paul says, "At midday, O king, I saw on the way a light from heaven, brighter than the sun, shining round me and those who journeyed with me," the light, of course, being Jesus. The words "at midday" represent the sun at its zenith, when it is doing its work in the Temple of the Most High, brighter than at any other time.

As expected, the early Christians were considered sun-worshippers, like their "Pagan" counterparts, although "sun-*worship*" is an inaccuracy, since the ancients did not "worship" the sun as the "one god" but revered it as one of the most potent symbols of the quality of divinity. For example, Krishna was considered not just the sun itself but the *light* in the sun and moon,[25] making him, like Jesus, brighter than the sun. Like their predecessor temples, many early Christian churches faced the east, or the place of the rising sun. In fact, as Doane relates, "Tertullian says that Christians were taken for worshipers of the Sun because they prayed towards the East, after the manner of those who adored the Sun."[26] Ex-Pagan and Bishop of Carthage Tertullian's actual words from his Apology are as follows:

> Others, again, certainly with more information and greater verisimilitude, believe that the sun is our god. We shall be counted Persians perhaps, though we do not worship the orb of day painted on a piece of linen cloth, having himself everywhere in his own disk. The idea no doubt has originated from our being known to turn to the east in prayer. But you, many of you, also under pretence sometimes of worshipping the heavenly bodies, move your lips in the direction of the sunrise. In the same way, if we devote Sun-day to rejoicing, from a far different reason than Sun-worship, we have some resemblance to those of you who devote the day of Saturn to ease and luxury, though they too go far away from Jewish ways, of which indeed they are ignorant.

In his protestations and refutations of critics, Tertullian further ironically admits the true origins of the Christ story and of all other such godmen by stating, "*You say we worship the sun; so do you.*"[27] Interestingly, a previously strident believer and defender of the faith, Tertullian later renounced Christianity.[28]

Christ was frequently identified as and/or with the sun by other early orthodox Christian fathers, including St. Cyprian (d. 258), who "spoke of Christ as the true sun (sol verus)," and St. Ambrose (@ 339-397), Bishop of Milan, who said of Christ, "He is our new sun."[29] Other Church fathers who identified Christ with, if not as, the sun include St. Gregory of Nazianzus (c. 330-c. 389), and St. Zeno of Verona (d. c. 375), who "calls Christ 'Sol noster, sol verus.'" Moreover, this overt Christian sun-worship was not a short-lived aberration, as Christian proponents would portray it. Wheless relates that "Leo the Great in his day (440-461) says that it was the custom of many Christians to stand on the steps of the Church of St. Peter and pay homage to the Sun by obeisance and prayers."[30]

As to such "insider" knowledge of the true meaning of Christianity, Doane remarks:

Many Christian writers have seen that the history of their Lord and Saviour is simply the history of the Sun, but they either say nothing, or, like Dr. Parkhurst and the Rev. J. P. Lundy, claim that the Sun is a type of the true Sun of Righteousness.

This "type of" sophistry has been used frequently in "religious" debate to squeeze out of a tight corner. Yet, the Christian conspirators cannot hide the fact that their "Lord's Day" is indeed *Sun-day*; hence, their Lord is the sun.

Even though this information has been well hidden, the early Christians were aware that Christ was the sun, as they were truly Gnostic and the solar myth was known all around them. When a member of at least one such Gnostic sect wished to become orthodox, he was compelled to renounce his "heresy" of equating Christ with the sun. Higgins relates of the influential and widespread Gnostic group called the Manichaeans:

> When a Manichaean came over to the orthodox he was required to curse his former friends in the following terms: "I curse Zarades [Zarathustra/Zoroaster] who, Manes said, had appeared as a God before his time among the Indians and Persians, and whom he calls the sun. I curse those who say *Christ is the sun*, and who make prayers to the sun, and to the moon, and to the stars, and pay attention to them as if they were really Gods, and who give them titles of most lucid Gods, and who do not pray to the true God, only towards the East, but who turn themselves round, following the motions of the sun with their innumerable supplications. I curse those persons who say that Zarades and Budas [Buddha] and Christ and Manichaeus and the sun are all one and the same."[31]

In his 2nd Apology, Justin Martyr acknowledges that the Gnostic-Christian Manichaeans were "sun-worshippers" and says:

> Accordingly, Menander seems to me to have fallen into error when he said: "O sun! for thou, first of gods, ought to be worshipped, by whom it is that we are able to see the other gods." For the sun never could show me the true God; but that healthful Word, that is the Sun of the soul, by whom alone, when He arises in the depths of the soul, the eye of the soul itself is irradiated.

In order to obfuscate the origins of Christianity, Justin is attempting to distinguish between the sun of the Gnostics, which was the solar orb, and the "sun (sol) of the soul" in the "person" of Jesus Christ. In fact, the sun of the Gnostics and other "sun-worshippers" also represented the cosmic and cellular "sun" found in living things, including human beings, who, it was perceived, by Gnosticism can become *illuminated*. Thus, both Gnostic and orthodox Christians were addressing the same "sun of the soul," but the orthodoxy insisted on putting a particular face and shape to it. One might also wonder how the *omnipresent* divine is separated out of its creation, such that it is "everywhere" but not in the sun, moon, stars, sky, earth and all of creation. To reiterate, the ancients were not just monotheistic, polytheistic and "atheistic"—as the Christians called and were called by their adversaries—but pantheistic, seeing the divine in everything, as is the definition of omnipresence.

It is clear that from early times Christ was correctly perceived by the Gnostic sects as the sun, a fact that the historicizing Christians were continuously compelled to combat, as is evidenced by the anti-Manichaean oath specifically designed to refute such assertions. Yet, as Higgins states, ". . . the Sun, Iao, and Jesus, were all taken for the same being by the ancients, and it will require more than the skill of the whole priesthood to disprove it."[32]

Furthermore, the adoption (or, rather, creation) of Christianity was not much of a stretch for the Roman conspirators:

> In the early Christian era, Roman emperors were routinely identifying themselves with the sun god and all his symbols: cross, eagle, fire, gold, lion, and so on. Constantine I, whom conventional history hails as the first Christian emperor, was actually a worshipper of the sun god, whose image he placed on his coins, dedicated to "the invincible sun, my guardian."[33]

In fact, a 100-lire coin issued by the Vatican depicts a woman, symbolizing the Church, holding a cup in her right hand, which represents the "pagan sunburst wafer god."[34] This "wafer" or host used in Communion by the Catholic Church as a symbol for the body of Christ is actually a very ancient symbol for the sun. The Catholic "monstrance" or "ostentorium," the device used to serve the "Lord's host," is also a sunburst, as admitted by Catholic authorities.[35] Christian art, like that of Buddhism and Hinduism, makes extensive use of the halo or *sunburst* behind its godman, mother of God, and saints. As Massey says, "The halo of light which is usually shown surrounding the face of Jesus and Christian saints, is another concept taken from the sun god."

The solar nature of Jesus Christ is thus reflected in art, explaining "nobody knew what he looked like" and why he was variously represented as a sun god, such as Apollo or Elias. As Biedermann says:

> In Christian iconography the sun, rising over and over again in the East, symbolizes immortality and resurrection. There are fourth-century mosaics showing Christ as a Helios-figure in a solar chariot surrounded by sunbeams, or surrounded by a solar nimbus. Since Christ is also triumphant over time (*chronocrator*),

he is frequently associated with the sun (which measures out the length of each day) in Romanesque art.[36]

The term "associated with" is a typical historicizing obfuscation, because Christ *is* the sun, which Christian artists have obviously known. The Apollo/Helios/Jesus image is often very light of complexion, with short blond hair, reflective not of an actual person but of the light and color of the sun. Other solar depictions include men with red hair, representative of the setting and summer sun, and black images symbolizing the orb in the dark underworld of night, which is the reason for the black bambinos and crucifixes in churches around the globe, not only of Jesus but also Krishna and other solar heroes. As stated, these black crucifixes have led some to posit that Jesus was black, i.e., African; however, despite this compulsion to make Christ "all things to all people," these images depict the black or nighttime sun. In fact, they are part of the mythos, which holds that the solar orb and night sky are a dual-natured god, represented by "twins" battling for supremacy.

Let us now see further how the solar mythos was passed to us as the Christian myth. To do so, we will also be following the sun's annual movements through the heavenly zodiac:

- According to legend, Jesus was born in a stable between a horse and a goat, symbols of Sagittarius and Capricorn.
- He was baptized in Aquarius, the Water-Bearer.
- He chose his first disciples, fishermen, in Pisces, the sign of the fishes.
- He became the Good Shepherd and the Lamb in Aries, the Ram.
- Jesus told the parables of the sowing and tilling of the fields in Taurus, the Bull.
- In Cancer, "the celestial Sea of Galilee,"[37] he calmed the storm and waters, spoke of backsliders (the Crab), and rode the ass and foal in triumph into the City of Peace, Jerusalem.
- Jesus was the Lion in Leo.
- In Libra, Christ was the true vine in the Garden of Gethsemane, the "wine press," as this is the time of the grape harvest.
- Jesus was betrayed by Judas, the "backbiter," or Scorpio.
- In Sagittarius, Jesus was wounded in the side by the Centaur, or centurion.
- He was crucified at the winter solstice between the "two thieves" of Sagittarius and Capricorn, who sapped his strength.

Roberts elaborates the solar drama:

> . . . the passage of the Sun, in its annual course through the constellations of the Zodiac; having his birth in the sign of the Goat, the Augean stable of the Greeks; his baptism in Aquarius, the John the Baptist in the heavens; his triumph when he becomes the Lamb of God in Aries; his greatest exaltation on St. John's, the beloved disciple's day, on the 21st of June, in the Sign of the Twins, the emblem of double power; his tribulation in the Garden of Gethsemane, in the sign of the rural Virgo; his betrayal in the sign of Scorpio, the malignant emblem of his approaching death in the stormy and adverse sign, Sagittarius, and his resurrection or renewed birth on the twenty-fifth of December in the same sign of the celestial Goat . . .

Regarding the mysterious Garden of Gethsemane, Wells says, "They went to a place which is called Gethsemane'. Nothing is known of such a place."[38] In fact, the Garden exists in the sky.

In addition, Jesus in the "upper room" symbolizes the sun in the "upper signs," as the two equinoxes divide the solar orbit into two halves, also represented by the two genealogies of Jesus in the gospels.[39]

Hazelrigg gives the astrological meaning of the annunciation of the divine one's birth:

> Directing our gaze to the right, we see rising on the eastern angle of the planisphere the constellation of the Virgin, the sixth sign of the Zodiac, or sixth month, reckoning from March (Aries). "And in the sixth month the angel Gabriel was sent from God . . . to a virgin espoused by a man whose named was Joseph, of the house of David; and the virgin's name was Mary."—Luke i. 26, 27.[40]

He further explains the Passion as it appears in the mythos:

> In due order, the next quarter introduces the Passion—a term appositely chosen and applied—prefaced under Aries, the first sign of the fiery triplicity, which is the Vale of Gehenna. . . . Thence comes Calvary, conformably with the crossification of the Sun of Nature at the gate of Libra, with the zodiacal Virgin recumbent next to this point of supreme sacrifice.[41]

The story of the sun is a daily, monthly, annual and precessional drama that takes place cyclically and over thousands of years. In order to change the mythos into the life of a man—in other words, to personify and historicize it—it was necessary to make the tale linear, such that there are discrepancies between the stories of the sun and that of the "historical" Jesus. For example, while the sun "dies" and is "reborn" or "resurrected" daily, monthly, annually and precessionally, as a "person" Jesus can only undergo such experiences once. In the early Christian period, when the story was still being formulated, yet another debate raged as to how long after beginning his ministry Christ was supposed to suffer his passion, with a common portrayal that it occurred "in the 12ᵗʰ month after his baptism," i.e., at the winter solstice, following his baptism in Aquarius, as acknowledged by Irenaeus, who wrote against the "heretics": "[T]hey affirm that He suffered in the twelfth month, so that He continued to preach for one year after His baptism." Irenaeus then insists that Christ "did not suffer in the twelfth month after his baptism, but was more than fifty years old when he died." Irenaeus's statements reveal not only Jesus's solar nature but also that by his time (c. 140-c. 200) the gospel story was not "set in stone," as it would have been, had it happened in history. In fact, some of the writings of the early Christian fathers demonstrate that they are discussing a number of different individuals, which is to be expected, since the Christ character is a composite of many.

These various debates reflect the complexity of the mythos, as further illustrated by Massey:

> When it was discovered that the moon was a mirror to the solar light, the sun-god as Osiris was reborn monthly in or of the moon! Thus, the resurrection in three days became that of the luni-solar god. . . . The Christ who rose again in three days for the fulfillment of scripture must be the Christ according to that scripture which contained the mythos, and the fulfillment of scripture was the completion of astronomical cycles, whether lunar, solar, or Precessional.[42]

As stated, the character of Jesus Christ was in fact created as the solar avatar or hero of the Age of Pisces, into which the sun was moving during the first centuries before the Christian era, an ill-omened time between ages of celestial "no man's land." Jesus as the Lamb of God was a remnant of the previous Age of Aries:

> And as it approached the "gates of Spring," "the Lamb of God," or the Lamb of March gathered up "the sins of the world," or the sins of the Winter, and bore them away. And thus was realized, astronomically, not only "the Lamb of God taking away the sins of the world," but also the death and resurrection of the Son of God, or the sun-God, more properly.[43]

Massey describes the changes of the ages:

> When Horus had fulfilled the period of 2155 years with the Easter Equinox in the Sign of Aries, the birthplace passed into the Sign of Pisces, when the Ever-Coming One, the Renewer as the Eternal Child who had been brought forth as a Lion in Leo, a Beetle in Cancer, as one of the Twins in Gemini, as a calf in the Sign of the Bull, and a Lamb in the Sign of the Ram, was destined to manifest as the Fish, in the Sign of the Fishes. The rebirth of Atum-Horus, or Jesus, as the Fish Iusaas, and the

Bread of Nephthys, was astronomically dated to occur in Beth-Lechem—the House of Bread—about 255 B.C., at the time the Easter Equinox entered the Sign of Pisces, the house of Corn and Bread.

Massey also states that "Horus in Egypt had been a fish from time immemorial, and when the equinox entered the sign of Pisces, Horus was portrayed as *Ichthys* with the fish sign of over his head." He further says, "The Messiah who manifested in this sign was foreordained to come as Ichthys the fisherman, or, doctrinally, the fisher of men."[44]

Thus, Jesus is the Piscean fish god, who, at Luke 24:11-2, upon his resurrection is made to ask, "Do you have any fish?", establishing the choice of communion food of the new age. Hence, the fish was ordered to be eaten in Catholicism. In addition, the early Christians were called "Pisciculi"—"little fishes."[45] As the solar hero of the Piscean Age, Jesus is also made to say, "I am with you always until the close of the age." It is now the close of the Age of Pisces, and the sun is moving into the Age of Aquarius, a "second coming" that signifies the changing of the guard.

1. Pike, 612.
2. Pike, 613.
3. Pike, 475.
4. Pike, 594.
5. Pike, 776.
6. Hazelrigg, 56.
7. Pike, 469.
8. Walker, *WDSSO*, 353.
9. Hazelrigg, 43.
10. Hotema, *EBD*.
11. Walker, *WEMS*, 127.
12. Graham, 74.
13. Leedom, 23.
14. Hazelrigg, 163.
15. Anderson, 206.
16. Massey, *HJMC*, 21.
17. Leedom, 27.
18. Pike, 465.
19. Massey, *EBD*, 50.
20. Doane, 472, 478, 492, 562.
21. Doane, 497-8.
22. A. Churchward, 226.
23. Massey, *EBD*, 9.
24. Higgins, II, 144.
25. Doane, 284.
26. Doane, 500-2.
27. Wheless, 147.
28. Wheless, 144.
29. www.christianism.com
30. Wheless, 30.
31. Higgins, I, 722.

32. Higgins, I, 325.
33. Walker, *WDSSO*, 15.
34. www.aloha.net/~mikesch/monstr.htm
35. www.aloha.net/~mikesch/monstr.htm
36. Biedermann, 330.
37. Hazelrigg, 161.
38. Wells, *DJE*, 136.
39. Hazelrigg, 120.
40. Hazelrigg, 105.
41. Hazelrigg, 165.
42. Massey, *HJMC*, 108-9.
43. Graves, *BS*, 81.
44. Massey, *HJMC*, 20.
45. Higgins, 568.

Image from Babain, Egypt, of priests
sacrificing to the Sun. (Hislop)

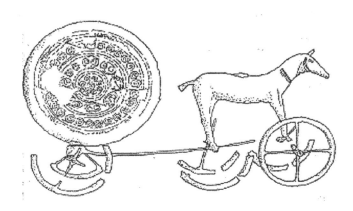

Bronze Solar Horse and Car
Denmark, c. 1000 BCE.
(Campbell, *CM*)

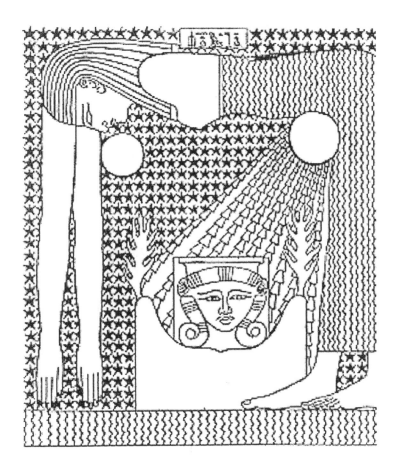

Nut (the Sky) gives birth to the Sun,
whose rays fall on Hathor.
(Campbell, *HWTF*)

Osiris as the Bull transporting his worshipper to the Underworld.
(Campbell, *HWTF*)

Medallion with Emperor Constantine
and Sol Invictus, the Roman Sun God,
313 CE. (I. Wilson)

Jesus as the Sun God in the Solar Chariot by white horses.
Mosaic from third century CE, found under the altar at
St. Peter's in Rome. (I. Wilson)

Image from Babain, Egypt, of priests
sacrificing to the Sun. (Hislop)

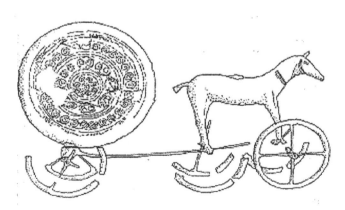

Bronze Solar Horse and Car
Denmark, c. 1000 BCE.
(Campbell, *CM*)

The Disciples are the Signs of the Zodiac

As we have seen, the son of God with the twelve disciples is not historical but an old mythological and astrological motif found around the globe for thousands of years and symbolizing the sun and its movements through the heavens, before it was carnalized, Judaized and historicized in the gospel tale of Jesus Christ. In reality, like Jesus, the famous biblical disciples are recorded nowhere in the works of any historian of their time. The only source for the disciples/apostles is in Christian literature, in which the stories of their "lives" are in fact highly apocryphal, allegorical and, therefore, inadequate as "history" or "biography." Of these various fables regarding the apostles, Walker relates: "Guignebert says 'not one of them is true . . . [T]here exists no information really worthy of credence about the life and works of the immediate Apostles of Jesus.'"[1]

As Wells states regarding the gospel tradition of "the twelve":

> The twelve disciples are often regarded as guarantors of Jesus' historicity, although we are told nothing of most of them except their names, on which the documents do not even agree completely. In Mk. and Mt. the list of names is also very clumsily worked into the text. All this makes it obvious that the *number* is an older tradition than the *persons*; that the idea of the twelve derives not from twelve actual disciples, but from other sources . . . [2]

And ben Yehoshua says:

> The first time that twelve apostles are mentioned is in the document known as the *Teaching of the Twelve Apostles* [Didache]. This document apparently originated as a sectarian Jewish document written in the first century C.E., but it was adopted by Christians who altered it substantially and added Christian ideas to it. In the earliest versions it is clear that the "twelve apostles" are the twelve sons of Jacob representing the twelve tribes of Israel. The Christians later considered the "twelve apostles" to be allegorical disciples of Jesus.

In fact, Eusebius himself gives the origins of "the Twelve" when he says, "At that very time it was true of His apostles that *their speech went out to the whole earth, and their words to the ends of the world*,"[3] an allusion to Psalms 19:4, which, as we have seen, refers to the starry configurations or constellations, whose "voice" or "line" penetrates the earth.

In reality, it is no accident that there are 12 patriarchs, 12 tribes of Israel and 12 disciples, 12 being the number of the astrological signs, as well as the 12 "houses" through which the sun passes each day and the 12 hours of day and night. Indeed, like the 12 Herculean tasks, the 12 "helpers" of Horus, and the 12 "generals" of Ahura-Mazda, Jesus's 12 "disciples" are symbolic for the zodiacal signs and do not depict any literal figures who played out a drama upon the earth circa 30 CE. The twelve disciples are thus the "sun's librarians, the treasure-scribes."[4]

Hazelrigg sums up the gospel tale thus:

> . . . the Romans . . . personified our sun, or centre of the solar system, as a living man, and the twelve signs of the zodiac as his twelve disciples; and the ingress of the sun through the different signs, as this man called Son of God, as going about doing his Father's work, or, rather, doing the will of the Father.[5]

Higgins elucidates upon the zodiacal role of "the twelve" in the mythos:

> The number of the twelve apostles, which formed the retinue of Jesus during his mission, is that of the signs, and of the secondary genii, the tutelary gods of the Zodiacal signs which the sun passes through in his annual revolution. It is that of the twelve gods of the Romans, each of whom presided over a month. The Greeks, the Egyptians, the Persians, each had their *twelve* gods, as the Christian followers of Mithra had their *twelve* apostles. The chief of the twelve Genii of the annual revolution had the barque and the keys of time, the same as the chief of the secondary gods of the Romans or Janus, after whom St. Peter, Bar-Jona, with his barque and keys, is modelled.[6]

Peter the Rock

The disciple, apostle and saint Peter, "the Rock" to whom so much of the Christian religion is entrusted, is easily revealed to be a mythological character and old motif:

> There is evidence that within some of [the secret] groups, long before Christian times, the "hierophant," or chief high priest and main spokesman for the son of God on Earth, was called by the title "PETR," or "Peter," meaning "the rock." To some, this has seemed too similar to the name Christ is said to have assigned to his strangely named prime disciple, Peter, also said to mean "the Rock," to have been a complete coincidence.[7]

This PETR was the rock of Vatican Hill upon which was built the Mithraic brotherhood. Walker relates the ultimate purpose of the insertion of the Peter character:

> The myth of St. Peter was the slender thread from which hung the whole weighty structure of the Roman papacy. . . . Unfortunately for papal credibility, the so-called Petrine passage was a forgery. It was deliberately inserted into the scripture about the 3rd century A.D. as a political ploy, to uphold the primacy of the Roman see against rival churches in the east. Various Christian bishropics were engaged in a power struggle in

which the chief weapons were bribery, forgery, and intrigue, with elaborate fictions and hoaxes written into sacred books, and the ruthless competition between rival parties for the lucrative position of God's elite. . . . Most early churches put forth spurious claims to foundation by apostles, even though *the apostles themselves were no more than the mandatory "zodiacal twelve" attached to the figure of the sacred king.*[8]

Jesus is made to give the keys of the kingdom to Peter, yet he then turns around and calls Peter "Satan," ironically implying that his church is to be built upon the "rock of Satan." Peter was thus the "gatekeeper" of heaven, likewise a role within the mythos. As Robertson relates: ". . . there is to be noted the remarkable coincidence that in the Egyptian Book of the Dead, Petra is the name of the divine doorkeeper of heaven . . ."[9] Massey expands upon Peter's role and counterpart in Egyptian mythology:

> . . . Kabhsenuf the hawk-headed is, as the name denotes, the refresher of his brethren, and this office is assigned to Peter as feeder of the sheep. It was Peter who rushed into the water to meet Jesus, and in the *Ritual*—when the dead Osiris has risen and come forth . . . *Kabhsenuf wets his limbs in the streams for them to guard Osiris . . .* [10]

"Peter" is not only "the rock" but also "the cock," or penis, as the word is used as slang to this day. As Walker says, "The cock was also a symbol of Saint Peter, whose name also meant a phallus or male principle (*pater*) and a phallic pillar (*petra*). Therefore, the cock's image was often placed atop church towers."[11] Higgins elucidates on the phallic nature of Peter the rock:

> On this *stone*, which was the emblem of the male generative principle, the Linga, Jesus founded his church. This sacred stone is found throughout all the world. In India at every temple. The Jews had it in the stone of Jacob, which he anointed with oil. The Greeks, at Delphi, like Jacob, anointed it with oil. The black stone was in the Caaba, at Mecca, long before the time of Mohammed, and was preserved by him when he destroyed the Dove and the Images. He not only preserved it, but he cause it to be built into the corner of the sacred Caaba, where it is now kissed and adored by all Mohammedans who make the pilgrimage to Mecca. . . . Mr. Bryant says, "When the worship of the sun was almost universal, this was one name of that deity, even among the Greeks. They called him Petor, and Petros, and his temple was styled Petra." Where the temples had this name . . . there was generally a sacred stone which was supposed to have descended from heaven. . . . Mr. Bryant observes, "Pator or Petor, was an Egyptian word; and Moses, speaking of Joseph and the dreams of Pharaoh, more than once makes use of it . . ."[12]

Furthermore, the veneration of the peter or lingam is reflective of the homoeroticism within the patriarchal cults. So fervent was this lingam-worship that the "cock" was considered the "Savior of the World":

> The cock was another totemic "peter" sometimes viewed as the god's alter ego. Vatican authorities preserved a bronze image of a cock with an oversize penis on a man's body, the pedestal inscribed "The Savior of the World." The cock was also a solar symbol.[13]

As stated, Peter was a remake of the Roman god Janus; thus, he was associated with the month of January, "when the sun entered the sign of Aquarius, symbol of both the gate of the year and the Pearly Gate of Maria-Aphrodite."[14] As Doane says:

> The Roman god Jonas, or Janus, with his keys, was changed into Peter, who was surnamed Bar-Jonas. Many years ago a statue of the god Janus, in bronze, being found in Rome, he was perched up in St. Peter's with his keys in his hand: the very identical god, in all his native ugliness. This statute sits as St. Peter, under the cupola of the church of St. Peter. It is looked upon with the most profound veneration: the toes are nearly kissed away by devotees.[15]

In addition to the canonical gospels, the Christianized Peter tales were not in existence at the time of Justin Martyr (100-165), who, as Blavatsky relates, "writing in the early part of the second century *in Rome*, where he fixed his abode, eager to get hold of the least proof in favor of the truth for which he suffered, seems *perfectly unconscious of St. Peter's existence!!* Neither does any other writer of any consequence mention him in connection with the Church of Rome, earlier than the days of Irenaeus, when the latter set himself to invent a new religion, drawn from the depth of his imagination."[16]

Judas the Betrayer

Although he is one of the most vilified characters in human literature, Judas was actually a key figure in "God's Plan" for salvation through blood-atonement and was charged by Jesus to betray him, an assignment which he obeyed, thus proving himself to be the best of the disciples. However, the gospel tale of the betraying kiss of Judas makes no sense as history. If such a wannabe king of the Jews existed and was famed throughout the land, there would be no need for Judas's kiss to identify him. And, we must ask why he needed to kiss Jesus at all—would not a simple fingerpointing or handshake have sufficed? The kiss is not only homoerotic but serves as a literary device, as it was part of an ancient ritual played out on a regular basis.

As noted, Judas is not a historical character but represents Scorpio, "the backbiter," the time of year when the sun's rays are weakening and the sun appears to be dying. Judas also serves as the last hour of the day, since the twelve disciples also symbolized the twelve hours of daylight.[17] In the Horus myth, the role of the betrayer is played by Set or Typhon, who is portrayed as having red hair, the color of the sun-*set*. When the mythos was Judaized, the betrayer became Judas, who was depicted with red hair.

Judas, of course, is yet another ancient god given historical dress, as Judas is the same word as Judah. As Walker relates:

> Formerly, Judas was an ancestral god, father of the nation of Judah and of Jews (*Judaei*). As Jude, or Jeud, he was the "only-begotten son" of the Divine Father Isra-El. Judas was a dynastic name for priest-kings of Judea for a hundred years after Judas Maccabeus restored ancient sacrificial customs to the temple of Jerusalem in 165 B.C. Thus the kingly name of Judas was commonly given victims sacrificed as surrogates for a reigning monarch.[18]

Indeed, as Judas betrayed Jesus, so did Judah betray his brother Joseph. It seems that the name Judas was used to put the onus of Jesus's death on the Jews and to cast aspersions on them for refusing to believe the newly created tale, thus betraying their own "brethren" who were promulgating it, some of whom were Jews and others Samaritan Israelites. Joseph also represented the northern kingdom of Israel, such that the OT story depicted the betrayal of the northern kingdom by the southern, as does the gospel tale. This type of personification of a nation or people as a character in a drama is common in mythmaking and has its precedent for the New Testament in the Old. Another example appears in the "Fragments of Papias," an early Church father who wrote an exegesis on the Logia Iesou, or Sayings/Oracles of Jesus, in which Papias gives an account of Judas's death, which also contradicts the gospel story:

> Judas walked about in this world a sad example of impiety; for his body having swollen to such an extent that he could not pass where a chariot could pass easily, he was crushed by the chariot, so that his bowels gushed out.

This tale is not historical but allegorical, representing the "bloated" Judah/Judea being crushed by the "chariot" of Rome, which dispelled its inhabitants outward. Furthermore, the gospel accounts of Judas's death are contradictory and allegorical, explainable only in terms of him being an ancient character within the mythos.

Judas has also been identified with the moon, which demonstrates once again the complexity of the mythos. At one point, the stellar cult was dominant, then the lunar cult, then the solar cult, and so on. The lunar cult was generally matriarchal, and the solar patriarchal. Thus, we have a battle between not only the sun and the moon but also the male and the female. As to Judas's lunar nature, Massey says:

> The French retain a tradition that the man in the moon is Judas Iscariot, who was transported there for his treason to the Light of the World. But that story is pre-Christian, and was told at least some 6,000 years ago of Osiris and the Egyptian Judas, Sut, who was born twin with him of one mother, and who betrayed him, at the Last Supper, into the hands of the 72 Sami, or conspirators, who put him to death. Although the Mythos became solar, it was originally lunar, Osiris and Sut having been twin brothers in the moon.[19]

Matthew the Scribe

Regarding the apostle Matthew, to whom was attributed the recordation of the "Oracles of the Lord," Massey describes his counterpart within the Egyptian version of the mythos concerning the Lord Horus:

> Taht-Matiu was the scribe of the gods, and in Christian art Matthew is depicted as the scribe of the gods, with an angel standing near him, to dictate the gospel. . . . The lion is Matthew's symbol, and that is the zodiacal sign of the month of Taht-Matiu (Thoth), in the fixed year. Tradition makes Matthew to have been the *eighth* of the apostles; and the eighth (Esmen) is a title of Taht-Matiu. Moreover, it is Matthias, upon whom the lot fell, who is chosen to fill the place of the Typhonian traitor Judas. So was it in the mythos when Matiu (Taht) succeeded Sut [Set], and occupied his place after the betrayal of Osiris. . . . It is to the Gnostics that we must turn for the missing link between the oral and the written word; between the Egyptian *Ritual* and the canonical gospels; between the Matthew who wrote the Hebrew or Aramaic gospel of the sayings, and Taht-Matiu, who wrote the *Ritual*, the Hermetic, which means *inspired* writings, that are said to have been inscribed in hieroglyphics by the very finger of *Mati* himself.[20]

Thomas the Twin

The disciple Thomas appears very infrequently in the canonical gospels, mostly in John, but he is a highly influential character, in that it was he who was chosen to verify Christ's resurrection by touching him. Of this incident, Walker states:

> . . . Later, an unknown Gospel writer inserted the story of doubting Thomas, who insisted on touching Jesus. This was to combat the heretical idea that there was no resurrection in the flesh, and also to subordinate Jerusalem's municipal god

Tammuz (Thomas) to the new savior. Actually, the most likely source of primary Christian mythology was the Tammuz cult in Jerusalem. Like Tammuz, Jesus was the Bridegroom of the Daughter of Zion . . .[21]

The Syrian and Jerusalemite god Thomas/Tammuz was given the role in the mythos of the "genius" of the time when the sun is at its weakest, during the winter solstice. As Carpenter states, ". . . the Church dedicates the very day of the winter solstice (when any one may very naturally doubt the rebirth of the Sun) to St. Thomas, who doubted the truth of the Resurrection!"[22] Indeed, the hierarchy of Jerusalem when Tammuz was worshipped there was composed of, as we have seen from Ezekiel, the elders "behind the hidden door," constituting the Zadokite/Sadducean priesthood, who, in fact, did not believe in the resurrection of the flesh. Tammuz's name is still retained in the Hebrew month of Tammuz.

Thomas is called Didymus, a name that "comes from the Greek word Didymos, the Greek equivalent of the Roman Gemini, the zodiacal twins."[23] "Thomas" itself also means "twin" in Aramaic/Syriac. Hence, Didymus Thomas is a redundancy that is not the name of any disciple but a rehash of the ancient story of the twin god. In fact, Thomas is also called "Judas Thomas," Judas likewise meaning "twin." As Walker says, "Judas and Jesus seem to have been traditional names taken by victims in whom the god Tammuz was incarnate,"[24] referring to the sacred king ritual enacted in Judea, as well as many other places.

It is said that "Thomas" preached to the Parthians and Persians, but what is being conveyed is that these groups were followers of Tammuz or Dumuzi, as was his Sumerian name. Although it was alleged that Thomas's tomb was in Edessa, tradition also claims that he died near Madras, India, where *two* of his tombs are still shown. This tale comes from the fact that when Portuguese Christian missionaries arrived in southern India they found a sect who worshipped a god named "Thomas" and whose religion was nearly identical to Christianity. So disturbed were the Christian missionaries that they created elaborate stories to explain the presence of the "St. Thomas Christians," claiming that the apostles Thomas and/or Bartholomew had at some point traveled to India, preached and died there.

The one aspect that truly perplexed the Christians, however, was that Christ was not the object of adoration in this sect. It was thus determined that this strange sect was heretical yet Christian, even though Christ was not its god. The reality is that these Indian "Christians" were worshipping Tamus or Tammuz, the sacrificed savior-god long prior to the Christian era.[25]

This Indian Tamus/Thomas sect evidently had a gospel written in ancient Chaldee, or proto-Hebrew, which identifies the partial origins of the gospel tale as being the "promontory of Tamus . . . in India, near to the settlement of St. Thomas Christians of Malabar,"26 rather than the other way around. In fact, these "St. Thomas Christians" of "Core-mandir-la" were Indian Nazarene-Carmelites,27 as were the Nazarenes of St. John, or Mandaeans. Of the Nazarenes, Higgins further asserts:

> . . . these Mandaites or *Nazareens* or Disciples of St. John, are found in central India, and they are certainly not disciples of the Western Jesus of Nazareth. . . . all Gnosticism came originally from India . . . the Mandaites or Nazareens are no other than the sect of Gnostics, and the extreme East the place of their birth.28

There are also traces of Tammuz/Thomas worship in China, where he was apparently considered to be an incarnation of Buddha.29

Paul the Apostle

In the gospel tale, Paul is not one of "the twelve" but the most influential convert after Jesus's death. Paul acted as a missionary and pastor, and had "an unshakable determination to collect money from his largely Gentile churches and to deliver the collection himself to the Jewish Christian Church in Jerusalem."30

Even though Paul claims in Acts, "My manner of life from my youth, spent from the beginning among my own nation and at Jerusalem, is *known by all the Jews*," like Jesus and the twelve he does not appear in any historical record, although some of the events in his life were fairly significant. For example, there is no mention in Josephus or anyone else of the "two hundred soldiers with seventy horsemen and two hundred spearmen" who allegedly went "as far as Caesarea" to bring Paul before the governor Felix. As Graham relates, the historian Seneca was "the brother of Gallio, proconsul of Achaia at precisely the time Paul is said to have preached there. While he wrote of many lesser things, no mention is made of Paul or the wonder-working Christ."31 Paul's life story has the same air of mythology as many great "men," changing to suit the teller. For instance, in the NT, there are three different (and apocryphal) accounts of his conversion (Acts 9:7, 22:9, 26:13ff).

Like so many other biblical characters, Paul is also fictitious. In fact, it has been claimed that "historical" details later added to the gospel version of the mythos were taken from the life of Apollonius the Nazarene. In this theory, Apollonius was also called "Apollos," or "Paulus" in Latin. Many elements of Paul's life agree with those of Apollonius, including the route of his journeys, which is almost identical to that of Apollonius according to Philostratus's account of his life. The fact that Paul was from a predominantly Greek town, Tarsus, and resembled a Greek more than anything else lends credence to this claim, as, according to Philostratus, the Greek Apollonius spent part of his youth in Tarsus. Like those of Paul, Apollonius's journeys originated in Antioch. Apollonius is also recorded as having traveled to India with his faithful disciple Damis (Demas) and visited the Brahmans. While on this journey, Philostratus reports, Apollonius "acquired from the Arabians a knowledge of the language of animals," an interesting story considering that Paul alleges in Galatians that he made a three-year visit to Arabia, during which time legend holds he learned various mysteries. Paul's purported visit to "Arabia," or the east, also corresponds with the claim that Apollonius went to the east, where he gathered various books, including those containing the story of Krishna.

Apollonius returned home from India, as Waite relates, "by going south to the sea, thence by vessel, up the Euphrates to Babylon, then, by way of Antioch, to Cyprus and Paphos."[32] The latter journey is exactly as was said of Paul. Apollonius then went to Ephesus, where the people flocked to him and where he did miracles, as he did afterwards in Athens, the same route taken by Paul, although purportedly in the opposite direction. Like Paul, Apollonius next went to Corinth, where he had a disciple named Lycian, or Luke. After traveling around Greece, he then proceeded to Rome, where he was accused of treason, after which went to Spain and Africa, returning to Italy and Sicily.

After traveling to Alexandria and down into Nubia, to an ancient Gymnosophic/Buddhist/Brahmanical community, Apollonius re-turned to Italy, Greece and on to the Hellespont, where he challenged wandering Egyptians and Chaldeans who were defrauding the people in a typical priestly manner. In passing through this area, Apollonius no doubt stopped at Samothrace, the island home of the exalted mysteries and one of the potent seats of the pre-Christian Iasios/Jesus cult, a journey also taken by Paul. Like Paul, Apollonius was summoned to Rome and put in prison, from which he escaped. Many other miracles were attributed to him, including an appearance in his hometown of Tyana after his death.

It was said that the Samaritan Apollonius was not fond of Judea and that he preached mostly to the Gentiles, just as was said of Paul, who according to the biblical tale preached to the Gentiles for 17 years before preaching to the Jews. It should be noted that many of these "Gentiles" were in fact Samaritans, who constituted the other 10 tribes of Israel, by their account.

Furthermore, as noted, a number of the "historical" details in the New Testament were taken from Josephus's histories, including elements of the life of Paul:

> Both Josephus and Paul made a disastrous sea voyage on their way to Rome. Both crews swam to safety after their ship was abandoned to the storm, which drove them into the Adria. Both crews boarded a second ship which took them to Rome, their destination. The purpose of the sea voyage, in both stories, was to deliver the priestly prisoners (Paul in the New Testament and an unnamed priest in Josephus) in bonds, to Rome to be tried before Caesar. In both stories the prisoners have been previously tried in Jerusalem by the procurator Felix.[33]

Like Jesus, Paul is a patchwork of characters, as it has been evinced that he is also a rehash of the Greek hero Orpheus, who, with his companion *Timothy*, travelled around the same area as later reported of Paul, preaching in the name of Dionysus, i.e., "IHS," "IES," "JES," "Iasios," "Iesios," "Jason," "Jesus," or other variant, the Savior of the Samothracian mysteries and pre-Christian Jesus cult. As the author of *The Other Jesus* says:

> There is an uncanny similarity between the legend of Orpheus and the story of Paul that has not escaped notice by researchers and scholars. Paul seems to have deliberately styled himself as a sort of second Orpheus. Many have pointed out parallels between Paul's thinking and Orphic ideas . . . Paul's teachings that each human being contains within them "two natures," sound very Orphic in character. Paul's idea that each human has a depraved, sinful nature within "the flesh" that is constantly at war with each person's higher "godly" nature, associated with their will . . . is essentially identical with the core of pre-Christian Orphic philosophy.
>
> The story of Paul and the story of Orpheus share other biographical details as well. For instance, one of Orpheus' closest associates was his brother named Linus, who seems to have been left in charge after Orpheus was murdered. Similarly, official Catholic doctrine maintains that the second Pope of Rome was someone named Linus, a friend of Paul, who was explicitly installed as Pope by Paul . . . and took over when Paul was murdered by Nero. The story is all the more strange because it is in direct contradiction to the rest of Catholic doctrine claiming that Peter, not Paul, was the first Christian Pope of Rome, and that all subsequent Popes derived their authority as successors of Peter, not Paul. Similarly, one of the most successful members of the lineage of priests founded by Orpheus at Eleusis was a man named Timothy. Timothy left Eleusis and became a missionary, helping to spread these mysteries abroad, and is credited with having left mainland Greece and traveled south to

establish the mysteries of Demeter in Alexandria, Egypt. Likewise, according to the New Testament, one of the most successful proteges of Paul was also a young man named Timothy, who . . . also became a missionary, being credited with such accomplishments as having left mainland Greece and traveled south to establish Christianity on the Greek island of Crete.

That the names of the close associates of Paul seem to be an exact match with great figures associated with the mysteries of Demeter in general and with Orpheus in particular is yet another of those issues that bothers people much less than it should. Another point they have in common is that Orpheus was famous as having been the first to compose and disseminate sacred literature connected with the mysteries. . . .

The similarity of roles that Orpheus and Paul are said to have played in their respective traditions is hard to dismiss. Let us examine the parallels: Orpheus, as a result of the pre-Christian son of God Jesus having "appeared" to him, . . . mounted a highly successful campaign to spread his version of the mysteries of Samothrace to mainland Greece. Paul, we are told, because the Christian son of God Jesus "appeared" to him, mounted a highly successful campaign to spread his version of Christian Jesus worship beyond Palestine and westward into mainland Greece.[34]

The Orphic rites were very similar to the successor Christian rites. One example of an Orphic scripture includes, "All things were made by One godhead in three names, and that this god is all things"[35]; thus Orpheus is a pre-Christian advocate of the Trinity, as well as pantheism. Walker elucidates upon the Orphic mystery cult and its similarity to Christianity, as well as to Buddhism:

> Orphism was a kind of western Buddhism, with escape from the karmic wheel effected by ascetic contemplation, spiritual journeys of the astral-projection type, and elaborate revelations. "Orphism was steeped in sacramentalism, which flooded the later Mysteries and flowed into Christianity. Salvation was by sacrament, by initiatory rites, and by an esoteric doctrine. . . . Orphism was the most potent solvent ever introduced into Greek religious life . . . [T]he Orphics sowed the seeds of distrust toward the national and hereditary principle in religion, and made the salvation of the individual soul of first importance. In this way Orphism had enormous influence upon the subsequent history of religion." . . . Orphism became one of the most serious rivals of Christianity in the first few centuries A.D., until the church devised ways to identify the Orphic savior with Christ. . . . The Orphic Gospel was preached throughout the Mediterranean world for at least twelve centuries. It contributed much to Christian ideology . . . The Orphic revelation was virtually indistinguishable from the Christian one . . . [36]

Thus Orphism was what could be called a "salvation cult," at the head of which was the savior, "IES." Orpheus has also been identified with Krishna[37] and with Horus, or Orus, as "Orpheus" could be translated as "voice of Or," "Or," appropriately, meaning "light" in Hebrew.

Furthermore, it was said of Apollonius that he had been given his master Pythagoras's travel journals, which he followed such that he gained access to the secret brotherhoods in the east. Upon his return, he follows virtually the same route as Orpheus and Paul, including passing through Samothrace several times. It would seem, therefore, that Apollonius was deliberately attempting to reproduce Orpheus's mythical teaching route.

John the Baptist/Baptizer

We have already seen that John the Baptist or Baptizer is a remake of Horus's Baptizer, Anup, both of whom lost their heads, among other similarities. There are varied astrotheological interpretations of John/Anup the Baptist/Baptizer, as is to be expected, since the mythos was ever-changing and evolving. As stated earlier, John the Baptist was the sign of Aquarius, into which the sun moves and is "baptized" after advancing to the "age" of 30°. As Walker relates:

> Medieval monks tried to Christianize the zodiac as they Christianized everything else, by renaming it the *Corona seu Circulus Sanctorum Apostolorum*: the Crown of the Circle of the Holy Apostles. They placed John the Baptist at the position of Aquarius, to finish off the circle.[38]

The Baptist's identity is also revealed by Goodman:

> . . . the greatest denouement awaits the investigator who makes use of the Julian calendar in the Roman Catholic calendar of Saints in connection with the large zodiac. He will find that the death of John the Baptist is fixed on August 29th. On that day, a specially bright star, representing the head of the constellation Aquarius, rises whilst the rest of his body is below the horizon, at exactly the same time as the sun sets in Leo (the kingly sign representing Herod). Thus the latter *beheads* John, because John is associated with Aquarius, and *the horizon cuts off the head of Aquarius!*[39]

In addition, eastern texts depict solar radiation as the "perpetual beheading of the sun."

As to the role of the Baptist in the Egyptian version of the mythos, Massey says:

> Anup was the crier of the way and guide through the wilderness of An, the black land. John's is the voice of one crying in the wilderness . . . John was decapitated by the monster Herod, and Anup is portrayed as headless in the planisphere just over the

Waterman. . . . The headless Anup is a type of demarcation: a sign of the division of the solstice. The river of the division is the Iaru-tana or Jordan. . . This can be seen in the planisphere, with the beheaded Anup as the original John.[40]

Massey further elaborates:

In the Zodiac of Denderah we see the figure of Anup portrayed with his head cut off; and I doubt not that the decapitated Aan or Anup is the prototype of the Gospel John who was above the river of the Waterman, the Greek Eridanus, Egyptian Iarutana, the Hebrew Jordan . . . [41]

The biblical story of John's birth is also an aspect of the mythos: Anna, the mother of John, became supernaturally pregnant in her old age and gave birth at the summer solstice, six months before Mary gave birth to Jesus. As Massey says, "The fact of John and Jesus being born six months apart shows a solar phase of the mythos . . ."[42] Furthermore, the double-headed Roman god Janus's mother was also known as Anna, and John the Baptist and Jesus would thus be the same double-headed god, i.e., "Jan-Essa," also an Indian savior name.

Higgins explains that John "the Forerunner" represents the six-month cycle from the winter solstice to the summer, decoding the mysterious passage at John 3:30:

Jesus came to his exaltation or glory on the 25th of March, the Vernal equinox. At that moment his cousin John was at the Autumnal equinox: as Jesus ascended John descended. John makes the Baptist say, chapter iii, ver. 30, *He must increase, but I must decrease.* . . . How can any one doubt that what was admitted by the fathers was true—that Christians had an *esoteric* and an *exoteric* religion?[43]

In other words, the fathers knew—have continued to know—what it is they truly represent, yet they have conspired to deceive the people.

Hazelrigg elaborates upon the passage, also demonstrating the complexity of the mythos:

The Baptism came at the thirtieth year, or after the Sun's passage through the thirty degrees of Capricorn and coincident with his entry into Aquarius, the Water Bearer, who is John the Baptist. The assertion of John (iii. 30) that "He (the infant Jesus) must increase, but I must decrease," corresponds with the fact that John's nativity was June 24th, when the Sun has reached its highest altitude and it declination begins to decrease; that of Jesus was December 25th, when the Sun accomplishes that first degree of its ascending arc, and is thence led up into the wilderness (winter).[44]

And Higgins relates:

> . . . the Baptist was Elias, that is, in plain Greek, the sun—Ἥλιος
> [Helios]. . . Now John the Baptist or the Prophet, Regenerator by
> means of water, who was also a revived Elias, was the immediate
> forerunner of Jesus—in almost every respect an exact copy of
> Bala-rama, the forerunner of Cristna. And John the Baptist, or
> Saviour of men by means of water, was the Oannes or Avatar of
> Pisces.[45]

The carnalized and Judaized John the Baptist was a
"Nazarene" or Nazarite, which is to say that he was a member of a
"brotherhood of the sun." As Hazelrigg says, "He was a Nazarite;
and it is a curious and striking circumstance that the fountain of
Aenon, where he baptized, was sacred to the sun."[46]

Andrew

Purportedly a fisherman from Bethesda, the apostle Andrew
was said to have been crucified at Patras, Greece, in an apparent
Paschal sacrifice: ". . . the springtime sacrifice of Jesus was
emulated by other heroes, such as Andrew, Philip, or Peter."[47]

"Andrew" was in a reality a local god of Patras, in all
probability ritually sacrificed as a sacred king on a periodic basis.
Concerning Andrew, Walker states:

> From Greek *andros*, "man" or "virility," a title of the solar god of
> Patras, in Achaea, where the apostle Andrew was supposed to
> have been crucified after founding the Byzantine papacy. St.
> Andrew's legend was invented to counter Rome's claim to
> primacy through its own legend of St. Peter. . . . Patras, the site
> of Andrew's alleged martyrdom, was an old shrine of the phallic-
> solar father-god variously called Pater, Petra, or Peter, whose
> name has the same basic meaning as Andrew.[48]

Hazelrigg elaborates on Andrew's astrological nature:

> The Sun as St. Andrew is the genius who presides over the
> autumn quarter that begins with the solar "crossification" into
> Libra; hence Paul's reference to his crucifixion in Romans, vi. 6.
> This is why St. Andrew is ever depicted as an old man holding at
> his back a saltier cross, goeniometer, indicative of this orbital
> angle in the Sun's passage over the equator.[49]

In the Egyptian version of the mythos Andrew is equivalent to
Hapi or Shu, one of the brothers of Horus.

Philip

The apostle Philip was born in Bethesda and was a follower of
John the Baptist, i.e., a Mandaean/Nazarene. He was present at
the feeding of the multitudes; thus, a "common symbol for Philip
is a loaf, reflecting the story of the loaves and fishes."[50] It may be,
therefore, that Philip represents the constellation of Virgo, the

goddess of the grain, although he was associated with Libra, which is also a time of harvest.

Bartholomew

Bartholomew is the "ploughman" in Hebrew. He was supposed to be a native of Galilee, and legend said that he went to India, Armenia, Mesopotamia, Ethiopia and Persia. Like the other disciples, however, Bartholomew is a mythical character, no doubt found in the aforementioned places. As Walker relates:

> Pseudo-saint based on a sacred king's title: Bar-Tholomeus, "son of Ptolemy." He was inserted into the Gospels as an apostle, but hagiographers gave him a different origin. He was called a son of "Prince Ptolemeus," crucified in Armenia, and flayed like the satyr Marsyas. . . An alternative history made Bartholomew a missionary to India, where he overthrew the idols of the oddly non-Indian deities Astarte and Baal-Berith. With many miracles, Bartholomew converted the king of that country to Christianity, but the king's brother was unaccountably permitted to crucify, flay, and behead the saint afterward.[51]

James the Brother

James, "brother of Jesus" and "brother of the Lord," is equivalent in the Egyptian version of the mythos to Amset, brother of Osiris and brother of the Lord.[52] As Massey says:

> James is also identified with the carpenter in the gospels . . . *This is the character of Amset . . . the carpenter.* Amset as devourer of impurity denotes the great purifier, and James has the traditional reputation of having been a great purifier.[53]

James is also the same word as Jacob, the supplanter, the title of Set, as in Am-*set*, the "brother" of Horus.

James the Greater and John the Evangelist, the Sons of Thunder

The brothers James and John are called "Boanerges," the "sons of Thunder," a mythical designation. The lightning and thunderbolts of Lord Zeus were called "Brontes" and "Arges," a role held by the brothers in Luke: "And when his disciples James and John saw this, they said, Lord, wilt thou that we command fire to come down from heaven, and consume them . . ."

As noted, John, the beloved of Christ, also is a rehash of Arjuna, the beloved disciple of Krishna: "In the Tibetan language John is called Argiun. This is Arjoon, (*Ar-John,*) the coadjutor of Cristna."[54] In addition, as Arjuna was the cousin of Krishna, so was John the cousin of Christ.[55]

Mark

Although many people think Mark was one of Jesus's original 12 disciples, he was not, and his main purpose was to serve as Peter's scribe. As one of the four evangelists, Mark represents one of the cardinal points of the zodiac, as is admitted by Irenaeus. The evangelists are depicted in Christian cathedrals as the four creatures of the apocalypse: the man, ox, lion and eagle, which, again, stand for the four cardinal points, or Aquarius, Taurus, Leo and Scorpio. In this cardinal designation Mark represents the summer, or Leo.

Luke

Luke also is not one of "the twelve" but attached himself to Paul. He was a "physician," that is, a *Therapeut*, as were all the "doctors" of the Church. Luke was said to have traveled to Greece, Macedonia, Jerusalem and Rome as a companion of Paul, yet "scholars doubt the strong connection between Luke and Paul." As ben Yehoshua says:

> We must also doubt the story of Luke "the good healer" who was supposed to be a friend of Paul. The original Greek for "Luke" is "Lykos" which was another name for Apollo, the god of healing.

Thus, Luke is yet another tutelary god whose name was used in order to include the people and priesthood of a particular culture in the "universal," i.e., Catholic, church.

Thaddeus/Jude and Simon the Zealot/Canaanite

Thaddeus is also called "Jude son of James" and sometimes Lebbaeus, although these associations are made simply because the gospel lists of the disciples contradict each other. Jude and Simon share a feast day on 10/28. Simon preached in Egypt and was joined by Jude in Persia. Simon was either martyred by being sawed in half or died peacefully at Edessa, a discrepancy that demonstrates his non-historical nature. Christian tradition associates Jude with Aquarius and Simon with Capricorn.

However, the zodiacal designations of the apostles vary from source to source as they are associated with different signs, and Judas the Betrayer, of course, was not included in Christian iconography but was replaced in the story by Matthias and in the zodiac by Jude/Judas Thaddeus, who evidently also at one point symbolized Scorpio. This confusion reveals the state of affairs when the different factions of the unifying brotherhood were being incorporated and doctrine was being violently debated. Of course, exoterically the zodiacal origin of these biblical characters was eventually severed, yet it continued esoterically, variants and all.

Regardless of how they were designated, the apostles and other disciples named herein were not real people. As Wheless says:

> . . . [T]he Holy Twelve had no existence in the flesh, but their "cue" being taken from Old Testament legends, they were mere names—*dramatis personae*—mask of the play—of "tradition," such as Shakespeare and all playwrights and fiction-writers create for the actors of their plays and works of admitted fiction.[56]

Indeed, they were part of the ubiquitous mythos and ritual enacted in many cultures long prior to the Christian era, constituting what later became the gospel story.

1. Walker, *WEMS*, 48.
2. Wells, *DJE*, 122.
3. Eusebius, 77.
4. Massey, *HJMC*, 162.
5. Anderson, 18.
6. Higgins, I, 781-2.
7. "The Other Jesus" website.
8. Walker, *WEMS*, 787. (Emphasis added.)
9. Robertson, 133.
10. Massey, *HJMC*, 144.
11. Walker, *WDSSO*, 397.
12. Higgins, I, 645.
13. Walker, *WEMS*, 79.
14. Walker, *WEMS*, 789.
15. Doane, 399.
16. Blavatsky, *IU*, II, 24fn.
17. Walker, *WEMS*, 483.
18. Walker, *WEMS*, 481.
19. Massey, *Lectures on the Moon*.
20. Massey, *HJMC*, 157-8.
21. Walker, *WEMS*, 467-8.
22. Carpenter, 51.
23. Graham, 318.
24. Walker, *WEMS*, 995.
25. Higgins, I, 663-4.
26. Higgins, I, 596.
27. Higgins, I, 808.
28. HIggins, I, 657-8.
29. Higgins, I, 755.
30. Funk & Wagnall's.
31. Graham, 292.
32. Waite, 105.
33. Holley, 40.
34. home.pacbell.net/gailk/iasius.html
35. Doane, 375.
36. Walker, *WEMS*, 745-8.
37. Higgins, 589.
38. Walker, *WDSSO*, 286.
39. Jackson, 185.
40. Massey, HJMC, 119.
41. Massey, *Lectures on the Moon.*

42. Massey, *HJMC*, 123.
43. Higgins, I, 647.
44. Hazelrigg, 119-20.
45. Higgins, I, 655-6.
46. Higgins, II, 66.
47. Walker, *WDSSO*, 153.
48. Walker, *WEMS*, 32.
49. Hazelrigg, 24-5.
50. Funk & Wagnall's.
51. Walker, *WEMS*, 92.
52. Massey, *HJMC*, viii.
53. Massey, *HJMC*, 147.
54. Higgins, I, 658.
55. Higgins, II, 137.
56. Wheless, 127.

The Gospel Story

In addition to the "lives" of Christ and the twelve, virtually the entire gospel story can be found in older mythologies as part of the ancient mythos revolving around the celestial bodies and movements. Many of these elements have already been discussed, and a thorough exploration would require another volume, but we can examine a number of such aspects of the Christian tale and doctrine in greater detail, beginning with the creation of the universe and the all-important fall that requires the saving grace of Jesus.

Genesis

It has long been known that the story of cosmic origins as found in the Judeo-Christian bible is a lift from more ancient versions, especially those of Egypt and Babylon. The tale can also be found in China, Japan, India, Scandinavia, and the British and Irish isles, to name a few. Obviously, then, no one culture has a lock on "God" or creation—a fact that cannot be emphasized enough. Nor has the biblical story ever been adequate to explain truly the origins of the cosmos; in fact, it is merely a mythologized, simplified explanation filtered through and for finite minds. Of the biblical Genesis, Walker says, "However absurd, these myths still maintain a hold on vast numbers of people deliberately kept in ignorance by an obsolete fundamentalism. Even educated adults sometimes insist that an omniscient god created the world for a purpose of his own."[1]

Adam, Eve and the Garden of Eden

Like other major biblical characters and tales, the fable of Adam, Eve and the Garden of Eden is based on much older versions found in numerous cultures around the globe. The Hindu version of the first couple was of Adima and Heva, hundreds if not thousands of years before the Hebraic version, as has been firmly pointed out by Hindus to Christian missionaries for centuries. Jackson relates that these myths "seemed to have originated in Africa, but they were told all over the world in ancient times. . ." Obviously, then, we will not find any historical Adam and Eve in Mesopotamia.

In the Sumerian and Babylonian versions of the Garden of Eden myth, from which the Hebrew one is also derived, the original couple were created equal in stature by the great Goddess. When the fervent patriarchy took over the story, it changed it to make women not only inferior but also guilty of the downfall of all mankind. Of this demotion, Stone says:

Woman, as sagacious advisor or wise counselor, human interpreter of the divine will of the Goddess, was no longer to be respected, but to be hated, feared or at best doubted or ignored. . . . Women were to be regarded as mindless, carnal creatures, both attitudes justified and "proved" by the Paradise myth. . . . Statements carefully designed to suppress the earlier social structure continually presented the myth of Adam and Eve as divine proof that man must hold the ultimate authority.[2]

Far from being literal, the Garden of Eden/Paradise story takes place in the heavens. According to Hazelrigg, the word "Paradise" means "among the stars," and he points out that the tale as taken literally by the "devoted biblicist" is a demeaning portrayal of "God," as it declares that "God" is vengeful towards his own flawed progeny, "the gullible pair whom He had created 'in His image' seemingly for the sole purpose that He might send a serpent of iniquity to tempt the weakness and depravity so inadvertently implanted in their godly-begotten natures. A monstrous doctrine, indeed, that can picture a God so sinister in purpose as to betray the innocence of His own offspring!"[3]

Yet, common sense has failed to prevail, as numerous theories have sprung up as to the "true" location of the Garden of Eden.

Walker further states:

Seventeen hundred years ago, Origen wrote of the Garden of Eden myth: "No one would be so foolish as to take this allegory as a description of actual fact." But Origen was excommunicated, and countless millions have been precisely that foolish.[4]

Adam

Adam is not a historical character, as the word "Adam" simply means "man" and is not a person's name. Adam is Atum or Amen in Egypt, the archetypal man and son of Ptah the Father.[5] In the Chaldean scriptures, from which the Israelite writings were in large part plagiarized, he is called "Adami," and in the Babylonian he is "Adamu." As in the Hebrew version, the Sumero-Babylonian Adamu was prevented by the gods from eating the fruit of immortality, so that he would not "be as a god." Adam is also "adamah," which means "bloody clay," referring to menstrual blood.[6] Walker explains that "the biblical story of God's creation of Adam out of clay was plagiarized from ancient texts with the patriarchs' usual sex-change of the deity," who was the Sumero-Babylonian "Potter" goddess Aruru.[7]

Eve

Eve is also not a literal figure who either caused the downfall of mankind or gave birth to it. Rather, Eve is the archetypal female and goddess found around the globe:

The biblical title of Eve, "Mother of All Living," was a translation of Kali Ma's title *Jaganmata*. She was also known in India as Jiva or Ieva, the Creatress of all manifested forms.[8]

As stated, earlier mythologies placed the created woman on the same par with the man, rather than as a mere "rib." In some of these ancient tales, Eve was superior to Adam and even to God, as his "stern mother."[9] According to one myth, before God made Eve he created Lilith as Adam's equal, but she proved to be too troublesome for the patriarchy, as she did not want to submit to Adam's sexual advances and demanded her own house. The liberated Lilith thus had to be killed off by both God and biblical scribes. One may suspect there was more to the story, as Walker explains: "Hebraic tradition said Adam was married to Lilith because he grew tired of coupling with beasts, a common custom of Middle-Eastern herdsmen, though the Old Testament declared it a sin."[10]

Eve is one with Isis-Meri and, therefore, the Virgin Mary and the constellation of Virgo, as well as the moon.[11] In the original astrotheological tale, as Virgo rises she is followed or "bitten on the heel by Serpens, who, with Scorpio, rises immediately behind her."[12] This astronomical observation is behind the passage at Revelation 12:14: "But the woman was given the two wings of the great eagle that she might fly from the serpent into the wilderness . . ." As noted, Scorpio is not only represented by the scorpion but by the eagle as well.

The Serpent

The serpent symbol is found around the world and represents divine wisdom, as is confirmed by Jesus, when he is made to say, "Be ye wise as serpents." The serpent was the "phallic consort" of the Goddess, and serpents were found under her temples, apparently used to induce prophetic and hallucinatory trances by their venom. The Egyptian queen Cleopatra may have died during such a ritual with an asp, if this is not an apocryphal story. These female priestesses were called "pythonesses" and, as receivers of prophecy and divine revelation, were reviled by Ezekiel for gaining knowledge "out of their own heads," as if their manner of revelation were different from his own.

The serpent's shedding of the skin and constant renewal made it a symbol of eternity and immortality, and thus of divinity and many gods. In fact, the title of "serpent" formerly conveyed sacerdotal duties, as opposed to being an aspersion. As Pike relates:

> In the Mysteries of the bull-horned Bacchus, the officers held serpents in their hands, raised them above their heads, and cried aloud "Eva!" the generic oriental name of the serpent, and

the particular name of the constellation in which the Persians place Eve and the serpent.[13]

This description reveals the origins of the New Testament exhortation to "take up serpents," and those who participate in such rituals are continuing an ancient tradition that dates back at least 4,000 years.

Although the serpent is portrayed as evil in the Judeo-Christian ideology, it was not always considered so by the Hebrews. As Walker relates:

> Early Hebrews adopted the serpent-god all their contemporaries revered, and the Jewish priestly clan of Levites were "sons of the Great Serpent," i.e., of Leviathan, "the wriggly one."[14]

The Hebrew veneration for the serpent-god is clear from Numbers 21:9: "Moses made a serpent of brass, and put it upon a pole, and it came to pass that if a serpent had bitten any man, when he beheld the serpent of brass he lived." Of this interesting fetish, which is also the caduceus of Aesclepius, the Greek god of healing, Stone says, "And in Jerusalem itself was the serpent of bronze, said to date back to the time of Moses and treasured as a sacred idol in the temple there until about 700 BC."[15]

As noted, Moses's serpent cult fell out of favor during the reign of Hezekiah, king of Judah, who "removed the high places, and broke the pillars, and cut down the Asherah. And he broke in pieces the bronze serpent that Moses had made, for until those days the people of Israel had burned incense to it; it was called Nehushtan." (2 Kings 18:4) Moreover, Walker relates:

> The biblical Nehushtan was a deliberate masculinization of a similar oracular she-serpent, Nehushtah, Goddess of Kadesh (meaning "Holy"), a shrine like that of the Pythonesses. Israelites apparently violated the sanctuary and raped its priestesses, but "Moses and Yahweh had to placate the angry serpent goddess of Kadesh, now deposed, by erecting her brazen image . . . . Mythologically, the serpent is always a female divinity."[16]

In addition, in the Bible the serpent, vilified "in the beginning," then venerated, then vilified again, is once more venerated as it is later associated with Christ, as a "type of" him: "And as Moses lifted up the serpent in the wilderness, even so must the Son of Man be lifted up." (Jn. 3:15) Indeed, the serpent was considered the savior of mankind for its role in bringing wisdom.

The serpent is, naturally, a celestial symbol, representing both the constellation of Serpens and the entire heavens, with the sun as one eye and the moon as another. The serpent was the "Prince of Darkness," the ruler of the night sky, and its vilification is also a rejection of the stellar cult in favor of the solar.

The Original Fall/Sin

The "original fall" or "sin" has been interpreted by literalists as meaning both the transgression of Adam and Eve in disobeying God and getting kicked out of Eden, and the manner in which humans procreate, i.e., sex. It has been admitted by Christians that without the concept of the original fall/sin of man and his expulsion from the Garden of Eden, there would be no need for a savior or for the Christian religion. For example, "reformed" ex-Father Peter Martyr said:

> Were this Article [of faith] be taken away, there would be no original sin; the promise of Christ would become void, and all the vital force of our religion would be destroyed.[17]

This fervent belief is why Christian proponents are so vehemently opposed to the theory of evolution, as it demonstrates the lack of an original fall or sin that requires a savior. Regarding the theory of evolution and its effect on Christianity, Walker relates:

> The American Episcopal Church said: "If this hypothesis be true, then is the Bible an unbearable fiction. . . then have Christians for nearly two thousands years been duped by a monstrous lie."[18]

Indeed, Jackson expresses his disgust at ". . . that damnable doctrine of original sin, which slanders nature and insults all mankind . . ."[19] And Higgins remarked, in the early 1800's:

> Perhaps we do not find in history any doctrine which has been more pernicious than that of Original Sin. It is now demoralizing Britain. It caused all the human sacrifices in ancient times, and actually converted the Jews into a nation of Cannibals, as Lord Kingsborough . . . has proved that they were.[20]

Like so many aspect of Christianity, the notion of original sin was unoriginal: "The *Indians* are not strangers to the doctrine of *original sin*. It is their invariable belief that *man is a fallen being*, admitted by them from time immemorial."[21]

Rather than representing the sinful nature of man, however, the "fall" never happened, as Gerald Massey affirms:

> The fall is absolutely non-historical, and the first bit of standing-ground for an actual Christ the Redeemer is missing in the very beginning, consequently anyone who set up, or was set up for, an historical Savior, from a non-historical fall, could only be an historical impostor.[22]

The Garden of Eden tale is not literal but allegorical, occurring in the heavens, as the Fall actually takes place when the sun passes through the autumnal equinox, in the sign of the Virgin (Eve). As the sun crosses into Libra, "he" descends or *falls* into "the winter quarter or 'fall' of the year—a title most consistent with the phenomenon itself," as Hazelrigg says. Hazelrigg further outlines the "deep astrology" of the celestial Garden of Eden drama:

> The serpent of iniquity, who plays the part of the Tempter, must therefore be viewed in an astronomical rather than an ethical or moral character, which, for purposes of allegory, has not been made an enviable one. He is the villain of the drama, and rather an elongated one at that, for, as found described on the planisphere "his tail drew after him a third part of the stars of heaven" (Rev. xii, 4), or from Cancer to Libra, which are four constellations, a third of the twelve. Going before, he leads the woman towards the setting point in the west, therefore his office is to "seduce" (Latin *seducere*, to lead on or go before), while the enamored Adam follows in true conjugal spirit towards the horizon, driven forth by the Power that causes the revolution of the heavens which carries them out of the Garden. At the moment of expulsion, or as the figures of Adam (Bootes) and Eve [Virgo] are sinking from sight below the western line, the constellation Perseus appears in the east, grim in armor and helmet, a being of vengeance holding aloft a flaming sword.[23]

Regarding the Garden of Eden tale, Graham spells it out:

> The world was not created by this God in six days or a million. There was no Garden of Eden or talking snake. There was no first man, Adam, or woman, Eve. They did not commit a moral sin and so we are not under condemnation for it. They did not fall from grace and so there is no need for redemption.[24]

Thus, Christianity's foundation is false, mythical and unoriginal, as is the gospel story itself.

The Virgin Mother of the Divine Redeemer

As demonstrated, the virgin mother and her divine child constitute a motif ubiquitous in the ancient world, long before the Christian era. In the solar myth, the "sun of God" was considered to be born of the new, or virgin, moon. The Virgin birth aspect also comes from the observation that during certain ages the constellation of Virgo rose with the sun:

> At the moment of the Winter Solstice, the Virgin rose heliacally (*with* the Sun), having the Sun (Horus) in her bosom. . . . Virgo was Isis; and her representation, carrying a child (Horus) in her arms, exhibited in her temple, was accompanied by this inscription: "I AM ALL THAT IS, THAT WAS, AND THAT SHALL BE; and the fruit which I brought forth is the Sun."[25]

Bethlehem

As was admitted by the early Christian doctor Jerome, the "little town of Bethlehem" was a sacred grove devoted to the

Syrian solar-fertility-savior god Adonis (Tammuz), who was born hundreds of years before the Christian era in the same cave later held to be that of the birthplace of Jesus. Like Jesus, Adonis was born on December 25th[26] of the Virgin Myrrha, who was:

> . . . a temple-woman or hierodule, identified with Mary by early Christians, who called Jesus's mother Myrrh of the Sea. . . . Syrian Adonis died at Easter time. . . Adonis died and rose again in periodic cycles, like all gods of vegetation and fertility. He was also identified with the sun that died and rose again in heaven.[27]

As noted, Adonis/Tammuz was a favorite Semitic and Hebrew god, and each year during his passion in Jerusalem, women "wailed for the dead savior Tammuz in the temple of Jerusalem, where Ishtar was worshipped as Mari, Queen of Heaven (Ezekiel 8:14)."[28] At this time, Adonis/Tammuz wore a "crown of thorns" made of myrrh. Walker relates of Tammuz:

> The *Christos* or sacred king annually sacrificed in the temple at Jerusalem . . . the Romans called Tammuz the chief god of the Jews. . . . A month of the Jewish calendar is still named after Tammuz . . . Tammuz was imported from Babylon by the Jews, but he was even older than Babylon. He began as the Sumerian savior-god Dumuzi, or Damu, "only-begotten Son," or "Son of the Blood." He fertilized the earth with his blood at the time of his death, and was called Healer, Savior, Heavenly Shepherd. He tended the flocks of stars, which were considered souls of the dead in heaven. Each year on the Day of Atonement he was sacrificed in the form of a lamb . . . Though Tammuz occupied the central position in the sacred drama at Jerusalem, the New Testament transformed him into a mere apostle of the new dying god, under the Greek form of his name, Thomas.[29]

As a fertility god, Adonis/Tammuz was representative of "the spirit of the corn," and "Bethlehem" means, the "House of Bread," "House of Corn," or "house of bread-corn, grain or wheat."[30] This motif is passed down in the Christian myth when Jesus, like his predecessor Horus, says, "I am the bread of life" (Jn. 6:48). Like so many other places in Israel, Bethlehem was first situated in the mythos and then given location on Earth.

Nazareth

The town of Nazareth did not appear on Earth until after the gospel tale was known. As Holley says, "There is no such place as Nazareth in the Old Testament or in Josephus' works, or on early maps of the Holy Land. The name was apparently a later Christian invention." In fact, the town now designated as Nazareth is near Mt. Carmel, indicating it was the Carmelites who created it.

Jesus, therefore, was not from Nazareth, which did not exist at the time of his purported advent. The real purpose for putting him there was to make of him a Nazarene or Nazarite, as he was the same as the most famous Nazarite, Samson, a solar myth. The title comes from the Egyptian word "natzr," which refers to "the plant, the shoot, the natzr. . . . the true vine," and Nazarite is an epithet for the sun, which gives life to the grape vine.[31] Nazarite is also translated as "prince," as in "prince of peace." The Nazarites/Nazarenes were the ascetics who were not to shave their heads or beards unless for ritualistic purpose, because their hair was a symbol of holiness and strength, representing in fact the sun's "hair" or rays, which is why the solar hero becomes weak when the woman cuts his hair. When the hair was long, the Nazarite would have nothing to do with the grape, vine or wine, but when the Nazarite was shorn in a ritual, he would then drink wine. This story reflects the time of the year when the grapes ripen and wine is made, as the sun's rays weaken.

Thus, we see that Nazareth is not the birthplace of Jesus but represents yet another aspect of the mythos. As Massey states, "The *actual* birthplace of the carnalized Christ was NEITHER BETHLEHEM NOR NAZARETH, BUT ROME!"[32]

The Manger and Cave, Birthplace of Many Gods

In Christian tradition, Jesus was said to be born variously in a manger, stable and/or cave, like many other preceding gods. As stated, the divine babe Adonis/Tammuz was born in the very cave in Bethlehem now considered the birthplace of Jesus, long before the Christian era. Regarding the Adonis cave, Christian apologist Weigall admits:

> The propriety of this appropriation was increased by the fact that the worship of a god in a cave was a commonplace in paganism: Apollo, Cybele, Demeter, Herakles, Hermes, Mithra and Poseidon were all adored in caves; Hermes, the Greek logos being born of Maia in a cave, and Mithra being rock-born.[33]

Like Jesus, the Greek god Hermes was also wrapped in swaddling clothing and placed in a manger, as was Dionysus.[34]

The cave/manger motif is part of the mythos, representing both the winter and the setting of the sun, when it appears to go underground or into the underworld, which is the womb of both the heavens and earth. Walker says, "The cave was universally identified with the womb of Mother Earth, the logical place for symbolic birth and regeneration."

The confusing stories regarding the solar babe being born in a cave, manger *and/or* stable reflect the changing of the heavens, specifically the precession of the equinoxes. As Massey states:

Thus the cave and the stable are two types of the birthplace at the solstice. . . . No Messiah, however, whether called Mithras, Horus or Christ could have been born in the stable of Augias or the cave of *Abba Udda* on the 25th of December after the date of 255 B.C., because the solstice had passed out of that sign into the asterim of the Archer.[35]

Herod and the Slaughter of the Innocents

The "slaughter of the infants" is yet another part of the standard mythos, an element of the typical sacred-king tradition found in many mythologies, whereby the reigning monarch tries to prevent from being fulfilled a prophecy that a new king will be born who will overthrow him. As Walker says, "Innocents were slaughtered in the myths of Sargon, Nimrod, Moses, Jason, Krishna and Mordred as well as in that of Jesus."[36] They are also slain in the stories of Oedipus, Perseus, Romulus and Remus, and Zeus. Doane states:

The flight of the virgin-mother with her babe . . . is simply the same old story, over and over again. Some one has predicted that a child born at a certain time shall be great, he is therefore a "dangerous child," and the reigning monarch, or some other interested party, attempts to have the child destroyed, but he invariably escapes and grows to manhood, and generally accomplishes the purpose for which he was intended. This almost universal mythos was added to the fictitious history of Jesus by its fictitious authors, who have made him escape in his infancy from the reigning tyrant with the usual good fortune.[37]

The Three Wise Men and the Star in the East

A favorite of children everywhere, the story of the three wise men or magi and the star in the east attending the birth of Jesus is also found in other mythologies. To reiterate, the three wise men or kings are the three stars in Orion's belt "whose rising announced the coming of Sothis, the Star of Horus/Osiris: that is, Sirius, the brightest star in the sky, whose coming heralded the annual flood of the Nile."[38] In addition, it would be very appropriate for the three kings worshipping the babe to be considered magi, since magi were sun-worshippers. Furthermore, the gifts of the wise men to the Divine Child are also a standard part of the mythos. As Higgins remarks, "It is a striking circumstance that the gifts brought by the Magi, gold, frankincense and myrrh, were what were always offered by the Arabian Magi to the sun."[39]

As concerns the famous star, Walker says, "Ancient Hebrews called the same star Ephraim, or the Star of Jacob. In Syrian,

Arabian and Persian astrology it was Messaeil—the Messiah."[40] Massey elaborates:

> . . . the Star in the East will afford undeniable data for showing the mythical and celestial origin of the gospel history. When the divine child is born, the wise men or magi declare that they have seen his star in the east. . . . The three kings or three solar representatives are as ancient as the male triad that was first typified when the three regions were established as heaven, earth, and nether-world, from which the triad bring their gifts. . . When the birthplace was in the sign of the Bull [@6,500-4,400 BP], the Star in the East that arose to announce the birth of the babe was Orion, which is therefore called the star of Horus. *That was once the star of the three kings;* for the *"three kings"* is still a name of three stars in Orion's belt . . .

The star in the east has also been associated with the planet Venus, which at times has served as the "morning star," heralding the arrival of the "sun of God," who is also the "morning star." Again, this appearance was not a historical occurrence but a recurring observation that preceded the Christian era for millennia. Furthermore, as Higgins says, "Every Amid or *Desire of all nations* had a star to announce his birth."[41] In this regard, the births of Abraham and Moses, among so many others, were also attended by stars.[42] As Doane says, "The fact that the writer of this story speaks not of *a star* but of *his star*, shows that it was the popular belief of the people among whom he lived, that each and every person was born under a star, and that this one which had been seen was *his star*."[43]

Jesus at age 12 and 30

As noted, like Jesus, Horus has no history between the ages of 12 and 30, "and the mythos alone will account for the chasm which is wide and deep enough to engulf a supposed history of 18 years."[44]

Jesus/Horus in the Temple in fact represents the sun of God at midday, 12 noon, its highest point, thus being the "Temple of the Most High." The story of Jesus being baptized and beginning his ministry at age 30 is a rehash of the identical tale of Horus, representing the sun moving into a new constellation at 30°. Jesus is alternatively depicted as beginning his ministry at 28 years, which represents the 28-day cycle of the moon, or the month, as reckoned by the Egyptians.

The Dove at the River Jordan

As depicted (only) in the Gospel of John, when Jesus is baptized at Jordan a dove appears to announce that he is the Son of God. This story is a repeat of the baptism of Horus in the River

Eridanus, or the Nile, and the dove represents the goddess Hathor, who brings Horus forth as an adult in a ceremony symbolizing rebirth. Higgins says:

> When Jesus was baptized by that very mysterious character [Joannes] in the Jordanus, the holy Spirit descended on to him in the form of a dove, and a fire was lighted in the river. Now I cannot help suspecting that a mystic union was meant to be represented here between the two principles—in fact the reunion of the sects of the Linga and the Ioni or Dove—which we yet find in Jesus and his mother in the Romish religion.[45]

The Forty Days and Temptation in the Wilderness

Many savior gods, including Buddha, Horus, Manu, Quetzalcoatl and Zoroaster, were tempted in the wilderness as a standard part of the mythos. As demonstrated, the Jesus-Satan story is a rehash of the tale about the Egyptian "twins" Horus-Set, and this temptation myth represents the struggle between light and dark, day and night, and winter and summer. Churchward explains these elements of the mythos:

> The Gospel story of the Devil taking Jesus up into an exceeding high mountain from which all the kingdoms of the world and the glory of them could be seen, and of the contention on the summit is originally a legend of the Astronomical Cult, which has been converted into history in the Gospels. In the Ritual . . . the struggle is described as taking place upon the mount, i.e. "the mountain in the midst of the Earth, or the mountain of Amenta which reaches up to the sky," and which in the Solar Cult stood at the point of the equinox, where the conflict was continued and the twins were reconciled year after year. The equinox was figured at the summit of the mount on the ecliptic and the scene of strife was finally configurated as a fixture in the constellation of the Gemini, the sign of the twin-brothers, who for ever fought and wrestled "up and down the garden," first one, then the other, being uppermost during the two halves of the year, or of night and day. . . . This contention in the wilderness was one of the great battles of Set and Horus. . . . Forty days was the length of time in Egypt that was reckoned for the grain in the earth before it sprouted visibly from the ground. It was a time of scarcity and fasting in Egypt, the season of Lent . . . The fasting of Jesus in the desert represents the absence of food that is caused by Set in the wilderness during the forty days' burial for the corn, and Satan asking Jesus to turn the stones into bread is a play on the symbol of Set, which in one representation was rendered as "a stone." The contest of the personal Christ with a personal Satan in the New Testament is no more historical fact than the contest between the seed of the woman and the serpent of evil in the Old. Both are mythical and both are Egyptian Mysteries.[46]

This battle between Set and Horus was also re-enacted upon the earth, as the stellar, lunar and solar cult priests and their followers have fought among themselves for millennia.

This particular part of the mythos was rejected by early Christian fathers as being "fabulous," but, like many other elements of the solar myth, it was later added in order to make the godman more competitive, "to show that Christ Jesus was proof against all temptations, that *he* too, as well as *Buddha* and others, could resist the powers of the prince of evil."[47]

The Wedding Feast at Cana/Turning Water into Wine

In the gospels, Jesus is claimed to have changed water into wine during the wedding at Cana as proof of his divinity. Once again, this tale is found in other mythologies and is part of the solar mythos. Long before the Christian era, Dionysus/Bacchus was said to turn water into wine, as related by A.J. Mattill:

> This story is really the Christian counterpart to the pagan legends of Dionysus, the Greek god of wine, who at his annual festival in his temple of Elis filled three empty kettles with wine— no water needed! And on the fifth of January wine instead of water gushed from his temple at Andros. If we believe Jesus' miracle, why should we not believe Dionysus's?[48]

As Walker says:

> The story of his miracle at Cana was directly modeled on a Dionysian rite of sacred marriage celebrated at Sidon; even the Gospels' wording was copied from the festival of the older god.[49]

In pre-Christian times, priests would turn water into wine to fool the gullible masses into believing they had miraculous powers. At Corinth, where "Paul" purportedly taught, there existed a water-to-wine device into which water was poured and then diverted by priests, who, hiding inside the covered parts of the sluice, would pour wine out the other end. Another such device was used at Alexandria.

As we have seen, the sun was considered to change water into wine when, following the rains, the grapes would ripen on the vine and ferment in the heat after picked.

Mary Magdalene

In the New Testament, the "whore" Mary Magdalene has a pivotal role, as despite her alleged unworthiness Magdalene holds the honor of anointing the new king, Jesus, with oil, an act that makes him the Christ and makes her a priestess. It is also Mary Magdalene, and not his male apostles, to whom Jesus first appears after the miracle of his resurrection. In the early Gnostic-Christian gospels Mary Magdalene is the most beloved disciple of

Jesus. Some traditions asserted that Jesus and Mary were lovers who created a bloodline, to which a number of groups have laid claim. Nevertheless, like Jesus and the twelve, Magdalene is not a historical character but an element of the typical solar myth/ sacred king drama: the sacred harlot. As such, she was highly revered, which explains why she is given top honors in the gospel story. As Walker states:

> Thus it seems Mary the Whore was only another form of Mary the Virgin, otherwise the Triple Goddess Mari-Anna-Ishtar, the Great Whore of Babylon who was worshipped along with her savior-son in the Jerusalem temple. The *Gospel of Mary* said all three Marys of the canonical books were one and the same. . . . The seven "devils" exorcised from Mary Magdalene seem to have been the seven Maskim, or Anunnaki, Sumero-Akkadian spirits of the seven nether spheres, born of the Goddess Mari. . . . The Gospels say no men attended Jesus's tomb, but only Mary Magdalene and her women. Only women announced Jesus's resurrection. This was because men were barred from the central mysteries of the Goddess. Priestesses announced the successful conclusion of the rites, and the Savior's resurrection. The Bible says the male apostles knew nothing of Jesus's resurrection, and had to take the women's word for it (Luke 24:10-11). The apostles were ignorant of the sacred tradition and didn't even realize a resurrection was expected: "They knew not the scripture, that he must rise again from the dead." (John 20:9).[50]

Walker also relates:

> Mary alone was the first to observe and report the alleged miracle. In just such a manner, pagan priestesses had been announcing the resurrection of savior gods like Orpheus, Dionysus, Attis, and Osiris every year for centuries. . . . Mary Magdalene was described as a harlot; but in those times, harlots and priestesses were often one and the same. A sacred harlot in the Gilgamesh epic was connected with a victim-hero in a similar way: "The harlot who anointed you with fragrant ointment laments for you now." . . . Under Christianity, priests soon took over all the rituals that had been conducted by women, declaring that women had no right to lead any religious ceremony whatever.[51]

Of course, this exclusion and degradation of women is in direct defiance of Jesus's rebuke of Judas, in which he is made to say that the woman who anointed him would be remembered in all the nations. And she should be remembered for good reason, for "the Christian derivate of Mari-Ishtar, is Mary Magdalene, the sacred harlot who said harlots are 'compassionate of all the race of mankind.'"[52]

The legends surrounding Mary Magdalene have led to claims of descent from her womb: For example, she and Jesus were lovers who sired a "royal family" in Europe, per the "Priory of Sion mystery." Walker says of the various Marian legends:

> Much Christian myth-making went into the later history of Mary Magdalene. She was said to have lived for a while with the virgin Mary at Ephesus. This story probably was invented to account for the name Maria associated with the Ephesian Goddess. Afterward, Mary Magdalene went to Marseilles, another town named after the ancient sea-mother Mari. Her cult centered there. Bones were found at Vézelay and declared to be hers. Her dwelling was a cave formerly sacred to the pagans, at St. Baume (Holy Tree).[53]

The Five Loaves, Two Fishes and 12 Baskets

In gospel tale, Jesus feeds the 5,000 with five loaves and two fishes. The two fishes are in reality the zodical sign of Pisces. The five loaves have been said to represent the five smaller planets. These, of course, would be the same five loaves requested of the priests by David at 1 Samuel 21:3. Later in the gospel myth, the number of the loaves is seven, representing the seven "planets" used to name the days of the week. "Jesus," the sun, "breaks up" the multiplied loaves into the 12 "baskets" or constellations, symbolizing the creation of the countless stars and the placement of them in the heavens.

Furthermore, as the sun was considered the "fisher," so was the Greek version of the Great Mother, Demeter, called "Mistress of Earth and Sea, multiplier of loaves and fishes."[54] Indeed, the loaves and fishes are pre-Christian communion foods eaten at sacred feasts, often following the resurrection of their god, as an initiation into an ancient mystical rite.

The Devils and the Swine

The story of Jesus exorcising devils out of the demoniac is also Egyptian in origin. As Massey states:

> The devils entreat Jesus not to bid them depart into the abyss, but as a herd of swine were feeding on the mountain they ask permission to enter into these. *"And he gave them leave."* Then the devils came out of the man and entered the swine, which ran down into the lake—exactly as it is in the Egyptian scenes of the judgment, where condemned souls are ordered back into the abyss, and they make the return passage down to the lake of primordial matter by taking the shape of the swine.[55]

Bringing Sword instead of Peace, Prince of Peace

The statement that Jesus, the "Prince of Peace," comes with a sword (Mt. 10:34) has always been a point of contradiction that has disturbed ethicists for centuries. Indeed, the sword bit has led to an atrocious amount of human suffering, as wild-eyed Christian fanatics descended upon the world, slaughtering millions under the banner of the "Prince of Peace."

This contradiction also can only be explained within the mythos. When the sun is being swallowed by the darkness, he must fight with the sword until he arrives the next day to bring peace.

The Transfiguration on the Mount

In the gospel story, Jesus is "transfigured" on a mountain in front of his disciples, Peter, James and John. The transfiguration is also a part of the mythos, as several other savior-gods were likewise transfigured on mountaintops. Massey explains the mythical meaning of the transfiguration:

> The scene on the Mount of Transfiguration is obviously derived from the ascent of Osiris into the mount of the moon. The sixth day was celebrated as that of the change and transformation of the solar god into the lunar orb, when he re-entered on that day as the regenerator of its light. With this we may compare the statement made by Matthew, that "after six days Jesus" went "up into a high mountain apart; and he was transfigured," "and his face did shine as the sun, and his garments became white as the light."[56]

The Ass

The riding of the ass into "Jerusalem," "City of Peace," or the "Holy City," occurs in Egyptian mythology, at least two thousand years prior to the Christian era. The ass is the totem animal of Set, who rides it into the city in triumph. Massey reiterates the astrological meaning of this episode:

> Neither god nor man can actually ride on the ass and her foal at the same time. Such a proceeding must be figurative; one that could not be humanly fulfilled in fact. We have seen how it was fulfilled in the mythos and rendered in the planisphere. The ass and its colt are described in the Book of Genesis as belonging to the Shiloh [king] who binds them to the vine . . . The vine to which the ass and foal were tethered is portrayed in the decans of Virgo, the ass and colt being stationed in those of Leo; the two asses in the sign of Cancer.[57]

Set, Horus's "twin," is sometimes represented as an ass-headed god, crucified and wounded in the side. Walker elaborates on the twin-god myth:

> Thus, Set and Horus were remnants of a primitive sacred-king cult, which the Jews adopted. The story of the rival gods appeared in the Bible as Seth's supplanting of the sacrificed shepherd Abel, evidently the same "Good Shepherd" as Osiris-

Horus (Genesis 4:25). Their rivalry was resolved in Egypt by having the pharaoh unite both gods in himself. . . . Similarly, the Jewish God uniting both Father and Son was sometimes an ass-headed man crucified on a tree. This was one of the earliest representations of the Messiah's crucifixion. Some said Christ was the same as the Jewish ass-god Iao, identified with Set.[58]

And Massey further elucidates:

In the pictures of the underworld, the ass-headed god is portrayed as bearer of the sun. . . In the Greek shape of the mythos, Hephaistos ascends to the heavens, or to heaven, at the instigation of Dionysus, and is depicted as returning thither riding on an ass. . . . The wine-god intoxicated him and led him heavenwards; in which condition we have the Hebrew Shiloh, who was to come binding his ass to the vine, with his eyes red with wine; his garments being drenched in the blood of the grape, and he as obviously drunk as Hephaistos. . . . [59]

As noted, Sut/Set was also the biblical Seth, son of Adam, or Atum, the primordial being. Like the Egyptian Set, the biblical Seth is the "enemy of the Egyptian gods." He is also the progenitor of the Hebrew people. In fact, Massey relates that the Jews were "Suttites" or Sethians "from the very beginning, and Sut was worshipped by the Christians in Rome."[60] Set was thus revered in ancient Palestine, which is in fact named after him, "Pales" being his Roman name. Regarding this ass-headed twin, Doresse explains:

It is upon certain monuments of Egypt that we find the most ancient proofs of the attribution of a donkey's head to a god, who was to become progressively identified with the god of the Jews. This originated from the Asiatic god Sutekh, whom the Egyptians assimilated to one of their own greatest gods: Seth, the adversary of Osiris. They represent Seth also, after the period of the Persian invasions, with a human body and an ass's head. Afterwards, this god Seth was definitely regarded by the Egyptians . . . as the father of the legendary heroes Hierosolymus and Judaeus—that is, as the ancestor of the Jews![61]

The Jews as Vipers and Spawn of the Devil

The designation by Jesus of Jews as vipers and the spawn of the devil is one of the sticking points of the gospel fable that have caused a great deal of trouble on this planet. If taken as a true story, this name-calling is ugly, and not a few "good Christians" have used these aspersions to justify their hatred and violence towards Jews, all the while worshipping some of them. But this tale has never been historical, and "the Jews" have been made to represent "the devils, vipers, and other Typhonian types" of the extant mythos. In the Egyptian story, Set, the enemy of Horus, commands the Apophis or deadly viper, as well as "the strangling snakes" and various demons and devils. The story is also reflective of the fact that the Jews were followers of Set, the serpent of the night sky.

The Last Supper/Eucharist

The Eucharist, or the sharing of the god's blood and body, has been a sacred ritual within many ancient mystery religions, and the line ascribed to Jesus, "This is my blood you drink, this is my body you eat," is a standard part of the theophagic (god-eating) ritual. While this cannibalistic rite is now allegorical, in the past participants actually ate and drank the "god's" body and blood, which was in reality that of a sacrificed human or animal, as the consuming of the flesh has been thought since time immemorial to bestow the magical capacities of the victim upon the eater.

The Christian form of the Eucharist is highly similar to the ritual practiced as part of the Eleusinian Mysteries, in detail, as was unhappily admitted by Christians from the beginning. The Eleusinian Eucharist honored both Ceres, goddess of wheat, and Bacchus/Dionysus, god of the vine.

In Tibet, the Dalai Lama was also known to celebrate a eucharist with bread and wine.[62] The Tibetan religious hierarchy is very similar to that of the Catholics, a fact that has disturbed Catholic proponents, as has the fact that the Eucharist was also found among the Mexican natives, long before the Christians arrived in the Americas. As Higgins relates:

> Father Grebillion observes also with astonishment that the Lamas have the use of holy water, singing in the church service, prayers for the dead, mitres worn by the bishops; and that the Dalai Lama holds the same rank among his Lamas that the Pope does in the Church of Rome: and Father Grueger goes farther; he says, that their religion agrees, in every essential point, with the Roman religion, without ever having had any connection with Europeans: for, says he, they celebrate a sacrifice with bread and wine; they give extreme unction; they bless marriages; pray for the sick; make processions; honour the relics of their saints, or rather their idols; they have monasteries and convents of young women; they sing in their temples like Christian Monks; they observe several fasts, in the course of the year, and mortify their bodies, particularly with the discipline, or whips: they consecrate their bishops, and send missionaries, who live in extreme poverty, travelling even barefoot to China.[63]

The Thirty Pieces of Silver & Potter's Field

According to the Gospel of Matthew, when Judas betrays Jesus for 30 pieces of silver, he is wracked with guilt and hangs himself, after which the priests who originally paid him off buy with his blood-money the "Field of Blood," or the potter's field. However, in Acts Judas is represented as having his guts explode in the field, thus its bloody name. Obviously, these accounts are not history; indeed, they are found in older mythologies. Walker relates an earlier version from which the biblical tale was molded:

> The Sumero-Babylonian Goddess Aruru the Great was the original Potter who created human begins out of clay. . . . The Goddess was worshipped as a Potter in the Jewish temple, where she received "thirty pieces of silver" as the price of a sacrificial victim (Zechariah 11:13). She owned the Field of Blood, Alcedema, where clay was moistened with the blood of victims so bought. Judas, who allegedly sold Jesus for this same price, was himself another victim of the Potter. In the Potter's Field he was either hanged (Matthew 27:5) or disemboweled (Acts 1:18), suggesting that the Potter was none other than the Goddess who both created and destroyed.[64]

In the luni-solar mythos, the 30 pieces of silver represent the 30 days of lunation.

Peter's Denial and the Cock Crowing

While discussing his betrayal, Christ claims that Peter, his "rock," will deny him three times before the cock crows. This element is found in other myths and earlier traditions. As Walker states:

> It is said in the *Zohar* that a cock crowing three times is an omen of death. . . . The Gospel story of Peter's denial of Christ, three times before cockcrow, was related to older legends associating the crowing with the death and resurrection of the solar Savior.[65]

"St. Peter," despite his denial, is considered the gatekeeper of heaven. The story is not historical but astronomical in origin, with Peter and the cock being one and representing the announcement of the morning sun, whom Peter "the gatekeeper/cock" finally allows to pass after denying him. As Walker relates:

> The resurrected god couldn't enter into his kingdom until dawn. The angel of annunciation appeared as a cock, "to announce the coming of the Sun," as Pausanias said. At cockcrow, the Savior arose as Light of the World to disperse the demons of night. But if he tried to enter into his kingdom earlier, disrupting the cycles of night and day, the Gatekeeper would deny him. The ritualistic denial took place also in the fertility cults of Canaan, where the dying god Mot was denied by a priest representing the Heavenly Father. This story made difficulties for Christian theologians, when the pagans inquired why Jesus should found his church on a disciple who denied him instead of a more loyal one.[66]

As the cock who announces the risen savior, Peter is associated with the sign of Aries, when the sun overcomes the night and starts its journey to fullness.

The Sacrifice of the Sacred King

The gospel story is basically yet another remake of the ubiquitous ancient sacred king drama and sacrifice already mentioned. This myth and ritual was common around the Mediterranean both at the purported time of Jesus and long prior, including in Greece, Italy, Asia Minor, the Levant and Egypt. As we have seen, the story was originally allegory, representing the celestial bodies and natural forces, but it became degraded as it was enacted upon Earth, with the solar hero who gives his life to the world represented by an actual flesh-and-blood sacrifice.

The sacred king drama is a scapegoating ritual in which the evils of the people are placed upon the head of a person or animal, such as a goat, often by shouting at him as he is paraded through the streets. Dujardin describes the scapegoat ritual:

> The sins of the community are magically reassembled in the person of the god, in slaying the god one is rid of the sins, and the god returns to life freed from the sins.[67]

Dujardin further relates the typical "scapegod" drama, which involved either an actual king or a proxy, criminal or otherwise:

> The god is anointed king and high-priest. He is conducted in a procession, clothed in the mantle of purple, wearing a crown, and with a sceptre in his hand. He is adored, then stripped of his insignia, next of his garments, and scourged, the scourging being a feature of all the analogous rites. He is killed and the blood sprinkled on the heads of the faithful. Then he is affixed to the cross. The women lament the death of their god . . . This happened at the third hour—namely, at nine o'clock in the morning. At sunset the god is taken down from the cross and buried, and a stone is rolled over the sepulchre. . . . Many of the sacrifices of the gods took place in the springtime, such as the death and resurrection of Attis, and conform to the gospel tradition which places the Passion of Jesus at the time of the Jewish Passover.[68]

During the sacrifice, the sacred king's legs may be broken, but the highest sacrifice—that for sin-atonement—calls for a blemish-free victim; thus, it is written that Jesus was spared this mutilation, so that "scripture might be fulfilled." At times, the victim was slain by having his heart pierced by a sacred lance; at others, he was wounded by the spear and left to die in the sun. Often it was necessary for the victim to be willing if reluctant, like Jesus. Sometimes the victims, who could also be unwilling prisoners of war, were given a stupefying drug such as datura or opium, the "vinegar with gall" or "wine with spices" given to Jesus.

This drama also served as a fertility rite, and the god-king was considered a vegetation deity. After his sacrifice, his blood and flesh were to be shared, sometimes in a cannibalistic eucharist and usually by being spread upon the crop fields so that they would produce abundance. In some places such ritual sacrifice was done annually or more often. Thus, it has never been a one-time occurrence in history, 2,000 years ago, but has taken place thousands of times over many millennia. As Massey says:

> The legend of the voluntary victim who in a passion of divinest pity became incarnate, and was clothed in human form and feature for the salvation of the world, did not originate in a belief that God had manifested once for all as an historic personage. It has its roots in the remotest part.[69]

The sacred king drama had already taken place in the Levant for thousands of years prior to the Christian era. As Frazer relates:

> Among the Semites of Western Asia the king, in a time of national danger, sometimes gave his own son to die as a sacrifice for the people. Thus Philo of Byblus, in his work on the Jews, says: "It was an ancient custom in a crisis of great danger that the ruler of a city or nation should give his beloved son to die for the whole people, as a ransom offered to the avenging demons; and the children thus offered were slain with mystic rites. So Cronus, whom the Phoenicians call Israel, being king of the land and having an only-begotten son called Jeoud (for in the Phoenician tongue Jeoud signifies 'only-begotten'), dressed him in royal robes and sacrificed him upon an altar in a time of war, when the country was in great danger from the enemy."[70]

Robertson elucidates on Jewish sacrifice:

> . . . hanged men in ancient Jewry were sacrifices to the Sun-god or Rain-god. It may be taken as historically certain that human sacrifice in this aspect was a recognized part of Hebrew religion until the Exile. . . . Hanging is not to be construed in the narrow sense of death by strangulation. The normal method of "crucifixion" was hanging by the wrists.[71]

In the gospels, while plotting Jesus's death, high priest Caiaphas ("rock" or "oppressor") says to the crowd, ". . . it is expedient . . . that one man should die for the people, and that the whole nation should not perish," a reference to the ritual of scapegoating that demonstrates Christ's was an expiatory and not punitive sacrifice.

The Passion

The scapegoat ritual is also the "Passion" of the sacred king. The Passion of Jesus is well known because it has been acted in plays or on the streets in many nations each year for centuries. The simple fact is that the Passion was also acted out in the same manner long prior to the purported advent of the Christ character, as there have been "Passions" of a number of savior-gods and goddesses. As Dujardin relates:

> Other scholars have been impressed by the resemblance between the Passion of Jesus as told in the gospels and the ceremonies of the popular fetes, such as the Sacaea in Babylon, the festival of Kronos in Greece, and the Saturnalia in Italy. . . . If the stories of the Passions of Dionysus, Attis, Osiris and Demeter are the transpositions of cult dramas, and not actual events, it can hardly be otherwise with the Passion of Jesus.

The following passion is not the story of Jesus but that of Baal or Bel of Babylon/Phoenicia, as revealed on a 4,000-year-old tablet now in the British Museum:

1. Baal is taken prisoner.
2. He is tried in a hall of justice.
3. He is tormented and mocked by a rabble.
4. He is led away to the mount.
5. Baal is taken with two other prisoners, one of whom is released.
6. After he is sacrificed on the mount, the rabble goes on a rampage.
7. His clothes are taken.
8. Baal disappears into a tomb.
9. He is sought after by weeping women.
10. He is resurrected, appearing to his followers after the stone is rolled away from the tomb.[72]

In addition, it is obvious that a number of the specifics of the Christian passion are lifted from the book of Psalms (22, 69:21), which in turn is based on older traditions, as Psalms in fact represents a reworking of Canaanite/Egyptian sayings. The passion play is in reality a very old device used in many mystery religions. Originally celestial, as noted, it is in no way a historical occurrence, except that it happened thousands of times around the ancient world.

The Passion as related in the gospels is easily revealed to be a play through a number of clues. For example, Jesus is made to pray three times while his disciples are asleep, such that no one is there to hear or see the scene, yet it is recorded. Robertson explains: "On the stage, however, there is no difficulty at all since the prayer would be heard by the audience, like a soliloquy."[73]

Another clue is the compression in time of the events, as well as their dramatic tone. The whole gospel story purports to take place over a period of a few weeks, and the entire "life of Jesus" represents about 50 hours total. Furthermore, Robertson states:

> The fact that the whole judicial process took place in the middle of the night shows its unhistorical character. The exigencies of drama are responsible for hunting up "false witnesses" throughout Jerusalem in the dead of night. . . . The Crucifixion and Resurrection scenes, even the final appearance in Galilee, are set forth in Matthew as they would be represented on a stage. The gospel ends abruptly with the words of the risen Lord. Where the play ends, the narrative ends.[74]

Carpenter says:

> If anyone will read, for instance, in the four Gospels, the events of the night preceding the crucifixion and reckon the time which they would necessarily have taken to enact—the Last Supper, the agony in the Garden, the betrayal by Judas, the hauling before Caiaphas and the Sanhedrin, and then before Pilate in the Hall of Judgment . . . then—in Luke—the interposed visit to Herod, and the *return* to Pilate; Pilate's speeches and washing of hands before the crowd; then the scourging and the mocking and the arraying of Jesus in purple robe as a king; then the preparation of a Cross and the long and painful journey to Golgotha; and finally the Crucifixion at sunrise—he will see—as has often been pointed out—that the whole story is physically impossible. As a record of actual events the story is impossible; but as a record or series of notes derived from the witnessing of a "mystery-play"—and such plays with *very similar* incidents were common enough in antiquity in connection with cults of a dying Savior, it very likely *is* true (one can see the very dramatic character of the incidents: the washing of hands, the threefold denial by Peter, the purple robe and crown of thorns, and so forth); and as such it is now accepted by many well-qualified authorities.[75]

And Dujardin concurs:

> The improbabilities of the accounts in the gospels are transparent . . . let us note only that Jesus is arrested, arraigned before two courts, and executed in the space of a few hours. The Jewish tribunal sits during the night, and this very night is the night of a religious feast, an absurdity which of itself proves how far the writer was from the events and place about which he wrote. No custom is respected; the Sabbath for instance, is again and again violated, and Jewish law and custom are ignored. As for Pilate, he is an inconceivable caricature of a Roman magistrate.

Thus, Christ's Passion is indeed a play, with its condensed time-frame, stage directions and ritualistic lines.

"Let His Blood Be Upon Us and Our Children"

As stated, the blood of the scapegoat was sprinkled upon the congregation or audience of the play, who would cry, "Let his blood be upon us and our children," a standard play and ritual line that was designed to ensure future fertility and the continuation of life. This ritual is reflected at Exodus 24:8, when Moses throws the oxen blood on the people to seal the Lord's covenant with them and was passed down in the Christian doctrine of being "washed in the blood of the Lamb of God." It is also displayed in the Epistle to the Hebrews, where the priests have even developed a "technology" to emulate the sprinkling of the blood.

Golgotha, "Place of the Skulls"

The site where Jesus is crucified is called Golgotha or Calvary, which is the Latin for "place of bare skulls." Walker relates:

> There were many Middle-Eastern peoples whose habit it was to preserve skulls of the dead for later necromantic consultation, especially the skulls of sacred kings. Their place of sacrifice called Golgotha, alleged scene of Jesus's crucifixion, meant "the place of skulls."[76]

According to Doane, the word Golgotha does not appear in Jewish literature, nor is there any evidence of such a place near Jerusalem. As Dujardin states:

> As in the case of Nazareth, no trace of [Golgotha] is to be found prior to the gospels. This is inexplicable, for the story places Golgotha at the gates of Jerusalem . . . These considerations suggest that the Golgotha which was the actual place of the sacrifice must have been situated elsewhere. Golgotha, Goulgoleth in Hebrew, was both a common and proper name, and one may infer that Jesus was crucified on one of the numerous hills in Palestine described as a goulgoleth. It would also appear that Goulgoleth was an expletive form of Golgola . . . and that Golgola is the same as Gilgal. Now, Gilgal is both a common name signifying a circle (applicable to the ancient megalithic circles that we call cromlechs—namely, the sacred or high places of Canaan) and also a proper name of several cities. If Jesus was sacrificed on a gilgal—namely, an ancient cromlech—we are face to face with the most ancient of Palestinian cults. . . . The Bible, in fact, narrates that a certain place called Gilgal was the principal centre of the patriarch Iehoshoua—namely, Jesus-Joshua. . . . Jesus-Joshua the ancient patriarch, who appears to have been a Palestinian god . . . At all events the fact remains that Golgotha of the gospels is a gilgal, that a gilgal is a sacred circle in Palestine, and that it was in a gilgal that the old Jesus-Joshua had his headquarters—namely, a sanctuary.[77]

Indeed, in the OT, there are only three cases of crucifixion, all of which are kings, seven in total, sacrificed by Joshua at the "high places" of Gilgal, Ai and Makkeda. These sacred kings are sacrificed not *by* Joshua/Jesus but in his name.

In addition, the Mexican savior-god and solar myth, Quetzalcoatl, was also crucified at the "place of the skull," long before contact with Christians. Skulls and necromancy are also a large part of Tibetan Buddhist religion, among many others over the millennia.

It should also be noted that there were "calvaries," i.e., sacred mounts where a cross was erected, in numerous places prior to the Christian era. These mounts were usurped by Christians, and the crosses made into Christian versions.

The Crucifixion

As we have seen, a number of savior-gods and goddesses have been executed or crucified in atonement for "sins" and/or as a fertility rite. As part of the standard sacred king drama, the crucifixion of the "King of Kings" is in no way historical, except that it happened thousands of times around the globe. In the ancient world, there were two basic types of crucifixion: punitive or expiatory. Although evemerists have tried to find in Jesus a "historical" criminal who was punitively executed, the fact is that his crucifixion is allegorical, not factual, and expiatory, not punitive.

Although the typical sacrificial victim was killed before being placed on the cross, tree or stake, in the expiatory sacred king drama, which was more important and ritualistic than the average sacrifice, the victim remained alive as part of the play, so he could utter mournful words and garner pity from the audience.

In addition, Jesus would have been crucified at the holy time of Passover only if he were an expiatory sacrifice. As Graham says:

> Now is it not strange that the crucifixion should take place during the Passover? Among the Jews this was a most sacred occasion. For them to crucify anyone at this time, they would have to break at least seven of their religious laws.[78]

Dujardin sums it up:

> The crucifixion was a reality, but it was not a judicial execution; it was a sacrifice. And there was not simply one historic sacrifice, but innumerable crucifixions of the god Jesus in Palestine.[79]

Although the ritual was reduced to a human drama, it is ultimately symbolic:

> The Christian doctrine of the crucifixion with the victim raised
> aloft as the sin-offering for all the world is but a metaphrastic
> rendering of the primitive meaning, a shadow of the original . . . [80]

Degenerate when reenacted upon the planet, the "crucifixion"
is properly the "crossification" of the sun through the equinoxes,
which is why there are differing accounts of the crucifixion in the
NT. In the first account Jesus's mother is absent from the scene,
actually representing the vernal equinox, when the constellation
of Virgo is not a factor. The crossification/crucifixion of the
autumnal equinox, however, takes place in the constellation of
Virgo; hence, the Virgin Mary is present.

There are also two dates of crucifixion, likewise explainable
only within the mythos: "The 14th of the month would be the
lunar reckoning of Anup=John, and the 15th, that of Taht-
Mati=Matthew in the two forms of the Egyptian Mythos. . . . Both
cannot be historically correct, but they *are* both astronomically
true."[81]

The Three Marys at the Crucifixion

In the autumnal crucifixion story, not only the Virgin Mary
but also the other two gospel Marys are present. In the Egyptian
version of the mythos, the three Meris appear at Horus's
crucifixion. Of the Jesus tale, Walker relates: "The three Marys at
the crucifixion bore the same title as pagan death priestesses,
myrrhophores, bearers of myrrh."[82] The three Marys/Meris are the
Moerae or fates:

> Three incarnations of Mari, or Mary, stood at the foot of Jesus's
> cross, like the Moerae of Greece. One was his virgin mother. The
> second was his "dearly beloved" . . . The third Mary must have
> represented the Crone (the fatal Moera), so the tableau
> resembled that of the three Norns at the foot of Odin's sacrificial
> tree. The Fates were present at the sacrifices decreed by
> Heavenly Fathers, whose victims hung on trees or pillars
> "between heaven and earth."[83]

The Spear of Longinus

Longinus was the name of the Roman soldier who stuck Jesus
in the side with a spear. Legend held that Longinus was blind and
was subsequently cured by Jesus's blood. Again, this is not a
historical event but part of the mythos and sacred king ritual, as
Walker relates:

> The true prototype of the legend seems to have been the blind
> god Hod, who slew the Norse savior Balder with the thrust of a
> spear of mistletoe. . . . March 15, the "Ides of March" when most
> pagan saviors died, was the day devoted to Hod by the heathens,

and later Christianized as the feast day of the Blessed Longinus.[84]

Walker also states:

> Up to Hadrian's time, victims offered to Zeus at Salamis were anointed with sacred ointments—thus becoming "Anointed Ones" or "Christs"—then hung up and stabbed through the side with a spear.[85]

In addition, the Scandinavian god Odin, and the god Marsyas of Mindanao in the Philippines were hung on a "fatal tree" and stabbed with a spear.[86] The Hindu god Vishnu (Bal-ii) was crucified with spear in his side, bearing the epithet "side-wounded".[87] The gods Wittoba and Adonis were also crucified and "side-wounded" saviors.[88]

Although a myth, many "authentic" "spears of Longinus" have been "found" in the Christian world. Indeed, Hitler purportedly spent a great deal of time, money and energy to track down the "true" spear, believing that it, like so many other "sacred" objects, held occultic powers.

As demonstrated earlier, the side-wounding in the mythos is due to the position of the sun near Sagittarius, the archer.[89]

My God, My God, Why Hast Thou Forsaken Me?

As noted, the pitiful and mournful words uttered by Jesus as he hung on the cross were another standard part of the mythos and ritual, found in older traditions such as in the sacrifice of Aleyin by his Virgin Mother Anath, "twin of the Goddess Mari as Lady of Birth and Death, worshipped by Canaanites, Amorites, Syrians, Egyptians, and Hebrews."[90] As Walker further relates:

> In the typical sacred-king style, Mot-Aleyin was the son of the Virgin Anath and also the bridegroom of his own mother. Like Jesus too, he was the Lamb of God. He said, "I am Aleyin, son of Baal (the Lord). Make ready, then, the sacrifice. I am the lamb which is made ready with pure wheat to be sacrificed in expiation."
>
> After Aleyin's death, Anath resurrected him and sacrificed Mot in turn. She told Mot that he was forsaken by his heavenly father El, the same god who "forsook" Jesus on the cross. The words attributed to Jesus, "My El, my El, why hast thou forsaken me?" (Mark 15:34), apparently were copied from the ancient liturgical formula, which became part of the Passover ritual at Jerusalem.[91]

The Rending of the Curtain of the Temple

When Jesus dies, he cries out with a loud voice and "yields up his spirit," after which, Matthew relates, "the curtain of the temple was torn in two, from top to bottom; and the earth shook, and the rocks were split; the tombs also were opened, and many bodies of the saints who had fallen asleep were raised, and coming out of the tombs after his resurrection they went into the holy city and appeared to many."

Obviously, this event did not happen literally and historically. Such a tremendous occurrence would hardly have escaped the notice of historians and scientists of the day, yet not a word is recorded of it anywhere. The same tale is told of a number of other sun gods and is only explainable within the mythos. In the Egyptian version, Horus rends the curtain or veil of the tabernacle or temple, which means that in his resurrection, he removes the mummified remains of his old self as Osiris. This scene represents the new sun being born or resurrected from the old, dead one. The refreshed spirit pierces the veil, with a loud cry of his resurrection and with the quaking of Amenta, "the earth of eternity." As Massey states:

> The [gospel] scene has now been changed from Amenta to the earth of Seb [Joseph] by those who made "historic" mockery of the Egyptian Ritual, and sank the meaning out of sight where it has been so long submerged.[92]

The Darkening of the Sun at the Crucifixion

The earth-shattering event of the sun darkening at Christ's crucifixion is also not historical; hence, it appears in no other writing of the day, a detail bothersome to believers and evemerists. As Hazelrigg relates:

> Thus, C. Plinius Secund, the elder, and Seneca, both worthy philosophers, wrote in the first century of our Era, dealing exhaustively in accounts of seismic phenomena, but nowhere do they mention the miraculous darkness which is said to have overspread the earth at the crucifixion; neither do they make mention anywhere in their voluminous texts of a man Jesus.[93]

Like the other contradictory and impossible events of the biblical narrative, this event is only explainable within the mythos. As noted, the same mythical darkening of the sun occurred at the deaths of Heracles/Hercules, Krishna, Prometheus, Buddha and Osiris.[94] The phenomena upon the death of Buddha are actually more impressive than those upon Christ's death, as not only did darkness prevail, but "a thousand appalling meteors fell."[95] This darkening is only natural, in that when the sun is "crucified," it goes out.

The Resurrection

As we have seen, numerous gods and goddesses have been depicted as having been resurrected, an ongoing, unhistorical event representing various forces and bodies in nature and the cosmos, largely revolving around the sun. As Dujardin relates:

> The word "resurrection" means today the return from death to life, but the resurrection of gods never takes the form of a simple return to life after the manner of Lazarus. In primitive religions resurrection expresses a re-commencement analogous to that of Nature in spring, and it is usually concerned with the renewal of vegetation and of the species. But it is not only a re-commencement, it is also a renovation. In the sacrifice of Elimination the god comes to life again rejuvenated. Thus, the resurrection is the completion—or rather, the object—of the sacrifice; the god is put to death in order that he may return to life again regenerated. . . Dionysus and Osiris are reborn renovated and also glorified; dead to life terrestrial, they revive to life divine. . . . The god dies and comes to life again only in order that through him the human society may renew itself.[96]

The Ascension on the Mount of Olives

As noted, several gods and goddesses around the world ascend to heaven in one way or another. Prior to Christianity, the Mount of Olives was used as a sacrificial site for the Red Heifer rite of the Hebrews,[97] who in turn took this rite from Egypt. As Churchward relates:

> Jesus rises in the Mount of Olives, but not on the Mount that was localized to the east of Jerusalem. The Mount of Olives as Egyptian was the mountain of Amenta. It is termed "Mount Bakhu," "the mount of the olive-tree," where the green dawn was represented by this tree instead of by the Sycamore. Mount Bakhu, the mount of the olive-tree, was the way of ascent to the risen Saviour as he issued forth from Amenta to the land of the spirits in heaven.[98]

Massey elucidates:

> And from the mount called Olivet, Jesus vanished into heaven— Olivet being a typical Mount of the equinox from which the solar god ascended.[99]

The ascension is significant, as without it much of the purpose for the Christian religion crumbles. Yet, as Graham remarks:

> The ascension of Christ is a very important part of Christian doctrine; it implies immortality, triumph over death, a heaven world beyond, and a possible Second Coming. Why then did Matthew and John ignore it? Luke mentions it only in one little verse of nineteen words, a sort of postscript not found in some manuscripts. And someone added to Mark a mere reference to it with the telltale little sign ¶.[100]

Like so many other biblical tales, the accounts of the ascension are contradictory, with Luke placing it three days after and Acts 40 days after the resurrection. These discrepancies are explainable not as history but within the mythos, representing the lunar resurrection at the autumnal equinox and the solar at the vernal equinox.

Many other elements, such as the flight into Egypt, the woman at the well, the pool of Bethesda, the cursing of the fig tree, the reapers of the harvest, Salome and the "Dance of the Seven Veils," the two sisters Mary and Martha, the Marys as mother of Jesus, the palms in Jerusalem, the purple robe, and the seven fishers in the boat are also found in other mythologies. The pool of Bethesda, for example, represents one of the mysteries of the secret societies and mystery schools.

Conclusion

It has been calculated that aside from the 40 days in the wilderness, everything related in the New Testament about what Jesus said and did could have taken place within a period of three weeks. The gospel story, then, hardly constitutes a "biography" of any historical value about the life of one of the world's purported great movers and shakers. What it does record is a "history" of the development of religious ideas and how they are usurped and passed along from one culture to another. The gospel is also reflective of a concerted effort to unify the Roman world under one state religion, drawing upon the multitudes of sects and cults that existed at the time. Most of all, however, the story records the movements of planetary bodies and the forces of nature in a mythos that, when restored to its original, non-carnalized, non-historicized grandeur, portrays the cosmos in a manner not only illuminating but also entertaining.

---

1. Walker, *WEMS*, 186.
2. Stone, 221-5.
3. Hazelrigg, 33.
4. Walker, *WEMS*, 292.
5. A. Churchward, 315.
6. Walker, *WDSSO*, 337.
7. Walker, *WEMS*, 815.
8. Walker, *WEMS*, 108.
9. Walker, *WEMS*, 291.
10. Walker, *WEMS*, 541.
11. Hazelrigg, 35.
12. Pike, 497.
13. Pike, 494.
14. Walker, *WEMS*, 905.
15. Stone, 209.
16. Walker, *WDSSO*, 387.

17. Wheless, 72.
18. Walker, *WEMS*, 292.
19. Jackson, 123.
20. Higgins, I, 255, 511.
21. Doane, 189.
22. Massey, *HJMC*, 185.
23. Hazelrigg, 35-36.
24. Graham, 234-5.
25. Pike, 455.
26. Doane, 364.
27. Walker, *WEMS*, 10.
28. Walker, *WEMS*, 1026.
29. Walker, *WEMS*, 970-1.
30. Massey, *HJMC*, 27.
31. Massey, *GHC.*
32. Massey, *HJMC*, 28.
33. Jackson, 206.
34. Jackson, 206.
35. Massey, *HJMC*, 41.
36. Walker, *WEMS*, 435.
37. Doane, 172.
38. Walker, *WDSSO*, 75.
39. Higgins, II, 96.
40. Walker, *WEMS*, 749.
41. Higgins, II, 95.
42. Higgins, I, 560.
43. Doane, 140.
44. Massey, *HJMC*, 58.
45. Higgins, I, 648.
46. A. Churchward, 387-9.
47. Doane, 175.
48. Leedom, 125.
49. Walker, *WEMS*, 464.
50. Walker, *WEMS*, 614.
51. Walker, *WDSSO*, 88-9.
52. Walker, *WEMS*, 496.
53. Walker, *WEMS*, 615.
54. Walker, *WDSSO*, 105.
55. Massey, *HJMC*, 63.
56. Massey, *HJMC*, 78.
57. Massey, *HJMC*, 121.
58. Walker, *WEMS*, 68.
59. Massey, *HJMC*, 123-7.
60. Massey, *HJMC*, 123-7.
61. Doresse, 42.
62. Carpenter, 66.
63. Higgins, I, 232.
64. Walker, *WEMS*, 815.
65. Walker, *WDSSO*, 397.
66. Walker, *WEMS*, 79.
67. Dujardin, 8-9.
68. Dujardin, 56.
69. Massey, *EBD*, 51.
70. Frazer, 340-1.
71. Robertson, 36.
72. viz. Jackson, 43-4.

73. Robertson, 49.
74. Robertson, 50-1.
75. Carpenter, 212.
76. Walker, *WEMS*, 988.
77. Dujardin, 58-9.
78. Graham, 345.
79. Dujardin, 57.
80. A. Churchward, 364.
81. Massey, *GHC*, 32.
82. Walker, *WDSSO*, 467.
83. Walker, *WEMS*, 469.
84. Walker, *WEMS*, 549.
85. Walker, *WEMS*, 469.
86. Frazer, 410-12.
87. Higgins, I, 572, 670.
88. Doane, 185, 218.
89. Anderson, 60.
90. Walker, *WEMS*, 29.
91. Walker, *WEMS*, 30-1.
92. Massey, *EBD*, 79.
93. Hazelrigg, 178.
94. Walker, *WEMS*, 393.
95. Doane, 207.
96. Dujardin, 70-1.
97. Robertson, 37.
98. A. Churchward, 376.
99. Massey, *HJMC*, 78.
100. Graham, 359-60.

Scene from the Temple of Luxor at Thebes, Egypt, dating to
around 1600 BCE and depicting the Annunciation by the God
Taht, the Word, to the Virgin Queen, of her birth to the coming
son; the Immaculate Conception by Kneph, the Holy Ghost; the
Birth of the Solar Babe; and the Adoration of the Child and
presenting of gifts by three men. (Massey, *HJMC*)

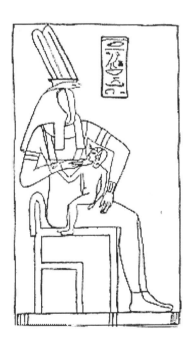

Pre-Christian Egyptian
Madonna and Child.
(A. Churchward)

Pre-Christian Indian
Madonna and Child
(Hislop)

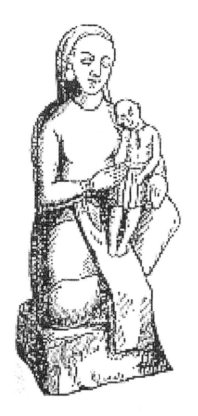

Pre-Christian Babylonian
Madonna and Child
(A. Churchward)

Indian virgin mother
Devaki with the infant
Krishna, the *black* god.
(Hislop)

Other Elements and Symbols of the Christian Myth

In addition to the multitude already examined are many other aspects of the Bible and the Judeo-Christian tradition that can be found in other, older cultures and mythologies. To outline them all would require another volume, which would include such concepts as Ash Wednesday, the Assumption of the Virgin, Gog and Magog, Son of Man, Immanuel and the Stations of the Cross, among others. However, some of the more important aspects are as follows.

The Alpha and Omega

In the gospel tale, Jesus is purported to be the "Alpha and Omega, the beginning and end," but these sentiments were plagiarized from older sources, including the Goddess Isis, in whose temple at Sais, Egypt, it was carved, "I am all that has been, that is, and that will be." As Walker says, "Alpha and omega, the first and last letters of the alphabet, were frequently applied to the Goddess who united in birth and death."[1]

Angels and Devils

The concept of angels and devils in no way originated with Judaism or Christianity but is found in many other cultures around the globe. The Jews, in fact, took the names of some of their angels from the Persians.[2]

Although Judaism and Christianity have portrayed them exclusively as male, a trend largely ignored by angel enthusiasts today, angels were originally considered female in several cultures, such as the Indian and Persian. Indeed, the seven archangels of Christianity are masculine remakes of the Seven Hathors of Egypt, which were female.[3]

As part of the mythos, the good and bad angels (devils or demons) actually represent the *angles* or aspects of the zodiac, whose influences were determined to be either benevolent or malevolent.

Antichrist

The term "Antichrist" has been applied to numerous rulers and dissidents over the centuries. Because of the hideous and evil abuses of the Catholic Church for centuries, a number of popes were deemed "Antichrists," including Clement VII. Anyone who claims that Jesus Christ never existed could also be called "Antichrist," a title that eminent philosopher Friedrich Nietzsche was proud to claim, because he viewed "Christ" as an oppression. Although many people have been persecuted for denying Jesus

Christ, Christ himself is made to say, "And every one who speaks a word against the Son of man will be forgiven" (Lk. 12:10).

It is clear from biblical writings that during the first centuries of the Christian era, numerous "Christs" were running about the Roman world, jockeying for position. These individuals were such a threat to the "true" Christ's representatives that they felt the need to dispense with the competition by forging the Epistles of John sometime during the second century: "Children, it is the last hour; and as you have heard that antichrist is coming, so now many antichrists have come." (1 Jn. 2:18)

Walker relates the true meaning of "antichrist":

> Antichrist was the Christian equivalent of the Chaldean Aciel, lord of the nether world, counterbalancing the solar god of heaven.[4]

In other words, it was the night sky.

Armageddon

In the earlier Persian version of the mythos, it was the devil Ahriman who was to bring his legions against the holy nation, which in this case was Persia, or Iran, where Armageddon was to be fought. Thus, Armageddon is yet another ages-old concept that did not originate with Judaism, Christianity or the Bible.

Baptism

Baptism is quite common around the world, long predating the Christian era, as is evidenced by the fact that it was already in practice when Jesus encountered John the Baptist. As Massey says, "Baptismal regeneration, transfiguration, transubstantiation, the resurrection and ascension, were all Egyptian mysteries."[5]

Baptism was done not only by the sprinkling of water but also by immersion into it. It was also by "holy wind/spirit" and by fire, the latter of which in actuality was popular in many parts of the world and is considered "Zoroastrian." In the baptism by fire, the participant, willing or otherwise, is generally passed through the fire unharmed. Baptism by fire was still practiced as of the last century in India and Scotland.[6]

Christmas

Many people today are aware that Christmas, December 25th, is the winter solstice and not the actual birthdate of the Jewish savior-god, yet they continue to look for some other birthdate, because this was one of the numerous significant "historical" facts conveniently overlooked by the gospel writers. Over the centuries, a number of birthdates had been put forth before the Western church decided to incorporate the December 25th element of the typical sun god mythos, in large part to usurp the followers of Mithra.

In addition, not a few people have noticed the irreconcilability of the December birthdate with the circumstances of the birth, which could not have taken place in the winter, with "shepherds tending their flock," etc. A date earlier adopted in Christianity and still maintained by the Eastern Orthodox church is January 6th, which would also not be correct according to the biblical tale, since it is also winter. ben Yehoshua relates the origins of the January 6th date: "Originally the eastern Christians believed that [Jesus] was born on 6 January. . . . Osiris-Aion was said to be born of the virgin Isis on the 6 January and this explains the earlier date for Christmas."

The early Western Church fathers assigned two birthdays to Jesus: One at Christmas (winter solstice) and the other at Easter (vernal equinox),[7] which is to be expected, since these dates are not historical but are reflective of the various stages of the sun. The dual birthdate is found in Egyptian mythology as well, as Horus was said to have been born as a babe on December 25th and to have been reborn as a man on March 25th, the same date traditionally held as the resurrection of the Savior Adonis, as well as of Christ, as is related by Byzantine writer Cedrenus:

> The first day of the month . . . corresponds to the 25th of March . . . On that day Gabriel saluted Mary, in order to make her conceive the Saviour. . . . On that very same day, our God Saviour (Christ Jesus), after the termination of his career, arose from the dead; that is, what our forefathers called the Pass-over, or the passage of the Lord.[8]

The "babe" aspect reflects the "smallness" of the sun in December (northern hemisphere), while the "man" born again or resurrected in spring signifies the sun passing over (Passover or "Crossification") the celestial equator, when the day and night are briefly equalized, and the day then begins to become longer than the night. Thus, it was said that the solar hero had two birthdays and two mothers.

Mangasarian concludes:

> The selection of the twenty-fifth of December as [Jesus's] birthday is not only an arbitrary one, but that date, having been from time immemorial dedicated to the Sun, the inference is that the Son of God and the Sun of heaven enjoying the same birthday, were at one time identical beings. The fact that Jesus' death was accompanied with the darkening of the Sun, and that the date of his resurrection is also associated with the position of the Sun at the time of the vernal equinox, is a further intimation that we have in the story of the birth, death, and resurrection of

Jesus, an ancient and nearly universal Sun-myth, instead of verifiable historical events.

The Cross and Crucifix

The cross and crucifix are very ancient symbols found around the world long prior to the supposed advent of the Christian savior. In the gospel story Jesus tells his disciples to "take up the cross" and follow him. Obviously, the cross already existed and was a well-known symbol, such that Jesus did not even have to explain this strange statement about an object that, we are led to believe, only gained significance after Jesus died on it.

The pre-Christian reverence for the cross and the crucifix, e.g., the cross with a man on it, is admitted by the "holy Father" Minucius Felix (211):

> As for the adoration of the cross which you (Pagans) object against us (Christians) . . . that we neither adore crosses nor desire them; you it is, ye Pagans . . . who are the most likely people to adore wooden crosses . . . for what else are your ensigns, flags, and standards, but crosses gilt and beautiful. Your victorious trophies not only represent a simple cross, but a cross with a man on it.[9]

The early Christians were actually repulsed by the image of a man hanging on the cross, which was not adopted by the Christian church until the 7th century. In fact, the crucifix with a man on it had been imported to Rome from India ages before the Christian era. Indeed, as Walker states, "Early Christians even repudiated the cross because it was pagan. . . . Early images of Jesus represented him not on a cross, but in the guise of the Osirian or Hermetic 'Good Shepherd,' carrying a lamb."[10] As stated, the original occupant of the cross was a lamb, not a man. Like the image of the man on the cross, that of the crucified lamb was also very ancient, preceding the Christian era by centuries. As Taylor recounts:

> On a Phoenician medal found in the ruins of Citium, and engraved in Dr. Clarke's Travels, and proved by him to be Phoenician, are inscribed not only the cross, but the rosary, or string of beads, attached to it, together with the identical *Lamb of God, which taketh away the sins of the world.*

The cross was also revered by the ancient people called the Pygmies. As A. Churchward relates:

> This primary Sign or Symbol, fashioned in the beginning by the African Pygmies to represent "The One Great Spirit," has been carried on by the various cults during human evolution, down to the present-day Cross of the Christian Doctrines; it has always represented the *One Great One.*[11]

Churchward thus reveals that the Pygmies were very early monotheists, evidently thousands of years before the Judeo-Christian era. He also reveals the true meaning of the cross:

> Fundamentally the Cross was astronomical. A Cross with equal arms denotes the time of equal day and night, and is a figure of the equinox.[12]

As Derek Partridge says, "What a cross with a circle in it . . . truly represents is the sun waning or dying on the zodiac, and not a man."[13]

The cross is the celestial emblem of the sun but it also serves as a phallic symbol. As Carpenter relates, "The well-known T-shaped cross was in use in pagan lands long before Christianity, as a representation of the male member . . ."[14] Walker reiterates, "The cross was also a male symbol of the phallic Tree of Life."[15]

Of the Pagan origins of Christianity and the cross, Higgins concludes:

> Mr. Ledwick has observed that the presence of Heathen devices and crosses on the same coin are not unusual, as Christians in those early times were for the most part Semi pagans. This is diametrically opposed to all the doctrines of the Protestants about the early purity of the religion of Christ, and its subsequent corruption by the Romists. . . . In fact it is mere nonsense, for there can be no doubt that the cross was one of the most common of the Gentile symbols, and was adopted by the Christians *like all their other rites and ceremonies* from the Gentiles . . . [16]

Easter

Easter celebrations date back into remotest antiquity and are found around the world, as the blossoming of spring did not escape the notice of the ancients, who revered this life-renewing time of the year, when winter had passed and the sun was "born again." Easter, of course, is merely the Passover, and Jesus represents the Passover Lamb ritually sacrificed every year by a number of cultures, including the Egyptians, possibly as early as 4,000 years ago and continuing to this day in some places. As ben Yehoshua relates:

> The occurrence of Passover at the same time of year as the pagan "Easter" festivals is not coincidental. Many of the Pessach customs were designed as Jewish alternatives to pagan customs. The pagans believed that when their nature god (such as Tammuz, Osiris or Attis) died and was resurrected, his life went into the plants used by man as food. The matza made from the spring harvest was his new body and the wine from the grapes was his new blood. In Judaism, matza was not used to represent

the body of a god but the poor man's bread which the Jews ate
before leaving Egypt. . . . When the early Christians noticed the
similarities between Pessach customs and pagan customs, *they
came full circle* and converted the Pessach customs *back* to their
old pagan interpretations. The Seder became the last supper of
Jesus, similar to the last supper of Osiris commemorated at the
Vernal Equinox. The matza and wine once again became the
body and blood of a false god, this time Jesus. Easter eggs are
again eaten to commemorate the resurrection of a "god" and also
the "rebirth" obtained by accepting his sacrifice on the cross.[17]

Easter is "Pessach" in Hebrew, "Pascha" in Greek and
"Pachons" in Latin, derived from the Egyptian "Pa-Khunsu,"
Khunsu being an epithet for Horus. As Massey says, "The festival
of Khunsu, or his birthday, at the vernal equinox, was at one time
celebrated on the twenty-fifth day of the month named after him,
Pa-Khunsu."[18]

The Easter celebration was so ubiquitous prior to the
Christian era that any number of sources are probable for its
inclusion in Christianity. As Jackson states:

> The Easter ceremonies still performed in Greek and Roman
> Catholic churches in Europe are so similar to the ancient rites of
> the Adonic cult that Sir J.G. Frazer has concluded that these
> churches actually derived these rites from the ancient
> worshippers of Adonis.[19]

And Walker relates:

> Christians ever afterward kept Easter Sunday with carnival
> processions derived from the mysteries of Attis. Like Christ, Attis
> arose when "the sun makes the day for the first time longer than
> the night." . . . But the spring Holy Week was not really
> Christian. Its origin was a universal Indo-European tradition of
> extreme antiquity, probably traceable to the Holi festivals of
> India which celebrated the rebirth of spring with joyous orgies.[20]

The Easter celebration was also found in Mexico, to the
astonishment of the invading Catholics:

> According to the Franciscan monk Sahagun, our best authority
> on the Aztec religion, the sacrifice of the human god fell at Easter
> or a few days later, so that, if he is right, it would correspond in
> date as well as in character to the Christian festival of the death
> and resurrection of the Redeemer. . . . Women came forth with
> children in their arms and presented them to him, saluting him
> as a god. For "he passed for our Lord God; the people
> acknowledged him as the Lord."[21]

In Anglo-Saxon, Easter or Eostre is goddess of the dawn,
corresponding to Ishtar, Astarte, Astoreth and Isis. The word
"Easter" shares the same root with "east" and "eastern," the
direction of the rising sun.

Furthermore, the fact that there is no set date for Easter is only explainable within the mythos and not as the historical death and resurrection of a savior-god. As Jackson relates:

> Everyone knows that Easter is a roving date in the calendar, since it is the first Sunday after the first full moon after the Vernal Equinox (the beginning of Spring). Easter, therefore, cannot be the date of the death of any historical personage. Two dates are given in the New Testament for the time of crucifixion, namely: the 14th and 15th of the month of Nisan. Why this discrepancy? The truth explanation was given by Gerald Massey:
>
> > "The Synoptics say that Jesus was crucified on the 15th of the month of Nisan. John affirms that it was on the 14th of the month. This serious rift runs through the very foundation! . . . The crucifixion (or Crossing) was, and still is, determined by the full moon of Easter. This, in the lunar reckoning, would be on the 14th in a month of twenty-eight days; in the solar month of thirty days it was reckoned to occur on the 15th of the month. Both unite, and the rift closes in proving the Crucifixion to have been astronomical, just as it was in Egypt, where the two dates can be identified."[22]

The date of Easter, when the godman was purportedly crucified and resurrected, was debated for centuries. One "distinguished churchman," as Eusebius calls him, Anatolius, reveals the meaning of Easter and of Christ, as well as the fact that astrology was a known and respected science used in Christianity, when he says:

> On this day [March 22] the sun is found not only to have reached the first sign of the Zodiac, but to be already passing through the fourth day within it. This sign is generally known as the first of the twelve, the equinoctial sign, the beginning of months, head of the cycle, and start of the planetary course. . . . Aristobolus adds that it is necessary at the Passover Festival that not only the sun but the moon as well should be passing through an equinoctial sign. There are two of these signs, one in spring, one in autumn, diametrically opposed to each other . . . [23]

Heaven and Hell

The concepts of heaven and hell were not introduced by the Judeo-Christian tradition but existed for millennia in other cultures, such as the Persian and Indian. The Tibetans depict several levels of heaven and hell, which is a temporary state of mind, rather than enduring torture. The afterlife was also a common theme in the Egyptian theology, which tended to be more upbeat and less focused on the torments of hell. As Massey relates:

The prototypes of hell and purgatory and the earthly paradise are all to be found in the Egyptian Amenta. . . . The Egyptian hell was not a place of everlasting pain, but of extinction of those who were wicked irretrievably. It must be admitted, to the honour and glory of the Christian deity, that a god of eternal torment is an ideal distinctly Christian, to which the Egyptians never did attain. Theirs was the all-parental god, Father and Mother in one whose heart was thought to bleed in every wound of suffering humanity, and whose son was represented in the character of the Comforter.[24]

The word "Hell" is also derived from the European goddess Hel, whose womb was a place of immortality. The Christians demonized this womb and made it a place of eternal damnation, and, since volcanoes were considered entrances into the womb of Mother Earth, it became a fiery hell. The original Pagan hell had no locality and was often situated in the same place as heaven.

The nature of hell has thus varied with the culture and era. Some cultures thought hell was the harsh winter; thus, it was located near the South Pole, the "bottomless pit," from which winter was thought to come. This hellish variety is reflected in the Judeo-Christian scriptures: Matthew and Jude both speak of a hell of darkness, while Matthew also refers to a hell of light/fire. Matthew also speaks of a hell where the body and soul are annihilated, and one where the soul is punished for eternity. In the Bible in general, hell is depicted as being limited yet endless; it is upper *and* lower. Hell is also biblically portrayed as a lake of fire and brimstone, yet a bottomless pit, etc.

The descent into hell by the savior is a common occurrence within many mythologies, found in the stories of Adonis, Bacchus, Balder, Hercules, Horus, Jesus, Krishna, Mercury, Osiris, Quetzalcoatl and Zoroaster.[25] This part of the mythos represents the sun entering into the womb of darkness, nightly and seasonally. The sun, of course, is the only expert on hell who has returned to tell about it; hence, it is the sun who is the immortal authority on the afterlife. Graves relates the meaning of hell within the mythos:

> The word astronomers use to indicate the sun in its high point of ascension is perihelion. Now you may notice there is a Hell in this word (peri-*hel*-ion); at least it can be traced to Hell, or Hell to it. *Hel*ion, the last part of this word was pronounced by the Greeks *Elios*, and is synonymous with Acheron, which is generally translated Hell. So that we have "peri," which means around, about, and "helion," *Hell*—that is, the sun roundabout Hell.[26]

Basically, the concepts of eternal heaven and hell have been utilized to suit the needs of the manipulating priests, who sell their wares by means of greed for heaven and fear of hell. As Doane says:

> *Heaven* was born of the sky, and nurtured by cunning priests, who made man a coward and a slave. *Hell* was built by priests, and nurtured by the fears and servile fancies of man during the ages when dungeons of torture were a recognized part of every government, and when God was supposed to be an infinite tyrant, with infinite resources of vengeance.[27]

The Holy Ghost

In many cultures, the Holy Ghost was considered female, as Sophia, Sapientia, or Hokmah—Wisdom—"but the patriarchy masculinized it."[28] As Christ was the sun, the Holy Ghost was also the moon, which was often considered female.[29]

Although the Holy Ghost is a cherished concept, representing God's very spirit and goodness, Wheless remarks:

> The "Holy Ghost" itself, it is claimed by the Bible and the Church, inspired and decreed by positive command all the bloody murders and tortures by the priests from Moses to the last one committed; and the spirit of them lives and is but hibernating to-day. The Holy God of Israel, whose name is Merciful, thus decreed on Sinai: "He that sacrificeth to any gods [elohim], save unto Yahweh only, he shall be utterly destroyed." (Ex. xxii, 20).[30]

The Holy Grail

The cup or chalice used by Christ in the biblical tale to convey "his blood" was, like so many other "relics," considered to contain magical powers of the highest kind. Thus, the "Holy Grail" became the object of much attention and many bloody "quests" for those seeking such powers. Of course, there was no "real" Grail, but this fact did not stop anyone from either looking for it or claiming they already possessed it. Of the frenzy surrounding the Holy Grail, Walker says:

> If the Grail was nothing more than the cup of Christ's blood, then there was no reason for the great Quest at all. The cup of Christ's blood was readily available to all, in every chapel; and even though it was called a holy sacrament, its discovery somehow lacked thrills. As matters turn out, to Christianize the Grail was to neutralize the magnetism of its secret nature.[31]

Naturally, the Grail myth existed prior to the Christian era. As Walker also relates:

> The real origins of the Holy Grail were not Christian but pagan. The Grail was first Christianized in Spain from a sacred tradition of the Moors. Like the Celts' holy Cauldron of Regeneration, which it resembled, the blood-filled vessel was a womb symbol

meaning rebirth in the Oriental or Gnostic sense of reincarnation. Its connotation was feminine, not masculine.[32]

The temple where the Grail was kept was in actuality not localized on Earth but in the heavens, surrounded by the 72 "chapels" or decans of the zodiac. Graham gives the "deep astrological" meaning of the Grail:

> The first decanate of Leo is the Crater, or Cup, the solar crucible; the second is Centaurus, the soldier on horseback. It was of this Cup the Sun of God drank, and it was this soldier that bound him and led him away to be crucified on Golgotha, Egypt, Earth.[33]

The Holy Land

Rather than being a designation of a particular place on Earth, the "Holy Land" is the direction of east, "the place of coming forth," where the sun god Horus appears.[34]

Ichthys, The Fish

As we have seen, Jesus is the solar avatar of the Age of Pisces, the Fishes. Dujardin relates the origin of the Fish and its identification with Jesus:

> This title [Ichthus, the Fish] was a survival of the primitive cults of the time when the gods had the form of animals . . . The following facts are significant: (1) Jesus is actually called the Fish, Ichthus. (2) He is represented in the form of a fish in the Catacombs. (3) Tertullian calls him "our fish." (4) Heretical sects worshipped him as "the serpent," into which animal Jahvehism transformed the primitive fish-god . . . (5) The cult of the fish is attested by the story of the loaves and fishes in the Gospels. . . . The patriarch Joshua, who was plainly an ancient god of Palestine and bore the same name as the god of Christianity, is called the son of Nun, which signifies "son of the fish."[35]

Augustine said of Jesus, "he is a fish of the living water,"[36] to which Massey might remark, "as was said of Horus."

The Lamb of God

As we have seen, a number of godmen around the world have been considered the "Lamb of God." This ubiquitous designation is not reflective of hordes of historical saviors but is another aspect of the mythos, dealing with the sun in the Age of Aries. As noted, during the Age of Taurus, the Bull motif was everpresent, while in Aries it was the Lamb: "Afterward the Ram or Lamb became an object of adoration, when, in his turn, he opened the equinox, to deliver the world from the wintry reign of darkness and evil."[37]

When the sun was in Taurus, the bull was sacrificed, and in Aries, it was the lamb or ram. Christianity was created as the sun moved into Pisces, hence the fish symbol and the fisherman motif. Yet, the old title of "Lamb of God" remained attached to Christ, and at Easter orthodox Christians still slaughter lambs, in holding with the ancient Pagan rituals. The slaughter of fish, apparently, is not bloody enough for blood-atonement purposes. Since the symbol of the coming Age of Aquarius is a "man carrying a pitcher of water" (Lk. 22:10), we certainly hope religionists will not begin to sacrifice bottled water deliverers or waiters.

The Logia (Sayings), Sermon on the Mount, Beatitudes and Parables

Over the millennia much has been made of the "Sayings" or Logia of Jesus, also known as the "Sayings of the Savior," "Sayings of the Sage" ("Logoi Sophon"), the "Gnomologue," the "Oracles of Jesus/the Savior," the "Hebrew Oracles," the "Oracles of Matthew," which are one of the two main subdivisions of the gospels, the other being the narrative. The sayings or logia constituted one of the many shared texts used separately by the evangelists in the creation of the gospels. This logia collection was eventually publicized as the "Gospel of Q," or just plain "Q," for "Quelle" in German, meaning "source." Q scholarship reveals the logia themselves are composed of three separate texts, Q^1, Q^2 and Q^3. Recognizing that virtually the entire gospel story is mythical, Q scholarship attempts to find the "real" Jesus in a handful of sayings represented by Q^1. It should be noted that the initial logia, constituting Q^1, do not have any Jewish affiliation except the word Solomon, and that Q^2 and Q^3 only mention the Pharisees and not Sadducees.

In finding a "historical Jesus" in Q^1, historicizers are thus left with a "man" who was "was first remembered as a Cynic sage and only later imagined as a prophet who uttered apocalyptic warnings."[38] However, in reducing Jesus to a handful of logia we are left with nearly verbatim sayings from manuscripts preceding the Christian era, demonstrating that this Q Jesus already existed, non-historically and mystically for centuries if not millennia. In other words, the Logia Iesou, as they are called in Greek, are not, as has been supposed, the "genuine" sayings of the "historical" Jesus but represent orally transmitted traditions common in the various brotherhoods and mystery schools long before Christianity was created.

The logia are in fact repetitions of the sayings of Horus, as the Word, or Iu-em-hept, 3,000 years before the Christian version.[39] As Massey states:

The "sayings" were common property in the mysteries ages before they were ever written down. . . . The "logia" in the twenty-fifth chapter of Matthew reproduce not only the sayings, but also the scenery of the Last Judgment in the Great Hall of Justice, represented in the [Egyptian] Book of the Dead.[40]

Just as the gospel writers and church fathers claimed the logia or "oracles" were recorded by Matthew, so were the sayings of Osiris recorded by the scribe Taht-*Matiu*. In addition, the logia are those of Dionysus, serving as part of "the mysteries" found at Samothrace, for one.

Some of the sayings constitute the famous "Sermon on the Mount," also not original with Christ. As noted, Horus delivered a Sermon on the Mount, and there is within the Egyptian Hermetic or Trismesgistic tradition a discourse called "The Secret Sermon on the Mount."[41] The Egyptian Sermon sayings also found their way into the Old Testament. As Robertson says, "As for the Sermon on the Mount, of which so much is made, it is no more than a patchwork of utterances found in the Old Testament."[42] Carpenter elaborates:

The "Sermon on the Mount" which, with the "Lord's Prayer" embedded in it, forms the great and accepted repository of "Christian" teaching and piety, is well known to be a collection of sayings from pre-Christian writings, including the Psalms, Isaiah, Ecclesiasticus, the *Secrets of Enoch*, the *Shemonehesreh* (a book of Hebrew prayers), and others . . . [43]

Potter adds:

Among the words of Jesus, you will recognize that much of the "Sermon on the Mount," especially the fifth chapter of Matthew, also the thirteenth of Mark and its parallels in the other gospels, sometimes called "The Little Apocalypse," seem almost verbatim quotations from the Books of Enoch, the Book of Jubilees, and the Testament of the Twelve Patriarchs.[44]

A number of the elements or beatitudes of the Sermon are found in the doctrines of the pre-Christian Nazarenes, such as "Blessed are the poor in spirit, for theirs is the kingdom of heaven." As Massey states:

And these, for example, are amongst the "sayings" in the Book of the Nazarenes. "Blessed are the peacemakers, the just, and 'faithful.'" "Feed the hungry; give drink to the thirsty; clothe the naked." "When thou makest a gift, seek no witness whereof, to mar thy bounty. Let thy right hand be ignorant of the gifts of the left." Such were common to all the Gnostic Scriptures, going back to the Egyptian.

The sayings of the Lord were pre-historic, as the sayings of David (who was an earlier Christ), the sayings of Horus the Lord, of Elija the Lord, of Mana the Lord, of Christ the Lord, as the divine directions conveyed by the ancient teachings. As the "Sayings of the Lord" they were collected in Aramaic to become the *nuclei* of the earliest Christian gospel according to Matthew. So says Papias. At a later date they were put forth as the original revelation of a personal teacher, and were made the foundation of the historical fiction concocted in the four gospels that were canonized at last.

No matter who the plagiarist may be, the teaching now held to be divine was drawn from older human sources, and palmed off under false pretenses. . . . Nothing new remained to be inculcated by the Gospel of the new teacher, who is merely made to repeat the old sayings with a pretentious air of supernatural authority; the result being that the true sayings of old are, of necessity, conveyed to later times in a delusive manner. . . . The most important proclamations assigned to Jesus turned out to be false. The kingdom of God was not at hand; the world was not nearing its end; the catastrophe foretold never occurred; the second coming was no more actual than the first; the lost sheep of Israel are not yet saved.[45]

Many of the concepts contained in the logia/sayings, which are held up by Christian defenders as the core of Jesus's teachings and a reflection of his goodness and compassion, can also be found in the Vedas as spoken by the compassionate Krishna and in the Dhammapada attributed to the equally compassionate Buddha, as well as in the Tao Te Ching of the Chinese sage Lao Tzu (6th century BCE).[46]

Likewise, a number of Jesus's parables were derived from Buddhism and from the very ancient Indian sect of Jainism, such as those of the prodigal son and the sower.[47] As Larson says, "We must thus summarize the basic teachings of Jesus, none of which were original to Him."[48]

The Logia Iesou constituted the sayings element of the mythos found in mystery schools that could be considered part of a "salvation cult," whose practitioners were "spiritual physicians" in the business of "saving souls." Once the code of secrecy regarding the logia had been broken, numerous books were written containing them. Bishop Papias purportedly published a five-volume "Exegeses/Expositions on the Sayings of the Lord," thus demonstrating that the sayings were a monolithic body separate from the narrative. It is inexplicable that such a monumental work by an early Christian father was "lost," except that it had to be destroyed because it revealed the Savior as absolutely non-historical.

The Lord's Prayer

As concerns the supposed originality of the "Lord's Prayer," which is presented as having come clear out of the blue from the very mouth of the Lord Himself, Wheless says it best:

> Like the whole "Sermon on the Mount," the Prayer is a composite of ancient sayings of the Scripture strung together to form it, as the marginal cross-references show throughout.

We might add that the "Scripture" referred to by Wheless is not only from the Old Testament but is part of the ancient mythos/ritual: ". . . the Lord's Prayer was a collection of sayings from the Talmud, many derived from earlier Egyptian prayers to Osiris."[49] Walker also relates that the Lord's Prayer was once the Lady's Prayer:

> The plea for daily bread incorporated into the Lord's Prayer must have been a plea to the Goddess in earlier times, for she was always the giver of bread, the Grain Mother . . . [50]

The Logos or Word

Jesus is called the "Word" or, "Logos," which, although it appears mysterious and mystical to the uninitiated, is actually commonplace in Greek parlance, as it has many meanings, including "word," "speech," "rumor" and "reason." The logos is in actuality a primitive concept, reflecting merely the way in which God created the world, i.e., through speech. The Logos concept is not new with Christianity but is applied to a number of older deities in mythologies from the Mediterranean to China. Pike relates:

> The Word is also found in the Phoenician Creed. As in all those of Asia, a Word of God, written in starry characters, by the planetary Divinities, and communicated by the Demi-Gods, as a profound mystery, to the higher classes of the human race, to be communicated by them to mankind, created the world.[51]

Of the Logos-Jesus concept in the Gospel of John, Wheless says:

> As there can be no more positive and convincing proof that the Christ was and is a Pagan Myth—the old Greek "Logos" of Heraclitus and the Philosophers revamped by the Greek priest who wrote the first chapter of the "Gospel according to St. John" and worked up into the "Incarnate Son" of the old Hebrew God for Christian consumption as the most sacred Article of the Christian Faith and Theology. . . Thus confessedly [in the *Catholic Encyclopedia*] is the Divine Revelation of the "Word made flesh" a Pagan-Jewish Myth, and the very Pagan Demiurge is the Christian Christ—"Very God"—and the "Second Person of the Blessed Trinity."[52]

Lucifer

Although much is made of Lucifer, the "fallen angel," his name only appears translated as such in one verse in the King James bible, at Isaiah 14:12, where he is called "son of the morning." "Lucifer" is also translated as "Day Star, son of Dawn." This passage describes the day star's "fall from heaven" after he attempts to "ascend to heaven; above the stars of God" to set his throne. From this single passage, an enormous tale has taken shape, with all sorts of speculation as to who Lucifer "really" was, including everything from the leader of the devils to that of evil aliens.

Despite all the political intrigue, Lucifer simply means "Light Bearer," and he was in earliest times a sun god, which is why he is called "Day Star, son of morning/dawn." The sun god Lucifer is "cast out of heaven" by the other angels, or stars, as night descends. This god/angel Lucifer is pre-Hebraic, found in Canaan, Egypt and Mesopotamia, and was not originally considered evil. In Dutch, a Lucifer is a match, a purely utilitarian object that brings light and fire. Like the many gods of other cultures, Lucifer was vilified by the Christians so they could raise their own god above him. Ironically, since both are the day or morning star, Jesus and Lucifer are in fact one and the same.

The Lucifer myth can also be found in the Greek story of the "son of the sun," Phaeton, who was cast out of heaven by his Father after committing the crime of hubris. The story of Vulcan, the Roman solar god, is similar to the Lucifer myth, as he too is cast out of heaven by the gods as darkness descends.

Melchizedek

The mysterious king of Salem, Melchizedek, or Adonizedek, as he is also called in the Book of Jasher, is mentioned in the OT as the priest of the Most High God (El Elyon) who blessed Abraham. In the Epistle to the Hebrews, Jesus is named as a mere priest "after the order of Melchizedek," a passage serving to establish the Order of Melchizedek as the ultimate authority, beyond Abraham and Jesus. In fact, the Christian Gnostics considered Melchizedek a savior-god higher than Jesus: "Melchizedek was the savior for angels, while Christ was only the savior for men."[53]

Like that of so many other biblical characters, the identity of Melchizedek can be found in the pre-Yahwist cultures of the Levant. As Walker states, "Jeru-salem was 'the House of Peace,' or of the god Salem, whose earlier city was ruled by Melchizedek (Genesis 14), the 'King of Light' called Melek or Molech in Phoenicia."[54] Molech is the sun and fire god, originally from Persia and India, and worshipped by the Canaanites.[55] The

Molech/Melek cult also flourished in Paul's purported hometown of Tarsus, as Heracles-Melkart.[56] As stated, Solomon and other Israelites worshipped Moloch/Molech/Melek/Milcom/Melchom:

> Moloch was a god of the Ammonites, also worshiped among the Israelites. Solomon built a temple to him, on the Mount of Olives, and human sacrifices were offered to him.[57]

Sacrifice to Moloch/Molech was by burning, and when the "sons of Judah" thus incinerated their children (Jer. 7:31), drums were beaten and instruments were played to drown out the screams.

Though vilified by the Yahwists, as Walker says, "For a while, Molech was identified with Yahweh . . . Levite priests eventually distinguished Yahweh from Molech and forbade the latter's worship (Leviticus 18:21)."[58]

The baptism of Molech or Melchom was likewise by fire, which is why Christ, as high priest of the Order of Melchizedek, was said to baptize by fire. It is this baptism by fire, as well as immolation by fire, as in burnt offerings, that distinguishes the Order of Melchizedek; hence, when mention of the Order is made in the Bible, it serves as a reference to these rites, the practitioners of which are considered the "true" priesthood. Indeed, offering to Molech is permitted to this day in the Talmud, although it is debated as to whether or not one may pass the child through fire.[59]

The Nativity

The birth celebration or nativity of the great savior existed as a ritual long prior to the Christian era. As Frazer says:

> The ritual of the nativity, as it appears to have been celebrated in Syria and Egypt, was remarkable. The celebrants retired into certain inner shrines, from which at midnight they issued a loud cry, "The Virgin has brought forth! The light is waxing!" The Egyptians even represented the new-born sun by the image of an infant which on his birthday, the winter solstice, they brought forth and exhibited to his worshippers.[60]

Hazelrigg explains the meaning within the mythos of the nativity and the rest of the sacred king drama:

> The Nativity, the Betrayal, the Crucifixion, and the Resurrection are but quarterly stages in the mystic journey, expressed as a geometrical ration in natural physics—ever the same whether applied to the four quarters of the day, the four lunar phases, the four cardinal points or seasons in the solar revolution . . . [61]

The Sabbath

The Sabbath predates the Jewish religion and is found in the Middle East and India, where it signified the seventh-day rest of the Goddess Durga.[62] Ignorant of its origins, the various Christian sects have been squabbling for centuries as to when the Sabbath should be observed, as ordained by the Jewish god Yahweh. The "purists" feel that Sabbath is to be observed on Saturday, rather than the "Pagan" day of Sunday adopted by the "corrupt" Catholic Church; however, Saturday is also a "Pagan" day, named for "Saturn." As Doane relates:

> The planet *Saturn* very early became the chief deity of Semitic religion. Moses consecrated the number seven to him . . . "The *Seventh* day was sacred to *Saturn* throughout the east." . . . "Saturn's day was made sacred to God, and the planet is now called cochab shabbath, 'The Sabbath Star.' The sanctification of the Sabbath is clearly connected with the word Shabua or Sheba, i.e., *seven*."[63]

The Second Coming/Day of Judgment

Although billions of people over the centuries have been waiting endlessly for the Second Coming of Jesus, believing that it is a very unusual event, the "second coming" has been expected of numerous savior-gods, including Krishna, Buddha, Bacchus, Quetzalcoatl and others around the world. The same can be said of the end of the world, the millennium and the Day of Judgment. Of the Day of Judgment, Doane relates: "Prof. Carpenter, referring to the Egyptian Bible—which is by far the most ancient of all holy books—says: 'In the "Book of Dead," there are used the very phrases we find in the New Testament, *in connection with the day of judgment.*'"[64] The "Second Coming," in fact, is the return of the sun in a new precessional age.

The Seventy/Seventy-Two

The number of disciples is represented variously in the gospels, from 12 to 70 to 72. This numerical trio can be explained by the mythos and not as history. To begin with, "72" was often rounded off to 70, so the two numbers are interchangeable. Tradition holds that there are 72 names of God,[65] which is appropriate, since 72 is yet another sacred number, the reason why there are also 72 nations in the 10th chapter of Genesis. Like Jesus, Confucius (6th century BCE) had 72 initiated disciples.[66] Furthermore, the 72 are the same accomplices of Set who plotted the death of Osiris.

The 72 actually represent the decans or dodecani, divisions of the zodiacal circle into 5° each, also considered constellations. In addition, it takes 72 years for the precession of the equinoxes to move one degree. As noted, the story of Jacob's Ladder with 72 ascending and descending angels is actually a reflection of the zodiac and the angles of the decans. Furthermore, the magical pentagram or pentacle is made from the division of the decans. Regarding the pentacle, the number 72 and the legendary 72 translators of the Hebrew bible into Greek, Walker says:

> To draw a pentacle, one divides a circle into five arcs of seventy-two degrees each. Seventy-two is the prime magic number . . . So magical was 72 that one of the most durable myths about the origin of the Bible called it the Book of the Seventy-Two (Septuagint), claiming that it had been translated from Hebrew to Greek in the third century B.C. by seventy-two scholars simultaneously, and that each version was precisely the same as all seventy-one others. This silly story was an article of Christian faith throughout the Middle Ages.[67]

In Gnostic texts, the chariot of Ezekiel is the wheel of the zodiac with the 72 decans, representing the "chariot of the Sun." Doresse relates the Gnostic interpretation: "The chariot, we are told, has been taken for a model by the seventy-two gods who govern the seventy-two languages of the peoples."[68]

Transubstantiation

The doctrine of transubstantiation, found at 1 Corinthians 10-12, represents the miraculous transformation of bread and wine into the body and blood of Christ. However, this sort of magical ritual was practiced around the world in a variety of forms eons before the Christian era and is, therefore, in no way original to Christianity:

> . . . the ancient Mexicans, even before the arrival of Christianity, were fully acquainted with the doctrine of transubstantiation and acted upon it in the solemn rites of their religion. They believed that by consecrating bread their priests could turn it into the very body of their god, so that all who thereupon partook of the consecrated bread entered into a mystic communion with the deity by receiving a portion of his divine substance into themselves. The doctrine of transubstantiation, or the magical conversion of bread into flesh, was also familiar with the Aryans of ancient India long before the spread and even the rise of Christianity.[69]

This practice has been considered barbaric and savage by non-Catholic Christians and other religionists, not to mention ludicrous by nonreligionists. The pre-Christian ancients knew that the transubstantiation was allegorical, not actual: "'When we call corn Ceres and wine Bacchus,' says Cicero, 'we use a common figure of speech; but do you imagine that anybody is so insane as to believe that they thing he feeds upon is a god?'"[70]

The Trinity

The trinity or triune deity is yet another aspect of the ubiquitous mythos, found in countless other cultures long prior to the Christian era. Obviously, then, the concept did not originate with Jesus; in fact, it was not adopted into Christianity until the Council of Nicea in 325. Like so many aspects of Christianity, the trinity was originally found in the Egyptian religion. As Churchward says:

> Such mysteries as the Trinity, the Incarnation, and the Virgin Birth, the Transfiguration on the Mount, the Passion, Death, Burial, Resurrection and Ascension, Transubstantiation and Baptismal Regeneration, were all extant in the mysteries of Amenta with Horus or Iu-em-Hotep as the Egyptian Jesus.[71]

Jacolliot notes that the Trinity is also of Indian origin: "The Trinity in Unity, rejected by Moses, became afterwards the foundation of Christian theology, which incontestably acquired it from India."

Over the millennia, the trinity took different forms: all-female, all-male and mixed. The earliest trinities in many places were all-female. As Walker relates:

> From the earliest ages, the concept of the Great Goddess was a trinity and the model for all subsequent trinities, female, male or mixed. . . . Even though Brahmans evolved a male trinity of Brahma, Vishnu, and Shiva to play these parts [of Creator, Preserver and Destroyer], Tantric scriptures insisted that the Triple Goddess had created these gods in the first place. . . . The Middle East had many trinities, most originally female. As time went on, one or two members of the triad turned male. The usual pattern was Father-Mother-Son, the Son figure envisioned as a Savior. . . . Among Arabian Christians there was apparently a holy trinity of God, Mary, and Jesus, worshipped as an interchangeable replacement for the Egyptian trinity of Osiris, Isis, and Horus. . . [72]

In the solar mythos, the trinity also represents the sun in three stages: Newborn (dawn), mature (full-grown at 12 noon), and "old and dying, at the end of the day (going back to the Father)."[73]

The trinity is even found in Peru, a fact that prompted the perturbed Rev. Father Acosta to remark:

> It is strange that the devil after his manner has brought a Trinity into idolatry, for the three images of the sun called Apomti, Churunti, and Intiquaoqui, signify Father and Lord Sun, the Son Sun, and the Brother Sun.

In reality these infamous "devil" comments are reflective of sheer cultural and racial bigotry, not to mention the appalling ignorance and stupidity of those supposedly entrusted by the "omniscient and omnipotent Lord God" with the instruction of the entire human race.

Thus, we discover the most important tenets, doctrines and other elements of the gospel story and Christian religion are unoriginal and mythological. Indeed, the onion of the "historical Jesus" has been peeled, and there remains no core to be found, only the pre-Christian mythos and ritual.

---

1. Walker, *WEMS*, 195.
2. Higgins, II, 88.
3. Walker, *WEMS*, 232-3.
4. Walker, *WEMS*, 40.
5. Massey, *EBD*, 80.
6. Doane, 824.
7. Massey, *HJMC*, 39.
8. Doane, 226.
9. Doane, 197.
10. Walker, *WEMS*, 188.
11. A. Churchward, 9.
12. A. Churchward, 363.
13. "The Naked Truth."
14. Carpenter, 183.
15. Walker, *WEMS*, 188.
16. Higgins, I, 219.
17. ben Yehoshua, (Emphasis added.)
18. Massey, *HJMC*, 35.
19. Jackson, 58.
20. Walker, *WEMS*, 78-9.
21. Frazer, 681.
22. Jackson, 197-8.
23. Eusebius, 252-3.
24. Massey, *EBD*, 107-9.
25. Doane, 214-5.
26. Graves, *BS*, 78-9.
27. Doane, 391.
28. Walker, *WDSSO*, 219.
29. Walker, *WDSSO*, 287.
30. Wheless, *IISGW*
31. Walker, *WEMS*, 354.
32. Walker, *WEMS*, 354.
33. Graham, 354-5.
34. A. Churchward, 290.
35. Dujardin, 53-4.
36. Higgins, I, 636.
37. Pike, 448.
38. Mack, 47.
39. Massey, *HJMC*, 151.
40. Massey, *HJMC*, 152-3.
41. Mead, *DJL*.
42. Robertson, 64.

43. Carpenter, 213.
44. Potter, 169-70.
45. Massey, *GHC*, 4-11.
46. Steele, "Was Jesus a Taoist?"
47. Larson, 349.
48. Larson, 411.
49. Walker, *WEMS*, 469.
50. Walker, *WDSSO*, 482.
51. Pike, 268.
52. Wheless, 155-6.
53. Walker, *WEMS*, 631.
54. Walker, *WEMS*, 885.
55. Higgins, I, 82.
56. Walker, *WEMS*, 1003.
57. Doane, 108 fn.
58. Walker, *WEMS*, 1003.
59. Sanhedrin, 64a-64b; Soncino Press, 437-441.
60. Frazer, 416.
61. Hazelrigg, 16.
62. Walker, *WDSSO*, 191.
63. Doane, 393 fn.
64. Doane, 245.
65. Higgins, I, 780.
66. Higgins, I, 789.
67. Walker, *WDSSO*, 73.
68. Doresse, 166.
69. Frazer, 568.
70. Frazer, 578.
71. A. Churchward, 393.
72. Walker, *WEMS*, 1018.
73. Leedom, 200.

 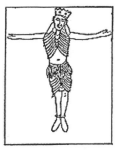

Pre-Christian Asian
crucifixes of Krishna
(Doane)

Hercules bending under
the Cross made of
the two pillars of Heaven
(Doane)

Christ as Lamb of God
(Biedermann)

The Patriarchs and Saints are the Gods of Other Cultures

As demonstrated, Christianity was built upon a long line of myths from a multitude of nations and basically represents the universal astrological mythos and ritual. In its creation was used a typical mythmaking device: To wit, when an invading culture takes over its predecessors, it often vilifies the preceding gods and goddesses or demotes them to lesser gods, patriarchs, prophets, kings, heroes and/or saints. Such mythmaking is found throughout the Old Testament as well, as previously noted regarding the "prophets" Daniel, Esther and Deborah, who were ancient gods of other cultures. As also demonstrated, prior to the vilification of the Baals of Canaan, Yahweh himself was a Baal. In fact, the Old Testament actually records the epics of Canaanite gods, as was evidenced with the discovery in 1975 of 20,000 clay tablets nearly 4,500 years old in the ruins of the large city of Ebla at Tell Mardikh in northwestern Syria. Of Ebla, John Fulton says, "It existed 1,000 years before David and Solomon and was destroyed by the Akkadians in around 1600 BC."[1] The language recorded on these tablets is old Canaanite, very similar to biblical Hebrew, written in the Sumerian cuneiform script. These tablets contain hundreds of place names, a number of which are found in the Old Testament, including "Urusalima," i.e., Jerusalem. They also contain the names of Hebrew "patriarchs" who, according to the Bible, would not exist for hundreds to over a thousand years later, such as "Ab-ra-mu (Abraham), E-sa-um (Esau), Ish-ma-ilu (Ishmael), even Is-ra-ilu (Israel), and from later periods, names like Da-'u'dum (David) and Sa-'u-lum (Saul)."[2] The tablets also contain the Canaanite creation and flood myths from which the very similar biblical versions were obviously plagiarized. In reality, the Israelites were mainly Canaanites, passing along the myths of their ancestors, which were corrupted over the centuries.

When the Yahwists imposed monotheism on both the Levantine peoples and their scriptures, they subjugated the wide variety of Canaanite Baals under their "one Lord" and turned these "foreign" gods into "patriarchs" and assorted other characters, good and bad. As Dujardin says:

> Where Judaism fully succeeded, the ancient Baals of Palestine were transformed into heroic servants of Jahveh; where it gained only a partial victory, they became secondary gods. . . . Many of the old Baals of Palestine were assimilated by Judaism, which converted them into heroes in the cause of Jahveh, and in fact many scholars agree that the patriarchs of the Bible are the ancient gods of Palestine.[3]

Dujardin further outlines the process by which "Baals" or "foreign" gods were changed into Hebrew patriarchs, kings, prophets and heroes:

1. The ancient divinities of Palestine are transformed by the Bible into historical characters and turned into servants of Jahveh.

2. Their sanctuaries are turned into sanctuaries raised by them to Jahveh, or into tombs where they are buried, or into monuments of their exploits. Sometimes, however, their names, or those of the animals that they had been originally, were given to a place, and were no longer used except to denote it.

3. The names of the clans, derived from these divinities and from the names of animals that they had originally been, became the names of persons, and were introduced into the interminable genealogies invented to glorify great families of the Jewish state. All this was by way of assimilation.

4. Proscription was effected by devoting to abomination all the cults that offered resistance.

5. Also by making impure such animals as had originally been ancient gods, by forbidding the eating of them, or by putting a curse on them.

6. And by transforming some of the rites and myths of these cults into historical legends.[4]

In this manner, ancient gods of other nations were mutated into not only biblical individuals but also tribes and nations.

Noah and the Flood

The fable of Noah purports to be the true story of the progenitor of the human race; however, like so many other biblical characters, Noah is a myth, found earlier in India, Egypt, Babylon, Sumer and other places. The fact is that there have been floods and deluge stories in many different parts of the world, including but not limited to the Middle East. As Churchward says:

> There was never any *one Great Deluge* as in the Biblical rendering. . . . at least ten Great Deluges have taken place at each glacial epoch, when the snow and ice have melted. . . . There was also a great inundation once a year—when the Nile came down in flood. There is a portrayal on the monuments where Num is in his boat or Ark waiting for this flood.[5]

Regarding the ubiquitous flood myth, Walker says:

> The biblical flood story, the "deluge," was a late offshoot of a cycle of flood myths known everywhere in the ancient world. Thousands of years before the Bible was written, an ark was built by the Sumerian Ziusudra. In Akkad, the flood hero's name

was Atrakhasis. In Babylon, he was Uta-Napishtim, the only mortal to become immortal. In Greece he was Deucalion, who repopulated the earth after the waters subsided [and after the ark landed on Mt. Parnassos] . . . In Armenia, the hero was Xisuthros—a corruption of Sumerian Ziusudra—whose ark landed on Mount Ararat. According to the original Chaldean account, the flood hero was told by his god, "Build a vessel and finish it. By a deluge I will destroy substance and life. Cause thou to go up into the vessel the substance of all that has life."[6]

Xisuthros or Ziusudra was considered the "10th king," while Noah was the "10th patriarch." Noah's "history" can also be found in India, where there is a "tomb of Nuh" near the river Gagra in the district of Oude or Oudh, which evidently is related to Judea and Judah. The "ark-preserved" Indian Noah was also called "Menu." Noah is also called "Nnu" and "Naue," as in "Joshua son of Nun/Jesus son of Naue," meaning not only fish but also water, as in the waters of heaven. Furthermore, the word Noah, or Noé, is the same as the Greek νους, which means "mind," as in "noetics," as does the word Menu or Menes, as in "mental." In Hebrew, the word for "ark" is *THB*, as in Thebes, such that the Ark of Noah is equivalent to the Thebes of Menes, the legendary first king of the Egyptians, from whose "history" the biblical account also borrowed.

Obviously, then, Noah's famous "ark," which misguided souls have sought upon the earth, is a motif found in other myths. As Doane relates, "The image of Osiris of Egypt was by the priests shut up in a sacred ark on the 17th of Athyr (Nov. 13th), the very day and month on which Noah is said to have entered his ark."[7] Noah is, in fact, another solar myth, and the ark represents the sun entering into the "moon-ark," the Egyptian "argha," which is the crescent or arc-shaped lunette or lower quarter of the moon. This "argha of Noah" is the same as Jason's "Argonaut" and "arghanatha" in Sanskrit.[8] Noah's ark and its eight "sailors" are equivalent to the heavens, earth and the seven "planets," i.e., those represented by the days of the week. As to the "real" Noah's ark, it should be noted that it was a custom, in Scotland for one, to create stone "ships" on mounts in emulation of the mythos, such that any number of these "arks" may be found on Earth.

Like Noah, the Sumerian Ziusudra had three sons, including one named "Japetosthes," essentially the same as Noah's son Japheth, also related to Pra-japati[9] or Jvapeti, son of the Indian Menu, whose other sons possessed virtually the same names as those of Noah, i.e., Shem and Ham. As Hazelrigg says, "These parallel the Hindu version of the same myth, wherein *Menu Satyvrah* figures as Noah, and *Sherma, Charma,* and *Jvapeti* are easily identified with the offspring."[10]

In the Bible, Noah's sons are depicted as the "fathers" of various nations and races: Shem is the progenitor of the Semites; Japheth, the Aryans; and Ham, the "Hamites," or Africans. The story has been turned into racist propaganda, as the Semites are considered the best and Japhethites suitable enough to "dwell in the tents of the Semites," while the Hamites are to serve as slaves to the other two, as a punishment for Ham ridiculing the drunken, naked Noah. Not only is such a punishment absurdly harsh, but Noah is not a historical character; thus, a fable has served to justify slavery.

The sons of Noah, of course, are also not historical, as Shem "was actually a title of Egyptian priests of Ra."[11] The three sons of Noah, in fact, represent the three divisions of the heavens into 120° each.[12] As characters in the celestial mythos, Noah corresponds to the sun and Shem to the moon, appropriate since the Semitic Jews were moon-worshippers.

Abraham and Sarah

Although Abraham is held up as the patriarch of the Hebrews and Arabs, the original Abraham and Sarah were the same as the Indian god Brahma and goddess Sarasvati, the "Queen of Heaven," and the story of Abraham's migration is reflective of a Brahmanical tribe leaving India at the end of the Age of Taurus. This identification of Abraham and Sarah as Indian gods did not escape the notice of the Jesuit missionaries in India; indeed, it was they who first pointed it out.[13] Concerning the patriarch and his wife, Walker states:

> This name meaning "Father Brahm" seems to have been a Semitic version of India's patriarchal god Brahma; he was also the Islamic Abrama, founder of Mecca. But Islamic legends say Abraham was a late intruder into the shrine of the Kaaba. He bought it from priestesses of its original Goddess. Sarah, "the Queen," was one of the Goddess's titles, which became a name of Abraham's biblical "wife." . . . In the tale of Isaac's near-killing, Abraham assumed the role of sacrificial priest in the druidic style, to wash Jehovah's sacred trees with the Blood of the Son: an ancient custom, of which the sacrifice of Jesus was only a late variant.[14]

Brahma and Sarasvati were apparently also turned into the Indian patriarch Adjigarta and his wife Parvati. Like Abram/Abraham, in the Indian version Adjigarta beseeches the Lord for an heir and eventually takes a young red goat to sacrifice on the mountain, where the Lord speaks to him. As in the biblical tale, a stranger approaches Parvati, who gives him refreshments, and tells her that she will bring forth a son named Viashagagana (Isaac), "the reward of Alms." When the child is 12, the Lord commands Adjigarta to sacrifice him, which the father faithfully begins to do, until the Lord stops him and blesses him as the progenitor of a virgin who will be divinely impregnated. Of the near-sacrifice by Abraham, Graham says, "This too is an old story and like so many others in the Bible, originated in India. Siva, like Abraham, was about to sacrifice his son on a funeral pyre, but his God, repenting, miraculously provided a rhinoceros instead."[15]

Abraham also seems to have been related to the Persian evil god, Ahriman, whose name was originally Abriman. Furthermore, Graham states, "The Babylonians also had their Abraham, only they spelt it Abarama. He was a farmer and mythological contemporary with Abraham."[16]

Hazelrigg relates that Abraham is also identified with the planet Saturn:

> "The Semitic name, Abraham," says Dr. Wilder, "appears to be made from the two words *Ab* and *Ram*, thus signifying 'The Father on High.' This, in astral theology, is a designation of the planet Saturn, or Kronos, and of the divinity bearing those names." . . . "Where, then, shall we find the difference between the patriarch Abraham and the god Saturn? Saturn was the son of Terra, and Abraham was the son of Terah." . . . "Our Father which art in heaven" was a direct prayer to this paternal principle, and for this reason Christ (Sun) is expressly denominated as the Son of Abraham, or *Son of the Father*, because the Sun is the center of a system about which Saturn describes an encompassing circle.[17]

Regarding details of the Abramic story, Walker says:

> The biblical mother-shrine Mamre at Hebron included a sacred oak in a female-symbolic grove. Old Testament scribes pretended it was the home of Abraham, although even in the fourth century A.D. it was still a pagan site, dedicated to the worship of "idols."[18]

Furthermore, Abram's "Ur of the Chaldees" apparently does not originally refer to the Ur in Mesopotamia and to the Middle Eastern Chaldean culture but to an earlier rendition in India, where Higgins, for one, found the proto-Hebraic Chaldee language.

Regarding Sarah, Walker relates that the "original name of Israel meant 'the tribe of Sarah.' Her name was formerly Sara'i, The Queen, a name of the Great Goddess in Nabataean inscriptions. Priests changed her name to Sarah in the sixth century B.C."[19] These stories serve not as chronicles of individuals but of gods and tribes, such that, as Walker further relates, "Sarah was the maternal goddess of the 'Abraham' tribe that formed an alliance with Egypt in the 3rd millennium B.C."[20] Hence the story of Abraham and Sarah in Egypt.

Moses, the Exodus, the Ten Commandments

The legend of Moses, rather than being that of a historical Hebrew lawgiver, is found from the Mediterranean to India, with the character having different names and races, depending on the locale: "Manou" is the Indian legislator. "Nemo the lawgiver," who brought down the tablets from the Mountain of God, hails from Babylon. "Mises" is found in Syria, where he was pulled out of a basket floating in a river. Mises also had tablets of stone upon which laws were written, and a rod with which he did miracles, including parting waters and leading his army across the sea.[21] In addition, "Manes the lawgiver" took the stage in Egypt, and "Minos" was the Cretan reformer.

Jacolliot traces the original Moses to the Indian Manou: "This name of Manou, or Manes . . . is not a substantive, applying to an individual man; its Sanscrit signification is *the man, par excellence*, the legislator. It is a title aspired to by all the leaders of men in antiquity."

Like Moses, Krishna was placed by his mother in a reed boat and set adrift in a river to be discovered by another woman. The Akkadian Sargon also was placed in a reed basket and set adrift to save his life. In fact, "The name Moses is Egyptian and comes from *mo*, the Egyptian word for water, and *uses*, meaning saved from water, in this case, primordial."[22] Thus, this title Moses could be applied to any of these various heroes saved from the water.

Walker elaborates on the Moses myth:

> The Moses tale was originally that of an Egyptian hero, Ra-Harakhti, the reborn sun god of Canopus, whose life story was copied by biblical scholars. The same story was told of the sun hero fathered by Apollo on the virgin Creusa; of Sargon, king of Akkad in 2242 B.C.; and of the mythological twin founders of Rome, among many other baby heroes set adrift in rush baskets. It was a common theme.[23]

Furthermore, Moses's rod is a magical, astrology stick used by a number of other mythical characters. Of Moses's miraculous exploits, Walker also relates:

> Moses's flowering rod, river of blood, and tablets of the law were all symbols of the ancient Goddess. His miracle of drawing water from a rock was first performed by Mother Rhea after she gave birth to Zeus, and by Atalanta with the help of Artemis. His miracle of drying up the waters to travel dry-shod was earlier performed by Isis, or Hathor, on her way to Byblos.[24]

And Higgins states:

> In Bacchus we evidently have Moses. Herodotus says [Bacchus]
> was an Egyptian . . . The Orphic verses relate that he was
> preserved from the waters, in a little box or chest, that he was
> called *Misem* in commemoration of the event; that he was
> instructed in all the secrets of the Gods; and that he had a rod,
> which he changed into a serpent at his pleasure; that he passed
> through the Red Sea dry-shod, *as Hercules subsequently did* . . .
> and that when he went to India, he and his army enjoyed the
> light of the Sun during the night: moreover, it is said, that he
> touched with his magic rod the waters of the great rivers Orontes
> and Hydaspes; upon which those waters flowed back and left
> him a free passage. It is even said that he arrested the course of
> the sun and moon. He wrote his laws on two tablets of stone. He
> was anciently represented with horns or rays on his head.[25]

It has also been demonstrated that the biblical account of the
Exodus could not have happened in history. Of this implausible
story, Mead says:

> . . . Bishop Colenso's . . . mathematical arguments that an army
> of 600,000 men could not very well have been mobilized in a
> single night, that three millions of people with their flocks and
> herds could not very well have drawn water from a single well,
> and hundreds of other equally ludicrous inaccuracies of a similar
> nature, were popular points which even the most unlearned
> could appreciate, and therefore especially roused the ire of
> apologists and conservatives.[26]

The apologists and conservatives, however, have little choice
in the matter, as there is no evidence of the Exodus and
wandering in the desert being historical:

> But even scholars who believe they really happened admit that
> there's no proof whatsoever that the Exodus took place. No
> record of this monumental event appears in Egyptian chronicles
> of the time, and Israeli archaeologists combing the Sinai during
> intense searches from 1967 to 1982—years when Israel occupied
> the peninsula—didn't find a single piece of evidence backing the
> Israelites' supposed 40-year sojourn in the desert.
>   The story involves so many miracles—plagues, the parting of
> the Red Sea, manna from heaven, the giving of the Ten
> Commandments—that some critics feel the whole story has the
> flavor of pure myth. A massive exodus that led to the drowning of
> Pharaoh's army, says Father Anthony Axe, Bible lecturer at
> Jerusalem's Ecole Biblique, would have reverberated politically
> and economically through the entire region. And considering that
> artifacts from as far back as the late Stone Age have turned up
> in the Sinai, it is perplexing that no evidence of the Israelites'
> passage has been found. William Dever, a University of Arizona
> archaeologist, flatly calls Moses a mythical figure. Some scholars
> even insist the story was a political fabrication, invented to unite

the disparate tribes living in Canaan through a falsified heroic past.[27]

Potter sums up the mythicist argument regarding Moses:

The reasons for doubting his existence include, among others, (1) the parallels between the Moses stories and older ones like that of Sargon, (2) the absence of any Egyptian account of such a great event as the Pentateuch asserts the Exodus to have been, (3) the attributing to Moses of so many laws that are known to have originated much later, (4) the correlative fact that great codes never suddenly appear full-born but are slowly evolved, (5) the difficulties of fitting the slavery, the Exodus, and the conquest of Canaan into the known chronology of Egypt and Palestine, and (6) the extreme probability that some of the twelve tribes were never in Egypt at all.[28]

As Churchward states, "Only one mention of the people of Israel occurs by name on all the monuments of Egypt. . . . There is no possibility of identifying this with the Biblical Israelites."[29] He continues:

Israel in Egypt is not an ethnical entity—the story represents the children of Ra in the Lower Egypt of Amenta, built or founded by Ptah, and entirely mythical. . . . The Books of Genesis, Exodus, and Joshua are not intentional forgeries; the subject-matter was already extant in the Egyptian Mysteries, and an exoteric version of the ancient wisdom has been rendered in the form of historic narrative and ethnically applied to the Jews. . . . The chief teachers have always insisted on the allegorical nature of the Pentateuch. Thus it is seen that "Biblical History" has been mainly derived from misappropriated and misinterpreted wisdom of Egypt contained in their mythological and eschatological representation as witnessed by the "Ritual of Ancient Egypt."[30]

The Exodus is indeed not a historical event but constitutes a motif found in other myths. As Pike says, "And when Bacchus and his army had long marched in burning deserts, they were led by a Lamb or Ram into beautiful meadows, and to the Springs that watered the Temple of Jupiter Ammon."[31] And Churchward relates, "Traditions of the Exodus are found in various parts of the world and amongst people of different states of evolution, and these traditions can be explained by the Kamite [Egyptian] rendering only."[32] Indeed, as Massey states, "*'Coming out of Egypt'* is a Kamite expression for ascending from the lower to the upper heavens."[33]

Churchward further outlines the real meaning of the Exodus:

The Exodus or "Coming out of Egypt" first celebrated by the festival of Passover or the transit at the vernal equinox, occurred in the heavens before it was made historical as the migration of the Jews. The 600,000 men who came up out of Egypt as Hebrew warriors in the Book of Exodus are 600,000 inhabitants of Israel in the heavens according to Jewish Kabalah, and the same scenes, events, and personages that appear as mundane in the Pentateuch are celestial in the Book of Enoch.[34]

Churchward continues, also explaining the notorious "plagues":

> If we wish to show that the Jews' version was a fable, we can obtain the proofs in Egypt, and nowhere else. The sufferings of the Chosen People in Egypt, and their miraculous exodus out of it, belong to the celestial allegory . . . The allegory of the Solar drama was performed in the mysteries of the divine nether-world, and had been performed by symbolical representations ages before it was converted into a history of the Jews by the literalizers of the Ancient Symbolism. The tale of the ten plagues of Egypt contains an esoteric version of the tortures inflicted on the guilty in the ten hells of the underworld.[35]

The exodus out of Egypt refers to that out of Amenta, which "is described in the Ritual as consisting of two parts called 'Egypt and the desert land or wilderness.'"[36] Of the ritualistic wandering in the wilderness, Churchward says:

> The Struggle of Set and Horus in the desert lasted forty days, as commemorated in the forty days of the Egyptian Lent, during which time Set, as the power of drought and sterility, made war on Horus in the water and the buried germinating grain. . . . These forty days have been extended into forty years, and confessedly so by the Jews.[37]

In addition, the miraculous "parting of the Red Sea" has forever mystified the naive and credulous masses and scholars alike, who have put forth all sorts of tortured speculation to explain it. The parting and destruction of the hosts of Pharaoh at the Red Sea is not recorded by any known historian, which is understandable, since it is, of course, not historical and is found in other cultures, including in Ceylon/Sri Lanka, out of which the conquering shepherd kings (Pharaohs) were driven across "Adam's Bridge" and drowned.[38] This motif is also found in the Hawaiian and Hottentot versions of the Moses myth, prior to contact with outside cultures.[39] The crossing of the Red Sea is astronomical, expressly stated by Josephus to have occurred at the autumnal equinox,[40] indicating its origin within the mythos.

Moreover, the famed Ten Commandments are simply a repetition of the Babylonian Code of Hammurabi and the Hindu Vedas, among others. As Churchward says:

> The "Law of Moses" were the old Egyptian Laws . . .; this the stele or "Code of Hammurabi" conclusively proves. Moses lived 1,000 years after this stone was engraved.[41]

Walker relates that the "stone tablets of law supposedly given to Moses were copied from the Canaanite god Baal-Berith, 'God of the Covenant.' Their Ten Commandments were similar to the commandments of the Buddhist Decalogue. In the ancient world, laws generally came from a deity on a mountaintop. Zoroaster received the tablets of law from Ahura Mazda on a mountaintop."[42]

Doane sums it up when he says, "Almost all the acts of Moses correspond to those of the Sun-gods."[43] However, the Moses story is also reflective of the stellar cult, once again demonstrating the dual natured "twin" Horus-Set myth and the battle for supremacy between the day and night skies, as well as among the solar, stellar and lunar cults. Churchward relates:

> The Jews strictly are of the Tribe, or Totemic Clan of Judah. The Israelites were not Jews, although some Jews may be Israelites. Moses and his followers have been termed Israelites, but there is no evidence that the "Israelites" were ever in Egypt except once when they made a raid, and were driven back with great slaughter. The Israelites, a mythological name, were a number of Totemic Tribes who originally left Egypt and went to the East during the Stellar Cult.[44]

Joshua

As noted, early Christian father Tertullian made the ridiculous claim that "the Lord" had "rehearsed his subsequent incarnation" as Jesus by becoming characters recorded in the OT. The major such character about which Tertullian and the other fathers write is the prophet and warrior Joshua, son of Nun, also translated as Jesus, son of Naue, who allegedly led the Israelites into the "promised land" and destroyed the city of Jericho, among other such pillage and slaughter. Of Joshua's purported adventures, *Time* reports:

> Historians generally agree that Joshua's conquest would have taken place in the 13th century B.C. But British researcher Kathleen Kenyon, who excavated at Jericho for six years, found no evidence of destruction at that time. Indeed, says Dead Sea Scrolls curator emeritus Broshi, "the city was deserted from the beginning of the 15th century until the 11th century B.C." So was Ai, say Broshi and others. And so, according to archaeological surveys, was most of the land surrounding the cities. Says Broshi: "The central hill regions of Judea and Samaria were practically uninhabited. The Israelites didn't have to kill and burn to settle."[45]

In reality, the patriarch Joshua was based on Horus as "Iusa," and the Joshua story represents the Horus cult in the Levant, when the stellar cult of the "sons of Seth" yielded to the solar.

Joshua is not only Horus himself but also his "brother," the Egyptian god "Shu," or "Shu-si-Ra," the "auxiliary" or son of Ra and "Uplifter of the Heavens," and Joshua was said to be the "preserver" or "deliverer" sun in Aries.[46] As Churchward says of Shu:

> He is the helper of Horus as the Solar God upon the horizon where the great battle is fought against the Apap of darkness . . . This has been rendered in the Hebrew as "Joshua helping to fight the battle of the Lord." . . . Shu was chief of the sustaining powers of the firmament, who were known in one phase as the seven giants. He then became the elevator of the Heavens that was imaged as the Cow of Nut. Lastly, he was the sustaining power with Atum-Horus in the Double Equinox.[47]

In Canaan, Joshua was Baal Jehoshua, the "Lord of Salvation," but when his cult had been suppressed by the Levites/Yahwists, he was demoted to a Hebrew patriarch and hero of the northern kingdom. However, his worship was continued "underground" atop Mt. Carmel, site of a pre-Christian temple of the Lord Jesus, Baal Jeshouah.[48]

Indeed, the Joshua cult was situated in basically the same area where the Christ drama allegedly took place, with Joshua mutating into Jesus.[49] In fact, the cult of the solar hero Joshua performed the sacred king drama at Gilgal, which in Greek is Galilee (Jos. 12:23), so "Jesus of Galilee" could read "Joshua of Gilgal," and vice versa. Like Jesus, Moses, Horus, Perseus and others, Joshua was a "fatherless hero born of 'waters' (Maria)."[50]

Furthermore, at 1 Corinthians 10:4 Paul claims that Christ "the Rock" followed the Hebrews at the time of their exodus out of Egypt, as did Joshua, according to the biblical myth. As Dujardin says, "The history of the ancient religion of Jesus goes back to the Stone Age and is prior to the settlement of the Canaanite tribes of Palestine."[51] Robertson states:

> The hypothesis that Joshua is the original Jesus—the origin of the myths which blended in a composite pattern mistaken for real history—solves many problems. . . . The association of Joshua with conceptions of Logos, Son of God, and Messiah is present in the Pentateuch.[52]

As noted, the association of Jesus with Joshua was admitted by early Christian fathers, particularly when they were trying to give scriptural authority to Jesus's alleged advent because the story was being challenged. In his 2nd Apology, Justin Martyr not only acknowledges but insists upon the Jesus-Joshua identification:

JOSHUA WAS A FIGURE OF CHRIST. . . . Jesus (Joshua), as I have now frequently remarked . . . when he was sent to spy out the land of Canaan, was named by Moses Jesus (Joshua). Why he did this you neither ask, nor are at a loss about it, nor make strict inquiries. Therefore Christ has escaped your notice; and though you read, you understand not; and even now, though you hear that Jesus is our Christ, you consider not that the name was bestowed on Him not purposelessly nor by chance. . . . But since not only was his name altered, but he was also appointed successor to Moses, being the only one of his contemporaries who came out from Egypt, he led the surviving people into the Holy Land; and as he, not Moses, led the people into the Holy Land, and as he distributed it by lot to those who entered along with him, so also Jesus the Christ will turn again the dispersion of the people, and will distribute the good land to each one, though not in the same manner. . . For I have proved that it was Jesus who appeared to and conversed with Moses, and Abraham, and all the other patriarchs without exception, ministering to the will of the Father; who also, I say, came to be born man by the Virgin Mary and lives for ever.

Martyr also relates the passage in the book of Zechariah in which Joshua, like Jesus, contends with the devil, comparing it with the "mystery of Christ," thus again virtually equating the Canaanite baal/Hebrew "prophet" with the Christian savior.

David

The great King David, from whose lineage Jesus, the "King of the Jews," was purported to have come, has been much exalted over the centuries. However, even though according to the biblical tale David was well known and "all the kings of the earth sought his presence" (2 Chron. 9:23), there is no record of David in non-Hebraic sources, such as the histories of Herodotus and Hesiod. Nor are there any archaeological finds to bear out his existence, despite recent claims that a plaque was found bearing the words "house of David," because not only is the plaque's language oblique but Bible proponents, among others, have been known to salt sites and fabricate artifacts. As Roberta Harris says in *The World of the Bible*, "Some of the best known Bible stories centre on King David, yet neither history nor archaeology can substantiate any of them."[53]

Like so many other major characters in the Judeo-Christian bible, David is non-historical. Massey evinced that David, "the eighth son of Jesse, whose thirty captains were changed, in keeping with the thirty days of the month, was the Hebrew form of the Kamite moon-god Taht-Esmun, the eighth, one of whose titles is '*the begetter of Osiris*, who was so called because the solar régime was subsequent to the lunar dynasty . . ."[54] In other words, Osiris/Jesus descends from Taht-Esmun/David, "as it is written."

As stated, even the well-loved biblical Psalms attributed to David are not original but are Canaanite/Egyptian. As Massey says:

> The Psalms of David contain a substratum of the *Muthoi*, parables and dark sayings of old, which belonged to the hermeneutical Books of Taht, the Kamite Psalmist, and scribe of the gods. Those who were not in possession of the gnosis searched these writings for prophecy—after the fashion of Justin—upon which to establish the history.[55]

These "dark sayings" and events were applied to Jesus, and their presence in Psalms has been loudly touted as prophecy regarding "the Savior." In fact, many of the psalms are, as stated, a paean to the sun, which is how they are applicable to the solar myth Jesus. As Massey also says:

> Such sayings do not relate to prophecies that could be fulfilled in any future human history. The transactions and utterances in the psalm are personal to the speaker there and then, and not to any future sufferer. They may be repeated, but the repetition cannot constitute history any more than it fulfills prophecy. The repetition of the words in character points to the reapplication of the mythos in a narrative assumed to be historical.[56]

Indeed, the fact that these sayings are repeated verbatim in the NT demonstrates that they were copied from older texts, rather than having been spoken by a historical character, unless he was a mere, unoriginal scriptural parrot. If so, he would have been an Egyptian parrot. In this regard, Potter reproduces the 14th-century Egyptian monotheist Akhenaten's "Hymn to Aten" and states:

> The reader who is familiar with the Psalms of David will have noted the many parallelisms between this hymn and the 104th Psalm, similarities in language and especially thought. The composition of the Hebrew Psalm is assigned by scholars to the Greek Period of Hebrew History, 332-168 B.C.; hence, the Egyptian hymn is at least a thousand years earlier. Even if David wrote the Psalm, as tradition has it, the Egyptian composition is over three centuries older. If anyone is guilty of plagiarism, it was not Akhenaten.[57]

Of David and his psalms-singing, Gaster says:

> . . . in a prominent position in the synagogue at Dura-Europus there is a fresco depicting an Orpheus-like figure by some identified as David; . . . a representation of the same scene occurs in a Jewish catacomb at Rome; and . . . in various manuscripts of the Psalter David is indeed portrayed as Orpheus.[58]

As a mythical character, therefore, David cannot be the progenitor of a historical Jesus.

Joseph, Father of Jesus

Jesus's lineage thus cannot be traced through his "earthly" father, Joseph, since Joseph was said to be a descendant of the mythical David. Naturally, Joseph also has his counterpart in older mythologies; for example, in the Egyptian version of the mythos, Seb is the earthly father of Horus. As Massey says:

> Seb is the god of earth, god the father on earth, therefore the especial father of the sun-god in the earth. . . . Thus Seb is the father of Osiris or Horus on earth. "My father is Seb . . . my bread on earth (is) that of Seb." In the same way, house and food for the Christ are found by Joseph. . . . Seb and Meri (Nu) for earth and heaven would afford two mythic originals for Joseph and Mary as parents of the divine child. . . *Aseb* is the name of a typical seat or throne of rule, in accordance with the Hebrew *Iosheb*, to sit, to be enthroned . . . [59]

Joseph is called "son of Heli," Heli or Helios meaning the sun. The name Joseph was also a title of a Hebrew priest. As Walker states:

> The priestly name of Joseph may have been bestowed upon Jewish counterparts of the priests known in Egypt as "fathers of the god." The function of such holy men was to beget, on the temple maidens [*almahs*], children who would be *sacer*: firstborn "sons of God" dedicated to the service of the deity. . . . The mythic proliferation of Marys and Josephs indicates that these were not personal names but characters in the drama: The chosen husband who was yet not a husband; the father-of-God who was yet not a father; the virgin-mother-Goddess-priestess-queen who was also a *kadesha* or "Bride of God." . . . It can be shown that Joseph was indeed a divine name in Israel. The Egyptian form was Djoser or Tcheser. . .[60]

Hazelrigg further demonstrates the antiquity of "Joseph," its existence in other cultures and its deep astrological meaning:

> And what of this espousal to Joseph, who was the Ioseppe of the Phoenicians, and Ananda of the Hindus, the Zeus—husband of Leto and the parent of Apollo—of the cosmogonic apologue? According to the Gospels: "Joseph went up to Nazareth, which is in Galilee, and came into the City of David, called Bethlehem, because he was of that tribe, to be inscribed with Mary his wife, who was with child." And here, in the City of David, or the celestial expanse, called Bethlehem, the sixth constellation, Virgo, the harvest mansion, do we discover Joseph (the constellation of Boötes, Ioseppe) and his wife Mary with the child. Here is personified a constellation whose very name (Ioseppe, the manger of Io, or the Moon) typifies the humble place of accouchement of all the Virgin Mothers, and, as related to Virgo, the genesis of all Messianic tradition.[61]

In fact, the Greek name for the constellation of Bootes, or Adam, is Ιοσεφ or Joseph.[62]

Mary, Mother of Jesus

As noted, the Virgin Mother motif is found around the globe, long before the Christian era, as was the name of the Goddess as "Meri," "Mari" or "Mary," representing the sea (Mer/Mar), which was governed by the Queen of Heaven, the moon. The Egyptian goddess Isis, for instance, was also called "Mata-Meri" ("Mother Mary") or just "Mari." As Walker says, "Mari" was the "basic name of the Goddess known to the Chaldeans as Marratu, to the Jews as Marah, to the Persians as Mariham, to the Christians as Mary . . . Semites worshipped an androgynous combination of Goddess and God called Mari-El (Mary-God), corresponding to the Egyptian Meri-Ra, which combined the feminine principle of water with the masculine principle of the sun."[63] Walker also relates that "Mari" was a name for the sun goddess in Buddhism.[64]

Like Mary, Isis was called "Queen of Heaven," "Our Lady," "Star of the Sea" and "Mother of God." The worship of Isis was spread throughout the Greco-Roman world, from Egypt to Britain, and was very popular in Rome during the first centuries before and after the beginning of the Christian era. In addition, Isis was the same as Ishtar, who was also called Mari and was worshipped in the Hebrew temple:

> Ishtar's priestesses apparently performed some version of the rite each year in the temple of Jerusalem, where the virgin form of the Goddess was called Mari, Mari-Anna, or Miriam, and her holy women annually wailed for the sacrificial death of Tammuz.[65]

It should also be noted that "the Savior" was at times considered female; in other words, there have been female saviors as well. In fact, the words Isis and Jesus come from the same root, meaning "salvation" or "savior." It is for this reason that Jesus is depicted in Revelation as having "paps." These multiple "paps" or breasts reflect the "Mother of All Living," who was also the "Great Sow" with many teats.

The Goddess is also the Great Earth Mother, who was worshipped for millennia around the world. As Jackson relates:

> The earliest important religious cult was the worship of the earth in the image of the Great Mother. Mother Earth was the first great terrestrial deity. Among other terrestrial cults were the worship of plants and animals. At a later date Sky Worship developed, and Father Sky became the consort of Mother Earth.[66]

And Carpenter states:

> There is ample evidence that one of the very earliest objects of human worship was the Earth itself, conceived of as the fertile Mother of all things. Gaia or Gê (the earth) had temples and altars in almost all the cities of Greece. Rhea or Cybele, sprung from the Earth, was "mother of all the gods." Demeter was honored far and wide as the gracious patroness of the crops and vegetation. Ceres, of course, the same. Maia in the Indian mythology and Isis in the Egyptian are forms of Nature and the Earth-spirit, represented as female; and so forth. The Earth, in these ancient cults, was the mystic source of all life, and to it, as a propitiation, life of all kinds was sacrificed. . . . It was, in a way, the most natural, as it seems to have been the earliest and most spontaneous of cults—the worship of the Earth-mother, the all-producing eternal source of life, and on account of her never-failing ever-renewed fertility conceived of as an immortal Virgin.[67]

When the Father Sky cult usurped that of the Mother Earth, the Goddess was demoted in a variety of ways, including eventually being made into "Saint Mary." Walker also says, "Biblical writers were implacably opposed to any manifestation of the Goddess . . ."[68] So completely was she purged that there is no word for "Goddess" in biblical Hebrew.

The Saints

Like Mary, many other Christian "saints" are not historical personages but are, in fact, the gods of other cultures, usurped and demoted in order to unify the "Holy Roman Empire." Of this saintmaking Walker says, "The canon of saints was the Christian technique for preserving the pagan polytheism that people wanted, while pretending to worship only one God."[69] The *Catholic Encyclopedia* itself admits, "It has indeed been said that the 'Saints are the successors to the Gods.' Instances have been cited of pagan feasts becoming Christian; of pagan temples consecrated to the worship of the true God; of statues of pagan Gods baptized and transformed into Christian Saints."[70]

In the saintmaking process, Christians took goddesses and gods such as Artemis (St. Artemidos/Ursula) and Dionysus (St. Denis), among many others, modified their names, and gave them great "historical" exploits. In addition, the Pagan temples or "tombs" of gods were converted into Christian churches. For example, the "tomb of Dionysus/Bacchus" was transformed into the church of St. Baccus.[71] As Higgins relates:

> On the adoration of saints Bochart says, "They have transferred to their saints all the equipage of the Pagan Gods: to St. Wolfgang the hatchet, or hook of Saturn; to Moses the horns of Jupiter Hammon; to St. Peter the keys of Janus. In brief, they have chased away all the Gods out of the Pantheon at Rome, to

place in their rooms all the Saints, whose images they worship with like devotion as those of the Pagan Gods sometimes were. They dress them up in apparel, they crown them with garlands of flowers, they carry them in procession, they bow before them, they address their prayers to them, they make them descend from heaven, they attribute to them miraculous virtues."[72]

All these phony saints were highly profitable, of course, as fake relics such as their hair, fingers and other bones and body parts proliferated. As Walker states:

> The church that slaughtered the heathen for worshipping false gods was itself guilty of worshipping false saints—which, sometimes, were even the same deities as those of the heathen. . . . The church never lost sight of practical common sense on one point, however; saints were leading sources of its income, thanks to the mandatory pilgrimage system, donations, and tithes. . . . The multitudes of phony or commercial saints are treated by modern Catholic scholars with a rather amused tolerance, as if the saint-makers' fantasies held something of the same charm as tales invented by bright children. It is rarely admitted that these fantasies were not intended to charm but rather to defraud. The saints were made up to earn money for the church, and many of the made-up saints are still doing so, for the church refrains from publicizing their spurious origins lest such publicity might disappoint the faithful—which, translated, means the donations might cease.[73]

St. Josaphat

In one of the more obvious of Christian deceptions, in order to convert followers of "Lord Buddha" the Church canonized him as "St. Josaphat," which represented a Christian corruption of the Buddhistic title, "Bodhisat." As Wheless says:

> . . . the holy Saint Josaphat, under which name and due to an odd slip of inerrant inspiration, the great Lord Buddha, "The Light of Asia," was duly certified a Saint in the Roman Martyrology.[74]

Walker elaborates:

> Medieval saintmakers adapted the story of Buddha's early life to their own fictions, calling the father of St. Josaphat "an Indian king" who kept the young saint confined to prevent him from becoming a Christian. He was converted anyway, and produced the usual assortment of miracles, some of them copied from incidents in the life story of Buddha. St. Josaphat enjoyed great popularity in the Middle Ages, an ironical development in a Europe that abhorred Buddhism as the work of the devil.[75]

St. Christopher

The beloved St. Christopher is another "Christian saint" who is a remake of an ancient god. As Massey states:

> The well-known story of Christopher shows that he was a survival of Apheru, a name of Sut-Anup. It is related that he overtook the child-Christ at the side of the river Jordan, and, lifting him on his back, carried him across the waters. But all the while the wondrous child grew, and grew, and grew, as they went, and when they reached the other side the child had grown into the god. The genesis of this is the passage of the annual sun across the waters, which reaches the other side as the full-grown divinity.[76]

As has been demonstrated, many of the great biblical heroes have been the "Baals" or gods of other cultures remade, as have been the Christian saints. This religion-making business utilized every bit of "technology" it could muster, building upon centuries of such behavior and bringing it to perfection.

---

1. "A New Chronology—Synopsis of David Rohl's book *A Test of Time*"
2. http://marlowe.wimsey.com/~rshand/streams/thera/canaan.html
3. Dujardin, 47-9.
4. Dujardin, 82-3.
5. A. Churchward, 353.
6. Walker, *WEMS*, 315.
7. Doane, 20 fn.
8. Higgins, II, 15.
9. Doane, 22-23fn.
10. Hazelrigg, 49.
11. Walker, *WEMS*, 902.
12. Hazelrigg, 48.
13. Higgins, I, 387.
14. Walker, *WEMS*, 5.
15. Graham, 125.
16. Graham, 111.
17. Hazelrigg, 14-15.
18. Walker, *WEMS*, 468.
19. Walker, *WDSSO*, 331.
20. Walker, *WEMS*, 890.
21. Graham, 147.
22. Graham, 146.
23. Walker, *WDSSO*, 441.
24. Walker, *WEMS*, 96.
25. Higgins, II, 19.
26. Mead, *DJL*.
27. Time, 12/18/95.
28. Potter, 27-8.
29. A. Churchward, 292.
30. A. Churchward, 294-5.
31. Pike, 466.
32. A. Churchward, 322.
33. Massey, *HJMC*, 28.

34. A. Churchward, 300.
35. A. Churchward, 324-5.
36. A. Churchward, 325.
37. A. Churchward, 325.
38. Higgins, II, 634.
39. A. Churchward, 323.
40. Anderson, 106.
41. A. Churchward, 304.
42. Walker, *WEMS*, 677.
43. Doane, 51.
44. A. Churchward, 291.
45. *Time*, 12/18/95.
46. Higgins, I, 325.
47. A. Churchward, 260-2.
48. Higgins, I, 329.
49. Dujardin.
50. Walker, *WEMS*, 676.
51. Dujardin, 82.
52. Robertson, 21-2.
53. Harris, 72.
54. Massey, *HJMC*, 105-6.
55. Massey, *HJMC*, 111-3.
56. Massey, *HJMC*, 113.
57. Potter, 18-19.
58. Gaster, 123.
59. Massey, *HJMC*, 51-2.
60. Walker, *WEMS*, 480.
61. Hazelrigg, 108.
62. Anderson, 126.
63. Walker, *WEMS*, 584.
64. Walker, *WDSSO*, 222.
65. Walker, *WEMS*, 453.
66. Jackson, 144.
67. Carpenter, 157.
68. Walker, *WDSSO*, 197.
69. Walker, *WDSSO*, 172.
70. Wheless, *IIGW*.
71. Higgins, II, 74.
72. Higgins, II, 81.
73. Walker, *WEMS*, 882.
74. Wheless, *FC*.
75. Walker, *WEMS*.
76. Massey, *HJMC*, 135.

Etymology Tells the Story

Throughout this book has been a recurring theme that essentially weaves a tapestry of human unity not widely perceived. In order to appreciate further this unity, we can turn to etymology, or the study of the origin and development of words, to demonstrate how closely cultures are related and how there has been basically one mythos and creed with many different forms. We will also discover, therefore, further evidence of what has been demonstrated herein concerning the Christ conspiracy.

Etymology is also significant because, to the ancients, words were magical, as it was believed that the "Word of God" created the universe. To the ancients, then, words were not, as Allegro says, "just vocalic utterances communicating ideas from one mind to another; they were expressions of real power in themselves. The word had an entity of its own; once released it could effect the desire of its creator. The god's or prophet's word was a thing to be feared, and if maleficent, 'turned back' as the Bible would say. Words which looked alike, we might think accidentally, were considered actually to be connected in some way."[1] Furthermore, the Hebrews, like other peoples, were fond of wordplay and used it extensively in their texts.

God the Father

Many people believe that the concept of God as Father originated with Christianity, but this assumption is erroneous, as numerous pre-Christian cultures had their God the Father as well. As it turns out, God the Mother has been a more popular idea for a longer period of time, but the Greeks, Indians and Egyptians, to name a few, also conceived of the male aspect of deity. In the Greek mythology, the sky-god father-figure, aka "Zeus Pateras," who is a myth and not a historical figure, takes his name from the Indian version, "Dyaus Pitar." Dyaus Pitar in turn is related to the Egyptian "Ptah," and from Pitar and Ptah comes the word "pater," or "father." "Zeus" equals "Dyaus," which became "Deos," "Deus" and "Dios"—"God." Dyaus also means sky, which is indicative of "God's" atmospheric and unhistoric nature. Dyaus Pitar also mutated into the Roman "Jupiter," likewise not a historical character.

Jesus Christ

Although most people think the name Jesus originated with the Christian godman, it was in fact quite common, particularly in Israel, where it was Joshua. As such the name appears in the Old Testament over 200 times. As demonstrated, the name Jesus also comes from the monogram of Dionysus, "IES," "Yes" or "Jes," among others. Jacolliot elaborates on these widespread names:

> As we have seen, all these names of Jesus, Jeosuah, Josias, Josue derive from two Sanscrit words Zeus and Jezeus, which signify, one, the Supreme Being, and the other, the Divine Essence. These names, moreover, were common not only amongst the Jews, but throughout the East.[2]

Higgins relates that the followers of Krishna shouted "Jeye" or "Ieue" during celebrations.[3] This "ieue," as we have seen, is the same as both YHWH and "Jesus," as admitted by Clement of Alexandria (153-214), who noted that "the Savior" had been represented by the letters "IE," the same designation found applied to Apollo on his temple at Delphi. The "Savior," of course, was not a carnalized, historical person but a spiritual construct that, as noted, was known to many mystery schools and sects, which could thus be termed "salvation cultists."

The title of Christos was applied not only to the kings and priests of Judah but also to a number of anointed savior-gods prior to the Christian era. As Walker says:

> "Anointed One," a title of many Middle-Eastern sacrificial gods—Attis, Adonis, Tammuz, Osiris—derived from Oriental cults of the sacred marriage. In the east, the god's *lingam* or the erect penis of his statue was anointed with holy oil (Greek *chrism*) for easier penetration of his bride, the Goddess, impersonated by one of the temple virgins. . . . Jesus became a *Christos* when he was *christ*-ened by Mary, the magdalene or temple maiden (Matthew 26:12), who also announced his resurrection (Mark 15:47).[4]

In other words, anyone anointed would be called "Christ" by the Greek-speaking inhabitants of the Roman Empire, who were many, since Greek was the lingua franca for centuries. As noted, in Greek Krishna is also Christos, and the word "Christ" also comes from the Hindi word "Kris," which is a name for the sun, as is evidently "Krishna" in ancient Irish.

In fact, in the face of criticism that his "new superstition" was fabricated, Eusebius protested that "the names Jesus and Christ [were] known and honoured from the first." Eusebius further insisted:

> Both Jesus and Christ were names honoured even by God's beloved prophets of old, as I must now make clear. . . For in describing God's high priest, the most powerful of men, *[Moses] called him Christ* . . . (Lev. 4:5, 16)

Eusebius continues:

> [Moses's] successor had not hitherto used the designation of Jesus [Joshua] but was known by another name, Hoshea . . . but

Moses calls him Jesus . . . for Joshua the son of Nun himself *bore the image of our Saviour* . . .

Eusebius's ruse of "bore the image of our Saviour" was a common argument by Christian apologists, who, when confronted with the truth that the gods and/or patriarchs of other eras and cultures had similar or identical "lives" as that of Jesus, sought to explain that these preceding individuals were either Pagan imitations created previously by the prescient devil or Hebrew/Jewish "archetypes" or "patterns," as Eusebius calls them, for the *real* Christ who was to come. As we have seen, Tertullian considers these archetypes to be God's "rehearsals" for his big role.

Despite the attempts of the Christian fathers to prove the antiquity of their savior, Hotema maintained that the name "Jesus Christ" was not formally adopted as a phrase until after the first Council of Nicea, i.e., in 325. Says he, "The name Jesus Christ was unknown until after the Nicean Council. It appeared in no writings before that time."[5] And Roberts says:

Prior to the Fourth Century, there was frequent and general mention of "Christos," and his worship to the east of Rome. But nowhere can be found any authentic mention at that time of a Jesus Christ. It was not until after the Nicean Council that the name Jesus Christ was ever known to the world.[6]

Satan, The Devil, etc

Many people today do not readily express belief in Satan, or the devil, as portrayed in Christianity, which in actuality depends upon the belief in such an absolute evil being for it to be "true." The devil was a very popular figure when the Church, Christianity and general hysteria reigned supreme, but in the time since secularism and freethought have become more influential, the devil seems to have dropped out of sight, save for the occasional hauntings and possessions. For example, before rationalism and science established their voice, lightning strikes and hurricanes were regarded as the devil's work. They are now often considered as "acts of God," leaving one to wonder where the devil has gone and if God is next.

Of course, the dualistic concepts of absolute good and evil did not originate with Christianity but are found long before the Christian era, particularly within Zoroastrianism. Satan is an adaptation of the Persian representative of evil "Ahriman," the twin brother of "God," the same as the Egyptian Set, Horus's twin and principal enemy, also known as "Sata," whence comes "Satan." Horus struggles with Set in the exact manner that Jesus battles with Satan, with 40 days in the wilderness, among other similarities, such as the revealing from the mount "all the kingdoms of Earth." This myth represents the triumph of light over dark, or the sun's return to relieve the terror of the night. Horus/Set was the god of the two horizons; hence, Horus was the rising sun, and Set the time of the Sun-*SET.*

As noted, Set is the biblical Seth, the progenitor of the Hebrew race, demonstrating the culture's stellar cult origins. While solar brotherhoods such as the Essenes and Nazarenes wore white, the priesthood of Set/Seth/Saturn/Sata wore black robes, "black as night"; hence, the black dress of Catholic, Jewish and Muslim clerics to this day.

In Hebrew, the name "Satan" or "Shaitan" merely means "adversary," not absolute evil being. The title of Satan as the "adversary," also at 1 Peter 5:8, refers to the sun as "Lord of the Opposite, which means a sign or constellation opposite to the sun at any given point."[7]

Moreover, Satan is called "the father of lies," yet it is Yahweh who claims to be the deceiver: "If a prophet is deceived, I the Lord deceived that prophet." (Ezekiel) This example is but one of the instances in which "the Lord" lies (1 Kings 22, Jer. 22:7), leaving one to speculate as to the true identity of the "Father of Lies."

The origin of the "devil" also can be uncovered through etymology, in that the word comes from the Sanskrit term "deva" or the Persian "daeva," both of which originally referred to angelic entities, usually female, who were demonized by Christian propagandists. In actuality, "devil" shares the same root as "divine." In addition, the word "demon" is a Christian vilification of the Greek word "daemon," which likewise referred to a divine spirit.

The devil was called "Baalzebub," but this word was also used for God, prior to its vilification. As Graves says, "Baal, as synonymous with Bel, was the Chaldean name for the Lord dwelling in the sun. Baal-Shadai was the sun in the zenith of his glory, and Baalzebub the sun while in the sign or constellation of the scorpion."[8] It also meant "Lord of the Flies," the god propitiated to keep flies away.

In fact, any number of names for the devil found within Judaism and Christianity are vilifications of the gods and goddesses of other cultures. The form of the devil commonly represented over the past several centuries, i.e., a man with horns and hooves, is in large part a demonization of the Greek god of Nature, Pan, who was wild and capricious. Several other gods were also involved in the creation of the Christian devil, such as Hades/Pluto and Dionysus/Bacchus. Massey elaborates:

The devil was of Egyptian origin, both as "that old serpent" the Apap reptile, the devil with a long tail, and as Sut, who was Satan in an anthropomorphic guise. Sut, the power of drought and darkness in physical phenomena, becomes the dark-hearted evil one . . . [9]

Jerusalem, the Holy City

The word "Jerusalem" simply means "City of Peace," and it is evident that the city in Israel was named *after* the holy city of peace in the Egyptian and Babylon sacred texts. As Graham says:

> The word Salem is not Hebrew in origin. In a Babylonian poem of 1600 B.C. we find a city called Salem, home of a might hero Daniel on whose exploits the scriptural Daniel is based. [10]

Jerusalem in the Egyptian mythos is "Arru-Salaam," or Salam, Shiloam, Siloam. Arru is the garden or fields where the wheat or barley is sown and harvested, the Elysian fields, where Osiris, the sun, takes his rest. It was said that in order to "reap" the Egyptian paradise or Arru-Salaam, one's "sowing" had to be in proportion to the reward; hence, "As you sow, so shall you reap."

Arru-Salaam is the celestial Holy City to which the "angels" ascend and descend the zodiacal ladder of Set/Jacob. The Holy City has no single location on Earth but appears first in the heavens and afterwards is constructed around the globe, being "the Eternal City, the City of the Blessed, the Holy City, the City of the Great King, the Heavenly City, the Eternal City that was the model of Memphis and Annu, Thebes and Abydos, Eridu and Babylon, Jerusalem, Rome, and other sacred Cities of the world." [11]

As Hazelrigg says:

> The "Holy City" is likewise a term essentially solar, being the same as the Phoenician word *hely*, and having its root in the Greek *helios*, Sun; whence Heliopolis, the city of the Sun. [12]

Bethany

"Bethany," site of the famous multiplying of the loaves, means "House of God," and is *allegory* for the "multiplication of the many out of the One." Any town of that designation was named for the allegorical place in the texts that existed centuries before the town's foundation. The Egyptian predecessor and counterpart was "Bethanu." That a "historical" or localized Bethany did not even exist at the time of Christ's alleged advent is attested to by Church father Origen, who "said he could find no trace of 'Bethany beyond Jordan.'" [13]

The River Jordan

There have been too many "Rivers Jordan" to name here. The Danube in Europe is one, as is the mythical Eridanus or Iarutana of Egypt. These bodies of water basically represent the "river of the sun," as can be demonstrated etymologically.[14] Without water, there would be no life, so it was quite common for migrating peoples to rejoice at the discovery of a potable body of water. Thus, rivers were venerated as "gifts from God" and named for "his" most visible proxy.

Solomon

The "great" king Solomon, so-called wisest man in the world, with his 1,000 wives and concubines, should today be considered an immoral criminal, were the story true. Obviously, this absurd tale is not historical. In fact, "Sol-om-on" refers to the sun in three languages: "Sol" is Latin, "om" is Eastern, and "on" is Egyptian. "On" means both "sun" and "lord," reflecting an association found in countless cultures. Solomon can also be traced to the same root as "Salvation," which is related to "Salivahana," the Indian savior-god.[15]

Much has been made of the great "Temple of Solomon," yet, as stated, this magnificent temple and the entire empire of Solomon were never found by ancient historians, nor did Alexander the Great pay heed to them. Furthermore, even if it had existed, the temple as outlined in the Bible would not be impressive, especially compared to the monuments of other cultures of the time. Such a blueprint was apparently followed, however, as, according to Higgins, the ruins at Persepolis indicate a temple similar to the biblical description of Solomon's temple.[16]

There are a number of other problems with the "history" of Solomon presented in the Bible. As Graham states:

> The Bible states in three different places that Solomon built the walls of Jerusalem, yet the historical Jerusalem was a walled city in the fourteenth century B.C., and the Jews as a distinct sect did not then exist . . . The statement that he began to build the temple some four hundred years after the Exodus from Egypt is also historically false. . . . The literature of the Jains of India tells this same story of their Solomon. Proverbs 22:17-23:11 is a nearly verbatim translation of the Egyptian book, *The Wisdom of Amenemope*, written about 1000 B.C.[17]

In reality, there have been numerous Temples or Mounts of Solomon, found largely in India and Persia, under a variety of spellings, such as Soleiman, Soolimana, Suleiman, Sulimon or Solumi. In fact, as noted, the entire story of Solomon can be found in India, as can be that of Genesis and David, among others.[18] This pervasiveness demonstrates that the temple of Solomon was originally allegorical, not literal. As Hazelrigg relates:

> As an example of the allegorical method used in the elucidation of these mysteries, take, for example, the story of King Solomon, deemed a personage of some importance in Holy Writ, whose temple "builded not with hands, neither with sound of iron or metal tool." Now, the word *Solomon* is a compound from three languages great in olden times—Latin, *Sol* or *Solus*, sun; Sanskrit, *Aum* or *Om*, heat; and Ethiopic, *On*, being—all pointing to solar principle in manifestation: *Sol-om-on*, the personification of wisdom, and described in his songs as of "brightness of the everlasting light, the unspotted mirror of the power of God, and the image of His goodness." Solomon's Temple meant nothing more nor less than the temple or vault of the heavens, of which Sol is king, or center . . . [19]

Anderson adds:

> The sun in Egyptian is Sire, Osiris, in Sanskrit, Aum, in Chaldean and Ethiopic, On, in other languages, Sol. And whether we call him Sol aum or On, or altogether Sol-om-on, it matters little, *since his temple has never yet been made by hands* and is eternal in the heavens. And though Herod's temple has been found and the remains of many others, no one has yet had the audacity to claim Sol-om-on's Temple as a discovery . . . [20]

Solomon's Temple is, in fact, the tent or tabernacle of the sun mentioned at Psalms 19, the same temple as Jesus's body. The "mounts of Solomon" are the 72 decans or divisions of the zodiac, reflected in the ancient Persian tradition that there were 70 or 72 Soleimans before the advent of Adam/Atum.[21] Traditionally it has been thought that the Knights Templar were designated for the "historical" temple of Solomon; however, they were in actuality named for the "templum of the heavens" or "starry vaults."[22] As Hazelrigg explains:

> The Holy Temple, Solomon's Temple, and the Temple of the Lord are all expressive of the celestial fabric that revolves around us, the altar in which is the constellation of Aries, the eastern sign.[23]

The temple as a symbol of what is above is reflected in the Letter to the Hebrews (9:24): "For Christ has entered, not into a sanctuary made with hands, *a copy of the true one*, but into heaven itself . . ."

Jonah

Incredibly, many people have believed the biblical tale of Jonah and the whale to be true. The fact that this belief can be rationalized, particularly since those selfsame believers roundly dismiss the "absurd" stories of other cultures, is an example of conditioning and cultural bias. In reality, the story of Jonah is itself found in other cultures, as Walker elaborates:

> Jonah's whale is described in the Bible as a "fish," because writers of that period (and for many centuries afterward) were unaware that whales are mammals. The whale of the original Jonah story was the Babylonian Sea Goddess Derceto, "The Whale of Der," who swallowed and gave rebirth to the god Oannes . . . Swallowing by the whale indicates an initiation rite, leading to rebirth. The Finnish hero Ilmarinen was similarly swallowed by a giant fish to be re-born. A variant of the story shows that the fish was really a womb . . . Biblical writers masculinized the image as Jonah, whose name means "Dove." The word *ionah* or *ione* may have descended from *yoni*, for the dove was a primary symbol of female sexuality.[24]

Far from being literal, the tale of Jonah is astrological, as "Jonah" in the "belly of the whale" for three days represents the sun in the "womb" of the earth. These three days are the "entombment" of the sun in darkness, nightly but also during the time between a new and old moon, as the "whale" is also the "moon-fish." As Doane says:

> There is a *Hindoo* fable, very much resembling [the Jonah tale], to be found in the *Somadeva Bhatta*, of a person by the name of *Saktideva* who was swallowed up by a huge fish, and finally came out unhurt. . . . In Grecian fable, Hercules is said to have been swallowed by a whale, *at a place called Joppa, and to have lain three days in his entrails.* . . . That the story is an allegory, and that it, as well as that of Saktideva, Hercules and the rest, are simply different versions of the same myth, the significance of which is the alternate swallowing up and casting forth of *Day*, or the *Sun*, by *Night*, is now all but universally admitted by scholars. The *Day*, or the *Sun*, is swallowed up by *Night*, to be set free again at dawn . . . The *Sun* was called Jona . . . Jonah, Hercules and others personify the *Sun*, and a huge *Fish* represents the *Earth*.[25]

Moreover, the words Jawna, Jon, Jona and Ionn are demonstrably the same as Baal, the Lord, or the "First Principle."[26] In addition, the Scandinavians purportedly called the sun "John," and in Persian the sun is "Jawnah." "Thus," says Doane, "we see that the *Sun* was called *Jonah*, by different nations of antiquity."[27]

In the New Testament, Jesus is identified with the solar hero Jonah: "For as Jonah was three days and three nights in the belly of the whale, so will the Son of man be three days and three nights in the heart of the earth." (Matthew 12:40) When Jesus is asked by the Pharisees and Sadducees for a "sign from heaven," he enigmatically answers, "An evil and adulterous generation seeks for a sign, but no sign shall be given to it except the sign of Jonah." (Matthew 16:4) The sign, of course, is the sun.

Thus, in studying the origins of words, we discover the fascinating fact that many of them can be traced to the same source, and that source is often the sun. In fact, as seen, the names of the various solar gods and heroes are often related to each other. For example, in the very ancient and mysterious Basque language, Dionysus is "Dunixi," which seems related to the "Dumuzi" of the Sumerians, which in turn became "Tammuz." Dionysus, or Bacchus, can also be traced to Yahweh, as Bacchus was also written "Iacchus," which in turn is related to "Iao" or "Jah." The Greek solar myth "Heracles" (Hercules) is the same as "Har-acles," referring to Horus, also called "Heru," while Krishna is called "Heri," the Sanskrit for lord, shepherd and savior. Buddha is also called "Heri-maya," which would correspond to Hermes. In old Irish, the word "Budh," as in Buddha, means sun, fire and universe.[28] Furthermore, the word "Baal," as in "the Lord," is found in India as "Bala" and is related to the word "Bull," reflecting that it was a common term in the Age of Taurus. The word "Bull" in turn can be traced to the same root as "syr," as in Syria, another term for the sun.

Like all other sciences, etymology is not exact or perfect, and etymological speculation at times may be faulty. Nevertheless, the theme demonstrated is too overwhelming to be dismissed. What such research reveals is that the various human cultures, nations and races have much more in common than they realize and that the focus of their religious attention was originally non-sectarian and non-racial, i.e., it was not a man of any particular ethnicity.

---

1. Allegro, *SMC*, 48.
2. Jacolliot, 301.
3. Higgins, I, 328.
4. Walker, *WEMS*, 167.
5. Massey, *EBD*, intro, 9.
6. Roberts, prologue.
7. Graves, *BS*, 47.
8. Graves, *BS*, 46.
9. Massey, *EBD*, 107-9.
10. Graham, 113.
11. A. Churchward, 276-7.
12. Hazelrigg, 22.
13. Graham, 325.
14. Higgins, I, 357, 530.
15. Higgins, I, 414.
16. Higgins, I, 411.
17. Graham, 226-233.
18. Higgins, I, 402.
19. Hazelrigg, 12.

20. Anderson, 50.
21. Higgins, I, 410-11.
22. Higgins, I, 703.
23. Hazelrigg, 22.
24. Walker, *WEMS*, 392-9.
25. Doane, 79-80.
26. Doane.
27. Doane, 80 fn.
28. Higgins, II, 287.

The Meaning of Revelation

Another biblical "code" in need of decipherment is the Book of Revelation, which has mystified and fascinated people for centuries with its bizarre imagery and purported prophecy. This fascination has led to endless speculation and interpretation of its "prophecy" by biblical literalists, who, being unable to do anything else with it, usually interpret Revelation allegorically. Needless to say, despite centuries of attempts to decode the text and to associate its players with a variety of world leaders, nations and organizations, Revelation remains a mystery, because it is, in fact, not prophecy, and its drama does not take place on Earth.

As to the question of who actually wrote Revelation, the *Encyclopedia Biblica* says, "The author of Revelation calls himself John the Apostle. As he was *not* John the Apostle, who died perhaps in Palestine about 66, he was a forger."[1] We would add that "died *perhaps*" is also accurate, in that John "lived not at all." Nor is the book unique, as it is purported to be. As Walker says:

> The Bible's *Book of Revelation* purports to be a doomsday-vision experienced by St. John the Divine, but it is in fact a collection of images and phrases from many sources. Literature of this kind was plentiful in the first few centuries A.D. . . . [2]

In fact, many apocalypses were written prior to and during the Christian era, as the apocalypse was a genre of writing:

> The Apocalypse, or Revelation, ascribed to John, seems to have been one of many productions of the kind which appeared early in the second century. It is similar to the Revelation of Cerinthus, and may have emanated from the same source.[3]

Even Eusebius calls Revelation "spurious" and further relates the words of Dionysius (c. 200-265), saint and head of the Alexandrian school after Origen:

> Some of our predecessors rejected the book and pulled it entirely to pieces, criticizing it chapter by chapter, pronouncing it unintelligible and illogical, and the title false. They say it is not John's and is not a revelation at all, since it is heavily veiled by its thick curtain of incomprehensibility: so far from being one of the apostles, the author of the book was not even one of the saints, or a member of the Church, but Cerinthus, the founder of the sect called Cerinthian after him . . . [4]

This devout and orthodox Christian writer Dionysius also admits that the author of the Gospel and Epistles attributed to John was not the same as that of Revelation. Says he:

To sum it up, anyone who examines their characteristics throughout will inevitably see that Gospel and Epistle have one and the same colour. But there is no resemblance or similarity whatever between them and Revelation; it has no connection, no relationship with them; it has hardly a syllable in common with them. Nor shall we find any mention or notion of the Revelation in the Epistle (let alone the Gospel), or of the Epistle in the Revelation.[5]

This debate over Revelation is a recurring theme in the early Christian writings, in which a number of fathers and doctors at one point or another express their doubts as to the authenticity of not only Revelation but also virtually every text in the canon. This skepticism is all the more peculiar considering it was claimed that the apostolic lineage was continuous and "unbroken," and that there were allegedly established churches all along whose authorities surely would have known for a fact whether or not any apostle had written biblical texts. It also reveals the tremendous amount of duplicity engaged in by clergy and biblicists who continue to present to the credulous populace that the books of the Bible were in fact written by those whose names are attached to them, knowing fully well that this assertion is false.

The book of Revelation was rejected by a number of churches, particularly the eastern ones, because they knew it was a spurious manuscript compiled from much older texts. As Pike says, "The Apocalypse or Revelations, by whomever written, belongs to the Orient and to extreme antiquity. It reproduces what is far older than itself."[6] Higgins concurs:

That the work called the Apocalypse of St. John . . . is of *very great antiquity* is clearly proved by the fact that it makes the year only 360 days long—the same length that it is made in the third book of Genesis . . . [7]

Based on its astrological imagery, Massey evinced that Revelation, rather than having been written by any apostle called John during the 1st century CE, was an ancient text dating to 4,000 years ago and relating the Mithraic legend of one of the early Zoroasters. The text has also been attributed pseudepigraphically to Horus's scribe, Aan, whose name has been passed down as "John." Jacolliot claimed that the Apocalypse/Revelation material was gleaned from the story of Krishna/Christna, an opinion concurred with by Hotema, who averred that the book was a text of Hindu mysteries given to Apollonius. In fact, the words "Jesus" and "Christ," and the phrase "Jesus Christ" in particular, are used sparingly in Revelation, revealing they were interpolated (long) after the book was written, as were the Judaizing elements. Indeed, it is admitted by Christians that the book was worked on by a number of hands, including those of Andrew, Bishop of Caesarea, who wrote parts of Revelation in the 6th-7th centuries CE.

Despite all the brouhaha surrounding it, Revelation is not a "book of prophecy." Hotema reveals the real meaning behind the book:

> It is expressed in terms of creative phenomena; its hero is not Jesus but the Sun of the Universe, its heroine is the Moon; and all its other characters are Planets, Stars and Constellations; while its stage-setting comprises the Sky, the Earth, the Rivers and the Sea.[8]

In fact, Revelation records the mythos of the precession of the equinoxes, or the "Great Year," and was apparently originally written to usher in the Age of Aries, which began around 4,400 years ago. As Churchward says:

> The drama appears as tremendous in the Book of Revelation, because the period ending is on the scale of one Great Year. It *is not the ending of the world, but of a great year of the world.*[9]

Churchward continues:

> The book is and always has been inexplicable, because it was based upon the symbolism of the Egyptian Astronomical Mythology without the gnosis, or "meaning which hath wisdom" that is absolutely necessary for an explanation of its subject-matter; and because the debris of the ancient wisdom has been turned to account as data for pre-Christian prophecy that was supposed to have its fulfillment in Christian history.[10]

Sacred Numerology/Gematria

The Book of Revelation is in fact an encapsulation of the ancient astrological mythos and religion, a part of which is sacred numerology. Indeed, several sacred numbers repeatedly make their appearance in Revelation, such as three, seven, 12, 24, etc. The "seven stars" or "spirits" are the seven "planets" that make up the days of the week and the Seven Sisters, which were variously the pole-stars or the Pleiades. These Seven Sisters corresponded to the Seven Hathors of the Egyptians, who were the "'seven beings who make decrees,' whom the dead would meet on their journey through the seven spheres of the afterlife."[11] The Seven Hathors were also considered the seven gates, as mentioned in Revelation, representing both the night hours and the "seven months of summer." The seven "torches of fire" or seven-branch lampstand symbolizes the sun in the middle, with the moon and five inner planets as satellites, corresponding to the days of the week. Concerning Jesus as the lamb with the seven horns and eyes, Wells says:

Revelation's figuring the heavenly Jesus as a lamb with seven horns and seven eyes "which are the spirits of God sent forth into all the earth" (5:6) is a manifold reworking of old traditions. Horns are a sign of power (Deuteronomy 33:17) and in Daniel designated kingly power. The seven eyes which inform the lamb of is happening all over the earth seem to be residues from ancient astrological lore . . . according to which God's eyes are the sun, the moon, and the five planets . . .[12]

The Great City in Revelation is the city of the Gods, located in the heavens, with the 12 gates of the zodiac. The "tree of life" in the city that bears "twelve manner of fruit" is also the zodiac.

In addition, the 24 elders in white garments around the throne are the 24 hours of the day "around" the sun. The four angels "standing at the four corners of the earth" are the four cardinal points or *angles* of 90 degrees each. The 144,000 elect are the 360 degrees of the zodiacal circle multiplied by the four minutes it takes for the sun to move one degree, times a factor of 10^2.[13]

The Four "Living Creatures"

Much has been made of the four mysterious creatures or cherubim found in Ezekiel and Revelation:

> And round the throne, on each side of the throne, are four living creatures, full of eyes front and behind: And the first animal was like a lion and the second animal was like a calf and the third animal had the face of a man and the fourth animal was like a flying eagle.

As noted concerning the same cherubim in Ezekiel, these four animals represent the four cardinal points of the zodiac. The throne is the sun, and the multitudinous "eyes front and behind" are the infinite stars. The three pairs of wings of each beast represent the three signs of each of the four zodiacal quadrants. These "living creatures" were also found in Egypt. As Walker says, "Spirits of the four points of the year were sometimes called Sons of Horus."[14]

Jackson relates that the four beasts also represent Noah and his three sons, i.e., the various races. In this scenario, the lion is the lion of Judah, or Shem, "father" of the Semites; the bull symbolizes the Hamites of Egypt; the eagle is Japheth, progenitor of the Aryans; and the man is Noah, who is of the "Adamic" or "Atlantean" race.[15]

The Four Horsemen

Concerning the frightening "four horsemen" endlessly interpreted and expected for almost two millennia, Jackson says:

In the Apocalypse we read about the four beasts, and the four horsemen; the beasts were the zodiacal constellations and the horsemen were the planets. . . .

1. The first horseman was a conqueror armed with a bow, wearing a crown, and riding a white horse. This was the planet Venus.

2. The second horse was red, ridden by a warrior with a sword. This was the planet Mars.

3. The third horse was black with the rider holding aloft a pair of balances. This was the planet Saturn.

4. The fourth horse was of pale-green or blue-green color, and his rider was death. This was the planet Mercury.[16]

Thus, the four horsemen, awaited for so many centuries, like the Second Coming, have been here all along, as has Jesus, the *sun* of God.

The Woman Clothed with the Sun

The "woman clothed with the sun" is both the moon, which reflects or "wears" the sun, and the constellation of the Virgin, who has the moon under her feet and the stars above her head. As Graves explains:

. . . St. John's marvelous figure of "a woman clothed with the sun, the moon under her feet and a crown of twelve stars upon her head" (Rev. xii), is easily understood when viewed through an astronomical mirror. More appropriately may the astronomical virgin woman be said to be clothed with the sun, than could be said of any other of the twelve signs of the zodiac, judging from her situation among the signs and her relative position to the sun. There she stands, right in the focus of the sun's rays in August, the hottest month of the year, and thus is clothed with the sun more brilliantly than that of any other sign. Of course the moon is under her feet, while the twelve months of the year, or the twelve signs of the zodiac form her crown of twelve stars.[17]

This motif is found in Persia, India and Egypt, among other places. In fact, in the Berlin museum is an engraving of the Goddess (possibly Ishtar) in nearly the same posture, clothed with the sun, with the moon and stars above and the twelve signs of the zodiac surrounding her.[18] At the Temple of Isis at Denderah was an image of a woman "seated at the center of a blazing sun crowned by twelve stars and with her feet resting on the moon. The woman was the symbol of Mother Nature; the sun represented creative strength; the twelve stars stood for the twelve signs of the Zodiac, and the Moon signified Matter and its domination by Spirit."[19] Walker relates the eastern custom regarding the woman:

According to Tantric tradition, the Goddess concealed herself behind the sun's brightness; it was "the mayik vesture of Her who is clothed with the sun." This image reappeared in the New Testament as "the woman clothed with the sun." (Revelation 12:1).[20]

As to the antiquity of this motif, it should be noted that the temple at Denderah has been averred to be possibly 10,000 years old, based on the astrology it depicts.

The Seven Seals

Regarding the mysterious "seven seals" opened by "the Lamb," i.e., the sun in Aries, Graham says:

> This part of the revelation is not from God but from Ezekiel, who got it from the Babylonians, the Assyrians and the Sumerians. The seven seals are identical with the seven decrees of Ishtar and Innana.[21]

These "seven decrees" are the same as those of the Seven Hathors mentioned above, which are also the seven gates through which the Prince of Light must pass, representing hours of the night and months of the year.

The "Sweet" Scrolls

Both Ezekiel and the Revelator are given "sweet scrolls" to eat prior to their visions. These scrolls evidently represent magical practices. As Walker relates:

> Eating instead of reading a piece of magical literature was a common Oriental method of absorbing the virtue of magic words even when one is unable to read. In Tibet, Madagascar, China, and Japan it was customary to cure diseases by writing the curative charm on paper and eating the paper, or its ashes. . . . The same notion was often found in the west. The modern pharmacist's Rx began as a curative symbol of Saturn, written on paper and eaten by the patient.[22]

It has also been suggested that these scrolls represented hallucinogenic drugs, which were commonly used in mystery schools and secret societies.

The Dragon and the Beast

The frightening dragon and beast of Revelation have intrigued people for centuries and caused much speculation as to what they were or would be. The favorite interpretation of the beast has been the Catholic Church itself, particularly when it was murdering people by the millions. Again, the book of Revelation is not prophetic, so this "beast" is not applicable to any earthly kingdoms, organizations, "Antichrists" or peoples, etc. Graves gives the astrological meaning of the dragon and beast:

St. John (Rev. 12) speaks of the Dragon having power to hurt the five months, and astronomically speaking, he does hurt the vegetable productions of the five principal prolific months of the year, with a vengeance. And St. John's monster, with the seven heads and ten horns, may find a solution in astronomy, or astrotheology, by assuming the seven heads to be the seven Summer months (as some nations divided the year in this way), and duplicating the five Winter months for the horns. And then, the story of the Dragon "pursuing the woman to destroy her male child," finds an easy explanation here. Turn to your almanacs, and you will notice that the Dragon or Scorpion is in pursuit of the woman, Virgin, sure enough, being the next sign in order in the zodiac; or direct your eyes to the heavens on a cloudless night, you will observe that just after the old maid (a virgin with a child in her arms, as the Persians show her) rises above the horizon in the East, up comes the old Scorpion called a serpent among the Persians; a Dragon in Phoenicia; Draco among the Romans, which is the Latin for Dragon. . . . The great Dragon, according to astronomical diagrams, is actually after the woman (Virgin) and her child, and was for thousands of years B.C., and until modern astronomers caught him, and cast him into a bottomless pit, and substituted the eagle in his place.[23]

Furthermore, Egyptian images of the Dragon were painted red; hence, "the great red Dragon."

The Mark of the Beast—666

The much ballyhooed number, 666, mentioned in Revelation as the "mark of the Beast," was in fact held sacred in the goddess-worshipping cultures as representative of female genitalia. When the Goddess was vilified by the patriarchy, she became the "Beast" and her sacred number the "mark." The number 666 was not held to be evil or a bad omen in Judaism, as is evidenced by the biblical story of Solomon possessing 666 talents of gold. In fact, it is a sacred number. As Higgins says:

> The Hexad or number *six* is considered by the Pythagoreans a perfect and sacred number; among many other reasons, because it divides the universe into equal parts. It is called Venus or the mother. It is also perfect, because it is the only number under X, ten, which is whole and equal in its parts. In Hebrew Vau is *six*. Is *vau* mother Eva or Eve?[24]

In addition, Anderson points out that "666" also corresponds to the sun rising at 6:00 a.m., reaching its height six hours later, and setting at 6:00 p.m.[25]

As "history" or "prophecy," the book of Revelation is not only incomprehensible but destructive, not merely boggling the mind but causing people to see "beasts" and "Antichrists" everywhere, thus creating prejudice and bigotry, and serving as a blueprint for

Armageddon and "end times." Understood as astrology, or astrotheology, however, Revelation is powerful and informative, as it represents a condensed narration of the universal mythos and ritual, found throughout the Bible and revealed to be behind the Christ conspiracy. Its true meaning, of course, has been lost to the masses, as they have been told that astrology is "evil," a deliberate device to prevent them from studying it, because, with such astrological knowledge, they would understand clues such as in Revelation (22:16), where the true nature of Jesus is clearly identified when he is called the "morning star," i.e., the sun, which is the real "revelation."

The Mysteries

It may be reasonably asked why, if the mythos and ritual are found around the world and thus in cultures not subjected to the censorship of the Catholic Church and Christian hierarchy, they are unknown. As noted, the mythos and ritual form part of "the mysteries" of secret societies, brotherhoods, priesthoods and mystery schools. As such, they were not to be revealed but dangled over the heads of the uninitiated. Of these secret societies, Allegro says:

> The whole point of a mystery cult was that few people knew its secret doctrines. So far as possible, the initiates did not commit their special knowledge to writing. Normally the secrets of the sect were transmitted orally, novices being required to learn direct from their mentors by heart, and placed under the most violent oaths never to disclose the details even under torture. When such special instruction was committed to writing, care would be taken that it should be read only by the members of the sect. This could be done by using a special code or cypher, as is the case with certain of the Dead Sea Scrolls. However, discovery of such obviously coded material on a person would render him suspect to the authorities. Another way of passing information was to conceal the message, incantations or special names within a document ostensibly concerning another subject.[26]

In reality, the Christian religion was a revelation of these mysteries, which had existed for millennia. Indeed, "Paul" himself attested that his preaching of Jesus Christ served to reveal "the mystery which was kept secret for long ages but is now disclosed and through the prophetic writings is made known to all nations" (Rom. 16:25-26). In fact, it was because of the criminal revelation of this secret that the Christians were persecuted.

As the author of *The Other Jesus* says:

> Much is made of the fact that Christians were supposed to have been severely persecuted just for "worshipping Jesus," (and for

other no reason) by the Romans during the first centuries AD. Although the degree to which Christians were actually persecuted by pagans has been wildly exaggerated, the truth is, early Christians did indeed seem to have evoked considerably more than their share of scorn and antagonism from pagan authorities. This is somewhat baffling because, as has often been pointed out, the official policy of the Roman Empire, both in principle and in practice, was one of permitting near total religious freedom. This extended even to the point of allowing many practices that even modern western nations would never permit in the name of religious freedom. But once you recognize that claiming you were about to "reveal the secrets of the Son of God Jesus" to the uninitiated public was a death penalty offense forbidden under the laws prohibiting people from "profaning" or "betraying the mysteries," you begin to at least partially understand why the pagan legal officials might have tended to take for granted that it was their duty to suppress "Christian" preachers. To them, certain aspects of Christian preaching represented blatant criminal activities. In the mind of the pagans, such sanctions against Christians were reasonable punishments for very definite, obvious and specific violations of the law, not unwarranted "persecutions" of people who were innocently worshipping God in their own way.

Thus, the Christian religion and founder were based on the ubiquitous mythos and ritual that served as the mysteries, which were eventually compiled and written down. These astrotheological mysteries, however, were later carnalized and historicized to hide them once again in the gospel tale.

---

1. Wheless.
2. Walker, *WEMS*, 856.
3. Waite, 36
4. Eusebius, 240.
5. Eusebius, 243.
6. Pike, 272.
7. Higgins, I, 577.
8. "Intro," Massey's *EBD*.
9. A. Churchward, 313.
10. A. Churchward, 366.
11. Walker, *WDSSO*, 76.
12. Wells, *WWJ*, 179.
13. Anderson, 85.
14. Walker, *WEMS*, 900.
15. Jackson, 187.
16. Jackson, 149-50.
17. Graves, *BS*, 74-5.
18. Wells, *WWJ*, 181-2.
19. Jackson, 137.
20. Walker, *WDSSO*, 39.
21. Graham, 366.
22. Walker, *WEMS*, 1033.

23. Graves, *BS*, 72-3.
24. Higgins, I, 221.
25. Anderson, 137.
26. Allegro, *SMC*, 42.

The Bible, Sex and Drugs

In our quest to ascertain the origins of Christianity and the nature of its founder, we have explored a number of themes and aspects of culture from around the globe. We have also briefly touched upon the controversial subjects of sex and drugs, which are usually omitted or avoided in the present type of analysis. However, these subjects are in fact very important in determining the development of human culture in general and religion in specific. Indeed, they constitute yet another part of the mysteries.

For centuries, the impression given by religionists is that to be a moral person, one must not only forgo but disdain sexuality, viewing it as if it were a curse from the devil rather than a "gift from God." The same can be said of drugs, at least of the variety that has anything to do with altering consciousness, even if such drugs are in the form of "God-given" plants. Hence, the picture of a religious or righteous individual is basically someone who must have (heterosexual) sex only with one person within a sanctioned marriage, if at all; to be in a constant state of procreation; and to remain as sober as "a judge." To those who think life is to be enjoyed, rather than endured, this picture represents a dull, robotic state, to say the least.

The reality is that there have been times on this planet when cultures have recognized sacred sexual practices and sacramental plants not only as gifts from "God" but also *paths to* "God," or "Cosmic Consciousness," as it were. Indeed, sex and drugs have been considered from time immemorial as devices to create union with the divine, which is a major reason behind the negative spin put on them by religionists, who insist that only they, "Jesus" or some other entity can be avenues to the divine. In actuality, it is the priest's task to create an artificial separation between human beings and the *omnipresent* "God." However, as even "Paul" says, "an intermediary implies more than one; but God is one"; thus, the priest as intermediary is contrary not only to common sense but also to Christian doctrine, which is one of the many reasons the masses were forbidden for centuries under penalty of death to read the Bible. These sacred sex and drugs practices have thus presented a threat to power-hungry priests and their political flunkies, because, as stated, they require no intermediary between the practitioners and the divine. If an all-powerful, dictatorial state religion was to succeed, it would need to destroy this concept of sacred sex and sacramental drugs from the human psyche and replace it with fear and guilt, such that those who had sex, for example, would be driven to cleanse themselves of their perceived sins by confession or other priestcraft. The exploitation of humanity's weakness regarding sex in particular worked nicely for priestly conspirators, since they could rail against it, knowing very well that people would continue to have it, such that the guilty would then be forced to return repeatedly to the Church for absolution from "sins."

Despite their best efforts, however, the various religionists could not eradicate the widespread spiritual practices utilizing sex and drugs, even under penalty of death. In reality, they held these practices for themselves while hypocritically preaching their evils to the masses and exhorting abstinence from them. As noted, along with the knowledge of astrology, the use of sex and drugs actually has formed part of the esoteric religion or "mysteries" hidden from the masses by the brotherhoods and secret societies that create exoteric and vulgar religions for the masses.

Indeed, these "sacraments" constituted a significant part of the mysteries, as many schools and cults have used sex and drugs in their initiation rites. One such widespread sex-related rite is circumcision, albeit it is an anti-sex one. Although it is widely perceived to be a Jewish custom, circumcision dates back to at least 2300 BCE in Egypt and is also found in other parts of Africa, as well as in Fiji, Samoa, Assyria, Phoenicia, Mexico and South America, prior to the introduction of Judaism and/or Christianity.[1] In Egypt, it was the priests only who were circumcised, but Israel was a "priestly nation," so all of its males were to be circumcised. In contrast to this anti-sex mutilation, however, have been a number of pro-sex, as well as pro-drug, rituals. Even though they have fervently attempted to set themselves apart from the rest, pretending to reject these concepts about sex and drugs, esoteric Judaism and Christianity have also utilized these rites and rituals.

Obviously, there is a downside to sex and drugs, as there is with virtually every human experience. However, mature cultures and individuals have possessed the ability to utilize these powerful devices wisely, and the taboo status itself makes them dangerous, in that they no longer come with the "instruction manual" of initiation. Also, there is an enormous difference between sacred sex and promiscuity, as well between the plant-drugs, or "entheogens" ("generating God"), and the potent extracted chemicals causing such turmoil today.

Sex and the Ancient World

Prior to its vilification, sex was venerated from the earliest times of human history, not only for erotic and spiritual or "tantric" reasons, but also because it was the act of reproduction. As it is today, fertility was very important to the ancients. In fact, the fecundity of the earth was identified with the fertility of the human being. Thus, the rain falling upon and fertilizing the womb of Mother Earth was considered the sperm of Father Sky. In effect, sex-worship was nature-worship, and nature-worship extended to the heavens, where the stars themselves were even named for trees, as noted. Nature was all-important to the ancients, as they realized they were not only dependent upon it but also inexorably linked to it. Jackson describes the nature-worship that developed from this perception:

> The Savior-God religions, Christianity included, are based on the worship of nature. Nature may be defined as the material universe and the forces at work in the cosmos, which operate independently of man. Among the varieties of natural religion were: the worship of the earth, of trees, and other plants; of volcanoes, mountains, water, and wind; of animals; of stars, planets, the moon, the sun, the sky, etc.[2]

The myths of the various human cultures, in fact, ubiquitously reflect this connection to and reverence for nature, especially in regard to the birth process, which was obviously the single most important event in a life and which introduced the human being into the natural world. The reproductive organs and genitalia have thus been a source of tremendous interest. In the ancient world, phallic and yonic symbols were seen everywhere in nature: a cave was a womb; a natural pillar was a phallus; mushrooms resembled both. Furthermore, many nonsexual words can be traced to roots meaning "womb," "menses," "vagina," "phallus," "penis," or "semen."

Sexual symbols were also reproduced abundantly in art, architecture and other cultural artifacts, including religion. In fact, it would probably not be an overstatement to say that every religion/cult has had something to do with sex, including the popular religions of today. Indeed, within organized religions such as Judaism and Christianity phallic and vulval symbols abound that are no longer properly understood by the people. Yet, these sexual symbols hold occultic power; hence, they have been profusely incorporated into temples and cathedrals.

Judaism and Sex

Many people today perceive such symbols, concepts and practices as odd if not deviant, because they have been taught that the polytheistic cultures who overtly practiced them were "bad" and "sinful." The common folk have also been taught to believe that the Jews and Christians have been very moral and have had little to do with sex. For example, it is erroneously perceived that the Old Testament heroes and patriarchs were impeccably moral individuals who never engaged in anything remotely smacking of sexual deviation and perversion. First of all, during the time of biblical peoples, humans were as obsessed with sex as they are now, particularly where they were repressed. Secondly, what is considered deviation or perversion has from the very beginning of humankind been dependent on cultural perspective, varying with different ages and places. Furthermore, often what has been approved by general consensus has also been considered to be "right in the eyes of God/dess." As noted, prior to the monopolizing patriarchy there were widespread matriarchal cultures, every bit as "godly," but with different interpretations of sexuality.

Peering between the biblical covers, we find that many of the book's characters are in reality depicted as engaging in behaviors that would be considered by current standards to be sexual deviation. From early on in the biblical drama we encounter incest, with even Moses himself being a product of it. Later, the righteous Lot is made drunk and then seduced by both his daughters, who bear sons from their incestuous trysts. Rape is another prominent biblical theme, engaged in frequently by the Yahwists, whose history according to the OT is based on the slaughter of other cultures and the kidnapping and rape of their young girls. In fact, a number of the "great" patriarchs and heroes have sex with "concubines," a fancy name for these young girls kidnapped and made into prostitutes. Of course, Solomon was the most conspicuous consumer, with 1,000 wives and concubines, not a true story but used to demonstrate the manliness of his purported progeny. But, if having so many wives and concubines is not adultery, we wonder what is and just what one would call Abraham's relationship with Hagar, his wife's handmaiden, by whom he has a child, or Jacob's various dalliances with Rachel, her sister Leah and their maids, by whom he has children. In the story of Jacob and Rachel, in fact, are found not only sexual deviation, by Christian standards, but also drug use, in that Rachel's "son's mandrakes" are "sex plants" or "fertility fruits."[3] In addition, adultery is practiced even by the great king David, as in the second book of Samuel. Like Noah, who got drunk and let it all hang out, we also find David exposing himself in front of a crowd. And, at Number 25:1-5, the Israelites even participate in an orgy.

Furthermore, although apologists have attempted to explain away its eroticism as having something to do with "the Church" and its "bridegroom," the Song of Solomon is indeed a sexual poem, with references to female genitalia, including as a "pomegranate":

Solomon himself impersonated the phallic god Baal-Rimmon, "Lord of the Pomegranate," when he was united with his divine bride, the mysterious Shulamite, and drank the juice of her pomegranate.[4]

Of the Song of Solomon, Walker further remarks:

We now understand that the whole poem is a work of sexual mysticism, modeled on traditional Sumero-Babylonian wedding songs that combined the erotic with metaphors of vegetable fertility—for this was the ultimate aim of the king's marriage to the priestess-queen who represented the earth and its fruit. The Song of Solomon was retained in the biblical canon only by a convoluted exegesis claiming that its lascivious double entendres represented the love of Christ for his church. . . . In the Song of Solomon it is no patriarchal deity that makes the decision to open the enclosure, but the priestess-queen herself who says, "Let my beloved come into his garden, and eat his pleasant fruits."[5]

The Song of Solomon, in fact, represents one of the saner perspectives of sex in the Bible. Indeed, despite the licentiousness by biblical heroes, so neurotic is the attitude towards sex that when Onan spills "his seed," God strikes him dead, a tale lampooned in the "Monty Python" song: "Every sperm is sacred, every sperm is great. If a sperm is wasted, God gets quite irate." Apparently, Onan's sperm was more valuable than Onan himself. So obsessed with the spilling of the seed is YHWH that it is prescribed that "no man who has had a nocturnal emission shall enter the sanctuary at all until three days have elapsed. He shall wash his garments and bathe on the first day . . ." Thus, "wet dreams" constitute a transgression against the Lord.

The Phallic Cult

One rather bizarre biblical perspective, also held by pre-Hebraic cultures, is "the Lord's" peculiar obsession with the foreskin, which is viewed as the most important token of the covenant between "him" and "his chosen." In fact, the word "circumcision" is used nearly 100 times in the Bible, and one must wonder at this obsession, as well as at the idea that either the Lord so screwed up in creating man that man needs to fix his handiwork, or the Lord finds this piece of flesh so significant as to base his most solemn vows upon it, thus revealing a homoerotic fetish. So obsessed are the biblical peoples with the foreskin that in exchange for the hand of his daughter, Saul demands the foreskins of 100 dead Philistines from David, who enthusiastically indulges the request by bringing Saul 200 foreskins.

The act of circumcision is all the more strange when its origins are not made clear. Among other reasons, including

purportedly serving to make men more docile and socially
acceptable, circumcision was said to be done in imitation of the
female's menstrual blood, "being performed on boys at the age
when girls first 'bled,' and even being described among some
peoples as 'man's menstruation.'"6 Another ritual used to create
such "femaleness" was castration, necessary for a man to
"assume religious authority among the priestesses of the
Goddess." As Walker explains, "All mythologies suggest that,
before men understood their reproductive role, they tried to 'make
women' of themselves in the hope of achieving womanlike
fertility."7 This phenomenon was widespread enough among the
Semites to warrant address by "the Lord," as was penile
amputation, such that those who had been thus mutilated,
evidently either naturally or artificially, were to be excluded from
God's elect: "He whose testicles are crushed or whose male
member is cut off shall not enter the assembly of the Lord" (Deut.
23:1). Yet, at Isaiah 56:4-5, the "infallible" Lord again contradicts
himself and says that eunuchs who keep his sabbath and hold
fast his covenant will be given a "monument and a name better
than sons and daughters . . . an everlasting name which shall not
be cut off."

Obviously, all this biblical talk about circumcision, foreskins
and testicles, as well as "members," "loins," "thighs," "stones,"
"secret parts" and "private parts," is a reflection of the true nature
of the patriarchal religions. As Potter says, circumcision is, in
fact, "a barbaric custom of primitive phallic religion."8 He also
states:

> There were undoubtedly phallic elements in Yahwehism up to
> the time of the prophets and later, some of which were adopted
> from Canaanite religion and some of which were original in it,
> but the central meaning which the name Yahweh had for Moses
> was evidently something like The Living God of Life. That
> included naturally a certain sponsorship of sexual relations, as
> numerous Old Testament passages indicate.9

Indeed, within the patriarchal religions the phallus has been
an object of worship, although this fact has been hidden for a
variety of reasons, not the least of which are its basic homosexual
or homoerotic implications. In fact, the male genitals were so
sacred to the Israelites that if, in defense of her husband, a
woman grabbed the "private parts" of his enemy, she would have
her hand cut off (Deut. 25:11-12). So important were the male
genitalia that solemn oaths were sworn by them, as is reflected at
Genesis 24:9, where Abraham's servant swears an oath by
"putting his hand under the thigh of Abraham his master." The
terms "thigh" and "hollow of thigh" used a number of times in the
OT are actually euphemisms for "penis," and the putting of one's

hand "under the thigh" and swearing an oath is a secret society "handshake":

> . . . an Israelite who was swearing an oath would customarily solemnize it by grasping the penis of the man to whom he was making the affirmation. . . . Before the death of Israel (Jacob), he called his son Joseph to his deathbed, and as Joseph grasped his father's penis, Israel made his son promise that he would take his remains out of Egypt [Gen. 47:29-31] . . . [10]

Regarding this practice, Walker elaborates:

> Patriarchal Semites worshipped their own genitals, and swore binding oaths by placing a hand on each other's private parts, a habit still common among the Arabs. Words like testament, testify, and testimony still attest to the oaths sworn on the testicles.[11]

Walker also explains another biblical phallic euphemism and custom:

> Biblical writers called the penis a "sinew that shrank," lying "upon the hollow of the thigh." This was the sinew that Jacob lost in his duel with "a man who was a god." . . . The garbled story of Jacob and the god-man was inserted chiefly to support the Jews' taboo on eating a penis (Genesis 32:32), formerly a habit of sacred kings upon their accession to the throne. The genitals of the defeated antagonist were eaten by the victor, to pass the phallic spirit from one "god" to the next.[12]

Furthermore, the "pillars" and "groves" of the biblical peoples were in fact lingams, or phalluses, and yonis, or vulvas, and the "household idols" of the patriarchs and heroes were smaller phallic symbols. For example, at Genesis 28:10 and 35:14 Jacob himself is represented as engaging in the very ancient practice of anointing the sacred "pillars," or phallic symbols, which was quite common in Israel.[13]

Hebrew Homosexuality

In addition to these episodes of fetishism and homoeroticism is the peculiar story in the first book of Samuel about the great king David and his enemy Saul's son Jonathan, who apparently falls in love with David:

> And Jonathan stripped himself of his robe that was upon him and gave it to David, and his garments, even to his sword, and to his bow, and to his girdle. . . . And Saul spoke to Jonathan his son, and to all his servants, that they should kill David. But Jonathan Saul's son delighted much in David . . .

Jonathan and David are then depicted kissing each other and weeping together. Later, it is not David who is killed but Jonathan, after whose death David moans, "I am very distressed for you, my brother Jonathan; very pleasant have you been to me; your love to me was wonderful, passing the love of women." The biblical passages certainly seem to be expressing something homoerotic. Of course, these scriptures must be overlooked by moralists, because the general biblical impression of homosexuality is extremely negative. Yet, we also discover that Israelites do in fact engage in "harlotry" with boys and that "male cult prostitutes" ("sodomites") are used even during Solomon's reign (1 Kings 14:24; 15:12) and remain in use centuries later when Josiah goes after them. The Hebrew word for these male cult or temple prostitutes, "qadesh," is the same as "qadash," which means holy, sacred and consecrated. Obviously, the pre-Yahwist Semites had a very different opinion of these "sodomites." Ironically, the term "sodomite" was used by detractors to describe phallus-worshippers, i.e., the patriarchy.

Semitic Bestiality

In addition to the phallus-worship, biblical peoples engaged in bestiality, such a temptation evidently a serious problem, since the Lord had to condemn it several times over a period of hundreds of years, demonstrating an ongoing habit of the "chosen" shepherd tribes. In other words, that this perversion was common is obvious from the fervid exhortations against it. As Akerley says in *The X-Rated Bible*:

> It is axiomatic that one can gain true insight into how prevalent a deviant sexual practice is in a given culture as well as how threatening it is to that culture by the degree of severity of the laws which exist against it. Judging by the fact that the Hebrew law decreed death for zoophilia, forbidden intimacies with animals were commonplace indeed among the Israelites.[14]

Judaism and Women

The problem with the sheep-loving and lingam-worshipping desert tribes was their extreme hatred of women, who have been slandered with the accusation of being sinful, sexual creatures who corrupt otherwise sinless men. Biblical misogyny is reflected in the stories of Lot and of the Levite in Judges, for example, where men are so important that, in order to protect them from bisexual mobs, Lot and the Levite throw out their women: in the case of Lot, his virgin daughters; and in the case of the "good" Levite priest, his sex slave, or "concubine," although his host initially offered the mob his own virgin daughter. The Levite's concubine, of course, is gang-raped and left for dead. Her "compassionate" master finds her on the doorstep, yells at her to get up and, when he discovers she is dead, sheds no tear but immediately cuts her body into 12 pieces and sends the parts to the various tribes. Now, this story must be taken literally, according to bible literalists, so we must conclude that the Levite did indeed engage this appalling behavior, which would be considered a heinous crime in today's society but is perfectly okay for one of God's ancient priests!

Furthermore, while exalting the male genitalia, the OT repeatedly portrays women as having defiling menstrual cycles, during which they must be isolated. Prior to this misogyny, however, the menstrual blood was considered sacred because women were viewed as the creators of life; in fact, as noted, the wine and cup of the Holy Grail were originally Pagan symbols of the blood and womb of the woman. Of course, the degradation of the woman accompanied the vilification of the Goddess, and the biblical attack on the Goddess and female sexuality was tireless:

> The religion of Astoreth, Asherah or Anath and Her Baal—and the accompanying female sexual autonomy—were the enemies. No method was considered too violent to bring about the desired goals.[15]

With this violence came horrendous, oppressive laws against women, who basically became property. Raping virgins was the preferred biblical way to acquire such property, but if the rape victim was already married or betrothed, she was killed. The oppression of women, of course, had much to do with men wishing to be certain of paternity, which evidently was, as Stone says, the "reason that the Levite priests devised the concept of sexual 'morality': premarital virginity for *women*, marital fidelity for *women*, in other words total control over the knowledge of paternity."[16]

Things did not improve much for the status of women with the introduction of the "new superstition" of Christianity, which continued the assault on women and which refined sexual repression.

Christianity and Sex

Because of such fervent repression, Christianity is perceived as having nothing whatsoever to do with sex. In reality, rather than the picture of peaceful, celibate devotees commonly portrayed, early Christians themselves were viewed as sexual deviants and perverts. That this perception was a problem is verified not only in the writings of the Church fathers but in the canonical Letter of Jude, in which the author is concerned with the impression given by men who were "blemishes" on Christian "love feasts":

> For admission has been secretly gained by some who long ago were designated for this condemnation, ungodly persons who

pervert the grace of our God into licentiousness and deny our only Master and Lord, Jesus Christ. . . just as Sodom and Gomorrah and the surrounding cities, which likewise acted immorally and indulged in unnatural lust, serve as an example by undergoing a punishment of eternal fire. Yet in like manner these men in their dreamings defile the flesh . . . These are blemishes on your *love feasts*, as they boldly carouse together, looking after themselves . . .

Walker explains the meaning and origin of these mysterious Christian "love feasts":

Agape or "love feast" was a rite of primitive Christianity, adapted from pagan sexual worship. Another name for the *agape* was *synesaktism*, that is, the imitation of Shaktism, which meant the Tantric kind of love feast involving sexual exchange of male and female fluids and a sense of transcendent unity drawn therefrom. Early church fathers of the more orthodox strain described this kind of worship and inveighed against it. Some time before the seventh century, the *agape* was declared a heresy and was suppressed.[17]

Some of the Gnostic Christian sects utilized ancient sex rituals considered vulgar by the orthodox Christian cultists and used by them to discredit Gnosticism. A number of these practices were in fact open to honest charges of lewdness, vulgarity and perversion, but the orthodox Christian movement certainly has not been devoid of such behavior, nor have been the adherents of any ideology known to mankind. Over the centuries many perversions have gone on behind monastery walls and church doors, including the ongoing abuse of young boys and girls, sexually assaulted or raped by "celibate" priests. This abominable behavior is actually a result of sexual repression, which produces obsession and sickness.

Furthermore, while the inhabitants pretended to be celibate, Christian nunneries were turned into whorehouses that serviced monks, among others. In fact, it was an apparently common practice for the compromised nuns' babies to be tossed into ponds near the nunneries or buried in basements. As Blavatsky relates:

Luther speaks of a fish-pond at Rome, situated near a convent of nuns, which, having been cleared out by order of Pope Gregory, disclosed, at the bottom, over six thousand infant skulls; and of a nunnery at Neinburg, in Austria, whose foundations, when searched, disclosed the same relics of celibacy and chastity![18]

While it may be argued that Luther was biased, apparently other such sites were discovered in Blavatsky's time in Austria and Poland.

Despite its antisex attitude and pretensions, Christianity incorporated many sexual images, including the ancient and ubiquitous lingam symbol, evident in the church steeple, and the yoni or womb, symbolized by the church nave. From the earliest times, in fact, temples and churches themselves served as wombs, into which the priest, with his phallus-shaped hat would enter, beseeching the Deity for fertility and fecundity. As Allegro says:

> The temple was designed with a large measure of uniformity over the whole of the Near East now recognizable as a microcosm of the womb. It was divided into three parts: the Porch, representing the lower end of the vagina up to the hymen, or Veil; the Hall, or vagina itself; and the inner sanctum, or Holy of Holies, the uterus. The priest, dressed as a penis, anointed with various saps and resins as representing the divine semen, enters through the doors of the Porch, the "labia" of the womb, past the Veil or "hymen" and so into the Hall.[19]

However, like Judaism, patriarchal Christianity was primarily a phallic cult. Walker describes the pervasiveness of the phallus in Christianity:

> A hint of the broad extent of phallic Christianity in England appeared after World War II when Professor Geoffrey Webb, of the Royal Commission on Historical Monuments, investigated a bomb-damaged altar of an old church and found a large stone phallus within it. Further researches showed that the altars of approximately 90% of English churches built before 138 had hidden stone phalli.[20]

The phallus was also called "perron" or "Big Peter" and represented, as we have seen, St. Peter, the "Rock" or stone lingam, of which the Christians were also anointers. As Walker says, "Christian phallus worship went on undiminished into the Middle Ages and beyond."[21]

Along with the phallus-obsession came the issue of circumcision, as well as castration, popular in the widespread cult of Attis/Cybele during Paul's time and given the green light by "Jesus," who is made to say of castration, "He who is able to receive this, let him receive it" (Mt. 19:12). In fact, a number of Paul's teachings revolved around the mutilation of the male genitalia. As Walker relates:

> Paul hinted that he was one of the "new creatures" in Christ, neither circumcised nor uncircumcised. A man would have to be one or the other, unless he altogether lacked a penis. . . . He scorned the "natural" (unmutilated) man for his lack of spirituality: "The natural man receiveth not the things of the Spirit of God; for they are foolishness unto him" (1 Corinthians 2:14). . . . Paul wrote to the Galatians: "I would they were even

cut off which trouble you" (Galatians 5:12). The word rendered "cut off" also meant "castrated."[22]

Indeed, over the millennia, many people have taken such exhortations to heart, believing that their mutilation would gain them special powers and favors in heaven. In Russia has existed for hundreds of years a cult called the Skoptsi, who in frenzied rituals brutally cut off their genitalia, including testes, penises and breasts. This mutilation predates Christianity in Russia but has been found within Christianity for centuries, justified by scriptures, and these Skoptsi are not an aberration, as castration was common among the early Christians, including some of the Christian fathers. As Akerley relates:

> Contemporaneous with Origen was a sect which was so enthusiastically addicted to the practice that, in addition to requiring castration of all its members, they also castrated any guest who was rash enough to stay under their roof. The sect, known as Valesians, performed their castrations with a hot piece of metal, referring to the act appropriately as a "baptism of fire." . . . The tonsure of the early priests of Christianity is a recognized symbol of castration and the skirted cassock worn by priests is, at least in part, an imitation of the many religions competing with early Christianity which required that their priests don female attire only after they were castrated.[23]

So enthusiastically did Origen embrace such concepts that he castrated himself, much to the admiration of several Christian proponents:

> Origen was highly praised for having castrated himself. Justin's *Apologia* said proudly that Roman surgeons were besieged by faithful Christian men requesting the operation. Tertullian declared, "The kingdom of heaven is thrown open to eunuchs." Justin advised that Christian boys be emasculated before puberty, so their virtue was permanently protected. Three Christians who tried to burn Diocletian's palace were described as eunuchs.[24]

Eusebius, however, called Origen's self-castration a "headstrong act" and said that Origen had taken Christ's comments about "eunuchs for the kingdom of heaven" in "an absurdly literal sense" and that Origen was "eager both to fulfil the Saviour's words and at the same time to rule out any suspicion of vile imputations on the part of unbelievers." Eusebius's comment about the castration serving to "rule out any suspicion of vile imputations" surely refers to sexual activity, possibly homosexual, imputations that over the centuries frequently were slung between competing sects, both Christian and Pagan.

At the same time as they were emulating women through castration, the Christians, like their predecessor Jews, were trying to destroy the Goddess:

> . . . Bible revisions tended to erase earlier deities, especially female ones. After the centuries of choosing and revising canonical books, nearly every trace of female divinity had been eliminated from Christian literature.[25]

As stated, however, temples and churches themselves represented the vulva and womb, and Christianity was not devoid of feminine symbolism, even though it tried to suppress it, except where it benefited the Christian hierarchy occultically. For example, one of the most common feminine symbols is the mandorla or vesica piscis, an almond-shaped symbol representing the female genitalia and used to frame images of Jesus, the Virgin Mary and assorted other Christian saints.[26] Likewise the rosary is an ancient symbol of the Goddess, the Queen of Heaven, as roses represent female genitalia.[27] In addition, female figures displaying oversized yonis were common on churches and cathedrals throughout Europe but were later obliterated by prudish church officials.[28] In reality, behind the scenes of the patriarchal cults, feminine symbolism is common, but it does not express an admiration for female *humans*; rather, Christian female symbolism is an attempt to usurp the supernatural powers of the "Goddess," or female aspect of creation. In fact, so obsessed was the patriarchy to "destroy the works of the female" that it declared an all-out war on them, the results of which were as tragic as they were absurd, as hundreds of thousands of "wise women" were tortured and murdered in the centuries that followed. Walker relates another result of this warfare:

> Suppression and concealment of the female sexuality is always a primary goal of patriarchy. Christian Europe even officially denied the existence of a clitoris and forgot the words for it, which is why the ancient Greek term is still in use. The church taught that women should not feel sexual pleasure, so the female organ of sexual pleasure became unmentionable.[29]

The Sacred Prostitute/Harlot

Prior to the demise of the matriarchal cultures and degradation of sexuality thus brought about by the patriarchy, priestesses of the Goddess frequently were teachers of love and sex; hence, they were given the moniker "sacred prostitutes." Ancient cultures often believed that the way to "God" was through the Woman, and they also knew that sexual repression was a social timebomb, such that they considered sexual expression an initiation into not only the mysteries but also society itself.

Echoing this wisdom, St. Thomas Aquinas said, "Take away prostitutes from the world, and you will fill it with sodomy."[30] For such essential duties, sacred harlots were considered holy women, the role, as we have seen, of Mary Magdalene. As Walker relates:

> Ancient harlots often commanded high social status and were revered for their learning. As embodiments of the Queen of Heaven, in Palestine called Qadeshet, the Great Whore, the harlots were honored like queens at centers of learning in Greece and Asia Minor. Some even became queens. The empress Theodora, wife of Justinian, began her career as a temple harlot. St. Helena, mother of Constantine, was a harlot before she became an empress-saint. . . . Temple prostitutes were revered as healers of the sick. Their very secretions were supposed to have medical virtue.[31]

Like their Jewish predecessors, the Christians denigrated this sacred sex practice, turning the Goddess's priestesses into "whores." As Walker further states:

> Because whores occupied a significant position in paganism, Christians vilified their profession. Churchmen didn't want to stamp out prostitution altogether, only amputate its spiritual meanings.[32]

In reality, some of the most exalted biblical women were sacred harlots. Indeed, the lineage of Jesus himself is traced to these priestesses and holy women:

> The four female ancestors of Jesus who are enumerated in the genealogies of Matthew are not only non-Hebrew, they are all four forms of the harlot. Thamar plays the whore with Judah to become the first female ancestor of Jesus, or the Lion of Judah. Rahab of Jericho is frankly designated the harlot, and she is the second female ancestor. Ruth, the Moabitess, whose history is so tenderly told, is the third. The fourth is Bathsheba, wife of Uriah the Hittite, the prostitute of David.[33]

The degradation of the sacred harlot and prostitution has taken a tremendous toll on the status of women over the centuries, reducing them to servants, babymachines and sex slaves. For example, Walker states:

> Outside the Judeo-Christian tradition, prostitution often became a fully legitimate lifestyle. Black Africans never fully accepted missionaries' views on the matter. White men's laws deprived African women of their property and their monopoly of farming, trading, and crafts by which they supported their children. African women suffered a devastating loss of self-respect, for in their society a woman without her own income was regarded with contempt.[34]

While many people think that the world has become more moral with the repression of sex, this notion is simply not true. Walker also relates the general end product of the denigration of sex and women:

A change in the attitude toward rape was one of the contrasts between the ancient world and the medieval one in western Europe. The Romans and Saxons punished rapists by death. Normans cut off a rapist's testicles and gouged his eyes out. The gypsies' Oriental heritage demanded the death penalty for the rapist. Hindu law said a rapist must be killed, even if his victim was of the lowest caste, an Untouchable; and his soul should "never be pardoned." The Byzantine Code decreed that rapists must die and their property must be given to the victim, even if she was no better than a slave woman. Christian laws changed the picture. Serfs' wives, sisters, or daughters were always sexually available to their overlords under the new regime. Peasant brides were raped by the baron before being turned over to their bridegrooms—probably to be raped again. The Church made it illegal for any wife to refuse sexual intercourse unless it was a holy day when marital sex was prohibited. Therefore, marital rape was encouraged. . . . From the Inquisition's torturers, who usually raped their victims first, to Victorian doctors who attacked female genitals with leeches, many kinds of rape could be traced to what has been called "virulent woman-hatred in fundamentalist Christianity." Recent studies show that most rapists were professed members of a religious sect and learned to regard sex as evil, in the traditional Christian manner.[35]

Furthermore, contrary to popular belief, the idea of a sacred marriage originated in pre-patriarchal, Pagan cultures and was anathema to the early Christian fathers, who abhorred matrimony.

The destruction of the "works of the female" also had the effect of propelling the world into centuries of bloodlust and warfare. As Walker further states:

[War is a] primary patriarchal contribution to culture, almost entirely absent from the matriarchal societies of the Neolithic and early Bronze Ages. Even when Goddess-worshipping was beginning to give way to cults of aggressive gods, for a long time the appearance of the Goddess imposed peace on all hostile groups. . . . Patriarchal gods tended to be warlike from their inception—including, or even particularly, the Judeo-Christian God. Stanton observed that the Old Testament's account of God's nature, purpose, and activities on behalf of his Chosen People boils down to "a long painful record of war, corruption, rapine, and lust." . . . But Christianity was never a pacifist religion.... All-male Christianity was disseminated by violence.[36]

The result of this degradation of the female includes the destruction of the planet itself, the Great Mother Earth. As Walker also relates:

> . . . the Middle East [is] a true Waste Land: the great desert which eastern mystics attributed to Islam's renunciation of the fertile Great Mother. Western pagans also maintained that if the Mother should be offended or neglected, she might curse the land with the same desperate barrenness that could be seen in Arabia Deserta and Northern Africa.[37]

Christianity and Homosexuality

As Aquinas said regarding the prohibition of prostitution, the repression of sex and the hatred of women have indeed led to one of the behaviors most outwardly despised by Judaism and Christianity: "sodomy," or homosexuality. In reality, in many places in the ancient world homosexuality was not considered a sin but was practiced for a variety of reasons. The Christian world, of course, has never been devoid of homosexuality, and Christianity's early representatives were compelled to address it, as in the Epistle of Barnabas. In Barnabas, the writer explains the "Laws of Diet" as laid down by Moses, including the following:

> Among other things, [Moses] also says, *you are not to eat of the hare* [Lev. 11:6], by which he means you are not to debauch young boys, or become like those who do; because the hare grows a fresh orifice in its backside every year, and has as many of these holes as the years of its life.

This paragraph is enlightening indeed, in that we discover not only that the debauching of young boys was a problem with the Christians but also that hares grow numerous orifices in their "backsides!" It is also interesting that this "dietary law" apparently does not prohibit the debauching of *older* men.

Eusebius relates a passage from the works of Christian father Tatian concerning the Cynic philosopher Crescens that gives further insight into the climate of the day: "Crescens, for instance, who made his lair in the great city, went *beyond everyone in his offences against boys* . . ."[38] The use of the term "everyone" is curious, in that it indicates that the writer himself and his compatriots were included in this category, rather than being outsiders. The statement also appears to express that this type of debauchery was common and socially acceptable, such that Crescens was evidently to be reviled not for his homosexuality itself but for his excessiveness.

As noted, the early Christians had some intriguing secret initiation rites, as also evidenced by the fragment of a letter purporting to be from Clement of Alexandria to one Theodore. In this letter, Clement repudiates the Gnostic-Christian sect of the Carpocratians and outlines secret scriptures that evidently had been originally in the Gospel of Mark, chapter 10, and contained "an account of the raising of a young man from the dead, a rite of initiation, and a brief excerpt of an encounter between Jesus and three women."[39] In response to Theodore's questions, Clement relates the contents of this "Secret Gospel of Mark" as follows:

> And they come into Bethany. And a certain woman whose brother had died was there. And, coming, she prostrated herself before Jesus and says to him, "Son of David, have mercy on me." But the disciples rebuked her. And Jesus being angered, went off with her into the garden where the tomb was, and straightaway a great cry was heard from the tomb. And going near Jesus rolled away the stone from the door of the tomb. And straightaway going in where the youth was, he stretched forth his hand and raised him, seizing his hand. But the youth, looking upon him, loved him and began to beseech him that he might be with him. And going out of the tomb they came into the house of the youth, for he was rich. And after six days Jesus told him what to do and in the evening the youth comes to him, wearing a linen cloth over his naked body. And he remained with him that night, for Jesus taught him the mystery of the Kingdom of God. And thence, arising, he returned to the other side of the Jordan.[40]

In response to Theodore's questions, Clement further relates:

> After these words follows the text, "And James and John come to him," and all that section. But "naked man with naked man," and the other things about which you wrote, are not found.

The suggestion is, of course, that Christ and his followers were alleged to have engaged in homosexual rites. As Akerley says, "In the secret gospel, Christ emerges as a teacher and practitioner of forbidden occult practices with strong erotic overtones."[41] However we wish to interpret this data, it would not be untruthful to assert that a measurable amount of homosexuality has gone on behind the doors of monasteries and churches from the beginning.

In fact, considering how much emphasis is placed on the male in patriarchal religion such as Christianity, in which monks are "married to the Church" and passionate lovers of Christ, it is ironic that homosexuality is overtly considered a terrible crime, with "those who have intercourse with males" being viewed as "blasphemers" who cannot enter into the "kingdom of heaven." Because of the vicious mentality towards homosexuality, which is purported to originate with the Deity "himself," homosexuals were driven to become monastics, in order to "purify" themselves of their overwhelming, "sinful" desires. This penitential sequestration has led to monasteries full of repressed homosexuals attempting to contain their urges but frequently failing, which is understandable considering the temptation all around. In other words, monasteries have served as "communal closets." In fact, this practice was common enough to warrant prohibition in the Secret Instructions of the Society of Jesus, i.e., the Jesuits:

> If two of ourselves have sinned carnally, he who first avows it will be retained in the Society; and the other will be expelled; but he who remains permanent, will be after such mortification and bad treatment, of sorrow, and by his impatience, and if we have occasion for his expulsion, it will be necessary for the future of it that it be done directly.

The orthodox Christian position towards homosexuality has been that it is a seductive temptation to be resisted at all costs, an interesting attitude, because homosexuality would in truth only be tempting to those who are initially inclined thus. Furthermore, a number of the Christian historicizers and conspirators also had serious problems with sex and women, such that it would not be farfetched to suggest they were homosexuals, repressed, closeted or otherwise, like the purported secret, rich, closeted homosexual fraternity of today called "Gamma Mu." One can find clues as to the homosexuality within their Christian brotherhood scattered here and there in the various writings of the early Church fathers, in secret gospels and allegedly in at least one unexpurgated canonical gospel, as noted. In any case, it can be argued with 100 percent certainty that monastic brotherhoods have often been the site of homosexual activity.

One of the most notorious of the "closeted" Christian homosexuals was in fact King James I, the patron of the King James Bible, which is so highly esteemed by evangelical Christians. As related by Otto Scott, King James "was a known homosexual who murdered his young lovers and victimized countless heretics and women. His cruelty was justified by his 'divine right' of kings."[42]

Carpenter sums up the attitude and destructiveness caused by the repression and vilification of sexuality, asking:

> How was it that the Jews, under the influence of Josiah and the Hebrew prophets, turned their faces away from sex and strenuously opposed the Syrian cults? How was it that this reaction extended into Christianity and became even more definite in the Christian Church—that monks went by thousands into the deserts of the Thebaid, and that the early Fathers and Christian apologists could not find terms foul enough to hurl at Woman as the symbol (to them) of nothing but sex-corruption and delusion? How was it that this contempt of the body and

degradation of sex-things went far into the Middle Ages of Europe, and ultimately created an organized system of hypocrisy, and concealment and suppression of sex-instincts, which, acting as a cover to a vile commercial Prostitution and as a breading ground for horrible Disease, has lasted on even to the edge of the present day?[43]

He continues, contrasting this pathology with the predecessor Pagan world:

When one compares a healthy Pagan ritual—say of Apollos or Dionysus—including its rude and crude sacrifices if you like, but also including its whole-hearted spontaneity and dedication to the common life and welfare—with the morbid self-introspection of the Christian and the eternally recurring question "What shall I do to be saved?"—the comparison is not favorable to the latter.[44]

Judaism, Christianity and Drugs

Also abhorrent to so-called moralists is the notion of "recreational" or "spiritual" drug use, even though the history of such drug use dates back many thousands of years, with numerous cultures utilizing herbs, plants and fungi for a variety of reasons, including medicinal and religious purposes. In fact, countless cultures have possessed sacred plants, herbs, fungi or other entheogenic "drugs" that allowed for divination and communion. Such sacred plant-drugs included the mysterious "Soma," which was personified as a teaching-god in the Indian text the Rig Vega, as well as Haoma, the Persian version of the teacher-plant. Opium, hashish and cannabis also have a long history of use within religious worship and spiritual practices. For example, on Sumerian tablets dating from about 5000 BCE are references to a "joy plant," believed to be the poppy, from which opium is derived.[45] The Chinese recorded the use of cannabis, hemp or marijuana as early as the 3rd millennium BCE, and cannabis use in India began at least 4,000 years ago. Furthermore, the magi and spiritual "physicians," or "Therapeuts," were wandering drug-peddlers and members of the fraternity network, in which drugs were used for initiation and divination. Indeed, there has been plenty of drug use in the Levant and Middle East, including by biblical peoples:

Although some historians are reluctant to attribute drug use to Semitic peoples, the Old Testament abounds with references to the cultivation and administration of medicinal herbs. There is, for example, a provocative inventory of favored plants in the Old Testament Song of Solomon (4:13-14). . . . While many of the apparent references to drugs in the Old Testament remain open to question, there is little doubt that an incident recorded in *Genesis* refers to Noah's drunkenness from alcohol.[46]

Alcohol, of course, is a potent drug, but is not frowned upon in Christianity because it is truly drugging and stupefying, whereas entheogens, including the "magic mushroom," have the ability to increase awareness and acuity. In fact, there have been many mushroom cults, going back at least as far as Sumeria, and, according to Allegro, et al., much of the world's sacred literature incorporated the mushroom in an esoteric manner. Indeed, it has been posited that the biblical "manna from heaven" actually refers to a psychedelic mushroom, a notion implying that Moses and his crew were on one very long, strange trip in their 40 years of wandering in the desert and living off manna. Regardless of whether or not manna is the magic mushroom, the mushroom cults have been real and influential in history. Moreover, Maxwell claims that the priests of Israel were known to use mushrooms:

> Many people are unaware that this kind of hallucinogenic mushroom-taking by the high priest of Israel was, in point of fact, a very integral part of the old Hebrew theology and the old Hebrew tradition . . . [it] still is used in the Middle East today.[47]

In fact, the high priest of Israel wore a mushroom headdress, as do officials of the Eastern Orthodox Church to this day, reflecting the esoteric veneration of this sacred fungus.[48] Thus, drug use did not end with the advent of Christianity. Like the Eastern Orthodox headdress, the ubiquitous architectural dome is also a reflection of the mushroom cult. In addition, in a ruined church in Plaincourault, France, is a Christian fresco dating to the 13th century that depicts the Edenic tree of knowledge as a stem with amanita muscaria mushrooms branching off it. Furthermore, drug use was rampant all over Christian Europe, and even Pope Leo XIII used a "coca leaf and red wine concoction."[49]

As Baigent and Leigh say:

> . . . there is little dispute today that drugs—psychedelic and of other kinds—were used to at least some extent among the religions, cults, sects and mysteries schools of the ancient Middle East—as indeed they were, and continue to be, across the world. It is certainly not inconceivable that such substances were known to, and perhaps employed by, 1st-century Judaism and early Christianity.[50]

In fact, Allegro's suggestion that "Jesus" was a mushroom god is not implausible, considering how widespread was the pre-Christian Jesus/Salvation cult and how other cultures depict their particular entheogens as "teachers" and "gods." However, this mushroom identification would represent merely one aspect of the Jesus myth and Christ conspiracy, which, as we have seen incorporated virtually everything at hand, including sex and drugs, widely perceived in pre-Yahwist, pre-Christian cultures as being "godly."

1. Doane, 86-7.
2. Jackson, 143-4.
3. Akerley, 209.
4. Walker, *WEMS*, 806.
5. Walker, *WDSSO*, 425.
6. Walker, *WDSSO*, 173.
7. Walker, *WEMS*, 142.
8. Potter, 214.
9. Potter, 45.
10. Akerley, 252-3.
11. Walker, *WEMS*, 793-4.
12. Walker, *WEMS*, 143.
13. Doane, 47.
14. Akerley, 295.
15. Stone, 189.
16. Stone, 161.
17. Walker, *WDSSO*, 168.
18. Blavatsky, *IU*, II, 58.
19. Allegro, *SMC*, 25.
20. Walker, *WEMS*, 796.
21. Walker, *WDSSO*, 321.
22. Walker, *WEMS*, 776.
23. Akerley, 300.
24. Walker, *WEMS*, 146.
25. Walker, *WEMS*, 184.
26. Walker, *WDSSO*, 10-11.
27. Walker, *WDSSO*, 13.
28. Walker, *WDSSO*, 104.
29. Walker, *WDSSO*, 101.
30. Walker, *WEMS*, 823.
31. Walker, *WEMS*, 820.
32. Walker, *WEMS*, 822.
33. Massey, *HJMC*, 81.
34. Walker, *WEMS*, 825.
35. Walker, *WEMS*, 842-5.
36. Walker, *WEMS*, 1058.
37. Walker, *WEMS*, 1064.
38. Eusebius, 125.
39. Barnstone, 339.
40. Barnstone, 340.
41. Akerley, 73.
42. Leedom, 120.
43. Carpenter, 184-5.
44. Carpenter, 191.
45."The History of Drugs and Man," Anonymous.
46."The History of Drugs and Man," Anonymous.
47."Symbols, Sex and the Stars."
48."Symbols, Sex and the Stars."
49."The History of Drugs and Man," Anonymous.
50. Baigent & Leigh, 61.

Bronze sculpture hidden in the Vatican treasury
of the Cock, symbol of St. Peter.
Inscription reads "Savior of the World."
(Walker, *WDSSO*)

Christian fresco showing the Amanita muscaria mushroom
as the tree of good and evil in the Garden of Eden.
(Allegro, *SMC*)

Essenes, Zealots and Zadokites

It has been established that the Christian religion is astrotheological, reflecting the mythos and ritual found ubiquitously long prior to the Christian era. The question remains as to how the Christian myth was created and by whom. In looking for the originators of Christianity, many people have pointed to the Essenes, the third Jewish sect besides the Pharisees and Sadducees in Jerusalem. Of course, because they cannot accept the nonhistoricity of virtually the entire gospel story and the Christian founder, such evemerists usually make the claim that beneath the countless layers of Pagan mythological lacquer there is yet a great master named Jesus who traveled around Palestine, ostensibly as a teacher of mysteries. The absolute dearth of evidence for such a master and his movement has perplexed researchers to no end, since, according to the gospel tales, not only had Jesus done wondrous works but so had his apostles, gaining fame near and far, and Christian churches with established hierarchies had popped up all over the Mediterranean during the first few decades after "the savior's" death. In their quest for such a leader and his organization, all these seekers have been able to find is mention of the brotherhood of Essenes. Thus, because so little of the "history" presented in the New Testament appears in the historical or archaeological record, historicizing scholars have insisted that the Christians were the Essenes and that Christ must have been an Essene master and "teacher of righteousness" who, like John the Baptist, another purported Essene, went out preaching, baptizing and spreading the word of the Essene doctrine.

Like the mythicists' arguments, the Essene theory of Christian origins is repugnant to fundamentalists, because it posits the pre-existence of the Church, which would mean that Jesus was not its founder. The Church, according to such Christians, was not already established at the time of Christ's alleged advent but, under Christ's supernatural power and inspiration, miraculously caught fire and was empowered beyond all expectations, to spring up out of nowhere into a full-fledged movement, with extraordinary influence and, apparently, a good deal of wealth. In swallowing this yarn, then, we are supposed to accept that, within a number of years of Jesus's purported death, a ragtag band of illiterate fishermen and semiliterate peasants questionable in their faith in Jesus was able to establish a full-blown church, with bishops, deacons, parishes and rituals. All this they supposedly did, despite the fact that Jesus was claimed to have said the end of the world was "close at hand."

The Myth of Primitive Christianity

In spite of this fervent belief, there remains no evidence for such a miraculous genesis, so scholars have been compelled to turn to the white-robed Essenes as the wellspring of Christianity. Within this theory, early Christianity was "pure" and "untainted" by corruption, which came only after it was institutionalized as the Catholic Church. Massey describes the "primitive Christianity" myth:

> Another popular delusion most ignorantly cherished is, that there was a golden age of *primitive Christianity*, which *followed* the preaching of the Founder and the practice of his apostles; and that there was a falling away from this paradisiacal state of primordial perfection when the Catholic Church in Rome lapsed into idolatry, Paganised and perverted the original religion . . . Such is the pious opinion of those orthodox Protestants who are always clamouring to *get back beyond* the Roman Church to that ideal of primitive perfection supposed to be found in the simple teachings of Jesus, and the lives of his personal followers . . . But when we do penetrate far enough into the past to see somewhat clearly through and beyond the cloud of dust that was the cause of a great obscuration in the first two centuries of our era, we find that there was no such new beginning, that the earliest days of the purest Christianity were pre-historic . . . [1]

There is little foundation for the assumption of a peaceful, ideal beginning, because from its inception "pure" Christianity was full of bickering and power struggles, as reflected in the Epistles and Acts. In fact, the Church started out in a contentious manner and continued in this way for centuries, as is evidenced by the endless forged texts and bloody battles over doctrine.

In reality, the so-called pure Christianity would have been abhorrent to the followers of a simple morality such as the Essenes. For example, in addition to the squabbling, threats and apparent murders of converts such as in Acts, where Peter is virtually depicted as having caused the deaths of a husband and wife over money, this "pure" Christianity included the exhortation of slaves to remain slaves, such as at 1 Timothy 6:1, where Paul says, "Let all who are under the yoke of slavery regard their masters as worthy of all honor, so that the name of God and the teaching may not be defamed." (Obviously God's name is more important than living, breathing and suffering human beings, whose wretched state in itself should be a stain on God's good name in the first place.) Again, at Colossians 3:22 Paul says, "Slaves, obey in everything those who are your earthly masters"; and, at Titus 2:9, he exhorts Titus to "bid slaves to be submissive to their masters and to give satisfaction in every respect . . ." As noted, early Christians, in fact, were both slaves and slaveowners.

As Pagels says, "Many Christians were themselves slave owners and took slavery for granted as unthinkingly as their pagan neighbors."[2] In other words, no egalitarian Christianity existed, and Christians were discouraged from inciting slaves to demand their freedom. As for the Essenes, "There is not a single slave among them," says Philo.

Thus, the "freedom-loving" Paul exhorts the Christians to submit to authority, not to rebel, as presumably his purported master would do and supposedly did do, according to the gospel story. Paul even claims that those same authorities who allegedly destroyed Jesus should be both obeyed "in everything" and basically equated with God Himself:

> Let every person be subject to the governing authorities. For there is no authority except from God, and those that exist have been instituted by God. Therefore he who resists the authorities resists what God has appointed, and those who resist will incur judgment. . . . For the same reason you also pay taxes, for the authorities are ministers of God, attending to this very thing. Pay all of them their dues, taxes to whom taxes are due, revenue to whom revenue is due, respect to whom respect is due, honor to whom honor is due. (Rom. 13)

Furthermore, the author of 1 Peter entreats:

> Be subject for the Lord's sake to every human institution, whether it be to the emperor as supreme, or to governors as sent by him to punish those who do wrong and to praise those who do right. . . . Fear God. Honor the emperor.

So much for the rebellious Jesus and his movement. No Essene would be preaching such things, but we can pretty much guess who would.

As to the real state of "pure" Christianity and its adherents, Fox relates:

> "In privated houses nowadays," claimed the pagan Celsus, c. 170, "we see wool workers, cobblers, laundry workers and the most illiterate rustics who get hold of children and silly women in private and give out the most astonishing statements, saying that they must not listen to their father or schoolteachers, but must obey them. They alone know the right way to live, and if the children believe them, they will be happy. They whisper that they should leave their teachers and go down into the shops with their playmates in order to learn to be perfect. . ."[3]

Most of the early Christians were of the lower, uneducated classes, a fact that was a thorn in the side of Christian proselytizers, who were always very interested in gaining converts of high social status, by bribes of one sort or another. In the early Christian book the *Octavius* by Minucius, the protagonist "complained that Christians assemble the 'lowest dregs of society' and 'credulous women, an easy prey because of the instability of their sex,' . . ."[4] And, as Origen stated, most of the "lowest dregs" and poor had "very bad characters."

As Keeler says, "It sounds strange to hear persons in these days express a desire for a 'return to primitive Christianity, when all was peace and love.' There never was such a time."

The Essenes

Not only was there no "primitive" Christianity of love and peace that can be traced to the Essenes, many of Jesus's own teachings were in contradiction to or non-existent in Essene philosophy, and Jesus's character and a number of his actions were contrary to the notion of him being an Essene master-healer. For example:

> A poor Canaanitish woman comes to him from a long distance and beseeches him to cure her daughter who is grievously obsessed. "Have mercy on me, O Lord," she pleads. But he answered her not a word. The disciples, brutes as they were, if the scene were real, besought him to send her away because she cried after them. Jesus answered, and said: "I was only sent to the lost sheep of the House of Israel." She worships him, he calls her one of the dogs.[5] (Mk. 7:25-27; Mt. 15:21-27)

In this passage, Jesus is not only uncompassionate, he is frankly rude, sexist and racist. Jesus is thus not the "gentle and loving son of God." Regarding Jesus's unmerited reputation as "Prince of Peace," Baigent and Leigh ask:

> Was Jesus indeed the meek lamblike saviour of subsequent Christian tradition? Was he indeed wholly non-violent? Why, then, did he embark on violent actions, such as overturning the tables of the money-changers in the Temple? . . . Why, before his vigil in Gethsemane, did he instruct his followers to equip themselves with swords? Why, shortly thereafter, did Peter actually draw a sword and lop off the ear of a minion in the High Priest's entourage?[6]

The zealous Jesus's rash and brusk behavior is, in fact, contrary to the restraint and discipline of the peaceful Essenes.

In addition, the Essenes were not followers of the Hebrew Bible, or its prophets; nor did they subscribe to the concept of the original fall that required a savior. They did not believe in corporeal resurrection or a carnalized messiah. In fact, it was possibly they, among innumerable others, who were being addressed in the Second Letter of John: "For many deceivers have gone out into the world, *men who will not acknowledge the coming of Jesus Christ in the flesh . . .*" The real Essenes, as described by Josephus, abhorred falsehood, and, unlike the Christian fathers, would not have mindlessly believed what is unbelievable.

Moreover, the Essenes were teetotalers and ate to live, whereas the assumed Essene Jesus appears to be a drunkard and glutton in comparison.

In fact, the forger of 1 Timothy, alleging to be "Paul," makes a scathing attack on individuals who seem very much like the Palestinian Essenes:

> Now the Spirit expressly says that in later times some will depart from the faith by giving heed to deceitful spirits and doctrines of demons, through the pretensions of liars whose consciences are seared, who forbid marriage and enjoin abstinence from foods which God created to be received with thanksgiving . . .

In assailing those who prohibit marriage and preach what is apparently vegetarianism, "Paul" is referring to the Buddhistic, monastic fraternity that proliferated around the known world and included the Essenes.

Moreover, the Essenes studied the writings of the ancients and, being widespread around Palestine, certainly would have known its geography and topography. However, as noted, the New Testament writers do not, making numerous mistakes in their geographical descriptions.

Yet, despite all these disparities, many people still wish to label the Essenes as the earliest Christians, because, according to the Christian tale, the church grew far too rapidly than was possible, with its hierarchy and organization shooting up all around the Mediterranean within a few years and decades, demonstrating pre-existence. No doubt certain aspects of the New Testament were modeled after the white-robed monkishness of the Essenes, who were eventually swallowed up by the newly created religion, as well as by Judaism and any number of cults. However, the Jewish aspects of the Christ character are mainly Pharisaic, not Essenic. As Massey asserts:

> In proving that Joshua or Jesus was an Essene, there would be no more rest here than anywhere else for the sole of your foot upon the ground of historic fact. You could not make him to be the Founder of the Essene, Nazarite or Gnostic Brotherhoods, and communities of the genuine primitive Christians that were extant in various countries a very long while before the Era called Christian. . . . Philo-Judaeus . . . was one of the Essenes— but does not seem to have met with the Gospel Jesus amongst them, or heard of him . . . [7]

Furthermore, Josephus was himself an Essene a few decades after the purported advent of the great Essene master who allegedly made such a splash, yet the historian never heard of the "historical" Jesus. In other words, the Essenes themselves never recorded the gospel Jesus as one of their own; nor did they create him. Nor did Josephus once mention the numerous Christian churches and well-established hierarchies that had purportedly sprung up all over the place.

Qumran and the Dead Sea Scrolls

The idea of a monolithic Essene community from which Christianity issued was nonetheless given fuel with the discovery in 1947 of the caches of scrolls in caves near the ruined site of Qumran along the Dead Sea in present-day Jordan. However, there is yet another debate as to whether or not Qumran was indeed an Essene community. In fact, Josephus and Philo reported that the Essenes had no centralized location but dwelled in many cities and villages in Judea. Pliny asserted that some Essenes did reside by the Dead Sea, but their settlement was near En Gedi, dozens of kilometers south of Qumran. Also, Pliny stated that there was not a woman among the Essenes, whereas at Qumran were found the graves of women and children.

In reality, the archaeological finds indicate Qumran was *not* an Essene community but a waystation for travelers and merchants crossing the Dead Sea. In *Who Wrote the Dead Sea Scrolls?*, Norman Golb evinced that Qumran was a fortress, not a monastery, as the site contains a large tower and a forge for weapons, both of which would be appropriate for the Jewish sect of the Zealots but not the Essenes. In addition, Golb posited that the scrolls were not written by any Essene scribes but constituted a collection from libraries in Jerusalem secreted in caves throughout eastern Palestine by Jews fleeing the Roman armies during the First Revolt of 70 CE. Of the theory that the scrolls represented only an Essene library, Golb says, "The necessary implication of the Qumran-Essene theory was that while several hundred works of the four-thousand-strong Essene movement had escaped destruction, virtually no shred of manuscript stemming from the first-century A.D. population of Judaea as a whole—numbering at least two million individuals at the beginning of the First Revolt—had been spared."[8] The Dead Sea collection is in fact eclectic, representing more than one sect or priesthood, competitors, in actuality.

Although the scrolls are thus not connected to "the" Essenes as such, they represent "intertestamental literature" and are extremely important in the quest for the origins of Christianity. Indeed, the absence of any early Christian writings or references to Jesus and his movement in this eclectic collection, some of which was no doubt from Jerusalem, serves as testimony that Christianity did not in fact yet exist when the scrolls were deposited, up to 40 and possibly more years after the purported death of Jesus. As Dr. Alan Snow states, "Some modern Biblical scholars and archaeologists believe that these scrolls could have

been hidden in the caves as late as the Jewish revolt of 132-135
A.D."9

As to the contents of the scrolls, not only is no variant of the
term "Essene" found in them, but they actually contain non-
Essenic and anti-Essenic ideas, as well as Hellenizing elements
that could have been produced only by Hellenized "Jews," i.e.,
Israelites both "zealous for the law" but also interpreting the law
to allow "foreign" influence, in this case Greek. The fervent tone
and warrior-stance of some of the scrolls also belie any Essene
origin and further indicate an attribution to the Zealots, who
were, per Josephus, the "fourth sect of Jewish philosophy, [of
whom] Judas the Galilean was the author," the term Galilean
itself being used to denote a Zealot. The association with the
Zealots is also confirmed by the presence of the scroll "Song for
the Holocaust of the Sabbath" at both the caves near Qumran
and the Zealot fortress of Masada. As Snow also says, "The
authors of the Dead Sea Scrolls were Zealots and believed in the
God-ordained destiny of the people of Israel."10

The Zealots

From their contents, it is thus evident that a number of the
more important original scrolls were written and deposited by
"Zealots for the Law." As such, the authors were reflecting their
history as representatives of the zealousness that emanated from
their deity himself, who was not only a *jealous* but also a *zealous*
god. In fact, although they are perceived as a separate sect, the
"Zealots" constituted anyone who was, like their god, "zealous for
the law," such as the various prophets, patriarchs, kings and
assorted other heroes. Such zealousness did not end with the Old
Testament, however, as "the" Zealots were overtly acknowledged
in the New Testament, with the disciple "Simon the Canaanite"
also being called the "Zealot," and with the fiery gospel Judas,
who resembles the zealous Judas mentioned by Josephus. As
noted, however, Judas was the name of the ancestral savior-god
of Judah, as well as of a number of Judaic kings and their
sacrificial proxies, many of whom could be termed "Zealots." In
any case, as is clear from his fanatical behavior and
megalomania, Jesus himself can be categorized as a Zealot and in
fact was called "Jesus the Galilean" (Mt. 26:69). As Waite says:

> Not only was Jesus surrounded by Zealots, but he was himself a
> Zealot. It was in execution of a Jewish law, called "the law of the
> Zealots," that, with a whip made of small cords, he scourged the
> money-changers and drove them from the temple.11

Peter was also called a Galilean, and his behavior in slicing off the servant's ear is certainly zealous. Paul is also obviously "zealous for the law," as seen.

According to Origen, "the" Zealots were a branch that broke off the Essenes, which would explain the confusion between the two sects, both of which were also claimed to be offshoots of the Hasidic/Levitical priesthood, which was itself zealous, representing the Zealous God. Of this confusion between sects, Baigent and Leigh related that, in their search for the "historical" Jesus, they found themselves "confronted by an apparently bewildering spectrum of Judaic cults, sects, and sub-sects, of political and religious organisations and institutions, which seemed sometimes to be militantly at odds with one another, sometimes to overlap. It became quickly apparent to us that the labels used to differentiate between the groups—Pharisees, Sadducees, Essenes, Zealots, Nazorenes—were neither accurate nor useful."[12]

The zealous followers of Judas the Galilean were called Sicarii, named for the daggers they carried and plunged into the "bosom" of victims. Obviously, though they may have come from the same seed, the Zealots were not Essenes, as, in fact, the Essenes abhorred such violent zealousness. However, other brotherhoods not only made use of such Zealots, they actually trained and funded them. "The" Zealots were, in general, lower-level initiates into secret societies, while the highest level were the sacerdotal class or Magi.[13] If the higher level initiates wanted something done, the Zealots were the foot soldiers to send out.

Galilee and Samaria

As stated, the name Galilean itself was used to designate a Zealot, and gospel characters such as Jesus and Peter were said to be Galileans. In fact, Galilee plays an important role in the Christian drama, as it was at Capernaum, on the border between Galilee and Syria that Christ was said to have "come down" and spent part of his time. Although at one point a part of Israel/ Samaria, Galilee was multinational, with a largely Syrian influence, and by the first century BCE was mostly Gentile. Galilee was also known to be a stronghold of the zealous Jewish priesthood, the Sadducees. As Lockhart relates:

> . . . the early "Penitents of Israel," composed of the purist Sadducees from the Temple in Jerusalem, left Judea and made their headquarters in the land of Damascus. Many sectaries founded settlements in the northern districts, and these "Elect of Israel" of the latter days interacted with like-minded spirits among the groups devoted to the old Nazarite way of life.[14]

Galilee was thus a site for Sadducees displaced from the temple of Jerusalem, going back to the split between the kingdoms of Judah and Israel, when the Sadducees were called "sons of Zadok." Some of the Sadducees, however, remained in Jerusalem, where they held the high priesthood for centuries until they were driven out of the Sanhedrin by the Pharisees in the first centuries before and after the beginning of the Common Era.

As noted, the definition of and division between of the various sects and priesthoods were not hard and fast. These groups' agenda or "interpretation of the law," in fact, depended on where they were located. Although they are deemed "purists" and "conservatives," the Sadducees were, in reality, Hellenizing Jews, and those who initially "repaired to" the northern kingdom of Israel became distinct from their counterparts in Jerusalem. The Israelite Sadducees apparently served as the "Jewish" priesthood not only in "Damascus," or Galilee, but also in Samaria, which is identified with Damascus at Isaiah 10:9: "Is not Samaria like Damascus?" Indeed, in Samaria, or Ephraim, were several important Israelite sacred sites, such as Shiloh, Shechem, Beth-El and Mt. Gerizim, operated by the northern Levitical priesthood, which included Zadokites/Sadducees who left Judah on various occasions.

Like so many "sons of Israel," Israel/Ephraim/Samaria was accused by the Judeans of "whoring after other gods" and was purportedly punished for worshipping the "Harlot," or Goddess, and "Baal," the "golden calf" of Horus/Moloch, i.e., the sun. Lockhart describes the religion of the northern kingdom:

> The Israelite religion of northern Palestine so dear to the Nazarenes seems to have absorbed much of the worship of the Syrians and Phoenicians. This older faith carried folklore and ideas and usages foreign to its southern neighbour, and the pre-Christian Nazarenes of the north are shown by Epiphanius to have had an affinity with the gnostically inclined Samaritans, and the Samaritans with the Essenes.[15]

Thus, the northern Israelite religion, although ostensibly Yahwistic, was also "Pagan," following the old polytheism "of the fathers" and having greater correspondence to Gnosticism and Christianity than the Judean religion.

In addition, the biblical story concerning the split between the kingdoms is related by members of the Jerusalem or Judean priesthood in the "books of the prophets," which were rejected by the Israelites/Samaritans, who accepted only the Pentateuch, also known as the Torah or "Book of Law."

According to these Judean books of the prophets, two centuries after the kingdom divided the entire Israelite population of Samaria was removed by the Assyrians and replaced with Persians or "Cutheans," who are portrayed by the Jews as the diabolical Samaritans. However, the Samaritans claimed they themselves were the original Israelites and true keepers of the law, and, like the Judeans, they maintained the right to interpret the Torah in their own favor. Lockhart describes the Samaritans and their side of the story:

> . . . the Samaritans were a mixed population of Israelites and descendants of Assyrian colonists, and although professing a form of Judaism, slowly broke religious ties with both Galilee and Judea over the centuries. This break with Judaism also meant a break with the Temple cult at Jerusalem, and resulted in the Samaritans' building an independent temple on Mount Gerizim at the time of Alexander. . . . Viewing themselves as of a single, homogenous race, they claimed that they were actually the descendants of the Ten Tribes, utterly denying that the latter were ever deported *en masse* to Assyria as the Old Testament relates.[16]

It seems that the "lost tribes" story was created by the Judeans to explain why the northern kingdom inhabitants, although "Jews," had a very different interpretation of Mosaic Law and worshipped after the manner of the original "Pagan" inhabitants. The story of the Israelite population being replaced also provided an excuse for the Jews to enslave the inhabitants of the northern kingdom, which, according to the scriptures, they did.

Furthermore, while the Jews considered the Samaritans to be "dogs," the feeling was mutual, and the Samaritans would claim their own right to serve as rulers over Israel, using the passage at Genesis 49:10: "The scepter shall not depart from Judah, nor the ruler's staff from between his feet, until *Shiloh* comes, and to him shall be the obedience of the peoples." Shiloh, as noted, is a northern kingdom sacred site, also referring to the Messiah. In fact, the Samaritan Israelites were expecting their own Messiah, who in Greek was called "Dositheus," or "Gift of God." In addition, the early Christian texts the Clementine "Recognitions" "state that Dositheus was the founder of the sect of the Sadducees, which means probably nothing more historically than that Dositheus, as was to be expected of a Samaritan, rejected all the subsequently canonical books, and held to the Pentateuch alone."[17] Thus, the Clementine Recognitions associate the Sadducees with the Samaritans, as does the Pharisaic Talmud. Indeed, after their explusion from the Sanhedrin, the remaining Judean Sadducees joined the Samaritans against the Judean Pharisaic priesthood.

The Zadokites/Sadducees

The rivalry between the priesthoods of Israel and Judah continued for centuries, extending into Galilee. At the end of the second century, Galilee was violently subjugated by the Judeans: "Conquered by Aristobolus I in 104-103 BCE, Galilee was forcibly converted to Judaism, even to the extent of its population's having to undergo compulsory circumcision."[18] Needless to say, like their Samaritan neighbors, the Galileans were not fond of the Judeans. In fact, Galilee was apparently a symbol of Judean oppression, which is evidently why Jesus was made to "come down" at Capernaum. After this invasion and forcible conversion, the ranks of the Herodian outpost Qumran supposedly swelled, evidently with Samaritans and Galileans, or Zealots "from Damascus," who also were the Sadducees, or "sons of Zadok," i.e., "the priests who keep the covenant," as the Zealots of the scrolls identified themselves. Indeed, Solomon Schechter, the discoverer of the Cairo edition of one important scroll also found at the Dead Sea—the "Zadokite Document," also known as the "Damascus Rule" or "Damascus Covenant"—considered the Dead Sea Zadokites an "offshoot" of the Sadducean sect, "possibly the Dosithean schism,"[19] thereby also equating this Sadducean offshoot with the Samaritans.

According to Josephus, the Sadducees/Zadokites rejected the Pharisaic traditions not contained in "the law," which ostensibly meant that they spurned everything but the Pentateuch, again identifying the Sadducees with the Samaritan priesthood. However, the Sadducees/Zadokites were not only Samaritans but also Levites, such that they did at least interpret the teachings of the prophets, in their favor, of course. In this manner, the Zadokites of the scrolls appear to interpret the prophets to favor Israel/Ephraim/Samaria over the "wicked priests of Jerusalem," as in the commentary on Nahum: ". . . when (eventually) the glory of Judah suffers dishonor, those in Ephraim who have hitherto been duped will flee from the midst of those men's congregations and, renouncing them that led them astray, attach themselves (once more) to (the true) Israel."[20]

In addition, one Zadokite commentator virtually identifies his Syrian/Samaritan affiliation when he interprets Habakkuk 2:17, which refers to "the violence done to Lebanon," as "'Lebanon' stands here for the Communal Council . . ." Concerning this statement, the author of *The Dead Sea Scriptures*, Theodore Gaster, notes, "The name Lebanon means 'white' (referring to the white cliffs). The point of the interpretation lies in the fact that the members of the Brotherhood wore white—as do the modern Samaritans and Mandaeans."[21]

The author of the Zadokite Document reveals his own Samaritan affiliation when he says, "Nevertheless, in all of their generations He has ever raised up for Himself duly designated men . . . And to these has He ever revealed His holy spirit at the hands of His anointed [Christ] and has ever disclosed the truth . . ." Of these designated men, Gaster notes, "I.e., the anointed priests, custodians and teachers of the Law, which is here called 'the Truth,' as regularly among the Samaritans and Mandaeans."[22] In fact, the Mandaeans were a Syrian pre-Christian brotherhood, one of the originators of Gnosticism whose high priests were called "Nasoreans," i.e., Nazarenes/Nazarites. This passage also sounds Christian, obviously, and in fact represents a seed of the Gnostic-Christianity that would emanate out of Samaria/Galilee/Syria.

Furthermore, the author of the Zadokite Document refers to the split between the kingdoms and cites Amos 5:26, wherein "the Lord" says to Israel, "I will exile Sikkuth your king and Kiyyun your image, the star of your God . . . beyond Damascus." The Hebrew also translates, "You have borne the *tabernacle* of *Moloch* and Chiun your images, the star of your Elohim . . . beyond Damascus." The tabernacle of Moloch/Molech is also that of Saturn/El, the old Hebrew god, as is the star-god Kiyyun/Chiun/Kaiwan, a name "used to symbolize Israelite apostasy," i.e., by Judeans against the northern kingdom. Of course, the goal of the Judean Amos's diatribe was to destroy Israel's high places and sanctuaries so its inhabitants would be forced to be involved in the centralized religion in Jerusalem. In addition, the objects of Amos's ire "hide themselves on the top of Carmel," which was a northern brotherhood stronghold or "monastery."

However, as Vermes says, ". . . the Damascus Rule transforms this threat into a promise of salvation,"[23] and the Zadokite author favorably interprets these passages by claiming that "Sikkuth your king" refers to the "Books of the Law" and "Kiyyun your image" to "the books of the prophets whose words the House of Israel has despised," i.e., the post-Pentateuchal texts written by Judeans. The "star of your God" the Zadokite renders as "every such interpreter of the Law as indeed repairs to 'Damascus,' even as it is written: There shall step forth a star out of Jacob, and a scepter shall rise out of Israel.'"[24] The author of Zadokite further claims that they will be judged who "rejected the Covenant of God and the pledge which they swore in 'the land of Damascus'—that is, *the new covenant.*" Thus, these Zadokites/Sadducees were Syrian/Israelite/Samaritan/Carmelite worshippers of El/Molech who considered themselves the inheritors of the New Covenant and who emphasized that it was out of Israel, not Judah, that the "scepter" or, as they called him, the "Prince of the entire congregation" would come.

The story of Israel's "betrayal" with the shrine of Molech is important not only to the Zadokites but also to the zealous Christian disciple Stephen, who, at Acts 7, repeats the episode in an allegorical recitation that in actuality represents the Hebrews' constant switching back and forth between the worship of the day and night skies. Stephen finishes off his speech with mention of the "Righteous One, whom you have now betrayed and murdered," purportedly referring to Jesus. This title "Righteous," also applied to Abraham and the disciple James, could be translated as "Zadok," as the meaning of that name is "just" or "righteous." In fact, according to the genealogy in Matthew, Jesus himself is a "son of Zadok."

The Maccabean Revolt

Indeed, there was a "son of Zadok" named *Jesus* purportedly persecuted by "the Jews," during the Maccabean Revolt of 167 BCE, long prior to the alleged advent of the gospel Jesus. At that time, the Jerusalem Zadokite priestly family was deposed when the traditionalist Hasmoneans sought to overthrow the Syrian leader Antiochus, who had captured the Jerusalem temple and, "determined to hellenize Judaea completely, forbade under penalty of death the observance of the sabbath and the practice of the rite of circumcision. In the temple he had a pagan altar, probably in honour of Zeus . . ."[25] While the Jews thus viewed him as a diabolical enemy, the Samaritans considered Antiochus a god and savior. Furthermore, according to Josephus, the Alexandrian historian Apion accused the Jerusalem Jews of being cannibals, relating that when Antiochus opened the temple he found being fattened a Greek captive whose entrails were to be shared among the Jewish elders, a ritual they were alleged to have performed annually with kidnapped foreigners. This story is possibly true, as according to Lord Kingsborough and others the Judeans were "horrible cannibals," which would explain why they were despised by their neighbors. However, this particular episode may also be an anti-Judean tale originating with any number of enemies, including the Samaritans.

The Hellenizing charge under Antiochus was led by the "modernist" Zadokite Jesus, a "sage from Jerusalem," and was opposed by the Hasmonean/Maccabean Mattathias and his sons, one of whom was named *Judas*. This story served as a prototype for the gospel drama, with a Jesus who attempted to abrogate the Jewish religion by introducing a "foreign" influence and who was stopped by a Judas in league with traditionalists. In this story and the gospel tale, in fact, are contained the ongoing rivalry between Israel and Judah. Furthermore, after the dethronement by the Maccabees, many of the remaining Jerusalem Zadokites scattered, some into Syria, Galilee and Samaria and others into Egypt, where the Zadokite high priest Onias IV, "in direct breach of biblical law erected a Jewish temple in Leontopolis with blessing of King Ptolemy Philometor (182-146 B.C.),"[26] an act that evidently scandalized the Palestinian priesthood and widened the rift.

In the story of the Maccabean Revolt is in fact a Jesus who can be considered the "teacher of righteousness" found in the Zadokite scrolls. However, the term "teacher of righteousness" is a title that could be applied to a number of individuals, past, present and future. "Teacher of righteousness" could also be translated the "teacher of Zadok," or "Zedek," and, conversely, the "sons of Zadok" could be called the "sons of righteousness."

The Order of Melchizedek

As noted, the "sons of Zadok" were the high priests, the only ones allowed to go to the north part of the temple to offer burnt offerings. The offering by burning is a mark of the cult of Molech, which, as we have seen, is being vindicated in the Zadokite Document. The cult of Molech has been demonstrated to be the same as the order of Melchizedek, whose name "king of Righteousness" could also be written "king of Zadok." As expected, Melchizedek takes an important role in the Zadokite literature. In one of the scrolls (11Q Melch), Melchizedek is depicted as the "savior-king who will bring peace and salvation to the faithful and condign punishment to the wicked and who will also mediate divine forgiveness for the former on the Final Day of Atonement"[27]:

> And Melchizedek will avenge the vengeance of the judgements of God
> . . . your *Elohim* reigns. . . . And your *Elohim* is Melchizedek . . . [28]

The Zadokite brotherhood thus considered Melchizedek, or "righteous Molech," to be *their* El or god. Molech, as noted, is the voracious deity to whom the Israelites sacrificed their children by burning, beating drums and playing instruments to drown out the screams. That the Zadokites were worshippers of the Elohim and Adonai is also demonstrated when the Zadokite author says, "No one is to take the oath by EL—or by AD—," abbreviations utilized out of respect for the Divinit(ies). As we have also seen, Molech, El and the various Elohim/Adonai represent aspects of the sun, and the esoteric sun-worshipping of the Zadokites/Sadducees of the scrolls is further evidenced by the fact that they used a *solar* calendar, as opposed to the Judean lunar calendar. It should also be recalled that horoscopes were found at the Dead

Sea, further demonstrating that the composers were esoteric adherents of the old religion. Also, as related, the synagogues of Galilee/northern Israel, whence evidently came at least some of these Zadokites, commonly had zodiacs in mosaics on their floors.

Moreover, in the Dead Sea "Invitation to Grace after Meals," the psalmist sings, "Although the Most High, forsooth, is Jacob's special Lord, yet does His majesty reach out over all that He has made . . ." The special "Lord" is Adonai; the "Most High" is Elyon or Helios, the sun; and Jacob the Supplanter is Set, the night sky. This passage, then, could read, "Although the sun is the lord over the night sky . . ." In addition, in the "Morning Hymn" the psalmist gushes, "Before Him goes a splendor; behind Him a surge of many waters." These verses refer to the sun as it rises in the morning, demonstrating the reverence the writer holds for the divine luminary.

Naturally, the Zadokite scroll writers also used the tetragrammaton, YHWH/IEUE, although sparingly, compared to the evidently Pharisaic compositions found at the Dead Sea. The tetragrammaton was used because it was believed that anything with the sacred name on it could not be destroyed; yet, the scrolls were ultimately shredded. Furthermore, as a typical priesthood attempting to dominate the world and procure total control over the people, the Zadokites were well trained to give an appearance of "monotheism" so they could claim to be "the Elect" and to hold the keys to the "one Jealous/Zealous God," the war god used to incite their soldier-Zealots. But, again, per Ezekiel, there was that "secret room behind the hole in the wall," which so angered the Jealous God and where the elders were no doubt engaged in the mysteries of "Righteous Molech," or Melchizedek.

The Zadokite Elect's predictions or intentions appear in another Dead Sea Melchizedek text, "The Last Jubilee," which reveals:

> The future king of Righteousness—that is, Melchizedek *redivivus*—will execute upon them God's avenging judgments, and at the same time deliver the [righteous] from the hands of Belial and all those spirits of his ilk.[29]

In this paragraph is another connection between the Dead Sea scrolls and the New Testament, in which Jesus is made a "priest after the order of Melchizedek," as the word "redivivus" is a Latin term meaning "second-hand" as in "building materials," which sounds very much like the "cornerstone the builders rejected," i.e., Jesus, as he is called in the gospel story. Hence, Jesus is "Melchizedek redivivus." This scroll does not serve as an astoundingly accurate "prediction," however, but as a *blueprint* for the creation of the ultimate godman.

Furthermore, the sons of Zadok, like Melchizedek, the priest forever, were the "priests whom God has chosen to keep His covenant firm for ever,"[30] which covenant was "now consummated" with "the church of the members of this Community," as was said in the scroll titled "The Messianic Kingdom."[31] Regarding the word "church" in this text, Gaster says, "It is interesting to find in the Hebrew the same word (*knst*), the Syriac cognate of which was later adopted by the Christians to designate their own communion."[32] Thus, we have yet another element connecting the Zadokites, Syria/Samaria and Christianity.

Joshua

The mention of Joshua in the scrolls provides another piece of the puzzle, since Joshua was a northern kingdom hero. In fact, he was the Carmelite/Israelite tribal sun god and savior, who admittedly served as a "type of Jesus" used in the creation of Christianity.

In discussing one of the "messianic expectation scrolls," regarding the "five Scriptural passages attesting the advent of the Future Prophet and the Anointed King and the final discomfiture of the impious," Gaster relates:

> The fifth is an interpretation of a verse from the Book of Joshua. An interesting feature of this document (not noticed by the original editor) is that precisely the same passages of the Pentateuch are used by the Samaritans as the stock testimonial to the coming of the Taheb, or future "Restorer". They evidently constituted a standard set of such quotations, of the type that scholars have long supposed to have been in the hands of New Testament writers when they cited passages from the Hebrew Bible supposedly confirmed by incidents in the life and career of Jesus.[33]

These statements themselves constitute a virtual acknowledge-ment that the scroll author is a Samaritan and that Jesus was a remake of Joshua by Samaritans. Furthermore, since the scrolls evidently for the most part were not written at Qumran but gathered from elsewhere, possibly over a period of two centuries, it is feasible that some of these Samaritan Zadokites emanated out of the ancient monastery at Mt. Carmel, site of a Temple of Jupiter or Iao (Pater) that also served as a temple of Melchizedek and of Joshua.[34] As noted, it was the apostate Israelites hiding on top of Carmel who so vexed Amos.

Their reverence for the sun and for solar gods and heroes, their solar calendar, overt astrological texts and zodiacs in their synagogues, as well as their white robes, all reveal that the Zadokites/Sadducees were remnants of the ancient priesthood of the sun. Furthermore, Gaster relates that the Dead Sea "sectarians" were expecting the end of the "Great Year":

> The [writers of the scrolls] were swept . . . by other winds. One of these was a widespread and well-attested contemporary belief that the great cycle of the ages was about to complete its revolution. . . . When major upheavals occurred, it was promptly supposed that the cycle was nearing its end, that the Great Year was at hand, and that the cosmos was about to revert to chaos. . . . Then the cycle would begin again; a new world would be brought to birth.[35]

The term "Great Year" usually refers to the precession of the equinoxes, of which the age then ending was Aries. According to Josephus, the phrase "Great Year" was also used to describe the 600-year "Phoenix" cycle,[36] which was called by others "Neros." In accordance with the age-old practice of establishing heaven on Earth, i.e., reproducing below what was above, the priest-astrologers worldwide were no doubt intent on creating any number of new solar incarnations for the end of both "Great Years," an auspicious and unstable time indeed. The race was on, and whoever arrived first would get the "Phoenix" as well as dominate the Age of Pisces. The "Jews" basically won, but, as the Zadokites said, "And when the present era is completed, there will be no more express affiliation with the house of Judah; every man will 'mount guard' for himself."[37] Which is to say that there would be no more overt Jews; rather, they would be priests of the "new covenant," or "new testament," as it would later be called.

The Zadokites and Christianity

It is evident that the Zadokites/Sadducees were attempting to produce a "future king of righteousness" to restore to them their traditional priestly role, a new Joshua/Jesus of the type of both the Old Testament and the Maccabean Revolt. Furthermore, the Zadokite Document says, the "scepter of Israel," also the "Prince of the entire Congregation," will destroy the "sons of Seth" (as at Num. 24:17). These "sons of Seth" were evidently the black-robed Pharisees, as mainly luni-stellar cult people, while the white-robed Sadducees were mainly solar cultists. These priesthoods and factions vying for supremacy thus reflect the same struggle that goes on daily and nightly, as well as annually and precessionally. Thus, the solar cultist Zadokite covenanters called themselves a church and were expecting "Melchizedek redivivus" out of Israel/Samaria/Galilee who would destroy the "wicked priests of Jerusalem." In this way, the new Joshua or Jesus was to overthrow the Pharisees, as was done in the New Testament.

In their writings, the Zadokites are certain of the coming Messianic Age and the advent of a "wondrous child" who would be precocious at the age of two or three and dazzle his elders, the same traditionally said of Jesus. As Gaster says of the treatise he calls "The Wondrous Child":

It is a prediction (one scholar has called it a horoscope) of the birth of a Wondrous Child, characterized as "the chosen of God" and of events which will ensue thereafter. The child will bear (like Krishna and Buddha) special marks on his body, and will be distinguished by precocious wisdom and intelligence. He will be able to prove the secrets of all living creatures, and no schemes against him will succeed.[38]

Along with these several correspondences between the Zadokites and Christianity are many others. As Golb says, "Scholars of the New Testament have demonstrated abundant parallels between ideas it contains and those found in the scrolls."[39]

The Christian origins can be seen further in the Zadokite Document: "And God will accept their atonement, and because they took refuge in His holy name they shall indeed see salvation at His hand."[40] This very Christian sentence is not an interpolation but reflects one school of thought that shaped Christianity, representing one zealous "Jewish" branch of the ubiquitous pre-Christian salvation cult.

The connection between the Zadokites and Christianity is also evidenced by a variety of concepts and terms, such as the "Holy Spirit," "Salvation," "sons of Light" and "the Elect," a term also used by the Mandaeans/Nazarenes. There is likewise a link between the Mandaeans' Book of John the Baptist and the Genesis Apocryphon found at the Dead Sea.

Furthermore, the author of the Zadokite Manual of Discipline refers to the "deliberative council of the community" in which "there shall be twelve laymen and three priests schooled to perfection in all that has been revealed of the entire Law." Of this council and community, Gaster comments:

No less interesting, and perhaps more exciting, than [the Dead Sea Scrolls'] connection with the Essenes are the many parallels which these texts afford with the organization of the primitive Christian Church. The community calls itself by the same name (*'edah*) as was used by the early Christians of Palestine to designate its legislative assembly as was used by that community to denote the council of the Church. There are twelve "men of holiness" who act as general guides of the community—a remarkable correspondence with the Twelve Apostles. These men have three superiors, answering to the designation of John, Peter and James as the three pillars of the Church.[41]

Regarding this deliberative council composed of "presbyters," the Zadokite continues:

> Any knowledge which the expositor of the law may possess but which may have to remain arcane to the ordinary layman, he shall not keep hidden from them; for in their case there need be no fear that it might induce apostasy.

Here is an admission of the existence of the mysteries, i.e., the mythos and ritual "behind the hidden door." It is also a confession of the conspiracy to keep such mysteries secret from the masses and of their possible effect on them, i.e., that the people would fall away from the faith if they knew such secrets.

The Zadokite further says of the council:

> When these men exist in Israel, these are the provisions whereby they are to be kept apart from any consort with froward [sic] men, to the end that they may indeed "go into the wilderness to prepare the way," i.e., do what Scripture enjoins when it says, "Prepare in the wilderness the way . . . make straight in the desert a highway for our God" [Isa. 40:3].[42]

As Gaster says, "The same quotation is used in the same sense by John the Baptist; Mat. 3:3; John 1:23," thus illustrating yet another important link between the Zadokites and Christianity.

Regarding the role of the "specially holy men," the Zadokite also states:

> Until the coming of the Prophet and of both the priestly and the lay Messiah, these men are not to depart from the clear intent of the Law to walk in any way in the stubbornness of their own hearts.

Gaster notes, "That is, the prophet foretold in Deut. 18:18, 'I will raise them up a prophet from among their brethren, like unto thee [Moses]; and I will put My words in his mouth, and he shall speak unto them all that I shall command him'."[43] The prophet who is supposedly predicted at Deuteronomy 18 is in fact Joshua—that is, *Jesus*, who is to act as a "mouthpiece of God." The priestly and lay Messiahs are, of course, *Christs*. The obvious conclusion is that when all else failed, i.e., when no such divine instruments were forthcoming, the conspirators rolled these exalted personages into one fictionalized character, i.e., Jesus the Christ.

Moreover, Gaster also points out that the Manual of Discipline and Zadokite Document are similar to the Christian texts called the Didache, the Didascalia Apostolorum, and the Apostolic Constitutions of the early Church organization.[44] The scrolls also contained Jewish apocrypha and pseudepigrapha, as well as texts with a Zoroastrian/Hellenistic Gnostic tinge, such as the

"Memoirs of Patriarchs," the Psalms and the "Litany of the Angels," indicating that these Zadokites were of the same brotherhood at Antioch, whence came Gnosticism and where "Christians" were first so called. The Book of Enoch was found at the Dead Sea, as were scrolls containing quotations identical to one in the Epistle of Barnabas and one in the works of Justin Martyr, thus proving the connection between the Christians and the Zadokites.[45]

It was not the Essenes who constituted the "Jewish" brotherhood from which Christianity issued but the Syro-Samaritan Gnostic "sons of Zadok," the authors of various Dead Sea scrolls who were determined to restore their priesthood to its proper place as spiritual leaders of Israel and of all mankind, and who occupied some of the most important places depicted in the NT: Jerusalem, Galilee and Antioch. The Zadokites/Sadducees were the Palestinian contributors to the Christ conspiracy, constituting a sect that "held by the way" of Abraham and Melchizedek, and that, while exoterically representing the "One God," nevertheless esoterically worshipped and propitiated after the manner of the old solar cult and polytheistic, astrotheological religion. As members of the white-robed brotherhood, these Zadokites were in opposition to the black-robed "sons of Seth" who also claimed to represent the Jealous/Zealous God.

In their many internecine battles, the Zadokites were deposed in Jerusalem by the Hasids/Hasmoneans/Pharisees, driven to Syria/Samaria and Egypt. With the destruction of Palestine, another wave of both Jewish and Samaritan refugees entered into the "foreign" brotherhood branches, especially that of Alexandria, one of the most important cities in the ancient world.

---

1. Massey, *GHC*.
2. Pagels, *AES*, 52.
3. Fox, 300.
4. Fox, 300.
5. Massey, *GHC*, 5.
6. Baigent & Leigh, xvi.
7. Massey, *GHC*, 6-7.
8. Golb, 58.
9. Leedom, 63-4.
10. Leedom, 63-4.
11. Waite, 517.
12. Baigent & Leigh, xv.
13. Jackson, 143.
14. Lockhart, 53.
15. Lockhart, 62.
16. Lockhart, 205.
17. Mead, *DJL*, p. 363.
18. Lockhart, 53.

19. Golb, 83.
20. Gaster, 316.
21. Gaster, 346.
22. Gaster, 108.
23. Vermes, 82.
24. Gaster, 76.
25. Wells, *WWJ*, 161.
26. Vermes, 22.
27. Gaster, 390.
28. Vermes, 301.
29. Gaster, 435.
30. Gaster, 97.
31. Gaster, 443.
32. Gaster, 470.
33. Gaster, 393.
34. Higgins, I, 329.
35. Gaster, 8.
36. Josephus, *Antiquities*, I, iii, 9.
37. Gaster, 71.
38. Gaster, 394.
39. Golb, 335.
40. Gaster, 79.
41. Gaster, 39.
42. Gaster, 61.
43. Gaster, 63.
44. Gaster, 40.
45. Baigent & Leigh, 65.

Alexandria: Crucible of Christianity

The confusion regarding the Essenes and early Christianity is understandable, because there was in fact a well-established organization, or "church," long prior to the Christian era, as has been demonstrated repeatedly with references to the numerous brotherhoods, priesthoods, sects and cults around the globe but also concentrated in the area in which the Christian drama is alleged to have taken place, i.e., Syria, Galilee, Samaria and Judea. In reality, as we have seen, like its savior and doctrine, Christianity's hierarchy was based on a variety of "Pagan" predecessors, such as the Mithraic and Brahmanical priesthoods, as well as on the Hellenistic-Jewish Zadokite/Sadducean model outlined in the Dead Sea scrolls.

Although such brotherhood and organization are pretended by Christians not to have existed, they are also revealed throughout the New Testament, in which the nascent Christian church is already presented as having, in the words of Taylor, "the full ripe arrogance of an already established hierarchy; bishops disputing for their prerogatives, and throne-enseated prelates demanding and receiving more than the honours of temporal sovereignty, from their cringing vassals, and denouncing worse than inflictions of temporal punishment against the heretics who should presume to resist their decrees, or dispute their authority."[1] Obviously, such an established institution could not have appeared overnight out of nowhere but was, in fact, pre-Christian. Concerning this pre-existing organization, Massey says:

> The existence of primitive and pre-historic Christians is acknowledged in the Gospel according to Mark when John says, "Master, we saw one casting out devils in thy name, and he followeth not us." . . . According to the account in Matthew, before ever a disciple had gone forth or could have begun to preach historic Christianity, there was a widespread secret organization ready to receive and bound to succour those who were sent out in every city of Israel. Who, then are these? They are called "The Worthy." That is, as with the Essenes, those who have stood the tests, proved faithful, and been found worthy. According to the canonical account these were the pre-historic Christians, whether called Essenes or Nazarenes; the worthy, the faithful, or the Brethren of the Lord.[2]

And Doherty states:

> Within a handful of years of Jesus' supposed death, we find Christian communities all over the eastern Mediterranean, their founders unknown. . . . Paul could not possibly account for all the Christian centres across the Empire; many were in existence

before he got there. . . . A form of Christian faith later declared heretical, Gnosticism, clearly preceded the establishment of orthodox beliefs and churches in whole areas like northern Syria and Egypt. Indeed, the sheer variety of Christian expression and competitiveness in the first century, as revealed in documents both inside the New Testament and out, is inexplicable if it all proceeded from a single missionary movement beginning from a single source. . . . Paul meets rivals at every turn who are interfering with his work, whose views he is trying to combat. The "false apostles" he rails against in 2 Corinthians 10 and 11 are "proclaiming another Jesus" and they are certainly not from Peter's group. Where do they all come from and where do they get their ideas? The answer seems inevitable: Christianity was born in a thousand places, in the broad fertile soil of Hellenistic Judaism. It sprang up in many independent communities and sects, expressing itself in a great variety of doctrines.[3]

This "other" Jesus being proclaimed by a rival group was in fact the ubiquitous, non-historical Savior of the numerous cults and religions of the pre-Christian brotherhood network, and his name was a secret spell used, among other things, to "cast out devils."

The existence of "Christian" churches before "Jesus of Nazareth" is also attested to by the author of the Epistle to the Philippians attributed to early Church father "Polycarp" (69?-155?), in which he says of Christ, "For he glories in you in all the churches *who then only knew God; for we did not then know him.*"[4]

The Therapeuts

As we have seen, the Zadokites/Sadducees of the scrolls constituted a major part of the eventual Christian edifice. However, as also demonstrated, there were numerous other religions, sects and brotherhoods, including and especially the Gnostics, whose earliest efforts to create a new religion were in fact non-historicizing and non-Judaizing, such that Christianity was not born solely of Judaism by any means. It was, in actuality, the creation of the Pagan priesthood, with a Jewish overlay.

In addition, the term "Essene" was used not only for the Palestinian sect, but, as Josephus says, there was "*another order of Essenes,*" and Walker relates that at "the Ephesian temple of Artemis, the *melissae* were accompanied by eunuch priests known as *essenes,* meaning 'drones.'"[5] In reality, there were several groups of "Essenes."

These pre-historic Christians were called by Philo not only Essenes but also Eclectics, Ascetics and Therapeuts, who were indeed members of a brotherhood that already had parishes, churches, bishops, priests and deacons long before the Christian era. Headquartered at Alexandria, this Therapeutan brotherhood also observed the same festivals as those of the "later" Christianity, and, like Christianity, pretended to have apostolic founders. Also like the historic Christians, these pre-historic "Christians" used scriptures they claimed were divinely inspired and had colonies at the same places claimed by the historic Christians, i.e., Rome, Corinth, Galatia, Ephesus, Philippi, Colosse and Thessalonica, as found in the Pauline epistles—all before the alleged advent of Jesus Christ.[6]

Like "Essene," the Greek word "Therapeut" means "healer" or "physician," as in "physician of the soul." The Therapeuts were, in fact, salvation cultists, but their savior was the "light of the world that every eye can see," because, also like the Essenes and so many others, they were "sun-worshippers." They were therefore no strangers to the ubiquitous solar myth, which existed in virtually every culture of the day in myriad forms and which previously had been historicized a number of times in the Old Testament. As Philo stated regarding the Therapeuts:

> They turn to the east, and, as soon as they espy the sun rising, they stretch aloft their hands to heaven and start praying for a fair day, and for truth and clear judgement in their vision.[7]

Like virtually the entire Mediterranean world, the Therapeuts also esteemed the Great Goddess, Isis/Mari, Herself a healer and savior. As Allegro relates:

> The Therapeutae . . . claimed Isis among their patrons. She was reckoned to cure the sick and to bring the dead to life, and she bore the title "Mother of God."[8]

Thus, the Therapeuts were basically "Pagan" "polytheists" and syncretizing Gnostics attempting to unify the solar, lunar and stellar cults. Doane says of this widespread and well-established brotherhood:

> For many centuries before the time of Christ Jesus there lived a sect of religious monks known as *Essenes, or Therapeuts; these entirely disappeared from history shortly after the time assigned for the crucifixion of Jesus.* There were thousands of them, and their *monasteries* were to be counted by the score. Many have asked the question, "What became of them?" . . .[9]

In short, they became the Christians, as it was they who created Christianity.

The Gospels in Egypt

In addition to the Church organization well in place prior to the Christian era was the pre-existence of the entire gospel story, in bits and pieces around the "known world," eventually put together by the Therapeuts at Alexandria. That the original gospels and epistles were in the possession of the Therapeuts is attested to by Church historian Eusebius. In his admission, Eusebius first relates what Philo said of the Therapeuts:

> They possess also short works by early writers, the founders of their sect, who left many specimens of the *allegorical* method, which they take as their models, following the system on which their predecessors worked.[10]

As noted, the Therapeuts were also the Gnostics, as is evidenced by the acknowledgment that their "short works" were *allegorical* rather than literal. The change from Gnostic to Orthodox Christianity, in fact, constituted the switch from knowledge of the allegory to blind faith in the literal. Eusebius goes on to say:

> It seems likely that Philo wrote this after listening to their exposition of the Holy Scriptures, and it is very probable that what he calls short works by their early writers were the gospels, the apostolic writings, and in all probability passages interpreting the old prophets, such as are contained in the Epistle to the Hebrews and several others of Paul's epistles.

Of the Therapeutan Church, Eusebius remarks, "These statements of Philo seem to me to refer plainly and unquestionably to members of our Church." Eusebius's assertions are more than just peculiar when one considers he was *the* church historian who was purporting to be recording a continuous apostolic lineage, such that, had it really existed, these important aspects of the history of the Christian religion surely would have been widely known by virtually everyone indoctrinated into it.

Concerning Eusebius's admissions, Taylor states:

> . . . Eusebius has attested, that the Therapeutan monks were Christians, many ages before the period assigned to the birth of Christ; and that the Diegesis and Gnomologue, from which the Evangelists compiled their gospels, were writings which had for ages constituted the sacred scriptures of those Egyptian visionaries.[11]

These pre-Christian gospels and epistles were those of the Gnostics, especially of Marcion, creator of the first New Testament, who was an "anti-Jewish" *Samaritan* member of the Therapeutan brotherhood, which constituted, Eusebius admits, the early Christians. Marcion's texts originated at Antioch, which represented the birthplace or cradle of Christianity. However, it was at Alexandria, the crucible of Christianity, where many key ingredients were combined, including the Indian/Egyptian narratives and mysteries, and where the allegorical and astrotheological characters eventually began to be carnalized and Judaized.

This Therapeut origin of the autographs or original "gospel" texts would seem to contradict the fact that Jesus and his church were not Essenic, since the Essenes are frequently identified with the Therapeuts. However, there are important distinctions between the monkish sect of Palestine and the mystery school at Alexandria. As Philo stated, the Essenic communities in Palestine and Arabia "did not soar to such a lofty height of philosophic and mystic endeavour as the members of the community near Alexandria. . ."[12] The Essenes of Palestine were much simpler and more contemplative than the worldly Therapeuts, who were profoundly engaged in the mystery religions, initiations and rituals. While both were called "healers," these were two different sects, although they were connected, as is the case with numerous brotherhoods and secret societies. The Therapeuts were, in fact, a major part of the brotherhood network that stretched from Egypt to China and up into Europe. Indeed, many of the aspects in the gospels attributed to "the" Essenes, such as prayer, fasting, celibacy, baptism, contemplation, cleanliness, healing, etc., were in reality practices common to the monkish fraternities around the world for millennia.

Regarding the confusion between the Essenes and Therapeuts, Waite says:

> By most writers the Essenes of Palestine and the Therapeuts of Egypt have been confusedly treated as the same people; or if not the same, it has been supposed that one was a branch or colony of the other. Later scholarship has shown, however, that neither of these theories is correct.[13]

Eusebius also makes the distinction between the Therapeuts and Essenes when he relates a passage from Hegesippus stating that the Therapeuts were basically Christians but the Essenes were of the "various Groups of the Circumcision, among the Children of Israel, all hostile to the tribe of Judah and the Christ."[14] Obviously, then, these Church fathers are acknowledging not only that the Therapeuts were the Christians and that the Essenes were not, but also that the Essenes were actually at odds with the Therapeuts.

Naturally, neither the Therapeuts nor the Essenes could be identified in the gospels, since that would serve to reveal the pre-existence of their Christian-like fraternities. Nevertheless, the Therapeutan ideology left its mark on the New Testament. In addition to the white-robed monkishness already discussed, the statements about the mysteries and the "kingdom of heaven" are references to initiation into the Therapeutan mystery school and doctrine. The Therapeutan network also included the Palestinian Nazarenes, which is why they are mentioned and why Jesus was claimed to be one of them, although the meaning was obfuscated to "Jesus of Nazareth" so that, again, the pre-existence of the brotherhood would not be known. As Wells says:

> In Acts 24:5 the hostile Jews describe Paul as a "ringleader of the sect of the Nazarenes"—which does not here mean "people from Nazareth" but "Christians". In the Talmud too the term is used as a Jewish term of abuse for Christians. . . . It is thus possible to hold that the adjective "Nazarene" originally designated a strict pre-Christian sect out of which Jesus and the Church emerged."[15]

These Nazarenes were also Mandaeans and Gnostics; thus, they were Syrians and Samaritans, enemies of the Judeans. Furthermore, in addition to being a Nazarene, Paul calls himself a deacon, which was already a low-level office of the Therapeutan brotherhood. The evangelist Luke was also made to be a physician, or *Therapeut*. In the gospel story, Jesus is also depicted in the temple as making fools of the elders and *doctors*, i.e., Therapeuts. The early Christians called the Lord himself a "devoted physician," or Therapeut. Christian father Epiphanius confirms the association between Christianity and the Therapeutan brotherhood when he says, "Jesus, in the Hebrew, signifies a healer or physician. However that may be, this is the name by which they were known before they were called Christians."[16] He is in fact referring to the "Jesseans" or "Essenes," i.e., "Therapeuts."

Furthermore, as noted, priests were considered "physicians of the soul," and the early Church hierarchy included "doctors," i.e., Therapeuts, who were also wandering drug-peddlers. In fact, the professions of medicine and divinity were inseparable, and those doctors or healers who received their degrees from the University of Alexandria were viewed as true apostles, while those who did not were deemed false. Of these priest-physicians, Higgins says:

> The Essenians were called physicians of the soul or Therapeutae; being resident of both Judaea and Egypt, they probably spoke or had their sacred books in Chaldee. They were Pythagoreans, as is proved by all their forms, ceremonies, and doctrines, and they called themselves sons of Jesse . . . If the Pythagoreans or Coenobitae, as they were called by Jamblicus, were Buddhists, the Essenians were Buddhists. The Essenians . . . lived in Egypt on the lake of Parembole or Maria, in *monasteries*. These are the very places in which we formerly found the Gymnosophists or Samaneans or Buddhist priests to have lived, which Gymnosophists are placed also by Ptolemy in North-eastern India.[17]

And Doane states:

> . . . Dean Milman was convinced that the Therapeuts sprung from the "contemplative and indolent fraternities" of India.[18]

Higgins continues:

> If the opinion be well founded, that their Scriptures were the originals of the Gospel histories, then it will follow almost certainly, that they must have been the same as the Samaneans or Gymnosophists of Porphyry and Clemen Alexandrinus, and their books, which they were bound by such solemn oaths to keep secret, must have been the Vedas of India; or some Indian books containing the mythoses of Moses and Jesus Christ . . . [19]

Of the gospel account, Taylor states that "the travelling Egyptian Therapeuts brought the whole story from India to their monasteries in Egypt, where, some time after the commencement of the Roman monarchy, it was transmuted in Christianity."[20] These books were from either the northeast of India or the coast of Malabar, or both, and were evidently first taken to Antioch and then to Egypt, by Apollonius, Marcion and/or others.

Like their eastern counterparts, the Therapeutan brotherhood had a savior-god and the attendant sayings and mysteries long before the Christian era. The Therapeuts were also followers of Serapis, "the peculiar god of the Christians," who had been created specifically to roll into one the various savior cults, thus providing the doctors with practice for their greatest creation. This savior-god of the brotherhood network extending from Britain to India was variously named IE, IES, Ieud, Judas, Joshua, Jason, Iesous, Iesios, Iasios, or other variant, which, again, represented a *secret spell*. Walker relates that "Iasus signified a healer or *Therapeuta*, as the Greeks called the Essenes, whose cult groups always included a man with the title of *Christos*."[21] Here again is the pre-existence of the words "Jesus" and "Christ" that Eusebius was forced to admit in the face of charges that Christ was a fictional character.

As stated, the early Gnostic Therapeuts were attempting to create a new "religion" that incorporated the teachings of virtually all the religions, cults, philosophies and mysteries then known, first setting about to record in writing the ubiquitous "Sayings of the Savior," or Logia Iesou, which had been orally transmitted for centuries and millennia. These texts constituted the earliest "Christian" writings, and were non-historicizing and non-Judaizing, consolidating sayings from India, Persia, Syria, Judea, Greece, Egypt, etc. The Therapeuts' original Gnostic-"Christian" efforts emanated out of the Antiochan branch of the brotherhood network; hence, that was where the first Christians were thus called. The Gnostic-Christian effort was, as noted, eventually taken over by the Alexandrian school.

The Alexandrian Jews

In the centuries before the Christian era, many Jews and other Israelites had migrated to Egypt, and by the third century BCE there was already a large Jewish community at Alexandria. As confirmed by Apion, the Alexandrian Jews were "from Syria," i.e., they were Antiochans, Galileans, Samaritans and Zadokites/ Sadducees, the latter of whom, as Levites, transcended nationality and developed affiliation with the nation in which they lived. However, Josephus claimed that the "Alexandrian Jews" fought with the Samaritans in Egypt regarding whose temple in Palestine was "according to the law," the one at Jerusalem or that at Mt. Gerizim. According to Josephus, who was a Jew and, therefore, not a Samaritan, the case was pled before Ptolemy (63-47 BCE), who decreed the Jews the winners and had the Samaritan representatives executed. While "the Jews," or Judeans, thus may have been powerful within Alexandrian Judaism, they were not so within the Alexandrian mystery school, since, as noted, the "Jewish" Therapeuts were in large part Nazarenes and Samaritans, both of whom were enemies of the Judeans.

In the second century CE, after the destructions of both 70 and 135, increasing numbers of zealous Jews, Samaritans and other Israelites migrated to Alexandria and joined the mystery schools, jockeying for position not only with each other but also with the non-Judaizing Gnostics, becoming ever more influential on the Gnostic effort. At that time, the salvationist literature started to become Judaized and Hebraicized, with the infiltration of the Yahwists and Joshua cultists, including and especially the Zadokites or Sadducees. In fact, the Zadokite-Therapeut connection is apparently confirmed by the use of the specialized "pentecontad calendar" by both groups.[22] The Zadokite-Therapeutan "Jews" were in fact Hellenistic, as opposed to traditionalist. However, within the Alexandrian school also were Judeans, such that the "Jewish" factions continued their centuries-long internecine squabbling. Yet, at this point, it was either do or die, because, according to Josephus, many of the Judeans had been wiped out, requiring various compromises from those within the Alexandrian school that shaped the gospel story. In this way, their combined efforts eventually produced the savior cult to top them all.

Why Make the Solar Myth into a Jewish Man

The question is not whether or not Jesus and his religion were created but why: Why was the ubiquitous solar myth turned into a "Jewish" man? As reflected in the Bible, the Israelites, particularly the tribes of Judah and Levi, considered themselves the chosen people of God and the spiritual leaders of mankind (Deut. 7:6). They were a "priestly nation" who had determined that other nations should serve Israel or utterly perish (Is. 60:10-12). The Israelites claimed that they had the right to kill the males of the enemy nations "but the women and the little ones, the cattle, and everything else . . . you shall take as booty for yourselves." (Deut. 20:13-14) In fact, throughout the Old Testament the god of Israel repeatedly commanded "his people" to exterminate other cultures and to commit genocide. The Israelites also insisted that they had the right to lend money with interest to the "foreigners," but were not to do so with their "brethren" (Deut. 23:19-20). As Larson says, "The Chosen People were to bind themselves together by bonds of mutual solidarity, but all others they might deceive and exploit at will."[23]

This supremacist mentality continued into the Christian era and can be found in the intertestamental literature, which includes the apocryphal and pseudepigraphical Jewish texts, as well as in the Dead Sea scrolls, one of which, the War Scroll, an evidently Judean text, calls for the destruction of the "Kittim," or "sons of Japheth," i.e., the Aryans, in this case the Romans. As another example, in the Jewish apocryphon Fourth Esdras, written after the destruction of 70 CE, the fanatical author bitterly complains to the Lord:

> [A]s for the rest of the nations which are sprung from Adam, you have said that they are nothing and are like spittle. . . . And now, Lord, behold, these nations . . . rule over us and devour us. But we, your people, whom you called your first-born, only-begotten, chosen, and beloved, are delivered into their hands. If it was for our sakes that the world was created, why do we not possess it as our inheritance?[24]

Larson elaborates upon the grandiosity of the Jews:

> The Jews considered themselves the chosen of Yahweh and attributed to Him their every victory, defeat, or chastisement. . . . No other people has ever been so conscious of ultimate primacy through supernatural intervention. This has given them cohesion and courage to persevere in the face of persecution and decimation. The conviction that every Jew will one day share in his divine destiny as a member of the world's ruling race has made him proud and has enabled him to survive unassimilated among the nations of the earth. . . . It was indeed a Judaeo-centric world.[25]

According to scripture, the Gentiles would embrace the Jewish religion, and the Jewish empire would extend to all ends of the earth. Included in the promised inheritance was a deliverer or messiah to bring about "the kingdom." This messiah would be either a temporal, human leader who with his armies would overthrow the enemies of Israel, or a supernatural being who would do likewise, establishing an "everlasting" Jewish kingdom as well. In this struggle, in fact, God Himself would appear:

> Moreover, in line with what the prophet Zechariah had foretold (14.3-5), it was held that the Lord Himself would come with His heavenly legions and fight on behalf of his people.[26]

Furthermore, the passage in Zechariah, the penultimate book before the New Testament, describes the Lord appearing on the Mount of Olives, obviously used as a blueprint in the creation of Christianity.

The Jewish imperialism would thus come as the awaited deliverer destroyed the enemies and gave their booty to Israel. As Larson says, "This Messiah shall bring judgment upon the Gentiles and they shall become the slaves of Judah . . ."[27] In order for the messiah to be considered genuine, he had to incorporate various characteristics described in the Old Testament, such as being of the seed of Abraham, the tribe of Judah, and the house of David. He was to be born in Bethlehem of a virgin or young maiden and would be called "Mighty God, Everlasting Father, Prince of Peace."

At the time of destruction of the temple in 70, the Jewish world had been in turmoil for centuries. In 332 BCE, Alexander the Great conquered Palestine, and after his death Israel came under the rule of the Greek Ptolemies of Egypt. In 175 BCE, Antiochus of Syria invaded Jerusalem and set up an altar to Zeus and other "foreign gods." Around 88 BCE, Judean king Alexander Jannaeus allegedly crucified 800 Pharisees and had the throats of their wives and children cut in front of them, while Jannaeus himself drank and lay around with concubines. During the vicious infighting between Pharisees and Sadducees under Jannaeus's rule, some tens of thousands on both sides were allegedly killed. Next, the Romans moved into Palestine under Pompey around 63 BCE, an invasion that crushed the Jewish nation and increased messianic fever, resulting in the appearance of swarms of alleged messiahs and christs. As Larson says, "The land was a boiling cauldron of Messianic expectation, and many were daily awaiting the Son of Man arriving upon the clouds and surrounded by myriads of angels, coming to establish the 'everlasting kingdom.'"[28] Of this era, Higgins relates:

About sixty years before Christ the Roman empire had been alarmed by prodigies, and also by ancient prophecies, announcing that an emanation of the Deity was going to be born about that time, and that a renovation of the world was going to take place. . . . Josephus says, "That which chiefly excited them (the Jews) to war was an *ambiguous prophecy,* which was also found in the *sacred books that at that time someone,* within their *country, should arise,* that should obtain *the empire* of the *whole world."* [29]

This messianic frenzy increased throughout the Roman occupation and was high during and after the purported advent of Christ. It is impossible to believe that, in such a desperate and fanatical environment, if Christ had been real, had done the miracles ascribed to him and—most importantly—*had satisfied all the scriptural requirements of the messiah,* the Jews would not have jumped with joy at his supernatural advent but would actually reject and cause him to be killed. But the Jews did not accept him, as messiah after messiah rose up thereafter, as if Christ had never existed at all. . . . As Jacolliot remarks:

One fact has always astonished me. Through all the sacred books of primitive times of Egypt and the East, the old tradition of the Messiah had passed into the Hebrew law. How is it . . . that the Jews refused to recognize this Redeemer whom they expected so impatiently—and whom, even today, they still expect? [30]

The Jews were literally dying for a supernatural deliverer and—lo and behold—an astounding, divine incarnation came along, with all the scriptural requirements of the messiah and the requisite miracles to demonstrate that he had the full power of God behind him, yet the Jews (and all historians of the day) completely ignored him—nay, they put him to death! In fact, *the world that followed Christ's alleged advent would have been impossible had he really existed at that time.*

Of course, in order to be saved by a deliverer, one has to have enemies, and the zealous Jews had created them everywhere by being extremely sectarian, arrogant and bigoted. The Jews as a whole were the only group exempt from a Roman law that compelled all subjects to conform to some degree to the state religion and political system, and their extreme sectarianism made them an annoyance to the empire. As Larson says:

Philostratus, agreeing with classical writers generally, declares that "the Jews have long been in revolt not only against the Romans but against humanity"; and that they are "a race . . . apart and irreconcilable." This separation stemmed from, and then intensified, the Jewish faith. At least half a dozen times in three thousand years, their annihilation has been decreed . . . It was experiences such as these which enabled the Hebrew genius to create a savior-cult which could defeat all others.[31]

Yet, the Jews were losing badly in their battle to maintain their separation, as they were being swallowed up by the Greek and Roman cultures, with their numerous cults and religions. In addition, many Jews disdained the oppressive Mosaic Law. These factors forced the priesthood to resort to its time-honored method of financing Zealots to re-establish its centralized religion. Larson describes the climate in Palestine during this time:

> Palestine was filled with robbers, and no man's life was secure. Any wild-eyed seditionists could procure a following through extravagant promises. The activities of the Zealots were supplemented by those of the Sicarii, a secret society of assassins who mingled with the multitude in the crowded streets especially during feast and holy days, and struck down their victims with daggers. . . . Roman indignation was aroused since the Jews alone were rebellious.[32]

In order to accomplish their ends, Jews and other Israelites such as the Levitical priesthood, which had split into two main, competing sects, the Sadducees and Pharisees, financed and organized military operations. Some of these operations no doubt emanated out of the fortress at Qumran, financed by the Zadokites/Sadducees, whose wealthy compatriots had a stronghold at Alexandria. During this time, several violent, zealous "messiahs" such as Judas, Theudas the Egyptian, and others burst forth and attacked each other, Romans and wealthy Jews, until they were put down, with the result of the loss of much Jewish blood. After the First Revolt, famine struck, and mothers ate their children, even though the Romans had attempted to prevent these abysmal circumstances: "Again and again Titus offered generous terms for capitulation, which were scornfully rejected by men hourly awaiting the apocalyptic Messiah."[33] Emperor Titus finally burned the temple and destroyed the city, during which time, Josephus claims, over a million Jews were killed or died from starvation, and hundreds of thousands more were enslaved. The two centuries around the beginning of the Common Era were, therefore, an utter disaster for the Jews. As Graham says:

> From about 100 B.C. to 100 A.D., the orthodox Jewish priesthood suffered an eclipse. The promises of their scriptures had failed them—Jerusalem was destroyed and Israel was dispersed. Thereafter many Jews fled to Egypt, Rome and Greece, and those among them who might have become priests joined the schools of the Mysteries, among them that of the Gnostics.[34]

Jerusalem was razed again under Hadrian in 135 CE after a revolt led by the Zealot Simeon Bar Cochba, who was appointed as the "star of Jacob" predicted in Numbers 24:17 and reiterated in the Zadokite Document found at the Dead Sea. But, say Baigent and Leigh, "Unlike the revolt of AD 66, Simeon's insurrection, commencing in AD 132, was no ill-organised conflagration resulting, so to speak, from spontaneous combustion. On the contrary, much prolonged and careful planning went into the enterprise."[35]

When their efforts to raise up the messiah failed and no such promised inheritance was forthcoming, in order to save Judaism and achieve its goals of world domination, zealous "Jews," i.e., "the Chosen," worked to concoct a story to demonstrate that their new covenant had indeed been kept by "the Lord." Just as a Moses was created to give divine authority to "his people" and to make them the elect of God, so Jesus was devised to prove that the Lord had indeed sent his long-awaited redeemer to his chosen as part of the new covenant. However, it could not be demonstrated that such a redeemer was a great warrior who physically usurped the enemies of Israel, because Israel had been destroyed; therefore, the messiah's advent was made solely into a spiritual usurpation. As Higgins says, "It has . . . always . . . been the object of Jesus to open the Jewish religion to the whole world."[36] For, as it says at John 4:22, "salvation is from the Jews." Translated differently, that passage would read, "Jesus is from the Jews."

With the final destruction of Israel, which drove out of Palestine not only the Jews but also the Samaritans, and with their subsequent entrance into the mystery schools, in particular at Alexandria, the push for the Judaizing of the Gnostic/Therapeutan Jesus sayings and narratives began in earnest. As Wheless says:

> It was at this critical juncture, to revive and stimulate the jaded hope of Jewish believers and to spread the propaganda amongst the all-believing Pagans, that the written Christ-tales began to worked up by the Christian propagandists. Before their admiring eyes they had for models the "whole literature" of Jewish apocryphal or forged writings, plus the Pagan Oracles. . .[37]

As noted, any number of the Jewish aspects in the canonical gospels and epistles betray that the writers were ex-Jews, half-Jews or non-Jews who were not expertly familiar with Jewish rituals and practices, did not know the geography of Palestine, and certainly did not write in the language of the Jews. However, the historicizing conspirators were also doubtlessly aware that Judea was a perfect place to set the story, since, as Andrew Laird says, "Set a story in a distant time, or clime, or both, and you are more likely to be believed."[38] And, since Judea was destroyed and its people scattered, it would be harder to disprove the tale.

In reality, much of the information about the Jews found in the NT was derived from the study of the OT and other Jewish books, such as Josephus's histories, as opposed to from the experience of the writers themselves. These inaccuracies serve as evidence that the gospel writers were simply sitting around with books, studying and copying passages, and throwing in an original phrase or two to link them all together.

The Library and University of Alexandria

In their creation of Christianity, the Therapeuts had at their disposal the university and library at Alexandria, which had been established by Alexander the Great as an international center of learning. Indeed, in its heyday the Alexandrian Library was a vast repository of some 500,000-700,000 manuscripts collected from around the world. Doane stresses the importance of Alexandria:

> In Alexandria in Egypt, there was an immense library, founded by the Ptolemies. . . . *There flocked to this great intellectual centre, students from all countries.* It is said that at one time not fewer than fourteen thousand were in attendance. Subsequently even the Christian church received from it some of the most eminent of its Fathers, as Clemens Alexandrinus, Origen, Athanasius, etc.[39]

Taylor describes the nature and climate of the library and university of Alexandria:

> The first and greatest library that ever was in the world, was at Alexandria in Egypt. The first of that most mischievous of all institutions-universities, was the University of Alexandria in Egypt; where lazy monks and wily fanatics first found the benefit of clubbing together, to keep the privileges and advantages of learning to themselves, and concocting holy mysteries and inspired legends, to be dealt out as the craft should need, for the perpetuation of ignorance and superstition, and consequently of the ascendancy of jugglers and Jesuits, holy hypocrites, and revered rogues, among men.
>
> All the most valued manuscripts of the Christian scriptures are *Codices Alexandrini.* The very first bishops of whom we have any account, were bishops of *Alexandria.* Scarcely one of the more eminent fathers of the Christian church is there, who had not been educated and trained in the arts of priestly fraud, in the University of *Alexandria*—that great sewer of congregated feculencies ["foul impurities"] of fanaticisms.[40]

Of the creation of Christianity by the Therapeutan brotherhood, Taylor says:

The Therapeutae of Egypt, from whom are descended the vagrant hordes of Jews and Gypsies, had well found by what arts mankind were to be cajoled; and as they boasted their acquaintance with the sanative qualities of herbs of all countries; so in their extensive peregrinations through all the then known regions of the earth, they had not failed to bring home, and remodel to their own purposes, those sacred spells or religious romances, which they found had been successfully palmed on the credulity of remote nations. Hence the Indian *Chrishna* might have become the Therapeutan head of the order of spiritual physicians.

No principle was held more sacred than that of the necessity of keeping the sacred writings from the knowledge of the people. Nothing could be safer from the danger of discovery than the substitution, with scarce a change of names, "of the incarnate Deity of the Sanscrit Romance" for the imaginary founder of the Therapeutan college. What had been said to have been done in India, could be as well said to have been done in Palestine. The change of names and places, and the mixing up of various sketches of Egyptian, Phoenician, Greek, and Roman mythology, would constitute a sufficient disguise to evade the languid curiosity of infant skepticism. A knowledge within the acquisition of a few, and which the strongest possible interest bound that few to hold inviolate, would soon pass entirely from the records of human memory. A long continued habit of imposing upon others would in time subdue the minds of the imposers themselves, and cause them to become at length the dupes of their own deception, to forget the temerity in which their first assertions had originated, to catch the infection of the prevailing credulity, and to believe their own lie.[41]

Taylor further summarizes the gospel work of the Therapeuts:

Some entire scenes of the drama have been rejected, and some suggested emendations of early critics have been adopted into the text; the names of Pontius Pilate, Herod, Archelaus, Caiaphas, etc., picked out of Josephus's and other histories, have been substituted in the place of the original *dramatis personae*; and since it has been found expedient to conceal the plagiarism, to pretend a later date, and a wholly different origination, texts have been introduced, directly impugning the known sentiments and opinions of the original authors. . . [T]hough they are to be received as the composition of Jews, contemporaries, and even witnesses of the scenes and actions they describe; those compositions do nevertheless betray so great a degree of ignorance of the geography, statistics, and circumstances of Judea at the time supposed, as to put it beyond all question, that the writers were neither witnesses nor contemporaries—neither Jews, nor at any time inhabitants of Judea. . . . The Therapeutae, we see, though not Jews, nor inhabitants of Palestine, were, says Eusebius, "it is likely *descended from Hebrews*, and therefore were wont to observe many of the customs of the ancients, after a more Jewish fashion."42

In creating their myth, the Hebrew/Israelite conspirators took one more Baal, Baal Jehoshua, the Savior, and carnalized him anew. Like his predecessor Joshua, Jesus was made to be an Israelite/Galilean/Samaritan, not a Judean, with his Bethlehem birthplace added later to "fulfill scripture." The Samaritan influence on and origins of the gospel tale is evident, firstly because its early contributors, the Gnostics Apollonius and Marcion were considered "Samaritans," as was Antioch. Furthermore, although Jesus is also made to call Samaritans "dogs," he himself is declared by the Jews a "demon-filled Samaritan," to which he is made to respond that he does not have a demon, without denying he is a Samaritan. In reality, the gospels actually serve to elevate the Samaritans above the Jews. For example, the most lasting memory of the Samaritans is the New Testament story of the "Good Samaritan," in which the Jews are made to look bad. Also, in the Gospel of John, Jesus is made to go against the Jews by welcoming a Samaritan woman, who, although she claims to have no husband is told by Jesus that she has in fact five, and "he whom you now have is not your husband." This "woman" with the "five husbands," however, is not a person but the northern kingdom of Israel, and these "husbands" are "her" foreign occupiers, Assyria, Persia, Egypt, Greece and Rome, who is nevertheless not Samaria's "husband," or "baal," or "lord."

In the Gospel of John, in fact, the Samaritans accept Jesus as the Messiah and "Savior of the world," but the Jews plot to kill him. As noted, John is an anti-Jewish text, with aspersions being cast *only* against the Pharisees, "priests and Levites," as well as "the Jews," but with *no mention* by name of the Sadducees, who constituted in large part the Samaritan priesthood. In fact, in the NT the Sadducees are mentioned by name only about a dozen times, while the Pharisees are named 100 times and bear the brunt of the blame for Jesus's death. In addition, the Pharisees disparaged the Samaritans for being "adherers to the Bible" and for interpreting it in a literal manner, just as Christians do to this day.43 In the Talmud, the Samaritans are lumped together with the Sadducees, "followers of Jesus" and other "Gentiles." Indeed, the Talmudic code word "Sadducees" refers to Gentiles.

It is clear that the individuals who Judaized the Gnostic/Therapeutan efforts were in the main not Pharisaic but Hellenizing "Jews" or Israelites, i.e., Samaritan Zadokites/Sadducees. Thus, the gospel story serves to elevate not only "the Jews" as God's chosen but also the northern kingdom over the southern kingdom, with the southern actually being castigated for its interpretation of the law. In this regard, the Samaritan Jesus's character is patterned after a Pharisee so that he can debate "the Jews" and usurp their power. Orthodox, Pharisaic Jews, in fact, have rejected the fallacious tale for 2,000 years, acknowledging in their Talmud that it was the Zadokites/Sadducees who created it and Judaized the books of the New Testament.[44] Regardless of the internecine fighting, the Christian myth was an outgrowth of "Jewish" thinking; it was the logical extension, in fact, of the group belief that "the Jews" or Israelites were the spiritual leaders of mankind, that their god and religion were superior to all others, that their land was blessed above all others, and that their history and destiny, and theirs alone, were guided and directed by God. The Israelite version of the savior religion and solar myth did indeed usurp all others in the West, as those others were consigned to their proper status as myths, while the Judeo-Christian version was, through centuries of violence and slaughter, eventually maintained as fact.

While Christianity "sprang up in a thousand places," its seed germinated in Antioch and grew to strength at Alexandria. But it would not become a force to be reckoned with until its roots took hold at Rome.

---

1. Taylor, 84.
2. Massey, *GHC*, 10.
3. "The Jesus Puzzle," Net.
4. *The Lost Books of the Bible*, 196.
5. Walker, *WDSSO*, 414.
6. Taylor, 70-76.
7. Allegro, *DSSCM*, 111.
8. Allegro, *DSSCM*, 157-8.
9. Doane, 419.
10. Eusebius, 52.
11. Taylor, 131.
12. Taylor.
13. Waite, 500.
14. Eusebius, 129.
15. Wells, *DJE*, 146.
16. Waite, 510.
17. Higgins, I, 747.
18. Doane, 423 fn.
19. Higgins, II, 43.
20. Taylor.
21. Walker, *WEMS*, 164.
22. Vermes, 48.
23. Larson, 199.
24. Larson, 199-200.
25. Larson, 195-197.
26. Gaster, 386.
27. Larson, 221.

28. Larson, 204.
29. Higgins, I, 187-9.
30. Jacolliot, 300.
31. Larson, 195.
32. Larson, 205.
33. Larson, 206.
34. Graham, 285.
35. Baigent & Leigh, 209.
36. Higgins, II, 253.
37. Wheless, *FC*, 96.
38. www.christianism.com
39. Doane, 438-40.
40. Taylor, 61.
41. Taylor, 63-64.
42. Taylor, 78-81.
43. *History of the Talmud*, Rod Kinson, 1.
44. Talmud, Sanhedrin 100a-100b, fn 9, Soncino ed., p. 680.

Enter Rome

Christianity was not created by a god who came to Earth 2,000 years ago but is a patchwork quilt of ancient motifs found in many parts of the world eons before the Christian era and spread mainly through fraud, fanaticism and force, as a deliberately contrived ideology. Christianity's earliest proponents, the Gnostics, were non-historicizers and non-Judaizers who were attempting to amalgamate the many religions of the Roman Empire and beyond. When the might of Rome crushed Palestine, into this Gnostic-Therapeut soup fell a multitude of Jews and Samaritans, including the Zadokites, who insisted upon supremacy and dominance, such that the allegorical and astrotheological Jesus became "Jewish." It was not until the Antiochan-Alexandrian efforts hit Rome, however, that they became locked into history, the result of the labors of the infamous church fathers, who were known liars, forgers and general psychotics whose brains were apparently afflicted by the lead in Roman pipes.

Why Carnalize and Historicize the Solar Myth

As the Christian myth was being formulated its proponents were, as noted, ridiculed and rejected by the Pagan intelligentsia, such that they were compelled to create forged texts and long rebuttals to dispute the various imputations against them. In this way, the Christian product became increasingly historicized for a variety of reasons, one of which was because of the charges that the conspirators had simply plagiarized older myths and legends. Indeed, historicizing their godman allowed the Christians to distinguish him from these more ancient mythological characters. For instance, when confronted with the fact that the various gods such as Krishna, Horus, et al., had the identical story as Jesus, Christian apologists argued that, while devilish "living realities," these "gods" were not flesh-and-blood incarnations and could thereby be dismissed, whereas Christ was historical and therefore must be accepted as who he said he was. An example of this usurpation is provided by the history of Mithraism, which was so important to Rome that in 307 the emperor designated Mithra the protector of the empire. Yet, Mithraism could not withstand the assault from Christianity. As Larson says:

> The power of Mithraism lay in its syncretism, its flexibility, its universality, its attractiveness to various classes. Its weakness lay in the fact that it could not point to an historical god-man savior . . . [1]

Because he really came in the flesh, the argument went, Jesus was the only valid one of these godmen, while the others were but phantoms, planted in the heads of the ignorant masses, centuries and millennia before Christ's alleged advent, in order to befuddle them and trick them into rejecting him. Of course, this argument is casuistic and ridiculous, but it has worked for those who have been bedazzled by the biblical tale. It should be remembered that, over the millennia, Krishna, Buddha and others have also been considered by a great number of people to have been real persons, so this debate also begs the question of why believers do not follow these other "historical" characters, since they too claimed to be the "alpha and omega," the "way, truth and light," etc.

It was because of these older godmen that Jesus had to be carnalized, to distinguish him from them, with Christian proponents at the same time working to demonstrate that the others were either diabolical, mythical or merely evemerized heroes. The incarnation was of key importance, as the Christians said, "Your gods are all fantasy, but our God is real, because he was here in flesh to tell us exactly what he wants of us and to reveal his true nature and Fatherhood." For example, in the Epistle to Diognetus, dating to the second century, the author asks, "Before his advent, who among mankind had any notion at all of what God is?" In other words, Jesus was also created to reveal the nature of God. However, the need for the incarnation was likewise not new, as previous cultures were always expecting one. Indeed, as Massey says:

> The doctrine of the incarnation had been evolved and established in the Osirian religion at least 4,000 and possibly 10,000 years before it was purloined and perverted in Christianity.[2]

And Wells says:

> . . . the Osiris worshippers of ancient Egypt believed, as did the early Christians (Hebrews 4:14-15) that "man cannot be saved by a remote omnipotent deity but by one who has shared the experience of human suffering". . . . Initiation into the pagan mystery religions involved a "personal meeting with the god" . . .[3]

In fact, while the mystical and supernatural apparition of Jesus to Paul on the road to Damascus is portrayed as a unique experience, it is not, either then or now, as over the millennia and during the era in question, many gods commonly appeared mystically to their followers. As Fox relates:

> The "presence" of Isis was invoked to help mortals in lawsuits and on journeys, and was experienced by adherents who gazed fondly on her statue. Very soon after his creation, the god Serapis had spread widely because he was accessible in dreams

and appeared and gave commands to people of all classes. Evidence for gods being thought to attend their own banquets and sacrifices is known from the sixth to fourth centuries B.C., yet it surfaces again for us in the small invitation tickets to the "couch" of Serapis, known to us from the second century B.C. onwards.[4]

Walker further explains the necessity for the incarnation:

From the Christians' viewpoint, a real historical Jesus was essential to the basic premise of the faith: the possibility of immortality through identification with his own death and resurrection. Wellhausen rightly said Jesus would have no place in history unless he died and returned exactly as the Gospels said: "If Christ hath not been raised, your faith is vain" (1 Corinthians 15:17). Still, despite centuries of research, no historical Jesus has come to light. It seems his story was not merely overlaid with myth; it was mythical to the core.[5]

In addition, Allegro states:

. . . . [T]he canonisation of the Joshua/Jesus legends focused so much popular piety and theological speculation on its central figure, that it became essential to historicize the myth, and successive generations of a largely non-Jewish Church were led to believe as fact the absurdly anachronistic and slanderously inaccurate picture painted in the Gospels of Jewish institutions in a Roman-dominated Palestine of the first century. Before long, pious pilgrims were scouring the Holy Land for relics of the Nazarene Master's life on earth, and erecting shrines to commemorate his activities and death in the most improbable places.[6]

He continues:

Unlike other eastern faiths, Christianity could "prove" by such relics the validity of its claim that God had entered history in the person of His Son, and had "so loved the world" that He had given His own Substance that He might redeem mankind.[7]

Furthermore, as noted, it was maintained by Irenaeus and other Christians that the belief was that "men" could not really "partake in salvation" if Jesus was merely imaginary. The author of the Epistle of Barnabas further illustrates this need for the carnalized Christ: "Then he clearly manifested himself to be the Son of God. For had he not come in the flesh, how should men have been able to look upon him, that they might be saved?"[8] "Barnabas" also gives a hint as to the identity of Christ in his next sentence: "Seeing if they beheld only the sun, which was the work of his hands, and shall hereafter cease to be, they are not able to endure steadfastly to look against the rays of it." In other words, looking at "Christ," some have seen "only the sun, which . . . shall hereafter cease to be . . ." And this was the charge of the conspirators: To make the "sun of God" disappear, so that its mythos would not be remembered and the person of "Jesus Christ" could be inserted in its place.

In *Against Heresies* V, Irenaeus expounds upon the need for the incarnation:

CHRIST ALONE IS ABLE TO TEACH DIVINE THINGS, AND TO REDEEM US: HE, THE SAME, TOOK FLESH OF THE VIRGIN MARY, NOT MERELY IN APPEARANCE, BUT ACTUALLY, BY THE OPERATION OF THE HOLY SPIRIT, IN ORDER TO RENOVATE US. . . . FOR in no other way could we have learned the things of God, unless our Master, existing as the Word, had become man. For no other being had the power of revealing to us the things of the Father, except His own proper Word. . . . Again, we could have learned in no other way than by seeing our Teacher, and hearing His voice with our own ears, that, having become imitators of His works as well as doers of His words, we may have communion with Him, receiving increase from the perfect One, and from Him who is prior to all creation.

The incarnation was established as doctrine in one of the most important of "Christian" councils, evidently held at Alexandria in the year after the Gnostic-Christian leader Marcion's death, 161, at which "Docetism," or the disbelief in the "historical" Jesus, was condemned as heresy.

As stated, many cultures were waiting for the mythos to become carnalized, just as people around the world today pray for any number of avatars, messiahs, maitreyas, mahdis and assorted other incarnations. In reality, this expectation can be found around the globe where the deep meaning of the mythos has been lost, as "the vulgar were taught to expect a new incarnation every 600 years."[9] As noted, in addition to the 2,150-year cycle of the precession of the equinoxes was this cycle of 600, the reason why Christ himself was compared to a phoenix, who rises from the ashes every 600 years, and why Mohammed appeared on the scene some 600 years later. The expectation of the incarnation, in fact, allowed for some places to be more easily conquered by Christian armies. Because of this past experience with the ongoing cycles and "incarnations," the ancient priest-astrologers were well aware that in order to create a new "faith" there had to be an obvious break from the past, which was rife with cults, sects and religions, with "someone" new to come along to found it, alleged to have been sent by the "Almighty Himself." The race was on as to who would produce this incarnation, one in a long line on a recurring theme.

Enter the Romans

While the Israelite Therapeuts had won the race and were seemingly in opposition to the Romans, having been displaced out of Palestine, their efforts were eventually combined with those of Rome. Indeed, in the decades between 170-90 was begun the push for Roman supremacy in the Gnostic-Therapeut-Christian Church, and the various gospel texts and epistles were reworked on behalf of the vested interests at Rome, producing the four gospels, based on manuscripts from the Alexandrian school and other branches/churches of the network. As Walker says, "The Gospels themselves were forged as required to uphold privileges and practices of the early church."[10] The Romanized gospels were thus slanted to bring the Jews into the fold by making them believe that their "Messiah" had bestowed his authority upon the Church, which would mean that the Jews were to follow the dictates of Rome.

It was also during this period that the canonical book of Acts was written, to invest the Roman church with hierarchical supremacy. In addition, the "lost" Gospel of Peter, purportedly the favorite of the Nazarites/Nazarenes, was clearly written to vindicate Pilate and, therefore, the Romans from the crucifixion and to cast the onus upon Herod and the Jews. This gospel was once considered as important as the canonical gospels—or, in the words of Rev. D.H. Stanton, "perhaps even higher than some of them"[11]—but it fell out of favor and was discarded. Furthermore, as noted, the Nazarenes were Samaritans and enemies of the strictly Yahwistic Jews, or Pharisees, and were obviously in cahoots with Rome at this point at least.

The Acts of Pilate was also written to place the onus of Jesus's death upon the Jews and away from the Romans. In this book, Pilate is even represented as making a pitch for the Jews to follow Christ, comparing him to Moses.

Rome's grab at supremacy, however, was not pleasing to the other Gnostic-Therapeut-Christian factions. Nor were the priests of other religions and cults thrilled by the "new superstition" of Christianity. Potter describes the religious climate in Rome at the time:

> In the century before the birth of Christ and in the century or two after, so many Eastern religions and mysteries entered Rome that very little was left of the original Roman religion. The great city was simply a hotbed of cults of all possible sorts which vied with one another for supremacy. From Egypt came the worship of Isis and Osiris, from Phrygia the cult of Attis, and from Persia via Asia Minor the powerful soldier religion of Mithra, dominant in the second century A.D.[12]

As noted, Christianity from the beginning was marked by warring priestly factions and endless bloodshed, as it expanded to engulf these various other cults. To unite these religions, sects, cults and mystery schools and to establish the doctrine of the new superstition, hundreds of texts were produced and various councils were called in different cities of the brotherhood.

The Council of Nicea

Rather than the advent and death a "historical" Christ, the single most important events in the history of Christianity were the "conversion" of the Pagan Emperor Constantine and the convening of the raucous Council of Nicea in 325, which in fact marked the true birth of Jesus Christ. Constantine, of course, "converted" to Christianity because it offered a "quick fix" to all of his heinous crimes, including the murder of several family members, removed simply by confession and "believing unto the Lord," absolutions he could not procure from other religions such as Mithraism, which did not cater to murderers.

At the Council of Nicea were not only Christian leaders from Alexandria, Antioch, Athens, Jerusalem and Rome but also the leaders of the many other cults, sects and religions, including those of Apollo, Demeter/Ceres, Dionysus/Bacchus/Iasios, Janus, Jupiter/Zeus, Oannes/Dagon, Osiris and Isis, and "Sol Invictus," the Invincible Sun, the object of Constantine's devotion. The purpose of this council was to unify the various competing cults under one universal or "catholic" church, which, of course, would be controlled by Constantine and Rome. As noted, Rome claimed the ultimate authority because it purported to be founded upon the "rock of Peter." Thus, the statue of Jupiter in Rome was converted into "St. Peter," whose phony bones were subsequently installed in the Vatican. In a typical religion-making move, the gods of these other cults were subjugated under the new god and changed into "apostles" and "saints."

As stated, it is maintained that during the Nicene Council the names Jesus and Christ were put together for the first time in the phrase "Jesus Christ" or "Christ Jesus," uniting two of the major factions, with Jesus representing the Hesus of the Druids, Joshua/Jesus of the Israelites, Horus/Iusa of the Egyptians and IES/Iesios of the Dionysians/Samothracians, and Christ representing the Krishna/Christos of India, the Anointed of the Jews and KRST of Egypt, among others. It is thus alleged that the phrase "Jesus Christ," which had never been a name, does not appear in Greek or Latin authors prior to the first Council of Nicea. Hence, just as the name "Hermes Trismegistus" "represents a tradition rather than a single man,"[13] so does "Jesus Christ." It is also purported that one Bishop Eunomius charged fraud and blew the whistle on the Council of Nicea, the record of which was never published, even though it was supposedly made and may be in the Vatican vault to this day.

Regarding the compilation of the Bible and the creation of Christianity, Roberts says:

> Every rational person might have known that the writings of the New Testament were the works of a man or a school of men who sought to blend such portions of the preceding creeds, doctrines, ceremonies, practices and religious formulas into a single religion, that would serve to harmonize and united mankind in one common effort to advance the welfare of all. . . . The religious systems of China, India, Persia, Egypt, Greece, Rome, Palestine, and even the Druidical system of Northern and Western Europe, were largely drawn from to make up the Eclectic system of religion . . . [14]

Walker states:

> Far-Eastern traditions were utilized too. The Roman empire was well aware of the teachings and myths of Buddhism. Buddha images in classic Greek style were made in Pakistan and Afghanistan in the first century A.D. Buddhist ideas like the "footprints of Buddha" appeared among Christians. Bishop Sulpicus of Jerusalem reported that, as in India, "In the dust where Christ trod the marks of His step can still be seen, and the earth still bears the print of His feet." Buddhist metaphors and phrasing also appeared in the Gospels. Jesus's formula, "Dearly Beloved," was the conventional way for Tantric deities to address their teachings to Devi, their Goddess. [15]

And Wheless relates:

> Cardinal Newman . . . says that Milman arrays facts "admitted on all hands," to wit: "that the doctrine of the Logos is Platonic; that of the Incarnation Indian; that of a divine Kingdom Judaic; that of angels and demons (and a Mediator) Persian; that the connection of sin with the body is Gnostic; the idea of a new birth Chinese and Eleusinian; that of sacramental virtue Pythagorean; that of Trinity common to East and West; and that of the rites of baptism and sacrifice equally ubiquitous"![16]

During the centuries after the purported advent of the Christian savior, at least 21 councils were convened to establish Church policy and doctrine, many of which were, as noted, bloody melees. It was a long, slow process that eventually unified the numerous warring factions to a large extent. The following is a partial list of the various religions, cults, sects, secret societies and mystery schools that contributed to the formation of the state religion called Christianity:

1. Buddhist/Gymnosophic/Sufic
2. Cabirian/Phrygian/Syrian
3. Dionysian/Bacchanal/Orphist/Samothracian
4. Druidic/Gallic/Teutonic
5. Egyptian/African
6. Essene/Nazarene/Nazarite/Ebionite/Therapeut
7. Greek/Eleusinian
8. Indian/Brahmanical
9. Mandaean/Manichaean
10. Marcionite/Valentinian
11. Mithraic/Zoroastrian
12. Neoplatonist/Stoic/Cynic/Eclectic/Peripatetic
13. Phoenician/Canaanite/Israelite/Samaritan
14. Yahwhist/Kabbalist/Pharisaic
15. Roman/Etruscan
16. Samanean/Magusean/Sampsaean
17. Sethian/Ophite
18. Zealot/Zadokite/Sadducean

In addition to these groups, many of which obviously overlap, are not a few other branches and even more esoteric designations such as the "Followers of the Eight-Pointed Red Cross," the "Sons of the Sun," the "Order of the Black Hand," the "Order of the Red Hand," and the famed "Order of Melchizedek." Other groups, such as the Marianites, or followers of the Goddess, were either excluded or given little empowerment at these councils.

The brotherhoods who were really in charge of the Therapeutan "churches" addressed in the Pauline epistles are as follows: Antioch was the seat of the Adonis cult; Ephesus was that of the Attis cult; Corinth represented the Greek gods and Eleusinian mysteries; Galatia was the locale of the Dionysian cult; and Rome had everything. The first Christians at Antioch were actually Gnostic Nazarenes, also Carmelites, who represented one of the oldest seats of the brotherhood and who were originally Egyptians/Canaanites/Phoenicians and later "Samaritans." These Nazarites/Nazarenes were also priests of Dionysus/Bacchus, who was the same as Joshua, Iasius, Iesius or Jesus, whose temple was found atop Mt. Carmel.

The Role of Masonry

As demonstrated, the Gnostic and Catholic endeavors in creating Christianity were eclectic and multinational, incorporating elements from around the world. Such a religion- and nationality-transcending cabal could only occur in one stratum of fraternity: that which is called Masonry.

Although the brotherhood of Masonry appears to be relatively new, it is in reality the oldest continuous network on the planet, dating back many thousands of years, beginning when stones were first dressed. Masonry today has a generally sinister reputation, because the people suspect that this powerful brotherhood has been manipulating and exploiting them. However, the average Mason has never been "in the know" and is, therefore, merely a member of a social club. Nevertheless, the higher-ups have indeed had their hand in creation on this planet on a large scale for a long time.

As stated, the ancient peoples considered God to be the Grand Architect of the Universe; thus, the Masons viewed themselves as imitators of God. The Masons were the first priests, and the word "minister" is related to "mason," as the root "myn" means stone.[17] The priestly ritual of circumcision has been from ancient times a Masonic rite of passage. Obviously, it is Masons who build the temples, cathedrals, mosques and sacred monuments around the globe, and it was Masons who developed writing, as they were fond of inscribing their monuments and buildings. Hence, Masonry and the creation of religions go hand-in-hand.

Where were these ubiquitous Masons when Christianity was being formed? Why is there so little mention of them in the texts of the time? They certainly existed, as it was they who were erecting massive and magnificent edifices all over the globe. The Masons are there, perpetually hidden behind the scenes, leaving clues to their existence as a brotherhood, some of which are evident yet still not seen. For example, the biblical Nimrod, the king who built the tower of Babel ("Bab-el"—"gate of God"), is considered the first Mason—and build a tower of Babel, the Masons certainly have done! Like so many other biblical characters, Nimrod is found in older tales, as the Assyrian god of war and the hunt, serving as a personification of the Assyrian empire. Another biblical character, Hiram, king of Tyre, is revered as a great mason for building "Solomon's Temple," although the temple actually is in the skies. In addition, the mysterious Urim and Thummim are Masonic symbols, as are the Jachin and Boaz.

As noted, Jesus is called the "very stone which the builders rejected. . . the head of the corner." Furthermore, this comment is prefaced by reference to the scripture where it is first written, Psalms 118:21: "I thank thee that thou . . . hast become my salvation. The stone which the builders rejected has become the head of the corner." As "Jesus" means "salvation," this OT passage could read, "I thank thee that thou has become my Jesus. The stone which the builders rejected . . ." The "chief cornerstone that the builders rejected" is an obvious Masonic symbol, referring to the peak of a pyramid, which is also the "all-seeing eye of Horus," the symbol of the sun who looks down upon the world, and which can be found on the back of an American dollar bill.

In addition, Peter "the Rock" and his keys are Masonic symbols. Church doctor/Therapeut Jerome relates that the man with the withered hand in Matthew 12 was "said to be a mason" and thus needed his hand for his livelihood.[18] When at 1 Corinthians Paul calls himself a "skilled master builder," "he is using a word pre-eminently kabalistic, theurgic, and masonic . . ."[19] At Hebrews 3:3-4, a Masonic calling card is left with the following passage (and notation), which was evidently interpolated: "Yet Jesus has been counted worthy of as much more glory than Moses as the builder of a house. (For every house is built by some one, but the builder of all things is God.)" In addition, Jesus is called "the rose of Sharon," also known as "Nazir," which, according to Higgins, who was a magistrate and Mason, refers to "the schools of the prophets which were on the mount of Carmel or the vineyard of God . . ."[20] Carmel, to repeat, was one of the earliest brotherhood strongholds and site of a temple of Jupiter, Melchizedek and Joshua, out of which emanated the monkishness that became the Nazarene brotherhood. As Nazarenes, Jesus and Paul were Masons as well. Furthermore, the "carpenter" label, also found in the stories of other solar heroes, is a Masonic designation, reflecting the sun's role as the great builder.

The Indian-Gnostic Nazarene-Carmelites were also Nestorians, Manichaeans, Samanaeans and Buddhists, Templars and Rosicrucians, "or followers of the eight-pointed Red Cross and Rose of Sharon, all the same under different names,"[21] serving to illustrate the complexity and pervasiveness of the international brotherhood of Masonry. The Masons were also Essenes, Therapeuts and Gnostics, and they are now Christians, Jews and Muslims. The Mithraites were also Masons, and the Kabbalists and Chaldeans were Master Masons. In fact, the Scottish Rite Masonry can be traced to the Chaldeans.[22] The Chaldeans, then, were also the Druids, who were likewise Masons. The Knights Templar were also Chaldeans, the same as the Culdees of India and as the Gnostic Manichaeans, who were followers of Bel/Baal.[23] The Culdees/Masons were the judicial astronomers of Rome,[24] and, as we have seen, the followers of Baal/Molech constituted the Order of Melchizedek, whose members were also Gymnosophs, as well as Zadokites. In fact, the fortress at Qumran was a Masonic enclave, since masons built it, particularly its large tower, a strong Masonic symbol. Likewise, the Dead Sea scrolls are abundant in "architectural metaphors," demonstrating their writers were Masons.

Furthermore, the mysteries of Isis and Serapis, which were models of those of Eleusis and Samothrace, are part of Masonry.[25]

The historian Josephus certainly knew of the Masons and allegedly was one, as well as being a member of the secret order called the "Sons of the Sun," to which also purportedly belonged Apollonius and the Emperors Claudius, Vespasian, Titus, Domitian, Nerva and Trajan.

Two centuries ago, no less an authority than the great Anglo-American philosopher, revolutionary statesman and lover of truth Thomas Paine clearly outlined the origins of Christianity and its connection to Masonry. Paine himself apparently was a Mason, as were his associates, George Washington, Ben Franklin and other American Founding Fathers. Why Paine's truthful admissions have been ignored by religionists, politicians and scholars alike can only be explained by the remarkably effective and disturbing system of concealment for profit that has been in place for thousands of years. In his treatise, "Origin of Freemasonry," Paine writes:

> The Christian religion and Masonry have one and the same common origin: Both are derived from the worship of the Sun. The difference between their origin is, that the Christian religion is a parody on the worship of the Sun, in which they put a man whom they call Christ, in the place of the Sun, and pay him the same adoration which was originally paid to the Sun . . .
>
> In Masonry many of the ceremonies of the Druids are preserved in their original state, at least without any parody. With them the Sun is still the Sun; and his image, in the form of the Sun is the great emblematical ornament of Masonic Lodges and Masonic dresses. It is the central figure on their aprons, and they wear it also pendant on the breast in their lodges, and in their processions. It has the figure of a man, as at the head of the Sun, as Christ is always represented.
>
> At what period of antiquity, or in what nation, this religion was first established, is lost in the labyrinth of unrecorded time. It is generally ascribed to the ancient Egyptians, the Babylonians and Chaldeans, and reduced afterwards to a system regulated by the apparent progress of the Sun through the twelve signs of Zodiac by Zoroaster the law giver of Persia, from whence Pythagoras brought it into Greece. . . .
>
> The worship of the Sun as the great visible agent of a great invisible first cause, "Time without limits," spread itself over a considerable part of Asia and Africa, from thence to Greece and Rome, through all ancient Gaul, and into Britain and Ireland. . . .
>
> . . . As the study and contemplation of the Creator in the works of the creation, the Sun, as the great visible agent of that Being, was the visible object of the adoration of Druids; all their religious rites and ceremonies had reference to the apparent progress of the Sun through the twelve signs of the Zodiac, and

his influence upon the earth. The Masons adopt the same practices. The roof of their Temples or Lodges is ornamented with a Sun, and the floor is a representation of the variegated face of the earth either by carpeting or Mosaic work. . . .

The Masons, in order to protect themselves from the persecution of the Christian church, have always spoken in a mystical manner of the figure of the Sun in their Lodges . . . It is their secret, especially in Catholic countries, because the figure of the Sun is the expressive criterion that denotes they are descended from the Druids, and that wise, elegant, philosophical religion, was the faith opposite to the faith of the gloomy Christian church.

The high festival of the Masons is on the day they call St. John's day; but every enlightened Mason must know that holding their festival on this day has no reference to the person called St. John, and that it is only to disguise the true cause of holding it on this day, that they call the day by that name. . . .

The case is, that the day called St. John's day, is the 24th of June, and is what is called Midsummer-day. The Sun is then arrived at the summer solstice . . . and it is in honor of the sun, which has then arrived at his greatest height in our hemisphere, and not any thing with respect to St. John, that this annual festival of the Masons, taken from the Druids, is celebrated on Midsummer-day. . .

As to what Masons, and books of Masonry, tell us of Solomon's Temple at Jerusalem, it is no wise improbable that some Masonic ceremonies may have been derived from the building of that temple, for the worship of the Sun was in practice many centuries before the Temple existed, or before the Israelites came out of Egypt. And we learn from the history of the Jewish Kings, 2 Kings xxii-xxiii, that the worship of the Sun was performed by the Jews in that Temple. It is, however, much to be doubted if it was done with the same scientific purity and religious morality with which it was performed by the Druids, who, by all accounts that historically remain of them, were a wise, learned, and moral class of men. The Jews, on the contrary, were ignorant of astronomy, and of science in general, and if a religion founded upon astronomy fell into their hands, it is almost certain it would be corrupted. . . . But to return to the worship of the Sun in this Temple.

. . . the description that Josephus gives of the decorations of this Temple, resembles on a large scale those of a Mason's Lodge. He says that the distribution of the several parts of the Temple of the Jews represented all nature, particularly the parts most apparent of it, as the sun, the moon, the planets, the zodiac, the earth, the elements; and that the system of the world was retraced there by numerous ingenious emblems. These, in all probability, are, what Josiah, in his ignorance, calls the abominations of the Zidonians. . . . Every thing, however, drawn from this Temple and applied to Masonry, still refers to the worship of the Sun, however corrupted or misunderstood by the Jews, and consequently to the religion of the Druids. . . .

The religion of the Druids, as before said, was the same as the religion of the ancient Egyptians. The priests of Egypt were the professors and teachers of science, and were styled priests of Heliopolis, that is, of the City of the Sun. The Druids in Europe, who were the same order of men, have their name from the Teutonic or ancient German language; the German being anciently called Teutones. The word Druid signifies a wise man. In Persia they were called Magi, which signifies the same thing.

"Egypt," says Smith, "from whence we derive many of our mysteries, has always borne a distinguished rank in history, and was once celebrated above all others for its antiquities, learning, opulence, and fertility. In their system, their principal hero-gods, Osiris and Isis, theologically represented the Supreme Being and universal Nature; and physically the two great celestial luminaries, the Sun and the Moon, by whose influence all nature was actuated." . . . In speaking of the apparel of the Masons in their Lodges, part of which, as we see in their public processions, is a white leather apron, he says, "the Druids were apparelled in white at the time of their sacrifices and solemn offices. The Egyptian priests of Osiris wore snow-white cotton. The Grecian and most other priests wore white garments. . . ."

"The Egyptians," continues Smith, "in the earliest ages constituted a great number of Lodges, but with assiduous care kept their secrets of Masonry from all strangers. These secrets have been imperfectly handed down to us by oral tradition only, and ought to be kept undiscovered to the laborers, craftsmen, and apprentices, till by good behavior and long study they become better acquainted in geometry and the liberal arts . . ."

I come now to speak of the cause of secrecy used by the Masons. The natural source of secrecy is fear. When any new religion over-runs a former religion, the professors of the new become the persecutors of the old. We see this in all instances that history brings before us. When Hilkiah the priest and Shaphan the scribe, in the reign of King Josiah, found, or pretended to find, the law, called the law of Moses, a thousand years after the time of Moses, (and it does not appear from 2 Kings, xxii-xxiii, that such a law was ever practiced or known before the time of Josiah), he established that law as a national religion, and put all the priests of the Sun to death. When the Christian religion over-ran the Jewish religion, the Jews were the continual subject of persecution in all Christian countries. When the Protestant religion in England over-ran the Roman Catholic religion, it was made death for a Catholic priest to be found in England. As this has been the case in all the instances we have any knowledge of, we are obliged to admit it with respect to the case in question, and that when the Christian religion over-ran the religion of the Druids in Italy, ancient Gaul, Britain, and Ireland, the Druids became the subject of persecution. This would naturally and necessarily oblige such of them as remained attached to their original religion to meet in secret, and under the strongest injunctions of secrecy. Their safety depended upon it. A false brother might expose the lives of many of them to destruction; and from the remains of the religion of the Druids, thus preserved, arose the institution which, to avoid the name of Druid, took that of Mason, and practiced under this new name the rites and ceremonies of Druids.

Thus, we have seen the remarkable history of Christianity and Masonry. Both are "brotherhoods of the Sun," the former exoteric and vulgar, and the latter esoteric and refined.

As Higgins says:

Every part of Christianity refers back to Abraham, and it is all Freemasonry. Jesus Christ at table, at the head of the twelve, offering the sacrifice of Bread and Wine, is Abraham and Melchizedek over again; such, in fact, it is acknowledged to be by the Romish Church; such is its esoteric religion . . . 26

Doane further illustrates the connection between Masonry and Christianity:

Masons' marks are conspicuous among the Christian symbols. On some of the most ancient Roman Catholic cathedrals are to be found figures of Christ Jesus with Masons' marks about him.27

Unbeknownst to the masses, the pope is the Grand Master-Mason of the Masonic branches of the world.28 Regarding this sordid partnership, Anderson remarks:

Freemasonry, corrupted by Roman Catholicism, has lost its ancient landmarks and been carried into captivity . . . Masonry not instituted by the ancient people is worthless and of no account. . . . Ancient Masonry is found all over the inhabitable world; modern Masonry in but a small portion of it. Ancient Masonry will last while the world endures; modern Masonry will die in derision as . . . the Catholic Church fades out; and it is rapidly dying in all places where science and knowledge prevail. A religion built upon a dream is not one to last; and Catholicism has for its authority, "and the angel appeared to Joseph in a dream."29

Masonry originally held, and still does at the higher levels, the knowledge that the Christ character was *the sun*. This knowledge has obviously been hidden from all but the few. In addition, as stated, the heliocentricity of the solar system and the roundness of the earth were known to the ancients eons prior to the Christian era, but these two facts, among innumerable others, were suppressed so that no one would apprehend the sublimation of the solar and celestial mythos. We must ask why the solar mythos, so significant and ubiquitous in cultures around the world for thousands of years, is now unknown, particularly when it is well understood that without the knowledge of the heavens we could scarcely function on Earth, time as we know it would not exist, and we would be unable to figure out when to plant and harvest our food, for one important example. What has happened to the ubiquitous celestial mythos? How is it that this information, so widely known in ancient times, is almost completely hidden from the masses today? The answer is that it has been *deliberately* suppressed, so that the masses would never realize the connection between their cherished gods and the celestial bodies.

As demonstrated by Paine, the Masons have known very well the true meaning and importance of astrology, which was considered a sacred science. Anderson explains this ages-old science and its relationship to Masonry and Catholicism:

> . . . [A]strology is the Word, and written from the beginning . . . an exact science, sublime and holy, which has existed longer than we have at present any history, and handed down by the great and wise of the past, those builders of the temples of the sun, or universe, until in its old age its ashes are buried in Roman Catholicism but yet burn in Freemasonry . . . [The] astrology of the ancients is the base of all and every science, either of the past or the future, and that it was at one time a universal religion, science, and language, the remnants of the sign language still held by the Masonic bodies, to whom it is as "shining in the darkness and the darkness comprehending it not."[30]

Astrology and astrotheology were not only known in the ancient world but have constituted an enormous portion of human civilization. Time and again, massive edifices around the globe have been built that are encapsulations of the heavenly story, serving as stellar "computers." But this astrotheological Masonry was corrupted, as the powermongering historicizers drove its true meaning and religion underground in a vicious quest to subjugate the world and acquire its wealth.

The Motive

It is obvious the conspirators were after power and money, and, as Pope Leo X quipped, they certainly have become wealthy from the fable of Christ. In fact, during the 500-year period of the Inquisition, which Walker calls, "a standing mockery of justice— perhaps the most iniquitous that the arbitrary cruelty of man has ever devised,"[31] the Church grew extremely rich. In reality, there is no other way to explain why the Romans would willingly worship a Jewish man as a god incarnate, a title and honor usually reserved for Caesars. As the Romans themselves said and as was admitted by Christians, they did not believe the tale, immediately recognizing it as a rehash of pre-existing myths, legends and rituals. Nor were they fond of the troublesome Jews, such that they would have exalted one in such a manner. The Romanized Jesus, in fact, was designed to castigate the Jews and, as noted, to give the Romans authority over them.

The gospel story was also designed to put the onus on the Jews for the destruction of their nation, which is why the story was placed at the time it was. The tale had to occur before the destruction of the temple in 70 CE, obviously, or the play would not have had a stage in which to set it. In fact, Church historian Eusebius makes it clear that Christ's advent must take place before the destruction of Jerusalem so that his Passion might be utilized as justification for that deed:

> To Pella those who believed in Christ migrated from Jerusalem; and as if holy men had utterly abandoned the royal metropolis of the Jews and the entire Jewish land, the judgment of God at last overtook them for their abominable crimes against Christ and His apostles, completely blotting out that wicked generation from among men. . . . Such was the reward of the Jews' iniquitous and wicked treatment of God's Christ.[32]

The editor of *The History of the Church* says of Eusebius:

> He regards the first Jewish War (66-73), with the destruction of Jerusalem, as a punishment for the crucifixion of Christ and for the continued persecution of His followers, especially James "the Lord's brother" . . . He records that since the second Jewish War (132-5) the "entire race has been forbidden to set foot anywhere in the neighbourhood of Jerusalem" so that "not even from a distance might Jews have a view of their ancestral soil". Eusebius clearly regards it as a just punishment . . . [33]

Eusebius, it should be noted, was from Caesarea, which would essentially make him a Samaritan, although not necessarily of "Jewish" blood. It is obvious that, while he considers Christ from the house of Judah, he is not fond of "Jews"; nor were many others in the Roman Empire. The author of *The Other Jesus* explains the prevailing attitude of the "Gentiles" towards the Jews during the Empire:

> We must remember that the New Testament was written at a time when Palestine had been under European domination for almost four hundred years. Europeans found Jews to be a very difficult people to deal with. To them, the Jews seemed to be the most stubbornly backward kind of barbarians they had ever encountered. Jews spoke an incomprehensible language (meaning that it was not at all like Greek or Latin). And Jews did many things that were intensely offensive to European sensibilities, like cut the tips off of male children's penises as a

matter of "religious" law. They were obsessed with "nonsensical" dietary superstitions and a seemingly endless set of "absurd" restrictions that seemed to prevent them from ever getting anything accomplished. The Greeks and Romans, both being steadfast believers in monogamous marriage and fierce defenders of the sanctity of the institution of the family, were morally outraged when they discovered that Jews allowed a man to have more than one wife if he wanted to. They were even more disgusted and scandalized by the Jewish practice of permitting men to divorce a wife for no reason other than he felt like doing so. In stark contrast to the general Greek and Roman attitude of religious tolerance, the Jews had an obnoxious tendency to denounce everyone's religion but their own in the most disrespectful ways imaginable, and sometimes spoke as if they had the right, or even the obligation to destroy the churches, altars, and holy shrines of other people. This last point, as you might imagine, created an acute antagonism among Europeans toward Jewish religion quite different from their usual policy of tolerating all foreign religions they encountered. The way this story is often told, the Romans and Greeks are typically presented as the "bad guys" without ethics or moral values, while the Jews are presented as the "good guys" on the moral high ground. But any such analysis is much too simplistic. For such a view ignores the fact that the pagan Europeans of that era were outraged and offended by the same Jewish ideas and practices that many contemporary Christians object to even today. Had the average modern Christian been in Palestine in the first century AD, they would probably have had more sympathy for the Greek and Roman position than for the Jews. . . . The Greeks, and their successors, the Romans, would need to create some kind of a "social movement," presumably with a heavy religious content, that would counteract the aspects of Jewish culture they perceived as most problematic. Such a campaign would loudly denounce practices such as circumcision, ridicule the strict adherence to Jewish dietary laws, preach against divorce and for monogamous marriage. European propaganda would need to preach against rigid interpretations of Jewish law, dispense with Jewish rituals in favor of European ones, and work to make free associations between Jews and non-Jews acceptable. Most importantly, Greek and Roman propaganda efforts would need to find something that would make Jewish submission to foreign authority acceptable within a Jewish religious framework. And since at the center of this dispute lay Jewish concepts of a Messiah who would free Palestine from evil foreign rulers, even a century or two before Christ, it would have taken no great prophetic powers to have guessed that the European propaganda campaigns would eventually be intertwined with arguments about who was and who was not the genuine Messiah.[34]

Furthermore, as the author of the Epistle of Ignatius to the Magnesians says, "To profess Jesus Christ while continuing to follow Jewish customs is an absurdity. The Christian faith does not look to Judaism, but Judaism looks to Christianity, *in which every other race and tongue that confesses a belief in God has now been comprehended.*"[35] Thus, Ignatius's statements constitute an admission that orthodox Christianity was formulated to abrogate the Judean religion and to roll all the competing religions into one.

The motives of those who composed and spread the gospel story were not entirely suspect. In fact, the composers had in mind the termination of the recurrent sacred king sacrifice/ scapegoat ritual with the final blood atonement prescribed in the Christian myth, as is stated in the Letter to the Hebrews, for example. As Dujardin says, "The sacrifice was in decadence in the first century in the official cults, scorned by Graeco-Roman society, and disparaged by the Rationalism of the intellectuals."[36] Walker elucidates the need for the Christian myth to change the habits of one of the last bastions of human sacrifice:

> The Jews however did retain a custom of human sacrifice, for special occasions, longer than any other people in the sphere of influence in the Roman empire. Out of this tradition arose the figure of the dying *Christos* in Jerusalem.[37]

As noted, the results of this effort to end human sacrifice have been far from satisfactory, as millions of humans have been sacrificed in the name of Christianity. In addition, the dreary image of the suffering Jesus has served as a constant reminder of gloom and doom, casting a somber pall across the world. It would have been much better for the world if the gnosis, or esoteric knowledge, had been made known in the first place.

When the Romans pulled together their state religion, they no doubt had in front of them the words of Josephus regarding Moses: "Now when once he had brought them to submit to religion, he easily persuaded them to submit in all other things . . ."[38] In addition, a favorite Roman adage was, "The common people like to be deceived—deceived let them be."[39] Thus, we see that the Romans were not mindlessly falling down to worship the Jesus character as an incarnation of God when they adopted the nascent religion, which they then changed for centuries to suit their own interests.

Furthermore, in order to pass off this doctrine of submission, there had to be inculcated a fervent belief in the "One God," such that it would be believed he had sent a messenger, prophet, son or other representative. This belief in an omnipotent supernatural being has not been difficult to sell, since it has existed from virtually the first moment man became cognizant of his surroundings. However, as Margaret Sanger said, "No God, no Master," and numerous freethinkers over the centuries have noted how the concept of an all-powerful, all-controlling god is used to create despotism, tyranny and fascism, which is, in the end, the motive for creating Christianity. Anderson describes the foundation of Christianity and its results:

> The Romans at that time were the worst of pagans or idolaters; but knowing well the power of state religion, strove to make from their original sun worship a religion which should embody Trinity; and so from the story of Buddha and Osiris, Isis and Horus, and the zodiacal signs, clothed the stories in new garments, and personified the sun into a *living* man, and the moon into a virgin mother, and the cross ♱ as the life-saving symbol, and then *forced the slaves of Rome by sword and wild beast, by inquisition and torture and auto-da-fe, to acknowledge as truth that which their souls abhorred*; forcing them to teach this to their children, established that abomination, the confessional, making spies and traitors in every household till, sinking deeper and deeper in despair and forced ignorance, generation after generation dared no longer even to think their soul was their own and given by God, but were led to believe that God the Father damned them from the beginning and delivered them over to the devil, to be saved (no matter how abominable their crimes) by this man called the Son of God . . . In fact, the whole story is incomprehensible; and as no one could explain it, the priests when questioned at once forbid such sacrilege as questions; and "It is a mystery" sufficed to stay all inquisitive minds.[40]

And Wheless says:

> Thus was the ultimate merger and total identity of Paganism with "the new Paganism called Christianity" finally established by law and Imperial policy of "One State and One Religion," to which conformity was enforced by laws of confiscation and death; all the other religions of the Empire were fused by fire and sword into a bastard Christianity.[41]

It was unquestionably these selfsame Roman authorities who put into the mouth of the fictitious Paul the exhortations that Christians obey the authorities "in everything." The honor that he exhorts them to give "to whom honor is due" is, of course, due to the Emperor, as are the taxes Paul also tells his followers to hand over. It makes little sense that Paul and other Christians would be persecuted as claimed if they were obeying these injunctions. Why would the authorities seize and execute Paul, when he was preaching to the Romans that they should give their money to, and obey in everything, those same authorities? And why would

Paul then grouse about being held prisoner, when he told his followers to submit to the authorities, for they are "from God?"

Furthermore, Christ himself is made to exhort his followers to despise "mammon," i.e., money, and to "render it unto Caesar." When sought for his sage advice by Roman soldiers, John the Baptist tells them to "be contented with their wages" (Luke 3:14). This injunction against money by the "rebellious" Jesus and his cohorts served the state and its religion very nicely, since it was they who ended up with the money. Such exhortations by "Jesus" beg the question as to why an omniscient and compassionate god would advise his followers to give away all their money and potentially starve to death. Such a god would not behave in this callous manner, but those who were to get the money would. Nor would any god need people to tithe to his priests and church if he were real and all-powerful, therefore having no need for the back-breaking labor of human beings to sustain him.

It is quite obvious who really wrote these passages, yet people still blindly submit to the authorities because of them, believing that there is indeed a single, omniscient, omnipresent and omnipotent being in charge at all times and that "he" has given authorities their power.

After centuries of killing millions around the globe and stealing their wealth, the Catholic Church became more "refined" in its extortionist policy, sending out its financial missionaries, the Jesuits. The Jesuits are the most effective proselytizers of Catholicism worldwide, for centuries envied by the other orders for their ability to acquire vast fortunes and properties. Over the past couple of centuries, the Jesuit handbook, "Secret Instructions of the Society of Jesus," has found its way into the hands of outsiders who have published it. This guidebook, or "Monita," focuses on how to defraud old ladies by telling them that they will receive grace if they submit to the confessor, who will then oversee how every penny of theirs is spent and make sure their wills are made out to the Order. The Monita also describes how to convince the rich that donating to the Church will "relieve the pains of purgatory." In order to secure these fortunes, the Jesuits appeal to the vanity of the donor by insuring that he or she will have his or her name on a college or university building. The Monita was written in Latin, of course, so that only the educated would have any chance of knowing what it contained and that it would therefore remain secret. One outsider who published the book was a Scottish Rite Mason, demonstrating how these societies compete with each other even though they are intimately linked, growing, in fact, out of the same root.

In reality, if we peek far behind the curtain of the secret societies and fraternities, we find traditional enemies working together to slice up the world for the benefit of the elite, creating nations and exploiting the masses. We discover they concoct conflict for profit, as many members have been weapons manufacturers—and there is for them to wield no more a contentious weapon than religion. Christianity, in effect, was a state religion devised to enrich and empower certain individuals and groups, who have since become among the most powerful on the planet.

---

1. Larson, 185.
2. Massey, *EBD*, 91.
3. Wells, *DJE*, 66.
4. Fox, 124.
5. Walker, *WEMS*, 470.
6. Allegro, *DSSCM*, 139.
7. Allegro, *DSSCM*, 230.
8. Chapt. IV, 13.
9. Higgins, I, 558.
10. Walker, *WEMS*, 320.
11. *The Lost Books of the Bible*, 283.
12. Potter, 464.
13. Barnstone, 568.
14. Roberts, 71.
15. Walker, *WEMS*, 469.
16. Wheless, 29.
17. Higgins, II, 279.
18. Eusebius, 70.
19. Blavatsky, *IU*, II, 91.
20. Higgins, I, 713.
21. Higgins, I, 809.
22. Higgins, I, 717.
23. Higgins, I, 745.
24. Higgins, I, 768.
25. Higgins, I, 719.
26. Higgins, I, 791.
27. Doane, 358.
28. Higgins, I, 823. See also the works of Jordan Maxwell.
29. Anderson, 11-12; viz. 13.
30. Anderson, iii-iv.
31. Walker, *WEMS*, 436.
32. Eusebius, 68-73.
33. Eusebius, xxv-xxvi.
34. "The Other Jesus" website
35. *Early Christian Writings*, 73.
36. Mead, *DJL*, 10.
37. Walker, *WEMS*, 878.
38. Josephus, *Antiquities*.
39. Doane, 271.
40. Anderson, 52.
41. Wheless, 31.

Egyptians wearing
Masonic aprons. Bronze
statuette (bottom) dates
from 3400 BCE.
(Bramley)

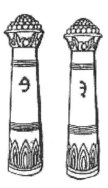

"Jachin and Boaz," the
Masonic pillars at the
entrance to Solomon's
temple. (Biedermann

George Washington wearing Masonic
regalia. (Bramley)

Masonic Emblem with
YHWH, ca. 1800 CE
(Biedermann)

The Making of a Myth

In creating their state religion, the Christian conspirators not only founded the world's greatest forgery mill but also went on a censorship rampage that silenced millions of dissident voices by murder and destroyed books, temples, statues, inscriptions and other traces of the previous cultures, eventually leading to immense ignorance and the virtual illiteracy of the Western world. As Roberts says:

> To get rid of the damning fact that there is no historical basis for their theological fictions, the Christian priesthood have been guilty of the heinous crime of destroying nearly all traces of the concurrent history of the first two centuries of the Christian era. What little of it they have permitted to come down to us, they have so altered and changed, as to destroy its historical value.

These censoring Christians were no doubt well aware what literacy and books really represented, as the words "library" and "liberty" share the same root, "liber," the Latin word for "book." Walker relates the Church's modus operandi:

> It was always important for religious authorities to control literature, and to gain the legal right to destroy books that contradicted their own teachings. Few people were so assiduous in this endeavor as Christians. In the third to sixth centuries, whole libraries were burned, schools and universities destroyed and citizens' books confiscated throughout the Roman world, on the pretext of defending the church against paganism. Under the early Christian emperors, people were framed by ecclesiastical investigators who planted "magical writings" in their houses, then legally confiscated all possessions.[1]

After the Council of Nicea, per the murderous Constantine's orders, the Christians turned up the heat on censorship, leading to the centuries-long orgy that obliterated millions of texts. One of the greatest crimes in human history was the destruction in 391 of the library at Alexandria perpetrated by Christian fanatics under Theophilus bent on hiding the truth about their religion and its alleged founder. Because of this villainy, we have lost priceless information as to the true state of the ancient world, with such desolation also setting back civilization at least 1,000 years. The portion of the Alexandrian library placed in the Temple of Serapis also perished, "as this very valuable library was wilfully destroyed by the Christian Theophilus, and on the spot where this beautiful temple of Serapis stood, in fact, on its very foundation, was erected a church in honor of the 'noble army of martyrs,' who never existed."[2] Of this nefarious demolition of the Serapion, Roberts asks:

> Will any Catholic or Protestant prelate, priest or clergyman tell
> us why the Christian emperor, Theodosius the First, should have
> ordered the destruction of the Serapeum Library of Alexandria, if
> not to destroy the evidence it contained of the spurious nature of
> the Christian religion and its heathen philosophical origin?[3]

Some decades later, the Christian patriarch of Alexandria,
Cyril, instigated mobs to terrorize Jews and to hideously torture
and murder the exalted female Pagan philosopher Hypatia (c.
370-415) by scraping the flesh from her bones with oyster shells.
For his evil acts, Cyril was later canonized by the "infallible"
Church. Hypatia was so esteemed and renowned for her wisdom
and brilliance that her murder has been considered the "death of
the Pagan world."

The destruction did not end there, however, as the ruination
of literacy and history became an all-consuming Christian
pursuit. As Graham states, "By the fifth century the destruction
was so complete Archbishop Chrystostom could boast of it thus:
'Every trace of the old philosophy and literature of the ancient
world has vanished from the face of the earth.'"[4]

At some point, a death penalty was enacted for reading
unapproved books, e.g., those that demonstrated the faith was a
sham. Pope after pope continued the assault on books and
learning. Gregory, Bishop of Constantinople (@ 540-604), the last
of the "doctors" of the Church, actively engaged in book-burning.
In the 11th century, "Saint" Gregory had the Library of Palatine
Apollo burned, and the Council of Trent (1545-63) reconfirmed
the policy against "heathen" learning.

Where the Christians did not destroy the works of the ancient
authors, they corrupted and mutilated them. Indeed, in order to
preserve their texts from these violent hands, the Gnostics
themselves were compelled to Christianize them, such that they
also had to historicize their mythical characters.[5] So extensive
was this practice of fraud that evidently no ancient author's work
maintains its original integrity.[6] Walker elaborates upon the
extent of the fraud:

> After burning books and closing pagan schools, the church dealt
> in another kind of forgery: falsification by omission. All European
> history was extensively edited by a church that managed to
> make itself the sole repository of literary and historical records.
> With all important documents assembled in the monasteries,
> and the lay public rendered illiterate, Christian history could be
> forged with impunity.[7]

As stated, in addition to destroying and mutilating books, the
Christians demolished and desecrated the temples, statues and
sacred sites of their predecessors and competitors. The erection of
Christian churches on the ruins of pagan temples and sacred

sites was not only common but de rigeur, serving to obliterate the evidence of the previous deity and worship. Walker relates the typical procedure used by Christians to usurp Pagan sacred sites:

> After temples were destroyed, monks and hermits were settled in the ruins to defile the site with their excrement, and to prevent reconstruction.[8]

Such were the efforts the "classy" Christians had to make for centuries to cement their fictions. The devastation of art and culture was appalling, yet some of the despoilers' efforts assisted in preserving evidence of the fraud:

> In some of the ancient Egyptian temples the Christian iconoclasts, when tired of hacking and hewing at the symbolic figures incised in the chambers of imagery, and defacing the most prominent features of the monuments, found they could not dig out the hieroglyphics, and took to covering them over with plaster; and this plaster, intended to hide the meaning and stop the mouth of the stone word, has served to preserve the ancient writings as fresh in hue and sharp in outline as when they were first cut and colored. In a similar manner the temple of ancient religion was invaded and possession gradually gained by connivance of Roman power; and that enduring fortress, not built but quarried out of sold rock, was stuccoed all over the front and made white a-while with its look of brand-newness, and reopened under the sign of another name—that of the carnalized Christ.[9]

Thus, these hieroglyphs have revealed the truth, because they contain the celestial mythos and ritual, and demonstrate that the Christian story is in large part Egyptian.

In addition to this odious Christian behavior was the Inquisition, the most ghastly period in all of human history, in which millions were tortured and murdered over centuries so that they or their descendants would conform to the dogma of the Catholic Church. During those many centuries, no dissenter was allowed to flourish and few to live at all. Anyone who dared to question the fairytales now being forced upon them—in other words, all the *honest* people—were forced to convert or die. Either way, the people would then become fiscally beneficial to the greedy, deceitful Church, by serving as slaves, tithing or forfeiting their assets through death, natural or otherwise.

Of this endless destruction, Doane remarks:

> Besides forging, lying, and deceiving for the cause of Christ, the Christian Fathers destroyed all evidence against themselves and their religion, which they came across. Christian divines seem to have always been afraid of too much light.[10]

Fortunately, they will not be able to escape the light today, as it is too bright. As Higgins says:

> Notwithstanding the strenuous exertions of the priests, for the last two thousand years, to eradicate every trace of the means by which their various doctrines, rites, and ceremonies have been established; yet they have not entirely succeeded.[11]

In fact, a number of important texts fortunately survived the purges intact enough to trace how Christianity was created and shaped. From these various surviving texts, as well as other archaeological evidence already examined, can be illustrated the development of Christianity as outlined herein. To recap, the early contributors to the Christian version of the ubiquitous celestial mythos were the Syrian Gnostics, who were attempting to create a syncretistic religion that would encompass the wide variety of cultures from around the "known world." By the end of the first century CE, at Antioch, for one, the Gnostics were already involved in committing to writing the various sayings and deeds of the characters of the celestial mythos and savior cult that had been transmitted orally within the brotherhood for millennia. Eventually, as Doresse says, "In the time of Hadrian (A.D. 110-38), Gnosticism passes over from Syria into Egypt . . ."[12]

Meanwhile, in Palestine, possibly emanating out of Galilee and/or the ancient monastery on Carmel, with an outpost at Qumran, the Jewish/Samaritan priesthood of Masons and astrologers, the Zadokites/Sadducees, had been anticipating the Great Year's end and agitating that they were the Elect, the inheritors of "the Lord's" kingdom on Earth, which would be brought about by a "wondrous child" and "restorer." After the destruction of Palestine, this group and others dispersed into various other brotherhood branches, including those at Antioch and Alexandria. The new influx reignited the centuries-old internecine struggle for supremacy over each other and the Gentiles. Thus began the conspiracy to set the ubiquitous solar hero sayings and narratives in Judea, with Jews as both protagonists and antagonists.

In the middle of the 2nd century, the original Gnostic schools began to dissent from the Judaizing and historicizing activity, objecting that their original work was not meant to be taken literally. At the end of the 2nd century, the historicizing push increased with the success of the Roman play for domination, and the canonical gospels were completed somewhat, although they were continuously reworked to agree at least superficially with other newly forged manuscripts. This tinkering went on for centuries until relative uniformity was achieved with dozens of councils as well. In fact, the mutilation continues to this day in translations that obfuscate original meanings.

The aim of this priestcraft, of course, was to create a new godman that would not only roll into one all the others but also unite the luni-stellar and solar cult priesthoods, as well as usher in the new age. As the mythical Moses had been utilized to inaugurate the new age of Aries, Jesus was created to do likewise with the age of Pisces. Thus, to the Krishna/Christos myth were added fish motifs from the Osiris/Horus myth, as well as numerous other elements of the Egyptian and other religions, such as the December 25th birthdate, which was established in the fourth century to usurp the cult of Mithra. So it went for centuries, as the fable was cobbled together and the texts overhauled, with ongoing purges.

In this effort, the largely astrological and mythological works of the eclectic Gnostics/Therapeuts were latched onto by historicizers of the second, third and fourth centuries, including Irenaeus, Justin, Tertullian, Origen, Clement Alexandrinus, Tatian and Eusebius. To the conspirators list can be added Ambrose, Augustine, Gregory and Jerome, the four "doctors," so-called because they had the highest degrees from the Therapeutan Alexandrian school. Other villains in the mythmaking included Lactantius, Constantine, Justinian, as well as basically all the popes, including Sylvester, who was pope during the Council of Nicea. Pope Innocent II created the Council of Basel (1431-49), in large part in order to call for bookburning. The first archbishop of York, Paulinus (d. 645), purportedly tampered with scriptures from Armenia and Upper Egypt newly discovered in his time. We can be certain that there are many others behind the scenes whose names have never made it into records books—at least not overtly. These individuals no doubt have been extremely wealthy and powerful.

The Intertestamental Literature and Christian Apocrypha

As seen, the Dead Sea scrolls dating to the centuries before and after the beginning of the Christian era survived unknown and untouched by the forgers, and reveal the Palestinian contributors to the Christian myth. In addition to the Samaritan Gnostic Marcion's New Testament, other texts utilized by the Christian conspirators included the intertestamental literature composed of the Jewish Apocrypha and Pseudepigrapha, as well as the Christian Apocrypha. Many of these books were originally canonical but were later removed and condemned, demonstrating how often "God's infallible Word" has been changed. A number of the Jewish Apocrypha, however, have been retained in the Catholic Bible, but not in the Protestant texts, illustrating that the latter is a corruption of the former and not a "return to primitive Christianity." Moreover, in the various texts either removed or kept out of the biblical canon may be found more truth about the origins of Christianity than in those made canonical. As the editor of *The Other Bible* says:

> Deprived of all scriptures between the Testaments, the common reader is left with the impression that somehow Christianity sprang self-generated like a divine entity, with no past, into its historical setting. Yet a reading of the texts between the Testaments shows how major eschatological themes of the New Testament—the appearance of the Son of Man, the imminence of the End, the apocalyptic vision in the Book of Revelation, the notion of salvation through the messiah—are all preoccupation of intertestamental literature. [13]

Indeed, the self-generating impression is contrived to cover up the ruse, yet there are enough of these ignored texts such that a thorough exegesis could fill a volume in itself.

The Book of Enoch

Among these texts was "The Book of Enoch," which was given scriptural recognition in the New Testament Letter of Jude and which was in the Christian canon for 500 years. [14] Copies of Enoch were found at the Dead Sea, demonstrating that the scrolls were not the writings of an isolated sect and that the Sadducean originators of Christianity used Enoch, which contained much of the story of "Jesus Christ" and which predated the alleged advent of the Jewish godman by centuries. Of this book Wheless says:

> The Book of Enoch, forged in the name of the grandson of Adam, is the fragmentary remains of a whole literature which circulated under the pretended authorship of that mythical Patriarch. . . . This work is a composite of at least five unknown Jewish writers, and was composed during the last two centuries B.C. . . . In this Book we first find the lofty titles: "Christ" or "the Anointed One," "Son of Man," "the Righteous One," "the Elect One,"—all of which were boldly plagiarized by the later Christians and bestowed upon Jesus of Nazareth. . . . [The Book] abounds in such "Christian" doctrines as the Messianic Kingdom, Hell, the Resurrection, and Demonology, the Seven Heavens, and the Millennium, all of which have here their apocryphal Jewish promulgation, after being plagiarized bodily from the Persian and Babylonian myths and superstitions, as we have seen confessed. There are numerous quotations, phrases, clauses, or thoughts derived from Enoch, or of closest of kin with it, in several of the New Testament Gospels and Epistles. . .[15]

And Carpenter states:

> In *The Book of Enoch*, written not later than B.C. 170, the Christ is spoken of as already existing in heaven, and about to come as Judge of all men, and is definitely called "the Son of Man." The Book of Revelations is *full* of passages from *Enoch*; so are the Epistles of Paul; so too are the Gospels. [16]

The Book of Enoch relates that the messiah will come and establish supremacy: "The Chosen One will have the sinners destroyed."[17] Of this judgment day, Wells says:

> Enoch's picture of the final judgement is strikingly paralleled at Matthew 25:31-46. Enoch says that "the Lord of Spirits seated the Elect One on the throne of his glory"; Matthew reads: "When the Son of man shall come in his glory . . . then shall he sit on the throne of his glory." Both writers go on to describe how the righteous are vindicated while the rest are banished to flame and torment.[18]

Enoch, of course, is not a historical character but is part of the mythos. As Massey says, "In the *Book of Enoch* one form of the Messiah is the '*Son of Woman*'; this was Enoch or Enos, the Egyptian Sut-Anush [Set], who had been twin with Horus but was superseded by him."[19] Hazelrigg elaborates:

> Then came Enoch, or Anûsh, words which mean knowledge; he was known as Ur-anous, and, according to a Hebrew manuscript, as Hermes, the inventor of astronomy, mathematics, and of divine worship. Aonac, an Irish word (pronounced Enoch), signifies a cycle of the sun. He was also known as Atlas, whence Atlantis, of which country he was the Supreme Pontiff. His symbol was the Bull, emblematic of the shepherd age.[20]

In actuality, the bull was the emblem of the *Taurean* age, which would mean that the book reflects a tradition 4,000 or more years old. The book is in fact highly astrological, as is to be expected since it contains the mythos. Regarding the Book of Enoch, Higgins relates:

> Here are all the leading doctrines which I have been contending for clearly maintained. The residence or birth-place of the theology, Upper India; the signs of the Zodiac; the change of the Equinox from Taurus to Aries; . . . the Hindoo Trinity, than which nothing can be more clear . . . and a history similar to the Jewish, but not copied from it; the prophecy of an *elect one* as described by all the prophets, including the prophecy of Virgil, and the elect one put to death, noticed by me in the cases of Buddha, Cristna, and him of the Apollo of Miletus . . . It has been the subject of this work to show that an universal system extended over the whole of the old world; and the principal facts for which I have contended are supported by this curious and unquestionably genuine document . . . [21]

Higgins avers that, based on the astrology, Enoch reflects it was originally composed around 2400 BCE in the latitude of Northern India.[22]

Another pseudepigraphic writing attributed to Enoch is the Book of the Secrets of Enoch, one of the "366 books" allegedly written by him, a number symbolic for the 365+ days of the year.

As in the OT, in the Secrets it was said that Enoch lived to be 365 "years"; in other words, he is the sun, and his "life" is the length of a year. In the Secrets, Enoch continues the solar imagery when he describes how the "angels," or *angles of the zodiac*, "bore me away to the east, and placed me at the sun's gates, where the sun goes forth according to the regulation of the seasons and the circuit of the months of the whole year, and the number of the hours of day and night."[23] This Enochian text is thus astrotheological, no doubt the reason it was eventually considered "apocryphal."

The Testaments of the Twelve Patriarchs

Although they are purported to be the products of the mythical "sons of Jacob," the Jewish Pseudepigrapha "The Testaments of the Twelve Patriarchs" were written likely between 137 to 107 BCE. Of the Testaments, the editor of *The Forgotten Books of Eden* says:

> When you look beyond the unvarnished—almost brutally frank— passages of the text, you will discern a remarkable attestation of the expectations of the Messiah which existed a hundred years before Christ. . . . The instances of the influence of these writings on the New Testament are notable in the Sermon on the Mount which reflects the spirit and even uses phrases from these Testaments. St. Paul appears to have borrowed so freely that it seems as though he must have carried a copy of the Testaments with him on his travels.[24]

Like the Dead Sea scrolls, these texts contain the blueprint for Christianity; however, some of them have been interpolated by conspiring Christians to give a semblance of "prophecy" of their pretended godman. As Barnstone says, "Indeed, because of the messianic nature of Jewish Pseudepigrapha, they were favorite readings of the early Christians and many of them were altered and 'Christianized,' falsified if you will, to make them reveal Christian truths."[25] In their cunning priestcraft, the mutilating Christians later accused the Jews of removing material from the originals. Nevertheless, some of the Christian-like passages are apparently genuine, such that they constitute proof that the forgers of Christianity were of the same school as the Testaments writers and used their texts.

These testaments were written and/or interpolated for the express purpose of: 1. raising the Semites over the other "sons of Noah"; 2. uniting the tribes of Levi and Judah as the rulers over other Israelites and over the Gentiles; and 3. laying the foundation for the coming king, who, in anticipation of the destruction of Jerusalem/Judea, was to be made into a spiritual "son of God" as well.

The Testament of Simeon, for example, seeks to raise the Semites, or "sons of Shem," over the Japhethites and Hamites. This book states: "Then the Mighty One of Israel shall glorify Shem. *For the Lord God shall appear on earth, and Himself save men.*" Thus, the Semites will subjugate all other races and God Himself will incarnate ostensibly *as a Semite,* according to the latter sentence, which is a Christian interpolation. As such, the Semitic godman will represent the tribes of Levi and Judah over the other Israelites, and provide salvation for all the nations, as Simeon also says:

> And now, my children, obey Levi and Judah, and be not lifted up against these two tribes, for from them shall arise unto you the salvation of God. For the Lord shall raise up from Levi as it were a High Priest, and from Judah as it were a King, *God and man,* He shall save all the Gentiles and the race of Israel.[26]

In this union of Levi and Judah is the spiritual "savior" plus the temporal "messiah," which is equivalent to "Jesus the Christ."

Furthermore, in the Testament of Levi, which was purportedly written between 109-107 BCE, appears this stunning blueprint for Christianity:

> And behold I am clear from your ungodliness and transgression, which ye shall commit in the end of the ages against *the Savior of the World, Christ,* acting godlessly, deceiving Israel, and stirring up against it great evils from the Lord. And ye shall deal lawlessly together with Israel, so He shall not bear with Jerusalem because of your wickedness; but the veil of the temple shall be rent, so as not to cover your shame. And ye shall be scattered as captives among the Gentiles, and shall be for a reproach and for a curse there. For the house which the Lord shall choose shall be called Jerusalem, as is contained in the book of Enoch the righteous.[27]

If this passage is not a shameless Christian interpolation, forged after the fall of Jerusalem, it is quite obviously a seed from which the Christ myth sprouted. It also verifies the importance of the Book of Enoch.

The Jewish Apocrypha and Pseudepigrapha provide a connection between not only Judaism and orthodox Christianity but also Judaism and Gnosticism, evidenced in such texts as the Wisdom of Solomon, the Haggadah, and the Wisdom of Jesus.

The Wisdom of Jesus, Son of Sirach, or Ecclesiasticus

For obvious reasons, the title of the pre-Christian "Wisdom of Jesus" is often represented without the "Jesus," as "Wisdom of Sirach" or "Ecclesiasticus." Purportedly written around 180 BCE by "Jesus" and translated into Greek by his grandson "Jesus," the text evidently represents the lineage of the pre-Christian

Joshua/Jesus cultists. The Wisdom of Jesus contains hundreds of wisdom sayings, including Old Testament aphorisms such as, "To fear the Lord is the source of wisdom." Here, as in Gnosticism, wisdom is identified as a female entity (Hokmah/ Sophia). This lengthy book also contains several New Testament Sayings of Jesus, or Logia Iesou, and is without a doubt Therapeutan, in that it prescribes the putting of oneself in the hands of a spiritual physician in order to "cleanse one's heart from sin." Like the gospel Jesus, the pre-Christian or Wisdom Jesus exhorts "faith and meekness" to win the approval of the Lord, excoriates hypocrites and admonishes his followers not to exalt themselves. The pre-Christian Jesus also exhorts his would-be servants of the Lord to "prepare yourself to be tried. Set your heart right and be firm . . . hold fast to him, and do not forsake him, so that you may be honored when your life ends," exactly as the followers of the gospel Jesus were told to be as "martyrs for the faith." Like the gospel Jesus, who entreats his followers to give away their belongings, the Wisdom Jesus says, "So charity will atone for sin" and urges his followers to do good works for those less fortunate, so that they may become like "sons of the Most High" (El Elyon). The Wisdom Jesus is also very similar to Paul in his sexist attitudes, saying, "A silent wife is a gift from the Lord," among other noxious and repressive comments. In this large collection may basically be discovered a significant portion of the wisdom sayings attributed to the gospel Jesus and his cohorts. Of the Wisdom of Jesus, Massey says:

> . . . the Book of Ecclesiasticus contains the logia of a pre-Christian Jesus. Here are two of *his* sayings: "Forgive thy neighbor the hurt that he hath done unto thee, so shall thy sins also be forgiven when thou prayest." "Lay up thy treasures according to the commandments of the Most High, and it shall bring thee more profit than gold." These are assigned to the Jesus of Matthew's gospel.[28]

Furthermore, the pre-Christian Jesus, like the gospel Jesus, calls God "Father" and says:

> He created me from the beginning before the world, and I shall never fail. . . . They that eat me shall yet be hungry, and they that drink me shall yet be thirsty. He that obeyeth me shall never be confounded, and they that work by me shall not do amiss.[29]

Obviously, either this text is interpolated, which would yet again demonstrate Christian fraud, or it serves as proof of the pre-Christian Jesus, eucharist and all.

Many of the exhortations in this book are for initiates into the brotherhood and are Buddhistic/Gymnosophic in nature. In fact, the Wisdom Jesus reveals his solar cult affiliation with his long homage to the sun, in which he states that the sun "has not permitted the saints of the Lord to recount all his wonders," i.e., to record in writing the mysteries of the solar mythos:

> The light-giving sun looks down on everything, and his work is full of the glory of the Lord. He has not permitted the saints of the Lord to recount all his wonders, which the Lord, the Almighty, has firmly established, so that the universe might stand fast through his glory. . . . The glory of the height is the firmament in its purity; The sight of the heavens with the spectacle of their splendor. The sun, when he appears, making proclamation as he goes forth, is a wonderful instrument, the work of the Most High; at noonday he dries up the country, and who can withstand his burning heat? . . . He breathes out fiery vapors, and shoots forth his beams, blinding men's eyes. (42:16-43:5)

In fact, the Wisdom Jesus's paean to the sun is about as close to Pagan sun-worshipping as it gets. Moreover, these sayings constitute one of several places where the pre-Christian Jesus exalts the sun, moon and stars and displays astrological/astrotheological knowledge.

The Teachings of the Twelve Apostles, or The Didache

The early Christian apocryphon "The Teachings of the Twelve Apostles," also called the "Didache," was utilized in the manufacture of the canonical gospels. ben Yehoshua states it was based on writings concerning the "12 tribes," and Larson say it combines the Logia Iesou, or Sayings, with the Manual of Discipline found at the Dead Sea. The Didache does not contain a narrative but provides explanation and instructions concerning baptism, the eucharist, tribulation and parousia, or arrival of "the Lord in the clouds."

The Gospel of the Hebrews and Syrians

Dating to around 115-125 CE, the Gospel of the Hebrews was reputedly used first and almost exclusively by the early Jewish-Christian church, and was also called by Eusebius the "Gospel according to the Hebrews and Syrians," "by which he meant it was used by the Jews in Syria, as elsewhere," a view confirmed by Jerome, who also affirmed that "the Gospel of the Hebrews was written 'in the Chaldee and Syriac languages.' It appears it was used by the Nazarenes residing in Berea, Syria . . ."[30] The Gospel of Hebrews was sometimes confused with the Gospel of Matthew, possibly because it represented the Egyptian "Oracles of Taht-Matiu." The Gospel of the Hebrews contained the "Logia Iesou" or Sayings of Jesus and was non-historicizing, containing no immaculate conception, genealogy "from Abraham to Christ" or childhood history.

The Gospel of the Egyptians or Diegesis

Another text utilized in the creation of Christianity was the "Gospel of the Egyptians," which predated the canonical gospels and was written by the Therapeuts. Of the Gospel of the Egyptians, Waite says:

> The original of this gospel may have been in use among the Therapeutae of Egypt, a long time before the introduction of Christianity, the passages related to Christ being afterward added. Or it may have been written in another country, and brought into Egypt, with the Christian religion. In either case it may be dated as early as A.D. 110 to 115. . . . The story of Joseph and Mary appears not to have been known when this gospel was written. Neither is any thing said, so far as we have information of its contents, of the miracles of Christ, or of the material resurrection.[31]

Taylor states that the "narrative" mentioned by Luke, i.e., the Diegesis, was the Gospel of the Egyptians:

> The first draft of the mystical adventures of Chrishna, as brought from India into Egypt, was the Diegesis; the first version of the Diegesis was the Gospel according to the Egyptians; the first renderings out of the language of Egypt into that of Greece, for the purpose of imposing on the nations of Europe, were *the apocryphal gospels*; the correct, castigated, and *authorised* versions of these apocryphal compilations were the gospels of our four evangelists.

The Gospel of Truth, the Gospel of Thomas and the Acts of Thomas

In addition, a number of the Gnostic gospels barely mention "Jesus" or "Christ," referring instead to the abstract "Savior," such as the Gospel of Truth (150 CE) and the Gospel of Thomas, which was composed primarily of the Logia Iesou and written in Aramaic/Syriac, representing the Tammuz faction. Furthermore, the apocryphal Acts of Thomas were likely forged to explain how the "Christians of St. Thomas" ended up in India; however, as demonstrated, these "Christians" were Tammuz followers already in India possibly millennia before the Christian era.

The Protevangelion, or Book of James

Used by the forgers of Matthew and Luke, the Protevangelion is one of the oldest Judaized narratives, written by a Hellenic Jew around 120-130 CE. The text was originally Indian and Egyptian, with the myth of Isis-Mari and Seb becoming Mary and Joseph, and was somewhat "historicized" with the mythical persecution by Herod, who is made to take the role of both the Indian Kansa and the Egyptian Set-Typhon.

Furthermore, into the portions of the Protevangelion used by the evangelists were interpolated phrases to "fulfill prophecy": For example, the verses at Matthew 1:22-23 about the "virgin" conceiving and bearing a son called Emmanuel are not found in the earlier Protevangelion. Also missing is Luke 4:24: "And he said, 'Truly, I say to you, no prophet is acceptable in his own country.'" This interpolation was made to make Jesus, the ubiquitous solar savior and wisdom genius, appear to be a Jewish man.

The Gospel of the Infancy

Dating to around 120-130, the Gospel of the Infancy was attributed by Jerome to "Matthew" but was "received by the Gnostics," thus not taken literally. The original Gospel of the Infancy was based on the Hindu story of Krishna's childhood, the Bhagavat Purana, apparently procured from the Indian Nazarene brotherhood, with Zoroastrian influence. This and other infancy gospels were used to construct the brief gospel accounts of Jesus's childhood. One interesting phrase may have been inserted as a clue to its allegorical nature, in a passage (vi. 18) following a description of the infant Christ's miraculous healing powers: "The people therefore said, 'Without doubt Joseph and Mary and that boy are Gods, for they do not look like mortals.'" Indeed not.

This book is quite obviously fiction, such that it was not included in the canon, snipped to reduce the roles of the gods Mary and Joseph. Also omitted are the tales depicting Jesus as a vicious boy and frightening sorcerer who changes other boys into kids, i.e., baby goats, so he can be their "shepherd," and strikes dead a Jewish boy who destroyed the young "savior's" fish pools because they had been built on the sabbath.

The Gospel of Luke

We have already seen that the Gospel of Luke was based on Marcion's gospel, with interpolations to historicize and Judaize it. In addition, the entire story of Jesus's entry into Jerusalem at Luke 19:29-48 is missing from Marcion; as demonstrated, this story is a part of the ancient mythos. The writers of Luke also interpolated the Masonic phrases regarding Jesus being "the head cornerstone the builders rejected" at 20:9-18, verses not found in Marcion. Furthermore, a number of passages were added "to fulfill prophecy."

Luke was not only interpolated but also expurgated to remove hints of the brotherhood. For example, at Luke 24, the "two men in dazzling apparel" were originally said to be "those in white clothing," i.e., monks or priests of the solar cult, or "Brotherhood of the Sun."

The Life of Apollonius

Accounts of the life of the Greek/Samaritan Nazarene/ Therapeut/Gnostic miracleworker Apollonius (c. 2 BCE-c 102 CE) purportedly existed during the second century, prior to Philostratus's composition in 210 at the request of Empress Julia Domna. One or more of these accounts was used in the creation of the New Testament narrative, as alleged by a number of accusers, including Hierocles, the pro-consul under Diocletian (284-305), who wrote the "Philalethes" (303) exposing the Apollonius-Jesus connection. It should be noted that Philostratus's account makes no mention of any Jesus Christ, not even as a rival to Apollonius, who purportedly lived precisely at the time alleged of Jesus.

Other Texts

Other texts originally non-Christian but later Christianized include the Apocalypse of Adam and the Paraphrase of Shem, as well as the Apocryphon of John, as Barnstone states:

> The *Apocryphon of John* (here called *The Secret Books of John*) was "originally composed as a non-Christian text" whose Christian thrust was added by a later Christian editor.[32]

The historicizers also used the works of Josephus and the teachings of the Gnostics Menander, Saturninus and Carpocrates, as well as those of the Neoplatonist Ammonius Saccas and others already mentioned.

In this mythmaking effort and religious conspiracy, hundreds of new texts were created, and these compositions produced turmoil among the warring priesthoods. The books of the NT, in fact, reveal how the warring factions developed and were counteracted. For example, in the synoptic gospels is the synthesis between the solar gods of the East and the West. The Gospel of John was compiled to debunk the second century Gnostics and to correct the errors of the other gospels revealed by Pagan critics. The Epistles of John served to excoriate those who claimed Christ never existed. In Acts, the battle between Simon Peter and Simon Magus represents the break between the Roman and Syrian Gnostic churches. Indeed, the confusion and fighting over Christ's life and doctrine within the Church has existed because the Christian plagiarists over the centuries were attempting to amalgamate and fuse practically every myth, fairytale, legend, doctrine or bit of wisdom they could pilfer from the innumerable different mystery religions and philosophies that existed at the time. In doing so, they forged, interpolated, mutilated, changed, and rewrote these texts for centuries.

Eusebius's Dirty Work

Besides Constantine, perhaps no single person had a greater hand in creating Christianity than Eusebius, who mutilated the New Testament books and works of the earlier Christian founders in a number of ways, including by allegedly inserting the newly coined phrase "Jesus Christ," as well as interpolating other instances of the single titles of "Jesus" or "Christ."

The question is, then, whether or not there are any genuine autographs prior to the fourth century that contain the phrase "Jesus Christ" or "Christ Jesus." In fact, in the canonical gospels, the word Jesus appears hundreds of times and the word Christ dozens, but the phrase Jesus Christ only five times altogether, twice in the first chapter of Matthew, once in the first verse of Mark and twice in John. A favorite trick used to interpolate the newly created name "Jesus Christ" was to tack it on at the beginning or end of a book or chapter, as was done in the gospels. In this way, if the interpolation was discovered by comparison with older versions (which were generally destroyed after copying) or writings in which the book had been quoted, it could be justified as a "copyist's note" to clarify the text. It must be remembered that there were no printing or copying machines, and all such reproduction was done by hand, such that few copies were ever made of many manuscripts. Thus, it would not be difficult to change text without discovery or censure, particularly if one had the full weight of Rome behind one's endeavor to squash dissension or whistle-blowers.

In addition, the Epistle of James makes no mention of any aspect of Christ's "life" or sayings and only mentions him by name at the beginning of chapters 1 and 2. This text is older than the canonical "history" or narrative and was written, for the most part, by an Egyptian Gnostic.

One example of how language was changed and interpolated to create references to "our Lord Jesus Christ" where there originally were none is found in the First Epistle of Clement, allegedly an early Christian text, but no doubt worked over by later forgers. In this epistle we find the following phrase: "This is the way, beloved, in which we may find our Savior, even Jesus Christ the high-priest of all our offerings . . ." In the footnote we discover that "our Savior" evidently was originally rendered, "*That which has the power to save us*,"[33] an abstract concept, rather than a person.

The Epistle of Barnabas

The Epistle of Barnabas provides several examples of the mythmaking obfuscation of texts. In the Latin version of Barnabas, for instance, we find the obligatory "our Lord Jesus Christ" interpolated at the beginning, yet in the Codex Sinaiticus, there is no such phrase. In this epistle, references to "Jesus" are in reality to "Joshua," the northern Israelite solar hero, also called the "Son of God." The verse in Barnabas regarding the Lord "delivering up" his body "to sanctify us by the remission of our sins; which is effected by the sprinkling of His blood," reflects the old sacred king drama, as performed by followers of Joshua in Palestine. In Christian scriptures, it was always a challenge to determine whether to translate "Joshua" as "Joshua" or "Jesus," and the identification between the two characters is clear, particularly in this epistle. For example, the following passage in the Codex Sinaiticus version is translated thus:

> Again, what has that other prophet, Moses, to say to them? Look, this is what the Lord God says: Enter into the good land which the Lord vowed he would give to Abraham and Isaac and Jacob . . . What it is, in fact, saying is, *Put your hopes in that Joshua who shall be shown to you in mortal guise.*[34]

The Latin version is translated thus:

> Moses also in like manner speaketh to them; Behold thus saith the Lord God; Enter ye into the good land of which the Lord hath sworn to Abraham, and Isaac, and Jacob . . . . It is as if it had been said, *Put your trust in Jesus, who shall be manifested to you in the flesh.*[35]

The editor of the Sinaiticus epistle notes in reference to this Jesus/Joshua confusion: "Joshua, who led the Israelites into the Promised Land, is a *well-known type of Jesus*. In Hebrew the two names are the same."[36] Also, references in the Barnabas epistle to "God's Son" are to Adam, not Jesus, but this fact is conveniently overlooked, with the excuse that Adam is also a "type of Jesus."

As stated, the Epistle of Barnabas serves as an illustration of the recurrent sacred king drama or "Passion" that preceded the Christian Era, complete with reenactment of the "blood upon us" ritual using scarlet wool on "wood," or branches that were then "sprinkled" on the faithful, a ritual also reflected in the canonical Letter to the Hebrews, as well as at Numbers 19:2-10. The Epistle of Barnabas, then, represented the Joshua cult, not the "historical" Jesus Christ, and served as instructions into the ages-old mysteries. As an initiate into those mysteries, Barnabas also admits that "IE," the designation of Apollo, is the same as "Jesus."

Barnabas further demonstrates his affiliation with the northern kingdom of Israel/Ephraim/Samaria when he mentions the story of Jacob's blessing of Joseph's son Ephraim, raising him above Manasseh. Says Barnabas, "So you can see who is meant by His decree that 'this People shall have the primacy, and inherit the Covenant.'"

The Shepherd of Hermas

An even earlier example of how "Christian" texts originally had nothing to do with "Jesus" or "Christ" is the noncanonical book "The Shepherd of Hermas," which was considered by Irenaeus and Origin to be divinely inspired and which was widely read in churches. As such, the book was included in the New Testament until the fourth century and deemed "apocryphal" thereafter.

Although the book is attributed to the "Hermas" who purportedly flourished around 140 CE, it is certainly an older writing and was asserted by Origen, Eusebius and Jerome to be the product of the "Hermas" referred to in the Pauline Epistle to the Romans. The *Encyclopedia Biblica* places the book to around 40 CE, and Fox to 90 CE. In any case, the book contains numerous Masonic and astrological references, indicating it was possibly a *Hermetic* writing of the *tradition* of Hermes Trismegistus. This lengthy text speaks many times of "God," "the Lord," "the Holy Spirit" and "the Holy Church," as well a number of times about "the devil," "salvation," and "sin," but, *in several dozen pages*, makes no reference whatsoever to "Jesus" or "Jesus Christ," names no apostle, and makes only one reference to Christians, an evident interpolation. Only twice, at the very end, is the word "Christ" used, also apparent interpolations. The book even refers to the "Son of God," who was the "rock" and "gate"— Masonic terms—but mentions no name. In fact, there are few if any references to a "historical" life of Jesus and no quotes from either the Old or New Testaments. In comparison, the later Epistles of Ignatius, for example, make reference in nearly every other sentence to "our Lord Jesus Christ." How Hermas escaped massive Christian interpolation can only be explained by the fact that it was so well known and publicly read in churches. Other prominent Masonic symbols in the Shepherd are the tower and vineyard, emblem of Carmel.

Why Place the Christian Myth at this Time

We have already seen reasons why the gospel tale was placed at the time alleged, including that it was a period of tremendous unrest and that the advent had to take place before Jerusalem's destruction, as asserted by Eusebius. In dating the gospel tale, in fact, Eusebius insists upon what should have been known, had it occurred:

> Herod, as I have said, was the first foreigner to be entrusted by the Roman senate and the Emperor Augustus with the Jewish nation. It was without question in his time that the advent of Christ occurred . . . [37]

This insistence is odd, because the gospel story was supposedly written down long before the fourth century, when Eusebius wrote, and the date of Christ's advent should not have been a factor that needed to be addressed. Furthermore, if it was "without question," why did Eusebius need to state it so definitively? As we have seen, many people *were* questioning it.

Eusebius further explains that the gospel fable had to occur at that particular time in order to fulfill the prophecy at Genesis 49:10: "The scepter shall not depart from Judah, nor the ruler's staff from between his feet, until he comes to whom it belongs," i.e., "Shiloh," or the Messiah, who, according to the next passage, would have garments washed in wine and eyes "red with wine." Eusebius states that Herod was the "first foreigner to become king of the Jewish nation," thus fulfilling this prophecy and ending the rule of Jewish leaders. This deposal, of course, spurred messianic fever, since it meant "Shiloh" would come. In fact, Eusebius is applying Jesus over the history of Herod, because, Herod himself was thought to be the long-awaited Shiloh. As Larson says, "Galilee teemed with fanatics, including Essenes, Pharisees, and Zealots, as well as Herodians, who believed Herod was himself the Christ . . ."[38] Obviously, Herod was not the messiah, but the historicizers in hindsight determined that Christ must appear to have come during his rule. In fact, the Shiloh passage refers to no "prophecy" at all, as Judah, the "lion's whelp," is in reality the constellation of Leo, and the wine-drenched ruler to whom Judah passes his scepter is that of Virgo, the time of the grape harvest.

Moreover, in attempting further to affix Christ's advent to this era, Eusebius later admits that there was a debate as to when it really occurred. What is the need of such debate and attestation if the tale found in the gospel depicted real history? Why so much confusion and murkiness, particularly after three centuries of alleged continuous apostolic lineage? Had Eusebius, the keeper of records, no testimonies of the many purported eyewitnesses who surely would have repeatedly talked about Herod and Pilate's dreadful actions? At the time of Eusebius, it was claimed that the Church had immediately sprung up with established hierarchies, a great deal of money and power, and a continuous lineage to his era, yet the Church's own historian evidently had no records at all except for the gospels, which were not sufficient to demonstrate when—and if—Christ's advent occurred. In his writings, Eusebius in actuality was fulfilling his task of creating the bogus history not only of Christ himself but of the Church. As Walker says, "The church never did have any continuous record of popes or 'bishops of Rome' from the beginning; most of the early popes were fictitious."[39] Regarding his forged history of the Church, Eusebius says, "As for men, I have failed to find any clear footprints of those who have gone this way before me; only faint traces, by which in differing fashions they have left us partial accounts of their own lifetimes."[40] Could there be any clearer admission that there was no "apostolic lineage" representing a "historical" savior?

Where the Bodies are Buried

We have already seen a tremendous amount of evidence as to the mythological nature of Christianity and its founder. Further proof may be found in a variety of places, although it may not be wise to make them public, because fanatics have forever destroyed such evidence, burning and looting temples and libraries, and desecrating and defacing sacred images and symbols. A number of these sites may also have been destroyed in various wars, including the two World Wars. In addition, some areas are so forbidding that it will even today be difficult both to access them and to convince the keepers of their secrets to release them. It is reported that priests, high-ranking Masons and members of other such brotherhoods are informed about the real origins of Christianity but are sworn to a blood oath against revealing the truth. Perhaps some of these individuals will be encouraged that others not thus bound are exposing this all-important information.

The evidence of the Christian myth may still be found in libraries in many parts of the world, clandestine and public, such as the Library of Ambrose at Milan, the Florentine library, and the library of Mt. Athos, the mysterious mountain of monasteries in Macedonia, although it would be very difficult to gain the evidence from such a place as Mt. Athos. Oddly enough, considering Athos takes its name from the Egyptian goddess Athor or Hathor,[41] Mt. Athos has been completely closed off to women for centuries. So terrified are these sexually repressed monks of all that is female, they will not allow even *female animals* in proximity of the monasteries.

It may also be difficult to obtain evidence from the Marionite monastery of Mt. Lebanon in Syria, but we are told that it is, or was, there. Such evidence in the form of texts may also be obtained, we are informed, in monasteries in what was Armenia, in the locale of Mt. Ararat. Evidence may also be procured from the "Cluny Abbey" and from "Mor Gabriel" in Turkey. The Vatican Library and the miles of tunnels of booty under the Vatican, of course, also provide a treasure trove of proof of the artifice. The churches of Russia likewise hold ancient manuscripts that would be valuable in our quest. Also, there may still be hidden texts in Jerusalem and other parts of Israel and Palestine, such as Mt. Carmel.

Such evidence can also be discovered in the ruins and statuary of pre-Christian cultures such as in Ireland, in the county of Armagh, or at Padua, Florence, Venice, Geneva and Rome, where there are, or were, statues of "the apostles" that were in reality Pagan gods made over. Such archaeological evidence may likewise be found at Heliopolis, the "City of the Sun," in Egypt, and in the sunken Phoenician city of Tyre, if it has not already been discovered and hidden or destroyed. Proof of the mythos also may be found in Upper Egypt, where arose one of the most ancient cultures and some of the original "Jews." India, of course, is rife with the mythos, and evidence of the life of Krishna/Christos can be found in the caves at Elephanta, for example.

Regardless of whether or not this evidence is extant in these places, there are many sites already well-known that provide proof of the ubiquitous solar and celestial mythos that was carnalized, historicized and personified in Jesus Christ. That the mythos once extended around the world in much the same form is *a fact* that cannot be disputed. Again, what happened to the ubiquitous solar mythos, if not as we have described? Where is it? Why did it disappear? The answer is, of course, is has been obscured; it is not gone but simply concealed beneath a surface of subterfuge and deception developed to enrich and empower a relative handful providing them with dominion over the "sheep."

Conclusion

After becoming aware of such "mysteries" revealed herein concerning Christianity and its alleged founder, many people may find the scholarship on this subject to appear less than satisfactory, to say the least, as it becomes clear that this information is known by the scholastic elite. This fact becomes evident from admissions such as the following, which appears in *Fiction as History* by GW Bowersock, a Professor of Ancient History at Princeton University in New Jersey. Says he:

> . . . in a series of Norton lectures, Frank Kermode also turned to the Bible, and in particular to the New Testament, to develop a sophisticated analysis of novelistic elements in the Gospels. He argued that the problem of historical truth is so elusive in the

Gospel narratives that those accounts are better viewed *simply as fiction* with a semblance of truth. The meaning, and obviously, the inspirational value of works of this kind *do not depend upon their historical veracity*, although apprehension of that meaning nonetheless does depend upon a provisional or temporary belief in their veracity. This is, in Kermode's words, a *"benign deceit"* that readers even today continue to countenance.[42]

Here we have the scholar Kermode admitting that the New Testament is fiction, and Prof. Bowersock relating the opinion that such "benign deceit" does not matter, because the book has "inspirational value." First of all, this deceit has not been benign but utterly malignant for almost 2,000 years, contributing to endless genocide and killing the spirit and mind. Secondly, how do deception and lying have any value in a spiritual quest or religious life? Is it not the complete opposite of such an experience? Is it not the goal in becoming a mature, spiritual human being to be rid of deceit and mendacity? It is clear that scholars have known about the mythological nature of the Bible, yet they have gone to immense lengths to hide it, including using sophisticated language, like the priestly counterparts who have utilized the dead language Latin to go over the heads of the uneducated masses. It is possible that any number of these scholars are also Masons or members of some such secret brotherhood who are under the blood oath. Or they may merely be products of their occupation, in that many universities and colleges are under the dominion of the fraternities and the grand master, the Pope, i.e., the Catholic Church. In any case, they have been pawns, unwitting or otherwise, in the Christ conspiracy, which has obscured ancient knowledge and wisdom under a false front of historicity, by the most thorough of methods, including secrecy, forgery, force and destruction.

---

1. Walker, *WEMS*, 122.
2. Walker, *WEMS*, 440.
3. Roberts, 267.
4. Graham, 281.
5. Doresse, 311.
6. Higgins, I, 593.
7. Walker, *WEMS*, 320.
8. Walker, *WEMS*, 208.
9. Massey, *HJMC*.
10. Doane, 438.
11. Higgins, II, 107.
12. Doresse, 12.
13. Barnstone, xix.
14. Book of Enoch, 3.
15. Wheless, 85-7.
16. Carpenter, 203.

17. Book of Enoch, 37-38; Wells, *WWJ*, 169.
18. Wells, *WWJ*, 170.
19. Massey, *HJMC*.
20. Hazelrigg, 96.
21. Higgins, I, 551-2.
22. Higgins, I, 544-5.
23. *The Forgotten Books of Eden*, 85.
24. *The Forgotten Books of Eden*, 220.
25. Barnstone, 202.
26. *The Forgotten Books of Eden*, 226.
27. *The Forgotten Books of Eden*, 230.
28. Massey, *HJMC*, 152.
29. *The Missing Books of the Bible*, II, 279-80.
30. Waite, 63.
31. Waite, 86.
32. *The Other Bible*, 52.
33. *The Lost Books of the Bible*, 129.
34. *Early Christian Writings*.
35. *The Lost Books of the Bible*, 150.
36. *Early Christian Writings*, 183.
37. Eusebius, 19.
38. Larson, 319.
39. Walker, *WDSSO*, 60.
40. Eusebius, 2.
41. Higgins, I, 583.
42. Bowersock, 123.

Out of Egypt or India?

As demonstrated throughout this book, the Christian religion and savior are not original but have their roots in the astrological mythology and religion of remote ages. Yet, those ages are cloaked in a mysterious shroud, such that it is difficult to determine where and when the roots themselves originated. The current orthodox paradigm places a significant part of cultural origins in Sumeria, starting around 4500 BCE. Nevertheless, there are other "Old World" archaeological sites worthy of note older than those of Sumeria, such as Catal Huyuk in Turkey, which is at least 9,000 years old; Jericho, the pre-Hebraic foundation of which goes back to around 9000 BCE; Lepinski Vir in the former Yugoslavia, which is 7,000 years old; and remains on Malta estimated to be 8,000 years old. In addition, a number of researchers have averred that the site of Stonehenge in England is much older than the orthodoxy allows for. Furthermore, as noted, there is evidence that some Egyptian temples may be thousands of years older than presently hypothesized, and the date of the Indian culture continues to be pushed back as well.

The present anthropological/evolutionary paradigm dictates that man first developed in Africa; hence, despite the current inclination towards Mesopotamia and Sumer, Egypt would seem to be the logical place to look for the origins of human culture. Yet, India also keeps beckoning for a closer look. Indeed, we have seen that the bulk of the Christian mythos and ritual was found in both India and Egypt millennia before the Christian era, and it is to these two nations that most research has pointed as the source of Christian origins. This fact has been recognized over the centuries, but the debate as to which came first has not been resolved, with erudite proponents and solid evidence on both sides, leaving the mystery intact. A number of these scholars were without modern archaeological knowledge; however, they made their assessments using sound scientific inquiry and methodology. In actuality, these pioneers had access to information and discoveries now destroyed or lost—and there have been plenty—and were closer to the events, such that at times their assessments were even more accurate than those of today. For example, archaeologists and other scientists 200 years ago were dealing with a Great Pyramid that had several feet of debris around it, such as alluvial sand, salt and sea shells that indicated the massive structure was at some time partly underwater. As Joseph Jochmans relates:

> The medieval Arab historian Biruni, writing in his treatise *The Chronology of Ancient Nations,* noted: ". . . The traces of the water

of the Deluge and the effects of the waves are still visible on these pyramids halfway up, above which the water did not rise." Add to this the observation made when the Pyramid was first opened, that incrustations of salt an inch thick were found inside. Most of this salt is natural exudation from the chambered rock wall, but chemical analysis also shows some of the salt has a mineral content consistent with salt from the sea.[1]

Since the Pyramid was cleared, however, too few modern analyses take this fact into account in determining the edifice's age.

Egypt

In reality, the antiquity and sophistication of Egypt are profound, and, as has been seen, the Egyptian culture was highly influential in the creation of Judaism and Christianity, both of which carnalized and historicized much of the mythos and ritual in their scriptures. Indeed, many scholars have insisted that the Bible is entirely Egyptian. Of the Egyptian influence on the Hebrews, A. Churchward says:

> The "Sacred historical documents" of the Hebrews are not historical at all, only traditions and copies from some other documents much older, which can only be traced to Egypt. . . . Modern research discovers in the Hebrew writings a composite work, not as the autogram of the Hebrew legislator, but as the editorial patchwork of mingling Semitic legends with cosmopolitan myths, which were copied from the Egyptians, either directly or indirectly, but without the gnosis.[2]

Furthermore, the Phoenician city of Byblos, whence comes the word "Bible," was an Egyptian colony as early as the 2nd Dynasty, i.e., 2850-2600 BCE. Churchward also states:

> The "Hebrew Scriptures," no doubt were written in *the Phoenician characters* for many centuries, *although they have not survived in this form,* and the Phoenicians were first Stellar Cult and later Solar Cult Egyptians. . . . The whole of the imagery of the Hebrew writings can be read and understood by the original Egyptian, but not from any other source. The secret of the sanctity of the Hebrew writings is that they were originally Egyptian. The wisdom of old, the myths, parables, and dark sayings that were preserved, have been presented to us dreadfully deformed in the course of being converted into history.[3]

Regarding the New Testament, A. Churchward wrote, "The canonical gospels can be shown to be a collection of sayings from the Egyptian Mythos and Eschatology." And Jackson reiterated Dr. Alvin Boyd Kuhn's assessment:

The whole Christian bible was derived from the sacred books of Egypt, such as: The *Book of the Dead, The Pyramid Texts,* and *The Books of Thoth.*[4]

Taylor shouted it out, "EVERYTHING OF CHRISTIANITY IS OF EGYPTIAN ORIGIN."[5] Massey, of course, concurred.

Jackson further relates Kuhn's words concerning the origins of the Hebrew scriptures and Christian religion:

The entire Christian bible, creation legend, descent into and exodus from Egypt, ark and flood allegory, Israelite history, Hebrew prophecy and poetry, Gospels, Epistles and *Revelation* imagery, all are now proven to have been the transmission of ancient Egypt's scrolls and papyri into the hands of later generations which knew neither their true origin nor their fathomless meaning. . . . [F]rom the scrolls of papyri five thousand to ten thousand years old there comes stalking forth to view the whole story of an Egyptian Jesus raising from the dead an Egyptian Lazarus at an Egyptian Bethany, with two Egyptian Maries present . . . Egypt knelt at the shrine of the Madonna and Child, Isis and Horus, for long centuries before a historical Mary lifted a historical Jesus in her arms. Egypt had from remote times adored a Christ who had raised the dead and healed the lame, halt, blind, paralytic, leprous and all afflicted, who had restored speech to the dumb, exorcised demons from the possessed, dispersed his enemies with a word or look, wrestled with his Satan adversary, overcame all temptation and performed the works of his heavenly Father to the victorious end. Egypt had long known a Jesus, Iusa, who had been born amid celestial portents of an immaculate parenthood, circumcised, baptized, tempted, glorified on the mount, persecuted, arrested, tried, condemned, crucified, buried, resurrected and elevated to heaven. Egypt had listened to the Sermon on the Mount and the sayings of Iusa for ages.[6]

These Sayings of Iusa are, of course, the Logia Iesou that existed in the mystery schools long prior to the Christian era.

India

The influence of Egypt is evident, but Higgins, Jacolliot and others have been equally insistent that culture emanated out of India, not Egypt, coming in waves beginning several thousand years ago, such as with Mitanni, the Indian kingdom in Syria (1400 BCE) whose inhabitants were called "Horites" in the Bible, and as otherwise noted, with a fresh infusion brought west by Alexander the Great three centuries prior to the Christian era. As Walker says, "From the time of Alexander the Great, Jain monks traveled westward to impress and influence Persians, Jewish Essenes, and later, Christians."[7] In fact, as we have seen, the correspondences between the Judeo-Christian mythology/religion and that of India are numerous and important.

That the culture and religion of India are very old is obvious. As the "celebrated Orientalist" Sir William Jones pointed out, the Indian scriptures, the Vedas, appear to be of an "antiquity the most distant."[8] Indeed, some scholars have posited that the Rig Veda contains mention of an astronomical configuration that could only have occurred 90,000 years ago. The Hindu chronology, in fact, goes back millions of years, and there has been effort to push back true human civilization, rather than man's apelike progenitors, to that era. Obviously, such "forbidden archaeology" is widely dismissed by the orthodoxy for seeming lack of solid evidence. Nevertheless, something certainly is amiss in the current orthodox paradigm, such that an overhaul is in order. Of course, conclusive proof of such antiquity would be difficult to provide, because millions of years have elapsed, during which there has been much cataclysm and scouring of the earth's surface.

As to the origins of Indian culture, the current theory of "Aryan invaders" has also been challenged, particularly by Indian scholars. The Aryan invasion theory posits that a caucasoid people from the northwest invaded India around 4,000 years ago and established civilization and the intricate sacerdotal law of Brahmanism. This theory presupposes that prior to the "invasion" the Indian natives were barbaric and uncivilized. However, Indian scholars maintain that India produced a high culture long before the Aryans purportedly arrived, a theory evidently validated by the archaeological and historical record.

There were, in fact, pre-Brahmanical cultures and religions in India, those of the rishis and the Jainists, who profess their religion to be the oldest in the world. Moreover, aspects of Brahmanism are in actuality similar to those of the Aryan Zoroastrianism, as well as of the Egyptian religion. Brahmanism represents, in reality, a degradation compared to the earlier rishi culture, much as later Egyptian culture never reached the heights of the Pyramid builders. Indeed, fanatical Brahmanism was as base as Catholicism during the Inquisition, and the Catholic inquisitors took their hierarchy and methods of torture from the Brahmans.

Larson traces the origins of monasticism and renunciation to India and alleges abject barbarism on the part of the Brahmanic priesthood:

> Just when ascetics and hermits became numerous, we cannot now know, but we may assume that it was at least six centuries before Christ. *Why* they arose is not difficult to comprehend; for in that heavily populated land, priest-ridden and ignorant, full of

misery and frustration, countless human hearts must have been bursting with pent-up despair. The joy of living reflected in the ancient *Rig* had long since departed; there was no hope or solace for the fettered millions, hemmed in on every side by rigid caste, denied all hope and pleasure in this world of frustration and despair. *This* life was a morass of slavery and starvation; and that beyond the grave was even more terrifying. . . . And so Mother India spawned the monster Renunciation, which has played so vast and spectacular a role in European and world history.[9]

Brahmanism introduced the racism that lighter skin was better than darker, such that caste was determined by color. Furthermore, women were horrendously treated, and the fervently sexist patriarchy evidently originated in Brahmanism.

Based on all the evidence, Jacolliot was adamant that western culture emanated out of India, not Egypt. Says he:

Enquirers who have adopted Egypt as their field of research and who have explored and re-explored that country from temple to tomb, would have us believe it the birthplace of our civilization. There are some who even pretend that India adopted from Egypt her castes, her language, and her laws, while Egypt is on the contrary but one entire Indian emanation. . . . The Sanscrit is itself the most irrefutable and most simple proof of the Indian origin of the races of the Europe, and of India's maternity.[10]

It is not definite that there is a single source of all human languages, but much western language certainly comes out of India, a fact known for millennia and now being revamped with the "Nostratic theory," which seeks to trace language to India around 12,000 years ago. This Nostratic language was possibly either "Chaldee," the ancient sacred lingua franca used by the brotherhood, or an even older version.

Jacolliot also states:

We shall presently see Egypt, Judea, Greece, Rome, all antiquity, in fact, copy Brahminical Society in its castes, its theories, its religious opinions; and adopt its Brahmins, its priests, its levities, as they had already adopted the language, legislation and philosophy of that ancient Vedic Society whence their ancestors had departed through the world to disseminate the grand ideas of primitive revelation.[11]

Higgins likewise says:

There is not a particle of proof, from any historical records known to the author, that any colony ever passed from Egypt to Indian, but there is, we see, direct, positive historical evidence, of the Indians having come to Africa.[12]

The various Indian migrations are further evidenced by the fact that Buddhism, far older than acknowledged, is found widespread beginning thousands of years ago. In addition to those examples previously explored, the Macedonians invoked Bedu (Buddha),[13] and the Egyptian Pharaohs or shepherd kings were Rajputs, or royal Buddhists.[14]

However, A. Churchward equally resolutely asserts, "The Buddhists and Brahmins in many of their religious ceremonies make use of words that are not Sanskrit, but are said to belong to a very ancient form of speech now dead. These words can be traced back to their Egyptian origins."[15] In addition, the very ancient Egyptian god Osiris was purportedly remembered in remote regions of India, where a legend existed about him arriving there many thousands of years ago and establishing his religion. In fact, in "Sanskrit *sat* means to destroy by hewing into pieces," and Osiris, of course, was cut into pieces by Set.

As can be seen, in our quest to establish the provenance of the mythos and ritual that became Christianity, we are at an impasse in choosing between Egypt and India.

Sumeria

In fact, as noted, the current paradigm favors Sumeria as the birthplace of human culture. While that may not be so, Sumeria has an important place in the debate, in that it serves as a crossroads between the cultures of Egypt and India. Like Egypt, Sumer had the god "Anu," and, as Stone says, the "inference that there was some contact between Egypt and Sumer at the time is confirmed by the presence of Jemdet Nasr type seals."[16] Stone also notes that the tombs of Egypt's 1st Dynasty were influenced by Mesopotamia, based upon brick-building evidence and other artifacts, and that a fish trap depicted in Egyptian tombs is identical to that used by northern Europeans, evidently the same race as the early Sumerians, who, it is claimed, consisted of the infamous "Aryan invaders." Of the Aryan/Iranian invaders, Larson says:

> These Iranians did more than drive the Semitic races into permanent eclipse: themselves descended from older Sumerians, they were the pre-historic conquerors of Egypt and India as well as the progenitors of the Greeks, the Romans, and the Teutons: in short, they have ruled most of the civilized world for two and a half millenniums.[17]

These Aryans were evidently the "Shemsu Hor" or "people of Hor" who invaded Egypt and apparently became the Horites, i.e., the Mitanni. As Stone relates:

> From the twentieth to the sixteenth centuries BC, the archaeology of Canaan shows continual nomadic disruption. This is generally attributed to local nomadic warfare. But as Professor Albright, who describes the entrance of the Indo-Europeans into Canaan

as a "migratory movement," tells us, "by the fifteenth century Indo-Aryan and Horite princes and nobles were established almost everywhere."[18]

As noted, the Hebrews/Israelites were a mixture of different peoples, as confirmed by "Ezekiel," who said of them, "your father is an Amorite, your mother a Hittite," which is to say an Aryan. Thus, the Israelites were a combination of "sons of Japheth" (Indo-European/Aryan) and "sons of Shem" (Semitic), as well as "sons of Ham" (Canaanite/African/Cushite). Indeed, as also noted, it is posited that the Levitical priesthood was Indo-European/Aryan, or Japhethite. In addition to their fiery mountain god and other factors, the Levitical marriage customs are similar to those of Indo-European peoples.[19] In other words, the Semitic desert peoples were Egyptians, Canaanites and others gathered under the direction of the priestly Levites, who were apparently in large part Indo-European/Aryans, some of whom were from Sumeria.

The Abramite Migration

Another inhabitant of the crossroads of Sumeria was purported to be the biblical "patriarch" Abraham, whose story in fact reflects the merger of the Aryan/Egyptian cultures. As demonstrated, the Abraham myth is paralleled in India, such that the "Ur of the Chaldees" apparently represents not the Sumerian city but an "Ur of the Culdees" in India, and the story of Abraham's migration to Harran reflects the movement of an Aryan Brahmanical tribe into the Levant. The Abraham myth evidently represents the fanatic patriarchal followers of Brahma leaving India during a war over gender brought about by the change of the equinoctial ages, i.e., that from Taurus to Aries. This Brahmanic tribe ostensibly migrated from the Indian region of Oudh (Judea), possibly from the village of Maturea, westward through Persia, ending up in Goshen, "the house of the sun," i.e., Heliopolis in Egypt, where it established a place named Maturea/Mathura. As the tribe migrated from India, it named various landmarks wherever it settled by the same or similar name as those of its homeland. The Abramites or Brahmans later moved back into Canaan from Egypt to create their own nation, dividing the land and extant peoples into the 12 zodiacal sections under "Jacob," or Seth the Supplanter, and his "sons," who were in reality tribal gods.

Among numerous other etymological examples to support this migration theory, many of which have already been provided, Higgins points out that Hebrews are called "Yehudi" and that the Sanskrit word "Yuddha" means warrior, which the Yehudi certainly professed to be in their sacred texts. In addition, the father of Krishna was Yadu/Yuda/Yudi, or Judi, and the word "Shaitan"—"adversary," whence comes "Satan"—is the same in Hebrew and Sanskrit. Higgins further states that the cradle of Buddhist and Jainist faith was in the Indian town of Jessulmer, evidently the same as Jerusalem, which, as we have seen, is also found in Egypt. The connection continues, as Higgins finds the Syro-Hebrew-Christian savior god/apostle Tammuz/Thomas not only in India but also in Egypt: "Tamus was the name of the chief Egyptian deity: the same as Thamus of Syria."[20]

It is likely that migrations between Africa/Egypt and India began occurring many thousands of years ago and that these cultures shared a common root. As Jackson says, "The ancient peoples of India were Asiatic Ethiopians, and it should not surprise us that they shared common traditions with their brothers in Africa." In the face of this confusion, Higgins stated matter-of-factly that the Indian and Egyptian cultures were the same and were split before the development of hieroglyphics.[21] The meanings of the mysterious Egyptian hieroglyphics were purportedly lost and only rediscovered with the unearthing of the Rosetta Stone by Napoleon's troops and his linguist, Champollion. However, Higgins averred that the Rosetta Stone is a fake. If this assertion is true, and it certainly could be, considering that fakery and forgery have been all too common, it would indicate that the meanings had never been lost and that the stone was made by members of the brotherhood, which had maintained the ancient knowledge. We may speculate that in releasing this hidden information these individuals either were interested in the glory of its discovery or wished for the hieroglyphics to become known, a "rediscovery," of course, that eventually led to the exposure of the Egyptian pre-Christian mythos and ritual echoed in the New Testament.

The Druids

The debate as to the origins of western culture does not end with Egypt and India but extends to the mysterious Druidic brotherhood, composed of ancient priests of the sun and masons who inhabited the British Isles. Like many others, A. Churchward averred that the Druids were an "exodus of Solar Cult people from Egypt."[22] As Pike also says:

> The first Druids were the true children of the Magi, and their initiation came from Egypt and Chaldea, that is to say, from the pure sources of the primitive Kabalah. They adored the Trinity under the names of *Isis* or *Hesus*, the Supreme Harmony; of *Belen* or *Bel*, which in Assyrian means Lord, a name corresponding to that of Adonai . . . [23]

The Druids, in fact, shared the same ancient "Chaldee" culture with the Egyptians, Indians and Phoenicians, including the proto-Hebraic sacred language. We have seen many demonstrations of the linguistical connection in cultures from Egypt to India, but the correspondence is also found in Britain. For instance, in Hebrew "Brith" means not only "covenant" but evidently also "holy land," the same as the Sanskrit "Bharata," meaning "pure or holy land," which in turn is related to the "Britain" of the Druids.[24]

Also pointed out by Higgins was the masonic connection between India and Europe, as masons built "gothic" buildings in India, thousands of years prior to the appearance of that form of architecture in Europe.[25] In addition, British Master Mason signs and signals are the same as in India.[26]

Pike further reveals the difficulty of disentangling the influences on the British Isles:

> The Druidical ceremonies undoubtedly came from India; and the Druids were originally Buddhists. The word *Druidh*, like the word *Magi*, signifies wise or learned men; and they were at once philosophers, magistrates, and divines. There was a surprising uniformity in the Temples, Priests, doctrines and worship of the Persian Magi and British Druids. The Gods of Britain are the same as the Cabiri of Samothrace. Osiris and Isis appeared in their Mysteries, under the names of Hu and Ceridwen. . . .[27]

And Hislop says:

> Some have imagined that the Druidical worship was first introduced by the Phoenicians, who, centuries before the Christian era, traded to the tin-mines of Cornwall. But the unequivocal traces of that worship are found in regions of the British islands where the Phoenicians never penetrated . . . [28]

Throwing yet another side into the debate, some authors, such as Conor McDari in *Irish Wisdom: Preserved in Bible and Pyramids*, have attempted to demonstrate that Western and Near Eastern culture emanated out of the British Isles, specifically Ireland, instead of the other way around. McDari's hypothesis recognizes that "the pyramids and the Bible, when properly deciphered, reveal that the oldest and truest religion is sun worship."[29]

The Mysteries

The worship of the sun, which became the Christian religion, constituted "the mysteries," or mythos and ritual. No matter how closely we examine these mysteries, we will nevertheless encounter the problem of provenance, which is the real mystery. As Pike says: "Where the Mysteries originated is not known. It is supposed that they came from India, by the way of Chaldaea, into

Egypt, and thence were carried into Greece."[30] Yet, Jackson argues that the "Mystery Schools of Egypt were the world's oldest universities."[31] Indeed, Albert Churchward stated that the Great Pyramid "was built to teach the seven Astro Stellar Cult Mysteries in symbolism and applied Eschatologically—also to record and register time and measurement."[32] Many others have perceived such a temple of sacred mysteries in the Pyramid's so-called King's Chamber. In fact, this temple served as an initiation center, with initiates passing through twelve gates or halls. James Churchward relates:

> Having passed through the second stage, the adept was allowed to enter the hall called the Tenth Hall of Truth, or Trial Scene, which was depicted in a black-and-white tessellated pavement— Right and Wrong, Truth and Falsehood.
>
> From this hall he was conducted to the Chamber of New Birth, or place of coming forth with regeneration of the soul. In this chamber were found emblems of mortality with the sarcophagus empty. A small opening admits the light of the bright morning star Sothis into the chamber. . . . [33]

Thus, the Great Pyramid is not and never has been a "tomb" except symbolically, as it was used to introduce adepts to the higher mysteries of death. It has also served as a celestial "computer," encoding the movements of many planetary bodies as well as much sacred math.

Black Buddhas and Pygmies

There is yet another mystery to be addressed, as, it will be recalled, in the caves of India have been found figures of Buddhas not only black in color but in feature, demonstrating that the black race had at some early point reached an advanced state of civilization. As Higgins said over a century and a half ago, thus using antiquated language:

> It was the opinion of Sir William Jones that a great nation of Blacks formerly possessed the dominion of Asia, and held the seat of empire at Sidon. These must have been the people called by Mr. Maurice Cushites or Cuthites, described in Genesis; and the opinion that they were Blacks is corroborated by the translators of the Pentateuch, called the Seventy, constantly rendering the word *Cush* by Ethiopia. . . . The religion of Buddha, of India, is well known to have been very ancient. In the most ancient temples scattered throughout Asia, where his worship is yet continued, he is found *black as jet*, with the flat face, thick lips, and curly hair of the Negro.[34]

And Jackson relates:

> A splendid era of Blacks seems to have preceded all the later races. There must once have been a tremendous Negro

expansion, since the original masters of the lands between Iberia and the Cape of Good Hope and East India were primitive and probably dwarfed Black men. We have long had proof that a primitive Negroid race of Pygmies once lived around the Mediterranean. Blacks were the first to plow the mud of the Nile; they were the dark-skinned, curly-haired Kushites. Blacks were masters of Sumeria and Babylon before it became the country of the four tongues.[35]

Indeed, into any fair analysis must be factored an overlooked people who, if the theory of evolution is correct, must constitute one of the oldest races on the planet: the Pygmies. In reality, the Pygmies provide a key piece of the puzzle, as many of their ancient traditions are basically the same as those of the cultures that succeeded them. We have already seen that they were pre-Christian monotheists who revered the cross. Belgian anthropologist Jean-Pierre Hallet, who has lived much of his life among the Pygmies, elaborates:

> My Pygmy friends have an Adam story of their own . . . It is the story of a god, a garden paradise, a sacred tree, a noble Pygmy man, who was molded from the dust of the earth, and a wicked Pygmy woman who led him into sin . . . The legend tells of the ban placed by God upon a single fruit, the woman's urging, the man's reluctance, the original sin, the discovery by God, and the awful punishment he laid upon the ancient Pygmy sinners; the loss of immortality and paradise, the pangs of childbirth, and the curse of hard work.[36]

Jackson reveals another surprise concerning the Pygmies that we may have expected:

> The Pygmies believed in a Father-God who was murdered, and a Virgin Mother, who gave birth to a Savior-God Son, who in turn avenged the death of his father. These later on became the Osiris, Isis and Horus of Egypt. The Pygmy Christ was born of a virgin, died for the salvation of his people, arose from the dead, and finally ascended to heaven. Certainly this looks like Christianity before Christ.

And the mystery continues, as the Pygmies claimed to have spread throughout the world thousands of years ago:

> Hallet's Pygmy friends told him that in the distant past they developed a highly technical and advanced type of material culture and that they built boats and traveled widely around the world, but that this technical excellence brought them nothing but bad luck, so, preferring happiness to misery, they finally gave up this high material civilization. There may be a lot of truth in these traditions, for Pygmy fossils have been found in all parts of the world.[37]

Thus, Pygmy remains and culture are found around the globe, including from Egypt to India. In fact, according to Higgins, "The numerous circles which are found in India are said by the inhabitants to have been erected by a race of people called Chaeones or Chaons, who are said to have been pigmies."[38] The Pygmies, in reality, were revered in ancient cultures, especially by the Egyptians, as A. Churchward relates:

> So closely were the facts of nature observed and registered by the Egyptians that the earliest divine men in their Mythology are portrayed as Pygmies, and the earliest form of the Human Mother was depicted with the characteristics of the Pygmy woman.[39]

Churchward further says:

> Ptah is represented in the form of a Pygmy, and his Ari are seven little Pygmies, the Egyptians having taken the type from the primordial, or first human evolved from the Anthropoid Ape in Africa.[40]

Although they may be the oldest race, the Pygmies are in fact true human beings and evidently reached an advanced state long before the "giants" existed in large numbers. The Pygmies represent an anthropological enigma, however, as they have been described as both negroid and caucasoid. Of this mysterious people, Walker relates:

> . . . pygmies are caucasoid people: thin-lipped, light-skinned, often blue-eyed. Anthropological investigations show the pygmies were not true primitives but remnants of a formerly sophisticated race, the proto-Berber people inhabiting what Hallet called "old white Africa." Pygmies have about the same stature as Egyptian mummies; the ancient Egyptians were not large people. . . . Not only are the pygmy myths and deities derived from those of the ancient world, but their traditional stories plainly speak of the time when their ancestors lived in a high state of civilization, in great cities, with wonderful tools to use, and skills that enabled them to work miracles.[41]

In the Pygmies can be found not only very ancient origins of human culture and religion but evidently a "missing link" between the black and white races as well. It should be noted that this extraordinary people is now in danger of becoming extinct.

It is obvious that no resolution can be made as to the origins of human culture in India or Egypt, or even Europe, as waves of immigrants and invaders moved between these areas over a period of millennia. In reality, the Pygmies, for one, represent an even older culture that contains the mythos and ritual. Indeed, in our quest as to the ultimate source of Christianity, we are led to conclude that claims made by the Pygmies and others as to a previous global civilization are true.

---

1. www.aa.net/~mwm/atlantis/issue8/ar8pyramids.html
2. A. Churchward, 305-6.
3. A. Churchward, 296-9.
4. Jackson, 115-6.
5. Taylor, 61.
6. Jackson, 116-8.
7. Walker, *WEMS*, 460.
8. Jacolliot.
9. Larson, 117-8.
10. Jacolliot, 24-5.
11. Jacolliot, 68.
12. Higgins, I, 54.
13. Higgins, I, 584.
14. Higgins, I, 612.
15. A. Churchward, 337.
16. Stone, 87.
17. Larson, 83.
18. Stone, 98-9.
19. Stone, 108.
20. Higgins, I, 584.
21. Higgins, I, 19.
22. A. Churchward, 304.
23. Pike, 103.
24. Higgins, I, 585.
25. Higgins, I, 725.
26. Higgins, I, 767.
27. Pike, 367.
28. Hislop, 103.
29. Wilson, 259.
30. Pike, 353.
31. Jackson, 131.
32. A. Churchward, 145.
33. J. Churchward, *LCM*, 326.
34. Higgins, I, 52.
35. Jackson, 174.
36. Jackson, 174.
37. Jackson, 175.
38. Higgins, II, 135fn.
39. A. Churchward, 7-8.
40. A. Churchward, 304.
41. Walker, *WEMS*, 831-2.

Evidence of an Ancient Global Civilization

> Civilizations have been born and completed and then forgotten again and again. There is nothing new under the sun. What is, has been. All that we learn and discover has existed before; our inventions and discoveries are but reinventions, rediscoveries.
>
> Col. James Churchward

As has been seen, it is virtually impossible to determine which nation is the progenitor of western culture and, therefore, the Judeo-Christian tradition, and we are left to ponder the idea of another source, such as the Pygmies, who claim to have been a global culture many thousands of years ago. The fact that the standardized mythos and ritual are found in detail around the world begs the explanation of at least one such global civilization long ago destroyed by cataclysms but preserved in both story and stone. Indeed, attempts to trace this commonality to India and/or Egypt do not suffice to explain how the same tales and rites came to be known and practiced in Mexico and in such remote places as Polynesia. Nor do they explain the enormous archaeological remains found around the globe, which serve as mysterious and inescapable reminders that at some ancient time so-called primitive men were able to do what, according to evolutionary and creationist theories alike, they were not supposed to be able to do.

These impressive ruins evidently go hand-in-hand with the global civilization revealed by the common legends and myths of the ancients, since, where there is such advanced technology and architectural skill as that which must have been used to work and move megaliths of 10-200 tons, or to produce the astoundingly precise Great Pyramid, there must also be advanced culture. As we have also seen, these traditions date back many thousands of years and eventually come increasingly closer to each other the farther back we go. Such similarities between cultures around the planet can be found in religion and mythology, customs, rituals and symbols, language, astrological and astronomical knowledge, and archaeological/architectural remains. In investigating such cultural commonality, it would reasonable to conclude that our current global civilization is not the first. The further we delve back in time, naturally, the more difficult it is to discover solid ground and the more speculative is the discussion.

Religion, Rituals and Customs

As revealed throughout this book, the doctrines and rituals of many religions are virtually identical to each other, and Christianity represents merely the end product of a long line of the same traditions. In this analysis, we have mainly treated the cultures of the Near/Middle East and Europe, because the Middle East is considered to be the "birthplace" of all human culture, the source of biblical tradition, the Garden of Eden, etc., and Europe is, of course, the adopted home of Christianity. We have also stayed in the "Old World," because it is widely believed that the Western and Eastern hemispheres arose separately, with little or no contact, until the last few centuries. As noted, however, many of humankind's most important traditions are found worldwide, in such matching detail as to demonstrate that contact had occurred beginning many thousands of years ago.

For example, in the Americas are found the Eden, flood and Jonah myths; the story of the sun standing still; the veneration of the serpent; the virgin birth; the crucifixion; the practice of circumcision; and ascetic monasteries and nunneries. As another example, natives of British Columbia called the sun/sky-god "Sin," like the Old World god, and represented Sin's mother as being married to a carpenter, who teaches his solar son his trade.[1] Furthermore, as Carpenter states: "The same legend of gods (or idols) being born in caves has, curiously enough, been reported from Mexico, Guatemale, the Antilles, and other places in Central America."[2] Also, the natives of Florida at the time of the Christian invasion were allegedly discovered to chant "Hosanna."[3]

Specific religious festivals and practices are found in diverse and widespread places. For instance, J. Churchward recounts the words of R.G. Haliburton, who, "in writing of the 'Festival of Ancestors,' says: 'It is now, as it was formerly, held at or near the beginning of November, by the Peruvians, the Hindus, the Pacific Islanders, the people of the Tonga Islands, the Australians, the ancient Persians, the ancient Egyptians and the northern nations of Europe, and continues for three days among the Japanese, the Hindus, the Australians, the ancient Romans and the ancient Egyptians.'"[4]

Robertson relates a sacrificial practice found in both Asia and America, remarking, "It is difficult to believe that the peculiar usages of sacrificing a 'messenger' or 'ambassador' to the Sun, painting him in red, and hanging up his and other victims' skins, stuffed, as possessing a sacred efficacy, were independently evolved in the two hemispheres."[5]

Furthermore, the very ancient Buddhist religion is found in many parts of the world, as noted. As Robertson says, "Singularly suggestive of Buddhist contacts . . . are a number of Mexican sculptures; many figures of Quetzalcoatl are practically identical with the established type of Buddha."[6] As we have seen, the religion of Quetzalcoatl is nearly identical in many aspects to that of Jesus, with a savior born of a virgin who is tempted and fasts

40 days, and who dies and is to return in a Second Coming—an expectation that led to the downfall of the Aztecs, when they mistook Cortes for the peaceful teaching god Quetzalcoatl, who actually long predated the bloodthirsty Aztecs.

Moreover, one of the Mexican gods was "Yao," the same as the Egyptian Iao and Hebrew Yah.[7] The early Hebrews and their neighbors such as the Phoenicians and Canaanites called their Lord "Baal," but, astonishingly, "*Bal* is a Maya word meaning 'Lord of the Fields.'"[8] The Aztec human sacrifice was the same as that of the Hebrews, Kingsborough's "horrible cannibals." Furthermore, the Adam tale is found in the Chimalpopoca manuscript of the Maya, which "states that the Creator produced his work in successive epochs, man being made from the dust of the earth on the *seventh day*."[9] So remarkable are the similarities between the Mexicans and the Semites that not a few scholars and researchers have wanted to call the Mesoamerican natives "Jews" and to find in them (and others) a "lost tribe" of Israel. However, as we have seen, according to the Samaritans there were no lost tribes, and, racially speaking that relationship is not indicated, at least not between the natives of the past few thousand years. But, in more ancient times there was indeed in Mesoamerica a race very similar to that of the Semites, i.e., bearded white men, resembling Phoenicians. In fact, there are purportedly Phoenician artifacts found in the port of Rio de Janeiro and other Brazilian sites, suggesting that the Phoenicians, for one, did cross the Atlantic at least 1,000 years before the arrival of the Europeans.

The traces of this particular typè of white race, as well as of a black one, are found in legends in Central America and in images on stelae, with the black race also immortalized in massive stone heads purportedly made by the Olmecs. In any case, the Mexicans are not colonies of the Semites in the Middle East, although it is probable there was ongoing contact and colonization by at least the time of the Phoenicians. Nevertheless, Mexican natives asserted their ancestors came over the ocean from the west, not the east.

The Mexican civilization resembles not only the Semitic, which is one reason it is clearly not an outgrowth of it. The Maya have much in common with the Indians as well. As to the similarities between the Mayan and Hindu religion and language, *Hinduism Today* says, "*Chacla* in Mayan refers to force centers of the body similar to the *chakras* of Hinduism. *K'ultanlilni* in Mayan refers to the power of God within man which is controlled by the breath, similar in meaning to *kundalini*. Mayan *chilambalam* refers to a sacred space, as does Tamil *Chidambaram*. *Yok'hah* in Maya means 'on top of truth,' similar to *yoga* in Sanskrit."[10] The Maya also had the same goddess Maya, mother of the gods and man, as in India.[11] Furthermore, the legendary founder of the Maya was the god Votan or Wotan, a name identical to the god of Teutonic tribes. There are many such correspondences between the Old and New Worlds.

It is not only in the Americas that we discover the global religion, which is, in the end, the mythos revolving around the celestial entities and their relationship with each other and Earth. The first couple story is found in such remote places as Tahiti, where the woman, "Ivi," is made from one of the man's bones, as well as on the Polynesian Island of Bowditch, where the myth is nearly identical to the Hebrew version, serpent, Tree of Life and all.[12]

As James Churchward says:

> Probably the most astounding of all is the fact that the Polynesians, who have been shut in from the rest of the world for over 12,000 years, should have among themselves traditions of the Creation identical with the Biblical account, such as the names of the first man and woman; and that the first woman was made out of the man's bones; that man was a special creation of God. The Marquesans and other Polynesians could not possibly have got these traditions from the outside world. The traditions of the Polynesians start from 12,000 years back, and how much more no one can surmise. The Biblical tradition started with Moses some three thousand years ago, which proves that it was handed down to Moses in some form. The Naacal and Egyptian show us in what form it was handed down and from whom.[13]

In addition, like the biblical tale of Cain and Abel, "Tonga tradition states that 'the son of the first man killed his brother.'"[14] Also, in Fiji "is still shown the site where a vast tower was built because the Fijians were curious and wanted to peep into the moon to discover if it was inhabited,"[15] a story reminiscent of the biblical tale of the Tower of Babel. As Walker says, "The Babel myth is found all over the world, including India and Mexico."[16] At least one group of South Sea islanders, the Melanesians, portrayed the sun as having 12 demi-gods or heroes, like the "helpers" and "disciples" of the Horus/Jesus myth. The South Sea island of Java, site of human occupation beginning many tens of thousands of years ago, also produces a number of pertinent mysteries, including that the last avatar there was to come riding on a white horse, exactly like the solar heroes Krishna and Jesus.[17] The Australian aborigines have a similar mythology to the Egyptian, and several Australian terms are nearly identical in Egyptian.[18]

Astrology/Astronomy

Thus, we see the mythos and ritual around the world. We also know that this knowledge constitutes not only religion but also science, representing detailed observations of the skies and their relationship to Earth, as well as natural forces upon the planet itself. In fact, in order for any civilization to have been global, it would have needed to possess the mythos, since such is in reality the story of astronomy. The detailed knowledge of astronomy, along with that of ocean currents, weather patterns and migratory routes of birds and fish, allowed early peoples to navigate all over the globe. In fact, the so-called primitive peoples of Polynesia are considered the "greatest navigators in the history of mankind" and successfully colonized a number of Pacific islands as early as 30,000 years ago. Such a feat required extensive knowledge of the stars, demonstrating that these peoples were master astronomers tens of thousands of years ago. This detailed knowledge is also exhibited in the celestial "computers" in stone the navigators left all over the world.

The evidence of a global civilization is found in shared astronomical and astrological peculiarities, such as the reverence for the Pleiades, the Great Bear and the constellation of Scorpio or "scorpion stars," a designation found from India to Greece and in Central America. Furthermore, as Walker states:

> Chaldeans believed the world would dissolve and return to its primordial elements when all the planets lined up in the constellation of the Crab. The same doctrine appeared in India, Egypt, Persia, China, northern Europe, and pre-Columbian central America.[19]

The antiquity of astrological/astronomical knowledge is in fact great. The zodiac in the temple of Denderah in Egypt begins with the sun in Leo, which would make it 10,000 years old, although the temple itself is evidently only a couple of thousand years old. Dupuis traced the origins of the zodiac to north Africa 15,000 years ago, and Volney pushed it back to 17,000 years ago. It is reasoned that Egypt at the time had excellent soil and a clear sky, serving as the perfect place for devising such a complex system. In addition, Massey stated that the astronomical mythology dates back 30,000 years at least.[20] A. Churchward thrusts it back much further than that.

Symbols

As noted, there are numerous symbols shared globally, including the cross, which, like so many others, was a symbol of the sun. One of the most ubiquitous symbols is the now-infamous swastika, or crooked cross, also an emblem of the sun, "termed the oldest symbol known to the world" and found around the globe, such as in Alaska, North and Central America, India, Russia and China.[21] The swastika was even a Christian symbol many centuries before its revival by the devout Roman Catholic Hitler. As Walker says:

> Swastikas appear on Paleolithic carvings on mammoth ivory from the Ukraine, dated ca. 10,000 B.C. Swastikas figure on the oldest coinage in India. . . . [The swastika] also represented many other deities from Iceland to Japan, Scandinavia to North Africa. . . . Early Christians adopted the swastika to represent Christ . . . [22]

Language and Etymology

As to the importance of linguistical evidence in detecting the origins of man, James Churchward says, "Language is admitted to be the most accurate guide in tracing the family relations of various peoples, even when inhabiting countries which are separated by vast expanses of water and extents of land."[23]

The linguistical/etymological evidence that connects the world is startling and has been demonstrated throughout this book. Mainly, however, our analysis has been confined to the "Old World." We have already seen some dazzling examples of how the languages of both worlds are related. As a basic example, the word "Mama" and/or "Ma" meaning mother is found in numerous cultures around the globe. A more complex etymological similarity can been found in the Mexican name Mexitli or Mesitli, meaning "the Anointed One,"[24] obviously related to the Egyptian Messu and the Hebrew Messiah. In Maya, "balaam" is a priest, while in Hebrew it is the name of a prophet. There are in fact numerous correlations between the ancient Mexican language and that of the Middle East, including the Sumerian. Indeed, the Mexican culture has close parallels in art, religion and language to Sumer as well.

Moreover, the Mayan creator god was called "Hurakan," and the Caribbean storm god was "Hurukan," both of which are nearly identical to the Tibetan wrathful deity, "Heruka," which in turn is related to Herakles or Hercules. It is from this stormy god that we get the word "Hurricane." Walker hypothesizes that "Horus" was "Heruka" of the East and notes that the Pygmies revered Heru, an archaic name for Horus. "Hul-Kin" in the Indian language of Naga-Maya and Hurki in Akkadian/Chaldean both mean "sunstroke,"[25] which would indeed be another wrathful aspect of the sun god.

Many more examples of correspondences exist between "Old" and "New" World words. Charles Berlitz cites, for example, the similarity between "teocalli," which means "house of the gods" in Aztec/Nahuatl, and "theou kalia," meaning "God's house" in

Greek. The word for "river" in Greek is "potamos," which is very close to the Potomac River in North America. In the South American language of Aymara, "malku" means "king," as does "melek" and "melchi" in Semitic languages. In both the American tongue of Araucanian and the Egyptian language the word "anta" means "sun," while a number of terms in Quechua are similar in form and meaning to Sumerian terms. The list goes on and includes cultures from the South Seas to North Europe as well.

Archaeological Evidence

The global civilization and its mythos are reflected in the amazing physical remains around the world, which have never been fully explained or addressed by mainstream authorities. Nevertheless, from Giza and Baalbek to Stonehenge, Tiahuanaco, China and Pohnpei are ruins of unexplained origins and resemblance, prompting John Keel, for one, to exclaim, "There *had* to be a single worldwide culture at one point in ancient history. . . . Some thing or someone inspired the ancients to perform incredible feats of construction."[26]

Robertson highlights some of these similarities:

> There is a remarkable, though perhaps not a conclusive, resemblance between the Aztec, pre-Aztec and Peruvian temple-pyramids and those of Mesopotamia which derived from the earlier Akkadians or Sumerians. Ruins of these still exist in Central American and Peru which can be compared with the records of those of Babylonia and the one example at Saqqara in Egypt.[27]

There is also a remarkable resemblance between Central/South American structures and those found in India, as has been noted by Indian architect Sri V. Ganapati Sthapati, who demonstrated that residential layouts at Machu Picchu were identical to those of the Harappan civilization at the ruined city of Mohenjodaro in the Indus Valley.[28] In addition, some researchers are now declaring the mysterious Mohenjodaro to be much older than the orthodox opinion, possibly as much as 8,000 years old. Interestingly, Mohenjodaro has been determined to have been a cosmopolitan area, with skeletons found of the following types: "Mediterraneans, Caucasoids, Armenoids, Alpines, Australoids and Mongoloids."[29] The age of Machu Picchu is likely thousands of years older than the orthodox date, as was asserted by its inheritors, the Inkas.

The architect Sthapati has also determined that the Mayan temple at Chichen Itza was "built according to the same design principles found in India's Hindu temples." J. Churchward posits that the fabulous structures at Chichen Itza, attributed by the orthodoxy to "the Maya" of a mere 1500 years ago, are in fact at least 11,500 years old. These structures and others worldwide were taken over by subsequent cultures, demonstrated by the fact that some of them show not only ancient repair work but also "improvements" in the form of encasements over the original ruins.

In studying the architectural remains of ancient civilizations, one category is particularly striking: The pyramid. As Keel says in *Disneyland of the Gods*:

> We know that pyramid building was once a universal practice throughout the world. Over six thousand years ago unknown peoples were assembling great pyramids in Mexico. Gigantic man-made mounds were constructed in China, Great Britain, North America, and on remote Pacific islands while the Egyptians were still living in mud huts along the Nile. During World War II pilots flying "the hump" reported seeing one or more massive pyramids standing silently in isolated Himalaya valleys.[30]

Of the ubiquitousness and similarity of pyramids, David Hatcher Childress states:

> Mayan pyramids are found from Central America to as far away as the Indonesian island of Java. The pyramid of Sukuh, on the slopes of Mount Lawu near Surakarta in central Java is an amazing temple with stone stelae and a step pyramid that would match any in the jungles of Central America. The pyramid is in fact virtually identical to the pyramids found at the ancient Mayan site at Uaxactun, near Tikal.[31]

In speaking of the global civilization, Keel elucidates the weaknesses of the current archaeological paradigm:

> All these things seem to be interrelated, as if they were once part of some great civilization—a common culture that spread throughout the world and then died. . . . We have a reasonably complete history of the past two thousand years, and a half-baked archaeological reconstruction of the past five thousand years. But there are so many gaps in our knowledge that most the popular archaeological theories really have very little merit. Indeed, we can't even be sure that the Egyptians built the Great Pyramid . . . [32]

In fact, the Great Pyramid is admittedly much more ancient than the Egyptians of history, as Hotema relates:

> When the most ancient Egyptians first saw the mysterious Sphinx and the great Pyramid of Gizeh, only their tops projected above the wind-blown sand of the desert. They knew no more about the purpose of these structures, their builders, or when they were built, than we do. . . . [The Great Pyramid] could not possibly have been the work of the Egyptian natives, nor has any one ever claimed that it was.[33]

In the word "pyramid," Anderson has detected "pyr-a-met," which he translates as "grand central fire."[34] The pyramid is the celestial "altar in the midst of Egypt." The pyramid, thus, was a worldwide symbol of an altar, being an encoder of "sacred knowledge."

Based on the "Records of the Past," A. Churchward stated that the Great Pyramid "must have been built at least 269,870 years ago."[35] Of course, the current paradigm dictates that such a date is absurd. What is not absurd is that the dates of artifacts worldwide are steadily being pushed back.

Although such a date is not allowed by the current paradigm, which places all civilization after the time of the Sumero-Babylonian cultures, the pyramid at Cuicuilco, Mexico, is evidently at least 2,500 years older than the earliest known Sumerian finds, as the Mexican structure was apparently unearthed under a lava field created by a volcanic eruption 8,500 years ago.

The city of Tiahuanaco on the shores of Lake Titicaca in Bolivia is one of the most enigmatic and stunning places on Earth. Lying in a desolate spot some 12,500 feet above sea level, Tiahuanaco has astounded and perplexed travelers for centuries. Although orthodox scholars deem this megalithic mystery an Inkan construction, the Inkas themselves insisted it existed long before their culture came into being. The city is dated by the orthodoxy to no earlier than the 5th century CE, but unorthodox scholars have opined that it may be as much as 15,000 years old. A number of observations lead to the conclusion of such antiquity, not the least of which are the astronomical alignments as found in so many ancient megalithic constructions around the globe, as well as the fact that the city was evidently once at sea level.

In addition to monumental structures indicating an advanced global civilization are numerous other "out-of-place artifacts" ("ooparts"), including Babylonian "batteries" and objects depicted on a mural at Denderah that look like glass tubes with "electric eels" inside them, leaving one to wonder if these devices could have been used for lighting in caves, tombs, pyramids or other buildings. The Ashoka Pillar in India is an enormous lingam made of iron and "expertly welded." Of the pillar, Jochmans says, "The mystery is that any equivalent mass of iron, subjected to the Indian monsoon rains, winds and temperatures for 1,600 years or more would have been reduced to rust long ago."[36] From a shipwreck in Greece of the first century BCE comes a navigational device or "astrolabe," which "calculated the annual movements of the sun and moon." Miniature model airplanes have been found in both the "old" world and the "new," and legends of diverse peoples speak of "flying machines." There are also the fabulous drawings at Nazca and elsewhere that can only be seen from above. Also in Peru have been found 50,000 engraved stones that "show people, extant and extinct animals, star maps, the star ring of the zodiac, and maps of unidentified land areas. The people are shown hunting or struggling with a variety of monsters that resemble brontosaurs, triceratops, stegosaurs, and pterodactyls, which properly belong to the Mesozoic era [225-65 million BP]. Even more surprisingly, human beings are portrayed as having domesticated animals that appear to be dinosaurs and are using them for transportation and warfare. People are shown using telescopes, looking at the stars, and performing surgery."[37] Although these baffling stones have been attacked as modern frauds, which some admittedly are, mention was purportedly made of their existence by a 16th century Spanish priest who sent some of them to Spain. In addition, the oxidation of the engravings would appear to demonstrate that many of the stones are at least several centuries old, dating to a time when neither native Americans nor anyone else were supposed to know about such things. In Central America, another technological anachronism appears in massive spheres almost perfectly round. In another apparent anachronism, pictures of horses and asses are frequently found in Mexican hieroglyphs,[38] even though the Americas were wiped clean of such fauna 12,000 ago.

The Enigma of North America

In the analysis of the ancient advanced global civilization hypothesis, North America still seems to remain part of the old paradigm with few signs of any advanced culture or outside influence, other than in legends. However, this perception is incorrect, as, in reality, North America was inhabited by one or more advanced cultures who did indeed leave their traces, traces sometimes so obliterated that they are certainly of a very profound antiquity. In actuality, it will come as a shock to many that the United States has numerous ruins and earthworks so old that the natives encountered by Europeans had no idea who built them. As Keel relates:

> [The experts] tell us that North America was uninhabited by anyone except Indians before the Europeans arrived. They overlook all the stone towers and structures found all over this continent (including miles of paved roads) when the Pilgrims arrived. Fort catalogued all kinds of metal objects from swords and axes to coins that have been found and dated as pre-Columbian. Somebody was mining ore and coal in this country, and pumping oil in Pennsylvania before Columbus set sail. Rather than tussle with the problem of identifying those

mysterious North Americans, the archaeologists have chosen to ignore these artifacts.[39]

J. Churchward relates the writings of Kentucky historian George Ranck as saying that under the modern city of Lexington is the "dead metropolis of a lost race . . . that these remains of a great city and a mighty people did exist, there can be not the shadow of a doubt. . . . Here they erected their Cyclopean temples and cities, with no vision of the red men who would come after them, and chase the deer and the buffalo over their leveled and grass-covered walls. Here they lived, and labored, and died, before Columbus had planted the standard of old Spain upon the shores of a new world; while Gaul, and Britain, and Germany were occupied by roving tribes of barbarians, and, it may be, long before imperial Rome had reached the height of her glory and splendor."[40]

In addition to the stoneworks in North America were the astonishing earthworks, some a mile or more long, constituting geometrical images such as circles, ellipses, octagons, rectangles and squares, as well as serpents and other animals, some of which were purportedly extinct by the time of humans in America. As Christopher Dun says, "My analysis reveals that: . . . There existed among the [Moundbuilders] a school of mathematics whose musings on geometric concepts differed from the Pythagoreans of ancient Greece only by degree."[41] Stone towers, walls, houses and other structures are, of course, built by masons, who are also skilled in the science of geometry. In other words, the individuals involved in these creations evidently were educated members of one or more schools.

Like the Great Pyramid, various edifices of North and South America were not built by the later cultures but either acquired by force or inherited by default because the buildings had been abandoned by earlier cultures. In fact, although Egypt is often given the honor of being the originator of much human culture, the Egyptians themselves recorded that they were the inheritors of a great civilization that came from elsewhere. Indeed, the Egyptian culture seemingly appeared out of nowhere at a high level of development, as did the Sumero-Mesopotamian and South American. This fact is explainable if the civilizers were advanced groups coming from elsewhere, from lands that had been destroyed by climatic change, war or other cataclysm.

Of the global culture, Keel says:

> It probably reached its zenith before the Ice Age ten thousand years ago, then deteriorated in the wake of the geological calamities. That early culture mapped the whole planet, and fragments of those maps were handed down over the centuries until they reached Columbus. The giants, who once tossed huge

blocks of stone around and built the puzzling monoliths that still stand on every continent, gradually reverted to a fierce, uncivilized state, driven by the urgent requirements of survival.[42]

Regarding these "Maps of the Sea Kings" made famous by Charles Hapgood, Zecharia Sitchin adds:

Indeed, by now a surprisingly large number of maps from pre-Columbian times have been found; some (as the Medicean map of 1351, the Pizingi map of 1367, and others) show Japan as a large island in the western Atlantic and, significantly, an island named "Brasil" midway to Japan. Others contain outlines of the Americas as well as of Antarctica—a continent whose features have been obscured by the ice covering it, suggesting that, incredibly, these maps were drawn based on data available when the icecap was gone—a state of affairs that existed right after the Deluge circa 11,000 B.C. and for a while thereafter.[43]

Evidence of Cataclysm

Throughout this demonstration of a global civilization has persisted a recurring theme, found in fact and in legend: cataclysm. The ruins scattered about the planet serve as evidence enough of a variety of catastrophes, such as flood, fire, earthquake, vulcanism, mountain-building, pole shifts, crustal displacement, and comet or meteor strikes. In fact, altogether these calamities have struck innumerable times throughout the history of the planet. During the Quaternary Period (2.5 million to 10,000 years ago), when man allegedly made his appearance, one-fourth of the land's surface was purportedly under ice, which certainly would have destroyed nearly all traces of any number of advanced cultures. The end of the Quaternary brought tremendous upheavals, with enormous floods produced by the melting of the glaciers, such glaciers and floods carving the earth's face like a clay sculpture and crushing life around the world. In *Fingerprints of the Gods*, Graham Hancock describes the impact on "New World" fauna during this great cataclysm:

In the New World . . . more than seventy genera of large mammals became extinct between 15,000 BC and 8000 BC . . . The staggering losses, involving the violent obliteration of more than forty million animals, were not spread out evenly over the whole period; on the contrary, the vast majority of the extinctions occurred in just two thousand years, between 11,000 BC and 9000 BC. To put this into perspective, during the previous 300,000 years only about twenty genera had disappeared.[44]

Berlitz relates the words of oceanographer Dr. Bruce Heezen regarding this tumultuous period:

Eleven thousand years ago the ocean level all around the world was perhaps three hundred feet lower than it is today. The eastern coastline of our United States, for instance, was some one hundred miles farther out in the Atlantic Ocean in that bygone era.

Then, suddenly, above eleven thousand years ago, the Ice Age was over . . . billions of gallons of ice and snow poured into the sea. The result was a dramatic, sudden, and terrifying rising of the sea level all around the world—an inundation which we have verified by half a dozen different types of research available to us today. The rise undoubtedly caused the flooding of many low-level seaside communities where primitive man had chosen to build his early towns and cities.[44]

This "man and his communities," however, were evidently not at all primitive, ostensibly representing an advanced, worldwide culture. This cataclysm and others apparently made it into the mythos, reflected by, as Giorgio de Santillana and Hancock evinced, "Hamlet's Mill" myths about the symbolic hourglass or mill shape made by the precession of the equinoxes and its "derangement." The mill motif is also found in the biblical tale of Samson, and, as Hancock says, "The theme resurfaces in Japan, in Central America, among the Maoris of New Zealand, and in the myths of Finland."[45]

Another aspect of the mythos seems to record a "derangement of the heavens," as in Hebrew mythology the god El is both the sun and the planet Saturn (the "Father on High"), a fact demonstrating that there were two "suns" in the ancient world's mythologies: The day orb and the "eternal" or unmoving pole star, around which all other celestial bodies appear to rotate. The planet Saturn was considered "the Heavenly Father" because it was the most remote of the inner planets and was thus viewed as being the overseer or parent. Velikovskian David Talbott says Isaiah "locates the throne of El in the farthest reaches north," i.e., El/Saturn is the pole star. When Saturn was no longer the "central sun," "El" became the daytime solar orb; hence, El/Saturn was both the planet and the sun. This change in the heavens could reflect a pole or axial shift.

Age of Mankind

Because of such ongoing destruction, it has been difficult to date and place the emergence of the true human being. This fact attests not only to the fragility of manmade artifacts and remains but also to the occurrence of natural processes—sometimes slow and gradual, sometimes quick and violent—that continuously shape the earth and "wipe the slate" clean of such remains. Regarding one such slate-wiping, James Churchward says:

> The remains of ancient man in Europe are limited because the mountains of ice which were brought down on the waters of the Last Magnetic Cataclysm ground everything to a pulp, leaving but few traces of life behind.[47]

As to the possible age of human culture, Albert Churchward makes this surprising assertion:

> The Solar Cult lasted about 100,000 years and the Lunar before this about 50,000 years. The Stellar Cult was anterior to these, and lasted at least 300,000 years; how much longer it is impossible to say, but from remains found of the Stellar Cult people in Pliocene Strata formations they were in existence at least 600,000 years ago.[48]

Based on archaeological, anthropological, astrological and mythological evidence, A. Churchward claimed that modern humans must have existed at least 2.8 million years ago.[49] While Churchward wrote several decades ago, and would thus seem to be outdated in the face of so many scientific discoveries and conclusions since then, his arguments are compelling. This estimation may not be so farfetched, in any case. In fact, in seeming accord with the Hindu chronology, which goes back millions of years, Keel reports that, "Human footprints and man-made objects were repeatedly turning up in coal mines and geological strata dating back millions of years."[50]

Keel also states, "Our planet is at least three billion years old and there is growing evidence that great civilizations existed here while our ancestors were still climbing trees."[51]

According to the current paradigm, the modern human only came into being 100,000 years ago, a figure that keeps being pushed back; however, for some reason, humans did not develop significantly for 70,000 years, when they began to paint beautiful images in caves, among other things. Nevertheless, if the human species can progress as far as it has in the past five hundred years, there is no reason it could not have done so tens of thousands of years ago. In fact, it makes no sense at all, if homo sapiens appeared 100,000 years ago, that it only reached an advanced degree of culture in the past 6-8,000 years.

The Evolution of Religion

However old it is or came to be here, the human species has a common culture going back many thousands of years. This culture included a religious and spiritual tradition that was simple and uniform, although highly detailed, because it was based on the complexities of nature. It was not, however, founded on the complexities of human beings, i.e., racism, sexism, general bigotry, warfare, etc., until humans brought themselves into it and imposed themselves on it. The proto-religion focused its attention not on any person, prophet, savior or saint of a particular ethnicity or gender but upon the "Architecture" of the Grand Architect, the Vault of Heavens and the Pillars of Earth. The Grand Architect was not only Father but the "Great Mother . . . the primeval waters and source of creation," a common theme in mythologies and cosmogonies worldwide, as is the idea of a self-generated male/female entity that separates itself into "the heavens and the earth." Another common concept is that "God" is One but is represented in and by the Many. The sun and moon are "his/her" eyes, for example, and the sky "his/her" abode. "S/He" is, indeed, both the daytime and the "serpent of the night." The Grand Architect demonstrated her/his masterful skills through the precise workings of the solar system, which were not only revered by the ancient global culture but imitated on Earth in massive stoneworks that are the domain of masons, who also kept the knowledge of the sacred geometry passed to them by the Architect. Evidently, these priest-masons passionately attempted to keep "the Architect's clock," wherever they went; thus, they built celestial "computers" worldwide, and they taught the celestial mythos so that the sacred knowledge would never be lost. So passionate were they, in fact, that they took enormous pains to preserve the mythos and sacred knowledge and to make it understandable; yet, it has been ignored, disparaged and historicized in the most vulgar manner in order to allow powermongers to compete with each other. Thus, we are inheritors of not only the physical ruins of the great global civilization but the spiritual wreck as well.

---

1. O'Hara, 57.
2. Carpenter, 25.
3. Higgins, II, 31.
4. J. Churchward, *LCM*, 310.
5. Robertson, 140.
6. Robertson, 141.
7. Higgins, II, 21.
8. J. Churchward, *LCM*, 80.
9. A. Churchward, 348.
10. *Hinduism Today*, vol. 17, no. 6.
11. J. Churchward, *LCM*, 78.
12. Jackson, 14.
13. J. Churchward, *LCM*, 300.
14. J. Churchward, *LCM*, 100.
15. J. Churchward, *LCM*, 100.
16. Walker, *WEMS*, 87.
17. Higgins, II, 38.
18. Massey, *EBD*, 115.
19. Walker, *WEMS*, 183.
20. Massey, *HJMC*, 201.
21. Hazelrigg, 135.

22. Walker, *WEMS*, 965.
23. J. Churchward, *LCM*, 311.
24. Sitchin, *LR*, 28.
25. J. Churchward, *CM*, 235.
26. Keel, 40.
27. Robertson, 139.
28. *Hinduism Today*, vol. 17, no. 6.
29. "Fixing History," *Hinduism Today*, 5/98.
30. Keel, 34-5.
31. "Top Ten Ancient Civilizations with Advanced Technology," *Atlantis Rising*, #1.
32. Keel, 110.
33. Massey, *EBD*, 18-22.
34. Anderson, 8.
35. A. Churchward, 152.
36. "Top Ten Out-of-Place Artifacts," *Atlantis Rising*, #5.
37. Berlitz, *AEC*, 193.
38. Higgins, II, 35.
39. Keel, 16.
40. A. Churchward, *LCM*, 223-4.
41. "High-Tech Agenda for the Mound Builders?" *Atlantis Rising*, #10, 12/97.
42. Keel, 13.
43. Sitchin, *LR*, 246.
44. Hancock, 213.
45. Berlitz, *AEC*, 72.
46. Hancock, 252.
47. J. Churchward, *CM*, 125.
48. A. Churchward, 149.
49. A. Churchward, 343.
50. Keel, 13.
51. Keel, 108.

The step pyramid of Sakkara, Egypt, built around 2900 BCE.

The sun pyramid of Teotihuacan, Mexico. (Muck)

Giant stone head with black features
from the Olmec culture of Mexico,
about 3,000 years ago. (Muck)

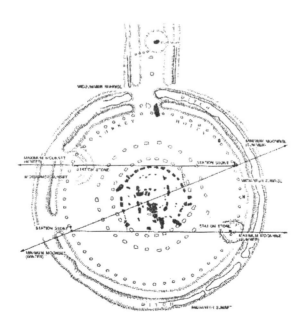

Stonehenge - celestial computer.
(*Mysteries of the Past*)

Conclusion

For nearly 2,000 years hundreds of millions of people have been taught that a historical "son of God" called Jesus Christ lived, did miracles, suffered and died as a blood-atonement especially established once and for all by God Himself, the Creator of the entire cosmos. In reality, the gospel story of Jesus is not a factual portrayal of a historical "master" who walked the earth 2,000 years ago but a myth built upon other myths and godmen, who in turn were personifications of the ubiquitous solar mythos and ritual found in countless cultures around the world thousands of years before the Christian era. As such, the tale served to amalgamate the numerous religions, cults and sects of the Roman Empire and beyond, to create a state religion that was promulgated through forgery, fraud and force.

Nevertheless, countless believers have insisted that the gospel tale happened, not because of any evidence, but merely because they have been told it was so and blindly accepted it, against common sense and better judgment. Furthermore, historicizing scholars and other evemerists, funded by the same agencies who created the myth, have thrown their scientific minds out the window and dishonestly begun their desperate work with the wrong premise, thereafter constantly trying to shore up the impossible, with endless tortured speculation where there are no facts at all. The actuality is that, had Jesus been real, the world would have developed differently than it did, particularly immediately after his alleged miraculous advent; yet, the world went on as if nothing had ever happened. Earl Doherty summarizes the problem with the gospel "history":

> If this man Jesus had had the explosive effect on his followers that is said of him, and on the thousands of believers who responded so readily to the message about him, such a man would have had to blaze in the firmament of his time. That impact would have been based on the force of his personality, on the unique things he said and did. There is no other way. And yet the picture we see immediately after Jesus' death, and for the next two generations in every extant document, flatly contradicts this. The blazing star immediately drops out of sight. No contemporary historian, philosopher or popular writer records him. There is no sign of any tradition or phenomenon associated with him. For over half a century Christian writers themselves totally ignore his life and ministry. Not a saying is quoted. Not a miracle is marvelled at. No aspect of his human personality, anchored within any biographical setting, is ever referred to. The details of his life, the places of his career: they raise no interest in any of his believers. This is an eclipse that does not even grant

us a trace of a corona! If, on the other hand, Jesus was simply an ordinary human man, an unassuming (if somewhat charismatic) Jewish preacher, who really said little of what has been imputed to him, who performed no real miracles, and who of course did not rise from the dead – all of which might explain why he attracted no great attention and could have his life ignored as unimportant by his later followers – what, then, is the explanation for how such a life and personality could have given rise to the vast range of response the scholars postulate, to the cosmic theology about him, to the conviction that he had risen from the dead, to the unstoppable movement which early Christianity seems to have been? This is an unsolvable dilemma.

When pressed, scholars and clergy alike will admit that the founding of the Christian religion is shrouded in centuries of intrigue and fraud. They will confess that there is not a single mention of Jesus by any historian contemporaneous with his alleged advent and that the biblical accounts are basically spurious, not written by their pretended authors and riddled with tens of thousands of errors, impossibilities and contradictions. They will even admit that such texts had been forged by the hundreds and later interpolated and mutilated. Such "experts" may even go so far as to concede that the historicity of Christ has been called into question from the beginning, with that fact itself being cloaked in euphemism and deceit. They may further confess that there is absolutely no physical evidence of the event or the man, and that the numerous relics, including the infamous Shroud of Turin, are fakes, as are the tourist spots where the drama allegedly took place. These scholars may even have the courage to admit that the Jewish religion, upon which Christianity claims to be based, is itself not what it is asserted to be but is basically a rehash of older myths and theologies, as, in the end, is Christianity.

In other words, like the Christian fathers, these scholars and experts will concede that the gospel tale and Christian ideology constitute a direct lift from so-called Paganism. They will even admit that the gospel story is fiction, cagily calling it "benign deceit." Yet, these scholars and researchers will continue in their quest to find a "historical" Jesus, endlessly pumping out tomes that would be better off as trees. Waite describes their futile endeavors:

> Many attempts have been made to write the life of Christ. But it is difficult to see where, outside of the gospels the material for such a work is to come from; while, if the gospels are to be taken as a basis, it is equally difficult to understand what is to be gained by rewriting what is contained in them. Any such attempt only brings out, in plainer light, the discrepancies in those accounts, and finally results in a mere display of ingenuity on

the part of the biographer, in his efforts to reconcile them; or, as in the case of some writers, in a sublime unconsciousness of any discrepancies whatever.[1]

Indeed, the efforts to find a historical Jesus have been pitiful and agonizing, based mainly on what he was *not*: To wit, the virgin birth is not history, and Jesus's parents were not called Mary and Joseph. Jesus was not from Nazareth, which didn't exist at the time, and the magi, star, angels and shepherds did not appear at his birth. He didn't escape to Egypt, because Herod was not slaughtering children, and he didn't amaze the priests with his teaching at age 12 in the temple. He did not suddenly at 30 reappear out of nowhere to mystify people who, if the birth stories had been true, would have already known him. The "historical" Jesus didn't do miracles or raise the dead. The sayings and sermons weren't originally his. He wasn't betrayed by Judas, since that would be illogical if he were already "world famous." There was no trial, no crucifixion and no resurrection.

Such are some of the numerous parts of the gospel story that have been thrown out by "skeptical" historicizers and evemerists over the centuries because they represent elements found ubiquitously in the myths of the solar heroes and in mystery rites. Tossing all these parts out, we might wonder, even more skeptically, where is the historical Jesus Christ? Have we found the core in the onion? The leap of faith even among evemerists is mindboggling. If 99 percent of this story is based on the myths and only one percent on any "history," what are people admiring and worshipping?

Although they are taught that "Jesus" represented a stunning break from the "old Pagan world," believers are worshipping basically the same deity or deities as the Pagans—in fact, practically all of them rolled into one. Yet, not knowing this, the faithful smugly set themselves apart in an atmosphere of superiority and pity, if not outright hatred, for so-called Heathens and Pagans, i.e., "those not of the faith." As Jackson says, "Many Christians denounce Paganism as a false religion. If this is correct, then Christianity is also false, for it is of pagan origin, and if one is not true, then neither is the other."[2]

To reiterate, as Robertson says, "There is not a conception associated with Christ that is not common to some or all of the Savior cults of antiquity."[3] And Carpenter states that "the doctrine of the Saviour is world-wide and world-old, and that Christianity merely appropriated the same (as the other cults did) and gave it a special flavor."[4] He also remarks:

The main Christian doctrines and festivals, besides a great mass of affiliated legend and ceremonial, are really quite directly derived from, and related to, preceding Nature worships; and it has only been by a good deal of deliberate mystification and falsification that this derivation has been kept out of sight.[5]

And Jordan Maxwell says:

All that we find in Judaism and Christianity—there is virtually not one concept, belief, or idea expressed in Judaism or Christianity, not one—that cannot be traced back many, many times to many different religions. It's a very old, ancient story. It's the greatest story ever told.[6]

Of this greatest story ever *sold*, Massey states:

In this way it can be proved that our Christology is mummified mythology, and legendary lore, which have been palmed off upon us in the Old Testament and the New, as divine revelation uttered by the very voice of God. We have the same conversion of myth into history in the New Testament that there is in the Old— the one being effected in a supposed fulfillment of the other! Mythos and history have changed places once, and have to change them again before we can understand their right relationship, or real significance."[7]

The gospel story, fought so widely from the beginning because it was misrepresented as true, has now become through constant force and proselytizing unhealthily lodged in the human psyche, a meme that has caused a large proportion of the human race to live in a world of awful fantasy and endless waiting for the miraculous, for the divine to step in, like "he" purportedly did 2,000 years ago. Yet this alleged "miracle" of Jesus's advent was no more factual than that of Osiris, Krishna, Horus, Quetzalcoatl or any of the numerous other myths and savior gods upon which the Christ character is predicated. To believe that the mythical is the historical is not only to be dishonest but also to destroy the meaning of the mythical and to ruin its real miracle. Indeed, the historicizing of the mythos removes its value and makes the mind idiotic; but, to understand the gnosis behind it is to become wise.

As Massey also says:

[I]t is the miraculous that shows the mythical nature of the history; the identical miracles of Christ the healer that proves him to have been the same character as the healer Iu-em-hept, or Aesclapius, and the caster-out of demons, Khunsu. It was the human history that accreted round the divinity, and not a human being who became divine. On the theory of an historic origin and interpretation the discrepancies may be paralleled for ever with no possibility of attaining the truth; the matter can never be moulded into coherent consistency. But the mythical origin explains all. . . . The mythical origins only can explain why there are two Marys both of whom are described as being the mother of Jesus. The mythical origins only can explain why Jesus should have been rebegotten as the anointed son at thirty years of age . . . The mythical origins only can explain why there is no history furnished from the time when the child-Christ was about twelve years of age to that of the adultship of thirty years. The mythical origins only can show how the Word, or Manifestor, from the first could be said to be made flesh. . . . The mythical Christ could have two birthdays like the dual-natured Horus, one at the solstice and one at the equinox.[8]

Massey further states:

The Christ of the gospels is in no sense an historical personage or a supreme model of humanity, a hero who strove, and suffered, and failed to save the world by his death. It is impossible to establish the existence of an historical character *even as an impostor*. For such an one the two witnesses, astronomical mythology and gnosticism, completely prove an *alibi*. The Christ is a popular lay-figure that never lived, and a lay-figure of Pagan origin; a lay-figure that was once the Ram and afterwards the Fish; a lay-figure that in human form was the portrait and image of a dozen different gods.

As to the hackneyed evemerist arguments in favor of these "dozen different gods" and any others being legendary heroes of old, rather than aspects of the celestial mythos, Higgins demonstrates their error and its consequences, obviously understood in his time over 160 years ago but suppressed:

The following is the state of ancient history given by Mr. Bryant, and nothing can be more true: ". . . it is evident that most of the deified personages never existed: but were mere titles of the Deity, the Sun; as has been in great measure proved by Macrobius. Nor was there ever any thing such detriment to ancient history, as supposing that the Gods of the Gentile world had been natives of the countries where they were worshipped. They have been by these means admitted into the annals of times: and it has been the chief study of the learned to register the legendary stories concerning them: to conciliate absurdities, and to arrange the whole into a chronological series—a fruitless labor, and inexplicable: for there are in these fables such inconsistencies and contradictions as no art, nor industry, can remedy."[9]

The Age of Darkness

There is indeed nothing new under the sun. And "Jesus" is, basically, the same old sun, the Hellenized Joshua, the Judaized Horus and Krishna, thought by the deceived masses to have been a native of the country in which he was worshipped. Is it mere coincidence that, after the celestial mythos and astronomical knowledge had become completely eclipsed and subverted, the Western world was plunged into the Dark Ages?

Jackson describes the results of this putting out of the light of the sun:

> [T]he Gnostic wisdom was not wholly lost to the world but its great, universal educational system was supplanted. It is a well-established historical fact, not denied by the church that it required about 500 years to accomplish this submersion of Gnosticism, and to degrade the new generations in ignorance equal to the state of imbecility. History again points its accusing finger at the living evidence. The horrible results of such a crime against nature and mankind are pictured in the Dark Ages . . . Not even priests or prelates were permitted to learn to read or write. Even bishops could barely spell out their Latin. During this period of mental darkness, the ignorant masses were trained in intolerance, bigotry, fanaticism, and superstitious fear of an invisible power secretly controlled by the church; all of which begat a state of hysteria and imbecility.[10]

Robertson explains why Christianity arose and what its purpose was:

> Religions, like organisms and opinions, struggle for survival and the fittest survive. That is to say, those survive which are fittest for the actual environment, not fittest from the point of view of another higher environment. What, then, was the religion best adapted to the populations of the decaying Roman Empire, in which ignorance and mean subjection were slowly corroding alike intelligence and character, leaving the civilized provinces unable to hold their ground against the barbarians? . . . Christianity . . . This was the religion for the Dark Ages . . .[11]

And Larson states:

> We believe that, had there been no Christianity, Greek enlightenment would, after a fierce struggle with Mithraism and its offspring Manichaeism, have emerged victorious. There would have been no Dark Ages. . . .[12]

During this appalling Age of Darkness without the Sun, learning and literacy were all but destroyed. Libraries were burned, in order to hide the horrible secret of the Christian religion, and a world that had been reaching for the stars, with great thinkers appearing in numerous places, was now subjugated in darkness falsely portraying itself as the "light of the world." As Pike says:

> The Church of Rome claimed despotism over the soul, and over the whole life from the cradle to the grave. It gave and sold absolutions for past and future sins. It claimed to be infallible in matters of faith. It decimated Europe to purge it of heretics. It decimated America to convert the Mexicans and Peruvians. . . .

The history of all is or will be the same—acquisition, dismemberment and ruin. . . . To seek to subjugate the *will* of others and to take the *soul* captive, because it is the exercise of the highest power, seems to be the highest object of human ambition. It is at the bottom of all proselytizing and propagandism . . .[13]

And, as Wheless declares:

Holy Fraud and Forgery having achieved their initial triumph for the Faith, the "Truth of Christ" must now be maintained and enforced upon humanity by a millennial series of bloody brutal Clerical Laws of pains and penalties, confiscations, civil disabilities, torture and death by rack, fire and sword, which constitute the foulest chapter of the Book of human history—the History of the Church![14]

The Origins of Cultural Bigotry and Racism

One of the most unfortunate aspects of the historicizing of this "oldest story ever sold" was that one particular ethnic group, and that one only, became esteemed above all others for being "God's chosen people," the "priestly nation" and the spiritual masters of mankind. Another calamitous aspect has been the vilification of these same people as "Christkillers" and foaming-at-the-mouth murderers of the Almighty Lord God himself. Thus, in believing the gospel tale Christians have been forced into a love-hate relationship with the Jews, who are to be perceived as "God's chosen" and "Christkillers" at the same time. Not only is this schizophrenic salvation plan and legacy not the product of any good god, it is utterly divisive, setting people against each other all over the world.

Furthermore, not a few people have wondered why these identical stories found outside of the Bible and revolving around "Gentile" or "Pagan" characters are "myths," while the biblical tales told about Hebrews and Jews are "history." As Jacolliot remarks:

We have repudiated Greek and Roman mythologies with disdain. Why, then, admit with respect the mythology of the Jews? Ought the miracles of Jehovah to impress us more than those of Jupiter? . . . I have much more respect for the Greek Jupiter than for the God of Moses; for if he gives some examples not of the purest morality, at least he does not flood his altar with streams of human blood.[15]

The gospel story constitutes cultural bigotry and does a disservice to the history of humanity. Contrary to popular belief, the ancients were not an ignorant and superstitious lot who actually believed their deities to be literal characters. Nor were they as a whole immoral or unenlightened. This propaganda has been part of the conspiracy to make the ancients appear as if they were truly the dark and dumb rabble that was in need of the "light of Jesus." As Massey says:

> The picture of the New Beginning commonly presented is Rembrandt-like in tone. The whole world around Judea lay in the shadow of outer darkness, when suddenly there was a great light seen at the centre of all, and the face of the startled universe was illuminated by an apparition of the child-Christ lying in the lap of Mary. Such was the dawn of Christianity, in which the Light of the World had come to it at last! That explanation is beautifully simple for the simple-minded; but the picture is purely false—or, in sterner words, it is entirely false.[16]

And Pikes asks, "Did the Deity leave the whole world without Light for two score centuries, to illuminate only a little corner of Palestine and a brutal, ignorant, and ungrateful people?"[17]

The reality is that the ancients were no less advanced in their morals and spiritual practices, and in many cases were far more enlightened, than the Christians in their own supposed morality and ideology, which, in its very attempt at historicity, is in actuality a degradation of the ancient celestial and terrestrial religion. Indeed, unlike the Christians, the true intelligentsia among the ancients were well aware that their gods were astronomical and atmospheric in nature. Even the much vilified Babylonians declared that their gods and those of other cultures and ages were the sun, moon, stars and planets, demonstrating that they were not only advanced but honest in this matter. In addition, the eminent Greek philosophers Socrates, Plato and Aristotle surely knew that their gods, such as Zeus, the sky-god father-figure who migrated to Greece from India and/or Egypt, were never real people.

These three great Greek luminaries were, oddly enough, highly esteemed by early Christian conspirators, who, as they had with so many preceding purveyors of wisdom and ideologies, falsely presented these savants' known accomplishments in philosophy as divine revelation to the Church. Such appropriation was recognized by the ancients themselves. For instance, Amelius, a Platonist of the 3rd century, "upon reading the first verse of St. John the Evangelist, exclaimed, 'By Jove, this barbarian agrees with our Plato.'"[18] Cardinal Palavicino is quoted as saying, "Without Aristotle we should be without many Articles of Faith."[19] It is amusing to consider that the omniscient "Lord," who came to deliver a "New Dispensation," needed the writings of Aristotle to determine doctrine for "his" Church. It is likewise interesting that, by constantly "borrowing from" and aligning themselves with exalted philosophers who were recognized as having penetrated the mysteries of the cosmos, the Christians themselves admitted just how advanced were their predecessors. Thus, we discover that the image of the ancient world as portrayed by Christianity is utterly false.

In fact, rather than serving as an improvement, Christianity has been a psychic trauma, uprooting ideas and deities that were worshipped since Neolithic times, particularly nature gods and goddesses. The sexist Judeo-Christian-Islamic ideology has been a war on all things considered female, including Nature and Mother Earth. The patriarchal age has represented the military campaign of the sky-god father-figure against the earth-goddess mother-figure. In the process, the Goddess's groves—so sacred to the ancients that to cut them down was sometimes a capital offense—have been plowed under and her creatures butchered in a vicious quest for riches and "heaven." The current culture is now headed for environmental cataclysm, because this ideology has served to disconnect human beings from the earth, to constantly focus their attention not on this life and this reality but on an afterlife and another world altogether.

Furthermore, as Graham says, "Such a story as the Gospels tell us is unworthy of man's respect; it is, we repeat, the greatest fraud and hoax ever perpetrated upon mankind."[20] No human culture can survive that bases its fundamental beliefs and perceptions on a hoax, particularly one in which the result has been the needless torture and slaughter of millions around the globe.

In reality, Christianity was the product of a multinational cabal composed of members of a variety of brotherhoods, secret societies and mystery schools, and was designed to empower and enrich such individuals and to unify their empire. To do so, these conspirators took myriad myths and rituals of virtually all the known cultures and combined them into one, producing a godman to beat them all. This unreachable fictional character has since been considered the "greatest man who ever walked the earth," to whom no one else can compare and besides whom nobody else deserves much recognition and appreciation. All others are, in fact, pathetic, born-in-sin wretches. But, he did not walk the earth, and we must hereafter allow the dignity of sanctity to be bestowed upon not just one "man" but all of creation.

The prejudice and bigotry promulgated by Christianity and other monolithic yet divisive ideologies have caused an atrocious amount of destruction of cultural diversity. It has been demonstrated what a wonderfully colorful and varied world it is in which we live. Around the globe for millennia has appeared a mythos, a core of understanding, that is cosmic and eternal in nature. It once had an infinite variety of flavors and incorporated much of creation in a divine and respectful play. To reduce all this glory to a handful of characters of a particular ethnicity who allegedly played out the cosmic drama one time in history robs us not only of the truth but also of our diversity and universality as well. Furthermore, by removing our ability to question "authority" and to develop our own individuality, this ideology homogenizes us in a way that it is not beneficial but ugly and sheepish. By understanding the terrestrial and cosmic mythos conveyed for millennia, we can move ourselves at last into an age of enlightenment and enjoy the multiplicity of the human mind, unfettered by controlling concepts and "thought police" that limit creativity and wisdom.

The New Age

It has been demonstrated that Christianity pretty much got it all wrong—except the end to its erroneous means: It succeeded in enriching and empowering its most effective proponents many times over. According to the same astrological system used to create Christianity, the age for such divisiveness, fascism and hierarchical exploitation is now drawing to a close, and lying, deceit, cheating and stealing will fall by the wayside. Included in this age in which "the truth will be shouted from the rooftops" is the exposure of Earth's "dirty little secret." As Jacolliot says:

> Apostles of Jesus, you have counted too much upon human credulity, trusted too much that the future might not unveil your manoeuvres and your fabricated recitals—the sanctity of your object made you too oblivious of means, and you have taken the good faith of peoples by surprise in re-producing the fables of another age, which you believed buried for ever.[21]

But the future is now, and the maneuvers are being unveiled. As far as Christianity's role in this "New Age," Carpenter states:

> Christianity therefore, as I say, must either now come frankly forward and, acknowledging its parentage from the great Order of the past, seek to rehabilitate *that* and carry mankind one step forward in the path of evolution—or else it must perish. There is no alternative.[22]

Despite the vilification of the so-called New Age movement, the fact is that we *are* entering into a new age. "I am with you always to the close of the age"—so ends the Gospel of Matthew. What does this mysterious statement mean, and why was this all-important book ended with it? The age referred to in the gospel tale is that of Pisces, and, through contrivance and duplicity, coercion and slaughter, the fish-god "Jesus," the Piscean Solar Avatar, has indeed been with us, but now it is the close of the age, and his time is over.

As Hancock says, "We live today in the astrological no man's land at the end of the 'Age of Pisces,' on the threshold of the 'New Age' of Aquarius. Traditionally these times of transition between one age and the next have been regarded as ill-omened."[23] Ill-omened verily, as the ongoing destruction of the earth and the endless warfare over ideology will indeed produce the "Armageddon" so long awaited and planned for by those who cannot live for today but must look towards an afterlife. By realizing the cultural unity revealed behind the Christ conspiracy, however, humanity can pull together and prevent this fall, to create a better world.

1. Waite, 22.
2. Jackson, 213.
3. Robertson, 52.
4. Carpenter, 130.
5. Carpenter, 19.
6. "The Naked Truth."
7. Massey, *Lectures on the Moon.*
8. Massey, *HJMC*, 182.
9. Higgins, I, 371.
10. Jackson, 122.
11. Robertson, 128-9.
12. Larson, 416.
13. Pike, 74.
14. Wheless, *FC*, 303.
15. Jacolliot, 119.
16. Massey, *GHC*, 2.
17. Pike, 102.
18. Wheless, *FC*, 33.
19. Wheless, *FC*, 33.
20. Graham, 356.
21. Jacolliot, 304.
22. Carpenter, 264.
23. Hancock, 240.

Bibliography

Aarons, Mark and Loftus, John, *Unholy Trinity*, St. Martin's, 1991

Akerley, Ben, *The X-Rated Bible*, American Atheists, 1989

Allegro, John, *The Dead Sea Scrolls and the Christian Myth*, Prometheus, 1992

Allegro, John, *The Sacred Mushroom and the Cross*, Doubleday, 1970

Anderson, Karl, *Astrology of the Old Testament*, Health Research, 1970

Atlantis Rising, http://atlantisrising.com/

Baigent and Leigh, *The Dead Sea Scrolls Deception*, Simon & Schuster, 1991

Barnstone, Willis, ed., *The Other Bible*, Harper, 1984

ben Yehoshua, Hayyim, *The Myth of the Historical Jesus*, www.inlink.com/~rife/jesus

Berlitz, Charles, *Atlantis: The Eighth Continent*, Fawcett, 1985

Bernard, Raymond, PhD, *Apollonius the Nazarene*, Health Research, 1956

Biedermann, Hans, *Dictionary of Symbolism*, Facts on File, 1992

Blavatsky, Helena, *Isis Unveiled*, Theosophical University Press, 1988

Blavatsky, Helena, *The Secret Doctrine*, Theosophical University Press, 1988

Book of Jasher, The, J.H. Parry Publishers, 1887

Book of Enoch, The, Artisan Sales, 1980

Bowerstock, GW, *Fiction as History: Nero to Julian*, University of California, 1994

Bramley, William, *The Gods of Eden*, Dahlin Family Press, 1990.

Campbell, Joseph, *Creative Mythology: The Masks of God*, Penguin, 1976

Campbell, Joseph, *The Hero with a Thousand Faces*, Princeton University Press, 1968

Carpenter, Edward, *Pagan and Christian Creeds*, Health Research, 1975

Charlesworth, James, *Jesus and the Dead Sea Scrolls*, Doubleday, 1995

Childress, David Hatcher, *Lost Cities* series, Adventures Unlimited

Churchward, Albert, *The Origin and Evolution of Religion*

Churchward, Col. James, *The Children of Mu*, BE Books, 1988

Churchward, Col. James, *The Lost Continent of Mu*, BE Books, 1991

Doane, T.W., *Bible Myths and Their Parallels in Other Religions*, Health Research, 1985

Doherty, Earl, *The Jesus Puzzle: Was There No Historical Jesus?* http://www.magi.com/~oblio/jesus.html

Doresse, Jean, *The Secret Books of the Egyptian Gnostics*, Inner Traditions International, 1986

Dowling, Levi, *The Aquarian Gospel of Jesus the Christ*

Dujardin, Edouard, *Ancient History of the God Jesus*, Watts & Co., 1938

Early Christian Writings, Penguin, 1987

Eusebius, *History of the Church*, Penguin, 1989

Fox, Robin Lane, *Pagans and Christians*, Alfred A. Knopf, 1989

Frazer, Sir James, *The Golden Bough*, MacMillan, 1963

Friedman, Richard, *Who Wrote the Bible?*, Simon & Schuster, 1989

Gaster, Theodore, *The Dead Sea Scriptures*, Doubleday, 1976

Golb, Norman, *Who Wrote the Dead Sea Scrolls?*, Scribner, 1995

Goodspeed, Edgar, tr., *The Apocrypha*, Vintage, 1989

Graham, Lloyd, *Deceptions and Myths of the Bible*, Citadel, 1991

Graves, Kersey, *The Biography of Satan*, Book Tree, 1995

Graves, Kersey, *The World's Sixteen Crucified Saviors*, University Books, 1971

Hancock, Graham, *Fingerprints of the Gods*, Crown, 1995

Harris, Roberta, *The World of the Bible*, Thames and Hudson, 1995

Haught, James, *Holy Horrors*, Prometheus, 1990

Hazelrigg, John, *The Sun Book*, Health Research, 1971

Helms, Randel, *Gospel Fictions*, Prometheus, 1988

Higgins, Godfrey, Esq., *Anacalypsis*, A&B Books, 1992

Hinduism Today, Vol. 17, No. 6, June, 1995

Hislop, Rev. Alexander, *The Two Babylons*, Loizeaux Brothers, 1959

Historical Atlas of the World, Barnes & Noble, 1972

Holley, Vernal, "Christianity: The Last Great Creation of the Pagan World," 1994

Jackson, John G., *Christianity Before Christ*, American Atheists, 1985

Jacolliot, Louis, *The Bible in India*, Sun Books, 1992

Keel, John, *Disneyland of the Gods*, Amok, 1988

Keeler, Bronson, *A Short History of the Bible*, Health Research, 1965

Keller, Werner, *The Bible as History*, Bantam, 1982

Kuhn, Alvin Boyd, PhD, *The Great Myth of the Sun-Gods*, http://magna.com.au/~prfbrown/ab_kuhn.html

Larson, Martin A., *The Story of Christian Origins*, Village, 1977

Leedom, Tim, ed., *The Book Your Church Doesn't Want You to Read*, Kendall/Hunt, 1993

Lockhart, Douglas, *Jesus the Heretic*, Element, 1997

Lost Books of the Bible, The, Crown, 1979

Maccoby, Hyam, *The Mythmaker: Paul and the Invention of Christianity*, Harper, 1987

Mack, Burton, *The Lost Gospel of Q: The Book of Christian Origins*, Harper, 1993

Mangasarian, MM, *The Truth about Jesus*, www.infidels.org

Massey, Gerald, *Gnostic and Historic Christianity*, Sure Fire Press, 1985

Massey, Gerald, *The Egyptian Book of the Dead*, Health Research

Massey, Gerald, *The Historical Jesus and the Mythical Christ*, Health Research

Maxwell, Jordan, "Symbols, Sex & The Stars" video series

Mead, GRS, *Did Jesus Live 100 B.C.?*, Health Research, 1965

Mead, GRS, *The Gospels and the Gospel*, Health Research, 1972

Mead, GRS, *Pistis Sophia*, Garber Communications, 1989

Missing Books of the Bible, The, Halo, 1996

Muck, Otto, *The Secrets of Atlantis*, Time Books, 1978

Mysteries of the Past, American Heritage, 1977

"Naked Truth, The" video series, IRES, 1990

New Larousse Encyclopedia of Mythology, Hamlyn, 1983

Notovich, Nicholas, *The Unknown Life of Jesus Christ*, Tree of Life, 1980

O'Hara, Gwydion, *Sun Lore*, Llewellyn, 1997

Pagels, Elaine, *Adam, Eve and the Serpent*, Vintage, 1989

Pagels, Elaine, *The Gnostic Gospels*, Vintage, 1989

Parker, Julia and Derek, *Parker's Astrology*, Dorling Kindersley, 1991

Past Worlds: Atlas of Archaeology, Harper, 1996

Pike, Albert, *The Morals and Dogma of Scottish Rite Freemasonry*, LH Jenkins, 1928

Platt, Rutherford, ed., *The Forgotten Books of Eden*, Crown, 1981

Potter, Charles Francis, *The Great Religious Leaders*, Simon & Schuster, 1958

Roberts, JM, Esq., *Antiquity Unveiled*, Health Research, 1970

Robertson, JM, *Pagan Christs*, Dorset, 1966

Sitchin, Zecharia, *The Lost Realms*, Avon, 1990

Sitchin, Zecharia, *When Time Began*, Avon, 1993

Steele, John, PhD, "Was Jesus a Taoist?"

Steiner, Rudolf, *Christianity as Mystical Fact*, Anthroposophic Press, 1972

Stone, Merlin, *When God was a Woman*, Dorset, 1976

Taylor Rev. Robert, *The Diegesis*, Health Research, 1977

Vermes, Geza, *The Dead Sea Scrolls*, Penguin, 1987

Waite, Charles, *History of the Christian Religion to the Year Two Hundred*, Caroll Bierbower, 1992

Walker, Barbara, *The Woman's Dictionary of Symbols and Sacred Objects*, Harper, 1988

Walker, Barbara, *The Woman's Encyclopedia of Myths and Secrets*, Harper, 1983

Wells, GA, *Did Jesus Exist?*, Pemberton, 1986

Wells, GA, *The Historical Evidence for Jesus*, Prometheus, 1988

Wells, GA, *Who Was Jesus?*, Open Court, 1991

Westerman and Lessing, *The Bible: A Pictorial History*, Seabury Press, 1977

Wheless, Joseph, *Forgery in Christianity*, Health Research, 1990

Wheless, Joseph, *Is It God's Word?*, www.infidels.org

Whiston, William, tr., *The Complete Works of Josephus*, Kregel, 1981

Williams, Sandra, "Sadducean Origins of the Dead Sea Sectarians," http://ddi.digital.net/~billw/Scrolls/scrolls.html

Wilson, Ian, *Jesus: The Evidence*, Harper, 1988

Wilson, Robert Anton, *Everything is Under Control: Conspiracies, Cults and Cover-ups*, Harper, 1998

Index

Acharya S
Greg Bishop
Len Bracken
David Hatcher Childress
Uri Dowbenko
Wayne Henderson
Jim Keith
Jim Martin
Adam Parfrey
Rob Sterling

The names of the world's best conspiracy culture researchers appear regularly in the pages of *Steamshovel Press*.

Steamshovel examines parapolitical topics in the tradition Mae Brussell, Jim Garrison, Ace Hayes and Danny Casolaro, exploring the many strange dimensions of the contemporary Con. From the UFO cover up to the politics of assassination, the religious hucksters and the corporate/military nightmare, *Steamshovel Press* covers it all with dependable and complete documentation.

"Feed that dark feeling in the pit of your belly."
--Arcturus Books

"...on the cutting edge--and a strange place that is...:
--*New Yorker*

Don't miss an issue--or the Conspiracy will close in on you! $6 per sample issue; $23 for a four issue subscription.

Checks payable to "Kenn Thomas" at POB 23715, St. Louis, MO 63121

On the web at www.umsl.edu/~skthoma

PHILOSOPHY & RELIGION

THE CHRIST CONSPIRACY
The Greatest Story Ever Sold
by Acharya S.

In this highly controversial and explosive book, archaeologist, historian, mythologist and linguist Acharya S. marshals an enormous amount of startling evidence to demonstrate that Christianity and the story of Jesus Christ were created by members of various secret societies, mystery schools and religions in order to unify the Roman Empire under one state religion. In developing such a fabrication, this multinational cabal drew upon a multitude of myths and rituals that existed long before the Christian era, and reworked them for centuries into the religion passed down to us today. Contrary to popular belief, there was no single man who was at the genesis of Christianity; Jesus was many characters rolled into one. These characters personified the ubiquitous solar myth, and their exploits were well known, as reflected by such popular deities as Mithras, Heracles/Hercules, Dionysos and many others throughout the Roman Empire and beyond. The story of Jesus as portrayed in the Gospels is revealed to be nearly identical in detail to that of the earlier savior-gods Krishna and Horus, who for millennia preceding Christianity held great favor with the people. *The Christ Conspiracy* shows the Jesus character as not unique or original, not "divine reve lation." Christianity reinterprets the same extremely ancient body of knowledge that revolved around the celestial bodies and natural forces. The result of this myth making has been "The Greatest Conspiracy Ever Sold."

431 pages. 6x9 Paperback. Illustrated. $16.95. Code: CHRC

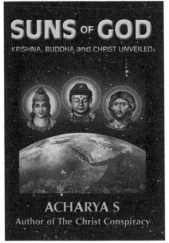

SUNS OF GOD
Krishna, Buddha and Christ Unveiled
by Acharya S

From the author of the controversial and best-selling book The Christ Conspiracy: The Greatest Story Ever Sold comes this electrifying journey into the origins and meaning of the world's religions and popular gods. Over the past several centuries, the Big Three spiritual leaders have been the Lords Christ, Krishna and Buddha, whose stories and teachings are so remarkably similar as to confound and amaze those who encounter them. As classically educated archaeologist, historian, mythologist and linguist Acharya S thoroughly reveals, these striking parallels exist not because these godmen were "historical" personages who "walked the earth" but because they are personifications of the central focus of the famous and scandalous "mysteries." These mysteries date back thousands of years and are found globally, reflecting an ancient tradition steeped in awe and intrigue. In unveiling the reasons for this highly significant development, multifaceted scholar Acharya S presents an in-depth analysis that includes fascinating and original research based on evidence both modern and ancient, captivating information kept secret and hidden for ages.

595 pages. 6x9 paperback. Illustrated. Bibliography. $18.95. Code: SUNG

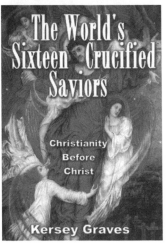

THE WORLD'S SIXTEEN CRUCIFIED SAVIORS
Christianity Before Christ
by Kersey Graves, Foreword by Acharya S.

A reprint of Kersey Graves' classic and rare 1875 book on Christianity before Christ, and the 16 messiahs or saviors who are known to history before Christ! Chapters on: Rival Claims of the Saviors; Messianic Prophecies; Prophecies by the Figure of a Serpent; Virgin Mothers and Virgin-Born Gods; Stars Point Out the Time and the Saviors' Birthplace; Sixteen Saviors Crucified; The Holy Ghost of Oriental Origin; Appollonius, Osiris, and Magus as Gods; 346 Striking Analogies Between Christ and Krishna; 25th of December as the birthday of the Gods; more. 45 chapters in all.

436 pages. 6x9 Paperback. Ilustrated. References. $19.95. Code: WSCS

PHILOSOPHY & RELIGION

JESUS, LAST OF THE PHARAOHS
Truth Behind the Mask Revealed
by Ralph Ellis
This book, with 43 color plates, traces the history of the Egyptian royal family from the time of Noah through to Jesus, comparing biblical and historical records. Nearly all of the biblical characters can be identified in the historical record—all are pharaohs of Egypt or pharaohs in exile. The Bible depicts them as being simple shepherds, but in truth they were the Hyksos, the Shepherd Kings of Egypt. The biblical story that has circulated around the globe is simply a history of one family, Abraham and his descendants. In the Bible he was known as Abram; in the historical record he is the pharaoh Maybra—the most powerful man on Earth in his lifetime. By such simple sleight of hand, the pharaohs of Egypt have hidden their identity, but preserved their ancient history and bloodline. These kings were born of the gods; they were not only royal, they were also Sons of God.
320 PAGES. 6x9 PAPERBACK. ILLUSTRATED. $16.00. CODE: JLOP

TEMPEST & EXODUS
by Ralph Ellis
Starts with the dramatic discovery of a large biblical quotation on an ancient Egyptian stele which tells of a conference in Egypt discussing the way in which the biblical Exodus should be organized. The quotation thus has fundamental implications for both history and theology because it explains why the Tabernacle and the Ark of the Covenant were constructed, why the biblical Exodus started, where Mt. Sinai was located, and who the god of the Israelites was. The most dramatic discovery is that the central element of early Israelite liturgy was actually the Giza pyramids, and that Mt. Sinai was none other than the Great Pyramid. Mt. Sinai was described as being both sharp and the tallest 'mountain' in the area, and thus the Israelite god actually resided deep within the bowels of this pyramid. Furthermore, these new translations of ancient texts, both secular and biblical, also clearly demonstrate that the Giza pyramids are older than the first dynasty—the ancestors of the Hyksos were writing about the Giza pyramids long before they are supposed to have been constructed! Includes: Mt. Sinai, the Israelite name for the Great Pyramid of Egypt; the biblical Exodus inscribed on an Egyptian stele of Ahmose I; the secret name of God revealed; Noah's Ark discovered, more.
280 PAGES. 6x9 PAPERBACK. ILLUSTRATED. COLOR SECTION. BIBLIOGRAPHY & INDEX. $16.00. CODE: TEXO

THOTH
Architect of the Universe
by Ralph Ellis
This great book, now available in paperback, is on sacred geometry, megalithic architecture and the worship of the mathematical constant pi. Ellis contemplates Stonehenge; the ancient Egyptian god Thoth and his Emerald Tablets; Atlantis; Thoth's Ratios; Henge of the World; The Secret Gate of Knowledge; Precessional Henge; Royal Planisphere; Kufu's Continents; the Ma'at of the Egyptians; ancient technological civilizations; the Ark of Tutankhamen; Pyramidions; the Pyramid Inch and Pi; more. Well illustrated with color photo sections.
236 PAGES. 6x9 PAPERBACK. ILLUSTRATED. BIBLIOGRAPHY. $16.00. CODE: TOTH

K2—QUEST OF THE GODS
by Ralph Ellis
This sequel to *Thoth, Architect of the Universe* explains the design of the Great Pyramid in great detail, and it appears that its architect specified a structure that contains a curious blend of technology, lateral thinking and childish fun—yet this design can also point out the exact location of the legendary 'Hall of Records' to within a few meters! The 'X' marks the spot location has been found at last. Join the author on the most ancient quest ever devised, a dramatic journey in the footsteps of Alexander the Great on his search for the legendary Hall of Records, then on to the highest peaks at the top of the world to find the 'The Great Pyramid in the Himalayas'; more.
280 PAGES. 6x9 PAPERBACK. ILLUSTRATED. COLOR SECTION. BIBLIOGRAPHY. $16.00. CODE: K2QD

THE DIMENSIONS OF PARADISE
The Proportions & Symbolic Numbers of Ancient Cosmology
by John Michell
The Dimensions of Paradise were known to ancient civilizations as the harmonious numerical standards that underlie the created world. John Michell's quest for these standards provides vital clues for understanding:
•the dimensions and symbolism of Stonehenge
•the plan of Atlantis and reason for its fall
•the numbers behind the sacred names of Christianity
•the form of St. John's vision of the New Jerusalem
•the name of the man with the number 666
•the foundation plan of Glastonbury and other sanctuaries
•and how these symbols suggest a potential for personal, cultural and political regeneration in the 21st century.
220 PAGES. 6x9 PAPERBACK. ILLUSTRATED. BIBLIOGRAPHY. INDEX. $16.95. CODE: DIMP

A HITCHHIKER'S GUIDE TO ARMAGEDDON
by David Hatcher Childress
With wit and humor, popular Lost Cities author David Hatcher Childress takes us around the world and back in his trippy finalé to the Lost Cities series. He's off on an adventure in search of the apocalypse and end times. Childress hits the road from the fortress of Megiddo, the legendary citadel in northern Israel where Armageddon is prophesied to start. Hitchhiking around the world, Childress takes us from one adventure to another, to ancient cities in the deserts and the legends of worlds before our own. Childress muses on the rise and fall of civilizations, and the forces that have shaped mankind over the millennia, including wars, invasions and cataclysms. He discusses the ancient Armageddons of the past, and chronicles recent Middle East developments and their ominous undertones. In the meantime, he becomes a cargo cult god on a remote island off New Guinea, gets dragged into the Kennedy Assassination by one of the "conspirators," investigates a strange power operating out of the Altai Mountains of Mongolia, and discovers how the Knights Templar and their off-shoots have driven the world toward an epic battle centered around Jerusalem and the Middle East.
320 PAGES. 6x9 PAPERBACK. ILLUSTRATED. BIBLIOGRAPHY. INDEX. $16.95. CODE: HGA

PHILOSOPHY & RELIGION

TIME AND THE BIBLE'S NUMBER CODE
An Exciting Confirmation of God's Time-Line
by Bonnie Gaunt

Bonnie Gaunt's latest research confirms the authenticy of the Bible's Number Code (Gematria) in this latest book of all new material. Gaunt delves into the fascinating patterns of time and numbers that reveal, she says, the master plan of the "Great Mathematician" to create the Kingdom of God on Earth. Confirming the time-line using the Number Code and the beautiful Golden Proportion is the exciting theme of this book. Chapters include: Finding a New Method; Why 6,000 Years?; The Year 1999 and 5760; The Pilgrim Festivals; Confirmation of Time Blocks; Jubilees—a Countdown; "Seven Times" (The Amazing Golden Proportion); Putting It All Together; more.
200 PAGES. 5X8 PAPERBACK. ILLUSTRATED. APPENDIX. $14.95. CODE: TBNC

THE STONES AND THE SCARLET THREAD
New Evidence from the Bible's Number Code, Stonehenge & the Great Pyramid
by Bonnie Gaunt

Researcher Bonnie Gaunt's latest work confirms the authenticy of the Bible's Number Code (Gematria). New evidence has been found linking its amazing pattern of numbers and its time prophecies with the sacred geometry of ancient stone structures such as Stonehenge and the Great Pyramid. In this, her previous eight books, and brings to light new evidence that a Master Plan involving man and his future on planet earth has been in the process from the beginning. She shows, through the Number Code, that the Bible's ancient story of the scarlet thread has been intricately woven through the history and future of man. This exciting book will open new vistas of understanding and insight into the marvelous works of the Master Designer.
224 PAGES. 5X8 PAPERBACK. ILLUSTRATED. APPENDIX. $14.95. CODE: SST

THE BIBLE'S AWESOME NUMBER CODE!
by Bonnie Gaunt

Researcher Bonnie Gaunt continues her research on Gematria and Bible codes. In this book, Gaunt details a new discovery of the numeric patterns in the Gematria of the Bible and their relationship to the 3:4:5: triangle, and the earth, moon and sun. Using the Number Code, it is found that the parable of the Good Samaritan is, in fact, a time prophecy, telling the time of Jesus' return. His miracles of healing and of turning water into wine have been encoded with evidence of the time and the work of the beginning of the great "Third Day." The Number Code takes us on a journey from Bethlehem to Golgotha, and into the Kingdom of Jesus Christ, the Kingdom of God and the building of the New Jerusalem. According to Gaunt, these awesome numbers also reveal the great "Third Day" as beginning in the Hebrew Year 5760 (AD 1999-2000).
220 PAGES. 5X8 PAPERBACK. ILLUSTRATED. $14.95. CODE: BANC

BEGINNINGS
The Sacred Design
by Bonnie Gaunt

Bonnie Gaunt continues the line of research begun by John Michell into the geometric design of Stonehenge, the Great Pyramid and the Golden Proportions. Chapters in this book cover the following topics: the amazing number 144 and the numbers in the design of the New Jerusalem; the Great Pyramid, Stonehenge and Solomon's Temple display a common design that reveals the work of a Master Designer; the amazing location of Bethlehem; how the process of photosynthesis reveals the sacred design while transforming light into organic substance; how the Bible's number code (gematria) reveals a sacred design; more.
211 PAGES. 6X8 PAPERBACK. ILLUSTRATED. $14.95. CODE: BSD

JESUS CHRIST: THE NUMBER OF HIS NAME
The Amazine Number Code Found in the Bible
by Bonnie Gaunt

Gaunt says that the numerological code tells of the new Millennium and of a "Grand Octave of Time" for man. She demonstrates that the Bible's number code reveals amazing realities for today's world, and gives evidence of the year of the "second coming" of Jesus Christ. The book reveals amazing evidence that the code number for Jesus Christ has been planted in the geometry of the Earth, ancient megalithic buildings in Egypt, Britain and elsewhere, and in the Bible itself. Gaunt examines the mathematics of the Great Pyramid, Stonehenge, and the city of Bethlehem, which she says bears the number of Jesus in its latitude and longitude. Discover the hidden meaning to such number codes in the Bible as 666, 888, 864, 3168, and more.
197 PAGES. 6X9 PAPERBACK. ILLUSTRATED. BIBLIOGRAPHY. $14.95. CODE: JCNN

STONEHENGE AND THE GREAT PYRAMID
Window on the Universe
by Bonnie Gaunt

Mathematician and theologist Bonnie Gaunt's study on the Sacred Geometry of Stonehenge and the Great Pyramid. Through architecture, mathematics, geometry and the ancient science of "measuring," man can know the secrets of the Universe as encoded in these ancient structures. This is a fascinating study of the geometry and mathematics encompassed in these amazing megaliths as well as the prophecy beliefs surrounding the inner chambers of the Great Pyramid, the gematria of the Bible and how this translates into numbers which are also encoded within these structures. Interest is high in ancient Egypt at the moment, with attention focused on how old the Sphinx and Great Pyramid really are. Additionally, the current crop circle phenomenon is centered around Stonehenge.
216 PAGES. 6X8 PAPERBACK. ILLUSTRATED. $14.95. CODE: SAGP

STONEHENGE ...A CLOSER LOOK
by Bonnie Gaunt

Like the Great Pyramid, Stonehenge is steeped in mystery and is a masterwork in stone. Gaunt decodes the megaliths and tells not only of 4,000 years of history, but of the timeless forces of the universe and of the future of this planet.
236 PAGES. 6x8 PAPERBACK. ILLUSTRATED. $9.95. CODE: SCL

CONSPIRACY & HISTORY

LIQUID CONSPIRACY
JFK, LSD, the CIA, Area 51 & UFOs
by George Piccard

Underground author George Piccard on the politics of LSD, mind control, and Kennedy's involvement with Area 51 and UFOs. Reveals JFK's LSD experiences with Mary Pinchot-Meyer. The plot thickens with an ever expanding web of CIA involvement, from underground bases with UFOs seen by JFK and Marilyn Monroe (among others) to a vaster conspiracy that affects every government agency from NASA to the Justice Department. This may have been the reason that Marilyn Monroe and actress-columnist Dorothy Kilgallen were both murdered. Focusing on the bizarre side of history, *Liquid Conspiracy* takes the reader on a psychedelic tour de force. This is your government on drugs!
264 PAGES. 6x9 PAPERBACK. ILLUSTRATED. $14.95. CODE: LIQC

INSIDE THE GEMSTONE FILE
Howard Hughes, Onassis & JFK
by Kenn Thomas & David Hatcher Childress

Steamshovel Press editor Thomas takes on the Gemstone File in this run-up and run-down of the most famous underground document ever circulated. Photocopied and distributed for over 20 years, the Gemstone File is the story of Bruce Roberts, the inventor of the synthetic ruby widely used in laser technology today, and his relationship with the Howard Hughes Company and ultimately with Aristotle Onassis, the Mafia, and the CIA. Hughes kidnapped and held a drugged-up prisoner for 10 years; Onassis and his role in the Kennedy Assassination; how the Mafia ran corporate America in the 1960s; the death of Onassis' son in the crash of a small private plane in Greece; Onassis as Ian Fleming's archvillain Ernst Stavro Blofeld; more.
320 PAGES. 6x9 PAPERBACK. ILLUSTRATED. $16.00. CODE: IGF

WHO KILLED DIANA?
by Peter Hounam and Derek McAdam

Hounam and McAdam take the reader through a land of unofficial branches of secret services, professional assassins, Psy-Ops, "Feather Men," remote-controlled cars, and ancient clandestine societies protecting the British establishment. They sort through a web of traceless drugs and poisons, inexplicable caches of money, fuzzy photographs, phantom cars of changing color, a large mysterious dog, and rivals in class and ethnic combat to answer the question, Who Killed Diana?! After this book was published, Mohammed El Fayed held an international news conference to announce that evidence showed that a blinding flash of light had contributed to the crash.
218 PAGES. 6x9 PAPERBACK. ILLUSTRATED. $12.95. CODE: WKD

THE ARCH CONSPIRATOR
Essays and Actions
by Len Bracken

Veteran conspiracy author Len Bracken's witty essays and articles lead us down the dark corridors of conspiracy, politics, murder and mayhem. In 12 chapters Bracken takes us through a maze of interwoven tales from the Russian Conspiracy to his interview with Costa Rican novelist Joaquin Gutierrez and his Psychogeographic Map into the Third Millennium. Other chapters in the book are A General Theory of Civil War; The New-Catiline Conspiracy for the Cancellation of Debt; Anti-Labor Day; 1997 with selected Aphorisms Against Work; Solar Economics, and more. Bracken's work has appeared in such pop-conspiracy publications as *Paranoia*, *Steamshovel Press* and the *Village Voice*. Len Bracken lives in Arlington, Virginia and haunts the back alleys of Washington D.C., keeping an eye on the predators who run our country.
256 PAGES. 6x9 PAPERBACK. ILLUSTRATED. BIBLIOGRAPHY. $14.95. CODE: ACON.

MIND CONTROL, WORLD CONTROL
by Jim Keith

Veteran author and investigator Jim Keith uncovers a surprising amount of information on the technology, experimentation and implementation of mind control. Various chapters in this shocking book are on early CIA experiments such as Project Artichoke and Project R H I C -EDOM, the methodology and technology of implants, mind control assassins and couriers, various famous Mind Control victims such as Sirhan Sirhan and Candy Jones. Also featured in this book are chapters on how mind control technology may be linked to some UFO activity and "UFO abductions."
256 PAGES. 6x9 PAPERBACK. ILLUSTRATED. FOOTNOTES. $14.95. CODE: MCWC

NASA, NAZIS & JFK:
The Torbitt Document & the JFK Assassination
introduction by Kenn Thomas

This book emphasizes the links between "Operation Paper Clip" Nazi scientists working for NASA, the assassination of JFK, and the secret Nevada air base Area 51. The Torbitt Document also talks about the roles played in the assassination by Division Five of the FBI, the Defense Industrial Security Command (DISC), the Las Vegas mob, and the shadow corporate entities Permindex and Centro-Mondiale Commerciale. The Torbitt Document claims that the same players planned the 1962 assassination attempt on Charles de Gaul, who ultimately pulled out of NATO because he traced the "Assassination Cabal" to Permindex in Switzerland and to NATO headquarters in Brussels. The Torbitt Document paints a dark picture of NASA, the military industrial complex, and the connections to Mercury, Nevada which headquarters the "secret space program."
258 PAGES. 5x8. PAPERBACK. ILLUSTRATED. $16.00. CODE: NNJ

MIND CONTROL, OSWALD & JFK:
Were We Controlled?
introduction by Kenn Thomas

Steamshovel Press editor Kenn Thomas examines the little-known book *Were We Controlled?*, first published in 1968. The book's author, the mysterious Lincoln Lawrence, maintained that Lee Harvey Oswald was a special agent who was a mind control subject, having received an implant in 1960 at a Russian hospital. Thomas examines the evidence for implant technology and the role it could have played in the Kennedy Assassination. Thomas also looks at the mind control aspects of the RFK assassination and details the history of implant technology. A growing number of people are interested in CIA experiments and its "Silent Weapons for Quiet Wars." Looks at the case that the reporter Damon Runyon, Jr. was murdered because of this book.
256 PAGES. 6x9 PAPERBACK. ILLUSTRATED. NOTES. $16.00. CODE: MCOJ

24 hour credit card orders—call: 815-253-6390 fax: 815-253-6300
email: auphq@frontiernet.net   www.adventuresunlimitedpress.com   www.wexclub.com

CONSPIRACY & HISTORY

TECHNOLOGY OF THE GODS
The Incredible Sciences of the Ancients
by David Hatcher Childress

Popular *Lost Cities* author David Hatcher Childress takes us into the amazing world of ancient technology, from computers in antiquity to the "flying machines of the gods." Childress looks at the technology that was allegedly used in Atlantis and the theory that the Great Pyramid of Egypt was originally a gigantic power station. He examines tales of ancient flight and the technology that it involved; how the ancients used electricity; megalithic building techniques; the use of crystal lenses and the fire from the gods; evidence of various high tech weapons in the past, including atomic weapons; ancient metallurgy and heavy machinery; the role of modern inventors such as Nikola Tesla in bringing ancient technology back into modern use; impossible artifacts; and more.
356 PAGES. 6x9 PAPERBACK. ILLUSTRATED. BIBLIOGRAPHY. $16.95. CODE: TGOD.

THE ORION PROPHECY
Egyptian & Mayan Prophecies on the Cataclysm of 2012
by Patrick Geryl and Gino Ratinckx

In the year 2012 the Earth awaits a super catastrophe: its magnetic field reverse in one go. Phenomenal earthquakes and tidal waves will completely destroy our civilization. Europe and North America will shift thousands of kilometers northwards into polar climes. Nearly everyone will perish in the apocalyptic happenings. These dire predictions stem from the Mayans and Egyptians—descendants of the legendary Atlantis. The Atlanteans had highly evolved astronomical knowledge and were able to exactly predict the previous world-wide flood in 9792 BC. Orion and several others stars will take the same 'code-positions' as in 9792 BC! For thousands of years historical sources have told of a forgotten time capsule of ancient wisdom located in a mythical labyrinth of secret chambers filled with artifacts and documents from the previous flood. We desperately need this information now—and this book gives one possible location.
324 PAGES. 6x9 PAPERBACK. ILLUSTRATED. BIBLIOGRAPHY. $16.95. CODE: ORP

THE HISTORY OF THE KNIGHTS TEMPLARS
by Charles G. Addison, introduction by David Hatcher Childress

Chapters on the origin of the Templars, their popularity in Europe and their rivalry with the Knights of St. John, later to be known as the Knights of Malta. Detailed information on the activities of the Templars in the Holy Land, and the 1312 AD suppression of the Templars in France and other countries, which culminated in the execution of Jacques de Molay and the continuation of the Knights Templars in England and Scotland; the formation of the society of Knights Templars in London; and the rebuilding of the Temple in 1816. Plus a lengthy intro about the lost Templar fleet and its connections to the ancient North American sea routes.
395 PAGES. 6x9 PAPERBACK. ILLUSTRATED. $16.95. CODE: HKT

SAUNIER'S MODEL AND THE SECRET OF RENNES-LE-CHATEAU
The Priest's Final Legacy
by André Douzet

Berenger Saunière, the enigmatic priest of the French village of Rennes-le-Château, is rumored to have found the legendary treasure of the Cathars. But what became of it? In 1916, Saunière created his ultimate clue: he went to great expense to create a model of a region said to be the Calvary Mount, indicating the "Tomb of Jesus." But the region on the model does not resemble the region of Jerusalem. Did Saunière leave a clue as to the true location of his treasure? And what is that treasure? After years of research, André Douzet discovered this model—the only real clue Saunière left behind as to the nature and location of his treasure—and the possible tomb of Jesus.
116 PAGES. 6x9 PAPERBACK. ILLUSTRATED. BIBLIOGRAPHY. $12.00. CODE: SMOD

DARK MOON
Apollo and the Whistleblowers
by Mary Bennett and David Percy

•Was Neil Armstrong really the first man on the Moon?
•Did you know that 'live' color TV from the Moon was not actually live at all?
•Did you know that the Lunar Surface Camera had no viewfinder?
•Do you know that lighting was used in the Apollo photographs—yet no lighting equipment was taken to the Moon?
All these questions, and more, are discussed in great detail by British researchers Bennett and Percy in *Dark Moon*, the definitive book (nearly 600 pages) on the possible faking of the Apollo Moon missions. Bennett and Percy delve into every possible aspect of this beguiling theory, one that rocks the very foundation of our beliefs concerning NASA and the space program. Tons of NASA photos analyzed for possible deceptions.
568 PAGES. 6x9 PAPERBACK. ILLUSTRATED. BIBLIOGRAPHY. INDEX. $25.00. CODE: DMO

WAKE UP DOWN THERE!
The Excluded Middle Anthology
by Greg Bishop

The great American tradition of dropout culture makes it over the millennium mark with a collection of the best from *The Excluded Middle*, the critically acclaimed underground zine of UFOs, the paranormal, conspiracies, psychedelia, and spirit. Contributions from Robert Anton Wilson, Ivan Stang, Martin Kottmeyer, John Shirley, Scott Corrales, Adam Gorightly and Robert Sterling; and interviews with James Moseley, Karla Turner, Bill Moore, Kenn Thomas, Richard Boylan, Dean Radin, Joe McMoneagle, and the mysterious Ira Einhorn (an *Excluded Middle* exclusive). Includes full versions of interviews and extra material not found in the newsstand versions.
420 PAGES. 8x11 PAPERBACK. ILLUSTRATED. $25.00. CODE: WUDT

ARKTOS
The Myth of the Pole in Science, Symbolism, and Nazi Survival
by Joscelyn Godwin

A scholarly treatment of catastrophes, ancient myths and the Nazi Occult beliefs. Explored are the many tales of an ancient race said to have lived in the Arctic regions, such as Thule and Hyperborea. Progressing onward, the book looks at modern polar legends including the survival of Hitler, German bases in Antarctica, UFOs, the hollow earth, Agartha and Shambala, more.
220 PAGES. 6x9 PAPERBACK. ILLUSTRATED. $16.95. CODE: ARK

24 hour credit card orders—call: 815-253-6390 fax: 815-253-6300
email: auphq@frontiernet.net   www.adventuresunlimitedpress.com   www.wexclub.com

MYSTIC TRAVELLER SERIES

THE MYSTERY EASTER ISLAND

THE MYSTERY OF EASTER ISLAND
by Katherine Routledge
The reprint of Katherine Routledge's classic archaeology book which was first published in London in 1919. The book details her journey by yacht from England to South America, around Patagonia to Chile and on to Easter Island. Routledge explored the amazing island and produced one of the first-ever accounts of the life, history and legends of this strange and remote place. Routledge discusses the statues, pyramid-platforms, Rongo Rongo script, the Bird Cult, the war between the Short Ears and the Long Ears, the secret caves, ancient roads on the island, and more. This rare book serves as a sourcebook on the early discoveries and theories on Easter Island.
432 PAGES. 6x9 PAPERBACK. ILLUSTRATED. $16.95. CODE: MEI

RARE ARCHAEOLOGY BOOK ON ER ISLAND IS BACK IN PRINT!

MYSTERY CITIES OF THE MAYA
by Thomas Gann

MYSTERY CITIES OF THE MAYA
Exploration and Adventure in Lubaantun & Belize
by Thomas Gann
First published in 1925, *Mystery Cities of the Maya* is a classic in Central American archaeology-adventure. Gann was close friends with Mike Mitchell-Hedges, the British adventurer who discovered the famous crystal skull with his adopted daughter Sammy and Lady Richmond Brown, their benefactress. Gann battles pirates along Belize's coast and goes upriver with Mitchell-Hedges to the site of Lubaantun where they excavate a strange lost city where the crystal skull was discovered. Lubaantun is a unique city in the Mayan world as it is built out of precisely carved blocks of stone without the usual plaster-cement facing. Lubaantun contained several large pyramids partially destroyed by earthquakes and a large amount of artifacts. Gann shared Mitchell-Hedges belief in Atlantis and lost civilizations (pre-Mayan) in Central America and the Caribbean. Lots of good photos, maps and diagrams.
252 PAGES. 6x9 PAPERBACK. ILLUSTRATED. $16.95. CODE: MCOM

SECRET TIBET
T. Illion

IN SECRET TIBET
by Theodore Illion
Reprint of a rare 30s adventure travel book. Illion was a German wayfarer who not only spoke fluent Tibetan, but travelled in disguise as a native through forbidden Tibet when it was off-limits to all outsiders. His incredible adventures make this one of the most exciting travel books ever published. Includes illustrations of Tibetan monks levitating stones by acoustics.
210 PAGES. 6x9 PAPERBACK. ILLUSTRATED. $15.95. CODE: IST

TIC TRAVELLER SERIES

DARKNESS OVER TIBET
by Theodore Illion
In this second reprint of Illion's rare books, the German traveller continues his journey through Tibet and is given directions to a strange underground city. As the original publisher's remarks said, "this is a rare account of an underground city in Tibet by the only Westerner ever to enter it and escape alive! "
210 PAGES. 6x9 PAPERBACK. ILLUSTRATED. $15.95. CODE: DOT

Danger My Ally

DANGER MY ALLY
The Amazing Life Story of the Discoverer of the Crystal Skull
by "Mike" Mitchell-Hedges
The incredible life story of "Mike" Mitchell-Hedges, the British adventurer who discovered the Crystal Skull in the lost Mayan city of Lubaantun in Belize. Mitchell-Hedges has lived an exciting life: gambling everything on a trip to the Americas as a young man, riding with Pancho Villa, questing for Atlantis, fighting bandits in the Caribbean and discovering the famous Crystal Skull.
374 PAGES. 6x9 PAPERBACK. ILLUSTRATED. BIBLIOGRAPHY & INDEX. $16.95. CODE: DMA

The true life adventure of F.A. Mitchell-Hedges

SECRET MONGOLIA

HENNING HASLUND

AUTHOR OF MEN AND GODS IN MONGOLIA

TIC TRAVELLER SERIES

IN SECRET MONGOLIA
by Henning Haslund
First published by Kegan Paul of London in 1934, Haslund takes us into the barely known world of Mongolia of 1921, a land of god-kings, bandits, vast mountain wilderness and a Russian army running amok. Starting in Peking, Haslund journeys to Mongolia as part of the Krebs Expedition—a mission to establish a Danish butter farm in a remote corner of northern Mongolia. Along the way, he smuggles guns and nitroglycerin, is thrown into a prison by the new Communist regime, battles the Robber Princess and more. With Haslund we meet the "Mad Baron" Ungern-Sternberg and his renegade Russian army, the many characters of Urga's fledgling foreign community, and the last god-king of Mongolia, Seng Chen Gegen, the fifth reincarnation of the Tiger god and the "ruler of all Torguts." Aside from the esoteric and mystical material, there is plenty of just plain adventure: Haslund encounters a Mongolian werewolf; is ambushed along the trail; escapes from prison and fights terrifying blizzards; more.
374 PAGES. 6x9 PAPERBACK. ILLUSTRATED. BIBLIOGRAPHY & INDEX. $16.95. CODE: ISM

N and GODS MONGOLIA

MEN & GODS IN MONGOLIA
by Henning Haslund
First published in 1935 by Kegan Paul of London, Haslund takes us to the lost city of Karakota in the Gobi desert. We meet the Bodgo Gegen, a god-king in Mongolia similar to the Dalai Lama of Tibet. We meet Dambin Jansang, the dreaded warlord of the "Black Gobi." There is even material in this incredible book on the Hi-mori, an "airhorse" that flies through the sky (similar to a Vimana) and carries with it the sacred stone of Chintamani. Aside from the esoteric and mystical material, there is plenty of just plain adventure: Haslund and companions journey across the Gobi desert by camel caravan; are kidnapped and held for ransom; witness initiation into Shamanic societies; meet reincarnated warlords; and experience the violent birth of "modern" Mongolia.
358 PAGES. 6x9 PAPERBACK. ILLUSTRATED. INDEX. $15.95. CODE: MGM

e 1935 book is back in print! ic Traveller Series

One Adventure Place
P.O. Box 74
Kempton, Illinois 60946
United States of America
Tel.: 815-253-6390 • Fax: 815-253-6300
Email: auphq@frontiernet.net
http://www.adventuresunlimitedpress.com
or www.adventuresunlimited.nl

ORDERING INSTRUCTIONS

✓ Remit by USD$ Check, Money Order or Credit Card

✓ Visa, Master Card, Discover & AmEx Accepted

✓ Prices May Change Without Notice

✓ 10% Discount for 3 or more Items

SHIPPING CHARGES

United States

✓ Postal Book Rate { $3.00 First Item
50¢ Each Additional Item

✓ Priority Mail { $4.00 First Item
$2.00 Each Additional Item

✓ UPS { $5.00 First Item
$1.50 Each Additional Item

NOTE: UPS Delivery Available to Mainland USA Only

Canada

✓ Postal Book Rate { $6.00 First Item
$2.00 Each Additional Item

✓ Postal Air Mail { $8.00 First Item
$2.50 Each Additional Item

✓ Personal Checks or Bank Drafts MUST BE

USD$ and Drawn on a US Bank
✓ Canadian Postal Money Orders OK

✓ Payment MUST BE USD$

All Other Countries

✓ Surface Delivery { $10.00 First Item
$4.00 Each Additional Item

✓ Postal Air Mail { $14.00 First Item
$5.00 Each Additional Item

✓ Payment MUST BE USD$

✓ Checks and Money Orders MUST BE USD$
and Drawn on a US Bank or branch.

✓ Add $5.00 for Air Mail Subscription to
Future *Adventures Unlimited* Catalogs

SPECIAL NOTES

✓ RETAILERS: Standard Discounts Available

✓ BACKORDERS: We Backorder all Out-of-

Stock Items Unless Otherwise Requested

✓ PRO FORMA INVOICES: Available on Request

✓ VIDEOS: NTSC Mode Only. Replacement only.

✓ For PAL mode videos contact our other offices:

Please check: ☑

☐ This is my first order   ☐ I have ordered before

Name	
Address	
City	
State/Province	Postal Code
Country	
Phone day	Evening
Fax	

Item Code	Item Description	Qty	Total

Please check: ☑

	Subtotal ➡
	Less Discount-10% for 3 or more items ➡
☐ Postal-Surface	Balance ➡
☐ Postal-Air Mail Illinois Residents 6.25% Sales Tax ➡	
(Priority in USA)	Previous Credit ➡
☐ UPS	Shipping ➡
(Mainland USA only)	Total (check/MO in USD$ only) ➡

☐ Visa/MasterCard/Discover/Amex

Card Number

Expiration Date

10% Discount When You Order 3 or More Items!